For
PRESIDENT CLAYTON
SPENCER,
WHO WILL BRING GREAT
THINGS TO BATES

The Culture Broker

& TO THE
"OTHER L.A." —
I hope you enjoy
& are inspired
by this story

— 2014 —

The publisher gratefully acknowledges the generous contributions to this book provided by The Ahmanson Foundation, the J. Paul Getty Trust, and the Skirball Cultural Center.

The Culture Broker

FRANKLIN D. MURPHY AND THE
TRANSFORMATION OF LOS ANGELES

Margaret Leslie Davis

UNIVERSITY OF CALIFORNIA PRESS
BERKELEY   LOS ANGELES   LONDON

University of California Press, one of the most distinguished university presses in the United States, enriches lives around the world by advancing scholarship in the humanities, social sciences, and natural sciences. Its activities are supported by the UC Press Foundation and by philanthropic contributions from individuals and institutions. For more information, visit www.ucpress.edu.

University of California Press
Berkeley and Los Angeles, California

University of California Press, Ltd.
London, England

Every effort has been made to identify and locate the rightful copyright holders of all material not specifically commissioned for use in this publication and to secure permission, where applicable, for reuse of all such material. Credit, if and as available, has been provided for all borrowed material on-page. Errors, omissions, or failure to obtain authorization with respect to material copyrighted by other sources has been either unavoidable or unintentional. The author and publisher welcome any information that would allow them to correct future reprints.

Library of Congress Cataloging-in-Publication Data

Davis, Margaret L.
    The culture broker : Franklin D. Murphy and the transformation of Los Angeles / Margaret Leslie Davis.
        p.   cm.
    Includes bibliographical references and index.
    ISBN 978-0-520-22495-7 (cloth : alk. paper)
1. Murphy, Franklin D., 1916–92.   2. Los Angeles (Calif.)—Biography.
3. Los Angeles (Calif.)—Cultural policy.   4. Los Angeles (Calif.)—
Civilization—20th century.   5. Arts—California—Los Angeles—History—
20th century.   6. Museums—California—Los Angeles—History—20th
century.   7. Cosmopolitanism—California—Los Angeles—History—20th
century.   8. Charities—California—Los Angeles—History—20th century.
9. University of California, Los Angeles—Officials and employees—
Biography.   10. Times Mirror Company—Officials and employees—
Biography.   I. Title.
    F869.L853M873 2007
    979.4'94053092—dc22
    [B]

                                                    2007011570

Manufactured in the United States of America

16   15   14   13   12   11   10   09   08   07
10   9   8   7   6   5   4   3   2   1

The paper used in this publication meets the minimum requirements of ANSI/NISO Z39.48-1992 (R 1997) (*Permanence of Paper*).

FOR ROGER VINCENT

CONTENTS

PREFACE

Art of the Trustee

Franklin Murphy? It is not a name that is widely known. In fact, the public knew little of him during his lifetime. He worked behind the scenes as confidant, family friend, and astute adviser to the founders and scions of some of America's greatest fortunes—Ahmanson, Rockefeller, Ford, Mellon, and Annenberg. He forged close ties to the legendary names of American collecting and philanthropy, and through his association with the wealthy founders of museums and art institutions and their families, he seized a moment that would never occur in American arts again.

Just at the time Los Angeles was establishing a dominant commercial position in the Pacific Rim, Murphy was on the scene as the key figure in the creation and shaping of the city's modern, cosmopolitan character. In the period between 1960 and 1990, Los Angeles grew from a cultural backwater to a vibrant center for the arts. Dubbed by one historian "the Doge of Los Angeles," Murphy was the powerful mystery figure at the heart of virtually every new cultural institution in the city.[1]

Los Angeles before 1960 had been a sunny, wayward place—boastful, even, of its disregard for civic responsibility. During the tumultuous era that followed, larger-than-life personalities came on the scene bent on bringing prestige and honor to their much-maligned city. There was Dorothy Chandler, who welcomed Murphy to Los Angeles and gave him his marching orders. He quickly observed her wiles and daring at work, as well as the clout of the family newspaper, as she relentlessly pursued her ambition to create a music center rivaling that of any other city. She had an equal fanatic in retail magnate Edward Carter, who was determined to see Los Angeles have a first-class art museum. Wealthy art collectors—among them Howard Ahmanson, Norton Simon, Armand Hammer, and Walter Annenberg—vied with one another for recognition, carving their names on museum wings and galleries or insisting on building their own vanity museums. Murphy also coped with the truly eccentric as he confronted the strange dynamics of the Getty family and attempted to hold together a great inheritance for the city.

Murphy was a man of great intelligence and energy, with a gift for psychological insight into the intricacies of power and personality. In the backstage manner in which he worked, he was privy not only to family resources but to family secrets as well. It was a delicate matter, Murphy found, to build close friendships with great collectors while simultaneously pursuing their collections for the institutions he served. As much as he valued his large and influential circle of contacts, he was never obsequious. He expected acceptance of himself and the Midwest from which he sprang—the very heart of America, as he liked to say. He was a welcome houseguest at some of America's most storied and sumptuous estates: Nelson Rockefeller's Hudson Valley home, Kykuit; Walter Annenberg's art-filled desert oasis, Sunnylands; Paul Mellon's splendid Brick House in Upperville, Virginia. He lunched with J. Paul Getty at Sutton Place near London and swam with oilman Ed Pauley in the lagoon of Pauley's private island in the Pacific. Yet there were times when he suffered cruel slights and bitter disappointments. In the obituary for Murphy in 1994, the *Los Angeles Times* wrote of this "family" of the wealthy and powerful, noting Murphy's ability to steer the recalcitrant toward worthy ends: "Whatever edge of calculation any of them brought into an exchange with [him] was quickly, mysteriously, caught up in something more exuberant."

Admirers spoke of Murphy's energy and persuasive charm; critics charged him with incessant blarney. He was at home on a dais; he was not an imposing figure—no more than average height—but with his total self-confidence, his forthright gaze, and the authority of his deep voice he readily won over an audience. "Dr. Franklin Murphy . . . is inconspicuous in a crowd," wrote the *Kansas City Star.* "But when he speaks, people turn to listen."[2] Earl A. Powell III, director of the Los Angeles County Museum of Art before going to the National Gallery of Art, was familiar with Murphy's techniques. When it came to watching Murphy in operation, he said, "one never knew for sure whether Franklin was in front of or behind the curtain." He found Murphy's skill mind-boggling: "He knew whom to pull and whom to push."[3] The young librarian Robert Vosper left Los Angeles to go to Kansas and build a library to Murphy's exacting standards and then followed Murphy back to UCLA, where together they created collections that garnered the university an international reputation. He observed Murphy in action for more than thirty years and thought that paramount to Murphy's success was "the sheer force of his personal conviction[,] . . . his utter impatience with dullness or the second rate, his innate sense of timing, his political acumen, and his administrative drive."[4]

Murphy had a keen analytic mind with a bent for the sciences, but he also possessed compelling charm and a way with a story. He reached adulthood in possession of natural gifts, an excellent education, and the grounding provided by a stable and cultured boyhood home. The only gifts he lacked were wealth and a prominent family name. Former University of California president Clark Kerr, who often found himself hard pressed to hold the line against Murphy's impatience and headlong drive, confessed himself amazed that "a man without wealth, family pedigree or connections could achieve so much."[5] He took on astonishing projects, many that he was warned against attempting. He was known to see a challenge through to the end, even if it meant dozens of years of excruciating negotiations or courtroom battles. He was a cyclone, his assistants said. His wife, Judith Murphy, herself a gifted juggler of multiple tasks, said that she sometimes felt she was sitting by the roadside, watching Franklin race by.[6]

Plans for art and culture in Los Angeles before Murphy arrived had been unorganized, almost always dictated by the whims and private aspirations of collectors and large donors. Murphy's genius for organizing the amorphous resource of art patrons and focusing on specific goals gave energy and direction to the cultural development of the city. He used the power and wealth of these patrons to build museums, acquire artistic masterpieces, open libraries, build public gardens, acquire rare books, and fund distinctive cultural venues for diverse ethnic groups.

This biography tells two stories. One involves how Los Angeles refashioned itself between 1960 and 1994, offering a glimpse of the workings of an inner circle in this remarkable period; the other reveals how it came to be that one man envisioned a paradigm of philanthropy for an adolescent city in which the arts and culture could flourish as it grew to take its place among the cosmopolitan centers of the world. In taking a dominant role in delivering to Los Angeles the array of distinctive cultural institutions that its citizens now enjoy, Murphy truly served as a culture broker.

As a trustee of the Los Angeles County Museum of Art, the Ahmanson Foundation, and the J. Paul Getty Trust, Murphy directed hundreds of millions of dollars in grants for the arts and humanities for Los Angeles. His decades-long stewardship of the National Gallery of Art and the Samuel H. Kress Foundation secured and enlarged art collections for the nation and produced notable achievements in art preservation around the world. He was chancellor at UCLA during the pivotal 1960s and corporate chairman and chief executive at Times Mirror at the advent of the communications explosion when the *Times* emerged as a newspaper of national importance; in his retirement years he continued to operate as citizen-steward of cultural assets in a maturing city. Murphy recognized early that there was a worldwide revolution under way in the 1960s that would deeply affect educational, religious, and cultural institutions. He did not fear or resist the coming changes; in fact, he accepted the role of mediator between the youthful rebels and the establishment as he advised donors on new ways of thinking and steered foundations to broaden their outreach. Some may disagree with Murphy's choices, with his self-appointed role as cultural curator, but his impact on Los Angeles cannot be denied.

The account essentially begins with Murphy's arrival in Los Angeles during the summer of 1960 and traces his career until his death on June 16, 1994, at the age of seventy-eight. It is not, then, a conventional birth-to-death biography; and yet if Murphy arrived in Southern California determined to accomplish great things, he did not arrive without a past. Like all of us, he was a child of the world into which he was born, in his case, an American Midwest that differed sharply from—yet in hidden ways resembled—the city where he would make his mark. He could have remained in medicine, his initial career, or pursued any number of other paths that would have been more financially rewarding. How was it that he came to put his talents in service to the arts—in Los Angeles, of all possible cities—and what explains the lifelong devotion of this man of science to the artistic expression of the world's cultures, particularly the artifacts of Western heritage? To what extent was he motivated by fear for the continued role of the arts in human experience in face of the hierarchical rigidity of modernity, and to what extent did he find the promotion of culture the means to position himself among the rich and powerful? This biography is an effort not only to describe the breadth and scope of Murphy's achievements but to describe as well why he chose trusteeship as the primary focus of his life's efforts. In any event, the obsession that gripped him proved fortuitous for Los Angeles as it moved through the anxieties of the cold war, through the social and cultural upheaval of the 1960s, and into world recognition as a player in the global economy.

In some distant, nobler era of enlightened understanding of the achievements and deficiencies of the world's cultural systems, there will exist for study artifacts of Western culture, superbly preserved because Franklin Murphy guaranteed that they would be preserved. In Los Angeles there will be art museums, cultural institutions, and philanthropic foundations that will function with purpose and direction, persevering into the future as strong, but flexible, institutions. They will accommodate the interests and needs of changing times and diverse cultural groups.

In garnering funds from the city's rich and powerful, Murphy worked in such an integrated fashion that it is impossible to separate the threads of his personal ambition from those of his mission. At a banquet to honor Murphy in 1992, two years before his death, Vartan Gregorian, then president of Brown University, described for the black tie crowd the breadth of Murphy's civic influence: "He will go down in the annals of this city as one of its great conspiratorial benefactors because he has forced all of you to make Los Angeles what it is now."[7]

He was not drawn to live in the East: as Dorothy Chandler liked to say, why live in the East where everything that needed to be done had long since been accomplished? "Los Angeles is a place for the kind of people who are willing to try something new. It's a place for people who want to build a new world."[8] Asked what had been meaningful to him about the part he played in the city's transformation, Murphy answered that Los Angeles's cultural coming of age had been an explosive moment in the artistic history of the nation: "Because all of this has happened in 30 years. Whereas in New York, you had 150 years."[9] The dynamics of the times, the forceful personalities involved, and the roadblocks barreled through to create an arts infrastructure, Murphy said, constituted "the great untold story of Los Angeles."[10]

Something to Prove

AS A YOUNGSTER IN MISSOURI, full of energy and wanting adventure, Franklin Murphy read his way to exploits with the novels of Sir Walter Scott and the Tom Swift series for boys. He could hardly have imagined that as an adult he would encounter a social and intellectual revolution as great as that facing the knights charging into battle in Scott's fiction. Nor could he foresee his own role in later years as a protector and a promoter of the valued works of the human spirit. Young Franklin, nurtured by a cultured family, would grow up unencumbered by the strictures of religious extremism that pervaded the Midwest. At some financial hardship to his parents, he was able to attend an elite boy's preparatory academy, where he moved among his youthful peers with self-assurance and a casual aplomb that continued to be a mainstay of his personality. The traits that made Murphy such a force in the transformation of Los Angeles had roots in his early years in the heartland.

Franklin was born into a family that valued rational thought over religious fervor.[1] His grandfather, Hugh Charles Murphy, had been the first in a generational sequence of doctors. Franklin's father, Franklin Edward, born in 1866 and neither baptized nor confirmed, continued both the family attitude toward religion and its medical tradition. He took pride in helping to persuade the Kansas legislature to establish a medical school at the University of Kansas, where he became a founding professor. Late in life, while in Germany working with medical colleagues, he met Cordelia Antoinette Brown, a gifted concert pianist, and convinced her to give up a successful European tour for marriage.[2] Both of Franklin's parents enjoyed fulfilling careers, though their chosen paths were not remunerative.

Franklin was born on January 29, 1916, the eldest of three children, followed by his brother, George Edward, in 1918 and their sister, Cordelia, or "Cordie," in 1922. Their parents had moved in with Franklin's grandmother in Kansas City, Missouri, and raised the children in the big, comfortable frame house built by Franklin's grandfather in 1883—a place where repairs were largely overlooked, as music and art took priority. The house was unpretentiously furnished, but its walls were covered with the paintings of Alice Murphy Gross, Franklin's paternal aunt. Aunt Alice's powerful and brooding landscapes ignited Franklin's imagination, and as a child he found himself mesmerized by her canvases. (Alice had studied in London with impressionist painter William Merritt Chase and was friends with Mary Cassatt.) Franklin's mother no longer performed in concert, but she played the piano every day, filling the Murphy home with music. Described by the *Kansas City Star* as a "free spirit often soaring in the clouds with vibrant enthusiasm," Cordelia actively campaigned for a fine philharmonic orchestra in Kansas City.[3] Franklin's father was something of an antiquarian, collecting rare medical books and antique medicine bottles.[4]

Franklin's boyhood afforded him a great deal of freedom, and his father, sixty years old when he was ten, infringed little on his youthful activities. Engrossed in his busy medical practice and civic interests, Dr. Murphy seldom interacted with his three children. Franklin remembered going on rounds with his father at the university hospital but recalled few other father-son activities.[5] Young Franklin is best remembered as a mischievous, fun-loving prankster, a "little hellion" as his grandmother called him. Franklin himself recalled that as a boy he was completely preoccupied with sports—baseball, tennis, golf, and especially football. Franklin's parents sent both their sons to the Pembroke Country Day School, a private elementary and preparatory school for boys. Franklin earned impressive marks with very little effort. At "Pem-Day," the most important part of school to Franklin was the football team on which he played quarterback. He was not a big youth—at his full height he would reach five feet, eight inches—but he was solidly built and fast, and he was extremely competitive. He was good-looking, with piercing blue-gray eyes and thick brown hair; and, with his outgoing nature, he was extremely popular among his classmates.

During a brief period of prosperity just before the Great Depression,

Franklin's parents built a house in an attractive neighborhood near the medical center. Cordie recalled that her brothers and their friends often gathered on the screened porch adjacent to their mother's music room where they played records on the Victrola and danced. Franklin's parents knew the value of not only a fine education but also the opportunity for their sons to associate with the scions of prominent local families. His mother and father moved easily among the affluent citizens of Kansas City, and Franklin found he too could hold his own in the classroom and on the playing field. As an adolescent he came to believe that no doors would be closed to him.[6]

In his junior year, Franklin was tackled during a football game against Pem-Day's big rival, Lee's Summit, and seriously injured a kidney. The following year he was eager to resume his position on the team, but his doctor father, who had no interest in football, was more concerned about the risk of permanent injury. Franklin beseeched his father for permission to play, and his father finally agreed on condition that Franklin wear special padding. That entire season, Dr. Murphy left his busy practice and attended each of the Pembroke games. Franklin was surprised to see his father sitting in the stands, but his mother explained that his father was afraid for him. "He wanted to be on hand if something should happen to you," she said.[7] He had a successful season without injury and was named Little-Six Conference Quarterback. At the end of his Pembroke years Franklin joined his fellow graduates, many from wealthy families untouched by the hardships of the depression, to enjoy a last summer of sports, cars, and parties before leaving for college. Cordie took special note of her brother's popularity and his dates. "He had some very rich girlfriends, I can assure you," she recalled.[8] He was moving into young adulthood caught up in the frivolity and leisure interests of his friends. But there were early hints that his keen intellect, social ease, and charisma would one day serve higher ends.

One Saturday during his high school years, while browsing in a bookstore downtown, Franklin was drawn to a woodcut print created in 1498 by the German Renaissance artist Albrecht Dürer, *The Four Horsemen of the Apocalypse,* depicting charging steeds and their riders with a dynamic quality of energy and purpose. In later years Murphy was unable to explain why Dürer's depiction of God's destructive force had appealed so strongly to him, but he persuaded the bookseller, Frank Glenn, to allow him to pay the $50 price in installments over several months. Franklin's hunger for a more intellectual life was also fed by his relationship with his maternal uncle, Russell Field, and his lifelong friendship with his cousin Lyman Field. The dinners at Uncle Russell's were built around word games and challenges for the young people at the table. "Today, boys, we're going to the capitals of the world!" Uncle Russell would announce and they would be off to a fast-paced competition in geography.[9]

In fall 1932 he said good-bye to classmates headed to Ivy League schools and entered the University of Kansas (KU), where he promptly took up athletics and skipped classes. He and Lyman pledged Beta Theta Pi and were roommates in the large stone fraternity house near campus. Lyman, an eager young idealist, was excited by the election of President Franklin D. Roosevelt and the inauguration of the New Deal. Franklin wrote witty articles for KU's *Jayhawker*, reporting sarcastically on Lyman's liberal politics and the make-believe world of student government.[10] He may have resented that he was not attending an East Coast school with his wealthy Pembroke classmates, but later he would take inordinate pleasure in comparing his achievements to those of the "Ivy Leaguers."

Murphy's father, now in his late sixties, was growing exasperated with both his sons. Franklin was not applying himself and had set no real goals for his future. Younger brother George had fallen into inertia over a faltering romance. Then, in 1933, Franklin's father died suddenly from coronary heart disease. Both sons were devastated by the loss. Cordie, eleven years old, vividly recalled that following her father's death, Franklin's personality changed completely.[11] Her brother instantly matured, offering comfort to their mother and patience and understanding to George, who took their father's death especially hard. Franklin became serious about school for the first time, in particular his science classes; the rational aspect of science, with its logical, prescribed procedures, provided an escape from grief and regret. His father's colleagues took him under wing, and he soon decided to make medicine his career. At this time he also had advice and emotional buttressing from Rabbi Samuel S. Mayerberg, a family friend and longtime ally of his father's in Kansas City civic reform.

Franklin was accepted at the University of Pennsylvania School of Medicine, his father's alma mater, but delayed entry for a year to attend the University of Göttingen in Germany where his father had studied. There, with the rector's help, he found his father's name in the old matriculation books and wrote to his mother that he was having the signature pages photographed: "two Franklin Murphys who worked in the same laboratories of the same German university."[12] Murphy's studies at Göttingen, however, were not to be the scholarly experience he had hoped for, bathed in warm remembrance of his father. Hitler was in power, and the professor with whom Franklin had his fellowship, Hermann Rein, a prominent vascular physiologist, was an outspoken critic of the Nazi regime. Six months into Franklin's stay, Rein was "taken away." Franklin left the university and set out to travel on his own, browsing cathedrals and museums and appreciating the flowering of human innovation that had characterized the Renaissance, responding with visceral excitement to the creativity that led to the European Enlightenment and the invention of the scientific method. "It was a mind-stretching, eye-opening experience," he said.[13] At a time of his own emotional reawakening, he embraced the art of this watershed era, and the fascination never left him. Studying the Renaissance became his lifelong avocation, and at various times, when he was in a position to direct acquisitions for cultural institutions, it gave him special pleasure to acquire fine books, paintings, and sculpture from the period.

At Warburg Castle, where Martin Luther had found refuge, Franklin was entranced by a sound-and-light performance and deeply moved by a choral rendition of Luther's hymn "A Mighty Fortress Is Our God." In a lengthy letter to his mother, he said that the event had brought him in touch with "the glory of that indefinable something that moved men to say, 'There is a God'—but . . . not the church's God surrounded by priestly robes, incense and illogic." He told his mother he perceived a deity "responsible for our being here" and that he recognized tribute was to be paid by living a life of purpose.[14]

In Europe, he was alone in a way he never had been before. As the initial shock of his father's passing lessened, he began to fully experience the responsibility of his own manhood. Returning home, he took up his medical studies at the University of Pennsylvania emotionally strengthened and fired with enthusiasm for science and research. He graduated first in his medical school class in 1941. "I was there with a lot of Ivy League types who had had their undergraduate work at Princeton and Harvard and Yale," he said. "It pleased me that a little ole Kansas boy could beat 'em to the wire."[15] Murphy had been surprised to find that wealth and family name were defining measures among his classmates at Penn. Though he responded to their gibes with good humor, their dismissive attitude toward midwesterners got under his skin. No honor later in his life could compete with the personal satisfaction he received from his medical school class standing.

At the time of the American entrance into World War II, Franklin was completing his residency. With senior physicians called to military service, he was given responsibility unusual for a medical resident. It was a rare chance to stretch his abilities and perform at full capacity. "It was the happiest year of my life," he said, reflecting on those hectic months at a jam-packed teaching hospital burdened with wartime shortages and dependent on initiative since personnel and equipment were "gone for the duration."[16] It was also the first year of his marriage to Judith Joyce Harris, a beautiful Vassar graduate who had made her own resolution to lead a productive and meaningful life. Statuesque and self-confident, Judy shared with Franklin a wide range of interests. Like Franklin, she was born in Kansas City, Missouri. She had been a gifted student at the private Barstow School for girls. Her father, P. Stephen Harris, an attorney, was the creator of Lucky Tiger Hair Tonic, which enabled the family to live in an affluent style, even through the depression. What appealed to her about Franklin, Judy would later say, was that he had plans, visions of work he wanted to do, and ideas about the world. "Franklin had a purpose in life," she said. "I had been accustomed to people who didn't seem to care what happened in the world, or they didn't seem to have any interest in really accomplishing anything. Franklin always did." Judy claimed that after only three dates she planned to marry him.[17]

The war years increased Franklin's enthusiasm for science. As an army captain he conducted accelerated research on drugs and worked on protocols for the first uses of penicillin and the creation of a synthetic quinine for troops in malarial jungles. His cutting-edge work gave him a glimpse into a future enhanced by scientific marvels in medicine, atomic energy, and biological engineering. Like many young scientists, he anticipated a rationalist era offering solutions to problems long thought intractable. He anticipated participating in this new, booming era of discovery, and though he had been promised a teaching post at Penn's medical school, he realized that it would be a long time before he held a position of authority. He turned instead to the medical school at the University of Kansas: from his experience at Penn he knew what was required to make an outstanding medical school, and he wanted to see the Kansas school that his father had helped to found become such an institution. The best Kansas students were leaving the state to study medicine, and few were returning.

After the war Murphy and his family returned to Kansas City. He and Judy now had two toddlers, Judith Joyce and Martha Alice; later they would have two more children. Murphy told his friend and mentor, Dr. Charles Mayo of the renowned Mayo Clinic, that when he and Judy considered where to settle, they decided on Kansas City because they felt an obligation to their home soil. Murphy said he had lived in the East long enough "to get completely sick and tired of hearing Kansas and the Middle West defined as a cultural desert or a grasshopper-ridden plain."[18] He was convinced that the trans-Mississippi West had greatness ahead, and he expected to play a significant role in bringing it about.

Murphy joined a private medical practice and began to round up support to prepare the KU medical school for the future in medicine he knew was coming. He was soon appointed dean and embarked on an ambitious program that promised country doctors for towns without medical service. The popularity of the Kansas Rural Health Plan won him the legislative votes he needed for a multimillion-dollar expansion of the medical school. It also won him attention in *Look* and *Life* magazines, and at the age of thirty-five a taste of celebrity. The plan he devised taught farmers and townspeople in rural communities how they could finance and build a clinic or provide a well-equipped medical office to rent to a young doctor— a doctor Murphy promised to send them from the medical school. What he solicited from them was their promise to press their legislators to provide construction funds for the expanded medical center and research facility he wanted to create. Murphy's plan was hailed as relying on free enterprise and providing a viable alternative to calls for socialized medicine.[19]

He became the darling of the American Medical Association, which was dead set against government medical programs. When Dwight Eisenhower prepared his run for president in 1952, he asked Murphy to brief him on the Kansas health plan. The young medical school dean was riding high— prominent in his profession and acknowledged in Republican political circles. Murphy counted midwestern energy and courage as vital to the nation's well-being; he particularly valued the social openness of the plains states in contrast to eastern snobbery and limits on access to status and power. Eisenhower's election to the presidency, taking Kansas spirit to the White House, was a great satisfaction to him.

During the immediate postwar years at KU's medical school, Murphy had worked with intensity, confident of his abilities as an administrator as well as a scientist. His enthusiasm for the cool rationality of scientific discipline shifted as the nation's best minds debated whether the United States should develop a hydrogen bomb. Murphy struggled with a reordering of his basic philosophy and devotion to science. As he sorted out his thoughts on the perils of the atomic age, he was alarmed to perceive among religious groups a seeming resignation to a nuclear apocalypse brought about by "godless science."

The framed Dürer print of the Apocalypse occupied a respected place on Murphy's university office wall, but the image he embraced was the dolphin and anchor symbol that identified the bound volumes from the press of the Renaissance master Aldus Manutius. The dolphin, a Christian symbol for the transporting of souls, was interpreted by Murphy as symbolizing the rescue of humanity through a balance of the intellectual and the spiritual. In public speeches he stressed that scientific advancement must be in the service of humankind. He urged art and the humanities as a counterbalance to the nonemotional intellectualism of science and pushed his medical students to nurture their spiritual lives with cultural interests. [20]

When Murphy was asked by the regents of the University of Kansas to accept the chancellorship, he was startled that at the age of thirty-five he would be considered for the position. "Ridiculous," he responded. "I'm a kid." And he was reluctant to leave medicine. "I like the laying on of hands. . . . I don't want to sit in an office and move paper around."[21] But after much discussion, he and Judy concluded that in the role of chancellor and chancellor's wife they could make a genuine contribution. The state of Kansas was settled by radical abolitionists who held great expectations for the university they established, and Murphy wanted to expand on their goals. In his travels through Kansas to promote the rural health plan, he had come face-to-face with a provincial, isolationist mind-set that had immobilized much of the state. There was an ongoing conflict between science and religion and a prevailing hostility to secular humanism, which was often equated with Communism. Dr. Karl Menninger of the Menninger Clinic in Topeka explained the Kansans' moral rigidity as rooted in profound feelings of inferiority, an emotional state resulting from "over-conscientiousness." When missionary zeal to bring about "the most idealistic and fruitful ways of life" falls short, Menninger said, Kansans retreat to bitterness, imagining that others have achieved what they cannot. [22]

Murphy was determined to restore optimism and a valid sense of pride in the Kansan tradition of moral commitment; after all, Kansas had been brought into the Union free of slavery as a result of the courage and dedication of its early settlers. Moral commitment continued to be a major characteristic of Kansans, and Murphy planned to expand that strength to include the spirit-enriching contributions of art and culture as well as an understanding of the merits of science. He did not realize how much of the unrealistic Kansan missionary zeal was in his own character as he set out to rescue the Kansan soul.

Murphy took up his duties as chancellor in the summer when seemingly endless rain led to the Great Flood of 1951. The Kansas River, surging eighteen feet above flood stage for twelve days, inundated all of north Lawrence and swept four blocks of businesses into its raging waters. The university was safe, high on its hill at Mount Oread, but with thousands of homes and farms destroyed throughout the plains, residents questioned the devastation and turned to their Bibles to compare their travail to the biblical deluge. When the flood was followed by years of drought, there was more talk of God's wrath. Murphy was embarking on his dream for the University of Kansas at a time when Bible Belt evangelicals saw evidence all about them that the end was near. With nation after nation sliding into Communism, they feared that Christianity could be wiped from the world. Reaction to Soviet expansion and the possibility of nuclear attack ranged from resigned acceptance of a coming apocalypse to demands for an arsenal of H-bombs.[23] The traumatizing fear and hysteria needed a scapegoat, someone to blame; and the hunt commenced for spies and traitors. In his inaugural address, Chancellor Murphy urged that history not be allowed to record the era with its terrible weapons as "setting back mankind's time table for a century or two." He endeavored to stir enthusiasm for the future and insisted that the best defense against "the Communist with his glittering lies" was commitment to the vitality of democracy in the free world. [24]

During his first five years as chancellor, Murphy expanded the campus, brought prestige to academic departments, and promoted a vibrant sports program. (Some of the most successful basketball teams in the university's history, with players such as Wilt Chamberlain, were assembled during the Murphy years.) Murphy also introduced the campus to his fascination with the Renaissance. He acquired a wood sculpture, *Madonna and Child,* by the German artist Tilmann Riemenschneider by soliciting a purchase gift from a university supporter so that the students would have the treasure, the real object, not a copy or some minor example.[25]

When he began the chancellorship, KU was a segregated institution. In Lawrence blacks were not permitted to eat in restaurants, take seats on the main floor of public movie theaters, or rent hotel rooms. On campus they could not join a fraternity or sorority, live in a campus dormitory, study medicine or nursing, or swim in the university pool. The major civil rights legislation of the 1960s was still well in the future. Murphy was not a radical like the abolitionists who had founded the university, and who had ear-

lier been willing to break the law and resort to violence to drive slavehold-
ers from the Kansas Territory. (Their shipments of rifles came concealed in
crates labeled "Bibles.") Murphy was not willing to act ahead of court orders, legislation, and public will, but he did take preliminary actions. He
saw his role as producing ethical citizens, who would then assume the responsibility of bringing about racial integration.[26] "We insist that man must
be measured by performance, not prejudice," he told students. "At KU, we
will not merely discuss human freedom and the dignity of all men—we will
put it into practice."[27] He embraced the visits of Thurgood Marshall and
Langston Hughes to the campus and invited the jazz artist Ella Fitzgerald
to perform in concert.[28] He encouraged the recruiting of black athletes for
the sports program and brought foreign students of color to KU as a way
to introduce racial integration. (In the pervasive illogic of the day, persons
of color from foreign countries were accepted and served in situations in
which African Americans were not.) Murphy paved the way for integration
of the KU faculty by hiring well-qualified African American librarians. Demanding religious diversity as well, Murphy ventured to the largest Jewish
temple in Kansas City to recruit outstanding students. "I want a Jewish
presence at the University of Kansas," he said.

He believed strongly that the presence of varying cultures was vital to an
exceptional institution and would prepare students for responsible citizenship. In the late 1950s Murphy toured the USSR and returned convinced
of the opportunity for dialogue with the Soviets through cultural exchange. In speeches he urged such programs as a vital dimension of foreign
policy and a counterbalance to Communist inroads; without these kinds of
contacts, he told audiences, tanks and bombs would not "win us either the
friendship and respect which we seek on the one hand, or security from the
threat of war on the other."[29] The concept was a hard sell in a region caught
up in the isolationist warnings of the late Senator Robert Taft and the jin-
goistic, anti–United Nations, anti-NATO rhetoric of Colonel Robert Mc-
Cormick's *Chicago Tribune*. Murphy's welcome of international students
subjected him to complaints from conservative alumni who felt such contacts opened the door to Communist subversion.

Murphy deplored the retreat from controversy exhibited by many university administrators in the wake of the House Un-American Activities
Committee hearings. As Senator Joseph McCarthy's hunt for Communists
became increasingly threatening to academic freedom, Murphy joined
forces in 1953 with Yale University's president, A. Whitney Griswold, to
write the American Association of Universities' public response. The state-

ment, printed in its entirety in *Time* magazine, made a well-reasoned case for academic freedom but nevertheless supported loyalty oaths: "Since present membership in the Communist Party requires the acceptance of principles and methods [that are contradictory to academic freedom], such membership extinguishes the right to a university position."[30] The statement brought protests from educators and teachers' unions that had long opposed loyalty oaths. In this crucial era Murphy developed close ties with Nathan M. Pusey, president of Harvard University, Harold Dobbs, president of Princeton, and Henry Wriston, president of Brown. He thus joined the inner circle of the nation's premier education leaders, sharing in the vast influence they commanded.[31]

THE MAD GOVERNOR VERSUS THE BOY WONDER

Murphy's ambitions for himself and for the university in Lawrence ended with the election of Democrat George Docking as the thirty-fifth governor of Kansas. The election took the chancellor by surprise. "This was a freak thing politically," he explained. A Democratic governor in Kansas in those years was "as rare as snow in June."[32] The Republicans were badly split at the time, the door was open, and Docking, president of a bank in Lawrence and a minor figure in local politics, seized his opportunity.

Murphy, who was acquainted with Docking, found him a "very peculiar man."[33] Evidently others thought so as well, for the officers of the Lawrence Chamber of Commerce had been in a running conflict with him for years. Always alert to promote harmony between town and gown, Murphy had become a familiar participant at breakfast meetings and business lunches. He was an impressive speaker, imposing not because of his physical appearance but because of his absolute self-confidence and desire to share his enthusiasm for the university with his audience. Docking quietly steamed as Murphy became a Lawrence favorite. Docking had his own reasons to resent the university crowd, but he discovered that going after the university with a vengeance was an effective vote-getting device. Kansans had always been divided politically, with the rural western part of the state suspicious and resentful of the cities in the eastern part and distrustful of the university on the hilltop at Lawrence.

Docking's demagogic campaign promised tax cuts and fiscal restraint; he proposed savings in nearly every area of state government, but he railed especially against extravagance in KU operations and a permissive environment that fostered campus immorality (panty raids were the high jinks of the era). He scoffed at Murphy's talk of a "distinguished" university; what Kansas needed, he told voters, was an efficient university. Once in office, Docking launched his hunt for waste; in the state capital he became known as "the Auditor" as he slashed one department budget after another. When the regents recommended a 10 percent pay hike for KU faculty and staff, Docking responded by publishing the name of every faculty member who made more than $750 a month (the average factory worker's salary then was less than $300 a month) and made sure to mention that Murphy earned more than anyone. Murphy was astounded by the venom of the governor's response. "This goddamned university," Docking shouted when Murphy traveled to Topeka to meet with him, "now they'll know who George Docking is."[34]

Murphy enjoyed first-name relationships with many of the state representatives—good, solid contacts he had made when he was promoting the Kansas Rural Health Plan. He felt he could count on the Republican majority to restore the budget as approved by the regents, but he knew Docking would veto it, and he was unsure if he could get enough votes to override the veto. Murphy dropped everything at the campus and set out to organize across the state; he mobilized the alumni and called on his friends in the press. Some of his undergraduate classmates were now heading their families' newspapers; he enlisted help from John McCormally, editor of the *Hutchinson News,* Marcellus Murdock, publisher of the *Wichita Eagle,* and his longtime friends, the McCoy family, at the *Kansas City Star.* When the legislature restored the cuts, Docking vetoed the bill, as anticipated. Murphy held his breath as the next set of votes were counted—enough to override the veto. Murphy's meddling infuriated Docking. "From that point on, he set out to get me fired," Murphy recalled.[35] In speaking engagements across the state, Docking accused Murphy of bilking Kansas with his $22,000-a-year salary, campus residence, and tax-supported international junkets. He told audiences that the state could get better chancellors for less.[36]

Every budget session now Murphy had to campaign to override Docking's vetoes. Docking declared that he would not fund the university's "clutter of courses" and suggested the school fire all those faculty members he saw "squeaking around." "The egghead[s]," Murphy replied, "ha[ve] been maligned by the short-sighted fatheads." He remembered it as an exhausting period when he was constantly driving through the rural counties, pumping up alumni, speaking to Rotary Clubs, keeping up the pressure on the representatives. At the same time, he took inordinate pleasure in defeating Docking's efforts. "It was a moment in my life that was exciting," he recalled; it was "a real struggle and a battle, and that keeps your blood boiling."[37]

Docking felt victimized by the press and by Murphy's smooth rejoinders and wit. Murphy interacted freely with people in high places, and as one colleague said, he actually loved opera and read dictionaries for fun. The governor's frustrated response was to tell associates, "I'm going to blow the hell out of that little punk."[38] Friends in the know advised Murphy to be scrupulous with his expense accounts and to be alert when traveling to possible attempts at entrapment, such as a woman arriving at his hotel room.

In political newsletters Docking was called the "Mad Governor," but his cost cutting had appeal to voters who did not mind if he was rude and insulting to his enemies and let his temper loose. Murphy deplored the governor's negativism. He did not want to build anything, Murphy complained—not roads, not schools, nothing for the welfare of the state. As for the university, "he hated it more than anything else."[39]

Murphy's plans to make the University of Kansas a leading U.S. educational institution may have had as much to do with his personal ambition, psychology, and family history as with Kansas or the university, but in the five years before Docking's election he had made tremendous strides in bringing recognition to the university. He had attracted government funding and hundreds of thousands of dollars in support from the Kansas City–based Hallmark Cards, as well as from the New York–based Samuel H. Kress Foundation. The alumni association was invigorated, and he had reshaped the Endowment Association, attracting pledges of $2 million in annual gifts—an increase of 300 percent.[40] In Topeka stories were told of his money-raising ability. Legislators were known to call out, "Watch your wallets, boys, here comes Murphy!"[41]

A superior library, Murphy knew, was essential to achieving a high rank for the university and vital to attracting fine scholars to the faculty. Murphy enticed a young specialist in acquisitions at the UCLA library, Robert Vosper, to leave Los Angeles and come to Kansas. He and Vosper doubled the size of the library holdings—to 920,000 volumes. Murphy told Vosper to do whatever was necessary. "I will find the money," he told him, which he did, later admitting to "parasitizing a budget here and shifting funds there."[42] Vosper called on his contacts in the book trade and acted quickly when he could buy collections en bloc. The two men—the tall, lean Vosper with his pipe and professorial eyeglasses and the shorter, high-energy, fast-moving Murphy—were frequently seen striding the campus together, always working on additional schemes for the library. When Vosper learned that an eccentric collector in Nebraska had died leaving a barn full of books (the famed Fitzpatrick hoard), Murphy commandeered a fleet of university trucks and Vosper hauled away thirty thousand volumes—twelve truckloads.

Vosper was impressed by the set of contacts Murphy maintained. In 1952 Murphy had joined like-minded moderate Republicans determined to dislodge the ultraconservative Senator Taft from leadership and invigorate the party with Eisenhower's presidential candidacy. Murphy took pride in his personal acquaintance with the Eisenhower family. (He had shared goals for Kansas higher education with Milton Eisenhower, who was president of Kansas State College at Manhattan when Murphy was dean of the University of Kansas medical school, and he had continued a close relationship with him as Milton became his brother's chief adviser.)

In addition to his rapport with regional business magnates and political figures, Murphy was well known by the Kansas City cultural elite. The Nelson-Atkins Museum of Art benefited from his relationship with the Samuel H. Kress Foundation, which presented the museum with outstanding works for their collection. Murphy was appointed a trustee of the Kress Foundation in 1953.

Vosper, in observing the growing conflict with Governor Docking, felt that its origin lay with Docking's character, something there "that wasn't straightforward."[43] Vosper, a Democrat, was often out in the Lawrence community and in contact with Docking. He knew that Docking was sensitive to slights and that he felt excluded from alumni groups. University administrator Raymond Nichols attributed Docking's animosity to feelings of insecurity about his education and background. "[Murphy] was well-connected and thoroughly respected across the state, and in many circles, across the country," he noted. "President Eisenhower and Winston Churchill were his personal friends. George Docking—even as governor—lacked everything that came to Franklin Murphy quite naturally."[44]

Vosper thought there was truth in Nichols's analysis. Murphy, who functioned in league with the heads of leading universities, traveled extensively to conferences on higher education in the United States and abroad (some forty thousand miles during one year). He had served on government commissions and had close contacts among both Republicans and Democrats. His speeches and travels were reported in Kansas newspapers in a steady stream of admiring coverage.

Having observed how effectively and naturally Murphy dealt with all kinds of people, Vosper was surprised that Murphy made no effort to bring Docking into university activities. Murphy had an intuitive understanding of the psychological needs of others—Vosper thought it accounted for much of his success—but he ignored Docking until suddenly Docking was governor and his simmering hatred of Murphy was all too apparent.

Murphy acknowledged that Docking was cunning in coming up with ways to turn the public against the university. "He was a kind of a shrewd animal type," Murphy said in describing how Docking stirred up the private colleges to complain that state-supported KU was tapping donors and foundations for funds private institutions needed.[45] Murphy's great success raising money for the university was now used by the sitting governor against him.

As Docking prepared his reelection campaign, Murphy became an active opponent, joining Joyce C. Hall, president of Hallmark Cards, and other business figures in support of Clyde M. Reed, a Republican who was the son of a former governor and who pledged full support for the university.[46] By becoming such a visible adversary in the campaign, Murphy risked everything—forfeiting any possibility of a working relationship if Docking won. The governor's bombastic campaign promising yet more tax cuts and stringent supervision of state spending brought results, and on November 4, 1958, he was returned to office. Murphy saw the vote as signaling the unwillingness of Kansans to tax themselves to support a superior university. Docking's reelection was in Murphy's mind "the crossroads—a crisis" that he felt ensured mediocrity for the education of Kansas youth. In a letter to the *Kansas City Star,* he wrote with great sadness, "This is no longer a temporary personal or political controversy—it is just a state tragedy."[47] Pundits predicted that Murphy would be the next Republican nominee for governor, though he denied any interest in the job. Long before, Murphy had decided to stay out of electoral politics—it was not the arena for him.

With Docking appointees now dominating the board of regents and Democrats in the legislature growing reluctant to incur the governor's wrath, Murphy was no longer able to protect the university. It was apparent that only two options, equally unappealing, were available: he must run for governor himself, or he must leave the state of Kansas altogether.

When Governor George Docking announced his decision to run for a third term, Murphy quietly traveled to Los Angeles, where he met with University of California president Clark Kerr and leading Southern California regents for preliminary discussions about the chancellorship at UCLA. In an emotional message to the chairman of the Kansas University

Board of Regents, Ray Evans, Murphy wrote, "I am only human. My patience has come to an end."[48]

IMPRINTED BY THE HEARTLAND

If everything had gone according to plan, Murphy would have lived the rest of his days in Kansas. The small town of Lawrence and the university were never far from his mind. "Everyone thinks Kansas is flat as a billiard table. As a matter of fact eastern Kansas is rolling hills," Murphy often pointed out. "Driving to Lawrence from Kansas City you begin to see the university ten miles away, rearing up high on a hill—Mount Oread. The buildings flow down the sides of this hill into Lawrence. It's absolutely beautiful." The campus occupied a thousand acres of green hills and dells, meadowlike lawns, and magnificent shade trees. As a little boy he went frequently with his mother and father to the campus and wandered with a youngster's delight over the grounds. "Lawrence and I were mutually imprinted," he admitted years later. "My whole life is bound up with that little town and long ago I fell in love with it." [49]

The chancellor's residence at the university was an imposing fifteen-room, nineteenth-century house on Lilac Lane at the southeastern edge of the campus overlooking the farms of the Wakarusa and Kansas River valleys. Such a beautiful setting was a gift Murphy felt he owed his children so that they could grow up, as he did, with roots to sustain them as they developed independence and self-confidence. On evenings when he was home, after the children were in bed, he and Judy would become night owls, eating a late supper and relaxing well past midnight listening to classical records and reading. As the decade came to an end, however, nightfall was given over to anxious debate about the future. The contacts that Murphy had made, his reputation and prestige, the opportunities that he had earned were now to be abandoned.[50] He was planning to start all over in a place where he was unknown. The most painful part of the experience for him was the realization that he had carried a vision of his native region, of the heartland, that perhaps was not true at all. On the other hand, maybe he could have made the vision true; he had achieved considerable progress with the medical school and the university, and he could have done more.

Leaving Kansas was a wrenching decision. He may have fantasized about an appointment to the Ivy League, but, in reality, he knew that such an invitation would not be extended to the administrator of a state university in the plains who had an M.D. degree, not a Ph.D., who lacked eastern establishment connections so necessary for fund-raising, and who, at forty-five, was still young for such a post. At UCLA he saw the opportunity to create a distinguished university and a chance to take part in the cultural structure of an emerging metropolis. He and Judy could not readily break into eastern elite circles, but he was sure they would be welcomed into the more open and fluid society of Los Angeles. They were right about that, yet not all doors would open at the first knock.

PART I

Chancellor

ONE

Into the Pastel Empire

THE DECISION WAS MADE: the Murphys would go to Los Angeles. They tried to keep the lid on the news until a proper announcement could be made, but on March 17, 1960, six hundred students, angered by the rumors, gathered on the snow-covered lawn of the chancellor's residence on Mount Oread, the Murphys' home for the past nine years. "We want Murphy! We want Murphy!" the students chanted. As they stamped their feet for warmth in the frosty evening air, they waved placards that read, "To Hell with Docking!" and "Stay Here Murphy." The mob hoisted up a life-size effigy of the Kansas governor made of straw and old blue jeans, with "GEORGE" painted on its chest. After hurling rock-hard snowballs at the figure swinging from a tree limb, they set "Governor Docking" ablaze.

Judy Murphy stepped to the front of the portico and told the students that her husband was in Topeka but was expected shortly. She spoke briefly about their regret at leaving Kansas and said the decision had been difficult. Just then someone spotted the chancellor's car, and the students rushed to line up along the slushy asphalt driveway. As soon as the car turned through the stone pillars of the gate, the crowd caught in its headlights cheered wildly and launched into "For He's a Jolly Good Fellow."

"This is St. Patrick's Day and my grandfather told me that a good Irishman can always talk if nothing else," Murphy told the crowd after making his way to the portico, "but I don't know if I'll even be able to talk much tonight." The usually well-composed chancellor had tears in his eyes as he spoke, his nine-year-old son, Franklin, standing at his side on the front steps. Murphy underlined his affection for the town of Lawrence and for the University of Kansas. "Ever since I've held this position here it hasn't been a job to me at all, but sort of a love affair," he said. "In the last year and a half, the student body has acted with such maturity it would put the adults of this state to shame."

Realizing there was nothing more they could do but bid farewell to their much-admired "Dr. Murphy," the tearful students burst into the Jay-hawks' anthem, followed by a vigorous rendition of KU's "Rock Chalk Chant," a rhythmic mantra that could unhinge the most stone-faced. Murphy thanked them all, said, "God bless you," and, deeply moved, walked hurriedly into the house.[1]

· · · · ·

On March 29, 1960, Clark Kerr, president of the University of California, wrote Franklin Murphy that the board of regents had formally approved his appointment as UCLA's chancellor. Murphy's duties as chancellor were slated to begin on July 1, 1960. He would receive an annual salary of $26,000, plus a contingent fund of $7,000 for entertainment expenses. On his arrival in Los Angeles, the regents would reimburse him for the cost of moving his family from Kansas to California and provide him with a house as well as a car for use on official business.[2]

"The committee of the regents and the faculty considered more than 100 leading American educators for this important post," Kerr told the *Los Angeles Times*.[3] Soon after the announcement, Murphy received an early-morning telephone call from former president Harry Truman, who said that he regretted "that the good doctor was leaving the Midwest" but wished him well in his new post.[4] Murphy was not prepared for all the congratulatory messages he received. Notes, flowers, letters, and telegrams kept arriving at his office, piling high on his desk. "I do not know when I shall ever get dug out," he said.[5]

In his farewell speeches to students and faculty Murphy did not soft-pedal his disappointment about Kansans' lack of support for the university. "The state of California, with its dedication to and central involvement in the great thrust to the future, is a compelling magnet," he said. "UCLA has the intense and active interest and support of Californians at all levels. The creative educational opportunities are unlimited."[6]

While the chancellor completed his good-byes to friends in Lawrence, powerful men in Los Angeles prepared for his summer arrival. Edward W.

Carter, a business magnate and university regent, approved Murphy's election to the exclusive Los Angeles Country Club and waived the $12,000 initiation fee; Norman Chandler, chairman of the Times Mirror Company and publisher of the *Los Angeles Times,* secured Murphy's nomination to the prestigious California Club; and Asa Call, a powerful insurance executive and the central figure in the redevelopment of downtown, arranged meetings with the city's movers and shakers.[7]

A CITY RETHINKING ITSELF

Franklin Murphy was coming to a city newly resolved on a daring makeover of its downtown core. City leaders were determined to have Los Angeles take advantage of the booming postwar economy. They feared that a failure of civic nerve now would condemn Los Angeles to stagnation as a minor though colorful West Coast town dependent on moviemaking and tourism.

The city council in 1960 focused its attention on a faded residential district occupying a downtown promontory known as Bunker Hill. During the flourishing 1880s and 1890s, Bunker Hill, at the edge of the civic center, had been the city's most fashionable address, noted for its exuberantly designed Victorian mansions. Wealthy families and city leaders exercised little restraint in building homes that featured the imaginative details of the Queen Anne and Eastlake architectural craze—cupolas, towers, turrets, and gabled roofs. A funicular railway called Angels Flight transported residents up and down the hillside in two fanciful cars, connecting the neighborhood at the top with the commercial district and city offices at the base.

As the whimsical architecture went out of style and the original owners moved to newer enclaves, the hilltop mansions lost their glory and were divided into rental units or turned into boardinghouses. The decaying neighborhood was occupied by recent immigrants, pensioners, and the down-and-out, although not quite the derelicts of skid row. The police often suspected that a criminal element now operated inside the parlors of the city's early elite. Angels Flight continued to descend to Hill Street, but the exclusive department store, the City of Paris, had long since been replaced by the Grand Central Market, a public grocery and produce bazaar. The quaint turn-of-the-century cars of Angels Flight were popular with tourists, who rode the "world's shortest railroad" to the top of the hill and bought postcards to prove it. From the hilltop, they could look out over an unobstructed vista of downtown. Franklin Murphy would arrive in a city with a skyline strangely limited to thirteen stories, an anachronism in an era of modern skyscrapers. The notable exception was City Hall, whose twenty-eight-story tower rose like a modern obelisk above the small-town skyline. Footings of the structure were said to stand in pools of mercury, the technology at the time for riding out an earthquake.[8]

The city was already deeply committed to the automobile, with a freeway grid intended to bring commuters to a central city curiously stuck in an earlier era. Except for the fact that the trolley tracks had been removed, Spring Street, the city's financial district of low-rise Beaux Arts bank and title company buildings, looked as it did in photos of the 1890s. The dilapidated Bunker Hill mansions with their eccentric details were popular with filmmakers when a gloomy, portentous setting was needed to suggest corruption underlying California's vaunted golden life.[9] City leaders, however, found noir films a betrayal of the idea of Los Angeles as a forward-looking, sunshine-bright metropolis: after all, when the new City Hall was completed in 1928, with its futuristic tower topped by the Lindbergh beacon, a revolving searchlight sweeping the night sky, it was meant to announce the arrival of modern Los Angeles. But the Great Depression and World War II intervened, putting further futuristic plans on hold.

In 1957, when new engineering technology ended the restrictions on building height, Los Angeles could at last erect sleek, efficient office towers, though developers still had to be convinced that the city had come of age and could attract corporate tenants. The optimistic city council ordered preliminary work on a master plan. High on the planning agenda was demolition of the disintegrating houses of Bunker Hill—Redevelopment Area No. 1—so conspicuously and incongruously close to the civic center. "Los Angeles passed Bunker Hill by and all but forgot about it for a quarter century," noted the *Times*.[10]

City leaders were determined that downtown would not become a blighted area of tenements and marginal enterprises. The Community Redevelopment Agency (CRA) envisioned Bunker Hill revitalized by luxury apartments and hotels, the Los Angeles version of San Francisco's Nob Hill. Subsequent financial realities, however, would lead to the planning of a mixed-use commercial and residential district with high-rise office towers, condominiums, and public plazas.[11]

Demolition of Bunker Hill was slated to begin in fall 1961, and it would take several more years for the city skyline to be redefined upward, with the thirty-five-story Union Bank Building rising as the first of the new towers.

Murphy arrived at a transitional moment in the city's history, and he witnessed the radical metamorphosis of both the city's skyline and the city's image of itself. Much of the city's changing philosophy would be played out on Bunker Hill.

· · · · ·

Everything about Murphy's initial visits to L.A. conspired to put the city in its best light—even the weather. The Kansas winter of 1959–60 had been one of the worst on record. Freezing ice and snow blanketed the farmlands of the Wakarusa and Kansas River valleys, and bitter temperatures lingered for months. On two whirlwind trips to Los Angeles in February and March, Murphy toured Los Angeles in his too-heavy overcoat, an outsider in what eastern journalists had taken to calling the Pastel Empire. Judy accompanied him on one of these trips, for although they were resigned to leaving Kansas, they were both apprehensive about starting life over in a place so different from what they had known.

The UC regents arranged for the Murphys to stay at the elegant Bel Air Hotel, a short drive from the UCLA campus. Its gardens were a dreamscape of tropical vegetation. The faded stucco walls brimmed with magenta bougainvillea, and the grounds were lined with banana trees, giant elephant ears, birds of paradise, and soaring palms. The scent of eucalyptus and jasmine was a welcome contrast to the biting midwinter air of the Great Plains.

Murphy was familiar with the Bob Hope jokes about freeways, traffic, and smog, and he had expected to see orange groves and movie lots, but he was surprised to find that Los Angeles was an industrial center, home to a vast labor force in the defense industries. Southern California was the leading beneficiary of cold war government contracts. Good-paying jobs enticed many former military people as well as eastern blue-collar workers, midwestern farmers, and African American laborers. Immigrants also came from Asia, Central and South America, and Mexico, the latter adding to California's already rich Mexican heritage.[12] White Protestants, however, were in the majority after World War II, and they persisted in thinking of Los Angeles as an Anglo city; in fact, immigration from the Midwest had been so heavy that the city was jokingly called "the Port of Iowa." Murphy's sister, Cordelia, and her husband, Lyman Ennis, were among the newcomer arrivals. After his discharge from the army air corps Lyman became an architect, and the couple built a handsome modern house in Pasadena.

Murphy had read about the idiosyncrasies of Los Angeles and its reputation as a cultural wasteland, but he found it curiously exciting, saying that he glimpsed a postwar city moving forward rapidly and transforming itself with its intellectual vitality. Invited to a dinner party in Beverly Hills, he found himself a guest at the home of the renowned violinist Jascha Heifetz and was captivated by an impromptu classical jam session with Heifetz, the celebrated composer Igor Stravinsky, and the cello virtuoso Gregor Piatigorsky. "We do pretty well, considering we only have local talent," Heifetz told Murphy at the end of the evening.[13] When Murphy related the story years later, he said that with their spirits lifted he and Judy returned to their hotel determined to put their hearts into their future in Los Angeles.

Indeed, as early as his first morning in Los Angeles, at a breakfast meeting with Clark Kerr and Ed Carter in the hotel's sun-drenched courtyard, Murphy had been swept off his feet, he admitted. Kerr and Carter arrived at the hotel in fine spirits and soon caught Murphy up in their celebratory mood. The long-awaited and much-touted Master Plan for Higher Education in California had finally come together, was assured of legislative approval, and would soon be on Governor Edmund Brown's desk for signature.[14]

Murphy knew Kerr from working closely with him at the annual conferences on education sponsored by the Carnegie Foundation. Both men were members of the foundation's board of directors. They shared similar ideas about the role of universities, but in most other respects they were notably different.

Kerr, reserved and soft-spoken, did not look the part of a strong-willed administrator. At forty-nine, he was of medium height, slim, and physically fit. He was bald, except for a rim of closely trimmed brown hair, and at a time when businessmen considered heavy, dark eyeglass frames a statement of power, Kerr wore rimless spectacles. As a former labor negotiator, he had cultivated a patient, low-key approach to administration. Yet Murphy knew his colleague was a superstar of American education, presiding over the nation's largest public university system, which had an annual budget of $450 million.

Murphy was not physically imposing either: he was five feet, eight inches, of average build, with regular features, a receding hairline, and a high forehead. Unlike Kerr, however, he possessed an outgoing manner and energy that drew people to him. He was also notably ambitious. On occasion, he could be brash and pushy, leading inevitably to a collision between the two men.

Their breakfast companion, Ed Carter, was a gregarious man with the double advantage of good looks and exuberant charm. Appointed to the board of regents in 1952 by Governor Earl Warren, Carter currently chaired its all-important Education Policy Committee. The square-jawed, dynamic businessman had made himself a multimillionaire by the age of forty. After graduating from UCLA and the Harvard Business School, he had risen from menswear salesman to president of the Broadway department store chain. During the postwar retailing boom, he had directed expansion into shopping malls to take advantage of the rush to the suburbs.

Kerr's negotiating skills and studied patience lay behind the achievement Carter and Kerr were celebrating: gaining a consensus to reorganize the California college system.[15] The master plan laid out three divisions of higher education in the state—the University of California, a separate state college system, and a network of junior colleges (later called community colleges). The top division, the University of California, would be a constellation of research universities (Berkeley and UCLA being the two major campuses) prepared to receive the upper tier of high school graduates.[16] With the colleges vying for prestige and status, the agreement was likened to a fair trade treaty for higher education. The most impressive part of the new master plan was the guarantee of access to a college education, tuition-free, for all California high school graduates. News of the innovative plan was drawing worldwide attention; no nation had yet attempted such a feat.[17]

Kerr predicted a golden age for U.S. higher education, with California leading the way. The national economy was entering a period of unprecedented prosperity, and funds were flowing to universities, with an added cold war boost in appropriations for science. The university regents had recently obtained legislative approval for construction funds to prepare the campuses for a tsunami in enrollment as the baby boomers reached college age. The university-wide population was expected to double within eight years.[18]

THE THREE POWERFUL SOUTHERN REGENTS

Though as president of the University of California Clark Kerr directed the operations of the multicampus university, three strong-willed Los Angeles regents had virtual veto power over many decisions. They were not only wealthy but also well connected, linked in a network of influence and authority. Edward W. Carter was a charismatic and powerful retail-chain tycoon; Edwin Wendell Pauley, a steadfastly conservative oil millionaire who had been a regent since 1940; and Dorothy Buffum Chandler, an obsessive doyenne, a driving force in the family that owned the Times Mirror Company and the *Los Angeles Times.* In addition to their statewide duties as regents, the three were intent on shaping Los Angeles into a new type of modern city. Murphy would find himself welcomed into their circle, and they would expect a great deal from him in return.

Edward Carter

Carter was the kind of man who was difficult to ignore, running a nationwide retail operation with sales in 1960 of nearly $180 million.[19] His wealth and success enabled him to pursue his grand civic and cultural ambitions. At their breakfast meeting at the Bel Air Hotel, Carter was candid in recounting to Murphy the doleful history of UCLA. It began as a teacher-training school on Vermont Avenue near downtown. In 1919, when adopted into the UC system, it was called the University of California, Southern Branch, and it had continued in that second-class status even after moving in 1929 to a new campus in Westwood. University-wide micromanagement from the Berkeley office of President Robert Gordon Sproul had meant years of stagnation for UCLA. (Sproul served as president from 1930 to 1958.) The Los Angeles regents and the Southern Branch alumni had agitated for greater autonomy, and finally, in 1952, decentralization was officially decreed: the southern campus would be called the University of California at Los Angeles. Its branch status was over, and the initials "UCLA" came into being. Clark Kerr, then a Berkeley faculty member, was named chancellor at Berkeley, and Raymond Allen (former president of the University of Washington) was chosen as UCLA's first chancellor.

Chancellor Kerr had fought strenuously for the promised decentralization, but in Los Angeles Allen had proved weak, much to Carter's exasperation. When Sproul retired in 1958, it was Kerr, not Allen, who was chosen to succeed him as president of the university. Acceding to pressure from Los Angeles, Kerr's first presentation to the board of regents contained language that the southern regents had been waiting to hear: the Berkeley and Los Angeles campuses were to be "comparable in size and have equal opportunities."[20] Carter, who claimed a hand in formulating the statement, wanted Murphy to understand that, as far as the southern regents were concerned, the directive for parity was his mandate.[21] They had waited a long time for UCLA to come into its own and were now determined to see it the equal of UC Berkeley.

The first wave of baby boomers would soon be entering college, and the university system was alarmingly underprepared. The university had seven campuses in 1960 and was hastening to add more.[22] UCLA and Berkeley were to have a maximum of 27,500 students each; the other campuses would pick up the overflow. Murphy was told to expect UCLA's enrollment to reach 27,500 by 1964; he would be under tremendous pressure to get the campus ready.

Carter laid out what the southern regents expected in UCLA's new chancellor: they wanted an administrator who was forward-looking but not problematically liberal, who valued both science and the humanities, and, above all, who could provide the strong leadership that had been lacking. Murphy later recounted that Carter assured him of the regents' full support for a truly distinguished university and also linked the university to the city's cultural venues, confidently predicting that Los Angeles was on the verge of an unprecedented cultural metamorphosis. UCLA, he promised, would be a significant component of the new Los Angeles.

In 1926 the journalist Henry L. Mencken wrote in the *Baltimore Sun*, "There are more morons collected in Los Angeles than in any other place on earth."[23] But now, Carter explained, he and a handful of others were on a crusade to change this assessment. They planned to remove the county's art collection from Exposition Park, where it was incongruously and shabbily exhibited with bones and fossils in a 1911 multipurpose facility—the Museum of History, Science and Art.[24] Such civic shortsightedness about art, Carter thought, had discouraged the oil tycoon J. Paul Getty, who initially gave the county some fine works, including the Ardabil Carpet, a masterpiece of Persian weaving, and Rembrandt's *Portrait of Marten Looten*, painted in 1632. But who would donate another Rembrandt to hang in a gallery displaying a saber-toothed tiger and an antique Pierce-Arrow? Getty chose instead to establish his own museum at his ranch house in Malibu.

In the past eighteen months, Carter reported, he had raised $4.8 million from private donors to build the county's first museum devoted solely to art. A site for the museum on Wilshire Boulevard was already under consideration—a county park located a few blocks west of La Brea Avenue. The Hancock family had donated the twenty-three-acre former oil field to the county for a science reserve, and though its official name—Hancock Park—honored the donors, it was popularly known as the La Brea Tar Pits, a place where the skeletal remains of ice age mammals mired in the tar could be found among the palm trees. Carter needed another $1 million, which he planned to get, if not from a single wealthy donor, then from a public campaign for smaller gifts.[25] In his opinion Los Angeles was ready to spend money on culture. "It is a center of artistic and musical activity, and spending money for their development is a prideful act. Besides, it tends to offset the image that the place is populated largely by kooks."[26] As Murphy listened to Carter's enthusiastic analysis, he was fully persuaded that if Los Angeles indeed was ready, Carter was the personification of that readiness.

Edwin Pauley

Edwin Pauley was the most senior, and the most vocal, member of the board of regents. Now fifty-seven and chairman of the university's board of regents, the wealthy oilman and Democratic Party politico had served as a University of California regent for more than twenty years. He took inordinate pride in the university and spoke of it in a proprietary way. He had been an influential force during the Truman administration both as a Democratic fund-raiser and as a presidential adviser. Pauley was from that patriarchal school of men of wealth and power who took pride in being a man's man, and he had more than a little difficulty accepting Dorothy Chandler as an equal power on the board. Pauley and Chandler were usually on the same side in their demands for recognition of UCLA, but there were other issues on which they sharply differed, and Pauley was known to grow exasperated when Chandler's vote canceled his. He underestimated her savvy; she counted votes ahead of time and then negotiated and bargained; she did not sell her support cheaply and always asked for her quid pro quo.

Kerr's observation of Pauley was that he was "an alpha male, par excellence."[27] The two men were frequently locked in conflict. Their differences began when Pauley, a fervent anti-Communist, had insisted on firing faculty members who refused to sign the prescribed loyalty oath and Kerr, then a professor of industrial relations, had been a forceful member of the faculty committee protesting the firings.[28] But Pauley proved a supportive ally in key moments of the negotiation concerning the Master Plan for Higher Education, and in 1960 the men shared a familiar if uneasy camaraderie.

Pauley had first met Franklin Murphy in May 1955, when Murphy delivered the banquet speech at the Hotel Muehlebach in Kansas City, Missouri, following the groundbreaking for the Truman Presidential Library. Pauley had been impressed by the youthful chancellor's moving tribute to Truman. Pauley was keenly aware of the leadership vacuum that existed at UCLA, and when Kerr reported to the regents that he found Murphy "bright, energetic, and full of ideas," Pauley heartily endorsed Kerr's selection. Murphy "seemed perfect for UCLA," Kerr said at the time.

During one of Murphy's visits to Los Angeles, as Cordie Ennis recalled, her brother was entertained by Pauley, and she and Lyman were invited. Pauley, a bear of a man, shook hands with Lyman and nearly crushed her (very pregnant with her first child) as he put an arm around her. He leaned close and told her that Murphy did not realize what an opportunity they were offering him at UCLA and that he wanted to know why her brother was so "awfully demanding." During dinner, Cordie listened with admiration to her brother's description of his vision for UCLA and noted that he was indeed very specific about what he needed and what he expected as the new chancellor for the Los Angeles campus.

Dorothy Chandler

Dorothy Buffum Chandler, the "Iron Lady," was widely acknowledged to be the most powerful woman in Los Angeles. Vivacious Dorothy Buffum of Long Beach, called "Buff" by her college friends, had married the quietly confident and very handsome young Norman Chandler on August 20, 1922, following their courtship at Stanford University. Norman succeeded his father, Harry Chandler, as publisher of the *Los Angeles Times* as well as chief executive of the Times Mirror Company. The city and the newspaper had long been entwined: inevitably, Norman and Dorothy became catalysts for the city's future, continuing the family's long-standing central role in shaping Los Angeles.[29]

Disciplined and organized, Chandler routinely started her morning with a plunge in the family pool, followed by a check of astrology charts. Dr. Murphy was an Aquarian, she noted. Those born under the sign of the Water Bearer were visionaries and humanitarians, showering the world with ideas. That boded well for the Kansan and for what Chandler expected of him. Aquarians can be inventive and original but also impatient and demanding. That was all right with her; the city needed shaking up.

Chandler, in her late fifties, possessed the spirit, energy, and ambition of a self-confident, savvy power player. She wore only moderate makeup, and her freckles and hazel eyes lent a hint of the pixie to an otherwise commanding appearance. Murphy, aware of his reputation for persuasiveness and his effectiveness with women, was confident he could charm her. What he did not expect was that she would totally charm him.

Chandler had come into her own on the board of the Southern California Symphony Association, a support organization for the Los Angeles Philharmonic Orchestra, and had won the appreciation of music lovers for her campaign to save the city's landmark Hollywood Bowl from financial collapse. The L.A. Philharmonic deserved a home of its own and the city deserved a prestigious concert hall, so she set her mind to building one. After three hard-fought campaigns for bond issues for a civic auditorium and opera house failed, in 1951, 1953, and 1954, she plunged briefly into despair but then became determined to raise private funds. She presented the board of supervisors with a proposal for a music center to be built and operated by a citizens' group on land leased from the county. A square block of land on Bunker Hill, soon to be cleared as part of the city's redevelopment plan, was available. Legislation was required for the lease arrangements and the mixed operation by the county and a private group, but Chandler had the bill drafted and expected to see the measure shortly on the desk of Governor Brown.

For his interview with Chandler, Murphy went to her Hancock Park home, whimsically named "Los Tiempos." In her well-known forthright manner Chandler told Murphy that the former chancellor, Ray Allen, had been a disappointment and that UCLA had suffered as a result. It had been a touchy matter, she confided, but in effect Allen was fired.[30] She told Murphy that he would find her accommodating in granting whatever UCLA needed. Tens of millions of dollars were approved and ready.[31] As chair of the Buildings and Grounds Committee, she was in a position to see that UCLA was not slighted. "All schematics [and] architectural plans come through my committee," she said.

There was an important condition for Chandler's support: UCLA must be brought into community life. She was convinced that the reason for UCLA's past failure to establish ties with the community was a lack of strong leadership.[32] For Dorothy Chandler and Ed Carter, UCLA was a means as well as an end; both wanted UCLA to play an important role in their plans.

Chandler never considered herself a feminist and disliked the term, but she asserted that the talents of women were underrecognized and underutilized. She did not mind if male colleagues called her Buff, but woe betide anyone who called her Buffie. Her own organizational abilities were demonstrated in the Music Center campaign, in which she sought the usual contributions from the area's influential old-money families but also turned to new-money sources in the city's show business Westside and among Jewish business leaders. This alarmed and distressed the old-guard elite, who had resisted community involvement with "movie people" and had quietly excluded Jews from their social life.[33] Chandler explained to Murphy that she had arranged meetings in a private dining room of a Wilshire Boulevard restaurant, since the California Club, the usual downtown meeting place for symphony supporters, denied Jews membership. "I wanted them to join me on the fundraising effort. I wanted them to feel a part of it and welcome on my team," she said. She had her reasons for describing her outreach methods to Murphy; she expected him to do the same. It mattered that UCLA was situated south of Bel Air and west of Beverly Hills, sections of the city with large, affluent Jewish communities.[34]

Chandler's goal for a concert hall was not just to provide good music for Los Angeles but also to resuscitate the heart of the city, the location of significant Chandler-owned real estate. She was working against the tide of the booming postwar economy, which was moving business to the suburban shopping malls. Demographics showed the central city increasingly populated by minorities and the poor while the suburbs were becoming more white and more prosperous.[35] Yet Chandler had an emotional as well as a financial interest in keeping the center strong. Members of the Otis-Chandler family had been major figures in Los Angeles since 1886, when the family patriarch, Harrison Gray Otis, acquired the Times Mirror Company.[36] Much of the character and promise of the city was credited to General Otis, his son-in-law, Harry Chandler, and the subsequent Chandlers. In keeping with this tradition, the *Times* editors threw the newspaper's support behind the extensive plans of the CRA to demolish blighted housing and promote the construction of modern condominiums and office complexes. The newspaper touted, as well, Chandler's plans for the grand concert hall.

As surprised as Murphy was by Chandler's shrewd analysis of her city and its cultural needs, he was even more impressed by her grasp of art and culture as a tool in foreign policy, a concept that Murphy had promoted as a member of Eisenhower's Advisory Commission on Foreign Exchanges.[37] Chandler told Murphy that she had become convinced of the importance of cultural exchange after a trip with her husband to the Soviet Union. In Moscow, civic and social leaders had taken little interest in Norman, the publisher, but they had all wanted to meet her as she was president of the symphony association and a university regent in a state that proposed offering a college education free of tuition. Murphy had returned from his Soviet junket, undertaken at the request of President Eisenhower, with a similar view on cultural exchange. In addition, he urged a policy of broad outreach—much like what later became the Peace Corps—in which Americans would commit to a period of service in underdeveloped countries.[38]

When Chandler mentioned that she had presented her ideas on cultural exchange to a receptive congressional committee, Murphy grasped that he was speaking with someone who not only shared his views but also had the contacts and dedication to make things happen. He later recalled that it was during this conversation that he recognized the potential for a very productive partnership. Chandler could charm and cajole wealthy donors, but when it came to convincing Los Angeles politicians and businessmen of the value of the arts for the city's growth, she was never afforded total credibility. She had pushed gender roles about as far as she could for the era; she was astute enough to know, for example, that however important her ideas were for the Times Mirror Company, she had to put them forward through her husband. In the domain of music and culture that had come to matter to her so deeply, she was in need of a partner; Norman Chandler, fully occupied with Times Mirror, was unavailable.

LURE OF AN ADOLESCENT CITY

After Murphy's final Los Angeles trip, his mood became brighter and his energy returned. During his last weeks in Lawrence, he was in constant motion, handling details and managing affairs in anticipation of the family's exit. As university colleagues came to his office to say good-bye, Murphy sat back in his chair with his arms crossed behind his neck, entertaining the callers with stories of his seduction by Los Angeles. He had come to terms with reality; his idealistic dreams for Mount Oread had ended. Clarke Wescoe, dean of the medical school and an able young administrator whom Murphy had mentored, was named his successor.

Murphy confided to his friend and colleague Robert Vosper that the feud was over, but he would never forgive or forget. He knew Docking would run for reelection in November but hoped his resignation as chancellor would prove the governor's undoing. "He was a very difficult human being," Murphy said. "I really wanted to destroy him in the process of my leaving."[39]

Judy Murphy had been deeply offended by the inflammatory accusations of the governor and uncomfortable with campus divisiveness. She knew that as the university's first lady her role was to "keep smiling . . . regardless of what happens." But frustration had overwhelmed her as she saw her husband ambushed at every turn.[40]

Every newspaper in the region carried accounts of Murphy's departure and recapped the bitter battle with Docking, calling Murphy's resignation a "lamentable loss," a "crying shame," and a "disaster to Kansas education." "There was no better man in American education," declared the *Kansas Star* in a front-page editorial. "The state of Kansas wasn't big enough to appreciate him. We'll never get a man so good."[41]

"It was a bloody tragedy," Vosper said of the turn of events.[42]

In Lawrence, Judy completed the packing and shipped the family's French provincial furniture to Los Angeles. She did her best to prepare the children for the coming change: Joyce and Martha, now college students, would come home for the holidays, not to their familiar home in Kansas, but to California. The two youngest, Franklin Lee and Carolyn, ten and eleven years old, would grow up in a Mediterranean-style mansion on the UCLA campus.

Judy and Franklin made the rounds of farewell parties given in their honor. A special "Letter to Judy Murphy" appeared in the local paper, bidding her adieu and praising her "unaffected manner, genuineness and naturalness."[43] For all the exasperation the couple experienced with the provincialism and isolationist mind-set of the Great Plains, it was where they felt most at home. But the enthusiasm and strong assurances of the powerful regents from Los Angeles had erased any lingering doubts about the decision to leave. "Almost from the beginning," Murphy wrote Ed Carter weeks before his departure, "my only hesitancy in the matter came out of the question as to whether I would really have the local administrative authority and flexibility to do the kind of strong and sound administrative job that quite obviously UCLA now requires." He added that his wife felt the same. "Judy, in effect, said that she was not only satisfied that she would be given the tools which she needs to do her part of the job, but she said that it would be almost impossible to turn down the opportunity of working under the influence of a person such as yourself."[44]

Although Murphy was satisfied with his decision, several Ivy League colleagues warned him that this UCLA post could ruin a brilliant career. Harold Dobbs, president of Princeton University, and Henry Wriston, recently retired as president of Brown University, urged him not to take the chancellorship of a *branch* campus of the University of California.[45] They said he would be ground like glass by the statewide administration at Berkeley and brought to his knees by a fractious and bitter Los Angeles faculty.

In spite of the well-meaning advice, Murphy was drawn to Los Angeles. He perceived the California mind-set as progressive and upbeat; he felt he and Judy would be warmly welcomed into Los Angeles's social circles. He had a vision of the city as a great new center of education and culture that in ten years would reach parity with the East. He predicted that his new campus in Los Angeles would someday emerge as the western anchor of a new East-West collegiate axis.[46]

· · · · ·

What was not apparent to Murphy in his early enthusiasm was that the same provincialism and disinclination to spend money on culture that George Docking exploited in Kansas had scarred Los Angeles as well. Early city planning for cultural venues and parklands had been cast aside as city leaders focused on industry and land development. At the time of Murphy's arrival, Los Angeles could boast of only a handful of cultural amenities. It was not just that the symphony orchestra lacked a proper concert hall and the county's art collection a proper museum; the large downtown public library was underfunded and short on books for the serious scholar. The University of Southern California (USC) was dismissively referred to as the University for Spoiled Children. Across town, the struggling UCLA was still thought of as an outpost of "Cal," the fabled campus of the north. Occidental College and the California Institute of Technology (Caltech), distinguished but small, commanded only perfunctory attention from city leaders who served as trustees on their boards.

Murphy attributed Los Angeles's cultural deficiencies to its status as an adolescent city, as Carter had described it, and it would be many years before he would realize that certain systemic factors, hard to overcome, had slowed the city's cosmopolitan development. Some of these factors were hinted at by scholars who had probed the region's history. In the first serious study of the California psyche, written in 1886, the philosopher Josiah Royce found not only promising vigor but also moral ambiguity and much to question in the founding of California, with its wild mix of individualism, spirituality, materialism, greed, and violence.[47] More than half a century later, Carey McWilliams, in his 1946 volume, *Southern California: An Island on the Land,* analyzed the much talked of "exceptionalism" of Los Angeles and examined the myths that the city harbored about itself. McWilliams found that the region's claim of openness and tolerance was contradicted by its history of race and class segregation and by orchestrated hostility to organized labor.[48]

The Pastel Empire was a city famously built on illusion. It advertised itself as tropical, when it was actually a semiarid coastal plain. By the 1950s the iconic orange groves featured on its postcards were not prized at all but were being bulldozed to make way for housing tracts.[49] City leaders boasted about the natural environment—that was their hook—but systematically favored the built over the unbuilt. As a result, the city that lacked museums also lacked public parks, scenic boulevards, and dedicated open space.[50]

Because Los Angeles had left its planning and growth to private developers, it was a fragmented city that came of age in the postwar period, unsure of its identity and confused as to its responsibilities. Still, Los Angeles was positioned favorably for the future. Even McWilliams admitted in the closing pages of his revealing work that Los Angeles was strategically located and had the potential to become the "great city of the Pacific," indeed, "the most fantastic city in the world."[51]

· · · · ·

To accommodate the postwar population boom, housing tracts extended in all directions, including to the San Fernando Valley, which was within the broad confines of the city limits. In an unincorporated section on the southern perimeter of Los Angeles, three land developers, Mark Taper, Louis Boyar, and Ben Weingart, set out to turn endless acres of beet fields into the largest suburban housing development in the nation—the biggest in the world, *Time* magazine said.[52] Lakewood was designed to be a self-contained community for seventy-five thousand people, with one hundred homes a day completed in the first phase of breakneck construction.[53] Two hundred sixty-four acres of the tract were given over to a shopping center and its immense, paved parking lot.

Workers at the nearby Douglas and Hughes aircraft plants and at the Long Beach Naval Shipyard queued up immediately, eager to purchase homes in the new, all-white, planned community. Taper called the tract an opportunity for blue-collar workers to become "enthusiastic owners of property" and thus "owners of a piece of their country."[54] Southern California tract developers liked to point out that they were creating Americans resistant to Communist propaganda, secure in their enclaves, bound by their mortgages. A mile-long delivery tunnel below the shopping mall was designated a Civil Defense fallout shelter, though in truth Lakewood, surrounded by defense plants and naval bases, was a potential ground zero. A twenty-megaton fusion bomb dropped on the military installations would leave no one alive in Lakewood.[55] It was not surprising that a survey of national attitudes found Southern Californians more worried about nuclear attack and more preoccupied with bomb shelters than other Americans.[56]

In spite of the tall stanchions bearing air raid sirens positioned among the palm trees along the city's boulevards, Murphy was hardly aware during his visit of the extent of cold war anxiety; to the contrary, he found a hearty optimism among civic leaders. The defense contracts that subjected the region to the threat of attack also contributed to the vibrancy of the local economy and created the opportunity for long-neglected development.

Murphy's conversations with Clark Kerr, Ed Carter, and Dorothy Chandler convinced him of the depth of the Southland's potential and the energy of its architects of education, art, and culture. "In Los Angeles, things will always need doing, things will always need to be made better," Chandler said.[57]

Chandler would prove a powerful ally in the years to come. Murphy would learn the intricacies of wealth that came from sources that had been totally foreign to him up to now: instead of the agrarian economy of Kansas, with its wheat fields and stockyards, it was oil, transportation, and land development that built great fortunes in Los Angeles, with additional roads to wealth from finance and the defense industry. In league with Dorothy Chandler, Murphy would have ready access to the secrets of the city. As Chandler once confided to him, she knew where the bodies were buried.[58]

• • • • •

While the Murphys were packing up the contents of their Lawrence home, Governor Brown signed the enabling legislation for construction of the Music Center, marking the last hurdle in Dorothy Chandler's two-decade effort. Murphy dictated a letter of congratulation. "Bravo!" he wrote Chandler. "I hope that I may be able to help in some small way to bring this important project to final reality."[59]

By the time the letter reached Los Angeles, Chandler had already hosted a press conference announcing details of the construction plan. Photographers and reporters crowded about as she and the architect, Welton Beckett, offered the first drawings of what promised to be "one of the greatest auditoriums in the world," in effect, three venues in one, meeting requirements for symphony concerts, world-class opera, and ballet. Becket said it was the most complex architectural problem he had ever undertaken.[60]

The county board of supervisors had agreed in 1959 to set aside six and a half acres adjacent to the Bunker Hill redevelopment project as the center's planned site. By spring 1960, as the self-appointed chairman of the Building Fund Committee, Chandler had collected more than $4 million in private donations. The county supervisors agreed to underwrite the remaining $6 million cost under a lease-back arrangement that permitted construction financing from private sources. Upon expiration of the lease, the Music Center would be publicly owned.[61]

Chandler provided to reporters a long list of her "Founder Members," those who had made generous donations. Chandler was well pleased, though the moment had been long in coming. "We have fulfilled our promise to the county of Los Angeles," Chandler told reporters. "We can start digging."[62]

THE INVESTITURE OF OTIS CHANDLER

An event that would be pivotal to Murphy's future took place in the interim between his acceptance of the chancellorship and his arrival in Los Angeles. Dorothy and Norman Chandler announced the installation of their son, Otis Chandler, as publisher of the *Los Angeles Times,* a milestone that Dorothy called the most important day of her life. The invitation sent to eight hundred guests read: "Come to the Biltmore Bowl Auditorium April 11, 1960, for an announcement of great importance." The leading figures of California—governor, mayors, legislators, county supervisors, business tycoons, and bankers—were invited, but no one, including Times Mirror executives, "knew what was in store."[63]

Inside the elegant Biltmore Bowl behind the speaker's platform were hung enormous black-and-white photographs of the four successive *Times* buildings—the bronze eagle dating from 1886 perched on the parapet of each succeeding building, wings spread and claws extended. *Times* columnist Bill Henry, whose tenure had begun in the days of General Harrison Gray Otis, ambled to the podium. In lighthearted, voluble remarks, he described General Otis with his thick mustache, goatee, and military bearing, who arrived in Los Angeles after the Civil War, entered into the newspaper business, and set about to turn the small dusty town with a part-time river into a thriving metropolis.[64] By the time of his death, Los Angeles had a teeming population, an amazing two-hundred-fifty-mile aqueduct bringing water from the Sierra Nevada snowmelt, and a harbor at San Pedro. The *Times* building was wrecked in 1910 by a bomb planted during a labor dispute, but the eagle was still on the parapet when the smoke cleared.

Bill Henry introduced the political editor, Kyle Palmer, who paid tribute to the general's successor, his son-in-law, Harry Chandler. Chandler advertised the city as a sun-drenched paradise, and as Palmer proudly pointed out, he was resolute in promoting conservative Republican leadership, quashing union organizing, and maintaining Los Angeles as an open-shop town. Unlike General Otis, who drove about in a black town car with a cannon mounted on the hood, Chandler kept a low profile: he was the able strategist of the Otis-Chandler dynasty.

The audience then gave a warm welcome to Norman Chandler, current *Times* publisher and eldest son of Harry Chandler. Norman was a strong executive and an authoritative voice in the business community. He told the audience that it had been his wish that they all be part of "this historic day." After a brief account of memorable moments in his thirty-eight years with the *Times,* he described the qualifications of the individual who was to succeed him as publisher. Then he abruptly announced, "I hereby appoint, effective as of this minute, Otis Chandler to the position of publisher of the *Los Angeles Times,* the fourth in its seventy-nine-year history."[65]

There was a missing beat as the audience took in the announcement, then loud and prolonged applause. Once the crowd settled down, Chandler related his son's steady, behind-the-scenes preparation for the position, his education at Stanford, and his seven-year apprenticeship during which he worked in each of the newspaper's departments. Chandler turned to address the tall, ramrod-straight young man seated at a table in the audience: "Otis, as my successor and as my son, I say to you—you are assuming a sacred trust and grave responsibilities. I have the utmost confidence that you will never falter in fulfilling these obligations. This trust is dearer than life itself."[66]

Otis Chandler, thirty-two, six feet, two inches, blond and suntanned— every inch the athlete—came forward to the microphone, took a deep breath, and said, "Wow!" In assuming his role as publisher, he followed, in direct descent, his father, Norman Chandler; his grandfather, Harry Chandler; and his great-grandfather, General Harrison Gray Otis.[67]

The moment was the fruition of Dorothy Chandler's hopes for her son and a turning point in the history of the Times Mirror Company. The rigid conservatism of the *Times* and its provincialism—there were no foreign bureaus and scant coverage outside of Los Angeles—were an embarrassment and a poor image for the booming city. The younger, more educated workforce of the future expected a newspaper of quality and substance. Norman Chandler had been stretched thin by his dual role as publisher of the *Times* and chairman and chief executive of the Times Mirror Company. He was shrewd in expanding and diversifying the company, but he had let the paper take care of itself. Dorothy pointed out that he could not both revamp the newspaper and run a corporation the size of Times Mirror. "For Norman's sake and for the sake of the *Times* which I cared so much about,

I had to push him. I did it with love, but I had to do it," she said about the change in leadership.[68]

Otis Chandler shared the far-reaching and ambitious plans that his mother and father had for Los Angeles—and for the *Times*. "A newspaper must be the image of a man, whether you agree with him or not," his father told the press following the banquet. That image belonged now to the Chandler heir. Franklin Murphy's first years in Los Angeles would coincide with the transformation of the *Times,* as the Chandler family readied the newspaper for the Los Angeles of the future. Murphy would soon join the Chandlers in bringing that future to fruition.

TWO

UCLA in Worldwide Terms

THE MURPHY FAMILY PULLED INTO the driveway of the chancellor's residence on the UCLA campus after midnight on July 1, 1960, at the end of a long, hot drive from Kansas. The house was dark, and there was no key. Furious, Murphy walked the campus in the moonlight until he found a security guard to unlock the door.

The red-brick Mediterranean villa was empty except for a piano and several abandoned mattresses. The electricity was working, but there was no hot water: a minor earthquake had knocked out the gas. The exhausted family slept in their traveling clothes and were awakened early by the ear-splitting sirens of fire trucks racing up the driveway to fight a brushfire on the hillside. In the morning light they set out to explore their new surroundings.

· · · · ·

The central quadrangle at UCLA, occupied by four Romanesque buildings of the original 1929 campus, was the result of a land developer's fantasy. The largely rural west side of the city was the prefecture of the Janss family, astute subdividers who designated the low rolling hills for affluent residential tracts. They offered an elevated, flat plateau for the new campus on condition of compatibility with their plans. The regents instructed the architects to create the ambience of a hillside university town so as to provide a fitting "European" view for the future upscale homes. The twin towers of Royce Hall, clad in construction scaffolding, were soon visible from miles around. Murphy saw in the grand hall and its graceful arches and arcades an evocation of the sixteenth century; he pictured students in their scholars' gowns gathered in animated groups participating in the Renaissance version of a "marketplace of ideas," a concept he would often invoke to describe the purpose of a university.

The campus was meant to be just such a distinct place, accorded elite status, tolerated, but separate from the community. Originally, access across a steep arroyo to the campus was by means of a bridge that, with its arched supports and fine brickwork, looked as though it too had come from Lombardy. The library, opposite Royce Hall, added a Spanish-Moorish touch to the Romanesque with an octagonal tiled dome. As time went by, intellectual change came to UCLA's quadrangle, and the optimistic faith of Josiah Royce, honored in the naming of Royce Hall, was displaced by student fascination with the existentialists. The fanciful bridge disappeared—buried when the arroyo was filled to make space for construction. By the time Murphy arrived, students strolled down the roadbed that crossed Dickson Plaza and rendezvoused at the flagpole with no idea they were walking across a buried bridge. The rolling, chaparral-covered foothills of the Santa Monica Mountains, inspiration for the school song, "Hail to the Hills of Westwood," had become the landscaped estates of Bel Air, Westwood Hills, and Holmby Hills.

When the Southern Branch, as UCLA was known in its early days, moved to its Romanesque quadrangle in 1929, it was a four-year college. Graduate studies were not authorized by the regents until 1933, and doctoral degrees were not awarded until 1936. The liberal campus counted among its students residents of the city's ethnic neighborhoods: the offspring of immigrant parents, a large contingent of Jews, and a few African Americans. Conservative citizen-watchdogs in the 1930s, who found the professors too liberal and ethnic inclusiveness an invitation to subversion, called UCLA "the little red schoolhouse" and Westwood, "Moscow by the Sea."

Beginning with the postwar hunt for Communists that lasted well into the 1950s, UCLA was repeatedly investigated by the state legislature's Un-American Activities Committee and subjected to public outcries for closer supervision by UC authorities and the board of regents. When Murphy took charge in 1960, the loyalty oath controversy had not been forgotten; in addition, research universities, in general, were subjected to scrutiny after the Soviets launched Sputnik in 1957. Murphy, not familiar with the history of UCLA, could not know how much the weight of its past would bear on its future and impinge on his plans.

Murphy had thought through his strategy and had his goals firmly in mind well before he arrived at the chancellor's residence. He had identified the critical elements needed at UCLA: it must be treated on par financially with UC Berkeley; it must obtain a unique identity; and—no small matter—it had to be tied more closely to the city of Los Angeles. He had noted Dorothy Chandler's concern in the last regard, and he was sure he could satisfy her by building community pride in UCLA and attracting financial support. He visualized UCLA as a prestigious institution and himself as well rewarded. If the previous chancellor had played his cards right, he might have been university president instead of Kerr.

Murphy was to administer 1,900 faculty members in 61 departments in 12 schools and colleges. He planned to use the summer to gather data to prepare UCLA for parity with Berkeley, to set his goals, and to draft budgets. He expected the current annual budget of $31 million to be increased to a figure comparable to that of the northern campus, but when he fired off a request for budget and planning information, he found his inquiry strangely ignored. He knew from his previous experience at the University of Kansas how important a top-notch library is to achieving the rank of a university of distinction, so he especially wanted information about the status of Berkeley's library and plans for its future. He was infuriated that even his query about the number of books the library held went unanswered.

Murphy soon perceived a system of overt control and a deliberate desire "up there" to keep Berkeley's "little sister" from getting too big and gaining strength and visibility.[1] When he brought the matter to the attention of Clark Kerr, knowing Kerr's enthusiasm for the master plan, he was baffled by Kerr's lack of interest. Murphy also found that he was being monitored in his UCLA office by President Kerr. He discovered that his secretary, fifty-four-year-old Hansena Frederickson, an organized and meticulous worker, also served as secretary to Kerr. He exploded, furious that his secretary's dual role made her nothing less than a spy for Berkeley. Only after his adamant protests was she relieved of her double duties.

Frederickson, in an oral history years later, recalled that Murphy summoned her to his office and explained that he would like her to stay on. "I have to tell you something, though," he confessed. "I have an awful temper. I'll yell at you and I'll throw things, but it won't be against you. It will be over in five minutes, and if you think you can take this, great." Frederickson agreed, and the two shook hands. On her first full day working with him, she discovered the new chancellor was a "cyclone." Frederickson, who in her thirty-two years at UCLA had assisted thirteen campus officers and observed many working styles, described Murphy as astounding in the amount of work he could move across his desk. She made sure he had a cup of coffee at his elbow and a cigarette within reach at all times. "When he wants to do something, he wants to do it right now. He can't wait." But when he got mad, she added, "he *really* got mad."[2] The discovery that most shocked Murphy was that he did not have full authority over faculty appointments, physical planning, budget allocation, research funds, and other key aspects of academic planning—all operational aspects that he controlled as chancellor at the University of Kansas.

While Franklin Murphy was engaged in a war with the statewide administration, Judy Murphy confronted her own problems on the home front. She was dismayed to find the university residence in shambles, with torn draperies and worn carpeting. Even the Murphys' furniture from their home in Kansas failed to provide familiarity and warmth, given the depressing state of the house. The previous chancellor's wife had painted everything gray, including the library paneling and the piano. Frederickson confided to Judy that Chancellor and Mrs. Allen had not entertained well (they did not serve cocktails) and were not popular with the faculty. Judy hoped to make the Murphys a welcome part of the UCLA family, but at one point she felt so overwhelmed that she retreated to the bathroom, exhausted and in tears. Given the difficulties they both were facing, Judy asked her husband, "Franklin, do you think we made the right choice?"[3]

That summer, as Franklin Murphy's frustration built over the situation at UCLA, another event revived unhappy thoughts of Kansas. Los Angeles's movers and shakers had lobbied long and hard to host the 1960 Democratic National Convention in the newly constructed Los Angeles Memorial Sports Arena.[4] Ed Pauley, one of the leading committeemen of the national Democratic Party, had played a key role in delivering the convention, the first ever held in Los Angeles. The tumultuous, fast-paced convention turned disconcerting for Murphy, however, when the Kansas delegation offered his nemesis, George Docking, as a favorite-son candidate.

On July 15 the nation watched as John F. Kennedy, senator from Massachusetts, was enthusiastically nominated on the first ballot. Kennedy then turned to the southern political giant Lyndon B. Johnson to add balance to the ticket.[5] Docking was dropped from national consideration, and later he would lose reelection in Kansas.

The Murphys found themselves in a bind. Murphy was feeling as dead in the water at UCLA as he had felt in his last years at KU. He was not inclined to eat crow and return to the Midwest after having made such an issue of the enlightened support for higher education in California. Equally embarrassing would be admitting to his Ivy League colleagues that they had been right to warn him against the UCLA chancellorship. He and Judy struggled to think through the problem to determine what was best for the family and for Franklin's career. They decided to stay at UCLA but with a firm condition: Murphy would demand—in no uncertain terms—that Kerr and the regents give him the tools and the authority he had been promised. In keeping with this resolve, Murphy sent a reasonable but insistent letter to Kerr requesting funds for the chancellor's mansion. The Murphys were not to live like poor relatives in the UC family.[6]

It infuriated Murphy every time he called his office and heard the operator announce, "University of California, *Los Angeles Branch.*" In short order he instructed the campus operators to say instead, "Thank you for calling UCLA." "From now on out," Murphy told his staff, "everything around here is UCLA. We will make those four letters just as visible and indelible as MIT."[7] When a Berkeley administrator complained, Murphy snapped, "I authorized it. And make it quite clear to everybody up there that if I can't authorize the telephone operators to identify the institution, I sure as hell shouldn't stay at UCLA because it would be my belief that my authority is zero." Almost overnight, stationery, signs, and campus vehicles were inscribed with a new insignia: the four block letters "UCLA."[8]

•　•　•　•　•

The summer's political conventions and the election campaigns would prove a critical part of Murphy's introduction to the way things operated in Southern California, affording him direct insight into the role of the Chandlers and the *Times.* Arriving delegates to the Democratic convention had been impressed by the new 16,700-seat sports arena but were not charmed by the welcome from the *Los Angeles Times.* "We are Republicans over here on First Street," a front-page editorial announced. "We're Glad You Came," editors declared in a bold headline but added: "In a few more days the Republicans in Chicago will nominate their man and we think they will choose their best one—Richard Nixon."[9] The newspaper continued its hearty endorsement of Nixon throughout the campaign, but the year 1960 marked the end of the Kyle Palmer era. The political editor, known widely as the kingmaker, was forced into reluctant retirement. Otis

Chandler was determined to apply journalistic standards to all reporting and leave behind the paper's ultraconservative past.[10]

Murphy struggled to establish his authority and create an effective relationship with the administration up north. Unhappily, his investiture on September 23, 1960, in the courtyard of the Dickson Art Building turned out to be a disorganized, badly handled event, one from which university president Clark Kerr was mysteriously absent.[11] Pauley hurriedly presided in Kerr's place, and Murphy's longtime friend Lee A. DuBridge, president of Caltech, obliged as the keynote speaker. A thrown-together buffet luncheon at the Bel Air Hotel after the ceremony was, Murphy said, the worst social occasion he had ever attended. "I don't give a damn personally—but for the image of this institution," Murphy said. "You know, this is not a little two-bit cow college." He insisted that if UCLA was to gain respect, the ceremonies and formalities of the academic world had to be taken seriously.[12]

At the inaugural ceremony, Murphy delivered a strong speech putting forward an ambitious vision for both UCLA and the city of Los Angeles. "My intention," he told the crowd, "is to build an institution of scholarly distinction in worldwide terms."[13] But despite the respectful applause, the chancellor received scant encouragement. In its description of Murphy's later career, *Time* magazine said that his initial plans were ambitious enough for an Ivy League school but were dismissed at the time as an impossible dream for a "soporific commuter college."[14]

TAKING COMMAND: HAIL TO THE HILLS OF WESTWOOD

Murphy's administrative style relied heavily on delegating responsibility; he believed that talented people like accountability. He appointed Foster Sherwood, a respected political science professor and chair of the academic senate, to serve as his administrative vice-chancellor. Sherwood, in his late forties, was respected by the faculty and knew the university and its operations. "He could keep me from . . . the sand traps and quicksand of the [academic] senate," Murphy acknowledged.[15]

His next move was to find an administrative deputy, a troubleshooter. His first pick was a disaster, someone who backed down in any conflict with Kerr or the statewide administration, telling Murphy there was no point in fighting since they couldn't win. After a few weeks Murphy fired him. He then met and recruited Charles "Chuck" Young, who worked in the president's office. Young was in his late twenties, a graduate of UCLA, a quick thinker, and a fast-paced manager. Murphy liked a no-news-is-good-news mode of operation, and Young could take an assignment and run with it. Recruiting Young proved a godsend. "I could communicate what I was interested in—in less than a sentence—almost with a look or gesture," Murphy said.[16] Soon, Murphy promoted him to assistant chancellor.

The third player on Murphy's administrative team was William "Bill" G. Young, a nationally known chemist, who served as Murphy's vice-chancellor of planning. Young, in his early fifties, could appear inarticulate and unfocused, but behind the scenes he was a dogged administrator who achieved spectacular results. It would fall to Bill Young to supervise the countless details connected with the campus expansion: dozens of new buildings, including an expanded medical school, as well as new roads and parking facilities—all told, a doubling of the university's physical plant. One essential component of construction was the provision for fallout shelters, the design requirement of the cold war. Young coordinated the work with the supervising architect, Welton Beckett, known as the "draftsman of modern Los Angeles," who had shaped much of the postwar cityscape.[17]

Murphy was well pleased with his administrative setup: with Foster Sherwood handling academic issues, Chuck Young taking care of administrative details, and Bill Young supervising new construction and university facilities, Murphy was free to focus on the larger elements of his plan.[18] He assigned himself the job of projecting UCLA's presence in the community, establishing an image of UCLA in the minds of the regents, and carrying the UCLA message head-on to Berkeley. Murphy was not about to seclude himself behind his desk in the chancellor's office; he was UCLA's traveling chamber of commerce.

The $120 million construction project taking place at UCLA, which it was now Murphy's responsibility to complete, was the largest educational building program in the nation's history.[19] Harking back to earlier centuries was no longer in vogue; intricate, red-brick masonry was out of style. White stucco, reinforced concrete, and industrial ceramic tile were favored—"the architecture of today" was the catchphrase. The pride of the campus would be a new $3.5 million graduate research library designed in the international style. An eleven-story social sciences building was to be the tallest structure on campus, elevated by engineering ingenuity on stilts two stories high to afford a dramatic thoroughfare to North Campus's garden court. North Campus was the domain of the humanities; the sciences occupied South Campus, which also was invaded by giant construction cranes. At the developing medical school, brick continued to be used as a building material but in a utilitarian, unadorned style.

· · · · ·

The fall semester coincided with the tumult of the presidential campaign. The *Los Angeles Times* endorsement of Nixon was expected, but there were other, surprising supporters—extremists whom Murphy took to be part of the "kook element" that Ed Carter deplored—who mounted a campaign of attacks against Democratic nominee John F. Kennedy. This ultra-right-wing faction, largely centered in Orange County and led by the John Birch Society, claimed Kennedy's election would mean the triumph of "collectivism" and a yielding to the Communists.[20]

Murphy attributed the red-baiting to campaign excess and was surprised that the rhetoric continued when the election was over. After a John Birch Society spokesperson claimed that Communists recruited many of their members from American college campuses, educators warned one another to be alert to Birch surveillance. (At the University of Texas, administrators discovered that a student cadre of the local John Birch Society was secretly taping professors' lectures and "tabulating subversion.")[21] When Murphy saw letters to the campus newspaper, the *Daily Bruin,* from Birchers taking issue with UCLA student editors, it reinforced his suspicion that UCLA was on their watch list.[22]

The ultraconservatives railed against foreign aid and cultural exchanges, but Murphy welcomed Kennedy's internationalism and his plans for the Peace Corps. When Kennedy asked him to serve on the President's Education Advisory Council, Murphy readily accepted, despite the fact that he was a registered Republican and had voted for Nixon.[23]

· · · · ·

With the battle for parity between the Los Angeles and Berkeley campuses under way, Murphy shared his strategic vision with Sherwood, Young, and Young, who took on their counterparts in Berkeley and fought as hard as he did.[24] The UCLA library became the focal point of Murphy's demand for the promised parity with Berkeley. He reiterated that equity between the two schools should not be at the expense of Berkeley but that the regents must fight to get additional resources. Murphy persuaded Robert Vosper, after his decade of accomplishment in Kansas, to pack up his household and return to Los Angeles to succeed UCLA's longtime librarian, Lawrence Clark Powell. At UCLA Murphy and Vosper continued to share their fanatical interest in books. As the two men pored over rare book catalogs together, Vosper chewed on his pipestem with slow deliberation while the high-energy, chain-smoking chancellor anxiously scanned the listings for prized volumes. Murphy was determined to expand the library from 1.5 million to 3 million volumes, which would make it one of America's major research facilities.[25] Once the new University Research Library on North Campus was completed, the original library building on the quadrangle was to be turned into an undergraduate library.[26]

After months of fruitless effort to get the facts and figures he wanted, Murphy felt he was forced to step outside customary channels. Soon, to Kerr's fury, Murphy began briefing the southern regents directly. By this time many regents had become Murphy's social friends. He played golf with Phil Boyd, a businessman; he had breakfasts with John E. Canaday, vice president of Lockheed Aircraft; and he socialized frequently with Ed Carter, Ed Pauley, and Dorothy Chandler.

Hansena Frederickson was helpful to Murphy as he built his personal network with the powerful university board. She took pride in the fact that she could reach any regent on Murphy's behalf almost immediately. Murphy was not inclined to obsequiousness, and when the situation warranted he could be extremely forceful, even belligerent. Frederickson said that she heard Murphy speaking sternly to the regents on more than one occasion. "Every time something was frustrated that he was aiming for, he would call up one of the regents, and he would *shout* over the phone at them," she said.[27]

Murphy accepted that taking his problems to the regents would alienate Kerr. He believed in administrative loyalty and chain of command, but he broke his own management rules. "I knew this was a dangerous game to play," he admitted.[28]

· · · · ·

On October 17, 1960, the lean, studious face of Clark Kerr with his rimless spectacles graced the cover of *Time* magazine. The lengthy cover story recounted California's educational goals and lauded Kerr as the "Master Planner." *Time* writers sketched Kerr's biography from farm boy with a college-educated but contrarian father to college at Swarthmore (A.B., 1932) and graduate study at Stanford University (M.A., 1933), and the University of California (Ph.D. in economics, 1939). His career as a respected labor negotiator was described, as well as his fast rise from Berkeley professor to president of the statewide university system. Although several column inches were given to predictions for the University of California, with Berkeley to have "more graduate students and an even more luminous faculty," nothing was said about plans for a magnificent university at UCLA—

the very reason Murphy thought he was brought to Los Angeles. Berkeley was represented as "the Buckingham Palace of Clark Kerr's empire"; Murphy was not mentioned.[29]

Conflict quickly arose when the man praised as the most prominent and effective figure in American education was faced with the "tantrums" of a defiant young chancellor challenging his authority. In one effort to maintain order, Kerr established a new rule that no chancellor could speak to a regent without his direct permission. Kerr's decree infuriated Murphy, reminding him of George Docking's refusal to allow him to talk to legislators. Murphy, in describing the incident, said he asked Kerr, "Are you saying that if they ask me about this or that or the other thing about UCLA, I'm to say, 'I'm sorry, you'll have to talk to Clark Kerr'?"

"Yes," Kerr said.

"If that's to be the policy," Murphy replied, "I'll have to tell you in advance I can't abide by it."[30]

Kerr, who remembered the conflict somewhat differently, described Murphy as paranoid and needing total control. "Without it," Kerr said, "Franklin felt threatened." Kerr said he found Murphy energetic and well organized, but inevitably he "challenged all authority but his own." As a former labor negotiator, Kerr was accustomed to complex discussions with results achieved step by step; Murphy's impatience, stubbornness, and vitriol were hard for him to understand. "I gave him the chance to take over one of the greatest universities in the world," Kerr said later, "and Franklin gave me nothing but antagonism."[31]

· · · · ·

With a budget approved for the chancellor's house and funds in hand, Judy set to work to have the grim paint stripped from the woodwork and the heavy drapes pulled down. With the help of a decorator from Cannell & Chaffin, she designed a warm, attractive home for the family and a gracious setting for entertaining. She settled her family into their routine: her youngest child, Franklin Lee, now ten, was enrolled at the University Elementary School; Carolyn, twelve, would be a seventh-grader at the Marlborough School; and Martha, seventeen, would leave for Stanford in the fall. Joyce, already eighteeen, had completed her first year at Bryn Mawr and would return as a sophomore in September. Also living in the chancellor's residence were the Murphys' two cocker spaniels, Toasty and Klinker.

The household was completed when Willia and Ted Roberts arrived from Lawrence. Willia had worked for Judy's parents from the time Judy was eighteen months old, and after World War II, when Franklin and Judy returned to Kansas City with their toddlers, Willia permanently joined their household. At UCLA Ted Roberts would serve as houseman and part-time driver, and the couple would live in the service apartment of the big brick house. Willia was the director-general of the house and strict with the children. Ted was more of a fun-loving conspirator with the youngsters, secretly meeting Franklin Lee after school to drive him home when his father said he was to walk.

Young Franklin took to his new surroundings and enjoyed jungle games with new friends, playing among the 48 species of trees and more than 125 varieties of plants on the grounds. It was an outdoor world that he would remember nostalgically years later. As Murphy knew would happen, his two youngest children came to associate their childhood with their Los Angeles home and recalled little of Kansas. Judy took up her demanding duties and managed to cope with grace and skill in a city completely new to her, one known for its bewildering individuality and progressive lifestyle.

After meeting the Chandlers, Judy realized that she and Franklin were expected to become more than university chancellor and wife. They were to help orchestrate the cultural and educational evolution of Los Angeles. She was impressed by Dorothy and Norman Chandler as a working team, deeply involved with their city. Though she had been apprehensive about meeting Los Angeles's most powerful woman, Dorothy had put her at ease; in fact, Judy discovered Dorothy could be absent-minded. She had a favorite piece of jewelry, a silver ID bracelet with "Buff" set in diamonds across a hinged top and a rolled up $100 bill inside, because, she admitted, "I sometimes forget to take money."[32]

· · · · ·

In March 1961 a controversial exposé of the John Birch Society was published in the *Los Angeles Times.* For some readers it was a startling revelation of extremism in their midst, but others saw it as a radical attack on traditional values and suspected it was Communist inspired. The more conservative members of the Chandler clan were outraged over the series and demanded the removal of Otis Chandler as publisher.

The series, written by Gene Blake, quoted liberally from the writing of Robert Welch, the retired Massachusetts businessman who founded the organization in 1958. Blake obtained a copy of Welch's privately circulated tract, "The Politician," in which Welch wrote: "In my opinion, the chances are very strong that Milton Eisenhower is actually Dwight Eisenhower's superior and boss within the Communist Party."[33]

Blake described the society—several thousand members, expected to reach one hundred thousand by the end of the year, with a goal of one million—as tightly controlled and disciplined. Small groups met in private homes for instructions on assignments that included taking over their local PTAs, establishing front organizations, disrupting civic meetings (by sharpening the "mean and dirty" question technique), threatening lawsuits (great for publicity), and bombarding the city council, newspaper editors, broadcasters, and theater managers with letter-writing campaigns.[34]

At the conclusion of the series, after fifteen thousand canceled subscriptions and a week of calls and letters accusing the *Times* of selling out to the left,[35] Otis Chandler set the record straight in an editorial. "The *Times* believes implicitly in the conservative philosophy," he wrote. But he insisted that by sowing suspicion and mistrust—using the Communists' methods—the John Birch Society did no credit to the conservative cause. "Subversion of the left or the right is still subversion."[36]

Murphy had suffered at the hands of ultraconservatives in Kansas and was pleased to see the Birchers taken to task, but the exposé did little to disenchant the organization's members. Birchers believed that traditional values and family structure were imperiled by pornography, sex education, school integration, liberal theology, and do-gooders in a Communist plan to weaken the moral fiber of the country. In the struggle against Communism, they set the battlefield as the domestic arena and claimed international negotiation for coexistence was a dangerous distraction. Murphy was familiar with the old-fashioned Taft-style, noninterventionist isolationism expounded in the Midwest, but the West Coast brand was unique in that it hyped military supremacy. Southern Californians, with their economy tied to the defense industry, were inclined to focus on weaponry as the means to their peace of mind.[37]

On campus, students who had grown up with duck-and-cover drills and the fear of imminent nuclear attack were moving into adulthood, questioning the cold war policies of the preceding generation and scrutinizing the civil rights hypocrisy of their elders. The first of the lunch counter sit-ins had occurred in North Carolina in February the previous year and provided the inspiration for UCLA students to look at merchant and landlord discrimination in Westwood. Murphy agreed to form a student advisory committee to assess religious intolerance and racism. "Discrimination is immoral," he told a reporter for the *Bruin*. "We are all God's children with merely different routes to our creator."[38]

By mid-spring the political crisis over Cuba had become a critically divisive issue. Headlines in April 1961 announced that Cuban exiles in Florida had attempted an invasion of the island and had been routed at the Bay of Pigs. Official U.S. involvement was soon disclosed, in spite of administration plans for plausible deniability. Students focused on the illegality of the invasion and at Berkeley took to the city streets to protest U.S. action (demonstrating on campus about off-campus issues was forbidden under university rules).[39] In the face of complaints from the public, the regents demanded that Kerr curtail "incidents that might cause unpopular public response."[40] Berkeley's acting chancellor, Edward Strong, nervous about the scheduled appearance of Malcolm X, canceled the campus event. As the NAACP sponsors hurriedly sought another venue, the American Civil Liberties Union launched a protest against Strong's action. In spite of their ongoing conflict over administrative procedures, Murphy and Kerr were in full agreement on the role of the university and the importance of free dissemination of ideas. Murphy placed no restraints on the *Daily Bruin* regarding articles about Cuba when John Birch Society letter writers claimed student editors were Communist dupes.

In the aftermath of the Bay of Pigs fiasco, Arizona's Senator Barry Goldwater, now heading the conservative wing of the Republican Party, lambasted Kennedy's ineffective action as cause for "apprehension and shame."[41] Kennedy called for a reassessment of Cuban policy and convened the Foreign Intelligence Advisory Board (FIAB), a little-known group of prominent citizen-advisers, to determine why the CIA had such unreliable information. Within a few months Kennedy restructured the CIA with John A. McCone as the new director. McCone, a Republican, who had been a major World War II industrialist (Bechtel-McCone Corporation) and had headed the Atomic Energy Commission under Eisenhower, was considered an authority on the Soviet nuclear threat. The issue of intelligence gathering, the FIAB, and the various roles of John McCone were elements that would figure time and again at crucial points in Murphy's career.

· · · · ·

The semester moved steadily toward June with UCLA functioning to Murphy's relative satisfaction. As the date for commencement exercises approached, marking Murphy's first year as chancellor, he was informed that diplomas conferred on UCLA students would be given, not by him as chancellor, but by the university's president, Clark Kerr. "This is ridiculous," Murphy fumed. It demeaned his role to sit on the stage, taking no part in the ceremony. Determined to maintain the prestige and authority of the chancellorship, he ordered the policy changed. On the date of the ceremony he stood at the center of the stage—while Kerr sat—and gave out the undergraduate diplomas. Kerr was called on to award the graduate degrees.

Perturbed to learn that he did not have the final decision in the appointment and promotion of tenured faculty, Murphy argued that such symbolic and important functions must rest with the chancellor. He conceded that statewide university policy should be centralized, but once basic decisions were made administration should be left to the individual campuses—especially with enrollment expected to increase to near-unmanageable levels.[42] Otherwise, he claimed, "you were in danger of creating a dinosaur with a huge body and a little nervous system that was incapable of managing this vast enterprise."[43] To Kerr's exasperation, Murphy persisted in describing this pin-headed dinosaur to reporters in press interviews.

Kerr felt that what Murphy and the UCLA faculty really wanted was not equal opportunity but equal distinction, "something else altogether." Distinction takes time, Kerr insisted, and it depended on factors that evolved slowly, such as the eminence of the faculty.[44]

FUNDING CULTURE IN THE COLD WAR

In November Ed Carter selected Murphy to be chairman of the county art museum's building fund campaign. Murphy's new role made him an increasingly visible figure in the community at large and ensured him ready access to Carter, who enjoyed significant clout among key regional movers and shakers and served on some of the city's most powerful corporate boards, including Pacific Telephone & Telegraph, Northrop, Southern California Edison, and United-California Bank.[45] Murphy told reporters at the press conference announcing his appointment that the art museum was another symbol of the coming cultural maturity of Los Angeles. "Our new Los Angeles County Art Museum will not be a monument to one titanic philanthropist," he said. "It will belong to everyone."[46] As he collected the checks, he spread the theme that Carter wanted the public to hear: the new Los Angeles County Museum of Art will make Los Angeles the artistic capital of the West.

The city's need for a new museum had become painfully obvious. The 1911 Museum of History, Science and Art located in Exposition Park was ridiculed as an "attic for archeology and science." The art curator, Richard "Ric" Fargo Brown, who later served as director of the new art museum, called the institution an anomaly, a "16th century Wunderkammer, with everything but a unicorn's horn and an ostrich egg."[47] Los Angeles art collectors were taking their collections elsewhere. In 1951 valuable works from the Louise and Walter Arensberg collection of French impressionists went to Philadelphia, and in 1957 the Edward G. Robinson collection was sold to the Greek shipowner Stavros Niarchos. The vanished collections emphasized the museum's shortcomings and gave rise to Los Angeles's reputation in the art world as a "city of lost opportunities."[48]

Carter devised an innovative public and private partnership for the new museum to appeal to wealthy donors, taxpayers, and city officials. The board of supervisors was to provide county-owned land while museum trustees, corporations, and individuals donated funds to build the new facility. Carter insisted that though staff salaries and maintenance expenses would be paid by the county, a private self-perpetuating and independent board should set policy and operate the museum. In 1961 a nonprofit group, the Museum Associates, was organized as a board of trustees for that purpose. Carter was appointed museum president, and Murphy was named a member of the board.

Hancock Park, a county-owned six-acre parcel along the Miracle Mile section of Wilshire Boulevard, was officially offered as a site. The smell of petroleum pervaded the air of the urban park, and the ground underfoot was saturated in spots with oil. The land was available for the museum, but county supervisors were reluctant to provide operating expenses (then estimated at $1 million a year). County Supervisor Kenneth Hahn opposed the building plans as too expensive, though he was repeatedly assured that powerful community leaders would provide private construction funding if the other conditions could be met.

The city's booming postwar economy had created new fortunes for entrepreneurs in aerospace, petrochemicals, tract housing, mortgage banking, and insurance who were not part of old-money Los Angeles. Just as Dorothy Chandler targeted this sector of wealth to finance the downtown Music Center, Carter intended to call on the city's new rich for support of the proposed museum. "The best way to raise lots of money," Carter said, "is to ask the people who have the most of it."[49]

Early on Carter managed to persuade the business tycoon Norton Simon, already an active museum trustee, to make an official pledge of $1 million. A self-made multimillionaire, Simon controlled colossal Hunt Foods and Industries, in addition to holding controlling interests in McCall's, among other companies. He was also a passionate collector who had assembled a fine collection of paintings and sculpture. Not an easy man to please, Simon directed the same interest and intensity to art as he did to business.

Carter also convinced the wealthy financier Howard Ahmanson to donate $2 million to the planned museum.[50] Ahmanson's ready cash and his influence with the board of supervisors were credited as the primary factors in securing the county's commitment.[51] When Ahmanson made his gift official, however, he stipulated that the museum be called the Ahmanson Gallery of Fine Art. Simon argued that naming the building for any one patron would undercut the public spirit of the project and deter other donors. To Carter's dismay, Simon angrily withdrew his million-dollar pledge. Eventually a compromise was reached in which the new museum would consist of three buildings, only one of which would bear Ahmanson's name. Simon committed $250,000 for a sculpture garden but declined to fund a Norton Simon building and did not revive his original million-dollar promise.

Bart Lytton, a former Hollywood agent and occasional scriptwriter, who was the colorful owner of Lytton Financial, a business empire he created through aggressive marketing of savings and loan deposits, stepped forward to fund the temporary exhibitions building. The Simon name was changed on the architectural plans to Lytton. The third building, the planned auditorium, was funded by Anna Bing Arnold, widow of the wealthy real estate developer Leo S. Bing.

The official groundbreaking was scheduled for the following year, but construction challenges had been woefully underestimated by all those involved.[52]

· · · · ·

United in the project to build the city's art museum, Carter, Murphy, and Ahmanson became close friends. As they juggled their respective day jobs, they moonlighted on behalf of the consuming civic project. Murphy and Ahmanson, in particular, developed a deep bond.[53] Murphy was a regular evening guest at Ahmanson's Hancock Park home. Ahmanson's wealth was enormous, and by the early 1960s Home Savings was reported to be the largest savings and loan in the country, the first to exceed $1 billion in assets.[54] The Nebraska-born Ahmanson, known for his affability and his taste for scotch, was a gregarious, good-looking man with steel gray hair and the sun-scorched face of a sportsman. Of stocky build, with Scandinavian features, wide-set eyes, and narrow lips, he had a genial smile but a determined jaw.

Ahmanson and his first wife, Dorothy, known in their circle as Dottie, were for many years a prominent couple on the Los Angeles social and civic scene. Howard was a key figure in the power structure of Los Angeles and an important player in the Republican Party.[55] At the time Murphy met the Ahmansons they were in the throes of ending their twenty-seven-year marriage. The last years of their union had been tumultuous, characterized by ugly clashes in which heavy drinking played a part. Dorothy filed for divorce in 1960. The Ahmansons' one child, Howard Ahmanson Jr., was close in age to Murphy's son, Franklin Lee. From the first months of his acquaintance with the Ahmansons, Murphy became a ready sounding board, called on for discreet advice. After their divorce the high-profile couple reached an amicable arrangement and rebuilt the rapport that had been at the root of their long marriage.

Dorothy Ahmanson made her residence at the couple's house in Newport Beach, where they had been part of the glamorous sailing crowd. Howard turned their Los Angeles home in Hancock Park into both his residence and his office. Following a heart attack in 1956 while at the helm of his yacht during a race, he was told by his doctor to take up safer exercise and reduce his stress. He moved his office to his home, where he could work in sports clothes and swim three times a day, stepping through the French doors of his office haven to dive into the pool. The home on tree-lined Hudson Avenue was a handsome structure built on a large city lot in an older, affluent neighborhood near the commercial district of Wilshire Boulevard; it was not the grand estate that a man of his wealth might have been expected to own, but it suited Ahmanson. He lived in comfort attended by a butler, a chef, secretaries, and housekeepers.

Murphy and Ahmanson spent evenings together in the wood-paneled library, surrounded by Ahmanson's art collection. Ahmanson was a shrewd and successful bidder at European art auctions, though some of his acquisitions were not well authenticated. In some instances, with additional research, he was able to verify the artist or improve the record of provenance—immediately increasing the value—but some of the works continued to have a clouded history, and a few turned out to be fakes. Impressive names in the collection included Vermeer, Titian, Velázquez, and Sargent. Suspended above Ahmanson's stone fireplace was Rembrandt's brooding seventeenth-century painting, *The Raising of Lazarus*. Three feet square, the canvas depicts Christ in the shadow-filled burial cave where the shrouded Lazarus lies in an open sarcophagus.[56] One guest remembered feeling uneasy with the somber scene in a room meant for conviviality. Nevertheless, it was an environment in which Murphy and Ahmanson relaxed, talked art and politics, drank heavily (fine Chivas scotch), and filled the room with smoke (both were chain-smokers). Carter lived nearby and frequently dropped in to add his colorful anecdotes to the conversation and take a hand in a round of Liar's Poker.

Longtime Ahmanson associate Robert DeKruif said that when Ahmanson and Murphy were seen together late in the night, a synergistic energy seemed to accompany the rise and fall of their voices and a deep affection infused the sound of their wholehearted laughter.[57] These two outgoing, high-energy alpha males were both men of superb intelligence who had known success early in their careers. Before the age of thirty-five Murphy had been celebrated nationally as the "wonder boy of medicine," creator of the Kansas Rural Health Plan; at the same age Ahmanson had a financial empire under way and was labeled a business genius. They could talk straightforwardly to each other about complex maneuverings in the worlds of business and politics, but they could also banter spiritedly: one charmer knows another. Murphy gave free rein to his bawdy Irish wit in competition with Ahmanson's droll observations. In their camaraderie they acknowledged a truth about themselves: they were not part and parcel of the ultrachic, sophisticated circle in which they functioned so well. The plains of Kansas are not far from the wheatfields of Nebraska; they recognized their roots in the hardy stock of the Midwest, which Murphy insisted was the actual, beating heart of America.[58] The geographic center of the country was also the energy hub, in his mind, in contrast to the effete sophistication that was admired in the East. Ahmanson and Murphy were accomplished, dynamic salesmen of ideas, but they would always feel separate from the people to whom they were selling.

Another characteristic they shared was a great appreciation of women. Howard admired women of beauty and competence and gave credit to Dottie, who had been a capable partner in the early years when he was getting a business under way. After the divorce, without a woman in residence, Ahmanson's Hancock Park house took on a distinctly men's club atmosphere that continued until his second marriage in 1965. Until then the poker table kept company with the art, and peccadilloes competed with civic plans.

·   ·   ·

The opening of the fall semester 1962 coincided with congressional election campaigns in which the crisis in Cuba was again the focus of debate. Shipments of Soviet military equipment had been observed on the island during the summer. From his Washington contacts, Murphy heard that behind-the-scenes arguments were raging, with hawks demanding a preemptive strike to take out Soviet-built missile sites and moderates urging negotiation with Khrushchev. On Monday, October 22, President Kennedy informed the nation that photographic surveillance had produced incontrovertible evidence of sites for ballistic missiles capable of striking American cities. He announced that the United States had ordered Khrushchev to remove Soviet missiles and was prepared to initiate a "full retaliatory attack upon the Soviet Union" if missiles were launched from Cuba.[59]

As Soviet ships steamed toward Cuba, U.S. bombers with nuclear warheads stayed aloft in coordinated relays ready to attack predesignated Soviet targets, and civil defense authorities prepared the country for attack. If a bomb hit downtown Los Angeles radiation would reach the UCLA campus within an hour, depending on weather conditions. The disaster preparedness supervisor instructed students to rush to underground shelters at the sound of campus sirens. They could not be saved from radiation if a nuclear blast was within ten miles of the campus but otherwise might have a chance of survival. Should there be no warning, students were instructed to drop to the ground until the shock wave passed and then dash to shelters. Two days after the blast the worst effects of fallout would be over, and the students could cautiously emerge.[60]

The terrifying suspense came to an end on October 28 when Soviet vessels halted and turned back. The Soviet Union agreed to dismantle missile sites in exchange for a U.S. pledge not to invade Cuba. Kennedy was the hero of the hour, widely acclaimed for his steadfast stand against Khrushchev—though there were pundits who felt Kennedy had brought on the crisis with his anti-Communist rhetoric and his earlier attempted invasion of Cuba. Murphy was a critic of provocative cold war rhetoric and the stockpiles of nuclear weapons. He stood with Eisenhower in the belief that with the United States armed sufficiently for defense and deterrence, Communism could be contained and ultimately defeated, though it could take decades. In his speeches Murphy held that the example of a stable, prosperous America playing a constructive role in the world was the best weapon against the Communists' blandishments and power grabs.[61] He lamented that with so much promise for humanity in a technological age, life on earth risked destruction in a rash confrontation.

THE TITAN CHANCELLOR

Much to the irritation of Clark Kerr, the chancellor at UCLA continued to interact with the regents on a regular basis. The massive building program kept Murphy in constant touch with Dorothy Chandler, chair of the re gents' Building and Grounds Committee. His role at the county museum put him in league with Ed Carter, with whom he conferred daily. Despite their opposing political views, Murphy had developed a warm friendship with board chairman Ed Pauley that stemmed from their mutual interest in UCLA athletics. Murphy was alert to send football or basketball tickets to Pauley and provide VIP parking. "Pauley had the habit of dealing directly with me," Murphy said later. "This infuriated Clark Kerr, but there was nothing he could do about it."[62]

As Murphy worked his civic wonders, his administrative team of Young, Young, and Sherwood picked up the tedious details of campus operations. As his prominence in the community grew and he was increasingly absent from campus, the three men were forced to become his surrogates, making critical decisions without him.

In April 1962 a day Murphy had eagerly looked forward to finally arrived—presentation of his carefully drafted academic plan to a meeting of the board of regents, a plan designed to transform UCLA into one of the world's finest universities. After pointing out that UCLA had grown from a provincial normal school into a large and complex urban university in less than half a century, Murphy predicted that by 1970 it would become known worldwide. He offered a prescient analysis of the needs of the Los Angeles of the future and the demands on UCLA. The growing city was destined to be a global crossroads; it was imperative that UCLA be prepared, and he urged that its centers for Middle Eastern, African, and Latin American studies be expanded.

Murphy offered a laundry list of needs: linguistics and interdisciplinary studies, a center of music composition, a graphic arts program, a school of theater arts, a school of architecture along with an undergraduate program of city and regional planning and doctoral-level programs in engineering. He also stressed the importance of a strong aerospace research program and urged significant expansion of the UCLA Center for Health Sciences. The insatiable demand of the region's research-based industries and the rise of a new technological culture created, in his mind, an obligation that UCLA must meet and a powerful stimulus to move forward rapidly. Murphy perceived that the direction of national power and influence was shifting. "As political, industrial and financial power flows from East to West," he explained, "so must cultural and intellectual leadership." Los Angeles could well be a powerhouse in the coming global economy.[63]

Given the need for a university of international stature, Murphy was surprised when he failed to obtain approval from the statewide offices at Berkeley for student exchanges and study abroad programs. He shared his puzzlement with Professor Charles Speroni of the Italian department, on whom he had grown to rely for his institutional memory and his witty descriptions of university personalities. Speroni and his wife had come to the Murphys' assistance after their dismaying arrival at the chancellor's residence, and the two families had become close friends. With his characteristic European aplomb, Speroni told Murphy that the powers that be had decreed no more programs abroad after a student had come home from Europe pregnant. An astounded and exasperated Murphy hit the roof and went to work immediately on foreign study programs.

· · · · ·

Clark Kerr had his own troubles with the southern regents, in addition to those Murphy stirred up. Ed Pauley, in particular, continued to challenge him. As the most senior regent, Pauley was determined to expand his power in spite of Kerr's efforts to constrain him. The moderate coalition of Chandler, Carter, and Simon were among Kerr's best supporters, but they pushed him hard for what they wanted. The board consisted of twenty-five members, eighteen appointed by the governor for sixteen-year terms and seven ex officio members, including the governor.[64] Most of the appointed regents were white men of substantial wealth and influence. Governor Brown likened the prestige of the appointment to "the Order of the Garter in England."[65]

But it was not an assignment for lightweights. The work was demanding; during the 1960s, meetings of the board were fraught with stress, and emergency sessions were common. The regents were under pressure to have the campuses ready for the coming college-age boom. Chandler especially felt the pressure during the site selection and construction of three new campuses and the gigantic expansion at UCLA.[66] She said that with so many details reviewed by the building committee, she could have been a professor of architecture.[67]

Chandler harbored a deep sense of public service and was dedicated to creating a first-rank university. It was her view that the board was the university's protector from assaults from either the left or the right. She perceived the academic community as removed from the interference of politics. It was a view shared with other members of the moderate coalition and with President Kerr. Unfortunately, in the course of events, when the test came their concept failed to hold. Chuck Young later remembered Chandler as the most courageous of the regents during the tumult of the 1960s. "She was one of the most remarkable people I have ever met," Young said. He watched her tire over the years, but her core values, especially when it concerned the university, remained steady. "In part because of her relationship with Franklin," Young indicated, "she came to understand what the university must be in terms of full academic freedom and free speech."[68]

The industrialist Norton Simon was appointed to the board of regents in 1960. He was the most liberal member of the board but also the most cantankerous. In his business career he had developed a pattern of seizing leadership in boardrooms by attacking management. University management proved no exception.[69] "You have to understand my strange style of working," Simon told the *Times*. "I'm operating from the position of not being 'one of the boys.'"[70] Simon was vociferous in his opposition to the university's acquisition of South Coast land from the Irvine Ranch, which he felt entailed conflicts of interest that were costly to the university. Finally the regents handed the sensitive negotiations over to Kerr, who after "heavy going" managed to secure a fair price, and the full board, including Simon, voted approval.[71] Chandler later recalled the memorable morning that she flew with architects over thousands of pastoral acres of Irvine coast to pinpoint the exact site for the new campus.

The regents were largely dedicated and hardworking, but they were subject to razor-sharp criticism and accusations of operating in secret. The "true interests" of the regents became a serious topic of debate. In the early 1960s more than $450 million in public funds was managed by the board.

In a tract by the counterculture activist Marvin Garson, the question was raised, "Just WHO are the Regents?" and are they in conflict with the stated aims of the university that they rule? "The Regents cannot help feeling responsible to the huge private corporations that dominate—indeed, constitute—the economy of the state of California," Garson wrote. "In their minds this is not corruption or prostitution; they cannot see that things could or should be any other way. . . . Taken as a group, the Regents are representatives of only one thing—corporate wealth."[72] The board of regents included key figures in the corporate world, among them, Samuel B. Mosher, chairman of Signal Oil and Gas Company; John Canaday, vice president of Lockheed Aircraft; Ed Carter, president of Broadway-Hale Stores and trustee of the Irvine Foundation; Ed Pauley, chairman of Pauley Petroleum and director at Western Airlines; Donald H. McLaughlin, chairman of Homestake Mining Company, the nation's largest gold producer, and director of United Nuclear Corporation; Catherine C. Hearst, wife of publisher Randolph A. Hearst; and Dorothy Chandler, wife of Norman Chandler, chairman of Times Mirror.

· · · · ·

Chandler ignored the attacks leveled against her as a university regent, and in Los Angeles she continued to focus her energies on building the city's grand new pavilion of culture. Her elaborate project was coming together: Los Angeles County had officially reserved nearly seven acres of hilltop in the downtown Civic Center, more than $10 million in private contributions had been received, and the County Board of Supervisors had unanimously approved expanded plans for a three-building complex.[73] The dramatic front entrance of the concert hall would face a courtyard with sculpture, reflecting pools, and a fountain. Welton Beckett referred to the planning as his "life work at the moment" and "the most exciting job [he had] ever undertaken."[74]

As the date for the groundbreaking neared, Chandler turned to Murphy to assist her in writing a letter to Jacqueline Kennedy asking her to speak at the ceremony dedicating the center as a "Living Memorial to Peace." Murphy wrote his suggestions in thick pencil strokes on the early draft. The letter, invested with Chandler's high hopes, was sent to the White House on March 3, 1962. "This is the most significant letter that I have ever written," she declared in the first sentence. She then described a community "glowing with joy and pridefully anticipating the historic groundbreaking ceremony which will be the most brilliant in the cultural history of the State of California." Chandler wrote that she was approaching Kennedy as a part of the "distaff world," since it was women volunteers (Chandler described herself as the catalyst) who were bringing the center to fruition. "Therefore nothing could be more fitting than that the woman who is The First Lady of Culture should come to crown our dedicated efforts."[75] Though Jacqueline Kennedy was unable to accept the invitation, a festive groundbreaking took place, with Chandler effusively acknowledging the women volunteers.

The cost of the complex had mushroomed to $25 million; Chandler and her team set their sights on collecting $12 million from private donations, to be followed by a matching $12 million from the county of Los Angeles. Still more funds were required for furnishings and operations. Asked about her fund-raising technique, Chandler said that her method was to be "intensely personal with the extremely rich." To that end she kept constant vigil on ten to fifteen very wealthy prospects. "You have to know the family situation at all times," she explained. "Divorce, illness, death—or just a routine change in the family financial situation—can inhibit contribution."[76]

By winter 1962 Chandler was nearing her immediate $12 million goal. Murphy watched with some amazement when on November 11 she announced the donation of $1 million from the wealthy financier Mark Taper, who was not known for openhandedness. The gift was earmarked for construction of an intimate 730-seat amphitheater, one of three planned units— the Memorial Pavilion, the Center Theater, and the Forum, which would now be called the Mark Taper Forum.[77] Exactly what transpired between Chandler and Taper remains private, but Taper's gift placed Chandler beyond 90 percent of her announced goal.[78] "We are the mecca, the paradise and dream of the world," Taper told the *Times* after the announcement of his million-dollar gift. "It is a wonderful thing to share in the fabulous life we are living here."[79]

While she was asserting her influence over Taper of American Savings and Loan, Chandler was courting Howard Ahmanson of the much larger Home Savings and Loan as well. "You've got to play one against the other," she said. "You've got to know when to push and when to shove."[80]

· · · · ·

Just as the ambitious goals for the Music Center had a tendency to grow larger, so too did plans for the forthcoming county art museum. When costs exceeded Ed Carter's original projections, a second fund-raising campaign was launched in February 1962. Murphy continued to serve as chairman of the drive with cochairs Sidney F. Brody and Mrs. Freeman Gates. By March 20 total pledges neared the $8 million needed for the three buildings. Revised plans called for more than twenty galleries to fill the new museum—each representing a gift of $125,000. "The generosity of these donors significantly hastens the cultural growth of our community," Carter said as he listed the new names to be inscribed on gallery walls—Firestone, Chandler, Hearst, Hope, Mosher, and Pauley.[81] On April 24 two more names were announced—Mr. and Mrs. Theodore E. Cummings and Mr. and Mrs. Norton Simon.[82] The three buildings making up the museum complex would carry the names of their generous million-dollar donors: Anna Bing Arnold, Bart Lytton, and Howard Ahmanson.

On Thursday, November 9, 1962, four generations of the Hancock family, who had donated the land, gathered at the museum site for the groundbreaking. As chairman of the fund-raising campaign, Murphy officiated at the event. Carter and Ahmanson were present for the celebration and warmly shook the hand of Captain G. Allan Hancock, all of them smiling for photographers. The city would soon witness the realization of a modern museum complex designed by the architect William Pereira with buildings grouped on a central raised plaza above a shimmering reflecting pool. Growth-giddy Los Angeles was poised to push toward maturity with its greatest boosters guiding its civic plans.[83]

· · · · ·

At UCLA Murphy was dedicated to the intellectual goals of the university as a marketplace of ideas, but to establish a strong identity, attract community support, and maintain alumni loyalty, he knew UCLA had to have outstanding sports teams. Pauley was an ardent sports supporter, and Murphy felt he could make good use of his interest. Because the men differed sharply in their political views, Murphy astutely kept his interactions with Pauley focused on athletics.[84] Legendary coach John Wooden had been at UCLA since 1948, and as head coach of the university's basketball team he achieved an unequaled win-loss record. Murphy and Pauley had watched with enthusiasm as Wooden won an AAWU championship for UCLA in 1962.[85]

The alumni had been talking about building a basketball pavilion for years, but they were unable to fund it.[86] As a result UCLA's basketball team played its home games at the Los Angeles Sports Arena. In April 1963 Murphy managed to persuade Pauley to pledge the money necessary to build UCLA's long-sought arena. One night over dinner and cocktails at the Claremont Hotel in Berkeley, with Pauley flanked by two other regents, Murphy nailed down a plan in which Pauley pledged $1 million, with an additional $4 million to come from alumni donations and state funds.

"It's going to be the finest indoor pavilion in Southern California, maybe one of the best in the United States," Murphy told Pauley. "And it will be called PAULEY PAVILION."

"Ed, I'll bet you that the name Pauley Pavilion, which already sounds good because it's alliterative, will be in the newspaper more than Royce Hall or the Dorothy Chandler Pavilion or anything else." The next day Murphy wrote Pauley, "The magnitude of the gift, and the crucial importance of the structure combined to make this one of the most remarkable events in the history of UCLA."[87]

After construction delays the thirteen-thousand-seat indoor arena designed by Welton Beckett was dedicated in 1965; televised sports made the name "Pauley Pavilion" synonymous with UCLA across the nation and the world. Under Coach Wooden's direction, the UCLA Bruins captured successive national basketball championships, and many of the team's most memorable games were played in the new building.[88] Pauley told Murphy more than once that the Pauley Pavilion was the only gift he ever gave where the performance matched the pitch. That was the kind of response Murphy worked for. "You match the man's interest with your need," Murphy said. "To me, that's constructive fund-raising."[89]

Pauley frequently invited Murphy and his family to visit his private retreat known as Coconut Island, a rustic tropical haven near the Hawaiian Islands. Murphy, wearing the local version of a straw hat made from palm fronds, readily adapted to beach life. Pauley had a pet dolphin corralled in the lagoon that was eager to swim with the humans. To his delight, Pauley managed to snap a photograph of the UCLA chancellor astride the dolphin.[90]

Kerr reported in his memoirs that he too had been a guest at Coconut Island. Thinking that Pauley had invited him for a visit in the spirit of reconciliation, he accepted. But he was gripped with second thoughts when he swam out into the lagoon and saw a dorsal fin approaching; he feared he had been set up for a shark attack. Pauley's dolphin would figure again in Kerr's discovery of Pauley's lesser-known emotional side. Kerr said that years later the power-driven oilman came to his office to tell him tearfully that the dolphin had died.[91]

· · · · ·

In 1963, days before the Thanksgiving recess, shattering news came from Dallas that President John F. Kennedy had been assassinated. When the news reached campus, Chuck Young and Murphy were together. It was the only occasion, Young said, on which he saw Murphy cry. Murphy was a critic of Kennedy's weapons-heavy conduct of the cold war, but to have a president—especially a young vibrant man—cut down by an assassin engulfed him with grief for the man and for the nation.

On November 24 Murphy was asked by city leaders to speak at the nationally televised memorial to the slain president held at the Los Angeles Sports Arena. Tens of thousands listened to Murphy's remarks broadcast by NBC News in which Murphy attributed to Kennedy a basic creed that was also his own:

Better than most men, he understood that the great scientific-technological revolution of the 20th century, with its cultural, economic and social impacts, had led to unprecedented problems requiring unprecedented solutions. Both the achievement of his life and the utter wastefulness of his death eloquently testify to the truth of his basic creed, namely, that man must proceed by way of reason as well as by way of faith.[92]

Chuck Young, though a Murphy loyalist, conceded that in clashes between the chancellor in Los Angeles and the university president, Murphy sometimes crossed the line: Kerr deserved far better from Murphy than he got. "It was almost as if Franklin had to create an antagonist," Young said. "It was like a Shakespearean drama in which the actors were distinguished educators."[93]

Charter Day at UCLA in 1963, nine months before Kennedy's assassination, turned into one such drama over the symbols of authority. Murphy, proud of his acquaintance with the Eisenhower family from his Kansas years, was pleased to have the former president as guest speaker. As the academic procession started, Murphy reportedly jumped forward so that he stood next to Eisenhower and Clark Kerr. As described by Harry R. Wellman, vice president of the university, Kerr stood to the left, Murphy was on the right, and Eisenhower was in the middle. "This was the first, and as far as I know, the last time that a chancellor of a UC campus assumed his rank was equal to that of the president of the university," Wellman said.[94]

For his part, Kerr said that he made no comment about the embarrassing situation to Murphy at the time or later. But in his memoirs Kerr offered a colorful psychological analysis of Murphy's compulsion:

> On our farm when I was a boy, we had a horse with the same kind of personality. Brownie had been a racehorse at county fairs early in his life . . . [and later] became one of our farm horses. But Brownie still needed to keep his head out in front of the other member of the team as a racehorse should in order to win. But this meant that he pulled more than his share of the load—commendable but suicidal—working against a much heavier draft horse. So I lengthened the chains in his harness: he could appear to be the leader while the swingletree behind the two horses stayed even (and they were pulling equally).[95]

Kerr's conclusion about Murphy's psychology was demonstrated in repeated clashes between the two men concerning protocol. Another incident erupted during the visit of President Lyndon Johnson at UCLA's Charter Day ceremony in 1964, arranged by Pauley.[96] On February 21, Marine helicopters carrying Johnson and the Mexican president Adolfo López Mateos landed on the UCLA athletic field. An audience of thirty-four thousand spectators waited to greet the two presidents. (Sproul Hall had been draped in red, white, and blue bunting on one side and in the green, white, and red colors of the Mexican flag on the other.) Presidents Johnson and López were Charter Day speakers and were to be awarded honorary doctorates of law by Kerr.

Regal functions such as Charter Day (the annual anniversary celebration of the University of California's founding in 1868) served an important purpose in Kerr's view; they created opportunities to present the university in historical perspective and to "burnish the cherished ideals." Kerr expected to be a familiar figure at such events, a "reminder that there was one university of several campuses with common interests."[97] Apparently Murphy again elevated his role by reducing Kerr's prominence in the ceremony. Because of the traditional purpose of Charter Day and the important role of the university president, Kerr was appalled at Murphy's squeezing him out. In recalling the incident, Chuck Young said that Murphy, unfortunately, lost a great deal with Kerr as a result. Afterward their relationship became increasingly cold and formal.

Young said that Murphy rarely had to fight for dominance. He seemed to come by it naturally, as if by birthright. He was never in awe of others because of their titles. "Some of us might have a difficult time marching up to someone of eminence as an equal," said Young. "Murphy never in his life had that problem." He was absolutely self-assured. But, Young added, he had the talent, experience, and background that fed his self-assurance. His analytic abilities as a physician and scientist, combined with his artistic and scholarly interests, made him a rare academic administrator. Young traveled extensively with Murphy on educational junkets and noted that Murphy never did anything second-class. Furthermore, whatever the continent or country in which Murphy found himself, "he had to see the President or the King!"[98]

・ ・ ・ ・ ・

The conflict with Kerr had grown so tense that in March 1964 Murphy penned an unusually candid eight-page letter to the UC president in the hope of clearing the air. Unfortunately, the letter, which he thought would be conciliatory, lent itself to interpretation as self-serving. Murphy told Kerr that he had come to UCLA against the advice of friends but that he had come with enthusiasm. He insisted that his decision was a "positive choice" and that he had not been forced to leave Kansas. "I still retain my enthusiasm and belief," he wrote, "that UCLA is destined one day to become one of the great university campuses of the world while, at the same time, being a part of a multi-university which already is unprecedented in all of the history of higher education."[99]

Kerr had accused Murphy of grandstanding, so in his letter Murphy stressed that he believed that by drawing attention to UCLA and enhancing its image and visibility, he had made a major, and practical, contribution to the statewide university system. "I cannot close this letter without reminding myself again of some of the conversations held prior to my coming here. At my breakfast meetings with you and Ed Carter at the Bel Air Hotel, as well as at meetings with others I repeatedly asked the question: 'What do you want in a Chancellor at UCLA?'" Murphy said that he was told that a strong leader was wanted and that was what he undertook to be. "All of this is not to say that I have not made mistakes. Indeed this is so tricky a job in such a complex situation that it is almost impossible not to." He said that he felt he had made real contributions and would continue to do so, provided he was given the tools to do the job.[100]

There is no record of Kerr's response to the letter. However, nearly four decades later at his home near Berkeley, Kerr remembered the entanglements with Murphy as a period of great frustration. He said he felt that Murphy's talents were extraordinary but that at the same time he was unpredictable, paranoid, and prone to unwarranted rages.[101] Kerr recounted that he had been warned beforehand by friends that Murphy was "brash" and "pushy," but he had discounted any apprehension, impressed as he was—as they all were—by Murphy's energy and drive.[102]

THE SCIONS PAUL MELLON AND HENRY FORD II

As the tug-of-war between Kerr and Murphy continued, Murphy's visibility in the Southland increased. It was not uncommon to find him photographed, quoted, or featured on a regular basis in the city's newspapers. He was often mentioned in the education section of *Newsweek* or *Time*. In spring 1965, after a full day with the mile-a-minute chancellor, the columnist Art Seidenbaum celebrated Murphy's drive in a front-page feature in the Sunday *Los Angeles Times* under the headline "UCLA's Man in Motion":

> In the compressed time-space and double-time pace of one working day,
> Franklin David Murphy, 49, started the morning worrying a way to get Ma-

tisses from Moscow, shifted to the subject of a new center for mental retardation research, jumped to a discussion of education with visiting administrators from Venezuela, huffed across the lawn to admire a historic collection of music scores, trotted over to huzzah through a gift of primitive art, discussed student activism with a student body president, chaired a meeting of the Academic Senate Council, charged to the new County Museum of Art to sit on a dais, wound up and unwound down during an informal dinner at the California Museum of Science and Industry.

Seidenbaum aptly summarized the talents demanded of the job: a "combination Renaissance man and glad-handing machine who must be able to beg millions, enrich thousands and lend dignity with each appearance."[103]

Murphy was now called upon in a wide variety of capacities. In 1964 Walt Disney sought his counsel on his cherished plan to found the California Institute of the Arts; and the business sector used his talent as well. At the request of Norton Simon he was appointed to the board of a Simon subsidiary, McCall's, Inc. After Simon merged McCall's with Hunt Foods, Murphy continued to serve on the new board. He was asked by Dorothy and Norman Chandler to join the board of directors of the Times Mirror Company. He was an intellectual workhorse; he said exactly what he meant, operated with tremendous energy, and stayed focused on the bigger picture.

Four years into his term at UCLA Murphy's rising status was reflected by invitations from the scions of two of the nation's most venerated family fortunes. In January 1964 he was asked to join the board of trustees of the National Gallery of Art by Paul Mellon, the only son of the financier Andrew Mellon. "Never before had a person west of Pittsburgh served on the board of a major cultural institution in the East," Murphy said of the rare nod to the West.[104] In September Murphy was appointed to the corporate board of the Ford Motor Company by Henry Ford II, eldest grandson of the automotive entrepreneur Henry Ford. Murphy came to the attention of Henry Ford II through Sidney Weinberg, an investment banker and a Ford board member. Weinberg had been instrumental in the financial rescue of the Samuel H. Kress Foundation at a time when Murphy was a newly appointed Kress trustee. He had been impressed with the way Murphy ably took over the chairmanship of the foundation in 1963 following the death of Rush Kress, younger brother of the founder.

Murphy, still in his forties, became the youngest Ford director, and as was true of his placement on the board of trustees of the National Gallery, he was the only noneastern member. The appointment to the Ford board positioned Murphy to be a decision maker in a watershed era in U.S. business as the nation moved through the tumultuous decades of the cold war into globalization and the worldwide reordering of industry. His role as a director also earned Murphy new Ford automobiles delivered to his doorstep each year. In January 1965 Murphy took delivery of a shiny black Lincoln Continental sedan and a Galaxy Country Squire station wagon. He also received assorted electronic products manufactured by Philco, then one of Ford's many subsidiaries. Feeling it was incumbent on him to evaluate company products, Murphy wrote frequent letters giving the company's development experts the benefit of his opinion.

The Los Angeles chancellor, who had been unable to assert his position against a ranting governor in his home state—although he bristled at any suggestion that he was driven out of Kansas—now served on the boards of major American businesses and moved in the social circles of the western power elite. He enjoyed the company of business magnates in the exclusive private California Club, but he was invited also into the homes of the Westside's leading entertainment industry figures, Harry Warner, Dr. Jules Stein, and Lew Wasserman; and among the literati, he enjoyed the company and friendship of best-selling author Irving Stone and writer, editor, and citizen-diplomat Norman Cousins.

Murphy's social calendar reflected his strong ties with many of the city's most visible and prominent figures. His directory of impressive contacts supported his theory that strong relationships are the primary driver in achieving results. He preferred to handle sensitive matters with a phone call or a quiet conversation before votes were counted. Often when a group was unable to reach consensus, he would end the meeting, then arrive at a resolution through back channels.

Murphy's rapport with Ed Carter proved invaluable to him in guiding UCLA policy, especially after Carter was appointed chairman of the board of regents in 1964. But the friend he most enjoyed was Howard Ahmanson. Murphy managed to circulate in Ahmanson's world despite the relatively modest income he earned as chancellor. When Ahmanson invited Murphy and his family to accompany him and his twelve-year-old son, Howard Jr., on a four-week European vacation, Murphy quietly secured a bank loan to pay for the airline tickets and hotel rooms for the Murphy family of six; he insisted on paying his own expenses, despite the fact that his traveling companion was one of America's wealthiest men. It was not widely known just how rich Ahmanson was, but his mushrooming financial empire was suspected at the time to be worth between a quarter-billion and a half-billion dollars.[105]

• • •

As Murphy's duties intensified his time was stretched thin. He was frequently traveling and away from home, leaving Judy to make family decisions without him. When the New York–based Kress Foundation, Washington, D.C.'s National Gallery of Art, or Los Angeles's county museum needed his presence, he was there. He was increasingly absent from campus as corporate responsibilities called him to Dearborn, Michigan, for the Ford Motor Company or to Kansas City for Hallmark Cards or when he was needed in downtown Los Angeles at the Times Mirror Company.

Despite his VIP status, the high-profile chancellor found his travels the target of scrutiny and adverse comment by the editor of the *Daily Bruin*. The dogged student journalist investigated Murphy's absences and launched a campaign in which he hoisted the university flag in front of the *Bruin*'s offices only on days when Murphy was present on campus. Those days were few in number.[106] "He accomplishe[s] so much when he's here, he doesn't deserve this reputation of neglecting his job, which he does not do," Frederickson insisted.[107] Hansena Frederickson, protective of her boss, engaged in deft maneuvers to hide his whereabouts. But despite her cagey efforts, the flag would be hauled down and Murphy would return in a fury over the *Bruin* editor and the flag.

Flag hoisted or not, Murphy's team of Sherwood, Young, and Young took care of the thousands of details involving the enormous campus and the massive building program. They proceeded with their work, unconcerned about Murphy's whereabouts. Each morning Frederickson arrived at the chancellor's office determined to outsmart the *Bruin*'s editor and keep the Stars and Stripes fluttering atop the campus pole.

• • • • •

Making good use of their contacts in the rare book trade, Murphy and Vosper assembled a valuable collection of Renaissance books bearing the dolphin-and-anchor emblem of the printer Aldus Manutius. Murphy's burning desire to acquire an Aldine collection came to fruition during this era of their great adventure, the "Golden Years" of UCLA's library.[108] The two built a distinguished collection in spite of restrictions that Vosper knew were bitterly frustrating for Murphy after the freewheeling manner in which he had operated in Kansas.

Murphy managed, nonetheless, to engage in high adventure in the book world. Irving Stone extracted an account from Murphy about smuggling from the Middle East books and artifacts relating to Persian, Arabic, and Armenian studies that could be obtained "only by dollars deposited to a Swiss bank."[109] Murphy confided to Stone that the UCLA library became, overnight, one of the most important sources of Judaica and Hebraica in the United States—through convoluted deals and unconventional procedures. On another occasion, when Vosper learned from scholars that the owner of a rare book shop in Jerusalem had died, Murphy rapidly raised funds from a private donor and an important collection was surreptitiously shipped to UCLA sidestepping the usual procedures of the U.S. Department of Customs.[110]

Murphy's interest in the European Renaissance, which took possession of him as a student traveling in Europe, was expressed throughout his life on occasions when he could promote the study and appreciation of that remarkable period in Western culture. In 1961 Elmer Belt, a professor emeritus in the UCLA School of Medicine who for sixty years had collected materials on the Renaissance, in particular those related to Leonardo da Vinci, donated his collection to the university. The Elmer Belt Library of Vinciana became an integral part of Murphy's plan to make UCLA a world center for Renaissance studies. When Stone undertook his mammoth biographical novel of Michelangelo, *The Agony and the Ecstasy,* Murphy offered encouragement for a project that would draw popular attention. In one campus event to determine "the Universal Man," Stone made the case for Michelangelo while Belt and Murphy argued for Leonardo.[111] Of course, Murphy, who was often described as a Renaissance man himself, would choose to advance the claim of Leonardo, the prototype. Murphy's interests, like those of Leonardo, spanned a wide range, from the scientific to the otherworldly, from medicine to art. On the other hand, Murphy may have had more in common with Michelangelo, who, judging from accounts of his jealous alertness to slights, was always on guard to protect his status. Murphy was no stranger to the vigorous assertion of prerogatives or to another quality ascribed to Michelangelo: *terribilità.*

THREE

Turmoil and Golden Moments

A new era in the cultural life of Los Angeles began on the evening of December 6, 1964, with the gala opening of the Los Angeles Music Center. The city's elite, in formal attire, strolled across the broad new courtyard to enter the pavilion designed by Welton Beckett, master of the pristine international style. In accordance with the serene orderliness of modernism, the five-level structure was sheathed in granite and glass and surrounded by a portico of slender white fluted columns.

The guests entered the grand hall for their first glimpse of the amber-hued onyx walls and massive crystal chandeliers (each seventeen feet high and weighing over a ton). Women lifted the skirts of their gowns to tread the dramatically cantilevered stairway and saw themselves reflected in the marble-framed, wall-sized mirrors that lined it. The grand flight of stairs led to the equally elaborate auditorium, with its sweeping curve of balconies, chief among them the Founders' Circle.

The velvet curtain with a gold sunburst pattern rose to the sound of the Los Angeles Philharmonic Orchestra conducted by Zubin Mehta. Jascha Heifetz was featured in a performance of Beethoven's Concerto in D Major. The audience knew they were part of an auspicious event. Mehta confirmed this belief when at the conclusion of the performance, his baton at his side, he told them, "This is the most unique city in the twentieth century. I do not think it is too late now, in mid-century, to begin a new cultural life." He motioned to the Founders' Circle, where Dorothy Chandler sat with her family. "I would like you all to join me in paying homage to the one person who is most of all responsible for the creation of this edifice. Unlike the princes of Florence and the pharaohs of Egypt, she is a dignified, simple lady."[1]

Franklin and Judy Murphy rose to their feet with the rest of the audience as Dorothy Chandler, radiant in white embroidered silk and a beautiful display of diamonds, took a slight bow. She rose reluctantly, nudged to her feet by her son, Otis. The audience accorded her a long, heartfelt ovation. No one in attendance would forget that emotional moment. Norman Chandler had tears in his eyes as he witnessed his wife's twenty-year ambition come to splendid realization.

Completion of the grand new pavilion atop Bunker Hill provided a much-needed centerpiece to the city—and a bold modern identity. "No single act had ever done more for a city," noted one appreciative critic. "It's impact on the Southern California psyche was fundamental. It gave pride to a city that, until recent years, had all but apologized for its existence." The new performing arts center may not have invented the cultural life of Southern California, observed Charles Champlin in the *Times,* "but it has revolutionized it, focused it and broadened it."[2]

Of the many letters of congratulation that Chandler received, perhaps none was more succinctly to the point than the one penned by Franklin Murphy the morning after the gala opening night: "I just want you to know that in forty-eight years of human existence, I have never seen such an extraordinary individual performance as yours, and I count it a unique privilege to know you both as a distinguished citizen, as well as a warm and sensitive woman."[3] Their friendship would grow to be a bond in which each held the other in high regard, but it would be a friendship sorely tested in the years to come.

· · · · ·

Dorothy Chandler was "bound and determined to bring culture to her much maligned city," wrote Hearst's *Herald Examiner* in a generous tribute. "In the course of raising money to build the Music Center she introduced San Marino to Hillcrest," observed Joan Didion. "She introduced the motion picture industry to the California Club. She mixed everybody up, woke up the drowsing and rearranged the seating."[4] "She brought people together who'd never been together and had never expected to be together," Otis Chandler told one interviewer.[5]

At the pavilion's dedication, Bob Hope quipped, "Just think; all the money for this beautiful center was raised by voluntary contributions—voluntary, that's when Buff stopped twisting your arm so you could write the check!" He added with a grin, "Extremism in the pursuit of the Music Center is no vice." (Hope, playing to the heavily Republican crowd, was alluding to a then-famous response by the 1964 Republican presidential candidate Barry Goldwater when he was accused of ultraconservative hawkish views: "Extremism in the defense of liberty is no vice.")[6]

Chandler had raised $45 million for what would be a three-building complex: the 3,200-seat music pavilion, later named in her honor; a 750-seat theater for innovative performances, which she persuaded Mark Taper, president of American Savings, to fund; and the 2,100-seat Ahmanson Theatre. The Ahmanson Foundation contributed a spectacular $1.5 million gift at the behest of Howard Ahmanson. *Time* magazine paid tribute to her virtuoso money raising and civic effort by putting her portrait on the cover of the December 18, 1964, issue.[7]

Murphy wrote an instructive essay for a special supplement of the *Los Angeles Times,* in which he explained why the Music Center should matter to the citizens of Los Angeles. The essay was written in the high moral tone that was as much a characteristic of the midcentury as the pristine modernist architecture that the Music Center exemplified.

> Spencer spoke of music as "the highest of the fine arts." Longfellow called it "the universal language." The composer Richard Strauss saw it as a "craft." But perhaps Martin Luther best described music in educational terms when he wrote: Music is a discipline, and a mistress of order and good manners. She makes the people milder and gentler, more moral and more reasonable.
>
> Completion of the magnificent Music Center is indisputable evidence that Los Angeles as a city has reached a degree of sophistication that puts it squarely among the great cities of the world.[8]

In calling the Music Center a monument to Dorothy Chandler's understanding of the relationship between music and the education of a people, Murphy took the opportunity to praise her work as a UC regent as well. The unusual relationship between the UCLA chancellor and Los Angeles's female dynamo was observed over many years by Vice-Chancellor Chuck Young. "Franklin became Buff Chandler's ally and counselor concerning the Music Center in a way never told," Young said.[9] His view is confirmed by notes found among Chandler's personal papers. To solve sensitive problems or plan key moments, she turned to Murphy for confidential advice and often ran important letters or announcements past him for his opinion and blue-pencil editing. Over the years he gave his assistance without hesitation.

• • • • •

Chandler's sweeping campaign to raise the funds needed for the music pavilion and her role as president of the Southern California Symphony Association generated raves but also snipes and criticism. "With the aid of the vast influence of the Chandler fortune (oil, ranching, television, insurance)," noted *Time* magazine in reporting the 1965 upheaval involving the departure of conductor Georg Solti and the arrival of Zubin Mehta, "Buff Chandler has established a near-dictatorship of culture in Southern California. Says one veteran of a Chandler-chaired board: 'A meeting with Mrs. Chandler is like a meeting with Mr. Khrushchev; you sit around a table, and she makes the decision.'"[10]

Despite the attacks, Chandler's great civic plans inched forward. After the December 6 gala, there were two more buildings to complete and funds to raise for the Music Center's continuing social, educational, and cultural activities. Chandler's all-woman Blue Ribbon Committee continued its peerless fund-raising. The women performed so well that Chandler renamed the group, "The Amazing Blue Ribbon 400."

Chandler rarely missed a target of opportunity, few could resist her cajoling and charm, and more often than not an appeal resulted in a check written on the spot. The Hollywood gossip columnist Hedda Hopper "popped one back to Buff" for her exasperating persistence with her handwritten notes: "If you ever send me another one, I'll punch you smack in the nose!" However, inside the envelope was Hopper's personal check. [11]

"The Music Center was the most educational experience of my life," Chandler told San Francisco women who had waited in line to hear her speak at a luncheon of the Junior League in 1966. The word *culture,* she said, was misused and abused, as it had nothing to do with class structure. "I think of culture as education, knowledge related," she told her audience. "Most importantly," she said, culture is to "be experienced as a vital part of making each person a total human being." Chandler and Murphy shared the belief that culture has an important role not only in the enrichment of individual lives but also in the promotion of civic harmony, a concept that would receive more attention in years to come in the debates over globalization.[12]

Clockwise from left. Franklin Murphy and Vassar student Judith Joyce Harris met on a blind date during their undergraduate years. "Franklin had a purpose in life," she said. The couple were wed on December 28, 1940, in Kansas City, Missouri. (Courtesy Franklin L. Murphy)

Franklin Murphy, ca. 1932–33. Following the unexpected death of his father in 1933, Franklin quickly matured and decided to make medicine his career. He attended the Pennsylvania School of Medicine, his father's alma mater. When he graduated first in his class, he noted with satisfaction that "a little ol' Kansas boy" had beaten the Ivy Leaguers to the wire. (Courtesy Franklin L. Murphy)

Franklin Murphy enjoyed a meteoric rise from private physician to dean of the medical school and then to chancellor of the University of Kansas at Lawrence. (Courtesy Franklin L. Murphy)

University of Kansas Chancellor Franklin Murphy with President Harry Truman in May 1955. At the request of the president, Murphy delivered the banquet speech at the Hotel Muehlebach in Kansas City, Missouri, following the groundbreaking for the Truman Presidential Library. (Courtesy Franklin L. Murphy)

Murphy with John F. Kennedy, then a senator, during a visit to the University of Kansas campus in October 1957. (Courtesy Franklin L. Murphy)

The young Murphy family photographed at the chancellor's residence in Lawrence, Kansas. From left to right: Franklin D., Franklin L., Joyce, Martha, Carolyn, and Judy. (Courtesy Franklin L. Murphy)

The annual Nightshirt Parade, a KU tradition that stretched back to the turn of the century, took place for the last time on September 27, 1957, while Franklin Murphy was chancellor. (Courtesy Franklin L. Murphy)

Franklin Murphy served as chancellor of UCLA from 1960 to 1968. As the intellectual upheaval of the 1960s gathered steam in universities around the world, Murphy warned educators that they were in the midst of "the most extraordinary revolution ever, and only revolutionary minds . . . can face it successfully." (Courtesy Franklin L. Murphy)

Left to right: UCLA Chancellor Franklin Murphy, President Dwight Eisenhower, and University of California President Clark Kerr at the Charter Day ceremonies in 1963. Despite their heated clashes, Kerr gave Murphy full credit for the transformation of UCLA into a world-class university. (Courtesy Franklin L. Murphy)

With tensions continuing across the country over voting rights, Murphy embraced the arrival on campus in April 1965 of Martin Luther King Jr. King's historic march from Selma to Montgomery, Alabama, had taken place in March under the protection of federal troops. Murphy supported King's visit despite legitimate fears over security, the potential for violence, and the adamant disapproval of some university regents. (Courtesy UCLA University Archives, University of California, Los Angeles)

Franklin Murphy and Jacques Lipchitz. When completed in 1967, the Franklin D. Murphy Sculpture Garden at UCLA was considered one of the most significant in the nation, featuring works by Henri Matisse, Alexander Calder, and Henry Moore, as well as Lipchitz. (Courtesy Franklin L. Murphy)

Norman Chandler and his wife, Dorothy Chandler, in front of their home, September 1968. The city and the *Los Angeles Times* had long been entwined: the couple were catalysts for the city's future, continuing the family's long-standing role in shaping Los Angeles. (Courtesy Franklin L. Murphy)

Opposite top, left to right: Franklin Murphy, Edwin Wendell Pauley, and Dorothy Chandler. As UCLA chancellor, Murphy worked closely with the strong-willed regents of the University of California, linked with them in a network of influence and authority. (Courtesy Franklin L. Murphy)

Opposite bottom: On April 12, 1960, Norman Chandler passed the role of *Los Angeles Times* publisher to his son, Otis Chandler. The Otis-Chandler family had been major figures in the city since 1886 when the family patriarch, Harrison Gray Otis, acquired the Times Mirror Company. Norman Chandler had succeeded his father, Harry Chandler, as publisher and also as chief executive of the Times Mirror Company. (Herald-Examiner Collection / Los Angeles Public Library)

Dorothy Chandler with Howard Ahmanson. Dorothy Chandler was "bound and determined to bring culture to her much maligned city." She had raised $45 million to complete the three-building Music Center complex. *Time* described her efforts as "the most impressive display of virtuoso money raising and civic citizenship in the history of US womanhood." (Courtesy The Ahmanson Foundation)

Opposite top: "We can start digging," Dorothy Chandler announced in 1960 when funding goals were met for the city's grand new music pavilion. Completed in 1964, the Los Angeles Music Center provided a much-needed centerpiece to the city atop Bunker Hill. Fountains graced the plaza in front of the concert hall, later renamed the Dorothy Chandler Pavilion. (Security Pacific Collection / Los Angeles Public Library)

Opposite bottom: When the Los Angeles County Museum of Art opened on Wilshire Boulevard in March 1965, it was the largest museum west of the Mississippi, forcing the *New York Times* to grant that it was an "impressive achievement" for the newly emerging cultural establishment in Southern California. (Courtesy The Ahmanson Foundation)

Howard F. Ahmanson, founder of the hugely successful Home Savings, in front of the Ahmanson Gallery at the Los Angeles County Museum of Art. He started the Ahmanson Foundation, which directed much of its philanthropy toward organizations and institutions based in Los Angeles. "Let's start with the idea that we are building a new way of life out here," he said. After Ahmanson's unexpected death, Murphy spent more than twenty years unraveling the foundation's complex financial and legal problems. (Courtesy The Ahmanson Foundation)

Robert H. Ahmanson, nephew of the financier Howard Ahmanson and president of the Ahmanson Foundation, photographed with a bust of Franklin D. Murphy. Established in 1952, the foundation endeavors to increase the quality of life and cultural legacy of the city of Los Angeles. (Courtesy The Ahmanson Foundation)

When the Los Angeles County Museum of Art opened on Wilshire Boulevard in spring 1965, it was the largest museum west of the Mississippi, forcing the *New York Times* to grant that it was an "impressive achievement" for the newly emerging cultural establishment in Southern California. The architectural plan by William Pereira called for three pavilions grouped together on a plaza surrounded by reflecting pools, creating the illusion that the museum's white, marble-clad buildings were afloat. Fountain jets installed in the shallow pools sent shimmering sprays into the air.

The formal reception for the museum's founding patrons took place on the evening of March 24, 1965, with a lavish dinner served in the dramatic three-story atrium of the Ahmanson Building. A beaming Ed Carter greeted guests with handshakes and kisses amid the "many-fountained splendor" of the forecourt. Benefactors Howard Ahmanson, Anna Bing Arnold, and Bart Lytton, the patrons for whom the three museum buildings were named, were welcomed by the museum director, Richard Brown, and the reception's hosts, Franklin Murphy, Sidney Brody, and David R. Bright.[13] The spectacular Ahmanson atrium was aglow with candlelight and flowers. From the gallery levels, strolling guests looked down to the floor of the atrium, where formal table settings and elaborate bouquets arranged in huge silver goblets complemented the sixteenth- and seventeenth-century paintings on display. When the dinner was under way, the serving staff moved among the tables offering patrons Beef Wellington and king crab legs prepared by the chefs of Perino's Restaurant. The evening ended with speeches, toasts, and accolades.

The museum opened its doors to the public a week later, on March 31, to great fanfare and publicity. Other names may have been on the museum buildings, but it was Norton Simon's collection, on loan only, that was the centerpiece.[14] Without Simon's paintings, the museum's collection, in the words of *Newsweek*'s art critic, was "little more than non-vintage wine in shiny modern bottles."[15]

The collection that had been moved from Exposition Park included works from major periods of Western art, along with a few Asian pieces. Collectors had been donating works to the county since 1918, and though there were some notable pieces, the local art community persisted in referring to the collection as "jugs and junk." The museum also suffered from a lack of art world respect for two of its major donors, J. Paul Getty and William Randolph Hearst. Getty had donated some fine works, including a Rembrandt, but he was criticized as a bargain hunter who acquired good deals in distressed times. Hearst gave the museum more than fifty old master paintings and sent thousands of objects from his castle on the California coast and from his various warehouses. In spite of his donation of more than $1 million to the museum for art purchases, the art world refused to credit him with a worthy interest in art, calling him an "accumulator," not a collector.[16]

Murphy knew that development of a truly fine collection was the only path to overcoming the museum's blighted reputation. Carter candidly admitted that the Los Angeles County Museum of Art, now dubbed LACMA, did not yet have a great collection of its own, but museum trustees were optimistic. With a handsome new building and Los Angeles's wealth to draw on, the two men were confident that fine paintings would come. Simon's extensive loan seemed such a grand symbol of his commitment to the museum that, for the time being, his withdrawn million-dollar promise was forgotten.

It was not only the collection that was criticized, however. Pereira's architectural plan had been influenced by Minoru Yamasakis's much-admired Pavilion of Science at the 1962 Seattle World's Fair, but reusing the concept was not applauded. The idea was derived from a "tired design," critics complained. The facade with its "disconcertingly close" columns was dismissed as "fussy, futuristic Gothic Revival."

Ahmanson had crossed swords with Brown, the museum's director, in contentious meetings to select an architect. Brown argued for Mies van der Rohe, but Ahmanson wanted the artist and architectural designer Millard Sheets.[17] Sheets had completed more than forty of Ahmanson's Home Savings and Loan buildings using mosaic tile, murals, and sculpture to highlight themes of home and family. The buildings were popular with the public and a drawing card for business.[18] Ahmanson wanted the same kind of visual attraction for the museum. After lengthy heated debate, the board of trustees settled the issue by selecting Pereira, an acknowledged master of design for large-scale building complexes. Ahmanson was familiar with Pereira's work: in the early 1960s Home Savings and Loan had engaged him to execute the master plan for development of a 6,300-acre parcel in Calabasas owned by the company.[19] In 1963 Pereira was featured on the cover of *Time* for his master plan of Irvine, California, expected to rise full-blown in the pastures of the Irvine cattle ranch.[20] Pereira's stylish, yet efficient, modernist approach would provide a dominant look for Los Angeles for the next thirty years, as seen in his designs for the Los Angeles International

Airport and CBS Television City as well as facilities for hospitals, air bases, and campuses, including the Dickson Art Center at UCLA.

Murphy was disappointed that Pereira's design for LACMA did not win acclaim, but he thought the architectural layout functioned well. The permanent collection was housed beautifully in the Ahmanson Building, and the Lytton Building for temporary exhibitions showcased the Norton Simon Collection. The Bing Auditorium complemented this with a promising schedule of programs.

The architecture, though important, was not the key element; the quality of the collection was what counted, and that was where Murphy intended to assert his full influence despite being caught in the middle between Brown and Ahmanson, his close friend and fellow trustee. Ahmanson had an exceptional understanding of why cultural venues were critical to a maturing city, and he had the willingness and resources to contribute heavily to building an arts infrastructure for Los Angeles; on the other hand, Brown was determined to establish the highest museum standards for the collection, an approach that Murphy did not want abandoned.

Less than eight months after the museum's grand opening, Brown handed in his resignation at the request of the trustees. His forced departure drew the ire of the art community and brought another round of unwelcome news coverage.[21] The *New York Times* lamented Los Angeles's cultural immaturity and quoted Brown's oblique references to misguided donors ignorant of museum standards.[22] *Newsweek* depicted the trustees as wealthy dilettantes bent on self-aggrandizement who micromanaged the staff and argued with one another over where to hang paintings.[23] *Time* referred to the acrimony as a case of growing pains and, in noting the stress caused by powerful benefactors pulling in different directions, paid a left-handed compliment to the collection as "a triumph of individualistic donations."[24] The *Nation* wrote that culture had become the latest bandwagon phenomenon: "men who have prospered by grabbing front seats on band wagons are jumping aboard the art wagon."[25] The editors of the Los Angeles–based *Artforum* doubted that any self-respecting museum official could be enticed to replace Brown as director.[26]

Murphy urged the board to reconsider, and at one point he succeeded in bringing in an independent business consultant to assess the situation. Against Murphy's recommendation, the board rejected the consultant's report. Even Brown's relationship with Norton Simon failed to mend the divide. The *Los Angeles Times* admonished the board for undercutting Brown's authority in his creative and administrative mandate, noting that thousands of citizens had contributed to the construction of the new museum and "all citizens shared the sense of community pride it inspired."[27]

The persistent bad press made LACMA seem the brat in the family of museums, juvenile and immature. "We would have preferred to see Ric go on the friendliest of terms," board president Ed Carter told *Time,* "with a big civic dinner and all flags flying." But the rift between the Harvard-educated scholar and the wealthy board was too deep to fix. Carter simply stated that the board's decision was based "on [Brown's] demonstrated inability to deal adequately with the administrative problems of a major museum."[28]

Once it was obvious that the board could not be swayed, Murphy accepted the situation, joining Carter in a public relations effort to restore morale and civic enthusiasm. In his comments to the press, Murphy said the crisis was merely an unfortunate case of "growing pangs" and the important work of the museum would march forward.

After leaving Los Angeles, Brown went to Fort Worth, Texas, where he was welcomed as the new director of a museum being planned to house the collection of the wealthy businessman Kay Kimbell. To design the museum building, Brown selected the Philadelphia architect Louis I. Kahn, who created a remarkable structure featuring dramatic cycloid curves. (The museum opened in 1972 and today is regarded as one of Kahn's finest architectural achievements.)

The search for a new LACMA director ended in June 1966, when the trustees gave the job to the museum's deputy director, Kenneth Donahue. Donahue, a scholar and specialist in seventeenth-century Italian art, was respected in art circles, and though he was not the energetic force that Brown had been—in fact, he was low-key and somewhat formal—he was appreciated by the staff, and, of great importance, the trustees were comfortable with him. Once museum operations were back on track, the board announced a campaign to match the $12 million they had previously raised for the building with a $12 million fund for art purchases. They were now determined to tackle head-on the sneers that the museum was all building and no art.

THE SHADOW BEHIND THE GOLDEN GLOW: THE WATTS REBELLION OF AUGUST 1965

Dorothy Chandler, Ed Carter, and Franklin Murphy, with vital help from Howard Ahmanson, had merged their talents and delivered to the city a striking new performing arts center, a futuristic county art museum, and an expanding and thriving university. Leaders before them, in the early fortune-making years of the city, had concentrated on population growth, industry, and trade. The commonweal commanded little attention. Early city planners favored the petroleum industry, car culture, and suburban tract development. The opportunity passed to have a magnificent civic center, and in a similar loss, the parks and scenic boulevards characteristic of great cities never developed.

Market forces largely drove city planning, with developers creating housing for their targeted segment—from two-bedroom "ranch houses" in Lakewood and the San Fernando Valley for white workforce families to châteaus in the foothills for the prosperous. Minority families and immigrants moved to the fringes of the city, into neighborhoods left behind by whites moving to the suburbs. The failure of planners to develop public space and create cultural resources had caused Los Angeles to grow without a sense of place, without a feeling of common community.[29]

The value of cultural amenities in developing pride in a city and a sense of cohesion was not lost on the new breed of cultural activists wanting a truly cosmopolitan city. Their city-in-process made headlines worldwide in the summer of 1965, not for the new museum in Hancock Park, but for the explosion of civil unrest in the South Central section of the city. Newspapers reported that in the mostly African American community of Watts, rioters shouting "Burn, baby, burn" were setting block after block of stores and businesses ablaze. Triggered by the arrest of a drunk driver the afternoon of August 11, the civil unrest and anarchy continued for six days, ending in the deaths of thirty-four people, the wounding of a thousand, and an estimated $50 million to $100 million in property damage.[30] Thousands of officers from the Los Angeles Police Department (LAPD), the Sheriff's Department, and the Highway Patrol were drawn into action, supported by National Guard troops.

The *Los Angeles Times,* with no black reporters on staff, called on a black classified ad salesman to enter the riot-torn neighborhood and bring back reports.[31] After three days of looting and arson and with uncontrolled fires spreading toward the civic center ten miles away, the National Guard moved forward in force to halt sniper fire and help the LAPD set up skirmish lines to bring the area under control. Police Chief William H. Parker and Mayor Sam Yorty deplored the uprising, blaming it on "propaganda" over civil rights. The chief told citizens the riot was a wake-up call, warning, "Next time they'll burn up the whole city." He said the country was being undermined through "destruction of its internal discipline," encouraged by liberal judges who were "protecting the criminal." President Johnson, warning of "Los Angeles–type" racial conflict in other cities, including the capital, dispatched a task force to help rehabilitate riot-torn areas and report on the reason for the violence. Governor Brown, suspecting outside agitators, appointed John McCone, a San Marino resident and the former head of the CIA, to investigate the persons and factors behind the disturbance.[32]

The underlying causes of the Watts rebellion had been brewing, unnoticed or unacknowledged, for years. Los Angeles prided itself on never having had Jim Crow laws; drinking fountains and public accommodations had never been segregated. However, until 1953 deed restrictions could be used to establish and preserve all-white enclaves; as a consequence modern Los Angeles developed as a de facto segregated city. Black families settled in the southern section of the city, and the area around Watts became one of the largest black ghettos in the country. Hispanics gravitated to the east side of the city.[33]

Housing discrimination had a long history in Los Angeles. Restrictive covenants had barred people of color from most new tracts, and even after racial restrictions in deeds were no longer legal, Federal Housing Administration appraisers downgraded loans for tracts with mixed races. The management of the huge Lakewood development of moderately priced homes protected its government loan guarantees by discouraging minority buyers and advertising the tract—in the code language of the era—as a "100% American community."[34] Appraisers who redlined minority neighborhoods gave even lower loan ratings to what they called "heterogeneous areas."[35]

In addition to the government studies under way, civic-minded business leaders went into action. Murphy was asked to join the downtown business group to assess the causes of discontent and plan for the future of the city's core. Asa Call formed the Committee of 25, established that winter "to determine the true Establishment position on civic matters."[36] Committee members found themselves divided over the issue of political leadership; the old guard largely supported the mayor and the police chief, while another faction, which included Murphy and Otis Chandler, felt that Chief Parker's brutal policing policies in minority communities were a hazard to the city and that Mayor Yorty's intractable support of the chief meant the city could not be at peace until both were replaced. Chandler brought the force of the *Times* into play, calling for the ouster of Yorty and the dismissal of Parker. Attention began to focus on Councilman Tom Bradley as a potential mayoral candidate. This black politician, known and respected in minority communities, had been a popular UCLA athlete, had studied law, and had then risen to the rank of lieutenant in the LAPD before running for public office.

After the explosion of civil unrest, city leaders realized that in preparing the downtown business district for the emerging global economy they had ignored the immense labor pool, now displaced, that had served Los Angeles during its heyday as an industrial center. The downtown skyline was being reshaped with the city's first soaring office towers, promising highly paid jobs in management and the high-tech sector, but job loss on the shop floor had left thousands of industrial workers unemployed in local industries such as steel, rubber, and automobile manufacture.

In addition to economic distress as a factor in the Watts eruption, goodwill had been shattered when racial animosity became blatant in the opposition of white citizens to the Rumford Fair Housing Act, passed by the California legislature in 1960. The subsequent campaign to repeal the act through the referendum process polarized communities. When the referendum, Proposition 14, passed in 1964, permitting continued discrimination in the sale and rental of housing, people of color felt they were seeing the manifestation of deep-rooted intolerance in the city. This revelation, coupled with the images on nightly television news of white resistance to black civil rights across the country, built a growing awareness of the depth of American racism. Implementation of Proposition 14 was blocked by the courts, and the federal Fair Housing Act soon settled the issue; but in the meantime, African American, Hispanic, and Asian Angelenos had learned an ugly truth about many of the white citizens of their shared city.

In the history of the city, the chamber of commerce and the Automobile Club were two powerful entities setting the rules for growth. Conservative business leaders opposed to federal programs shut the door on assistance to minority communities that might have been available through government grants. Prosperous whites, grounded in the values of strict morality and individualism, held firm beliefs about local control, private property, and private development, seemingly unaware of the need to consider the city as a whole in order to make it viable and livable.

Murphy, the Chandlers, and other members of the coalition seeking new city leadership hoped to institute a sense of obligation to the entire city. Watts now had everyone's attention. In the aftermath of the uprising, the *Los Angeles Times* would win a Pulitzer Prize for its coverage, task forces would scour Watts for data, and Murphy would be among the civic leaders the stunned city would look to for solutions. The long-accepted silent segregation of Los Angeles was now revealed. A first step toward change was acknowledgment of the dark shadow behind the city's golden glow.

UNIVERSITY IN TURMOIL

The previous fall the Berkeley campus gave birth to the Free Speech Movement, in which students won the right to hold discussions and conduct campaigns dealing with off-campus issues. The student protests at Berkeley had been disorderly and volatile but not entirely unexpected. Kerr had earlier returned from a two-month trip to Europe and Asia, where he had seen an explosion of student opposition to authority. He had warned the California regents that it was only a matter of time before American universities would erupt as well. "Elements of youth, as never before, were rising in rebellion against the civilizations they had inherited," he told them.[37]

Worldwide, the generation coming to maturity had serious questions about their elders' decisions as they faced a world divided rigidly by ideology and threatened with nuclear destruction. Youth in the industrialized countries were questioning their personal options in a highly technological age. Efficiency and productivity had become such overriding goals that modern homes were described as "machines to live in" and universities were seen as part of the "knowledge industry." The modern era at midcentury seemed regimented, hierarchical, and unsatisfying and, despite technological promise, ineffective in redressing poverty and racism, attending to the environment, or achieving peace among nations.

Kerr had been apprehensive about the 1964–65 school year. He knew that UC students outraged by their experience in the Mississippi Summer voter registration campaign would be returning to campus as dedicated activists schooled in civil disobedience. In addition, the nomination of conservative hawk Barry Goldwater as the Republican presidential candidate augured a fierce campaign, made all the more passionate after President Johnson secured passage of the Gulf of Tonkin resolution authorizing U.S. bombing of North Vietnam. In California the November election had the added tension of Proposition 14, which threatened to repeal the state's recently enacted Fair Housing Act.

Students demanded the right to be a part of the debate and resented campus rules that restricted political advocacy. Following the arrest of a former graduate student for handing out leaflets at Sproul Plaza, the Berkeley campus became the scene of a fierce struggle between the young activists and the university administration. Rallies and demonstrations were staged as students held to their position that speech that is constitutionally protected off campus should be protected on campus. On December 7 a raucous protest at Sproul Hall resulted in eight hundred student protestors being arrested, dragged from the building, and taken to detention centers. Enshrining the event was the statement of Mario Savio, a philosophy student and activist who had spent the summer in Mississippi registering black voters: "There is a time when the operation of the machine becomes so odious, makes you so sick at heart, that you can't take part; you can't even passively take part, and you've got to put your bodies upon the gears and upon the wheels, upon the levers, upon all the apparatus and you've got to make it stop."[38]

Students released on bail showed up on campus with cardboard name tags made to look like IBM punch cards that read: "I am a student: Do not Fold, Spindle or Mutilate." In a huge noontime rally more than five thousand persons filled Sproul Plaza to hear protest leaders, now joined by a number of faculty members, condemn the action of the administration. Kerr had attempted to assist Berkeley Chancellor Edward W. Strong and had urged him to mediate the crisis, but Strong, who was outraged by the student protests, had called police to campus. For their part, the students took a Goldwater-like stance that extremism in defense of their rights was no vice.

After an uneasy Christmas break, students returned to classes in January 1965 to learn that the regents had revised previous policy, and political and social advocacy dealing with off-campus issues would now be permitted on campus. Directives were drawn as to time, manner, and place. At UCLA, Murphy and Chuck Young assembled student committees to designate locations and work out rules for free speech activities.

In addition to political advocacy, students registered complaints about campus conditions and the quality of their education. They were angry about instruction in huge auditorium classrooms, long registration lines, and the impersonal, bureaucratic regimentation represented by the IBM cards that had come to rule their lives. Murphy was ready to let students have their say and was supportive of their desire to involve themselves in campus decisions. What he would not allow, however, was the kind of disruption the world had seen at Berkeley.

Murphy observed in the goals of the student activists the embodiment of a far-reaching revolution. He saw genuine interest on the part of young people to create a better world, one that called for new ways of thinking and new approaches to problems. He knew the battleground for this revolt would be the university, as it should be, and he knew that the youthful warriors would bring energy and imagination to the conflict. He acknowledged the coming of a social and political storm but did not fear it. Any institution worthy of being called a university was destined to be in tension with the society that supported it. "If there is not tension, it is not a university," he said. "It is a trade school." As chancellor, he had often said that the primary function of the university is the examination of presumed truth; students were now taking a hard look at the truths they had been expected to take for granted.[39]

As perceptive as Murphy was in acknowledging that student protest was part of a larger philosophical critique of the quality of postwar life and the tenets of modernity, he seemed blind to the battle under way by another, older segment of the population. The religious fundamentalists and the ultraconservatives—the John Birchers and others—felt they, too, were at the mercy of factors over which they had no control. They protested that an expanding government encroached on their lives, that their property rights were infringed by taxes supporting a creeping socialism, and that they were victimized by laws that forced open housing and school integration. They were losing control of their communities and their families; their children were subjected to progressive education and the values of secular humanism. They felt bombarded by pornography and indecency, and found their wishes ignored over such issues as sex education in the schools. They suspected that the call for racial equality, the sexual revolution, and the "do your own thing" cultural imperative were all part of an underlying Communist strategy to disrupt "family values" and ultimately destroy the free enterprise system. With the problems of the university commanding his full attention, Murphy was unaware at the time of growing discontent in other quarters.

· · · · ·

Though he knew the public had little patience with the rowdy demonstrators, Murphy felt student demands at UCLA could be handled fairly and effectively. The board of regents established the Special Committee to Investigate Basic Causes of Recent Disturbances on the Berkeley Campus, chaired by William E. Forbes. At the suggestion of Dorothy Chandler, a Los Angeles attorney, Jerome Byrne, was selected to write the report.

Murphy spent so much time with Byrne that the resulting document, the Byrne Report, came to be referred to as the "Murphy Report." Byrne was largely sympathetic to the Free Speech Movement and supported the right of students to engage in social and political advocacy. Byrne's analysis also proposed a somewhat radical and far-reaching reorganization in which the University of California would be divided into "separately chartered" universities. Under Byrne's plan, chancellors would have complete responsibility for each campus. This last provision was Murphy's hand at work, since the autonomy he felt he had been promised had not materialized.

Murphy applauded the report, but it was flatly rejected by the board of regents who dismissed Byrne's recommendation for restructuring the sprawling university system.[40] The regents' decision was a relief to Clark Kerr. "What I thought of as Murphy's rebellion had been put down," Kerr wrote in his memoirs. "Murphy's attempt to turn the . . . University of California into a confederation of nine independent campuses had failed."[41] However, the report may not have been without effect. As university president, Kerr undertook greater decentralization during this period, and chancellors were given more control over personnel actions and the authority to approve research grants, contracts, and budget transfers. Kerr insisted the changes were part of a long-established overall plan and were not the result of pressure from the ambitious UCLA chancellor.[42]

Murphy nevertheless managed to declare the result a personal victory, for the *Times* education writer, William Trombley, credited the Los Angeles chancellor for the new procedures in an article headlined, "UCLA Autonomy Fight Believed Won." "In the past Dr. Murphy frequently has compared the University of California to a dinosaur, with a central nervous system unable to cope with its anatomical growth," wrote Trombley. "However, in a recent interview [Murphy] said, 'What we are seeing now is a splendid and successful attempt to match the nervous system to the body.'"[43]

For Clark Kerr, the incident was another example of Murphy's manipulative style. "He preferred to work the phones, the halls and the social gatherings in advance," Kerr groused, "rather than engage in direct confrontations." Kerr found Murphy almost impossible to manage. Noting that Murphy dropped his idea to reorganize the university, he said that Murphy had a deep-seated need to be on the right side of an issue and was always quick to abandon lost causes.[44]

· · · · ·

The UCLA chancellor put into effect the regents' new free speech policy. He opened the campus to a wide range of speakers, even though he was accused of allowing the dissemination of dangerous ideas. "The University exists *not to protect* students, *but to prepare* them," Murphy responded. "This is not a playpen. It is a university."[45]

In April 1965, four months before the uprising in Watts, Murphy embraced the arrival on campus of Martin Luther King Jr. In March, King had led a historic march from Selma to Montgomery, Alabama, with the protection of federal troops. Murphy approved King's visit despite legitimate fears over security, the potential for violence, and the adamant disapproval of some regents.[46] King visited with Murphy at the chancellor's residence and then was escorted by Murphy on a brief tour of the campus to come, where buildings encased in scaffolding promised to welcome a record number of students under the university's master plan; both men were looking to a future they hoped would bring enlightenment and tolerance.

More than five thousand students gathered at the Janss Steps to hear King's address on race relations, poverty, and nonviolence. They heard King declare that the strength of American blacks was undaunted. "We will match your capacity to inflict suffering by our capacity to endure suffering," he said.[47]

COLOSSAL CONSTRUCTION

Murphy continued to be fully occupied with the final phases of what was described as the greatest construction effort undertaken to date by any American university. Vice-Chancellor Bill Young supervised the day-to-day details of erecting eighteen new campus buildings at a cost of more than $100 million.[48] Cranes, bulldozers, and earthmovers were visible in every corner of the campus, and students and faculty were forced to endure the thud of jackhammers and the high-pitched whine of power saws. Completing buildings for a fast-escalating enrollment and maintaining a unified architectural style challenged an army of specialists.

Murphy established an excellent rapport with Welton Beckett, whose instructions were to build in a contemporary idiom but to respect the university's original Romanesque architecture. Royce Hall, the university's enduring trademark, had established the original design for the central campus. But the cost of materials and craftsmanship to continue the bricklayer's art expressed in the older buildings was no longer feasible. The regents committed to a departure from the Romanesque theme when they engaged Beckett, whose solution was to give the new modernist buildings of the North and South Campuses integrity of their own while leaving the original quadrangle intact.[49]

Murphy took a particular interest in planning the outdoor area of North Campus, site of the humanities departments. For North Campus, he was unwilling to accept the concrete courtyards that dominated South Campus, home of the sciences; he wanted trees and greenery—sycamore, eucalyptus, jacaranda, and coral trees under which students could stroll and study. He conceived a four-and-a-half-acre outdoor sculpture court dotted with lush plantings. The garden was widely praised when it was completed. "The garden nestles amid a cluster of spanking new buildings," wrote *Time* magazine, crediting Murphy with the idyllic spot amid the frenzy of new construction.[50]

The landscape architect Ralph D. Cornell worked for several years with Murphy on the project. At the garden's dedication Murphy told guests, "There cannot be beauty of spirit without beauty of environment."[51] It was a truism he expressed often and a concept he sought ways to fulfill. The assembled artwork by Jacques Lipchitz, Henri Matisse, Alexander Calder, and Henry Moore, one of the most significant installations of twentieth-century sculpture in the United States, had been made possible by private gifts from Anna Bing Arnold, Mrs. Charles Ducommon, Sidney F. Brody, Norton Simon, and the estate of David E. Bright. It was appropriately noted that Murphy's garden was one of the few places in the world where a student could walk out of a sculpture class and see a work by Auguste Rodin or Tony Rosenthal.[52]

• • • • •

During the hectic years of construction on campus and student demonstrations, Murphy escorted his oldest daughters, Joyce and Martha, down the aisle. Joyce, who had graduated from Bryn Mawr College and was teaching at a high school near Los Angeles, married attorney Walter "Chip" Dickey on June 26, 1965. At twenty-two, Joyce looked very much like her mother, with strong cheekbones and blue eyes. She had a tall, slender frame and wore her clothes like a fashion model. However, Murphy was not enthusiastic about the match. He was forthright in his complaints to Judy, but the wedding plans had momentum of their own. For the couple's wedding reception, Judy transformed the grounds of the chancellor's residence into a garden world where flowers, music, and the laughter of several hundred guests gave the young couple a memorable send-off.

Martha's wedding followed two years later, on June 24, 1967. At twenty-three, Martha married UCLA law student Craig Crockwell. The couple had met when they were students at Stanford University. Following her graduation from Stanford, Martha had earned a master's degree in social work at UCLA. She was an avid reader and an exceptional student, and, according to her aunt, Cordie Ennis, if she had been born male, she would have made a fine doctor. She was organized and energetic and shared many of her father's best traits. Martha, not as interested in high fashion as her sister, chose silk organza for her wedding gown and carried an old-fashioned bouquet of mixed wildflowers. Judy saw to it that the wedding service was beautiful and traditional—nothing of the hippie, counterculture-type celebration that was then becoming popular. Martha's cousins Rebecca and Kevin Ennis, five and seven years old, served as flower girl and ring bearer. Over the years Murphy grew close to Craig and often relied on him for legal counsel. Martha had always enjoyed good rapport with her father, though she was the most outspoken of the four children.[53]

With Joyce and Martha married, Judy and Franklin had completed the rearing of the first contingent of their family. The next group, Carolyn and Franklin Lee, would soon be in college. They remembered that during their teenage years they were largely supervised by Willia and Ted Roberts. Franklin Lee recalled his father as a figure of great authority who entered the house at the end of the day like a thunderclap, gave orders, and was gone the next morning.[54] He observed his father's civic reach during his years at UCLA. "It seemed like anything important to the city came through Dad," he said. "He was always on the telephone speaking to somebody famous. As a young boy, I thought he was God."[55]

A THREAT TO CLARK KERR

In summer 1965, as another call-up of the draft loomed, Berkeley students used their newly won free speech prerogatives to mount campus demonstrations against the war. They staged student marches for peace and blocked the doors to army induction centers. Throughout the nation large demonstrations and public burnings of draft cards became commonplace. Kerr conceded that the once-serene campus at Berkeley had become "ground zero" for the burgeoning peace movement.

Television images of hippies with daisies in their hair and determined demonstrators at Berkeley were broadcast to a national audience. The steady stream of pictures was humiliating to the university regents, who feared that Kerr lacked the strength—or the will, Pauley claimed—to bring an end to the chaos. The regents demanded to know why the jewel of the California education system was under the control of student activists.

Also that summer the state senate's Burns Committee, which investigated un-American activities, released a report accusing Kerr of fostering a subversive atmosphere on campus. While the Burns Report was still front-page news, Pauley sought to round up support for Kerr's dismissal. It was well known that Pauley, infuriated over the student protests, believed the campus disturbances were Communist directed. (Later, in explaining Pauley's vendetta, Kerr said he felt that power was the real issue for the wealthy oilman, and fighting Communism was simply his chosen tactic.)[56]

Murphy learned of the depth of Pauley's effort against Kerr soon after his arrival in San Francisco for a scheduled meeting with the university regents. In the hotel cocktail lounge he encountered several regents who had just concluded a heated private session. "There's a movement afoot tomorrow to fire Clark Kerr," Dorothy Chandler told him. "And it's touch and go. There are a group that absolutely are determined that he should go and go now; there are a small group that are absolutely determined that he stay; and then there's a large group of us in the center."[57]

When she asked Murphy what he thought, he insisted that firing Kerr would not solve the Berkeley problem and would only lead to greater agitation. He felt so strongly that such action would be detrimental to the university that he made hurried arrangements to meet Norton Simon for breakfast before the regents' meeting in an effort to swing the vote in Kerr's favor. Murphy told Simon that firing Kerr would be throwing "a stick of dynamite into the whole statewide university problem."[58] In the hallway just before the meeting was about to begin, Murphy found an opportunity to make a similar appeal to Phil Boyd, a member of the moderate faction.

Murphy was not privy to the actions the regents took behind closed doors, but recorded minutes show that the meeting opened with a motion by Chandler expressing appreciation of Kerr's administrative skill and moved on to other matters.[59] Murphy went back to Los Angeles badly shaken; he knew there was friction, but he had not realized there was the possibility of Kerr's involuntary removal. Murphy's first instinct was to warn him. "If he and I had had a relationship, he was the first one I'd have gone to," Murphy recounted later, saying he did not feel able to talk to Kerr directly. "At that point I had more influence than he did, and that's a humiliating thing for a proud man to realize."[60] For the time being, Kerr was retained as head of the university, but Murphy knew Kerr's position was tenuous.

Ronald Reagan announced his candidacy for governor of California on January 4, 1966, pledging to clean up the mess at Berkeley and calling for the dismissal of administrators and professors who contributed to the degradation of the University of California. Reagan's pronouncements landed him on the cover of *Newsweek,* but Democratic governor Edmund Brown failed to fully comprehend the threat both to his reelection to a third term and to the well-being of the university.

Shortly after Labor Day Reagan promised voters that he would immediately investigate Berkeley's student activism with help from John McCone, who had written the report on the Watts civil unrest and now served Reagan as a policy adviser.[61] Reagan's campaign rhetoric was deeply disturbing to Murphy. Chandler was equally dismayed, although her social circle supported Reagan's candidacy. Regent and former UCLA Alumni president H. R. "Bob" Haldeman tried, with only moderate success, to persuade Reagan campaign strategists to back off on diatribes against the university.[62]

In one burst of campaign oratory Reagan described the university at Berkeley as a hotbed of Communism and sexual deviance.[63] Murphy thought such sentiments would lose Reagan credibility, but he was wrong. Voters responded overwhelmingly in Reagan's favor, and on November 8 Reagan defeated the incumbent by more than one million votes. Staunch support for Reagan came from conservative groups that had quietly organized their forces, reactivating over one hundred former Goldwater precinct organizations in Southern California. They saw Reagan as the candidate who would get government off their backs, restore local control, protect free enterprise, bring a halt to social engineering, and end the permissiveness at Berkeley.[64]

Filled with dread at Reagan's election, Murphy took solace in the fact that, at least for the moment, he was blessed with a quiet campus. The regents questioned him about why Berkeley was torn by student activism and UCLA was not. "Look," Murphy told them during one heated meeting, "you're talking about apples and oranges." The universities are in completely different environments, he pointed out. The Westwood campus was never the kind of magnet the Bay Area was for "the drug kids and the runaways and the great unwashed." "If I were at Berkeley," Murphy said, "I don't think I'd be doing much better. I think you've got an impossible problem, really."[65]

Nevertheless, Murphy took pride in maintaining calm at his campus, feeling that he understood the attitude of the students and that he had made preparations. It remained to be seen if Murphy's campus would remain quiet when confronted with the increasingly defiant antiwar demonstrations that followed on the heels of the Free Speech Movement.

· · · · ·

The newly elected governor was infuriated that student demonstrations attracted tourist buses to Berkeley's Sather Gate to watch the motley assortment of students and drifters in outrageous dress, carrying signs criticizing the government. In his inaugural speech, Reagan warned students that university rules would be strictly enforced. He intended to use whatever means were necessary, including armed police.

Following the gubernatorial election, Chandler asked Kerr to visit her in Los Angeles. She was then the board of regents' vice-chair. She told Kerr that she had backed him throughout his career and that he had been an outstanding university president; however, she said with regret, she was forced to support Governor Reagan in his goal to appoint a new university president. The board of regents had to acknowledge that the governor had won the election by a wide margin, reflecting the desire of voters for substantive change. Chandler did not ask Kerr to resign, but she informed him, with grace and diplomacy, that she would vote for his dismissal when the time came. (Chandler later said that telling Kerr this news was the second-hardest thing she had ever had to do in her life; the first, she said, was when she had to tell her husband, Norman, that it was "time for him to step aside" and let Otis replace him as publisher of the *Times*.)[66]

About this same time, Murphy revealed to Kerr that soon after the election four members of Reagan's kitchen cabinet had approached him to ask if he would accept the position of university president. Murphy told the delegation that he would be interested in the job but only on condition that Kerr was treated with dignity.[67] Kerr enjoyed great respect in higher education circles, and Murphy did not want to be seen as participating in a coup.

On November 17 Kerr attended a dinner at the Los Angeles home of regent Bob Haldeman in honor of the governor-elect. The self-confident, hard-driving Haldeman, a successful advertising figure and Nixon campaign official, had been devoted to UCLA and its alumni program. On the evening of the party Ed Pauley subjected the guests to a tirade on the antiwar activities of faculty members, which he called "treasonable." Reagan reportedly replied that, as governor, he personally would see to it that no one would be appointed to the faculty who lacked "moral standards." Later that night, Norton Simon, one of only a few regents who openly opposed Reagan and his administration, approached Kerr and warned him: "Before this is all over, you're going to be covered in blood."[68]

· · · · ·

In January, after his inauguration, Governor Reagan conducted a meeting of the board of regents, assembled in Berkeley. Six of the regents had already expressed their lack of confidence in Kerr, and eight who remained neutral switched their position during the closed-door two-hour session. In the end the vote was fourteen to eight, and Kerr was out. Chandler voted in favor of dismissal, but Simon vehemently opposed it.

When the closed session was concluded and the public meeting resumed, Kerr walked toward the door, where an assistant to the board stopped him. She placed her hand on his chest and said he was not allowed inside.

"It's a public meeting," Kerr told her.

"It's public to everybody but you. You're not to come in," she said.[69]

When the door was opened again the meeting was called to order by the chairman, who announced, "Clark Kerr has been dismissed as president of the university effective immediately."

Kerr saw Chandler seated directly across the long oblong conference table with a stiff, sad expression. He attempted a small smile to let her know that he understood why she voted against him. "I admired him very much and I didn't want to see him fired," Chandler said later. But, she admitted, she was a realist.[70]

As portentous as the regents' meeting was, Murphy was unable to stay for the outcome; in pain from an ear infection, he had to leave early to go to the airport, where on his arrival in Los Angeles he drove immediately to the UCLA Medical Center. As he was driving to the doctor's office, he heard on the car radio that Kerr had been fired. UC Vice President Harry Wellman was appointed acting president until a replacement for Kerr could be selected.

That night, with a throbbing pain in the side of his face, a saddened and shocked Murphy tried several times to telephone Kerr at his El Cerrito residence but was unable to reach him. Indeed, inside the Kerr family home, with its sweeping vista of San Francisco Bay, the telephone rang for hours. The four calls Kerr appreciated most came from other university giants: Nathan Pusey of Harvard, Wallace Sterling of Stanford, and Courtney Smith of Swarthmore each invited Kerr to join his institution; and from Alan Pifer, president of the Carnegie Corporation of New York, came a job proposal.[71]

The fall of Clark Kerr made front-page headlines nationwide. Kerr was diplomatic in his comments to the media. At an impromptu public assembly and press conference he received a prolonged standing ovation. It was the only moment during the ordeal, he said, when he came close to tears.

"I left the presidency just as I entered it—fired with enthusiasm," he told reporters and well-wishers. Later he acknowledged that his dismissal, especially the abrupt, immediate order lacking any courtesy and without any acknowledgment of his considerable contribution to the university, was the most painful event of his professional life.[72]

Later, facts emerged that showed a hidden dimension to Kerr's dismissal. The student chauffeur who drove the regents from the Sacramento airport to meet the governor revealed that he had overheard a historic strategy session in the backseat of the car. Several regents, including Dorothy Chandler, had resolved to ask for concessions from the governor in exchange for their vote of dismissal. The first condition was that Reagan restore the university budget to at least its previous level (restoring roughly $24 million). The second condition was that Reagan call off the McCone investigation into campus subversion. During the return trip, the student driver said, he discovered that the regents had been successful; the governor had agreed to the bargain. "When I learned of the two demands," Kerr later said, "I agreed with the regents' reaction. They were not settling for my dismissal without getting substantial concessions." In the end, Kerr told the *Los Angeles Times*, "I wasn't sold all that cheaply."[73]

· · · · ·

The obvious front-runners to replace Clark Kerr were the gifted chancellors of three UC campuses: Roger W. Heyns (successor to Edward Strong) of Berkeley, Daniel Aldrich of Irvine, and Franklin Murphy of Los Angeles. Murphy claimed that various regents approached him about the presidency, but he replied that he was not interested. Indeed, Murphy seems not to have campaigned for the job, feeling that the prevailing climate of dissension, budget cutting, and student unrest would thwart any plans he might have for achieving distinction for the university and credit for himself. Charles J. Hitch, vice president of university administration, was appointed president in 1968, and Murphy supported the selection. He felt Hitch had the skills and administrative background needed, and he was not identified with any one campus. His management style was low-key, and he enjoyed a reputation for integrity. The presidency was a great honor for the talented Harvard-educated administrator, but he would have little time to relish it; he would soon face the severest economic assaults on education ever to emanate from a governor's office. Murphy's ambition of someday heading the University of California and joining the ranks of presidents of prestigious universities as a renowned and innovative figure in U.S. education had come to an end.

· · · · ·

When Clark Kerr was asked later to reflect on the tumultuous era, he said that he saw the student uprising in a different light from many of the regents. He insisted that the campus protests were not Communist dominated and were not the beginning of a political revolution. "This was not the storming of the Winter Palace," he asserted. "To me, controversy was the world you lived in. When it hit, the Free Speech Movement, I just took it as part of life—an episode, a problem to be handled."[74]

Murphy also had a long-range view of the tumultuous events. "I believe that the whole Kerr episode was a tragedy. And I think when the dust has settled and people can get a little perspective on that, Clark will go down as a strong and gifted president," he conceded. "But in spite of everything, my job was to build UCLA and I wasn't about to let *anybody* prevent that from happening."[75]

· · · · ·

Thirty-five years after the fall of Clark Kerr a resourceful San Francisco reporter gained access to secret FBI files and learned the extent of covert activities conducted by the FBI and the CIA during the Free Speech Movement. For his groundbreaking exposé, *Chronicle* staff writer Seth Rosenfeld obtained thousands of pages of FBI records revealing that the FBI "unlawfully schemed with the head of the CIA to harass students, faculty, and members of the Board of Regents." The documents also confirmed that the agency mounted a concerted campaign to destroy the career of Clark Kerr.[76]

The records revealed that after the first large-scale protests at Berkeley, the FBI's director, J. Edgar Hoover, ordered agents to locate damaging intelligence on students, administrators, and faculty and find links with the Communist Party or other subversive groups. According to Rosenfeld, the bureau's investigation rapidly extended past gathering intelligence to manipulating public opinion. News stories were planted in the press calling the peace movement a "Marxist-dominated plot." Such stories had a broad political impact, casting Clark Kerr and Governor Brown as incompetent and a threat to national security.

According to information in the files, CIA director McCone met with Hoover and together they arranged to leak derogatory FBI reports to Ed

Pauley to stir him to action to "curtail, harass and at times eliminate" liberal university faculty. The documents also revealed the sweeping nature of the FBI's activities into the realm of California state politics. The agency fed Reagan information and catalyzed his transformation, as Rosenfeld said, "from liberal movie star to the staunch conservative who became one of the 20th century's most powerful figures." Rosenfeld's inquiry confirmed that the FBI wrecked any chance of Kerr serving in a government post (President Johnson had considered him for secretary of health, education, and welfare) by releasing accusations that he was disloyal and "pro-Communist," despite the fact that the bureau knew the charges were false. Kerr was never offered a White House appointment. Later he served as chairman of the prestigious Carnegie Commission on Higher Education. Until Rosenfeld contacted him in June 2002, Kerr was unaware of any of the FBI's unlawful campus activities or its campaign against him. "Maybe I was too naive," Kerr said when asked for his reaction.[77]

· · · · ·

In early February 1967 Murphy attended another hair-raising session with the board of regents. Ed Carter, as chair, pushed a divided body to propose realistic solutions to the economic threat to the university. "If Reagan is incapable of bending to match the unprecedented willingness of the Regents to help him out," a weary Murphy wrote Carter, "the future will look very gloomy indeed. This can only lead to enormous damage to the University over the next four years, and, in my view, to the destruction in the long run of any political aspirations that he may have."[78]

Again Murphy misjudged Reagan's political prospects. In spite of Carter's efforts, the university's request for a $278 million state appropriation was cut to $231 million. An angry and bewildered Murphy told the collected regents brusquely, "I do not intend to be present at the liquidation or substantial erosion of the quality that 50 years of effort have created."[79] Even Murphy's fans among the proud university regents bristled when they read the chancellor's bitter remarks in the September issue of *Time*. "It's a demeaning thing to run around with a tin cup, pleading with people to help their children," Murphy said of the regents' failure to protect the university's funding.[80]

Paradoxically, the removal of Clark Kerr proved a terrible setback for Murphy. Though the men had jousted with each other for power, they shared a deep commitment to the university's overall purpose. Murphy now had few allies in his efforts to fight tuition fees and the erosion of quality education. Sensing that his dreams for UCLA and for his own advancement were fading, Murphy grew increasingly short-tempered and irascible. The rise of Ronald Reagan awakened in him memories of his losing battle with George Docking, and he said he simply could not live through the experience again.[81]

Murphy would find his plans for UCLA during the final two years of his chancellorship repeatedly thwarted. In addition to severe funding cuts, he would be hard hit by assaults from the student body in ever more vigorous anti–Vietnam War protests and student actions designed, as the *Daily Bruin* put it, to "disturb the functions of the establishment."[82]

· · · · ·

Despite the campus chaos, for Murphy the world outside the university was one of pleasurable invitations and acknowledgment. In 1967 Murphy was named one of the ten most powerful men in Los Angeles. The list, a who's who of influence and civic authority, included men whom Murphy considered part of his widening circle: Ed Carter, Asa Call, Howard Ahmanson, Lew Wasserman, Charles B. "Tex" Thornton (Litton Industries), Harry Volk (Union Bank), A. C. Rubel (Union Oil), Norton Simon, and Otis Chandler.[83]

For the first time Murphy considered leaving the arena of academic administration. He was offered the chairmanship of Home Savings and Loan by Howard Ahmanson, but he declined; banking was not his field. However, the offer added to Murphy's growing sense of self. Other offers came his way, but Murphy said he was not interested.

In April 1967 Judy and Franklin Murphy accompanied Howard and Caroline Ahmanson to the opening of the handsome new 2,100-seat Ahmanson Theatre. It was the second of three planned theaters at Dorothy Chandler's Music Center complex. For the opening, the theater mounted a lavish production of *Man of La Mancha*. The evening was a triumphant celebration of Ahmanson's civic contribution to the cultural arts and a source of pride and satisfaction to the hard-driving financier. Murphy took pleasure in sharing Ahmanson's moment and looked ahead to working with him on the creation of other cultural landmarks.

Also in April came the opening of the 750-seat Mark Taper Forum. Welton Beckett's modern theater proved popular among Los Angeles theatergoers; by the end of April the Taper had virtually sold out its first season. The completion of the three-theater Music Center provided Los Angeles with one of the most versatile performing arts centers in the country. Dorothy Chandler's music and theater complex cost $34 million, less than half the $91 million price tag for New York's four-theater Lincoln Center.[84]

Live theater and music in Los Angeles that would rival Broadway's best was fast becoming reality.

As the year drew to a close, Murphy came to the hard personal realization that the university was not going to be the vehicle he had anticipated for cultural advancement. He became reluctant to engage himself further in the struggle between the board of regents and the governor. In addition to his outrage over the shortfall in funding, Murphy was apprehensive about scrutiny into the university's internal affairs in a search for subversion, and he feared a new round of witch-hunts and threats to academic freedom.

FOUR

1968—Year of Crisis

THERE WAS LITTLE ANY ADMINISTRATOR could do to stop the wave of student dissent as the nation became mired in the Vietnam War. Soon after the academic year 1968 began UCLA students staged a massive sit-in at the Administration Building, protesting campus recruitment by Dow Chemical Company, manufacturer of napalm.[1] Murphy was absent from campus as the incident erupted, and Chuck Young frantically telephoned him for instructions on how to proceed. The LAPD arrived but were sent away when Young persuaded the demonstrators to disband, promising to arrange a meeting with the chancellor.[2]

The protests, however, continued. Students for a Democratic Society (SDS) and the Vietnam Day Committee (VDC) marched through campus with megaphones, disrupting classes and urging militant resistance. Students worked up a case against the university for war complicity; the *Bruin* editorialized against university research "for the Feds"; and Murphy was accused of supporting war-related activities as a director of the Ford Motor Company, which had numerous defense contracts.[3] Students became increasingly at odds with the UCLA chancellor and on campus called him "Big Daddy," mocking his paternalism and caution.[4]

On the other side, conservative alumni complained that Murphy was losing control; Ed Pauley, calling the war protesters cowards, pressed Murphy to get a grip on campus activism; and an Alumni Association resolution condemned campus disruption and called on Murphy to explain his lax policies.[5] He was repeatedly pressed by downtown business leaders for his assurance that campus demonstrations could be contained.

The university board of regents' meetings proved chaotic and ineffective. When Governor Reagan announced plans to institute tuition fees for the first time, ten thousand angry students marched to Sacramento.[6] Norton Simon was the most vocal regent in opposition to Reagan and the cost-cutting legislature, but he emerged as a gadfly in a continuing struggle with Pauley over university investments. Longtime regent Katherine Hearst dedicated her efforts to a campaign to stop marijuana use; Bob Haldeman busied himself with Richard Nixon's presidential campaign; and an exhausted Dorothy Chandler succumbed to a sense of hopelessness, frustrated by the lack of substantive board action.[7]

THE EMBATTLED CHANCELLOR

Early on Murphy had grasped the social complexity of Los Angeles's cultural mix. He had taken a forceful interest in diversity plans, but he was unable to satisfy minority groups such as the Union of Mexican-American Students (UMAS) and the Black Student Union (BSU), whose proposals seemed to him weakly formulated and ineffective but nevertheless consumed his time and patience.[8]

The catch term *relevance* dominated student rhetoric in demands to change the humanities curriculum. Students complained that Western Civilization classes focused on achievements emanating from the European Enlightenment and therefore privileged the values of Western culture. Many younger faculty members joined the call to examine and revise the canon. Some of the faculty challenged the chancellor's decision not to issue a moratorium on recruiting by Dow Chemical Company pending a campus referendum; one professor told the *Daily Bruin,* "This could be the end of Murphy if every card is played correctly."[9]

Murphy attempted to convey to the fractious Academic Senate that he was willing to see the curriculum expanded to make it more inclusive, but such changes had to be developed with care and conscientious scholarship. He had moved UCLA steadily through hoops of rating requirements to a level of prestige, and he feared that hastily conceived courses could cost UCLA its academic standing. He tried to maintain an open-door policy for student groups with proposals, but he lacked confidence in their groundwork and was exasperated with their style of protracted wrangling. In the end, he turned over the chore of meeting with students to Chuck Young.

Murphy tried with little success to get students to accept the principle that freedom of speech also meant freedom not to listen and that those who wanted to continue with the normal business of the university should be able to do so. "We cannot survive in the presence of anarchy," he told them.[10] Murphy lacked student deputies who could rally others to his point of view, and he found he could not work through elected student representatives, since vocal activists dismissed student government as irrelevant. The *Daily Bruin* granted extensive coverage to demonstrations and was consistently hostile to the chancellor.

In mid-January 1968 Murphy shared his perspective on the year ahead with readers of the *Saturday Review;* in a guest editorial he urged acceptance of the fact that "we live in the midst of revolution—a period of unprecedented and rapid change without end in sight." He urged openness to new solutions, for "there is no going back to a time when the world seemed to be of simple construction."[11] In speeches before civic groups he delivered the same message: there was much merit in the goals of the young activists, though their tactics might be appalling. It is time to make fundamental assessments of our attitudes to civil rights, war, poverty, the environment, and the role of our institutions, he stressed.[12]

As pressures increased, he found he was not his genial self; he lost his temper easily and suffered from insomnia and depression. For a time he resorted to antidepressants. He drank heavily. Lunch meetings that started with cocktails would include several glasses of wine, and at night his favorite scotch was poured plentifully. He was under attack from all sides and found reasons to escape from campus. The Reagan administration and key legislators were now bent on punishing the university for campus chaos, which they felt discredited the image of the state and which many believed was Communist directed. Murphy had been blindsided by Reagan's rise and the alarming hostility of the electorate to the university. He admitted he was unable to cope, and his disappearing act became more the norm than the exception.[13]

"I was getting short tempered with the students," he acknowledged. "Chuck Young and others would say, 'Franklin, you've never been like this before.' And I'd say, 'You know, you're right.' And I knew the time was ripe. I'd run out of gas."[14]

Murphy's favorite escape was to spend time with Dorothy and Norman Chandler at their home in Hancock Park. The 1920s mansion was designed by Julia Morgan, the same architect who created William Randolph Hearst's fabled castle at San Simeon. The serene residence with its lavish interior (including a music room with a harpsichord once owned by Wolfgang Mozart) must have seemed a million miles from the university chaos. One relaxing candlelit dinner in the formal dining room was followed by an offer to Murphy to leave UCLA and take the helm of the giant Times Mirror Company, as chairman and chief executive.

Sixty-nine-year-old Norman Chandler said that he felt the time had come for him to be less active. He had succeeded in launching the company's diversification program, and revenues and earnings had reached an all-time high (1967 sales were $301 million). The Chandler's son, Otis, was doing a fine job as the publisher of the *Los Angeles Times,* and Norman said he was now comfortable bowing out.[15]

According to *Fortune* magazine, the family had considered at least six other candidates for the chairmanship. Precisely how the decision was reached was a family matter, but it was widely believed that Dorothy Chandler had pressed for Murphy's selection.[16] Years later she confirmed she had lobbied hard for Murphy to succeed her husband, convinced of his talents, experience, and loyalty.[17] Otis Chandler was said to applaud Murphy's selection as well, telling his biographer that Murphy "sensed the future of Southern California."[18] The offer to lead one of the nation's major publishing enterprises was an enormous life-changing opportunity. Everything came together for Murphy: he wanted to stay in Los Angeles, and though he wanted to exit the arena of higher education, he was not attracted to an industrial post—he did not want "to make canned tomato juice or steel"—and he was not interested in running a financial institution. If he were identified with an influential publishing enterprise, he would have national prominence and wider opportunities. Financial reward figured into his decision, but the primary consideration was the opportunity to expand his influence and enjoy life.[19]

Rumors spread that Murphy would be leaving UCLA, but no one predicted he would launch a third career in business. Instead it was assumed that he was headed to Washington, D.C., perhaps as secretary of health, education, and welfare, or that he would head a large philanthropic foundation.[20] Others thought he might enter politics; it was common knowledge that he had been urged to run for governor of California or for the U.S. Senate.

Official word came on February 17, 1968, when the *New York Times* announced that Murphy was taking the CEO post at Times Mirror.[21] The *Los Angeles Times* ran a long profile of Murphy, describing his career and achievements. On February 19 the news appeared on the front page of the *Wall Street Journal,* followed by prominent features in *Time, Newsweek,* and other national magazines.

On campus student reaction was mixed. One editorial in the *Daily Bruin* expressed hope that the next chancellor would be willing to subordinate his personal interests and ambitions to the general well-being of the university.[22] A group of undergraduates awarded him an "F" for his performance and criticized his evasive speechmaking and obfuscation. They nailed him on two of his favorite (probably overused) expressions—"meaningful dialogue" and "marketplace of ideas."[23] Little reaction, positive or negative, concerning his impending departure came from the faculty, but Murphy's friend and colleague Sherman Mellinkoff, dean of the UCLA Medical School, told reporters, "There couldn't be a worse blow at this time."[24]

Conjecture soon focused on the identity of Murphy's successor. When rumors hinted that Vice-Chancellor Charles Young would be selected, Murphy told the *Bruin* that if the regents were smart they would appoint him immediately. "The students couldn't find a better friend in court than Chuck Young—even better than I. He's often served as a restraining influence on my Irish temper."[25]

It was widely believed that Murphy's decision to leave UCLA was due to Governor Reagan's massive budget cuts or, perhaps, to disappointment that the university presidency was not to be his. Murphy repeatedly stated that neither reason was the basis for his decision. However, the facts surrounding his departure gave credence to the speculations he denied.[26]

Murphy would assume his new post in September, leaving six months to wind down his university obligations and take a much-needed vacation. Not long after his new post was announced, he disappeared from campus once again. He traveled to Dearborn, Michigan, to celebrate with Henry Ford II as the millionth Lincoln Continental rolled off the line. Murphy had developed great affection for the Ford scion in spite of his stubbornness, erratic behavior, and devotion to the Democratic camp.[27]

Murphy was headed for corporate life at the top, but university problems continued to fall like bombs. By March the Johnson administration was considering a major escalation of the war, which could mean a call for as many as two hundred thousand additional troops. Murphy expected a surge in antiwar protests and campus turmoil. The nationwide student network designated the last week of April as a period of massive strikes and sit-ins.[28] Murphy gave directions to open the campus to dialogue and peaceful demonstrations and hoped for the best.

• • • • •

During these turbulent months, Murphy and other city leaders, alarmed by the polarizing tactics of the controversial mayor, Sam Yorty, worked to have a candidate in place to defeat Yorty by 1969. Tom Bradley, the first African American to win election to the city council, was favored for his potential to reconcile racial groups. Murphy's Westside contacts proved helpful in creating a viable coalition that included leading Westside liberals and African American leaders in South Central Los Angeles, as well as reform-minded downtown business figures.

Fears for the city escalated with news of the assassination of the Reverend Martin Luther King Jr. on April 4. Riots erupted in forty U.S. cities, and Los Angeles's police and fire personnel were placed on full alert. Murphy was shocked by King's murder. He organized a memorial service at UCLA, but Black Student Union members refused to participate. As the atmosphere on campus grew volatile, he implored Bradley to rush to campus and speak to students in an attempt to relieve the tension. Bradley arrived immediately, an action Murphy deeply appreciated. "I shall never forget your instant willingness to come to UCLA and participate in the memorial service in Royce Hall," he told Bradley. "It was a critical moment on the campus and your measured, deliberate and meaningful comments set the tone which brought us through what could have been a destructive and traumatic moment."[29]

• • • • •

Murphy's worst fears for the future of the university came to pass when Reagan slashed the regents' budget for 1968–69 by a staggering $31.8 million. Chandler confided to Murphy that she was fed up with Reagan, and she planned to resign from the board of regents by the end of the year. Robert Vosper came to Murphy to warn him that UCLA's hard-won library standing was imperiled by the budget cuts, but this time Murphy found himself with no possible solution.

As the nerve-wracking year moved through spring, Murphy looked ahead to his new position at Times Mirror, where he could escape student emotionalism, political and bureaucratic struggles, and academic infighting. He was in unusually good spirits on the evening of April 21 at the lavish farewell dinner at the Beverly Wilshire Hotel, where he was toasted by Ed Carter, Ed Pauley, and the other regents who had welcomed him to Los Angeles in 1960. His fellow chancellors were on hand to bid him adieu: Daniel Aldrich of Irvine, Ivan H. Hinderaker of Riverside, John Galbraith of San Diego, and Vernon I. Cheadle of Santa Barbara. Also present that evening were UC president Charles Hitch and USC president Norman Topping.

Regent John Canaday stood to raise a glass in recollection of Murphy's arrival at UCLA. "We toasted then a man of vision, thinking way ahead of the times," he said, "and now we toast a man behind the *Times*."[30] With a broad smile Murphy stood to accept the accolade, and in his entertaining style, familiar to all, he recounted his 2:00 A.M. arrival from Kansas with his road-weary family to find they were locked out of the chancellor's mansion and had just missed an earthquake. The next morning, he related, they were put in fear of their lives when fire trucks raced up the driveway to battle a brushfire. In his anxiety and bewilderment, he said, he realized he did not know "one single person from Tehachapi to the Mexican border." He paid tribute to the fabled spirit of Californians and expressed appreciation for the many friends gathered in the room, friends made during the past eight years, and thanked them for including him in important undertakings for Los Angeles and for California.

Among the hundreds of congratulatory messages the newly designated chair of the Times Mirror board received were letters from President Lyndon Johnson, New York Governor Nelson Rockefeller, Henry Ford II, and Paul Mellon. One note written by former Vice President Richard Nixon bore the salutation, "Dear Frank," but Nixon's intended cordiality missed the mark. Anyone who knew Murphy knew that he disliked the nickname. In fact, if a voice on the telephone asked for "Frank," he would hang up.[31]

But of all the letters he received, Murphy took particular delight in the one sent by Los Angeles television news director Grant Holcomb, who wrote to congratulate him on his new role as a media chief. "Welcome to World War III!" he said.[32]

· · · · ·

With his network of operation expanding, Murphy's concern went beyond disruptions at UCLA to the safety and future harmony of the city at large; if the perception of a city in turmoil continued, the expensive downtown towers of the new financial center then under construction would stand empty. Events again turned tragic when on June 5, 1968, the city—and the nation—was shocked by the murder of Robert F. Kennedy at the Ambassador Hotel following his triumphant victory in the California primary.

City officials and church leaders organized memorial services in the torn and apprehensive city. Murphy delivered a moving speech at Pauley Pavilion to the bewildered, grief-stricken student body. "The hour is late," he said. "The time for both action and restraint is now."

· · · · ·

On the eve of his departure from UCLA, Murphy was asked what he considered the essence of the university's spirit. "We are on the go," he replied diplomatically. "The distinguished university in worldwide terms is not a cliché. . . . [I]t is possible of achievement, and we are closer to it than we realized."[33] Murphy was not one to hand out sour grapes, but the truth was that he was bitterly disappointed that his plan for UCLA had not been realized.

In terms of his reputation and career, fortunate timing had been key for Murphy, both in his arrival and in his exit. He came to Los Angeles during an era of explosive growth, when business, industry, and government were demanding men and women with high-quality educations and when funds were available for a massive campus expansion.[34] Murphy's departure from UCLA was equally well timed; he removed himself from the scene before the university became immobilized by agitation, starved for funds, and threatened with the loss of public regard and support.

As he was making his escape, Murphy seized a last opportunity to put student agitation in context for the bewildered older generation as well as for the students themselves. In his final commencement address on June 16, he told the audience that what they were witnessing was a revolution, a worldwide explosion in which young people were taking the lead. He said he thought the magnitude of the change would be akin to the Enlightenment's rejection of metaphysics and faith in favor of the independent intellect, as in Descartes's dictum *Cogito ergo sum*. By the nineteenth century, Murphy told his listeners, the advent of the industrial revolution had brought a new concept emphasizing work, a concept Murphy called *Facio ergo sum*—I make, therefore I am. The "production, possession and distribution of goods and services became the guiding principle," he said. He described the mid-twentieth-century revolution of activist youth as proposing a new philosophy of moral commitment and feeling. Murphy tagged this new ethos *Sentio ergo sum* and described it as "the basic philosophy of our youth . . . I feel, therefore I am." This viewpoint, in its rejection of the tenets of modernity, would be a turning point, he predicted, in Western thought and culture. He told the assembled students that he accepted and applauded "the increasing concern of [their] generation with moral imperatives." But, he said, "I must remind you that you cannot build a society on feeling alone." He cautioned that reason and patient negotiation were still worthwhile tools and could be useful in working toward the society they desired.[35]

. . . . .

Charles Young was named Murphy's successor, becoming the first UCLA graduate to lead the institution and, at thirty-six, the youngest administrator ever to head a UC campus. Young would spend the rest of his career at UCLA fighting, like Murphy, for parity with Berkeley but using a less confrontational style.[36]

Murphy folded away his academic robes. At fifty-two he had come to the disappointing realization that the university as an institution, susceptible to erratic funding and academic conflict, could not serve as the cultural catalyst he had once hoped. He confided to his closest friends that he feared he was permanently scarred from his battering in academe. He had been at it for twenty years, and he and Judy had not owned their life for one minute of that time. "There is no more demanding job in American society today than running a large, complex university," he remarked. "You belong to everybody; your time is not your own. Your house is not your own; it belongs to everybody but you."[37] Murphy now sought escape from belonging to the public. He wanted a private life.

THE DEATH OF HOWARD AHMANSON

Murphy anticipated that his position as CEO of Times Mirror would catapult him to a level of power and influence where he could collaborate with wealthy city leaders—his friend Howard Ahmanson, in particular—to truly affect the future of Los Angeles. His optimistic plans ended on June 17 with tragic news from Belgium. Ahmanson, his eighteen-year-old son, and his wife, Caroline Leonetti Ahmanson, had been on an extended vacation in Europe, touring in a motorcade with friends through the rural countryside of southeastern Belgium, when Ahmanson was seized by a massive heart attack.[38] The news was flashed to the United States, and many who knew Ahmanson learned of his death from the *New York Times* morning headline: "Howard F. Ahmanson, 61, Dies; One of Nation's Wealthiest Men."[39]

Ahmanson had seemed in such robust health that associates had forgotten the warning of a previous heart attack, and his death came as a tremendous shock. Murphy was emotionally undone by the news. He and Ahmanson had enjoyed a deep friendship. He had known Ahmanson since he took up his post at UCLA in 1960; together they had weathered many crises during the building of the new Los Angeles County Museum of Art and had celebrated its opening only three years before. Ahmanson, having gained his wealth from mortgage financing in Southern California, had a vested interest in the region and definite ideas about what it took to create a prosperous, expanding city.[40] Murphy had anticipated joining forces with him in the building of Los Angeles's cultural infrastructure, having at hand not only the resources of Ahmanson's fortune but his political contacts as well.[41]

Friends who observed Murphy and Ahmanson's relationship said they had a warm and lively rapport, despite a ten-year difference in age and the enormous contrast in their net worth. The barrel-chested, high-living tycoon and the stocky, ebullient university chancellor simply clicked. The men's club evenings at Ahmanson's Hancock Park house had changed after Ahmanson's friend Art Linkletter introduced him to Caroline Leonetti, a dark-haired, vivacious beauty. Romance overcame age when Ahmanson, fifty-eight years old, married the thirty-something California native in 1965.

Murphy and Ahmanson had realized that it would be very difficult to promote cultural development when city leaders were dealing with a community in turmoil and a contentious mayoralty election ahead. Now Murphy faced the task without Ahmanson, and, caught at the moment of his metamorphosis from chancellor to corporate officer, he was immobilized by the loss. Murphy felt he had been present at the beginning of a cultural renaissance fostered by a group of enlightened, enthusiastic civic leaders, and now his key ally was gone.

The lengthy obituary in the *Los Angeles Times* listed Ahmanson's contributions to the city and revealed to the surprised fascination of many in the financial world the immense size of his fortune. On the day of his funeral flags on all county buildings were flown at half staff. Mayor Yorty spoke of Ahmanson's dreams for Los Angeles, saying, "It's unbelievable that we won't have Howard Ahmanson here among us—this is a great loss to our city."[42]

Ahmanson was laid to rest in the Great Mausoleum at Forest Lawn Memorial Park in Los Angeles. More than twenty-five hundred mourners attended the funeral on Saturday morning, June 22. Murphy and Norman Topping, president of USC, delivered eulogies for their friend who had achieved such remarkable success and had lived with such zest for life. "He wedded his energy and his genius to the dynamics of the west—Southern California," Murphy told the mourners. "He was a friend whom we loved and whom we trusted and whom we will deeply miss."[43]

· · · · ·

In Ahmanson's last will and testamentary trust, signed and executed only two weeks before his death, he named the Ahmanson Foundation the residuary beneficiary of his estate after providing for the lifetime support of his first and second wives and his son. Shortly after Ahmanson's death, his first wife, Dorothy Grannis Sullivan (who had remarried in 1966; her new husband was the businessman Denis Sullivan), was reelected president of the Ahmanson Foundation. She was originally in charge of the foundation when the couple established it in 1952, and after their divorce she continued to take a role in distributing grants. In the difficult months after the funeral, Sullivan called on Murphy to help with the baffling and conflicting reports about the foundation's assets and the stringent legal requirements that had to be met. Ahmanson's will had been constructed prudently, but his carefully considered dispositions were thrown into limbo by a complication not contemplated and therefore not addressed in the will. His death came just at the time Congress was formulating the 1969 Tax Reform Act promulgating requirements that had potentially perilous consequences not only for the foundation but for Los Angeles as well. The directive Ahmanson had given the foundation was broad, to administer funds for the "public welfare and for no other purpose"; though there was no specific requirement to do so, grants had favored Los Angeles and Southern California.[44]

Ahmanson, early on, had urged Los Angeles leaders to formulate a cultural master plan: "We have to find out how many art galleries we're going to need, how many symphony orchestras and theaters. There is a growing enthusiasm about culture, and we're going to have more leisure for culture."[45] He intended that the foundation would have an important philanthropic role in the cosmopolitan metropolis of the future. It was now up to Murphy to rescue Ahmanson's plan; it was a responsibility he accepted in memory of his friend and their shared vision. Ahmanson's faith in Murphy's skill as an administrator would be tested in a twenty-year struggle to preserve the enormous, now imperiled, assets of the foundation.[46]

The Los Angeles Times speculated that the entire empire built by Ahmanson from a small insurance company could be as much as $3 billion.[47] Unlike other entrepreneurs, Ahmanson never took his company public, and as a result he owned substantially all the Ahmanson-related stock at the time of his death. A teenager when his father died in 1925, Howard watched as other stockholders seized control of the company his father had founded. The experience not only drove him to regain National American Insurance, his father's company in Omaha, but also fueled his resolve to maintain control of his enterprises. "Home Savings and Loan has one stockholder— Me," he liked to say.[48]

Although Ahmanson acknowledged that after the war he knew there was opportunity in home financing, he readily admitted he was surprised by the spectacular growth of Home Savings and Loan.[49] With Southern California's phenomenal building boom under way, H. F. Ahmanson and Company was prepared to offer both mortgages and insurance to eager home buyers. Home Savings and Loan became the largest such business in the country.

"It was a marvelous era," recalled Robert H. Ahmanson, the financier's nephew, who began his career with his uncle when he was a student at UCLA. "Large tracts went up—in the San Fernando Valley, in Torrance, in Lakewood—and we were there financing thousands upon thousands of houses through construction loans on big tracts, and mortgages on individual homes."[50] Home Savings also financed rapidly growing land subdivisions, among them Baldwin Hills in 1951 and Laurelwood in 1958. With FHA-guaranteed loans requiring low down payments and Veterans Administration loans requiring no down payment at all, middle-class families of modest means and workforce families could buy homes in the postwar boom.

What Ahmanson had created was a vast financial organization under his holding company, H. F. Ahmanson and Company—a successful strategy for singular control but one that would prove a handicap to a smooth succession. As events unfolded, Ahmanson's one-man structure soon put the company and the Ahmanson Foundation in jeopardy. It seemed unlikely to Murphy that one individual could step into the shoes of the business giant; instead, he felt, a new operating structure had to be created, a daunting proposition and a legal nightmare.[51]

· · · · ·

Murphy had become an intimate family friend, privy to the worries and concerns that not even great wealth could avoid. One matter now involved Ahmanson's only child, Howard Jr., called "Steady," who was devastated by his father's death. Howie had been an imp of a youngster who totally captured Howard's heart. It was soon apparent, however, that the child would not be the sports enthusiast that his father was, as he had poor coordination and needed glasses from an early age. He started reading very young, and his father recognized that he was exceptionally bright and avidly curious. To the delight of his father he gave free rein to his thoughts, speaking in a spontaneous, unfiltered manner that set his father off into gales of laughter. But young Howard did not cope well with stress; he succumbed to obsessive movements, tics, and unintelligible mumbling. At such times his father put his arm around him to comfort and bolster him, and the youngster responded to his calming influence.

Ahmanson and Murphy, each with an only son, had talked about their goals for their boys. Both felt their own boyhoods had prepared them for the roles they would assume later in life, and they credited their fathers with perceptive parenting. Murphy said it was a gift to him that his busy doctor father let him run free to explore his surroundings, take the measure of his options, and find his own identity. Ahmanson remembered his satisfaction when his father took him as a young boy to business meetings, where he sat in one of the big chairs at the conference table, his feet not reaching the floor. He observed the backslapping rapport of the men and watched with fascination as they argued with one another across the table. Wanting to give his son the same experience, Ahmanson included young Howard at meetings. But the child grew restless, slipped out of his chair, and crawled under the table. As he reached adolescence, his behavior became more perplexing. Murphy perceived young Howard as extremely intelligent and suspected that a neurological impairment accounted for the sudden outbursts and involuntary movements that beset him. Confident of the boy's intellectual ability, Ahmanson searched for a school for his son and selected Black Fox Academy; Ahmanson took a great interest in the school and its programs and became its major benefactor. It would be the 1970s before Tourette's syndrome was defined and the neurological nature of Howard's symptoms diagnosed. In the meantime, in his teen years his condition puzzled his father, who, as could be expected, wanted his son to enter the business he had founded.

Murphy had known the sons of wealthy tycoons, and he knew how difficult it was for them to meet the expectations placed on them. He was able to share with the Ahmanson family the example of Paul Mellon, who had no enthusiasm for a role in the Mellon financial empire but won his father's respect as an able supporter of his father's plan to give the nation an art museum. In bringing the National Gallery of Art to fruition, Paul found fulfilling work for himself and created a close bond with his father. The story of the Mellons offered a possible pattern for the Ahmansons. To that end, one year before Ahmanson's death, when Howard Jr. turned eighteen, the family elected him to the board of directors of the Ahmanson Foundation. But now with the foundation facing a long period of complex restructuring to stay afloat, Howard was too shaken by his father's death to participate. Dorothy Sullivan sought Murphy's advice, and at his recommendation Howard was taken to the highly respected Menninger Clinic in Topeka, Kansas, where he could work closely with a psychiatrist and take courses at nearby Washburn University.[52] His condition was still not understood at this time, and grief had aggravated his symptoms.

· · · · ·

During the summer of 1968, more rioting erupted, this time on Berkeley streets, resulting in police action in which officers in protective gear lobbed teargas at student demonstrators in the "Battle of Berkeley." All across the country campus life gave way to demonstrations as presidential candidates prepared for the national nominating conventions. Vice President Hubert Humphrey heatedly debated Richard Nixon over the Vietnam War, and Governor George Wallace of Alabama mounted a campaign opposing civil rights legislation, capitalizing on southern racism.

In August, just days before Murphy was to join Times Mirror, bloody antiwar protests at the Democratic convention ended with the arrest of the Chicago Seven. In other radical encounters, women's movement protestors picketed the Miss America contest in Atlantic City; the Black Panthers mounted a fight to free Huey Newton from jail; and Eldridge Cleaver, to the consternation of alumni and city leaders, gave a fiery address to students at UCLA. On the eve of the Olympics in Mexico City, student demonstrators were fired on and more than one hundred killed by military riflemen. African American athletes at the Olympics captured world attention with a defiant Black Power salute as they received their medals. In Prague Soviet tanks crushed the Czechoslovakian reform movement, and farmers in Japan joined forces with students to halt expansion of an airfield for U.S. military craft. Rioting erupted in country after country: Brazil, Pakistan, China, Portugal, Spain, Northern Ireland, and Italy. At Times Mirror Square in Los Angeles, Murphy would direct a media conglomerate charged to cover a world enmeshed in turmoil.

PART II

Chairman

FIVE

The Chancellor Becomes CEO

FRANKLIN MURPHY ARRIVED IN SEPTEMBER 1968 to take up his duties in the historic Times Mirror building at First and Spring Streets. The imposing streamline modern structure designed by Gordon B. Kaufman in 1934 was described by one executive as "prison modern." The focal point of the lobby, a revolving globe measuring five and a half feet in diameter, signified the worldwide coverage of the *Times*. The bronze eagle perched on a pedestal in the elevator lobby was the same ominous raptor that had "stood guard atop three successive Times buildings from 1881 to 1935."[1] Murphy rode the nickel-plated elevator to the fourth floor and exited to face a large wood panel bearing the motto of the family patriarch, Harrison Gray Otis: "Stand Fast, Stand Firm, Stand Sure, Stand True." Murphy settled himself in the wood-paneled suite that had previously belonged to Norman Chandler and assumed his role in a culture of established power and influence.

As a member of the board of directors of Times Mirror since 1965, Murphy was familiar with the boardroom interests of Chandler family members. Because he would be the first non-Chandler to manage the company, however, he asked that Norman Chandler stay at Times Mirror in some capacity for at least five years. "I felt I simply had to have the senior member of the Chandler family around because I was uncertain how the family would react to some of my initiatives. [Norman] agreed to do that," Murphy told an interviewer.[2] Norman Chandler took the title of chairman of the Executive Committee, and Otis Chandler assumed a newly created position, vice-chairman of the board, in addition to his role as publisher. Albert V. Casey, forty-eight, who had been with the company since 1963, continued as president of Times Mirror, directing the company's many divisions and subsidiaries throughout the United States and Europe. Dorothy Chandler, whose title was assistant to the chairman, was to make herself available to Murphy and continue her duties in public relations as well as her responsibility for the design and allocation of Times Mirror facilities.[3]

A BEAUTY TO BEHOLD

The selection of the chancellor to serve as chairman and chief executive stunned some company officials. One executive recalled that Albert Casey ran into his office white-faced and breathless to announce the news.[4] Although Murphy had been active on various corporate boards, he had never run a business, and he had no experience managing a for-profit enterprise the size of Times Mirror. The decision to choose Murphy, called "bold and unexpected" by *Fortune,* caused apprehension among Wall Street insiders.[5] When Otis Chandler was asked to explain the choice of an educator to head the communications empire, he flatly told *Newsweek,* "We're dealing with thoughts . . . and great social problems. So we need a planner and an innovator as well as a man capable of handling the chickens in the barn."[6] *Time* echoed Chandler's sentiments, reporting that Murphy's work experience at UCLA—running an enterprise the equivalent of a small nation-state—rivaled that of the best managers of corporate America.[7]

For Murphy, it was an auspicious moment to be put in charge. All-time high revenues and net income were expected at Times Mirror, and 1968, as frustrating and disruptive as it was for civic leaders, would prove an extraordinary year for those in the news business. At the time he was named chairman, Times Mirror was an outstanding business, superbly run. "It was a beauty to behold," recalled one executive.[8] As chief executive officer of the Times Mirror Company, Murphy would preside over a publishing and printing conglomerate ranking in size below only Time, Inc., and McGraw-Hill Book Company. The company had embarked in 1960 on a long-range diversification program to seize a major position in the rapidly growing billion-dollar "knowledge industry." Its acquisition strategy aimed at reducing the company's dependence on the *Los Angeles Times.* Over the next twenty years, newspaper publishing would come to constitute no more than 25 percent of the company's revenue. (In 1959, one year before Otis Chandler was named publisher, Times Mirror earned nearly 75 percent of its income from newspaper operations.)[9]

To execute this change of focus, Norman Chandler had recruited the talented Albert Casey, who had been vice president and treasurer of Railway Express. Casey was a fidgety, impatient workhorse, with a mind that "sliced through ideas like an automated lathe." He set out to revise the company's capital structure; by taking on $50 million in long-term debt, he acquired cash to supplement company stock for rapid acquisitions. Under Casey's supervision, Times Mirror joined the Big Board to great success in 1964 and during the following year achieved a $40 million bond offering. That was soon followed by a successful $15.5 million secondary stock issue. One market analyst declared Casey's strategy "flawless."[10]

Under the stewardship of Norman Chandler, Times Mirror had boosted revenues in seven years from $112 million to $301 million, purchased twenty-two companies, and expanded operations into dozens of new fields. The company was the nation's biggest publisher of paperback books with New American Library, which the previous year had published Truman Capote's *In Cold Blood,* a blockbuster that sold over two million copies. In addition, the company was one of the largest producers of Bibles, roadmaps, and telephone directories in the world. Ranking 273rd on the *Fortune* 500 list, Times Mirror was considered well managed and aggressive.

At the last meeting he conducted as chairman and chief executive, sixty-nine-year-old Norman Chandler, still strikingly handsome, with thick white hair and chiseled features, assured shareholders of his complete confidence in the new management. "I refer to Otis Chandler, Albert V. Casey and Dr. Murphy," he said. "These men will make a great trio."[11]

Franklin Murphy was alert to the implications of the wait-and-see attitude expressed in *Fortune;* analysts were enthusiastic about the Times Mirror diversification plan and expansion into additional areas of the newly labeled knowledge industry but less sure of the company's new leader:

> When Murphy takes over Times Mirror this month, he will be taking on one of the toughest assignments of his career. On the one hand, he must prove that a man from an academic background can maintain the profit record of one of the most successful corporations in the country. On the other, he must be ready to accept very large risks in an industry so full of unknowns that even its definition is still being debated.[12]

Murphy's career trajectory warranted admiration, but it remained to be seen whether he could adapt to an environment that lived by the rise and fall of a stock price and the swings of a volatile economy.[13] Murphy seemed unaffected by the scrutiny into his résumé. "After all," he told one business writer, "running a university is really about the same as running a conglomerate, once you have defined how to produce a return for the shareholders."[14]

THE INTERLOCKING DIRECTORATE

Otis Chandler proved his mother's intuition right: he had what it took to transform the newspaper. He insisted that partisanship yield to objectivity, and he demanded that his editors seek out and hire America's finest reporters. The *Times'* historic opposition to labor unions caused some journalists to hesitate, but the handsome salaries he authorized provided incentive to join his effort to revoke the paper's notorious conservative bias. With Chandler as publisher, the *Times* won nationwide recognition for its coverage of the assassination of Robert Kennedy, the lunar-orbit mission of Apollo 8, two political conventions, and the election of Richard Nixon. The newspaper's main competitor, the *Herald Examiner,* struggled to survive a prolonged labor strike. As the strike wore on, many of the *Examiner*'s advertisers switched their business to the *Times.*

Shortly after accepting his post, Murphy organized the responsibilities of the three-man team that Norman Chandler had described to stockholders: Otis Chandler, in charge of the newspapers; company president Albert Casey, in charge of other subsidiaries, new acquisitions, and day-to-day operations; and Murphy himself, focusing on the image of the company and long-range strategy for growth. Murphy intended to insulate professional management from time-consuming family issues and Chandler family board politics. This high-powered Troika, as one observer called it, set the management tone and provided the leadership that would generate one of the best economic periods in the company's history.

A number of significant management changes coincided with the arrival of the company's new chairman. Two new directors were elected to the board: Simon Ramo, vice-chairman of TRW, Inc., and Robert Erburu, Times Mirror vice president, secretary, and general counsel. Dorothy Chandler continued as a director, but in the newly devised position of assistant to the chairman she also functioned at the elbow of the CEO she had hand-picked. Harrison Chandler (Norman Chandler's younger brother) retired as vice president of Times Mirror and president of Times Mirror Press but remained as a board member.[15]

In a note to his friend and publisher Walter H. Annenberg, Murphy acknowledged the talented crew that was drawing attention in the national business press: "My new job is proving to be fascinating, exciting and personally rewarding primarily because of the able and attractive young team which Norman put together and which I inherited and which is the main reason, although not the only one, that the growth and vitality of this company is magnificently assured."[16]

· · · · ·

Board chairman Murphy underwent a sartorial transformation as he eased into his powerful role. Gone were the blazers that had been his uniform as chancellor. In their place were finely tailored wool suits, with a selection of executive ties from Neiman Marcus in Beverly Hills. The former chancellor now operated at the same level of power and prestige as many of those who previously had been targets of his fund-raising and boostering pitches.

The lucrative invitation to head Times Mirror not only rescued Murphy from the battleground at UCLA but solved concerns over family finances. Murphy's two eldest daughters were married, but Carolyn was a freshman at Berkeley and Franklin Lee was a senior at the Harvard School for Boys, with years of educational expenses still ahead. Judy was elated. "Frankly, I was just delighted to have him leaving UCLA," she said. "I've never been so happy to get out of a place in all my life. Much as I loved [the university] . . . [living on campus at UCLA] was just like having the FBI on your tail all the time. It was a joy to get out."[17]

The Murphys could now purchase a home of their own after nearly twenty years of campus living. They selected a handsome 7,200-square-foot house north of Sunset Boulevard at 419 Robert Lane, in an attractive planned development in Beverly Hills. The house, previously owned by Norton Simon's sister, had been recommended to Murphy by Norman Chandler. The contemporary, single-story gated residence had oversized sliding glass doors opening to a large patio, a swimming pool, and a garden. Norman Chandler arranged a low-interest loan for Murphy to enable the purchase.[18]

Visitors were most surprised by the living room, which was filled floor to ceiling with books and displays of African, pre-Columbian, Northwest Coast Indian, and Oceanic works of art. Murphy's library shelves held first editions and rare books, including venerable medical volumes from his father and cherished works of the Irish author Sean O'Casey. The warm and welcoming home reflected the tastes of a cosmopolitan family with wide-ranging interests in literature and art.

· · · · ·

Almost immediately after his arrival at Times Mirror, Murphy was asked by Dorothy Chandler to act as a facilitator in another fracas with the Los Angeles County Board of Supervisors involving the Music Center's parking structure. He deftly took on Chandler's nemesis, Howard Jarvis (later famed for the tax revolt known as Proposition 13), who infuriated her with his verbal attacks and opposition to any use of public funds for the Music Center. Calling on his friendships with supervisors Ernest Debs, Kenneth Hahn, and Warren M. Dorn, Murphy speedily resolved the issue. He wrote Dorothy, on a family vacation in D'Agaro, Spain, with the good news: "So now you and Norman can have a completely restful vacation with your only concern being whether Otis, Al [Casey] and I give the company away in your absence."[19]

Such civic firefighting was precisely the kind of performance Norman and Dorothy Chandler expected from their new chairman. Murphy's world rapidly expanded locally and nationally. He was asked to join numerous civic organizations and corporate boards. In October he turned down an invitation to join the board of North American Rockwell because of the conflict it presented with his role at Ford; he turned away an offer from Crocker Citizens Bank and a (second) offer from Security First National Bank because of the conflict with his directorship at Bank of America. But he continued his membership on the boards of the Institute of International Education, the Board of Visitors of the National War College, and the President's Advisory Committee on Foreign Aid.[20] In the cultural arena, of special importance to Dorothy Chandler, Murphy served as president of the Kress Foundation and as trustee at the National Gallery of Art. He maintained close ties with Ed Carter as board member of both the county art museum and the California Museum of Science and Industry as well as the Performing Arts Council. He was also a member of the Urban Coalition, the civic committee formed by business leaders following the Watts uprising.

Continuing his active role as adviser for Dorothy Ahmanson Sullivan and the Ahmanson Foundation, Murphy faced troubling complications in helping the family to preserve foundation assets, now beset by challenges from heirs and scrutiny from the Internal Revenue Service. In an emotional board meeting on September 30, only weeks after Murphy's start at Times Mirror and the first after Ahmanson's death, new officers were elected and the charter amended to add new trustees. Murphy, who had earlier responded to Dorothy Sullivan's request for assistance, took a seat on the board, as did Robert DeKruif, president of H. F. Ahmanson and Company and later its vice-chairman.

Murphy found himself assuming the delicate task of helping Sullivan to select family members to step into a difficult situation. Ahmanson's nephews, Robert H. Ahmanson and William H. Ahmanson, who were executives at H. F. Ahmanson and Company, were elected vice presidents of the board. Howard Ahmanson Jr., now at the Menninger Clinic, was not available to participate, and because of his youth and precarious emotional health, it was not clear what role he could play. Murphy turned to the Ahmanson nephews and worked with them and Sullivan to plan a strategy to satisfy the probate court, the IRS, and the state of California in an effort to safeguard the foundation. The foundation had immense potential and importance for Los Angeles, but with seemingly intractable legal issues ahead the foundation's assets and its mission remained uncertain. Murphy missed Ahmanson greatly, professionally and personally. There were few people with whom Murphy could share the depth of his loss. Forced to hold his emotions in check, he compartmentalized his grief and moved forward.

Increasingly, leading figures in business, government, entertainment media, and the arts sought the chance to become better acquainted with the new chairman. Murphy found himself in constant demand as a speaker, and as the beleaguered city reeled from protests and demonstrations, he offered variations on his popular address "Over 50 Looks at Under 30," telling anxious parents and business leaders that far from simply acting out, young adults worldwide were demanding a reordering of priorities—calling for attention to human rights, participatory government, cultural respect, and commitment to the environment. "Now why don't we join them, give them some of our wisdom and experience," Murphy urged, adding, "We should be helping them not just to preserve our world, but to build their own, which I most earnestly hope will be a better one."[21]

He encouraged audiences to look beyond the radical fashions and the sometimes-inexplicable behavior and listen to what young people were saying. Ignore the long hair, he told them—it's their hair. And if miniskirts are "too stimulating to some of you, then wear dark glasses." He urged the over-fifty group to engage in dialogue with the young revolutionaries, who were involved in a serious philosophical rethinking of human purpose with much potential value. What youth do not realize, he argued, is that all the things they want for human society and the environment "cannot come to pass without their understanding the elementary facts of how a free enterprise society generates and distributes the capital required to do these things." Conveying this information is the responsibility "of those of us who have to do with the creation of capital," Murphy said.[22] Yet even as he urged the successful men at his breakfast meetings to sit down and talk to the young people in their lives, he admitted to himself that he had become exasperated with the activists at UCLA: it was not all that easy to talk to them.

· · · · ·

One secret to Murphy's juggling act was his dedication to certain established routines. Immediately on returning to his office from business trips he dictated his thank-you notes and compiled his expense report, a ritual he began during his days as chancellor at the University of Kansas. Only then did he permit himself to plow through the stack of mail and pressing papers that had collected during his absence. In addition to his corporate and cultural obligations, he received a steady stream of requests to comment on educational issues, recommend and recruit faculty, or advise educators on dealing with the tumult of the campuses.

Imogene "Imy" Butterfield and two other secretaries were kept fully engaged in the flow of carbon-copied correspondence. Examination of his papers reveals that Murphy was strict about his personal correspondence: he answered every letter within seven days and consistently returned telephone calls within twenty-four hours. Under no circumstances did he permit a personal letter to go unacknowledged.

Murphy's routines also produced a renewed balance in his personal life. Judy's experience as an executive wife was a "wonderful time," she said. "I was free to do what I wanted to do whatever that might be."[23] The Murphy children recalled this period as the most idyllic in their parents' marriage. They were amorous and affectionate and typically spent Sundays in their pajamas reading in bed. The fine house offered Judy some of the elements she had missed when she left her parents' well-appointed home for life on an educator's salary. Although she had a modest trust fund, carefully preserved, Judy was prone to an exaggerated fear about finances. Their new affluent status was a great relief. Murphy earned a salary of $208,731 plus a deferred incentive bonus during his first year as company chairman.[24]

After the family moved into the new house, Judy set to work with decorators to complete its interior. Murphy took satisfaction in assembling his Peruvian ceramics in the custom-built glass cases in the living room and installing a carved wooden screen from Chorrillos, Peru, commissioned from a local artist during one of his trips to South America. Judy enjoyed swimming in the aqua pool, and many mornings Franklin did his paperwork seated in the sunshine at the patio table.

Carolyn worried about the family's aging cocker spaniels Toasty and Klinker, but on her first visit home from Berkeley the dogs happily greeted her, completely at home in their new yard. Judy had outdone herself decorating Carolyn's new room, which had its own pink marble bath. "It was pretty darn fancy," Carolyn remembered. Willia and Ted also resided at Robert Lane. Willia cared for Franklin Lee and did housework and much of the cooking; Ted acted as houseman and part-time driver, frequently picking up or dropping off Murphy at Los Angeles International Airport.

Over time, however, frequent absences began to take a toll on the marriage. Murphy's many business trips became opportunities for him to enjoy the company of other women. Colleagues close to him were aware of various romantic affairs, and others heard rumors. Little had been said, but Murphy had already garnered a reputation as a womanizer. For some time he had had a relationship with an attractive and ambitious scholar who had earned her Ph.D. at UCLA, and it continued even after she left California for an associate professorship in another state. At about the time Murphy became chairman of Times Mirror, however, she hastily broke off their arrangement, and Murphy received a note warning him that she would not be at the airport to greet him. Murphy, for his part, was not to be deterred. He wrote that he was coming anyway. "Let us not worry about nuances," he told her.[25]

It is not clear if Judy knew of this specific romance, but one family member recalled a shouting match between the couple over a liaison of Murphy's, and many years later a longtime friend delicately confirmed that Judy knew of her husband's propensity for romantic affairs. Yet Judy must have come to terms with her husband's susceptibility to interesting and appealing women, for she and Franklin settled into a workable domestic routine. Although Judy had announced herself happy to escape the demands of UCLA, her life as a corporate wife lacked the stimulation she had known partnering with her husband in campus responsibilities. She now had no precise role, and she began to suffer, without fully realizing it, a loss of identity. Her old fears about lack of money occasionally resurfaced. She eased her anxiety with smoking and often an extra cocktail or two. She always pulled herself together, however, when her husband needed her.

• • • • •

Murphy continued to cultivate his contacts on the national political scene. Following the 1968 nomination of Richard Nixon as the Republican candidate for president, Murphy stayed in close touch with his friend Bob Haldeman. As the campaign got under way to restore the Republican Party to power, Murphy wrote Haldeman that he could call on him for "maximum help to the new administration before the inauguration and afterwards, in terms of advisement—formal or informal—serving on commissions or doing any other trouble shooting either here or abroad."[26] Taking him at his word, Haldeman enlisted Murphy's aid in assembling an early roster of possible candidates for a number of posts, ranging from ambassadorships to secretary of state.[27]

Later, while in Washington to wait for the election returns, Murphy received a telephone call in his hotel room during which Haldeman informed him that the president-elect wished to speak with him. According to Murphy, Nixon asked him to serve as his undersecretary of state. Surprised, Murphy said he was flattered but had to decline: "I just came down to Times Mirror. I can't tell these people that I'm leaving. No way."[28]

There had been widespread rumors at Times Mirror that Murphy had been considered for the vice presidency early in the campaign, when he was still chancellor at UCLA. Apparently the rumor was true. "Nixon had been convinced that he should get, as a Vice President, someone who had respectability in the intellectual community and I was the person he chose," Murphy acknowledged to an interviewer years later. He said that he and Judy were leaving for a Mediterranean cruise aboard the yacht of friends when Haldeman told him to be available by phone. "Then, Reagan made a very serious run at him and he needed the south and he realized that he had to get somebody, a visible southerner . . . that's when he chose [Spiro T.] Agnew, who was Governor of Maryland." (Murphy said he thought at the time that the decision to pick Agnew was ill advised.) "So I never got the call and I never expected the call," Murphy said.[29] He anticipated that Haldeman would be given an important position in the new administration and that in Haldeman he would have a valuable liaison to the White House and the Republican administration.

POLITICS AND THE MIGHTY CHANDLERS

Nixon's ties to the Chandlers had been crucial to his political ascent,[30] but the relationship significantly cooled after his unsuccessful run for the White House in 1960 and his defeat in the controversial race for the governorship of California in 1962.[31] The *Times* had supported Nixon's reelection to Congress in 1948 and had praised his performance on the House

Un-American Activities Committee during televised hearings. Throughout the 1950s the Chandlers had supported Nixon's rise to the upper echelon of the Republican Party. In that era the newspaper's political clout was wielded by the *Times'* longtime, all-powerful political editor, Kyle Palmer, who purportedly masterminded Nixon's triumphant 1950 U.S. Senate campaign against Democrat Helen Gahagan Douglas. Following the "Checkers" speech, in which Nixon defended himself against charges of receiving illegal campaign contributions during the Eisenhower-Nixon 1952 presidential campaign, the *Times* printed a rare front-page editorial headlined, "We Stand by Nixon."[32]

Dorothy and Norman Chandler attended the 1964 Republican convention in San Francisco, where a defiant Nelson Rockefeller barely made himself heard over the shouts of a hostile crowd as the party prepared to nominate Barry Goldwater. Nixon knew 1964 was not the time for him to run; he brushed off a "Draft Nixon" movement early in the convention and pledged his support to Goldwater. The Chandlers watched with interest as Nixon delivered a memorable speech of withdrawal. Palmer, the *Times'* political kingmaker, had died of leukemia two years earlier; Otis Chandler was now publisher of the *Times;* and Nixon was no longer a favorite.

Dorothy Chandler had wanted Rockefeller as the nominee and had persuaded Norman, who favored Goldwater, to join her in supporting the more liberal segment of the party. After Goldwater won the nomination, the *Times,* in line with its established policy of support for the Republican presidential candidate, endorsed Goldwater. Murphy was distressed that Rockefeller, whom he had grown to appreciate from their work on government commissions, had been forced from the running. Furthermore, he was surprised by the vehement opposition to Rockefeller and the boisterous support of Goldwater by delegates belonging to conservative organizations, among them the John Birch Society, in Orange County.[33] They saw in Goldwater a strong advocate and a fierce foe of the Soviet Union. Southern California conservatives readily embraced militaristic anti-Communism as their sense of safety—and the local economy—relied heavily on the military installations and defense industries in their backyard.[34] Murphy misjudged the depth of their concern and their grassroots power. Goldwater's resounding defeat led Murphy to believe the party had seen the end of this swarm of hornets, but two years later a dismayed Murphy would find the same groups—now even better organized—helping to catapult Ronald Reagan to the governorship.

After Lyndon Johnson's victory in the 1964 presidential race, the Chandlers maintained a cordial association with him, fostered by Otis Chandler. On one occasion, relating to Dorothy Chandler that her son had become a valued personal friend, President Johnson wrote: "You and Mr. Chandler have every right to be proud of him . . . the making of a boy into a man is one of the most sensitive and rewarding of all parental achievements. Your paper is in good hands."[35]

· · · · ·

That the Times Mirror Company had become a communications force responsible for leadership in the most influential part of an increasingly influential state was apparent as *Times* reporters covered the heated 1968 presidential campaign that roared from one incendiary incident to another. The centerpiece of Nixon's campaign was a series of commercials with photomontages and jarring music intended to create an image of "a country out of control, with crime on the rise, violence in the streets and an unwinnable war raging overseas." The most controversial ads used photographs of a smiling Hubert Humphrey juxtaposed against flashing violent images of Vietnam and the Chicago Democratic convention.[36]

Republicans celebrated victory with a sense of relief, believing the new administration would get a grip on the chaos that had enveloped the nation. Murphy was happy to see the Republicans restored to power and welcomed a turning away from the Democrats' favored solutions of ever more bureaucracy, but he knew there was to be no return to tradition. He sensed that behind the demonstrations there was profound change. The young people's revolution was not over; and as he told audiences time and again, the generation coming to adulthood was bringing with them a moral commitment that would forever alter every social institution. Already their revolution had shaken established authority, weakened class distinctions, radicalized race and gender, and reordered attitudes toward sex. There would be no turning back the clock.

· · · · ·

A month after the 1968 election, Dorothy Chandler made headlines throughout the state when she resigned her position on the University of California Board of Regents. Former Governor Edmund G. Brown wrote Chandler that he hated to see her leave:[37] "I had hoped you would use your superior intelligence, courage and position to fight the battle for higher education in our state. You have exercised more good judgment educationally and business wise, as a regent of the university than any single person I know. You and I didn't always agree, but I think both of us understood the need for investing in the *brains* of our country."[38]

Chandler had been both praised and criticized for her actions as regent. She was repeatedly accused of feeding stories to the *Times* education reporter, William Trombley, although she insisted she did not. She pointed out that she served as a regent, not as "Mrs. Chandler of the *Times*. . . . I was there as Dorothy Chandler, citizen of the State of California."[39]

During her last year on the board of regents, Chandler saw the demise of the dream she and Murphy had for UCLA, and she witnessed firsthand the damage inflicted by Governor Reagan's slashing the state's education budget. She accused the governor of using university students' rebellion as a scapegoat in the election campaign and of continuing to do so after his election. Chandler's resignation signaled what one observer called a turning point "in the history of the university, perhaps on par with the exit of Clark Kerr."[40] She was a pivotal figure in the board's moderate-liberal coalition that was credited with defusing the free speech crisis "by granting reasonable concessions to students and giving more authority to chancellors to deal with student demands."[41]

From his hilltop home in El Cerrito, Clark Kerr sent a handwritten letter to Chandler to tell her how sorry he was to hear of her departure. He noted that the years in which they worked together had been "a period of substantial accomplishments."[42] (Chandler held Kerr in high esteem and saved this note from him in her file titled "VIP Letters" containing correspondence from eminent world leaders, U.S. presidents, and celebrated artists.) Whatever her real reasons for leaving, when asked for a comment by reporters she would say only that fourteen years was long enough.[43]

· · · · ·

Though she was a corporate vice president of a burgeoning conglomerate, Dorothy Chandler inevitably was scrutinized more for what she was wearing than what she was thinking. She was praised for her sense of style, and her name appeared frequently on many of America's best-dressed lists. Minimal makeup and a year-round tan were staples of the Chandler look. The fashion press called her a "dynamo who concentrates on vitalizing that cultural wasteland, the West Coast."[44]

Chandler may have given sincere attention to dressing for her role—fashion was also a component of the city's image—but she was all business. In her fifth-floor office at Times Mirror Square, the files on her desk were carefully stacked in order of priority. She was extremely organized, refusing to jump back and forth among unrelated activities. Her longtime administrative assistant, Marion Burke, marveled at the work she accomplished: "One thing about working for Mrs. Chandler, you are always busy. As soon as one project is near completion, we move on to another."[45] Chandler expected perfection from herself and from others. "There's something about Mrs. C," one executive said of her, "that makes everybody shake. Even top management jumps when she's around."[46]

"I fix the facilities, but I don't tell them what to put in the paper," she told *Women's Wear Daily* in describing her company responsibilities for architecture and design. Regarding the newspaper, she said, "If I have an opinion, I send a memo, just like any employee, but I never go below top management to express my views."[47] Some seasoned reporters at the *Times* told a slightly different story. One editor commented, "We never actually see Mrs. Chandler on the floors, but she lurks in every corner. When I write something, I can feel her peering over my shoulder, questioning, analyzing and criticizing."[48] The truth, perhaps, was somewhere in between. When Norman was publisher, she stayed close to the newspaper, but after her son assumed that role she claimed she scrupulously stepped away.

When asked what woman she most admired in the publishing world, Chandler singled out Iphigene Sulzberger, wife of *New York Times* publisher Arthur Hays Sulzberger. "[She is] the most influential woman I have ever known," Chandler said. "In her quiet strong way, she didn't have to be sitting on the *New York Times* editorial board to get her thoughts across. She guided major policy decisions, especially political ones." Chandler did not name Katharine Graham, publisher of the *Washington Post,* a woman who put herself too much in the limelight, Chandler thought. Furthermore, Graham was not able to augment her influence by acting through a husband, the well-honed skill of Dorothy Chandler and Iphigene Sulzberger.

After her election to the vice presidency of Times Mirror in 1961, Chandler had been a prime mover in the company's diversification effort and the decision to take the company public. Her personal papers during this period reveal her keen understanding of business practices, rare for a woman of her era. (Ironically, though she was a Times Mirror executive, when she was present in New York to celebrate the company's IPO in 1964, she was denied entrance to the New York Stock Exchange because women were not allowed on the trading floor.)

The years spent implementing the diversification plan and expanding the company were Chandler's most influential and potent ones, when she worked in tandem with her husband and then assisted Murphy, whose appointment she was said to have engineered. Her working relationship with Otis was formal, appropriate to the workplace. "We're very close," she told

Women's Wear Daily, but at work "you'd never know we were related. He calls me 'Mrs. C.' . . . I call him 'O.C.' or 'Oates' just as everybody else does. We never discuss anything personal here."[49]

As 1968 drew to a close, she took quiet credit for a company structure that was sound and held great promise for the future: Otis was functioning well up to her expectations, garnering prestige and respect for the newspaper; Norman was quietly serving as the éminence grise; Murphy was projecting the image she wanted for the company and was proving an effective civic leader, marshaling resources for a heated mayoral campaign ahead; Casey was serving as company president in the role she felt best suited him, though she was aware that he had expected to be CEO; and the flock of new young executives heading the recently acquired companies worked hard and were quick to respond. She had attended nearly every meeting of the Times Mirror board since 1955, and as a director she was an astute observer, critic, watchdog, and questioning nuisance.

JUBILANT REPUBLICANS AND THE FOREIGN INTELLIGENCE ADVISORY BOARD

On New Year's Eve, 1968, the Murphys hosted a party at their home for the men and women of the Washington press corps. The talented, high energy guests topped one another with stories of the presidential campaign and in the festive atmosphere made lively predictions for the new administration. Nixon's new press secretary, Ron Ziegler, joined Murphy and *Times* staff writers dining and enjoying the champagne. Ziegler, a former J. Walter Thompson marketing executive, was well known in California politics as press secretary to the California Republican legislative caucus, and he had worked on Nixon's unsuccessful gubernatorial campaign. As the clock struck twelve, Franklin and Judy Murphy's new Beverly Hills residence reverberated with witty toasts, laughter, and high-level political and media gossip.

In January Murphy flew to New York to attend the Fifth Annual Dartmouth Conference, a gathering of prominent citizens of the United States and the USSR who maintained nongovernmental channels dedicated to avoiding nuclear confrontation. In New York he socialized with Norman Cousins, Buckminster Fuller, Arthur Miller, Norton Simon, and David Rockefeller. After the conference Judy met Franklin in Washington, D.C., where they attended the inauguration as guests of the White House with tickets provided by Bob Haldeman, now Nixon's chief of staff. Hotel accommodations were in short supply, so they stayed at the Washington home of John Walker, director of the National Gallery.

The Murphys watched the swearing-in ceremony on a cold Washington morning and heard President Nixon speak of peace: "The greatest honor history can bestow is the title of peacemaker. This honor now beckons America." Murphy wrote Norman Cousins, editor of the *Saturday Review,* with whom he had a deep rapport, "Inaugurals are like Las Vegas—you ought to see it once but once is quite enough."[50]

· · · · ·

In March 1969, by executive order, President Nixon reconstituted an advisory board on national security and foreign relations. The board had been established by President Eisenhower in 1956 and had been continued during the administration of John F. Kennedy as the President's Foreign Intelligence Advisory Board (PFIAB, later FIAB).[51] Murphy was asked by the president to accept appointment to the board. "I have established this Board for the purpose of providing me with independent, continuing assessments of the objectives and conduct of the overall U.S. foreign intelligence effort and of the performance of the several civilian and military agencies engaged in that effort," Nixon wrote Murphy in Los Angeles. "Your willingness to serve in this capacity is much appreciated . . . [and] you will make substantial contributions to the national interest by your service."[52]

Murphy joined the reactivated FIAB just six months after assuming his post at Times Mirror. The participants, "a non-partisan group of distinguished private citizens,"[53] as the president described them, constituted a roster of men largely from American big business, many with military connections: Maxwell D. Taylor, president of the Institute for Defense Analysis; George W. Anderson, former chief of naval operations; William O. Baker, vice president of research at Bell Telephone Laboratories; Gordon Gray, former special assistant to the president for national security affairs; Edwin H. Land, president of the Polaroid Corporation; Robert D. Murphy (no relation to Franklin Murphy), chairman of the board of Corning Glass International; and Nelson A. Rockefeller, governor of New York. These citizen-statesmen met two days each month in Washington for briefings by the CIA. The extent of real power wielded by the FIAB was a subject of debate in the intelligence community; some considered the board "more of a nuisance than a true control mechanism."[54] Nevertheless, the board membership represented a towering level of brainpower and corporate clout.

Time described Nixon's selection of Henry Kissinger as national securty adviser as an "improbable partnership," noting with surprise that Nixon, a secretive, aloof, old-fashioned politician, had chosen a Harvard professor of cosmopolitan outlook and urbane intelligence. As foreign policy adviser in the Kennedy and Johnson administrations, Kissinger had advocated both nuclear and conventional force in response to Communist aggression. Under the Nixon administration, he modified his recommendations to urge that the United States recognize the USSR as a rival superpower and seek global balance through détente, a conciliatory stance that upset the far-right Goldwaterites.

With a foreign relations approach focusing on coexistence, it was essential to have good intelligence. When President Nixon, in promoting an antiballistic missile system, announced that the FIAB would make annual assessments of the "developing Soviet and Chinese threat,"[55] nationwide attention suddenly zeroed in on this little-known group. Joseph Kraft of the *Washington Post* wrote in April that the list of board members read like a mini-roster of the military-industrial complex: "Only two—Gov. Nelson Rockefeller and former UCLA [chancellor] Franklin Murphy—can be said to have a primary commitment to internal public affairs. . . . Not a few Government officials think of the Board as a protective agency—a kind of public relations cover—for the intelligence community. Plainly, the Intelligence Advisory Board is in no position to do any serious independent review of how changing international conditions affect the relative priorities to be attached to deploying an antiballistic missile."[56]

It is not known how Murphy reacted to Kraft's criticism, but in June he wrote Kissinger that the board seemed well balanced in terms of ideology, professional background, and experience. "I am convinced," Murphy told Kissinger, "that it represents one of the best bits of human resources the President has at his command."[57] Late that summer Kissinger visited Los Angeles, where he met with Murphy and editors at the *Times*. Murphy wrote Haldeman at the western White House in San Clemente to say that Kissinger did a superb job: "All of our people (including the few who might have been critical) were highly impressed."[58]

Murphy's dual role as a member of the FIAB and chairman of the board of a media conglomerate was loaded with potential for conflict. Murphy wrote Maxwell D. Taylor, general of the army and FIAB chairman, regarding his concerns. He insisted that Taylor understand he had no direct responsibility for the newspaper, and if its "large and competent investigative staff" unearthed national security information, he would not be the source.[59] Later, when Richard Helms, director of the CIA, wrote Murphy about his concern over a feature in the *Times* that disclosed the identity of agency operatives in Laos, Murphy refused to get involved.[60] At the time Otis Chandler had embarked on an extensive trip to India, and Murphy turned the matter over to *Times* editor Bob Donovan. Murphy informed Helms that he would not interfere in editorial operations: "My responsibility is to the total company and when I came I made it quite clear that Otis Chandler would publish the newspaper."[61]

In spite of Murphy's resolve not to meddle in the editorial arena, he often encountered demands from leaders in the arts, business, government, and entertainment.[62] He negotiated these moments of conflict as though he were whitewater rafting. At times, when politicians and business leaders who dined socially with Murphy at night found themselves pilloried in the pages of a Times Mirror newspaper in the morning, Murphy had to make sunrise telephone calls to deny that he was the reporter's source for a sensitive story. In one incident Murphy hastened to inform Robert O. Anderson, chairman of the board of Atlantic Richfield, that he was not an unnamed source after the oil executive hosted a luncheon for George Bush. "When I go to luncheons of this sort, I do so as a private citizen and lean over backwards to keep the confidentiality," Murphy assured Anderson.[63] Despite his steadfast clarity about his role, Murphy was often mistakenly introduced at engagements and civic functions as "publisher of the *Los Angeles Times*" rather than chairman of the Times Mirror Company—even when his secretary had sent a letter in advance giving his exact title. Murphy would then feel obliged to explain that he was chairman of a company that included not only the *Times* but also other newspapers, as well as television stations, a large book publishing operation, an information services division, and a very large forest products group. As chairman, he presided over the entire enterprise and "*never* acted as publisher."[64]

· · · · ·

American publishing companies were hunting for valuable media properties and moving swiftly to make promising acquisitions. During one rare visit to Los Angeles in March 1969, Katharine Graham, chair of the Washington Post Company, spent the day with Murphy discussing the prevailing business climate. She toured the company's printing facility in Orange County and was entertained at a private dinner that Murphy hosted. Otis Chandler accompanied the Washington guest during the afternoon tour.

Chandler seemed uneasy after Graham's visit. He told Casey and Murphy that Times Mirror was lagging behind in acquiring critical television and cable operations. He was frustrated watching competitors buy the remaining few good media properties. "We really have not had the guts to move when the opportunity came along," he complained. "Since apparently none of the large television chains are available to us, I would think we would have to go out and pay the price to create our own chain even if they were not primary network stations." Further delay risked encountering future government regulations that could preclude expansion as the *Times* was so dominant in its market. Chandler's insistence resulted in a new strategic move: Times Mirror established a foothold in broadcast media and cable outlets once management "bit the bullet," as Chandler urged, and yielded to paying what seemed like exorbitant prices.[65] Much of Murphy's time over the next few years would involve pursuing potential media acquisitions.

At the same time that he presided over an expanding international media conglomerate that reached into more than twenty cities and ten states, in addition to holdings in Amsterdam, Tokyo, Frankfurt, and London, Murphy continued his activities on behalf of the city's cultural institutions. On March 16 he boarded a TWA B-727 to Washington for a breakfast meeting with President Nixon at the White House. As he opened a copy of the *TWA Ambassador* stuffed in the seat pocket near his knees, a smile of satisfaction crossed his face. The magazine presented its readers with a pressing question: "Has Los Angeles REALLY morphed into the Athens of the West?" Take a TWA flight and see for yourself, the article urged, "but don't be surprised if some of your cherished illusions about Smog City are broken on the wheel of the Los Angeles cultural revolution."[66]

SIX

The Chandler Empire in the Watergate Years

U.S. BUSINESS WOULD INCREASINGLY SUFFER over the next decade, but 1971 was still bright as Murphy opened the Times Mirror Company annual report and studied his photograph and his commentary as chairman. The company's year-end record affirmed that he had performed well; three years into his new role, he was wearing it like a suit of clothes, tailor-made. The sleek report announced earnings for the year of $34.9 million, equal to $2.08 per share. At the start of the 1960s the company achieved a benchmark goal of $200 million in revenues for the first time; it finished 1971 with revenues totaling $523.8 million. "We have become a major force in the world of communication," Murphy told stockholders at the company's eighty-eighth annual meeting on May 26. However, he wanted the mark he left on the company to be more than monetary: "Times Mirror has never operated on the principle that the only value is the value of its stock. We are an *aware* company, and we shall continue to strive for excellence."[1]

The team of Murphy, Otis Chandler, and Albert Casey was functioning well. Times Mirror made two of its most important acquisitions—Long Island's *Newsday,* the nation's largest suburban daily, and the *Dallas Times Herald.* Purchase of the *Herald* also included the television station KDFW-TV, which added a Texas television outlet to Times Mirror's cable operations in California and New York. William Attwood, former editor in chief, vice president, and director of Cowles Communications, was appointed president and publisher of *Newsday;* David Laventhol was promoted to editor. Times Mirror's book-publishing division scored a bonanza with the sales of Erich Segal's *Love Story*—nearly nine million copies, the highest figure ever for a single title by New American Library. Record revenues were produced by the legal books from Matthew Bender and Company and the medical texts from C. V. Mosby Company.

Operations at the *Los Angeles Times* were fast-paced and sophisticated, "a miracle of organization and co-ordination," Murphy liked to say.[2] He was elated when the *Times* passed the one million mark in weekday circulation, making it the only standard-size metropolitan newspaper in the United States reaching such a large audience. What pleased him most was that the *Times* continued to win national recognition for editorial excellence. Jim Murray was named America's outstanding sportswriter for the fifth consecutive year, and Paul Conrad received his second Pulitzer Prize for his work as an editorial cartoonist. Conrad, who had early suspicions about Nixon, was soon stretching the bounds of the single-panel medium with his depictions of the slope-nosed president and generating both praise and protest. "Let me say," Murphy congratulated Conrad, "on your bad days you are good; on your good days you are, in fact, incomparable!"[3] (Murphy was also a fan of the legendary *Times* columnist Jack Smith, known for his engrossing first-person vignettes. "Keep them coming," he wrote Smith, "for the greater glory of the *Times* but more importantly . . . for the pleasure of your readers such as myself.")[4]

The year 1971 marked the retirement of the celebrated *Times* editor Nick B. Williams after forty years of service. Williams had joined the *Times* as a copy editor in 1931 and worked his way to the editorship in 1958. Two years later, when Otis Chandler was named publisher, the two men began to remake the *Times*. Talented and tough, Williams had been called one of the finest newspaper editors of his generation. "Nick was one of the closest friends I ever had," Chandler said. "He probably helped me more than any other single person in my life."[5] Murphy praised the diligence and diplomacy of an editor who had known intimately three generations of Chandlers and had "shepherded the newspaper from mediocrity to excellence."[6]

Chandler named William F. "Bill" Thomas the seventh editor of the *Los Angeles Times*. Thomas had big shoes to fill, but he was up to the challenge. "Bill Thomas and Otis Chandler delivered an intense, thorough and frequently surprising brand of daily journalism rarely matched by any other newspaper in the country," Dennis McDougal wrote in his account of the Otis Chandler years. "Two succeeding subscription campaigns were designed around the accurate, if arguably pretentious slogan, 'Stay on Top of the World,' followed by 'A Special Kind of Journalism.'"[7]

Although in his Times Mirror office Murphy seemed far from the turmoil of the university campus, he had not turned his back on the young revolutionaries. He watched closely as the 1972 presidential campaign got under way, and Nixon promised to decrease U.S. involvement in the Vietnam War. In his public speeches Murphy attempted to explain the wider goals of the antiwar activists. "Let me have the temerity to try to be a spokesman for the vast majority of our decent, committed youth," he told audiences. "I do not speak for the exhibitionistic Jerry Rubins and Abbie Hoffmans. A good psychiatrist should represent them. I cannot speak for the arsonists and the bombers and the snipers. Only a criminal lawyer can handle their case." Murphy said he wanted to address the concerns of "young people who want to see the system work, but want to see it working effectively and responsibly *now.*" The gap between the generations was growing, Murphy said, and most of the effort to bridge it must come from the older generation. "At stake is not just the survival of our institutions, our cities and our systems but, much more important, the quality, commitment and future of a generation—the generation of our children."[8]

A TIME OF SCANDAL

In February 1972, after twenty-five years of animosity between the United States and China, Nixon traveled to Beijing for a historic meeting with Chairman Mao Tse-tung. The diplomatic breakthrough, implemented with great secrecy by Henry Kissinger, astounded U.S. citizens and surprised the world. An exhilarated Murphy wrote to Bob Haldeman: "I stand in awe of the approach to China from the point of view of daring, timing and creative courage. In many ways I think it is one of the most remarkable diplomatic achievements within my lifetime—and I say this knowing full well that the path ahead is long and tortuous."[9]

Murphy continued his close association with Haldeman. "It is good to see you so relaxed under the circumstances of your pressurized life," Murphy wrote after a comfortable visit with his former comrade-in-arms in the battles for UCLA.[10] The men spoke often, and when Murphy traveled to Washington, they would frequently meet for lunch. When Judy accompanied her husband, they were joined by Haldeman's wife, Jo, and attended the theater or enjoyed a nightcap in Georgetown or at the Haldemans' Chevy Chase home.

On June 1, 1972, Murphy returned to Washington to attend two full days of meetings of the Foreign Intelligence Advisory Board. On Saturday, June 17, the capital was buzzing with rumors: five men had been caught by police burglarizing the Democratic National Headquarters at the Watergate complex. Speaking for the Nixon reelection campaign, the self-assured, pipe-smoking John N. Mitchell, who had resigned his post as attorney general to head the campaign, publicly denied any administration link to the operation. But surprisingly, on July 1 Mitchell abruptly gave up his job as campaign manager, telling reporters that he needed to spend more time with his family. Members of the FIAB and other Washington insiders were dumbfounded as to why the Nixon loyalist would bail out of the campaign with the election only months away.[11]

On Saturday, July 29, Murphy flew to Aspen, Colorado, for seminars at the distinguished Aspen Institute, before returning again to Washington for the monthly FIAB meeting. The administration dismissed the incident at the Watergate as a "third-rate burglary" having nothing to do with the election campaign. Murphy embarked for London, for a rendezvous with the Hollywood producer Hal B. Wallis at Park Lane's Dorchester Hotel. As planned, Wallis and Murphy met the oilman–art collector Armand Hammer and his wife, Frances, at the Westminster Pier for a Thames cruise on the Ford Motor Company launch. The next morning Murphy flew aboard the Hammers' private plane (OXY 1) to Dublin for a black-tie reception and dinner in honor of the Hammer exhibition at the National Gallery of Ireland. On the London and Dublin trip, Murphy's mind was fixed on the goal he had set for himself—winning Hammer's collection for the Los Angeles County Museum of Art.

On his return to Los Angeles, Murphy was shocked to read in the *Washington Post* that $25,000 earmarked for the Nixon reelection campaign had been deposited in the bank account of one of the five men arrested by police in the bungled break-in at the Democratic National Headquarters. Suddenly the so-called third-rate burglary threatened to become a full-blown scandal, one in which campaign chairman Mitchell might have had a part.

· · · · ·

At the same time the Watergate affair was drawing attention in Washington, a disturbing problem was surfacing at Times Mirror. Otis Chandler was confronted with embarrassing questions as details of a questionable financial venture known as GeoTek trickled to the surface. Chandler had purportedly solicited investors for GeoTek Resources Fund, a consortium of oil and gas partnerships founded by his longtime friend Jack Burke. Chandler had secured significant investments from members of the Los Angeles establishment, including his cousin, Otis Booth, and his sister's first husband, Kelly Spear, as well as such celebrities as Nancy Sinatra, Kirk Douglas, Natalie Wood, and Jack Kent Cook, owner of the Los Angeles Lakers.[12] The Securities and Exchange Commission (SEC) accused Burke of scamming investors by using dollars intended for oil exploration to support his lavish lifestyle, and investigators had uncovered various bogus partnerships and corporations. Chandler reportedly received lucrative finder's fees from Burke and blocks of GeoTek stock.

The *Wall Street Journal* was the first to expose the scandal and Otis Chandler's alleged complicity in it. Murphy was horrified to see the prominently printed four-deck headline appear on the *Wall Street Journal's* front page:

PRICE OF FRIENDSHIP

How Rich Acquaintances
Of California Publisher
Evidently Lost Bundle

Otis Chandler "Opened Doors"
For College Pal Who Ran
Oil Fund SEC Now Probes

$30 MILLION DOWN THE HOLE?[13]

According to Chandler's biographer, after the *Wall Street Journal* story ran Chandler was viewed by friends, family, and his own journalists as either Jack Burke's dupe or his fellow conspirator. "Otis might have sidestepped further humiliation," wrote Dennis McDougal, "if he hadn't denied accepting finder's fees from Burke. At first, Otis Chandler stonewalled both the SEC and the media. But his old mentor, editor Nick Williams, joined Franklin Murphy, Times Mirror President Al Casey, and other ranking Times Mirror leaders in urging him to come clean."[14]

Suddenly it seemed possible that Chandler might face federal indictment and even prison time. The ordeal produced considerable anxiety for Murphy, who not only had to safeguard the operations of the *Times* and the Times Mirror Company, but also protect and counsel Chandler. Norman Chandler's deteriorating health made Murphy's assistance even more essential. The complex chronology that led to the disastrous affair was difficult to sort out. As McDougal noted, the "gloom of GeoTek hovered over each business day like a pox . . . it was hard to imagine how things could get much worse." On May 17, 1973, Burke was indicted, charged with defrauding more than two thousand investors through sales of $17 million of worthless GeoTek stock. In tense discussions with lawyers behind the scenes, Murphy attempted to fashion a legal strategy. Dorothy Chandler counseled "a stiff upper lip and absolute attention to attorneys' advice."[15] She was steadfastly loyal to her son but did not hesitate to chide him. Norman Chandler was probably unaware of the full extent of the legal peril that faced his son. A lifetime of pipe smoking had brought on cancer of the throat and jaw, and with his condition worsening, he was rarely seen outside Los Tiempos.

The Chandler dynasty had not been immune to scandal in the past. Otis's grandfather, dynamic, larger-than-life Harry Chandler, had faced federal indictment in 1917 and at the time quipped to reporters, "You're not a man until you've been indicted at least once." Dorothy Chandler took a more serious view of the ramifications and could barely contain her alarm and exasperation. Early on she had asked Nick Williams what it would take to transform the *Times* into a world-class journalistic enterprise. She had worked hard to see that the paper gained respect, and she was gratified by the acclaim her son had received for turning the paper around. Now the achievement seemed needlessly jeopardized. Such a scandal was hard to overcome in the business of journalism, where reputation and integrity were essential.

Several years after the incident Dorothy Chandler was asked her view of the GeoTek episode: "I wasn't surprised, but I was so mad at my son for not having listened to me and having been so taken in. I told Otis when I first met [Jack Burke] that I did not trust him. I didn't like him at all. I told Otis, 'You're going into the business with the wrong man.'" She asserted that she had believed in her son the entire time. "I knew that Otis was in no way crooked," she said. "If it hadn't been a Chandler, it never would have gone where it did."[16]

At the height of the crisis Otis Chandler became suspicious that the Geo-Tek investigation might be politically motivated. White House tapes released later confirmed that Nixon was furious over the Watergate coverage in the *Times;* he had thought that in view of his past relationship with the newspaper, it would have cut him some slack. The tapes reveal Nixon ordering Attorney General Mitchell to direct the Immigration and Naturalization Service to raid the *Times* for "illegal aliens" and investigate the citizenship status of Otis Chandler's home gardener. The president's voice can be heard ordering Haldeman to instruct Secretary of the Treasury John B. Connally Jr. to "turn the IRS loose" on every member of the Chandler family. "There's one thing I want done. . . . Look over all the activities of the *Los Angeles Times*—all," said Nixon. "I want this whole goddamned bunch gone after."[17]

Chandler was advised by his lawyers that he could avoid federal charges if he provided information against Burke, and after many sleepless nights he agreed to do so. Burke pleaded guilty to making false statements to the SEC and was sentenced to thirty months in prison. Chandler still faced years of civil lawsuits, and his legal bills would exceed $1 million. The drama had reached a satisfactory conclusion, based in part on the efforts of Chairman Murphy, but Mrs. C did not credit him; instead, she said she thought Murphy "took a little bit of pleasure out of Otis' discomfort."[18] She complained that Murphy was always trying to psychoanalyze Otis for her, which was no doubt true. Murphy had often observed the struggles of sons to find their identity and purpose when they were preceded by a powerful father, or, in Otis's case, by father, grandfather, and great-grandfather.

• • • • •

Murphy was unaware of Haldeman's complicity with President Nixon regarding threats to the Chandler family when he returned to Washington in October to meet with Nelson Rockefeller and other members of the FIAB for their monthly two-day session. In mid-October the *Washington Post* published a startling exposé asserting that FBI agents had established that the Watergate bugging incident stemmed from a "massive campaign of political spying and sabotage directed by officials of the White House and the Committee for the Re-election of the President (CREEP)." According to FBI and Department of Justice files obtained by the *Post,* significant funds from Nixon campaign contributions were being used in secret schemes to harass and discredit Democratic presidential candidates and disrupt their campaigns. Reporters Carl Bernstein and Bob Woodward found the breadth of intrusive activity "unprecedented in scope and intensity."[19] The reporters' revelations, though infuriating to Republican campaign strategists, had little impact on the electorate. The campaign slogan, "President Nixon Now More than Ever," pervaded the campaign, and Richard Nixon was reelected on November 7 in one of the largest landslides in American political history.

With the Watergate scandal seemingly in abeyance, Washington prepared for another inaugural ceremony. Franklin and Judy Murphy attended the event with their daughter Carolyn and her fiancé, Stanford law student

Reese Llewellyn Milner II. Bundled in winter coats, the family watched from the grandstand on the morning of Saturday, January 20, as Richard Nixon delivered his second inaugural address before onlookers huddled in near-freezing temperatures. "As we meet here today, we stand on the threshold of a new era of peace in the world," he told the appreciative crowd.[20]

Republican celebrants moved from one festive party to another through the day and evening. The euphoria did not last. On January 30, former Nixon aide and FBI agent G. Gordon Liddy and CIA and FBI veteran James W. McCord Jr. were convicted of conspiracy, burglary, and wiretapping. By spring a variety of congressional and federal investigations into the scandal were taking place. The administration was forced to answer new questions about Watergate. Haldeman, as Nixon's chief of staff, routinely kept close guard over access to the president. One observer said that Haldeman relished his role in the White House and called himself "the president's son-of-a-bitch." The *Washington Post* reported that critics "made fun of his German name, short haircut, arrogance and capacity for detail."[21] Haldeman, aloof from snipes and criticism, was privy to almost every decision made by the president, and his meticulous and extensive handwritten notes later provided a shocking glimpse into the inner workings of the administration. Murphy, like everyone in Washington, knew that Haldeman exercised influence in the White House, but only later would he come to understand the extent of his friend's dedication to self-aggrandizing power, power for its own sake.

For a brief period, Los Angeles turned from Watergate to a heated mayoralty race that resulted in a record-breaking turnout at the polls. The coalition that Murphy and the Chandlers had helped to assemble to support the candidacy of Tom Bradley had regrouped after failure in the 1969 election. Downtown leaders who had withheld support in the previous election now came on board, assured that Bradley would continue redevelopment of the Central Business District. When the 1973 votes were counted, Bradley had defeated Mayor Samuel Yorty, sending the old guard from office. A new, more inclusive administration moved into City Hall. "Your smashing victory was greeted with great jubilation in Times Mirror Square and no one was made happier than I," Murphy wrote the mayor-elect on May 31. "I hope you realize that within my limitations I stand ready to assist you in all possible ways. Best of luck as you embark on this terribly important new epoch in your already remarkable life."[22]

The Watergate scandal, however, was consuming America's attention as revelation followed revelation. Presidential advisers Bob Haldeman and

John Ehrlichman and Attorney General Richard Kleindienst resigned on April 30. White House Counsel John Dean, whom Haldeman and Ehrlichman said had directed the cover-up, was fired. Two weeks before the Senate Watergate Committee began nationally televised hearings, Murphy sent a brief note to Haldeman with words of commiseration: "I am writing to say that I am sorry—desperately saddened—it all seems so damned unfair."[23]

Like everyone else in America, Murphy watched the hearings week after week, month after month, as Senator Samuel Ervin deftly guided the proceedings in a search to determine who had participated in the cover-up. There was still no smoking gun that implicated the president. Murphy felt sorrow and bewilderment. He knew most of the actors involved in the Watergate saga, but Haldeman was more than an acquaintance; he was a person Murphy knew well—or thought he knew well.

In his second inaugural address Nixon had pledged to continue initiatives for peace, a foreign policy approach that was of great interest to Murphy. He had followed the progress of détente with the Soviets with increasing optimism and had been heartened by Nixon's opening of a forward-looking relationship with China. He felt that the forthcoming LACMA exhibition of paintings from the USSR, arranged by museum trustee Armand Hammer, was in keeping with Nixon's call for new patterns of world relationships. Indeed, the idea occurred to Murphy that Nixon could get a welcome boost in image if he visited the exhibition with Soviet leader Leonid Brezhnev. It could provide worldwide exposure to the cultural exchange between the two nations and at the same time handsomely promote the Los Angeles museum. The Soviet official was scheduled to be the president's guest in San Clemente in late June, precisely the time the masterworks on loan from the Hermitage Museum and the Pushkin Museum of Fine Arts were to be exhibited in Los Angeles. "If President Nixon accompanied Brezhnev," Murphy told Nixon advisers, "it would provide a very visible and constructive appearance."[24] The museum was located in a large park on Wilshire Boulevard where a presidential helicopter could safely land, Murphy assured the White House, and if that were not sufficient for security purposes, there was a heliport on the roof of the California Federal Savings and Loan Building two blocks away. Murphy's proposal suddenly stalled when Elliot Richardson, the attorney general–designate, announced that he was appointing a special prosecutor, former solicitor general Archibald Cox, to investigate the Watergate charges. The Soviet leader's field trip was abruptly canceled.

As the congressional hearings dragged on and the depth of Haldeman's involvement with President Nixon in the illicit cover-up became apparent, Murphy expressed his dismay in correspondence with Theodore White, posing the question "Why?"[25] But he did not have long to dwell on his friend's legal woes. He soon found himself, along with other members of the FIAB, targeted in the widening investigation. He was shocked to learn that allegations had been levied against the FIAB with regard to several phases of the so-called Watergate cover-up. The suggestion had been leaked that the Watergate burglars were somehow connected with foreign intelligence activities. Members of the FIAB were called to Washington for an emergency session in June to discuss launching an investigation of their own.

The urgency of the FIAB meeting caused Murphy to cancel his appearance at the long-planned retirement tribute for Robert Vosper, university librarian at UCLA. His affection for Vosper ran deep, and he was so distraught at the thought of disappointing Vosper that he took him into his confidence. Asking Vosper to keep the information confidential, he explained that a situation of the greatest urgency involving the FIAB was calling him to Washington. "Hence, 'the best laid plans of mice and men' phenomenon gets even in my way," wrote Murphy. He recalled the exhilarating, productive years they had shared assembling a rare book collection for UCLA as among "the most meaningful [memories] I possess." He noted, "Judy will be present, and I hope that you will recognize that I shall be there in spirit as well."[26]

· · · · ·

Internal discussions among FIAB members concerning Watergate remain secret, but by mid-June Murphy abruptly resigned, blaming his departure largely on his frustration with the actions of National Security Adviser Kissinger. Murphy told George Anderson, chairman of the FIAB, that he regretted the necessity for his decision because of the admiration and affection he had for other members of the board, but he could no longer tolerate Kissinger and the "smoke screen" he erected between the office of the president and members of the board. "I will always be saddened that President Nixon did not see fit to take the fullest advantage of the combined experience and wisdom of a really extraordinary group of men," he wrote Anderson. "I know that Henry Kissinger will be much more comfortable now that I have left the board, and in some ways so will I. The potential conflict of interest between our newspapers and what they might publish on the one hand and my position on the Board on the other hand has worried me some and in these latter days my worries had increased substantially."[27]

Before his resignation and before Watergate was seared into the public consciousness, Murphy had written the president expressing his anxiety regarding national security. He noted that intelligence gathering had come to rely most heavily on the "hard" intelligence obtained by technological means, such as satellite photography and telemetry, and had failed to develop adequate resources in "human intelligence." This trend had started in the Eisenhower years with the development of the U2 spy plane and continued as subsequent administrations put resources into technology and gadgetry. Murphy urged that "a *special* effort now be mounted to extend the reach and depth of our activity in *human* or agent intelligence gathering." After the catastrophic attacks, nearly thirty years later, on the World Trade Center in New York City on September 11, 2001, Murphy's message regarding the essential value of human intelligence-gathering appears alarmingly prescient.[28]

· · · · ·

Drawing on his talent at putting pieces of his life into separate compartments, Murphy turned his attention to the wedding of his youngest daughter, Carolyn, to Reese Milner II on June 16. The large wedding, attended by many of the city's VIPs and Times Mirror executives, took place two weeks after John Dean told Watergate investigators that he had discussed the cover-up with President Nixon at least thirty-five times, including times when Nixon gave him directions on action to take. As Dean had no hard evidence of the president's involvement, investigators treated the revelations with a degree of skepticism. In another strange development, Watergate prosecutors unearthed a memo to John Ehrlichman describing detailed plans to burglarize the office of Daniel Ellsberg's psychiatrist after Ellsberg had passed the Pentagon Papers to members of the press.

Yet all the burning political suspense was set aside as Murphy walked his lovely daughter down the aisle at All Saints' Episcopal Church in Beverly Hills. Bride and groom had been steady companions since their high school days, but when the music started and faces in the crowd turned her way, Carolyn became nervous. "I'm here," her father whispered as he slipped an arm around her waist. "There is no need to worry."[29]

THE PICASSO ROOM

On June 28, four weeks after Bradley's election as Los Angeles's first African American mayor, Chairman Murphy brought the downtown community together to celebrate a grand new addition to Times Mirror Square. A who's who of the region's foremost personalities in business and local government, as well as executives from the company's far-flung divisions, were invited to inaugurate a new four-story, 78,000-square-foot building sheathed in sleek black glass that now adjoined the landmark 1934 *Times* building. Murphy and Dorothy Chandler had worked closely with architect William L. Pereira and designer Charles Kratka to create a unique space for the company. Chandler wanted the design to showcase the image she envisioned for the Times Mirror Company and at the same time provide space for the meetings and receptions of her extensive civic activities.

The top-floor atrium, covered by a huge skylight, was an unusually striking place: four stories above the street, it was like a high-tech secret garden, with ceramic tile flooring, a splashing fountain, and green shrubs. Surrounding the central court were the glass-fronted executive offices.[30] Included in the new addition was the huge glass-walled directors' suite, fifty-five feet long, with a spectacular view of the city; it was designed to accommodate the board of directors' meetings as well as to function as an impressive site for entertaining.

Chandler had spent hundreds of hours in a hard hat conferring with Pereira and Kratka amid the dust and debris of construction. Although Murphy contributed considerably to completion of the aesthetic triumph, in characteristic fashion he gave full recognition to Dorothy Chandler and Kratka "What you and your staff and Mrs. Chandler have finally pulled together is not only exciting—but exceedingly tasteful," Murphy wrote Kratka. "There is also a great deal of heart 'over and beyond the call of duty.' We are grateful indeed."[31]

Otis Chandler's glass-walled office as seen from the atrium was spare, with an oak desk and credenza and clusters of Mies van der Rohe chairs. Animal heads and trophies from Chandler's hunting expeditions, including the large mounted head of an elk, hung on the wall. Like Chandler's office, Murphy's suite was separated from the atrium by a wall of glass through which visitors could see in and he could see out. He had fine art hung on his walls, and his shelves were filled with photographs and first-edition books. Secretarial stations with sleek cherry-wood partitions were nearby, but the courtyard atrium was the province of the executives. Murphy was well pleased with the new corporate headquarters, feeling the design expressed a fresh, active, forward-looking spirit for a company that also had a long, vibrant history. The downtown location was an essential part of that history, and it was important that the new building express the company's commitment to the revitalization of the city's core.

The art displayed in the new corporate headquarters reflected the merger of the demanding tastes of Murphy and Chandler. They had indulged in a companionable experience selecting contemporary European and American sculpture, paintings, and lithographs—works by Milton Avery, Richard Diebenkorn, Helen Frankenthaler, Jacques Lipchitz, Ellsworth Kelly, Kenneth Noland, and Henri Matisse, as well as a small group of African pieces.

The executive dining room was designated the "Picasso Room," named for a collection of twenty-nine signed Picasso prints of Shakespearean characters handsomely mounted and displayed on the walls. Chandler and Murphy wanted a stunning impact when visitors entered the room. The vivid color of the artworks was repeated in the red, blue, and red-orange upholstery of sleek modern chairs designed by Cesca. A five-star chef was recruited to run the kitchen, and the experience of fine dining among the Picassos was a delight to the palate and the senses, an experience reserved for VIP visitors and top Times Mirror officials.

The executive office space won praise from *Interiors* magazine: "For all its munificence of space, for all its beautifully wrought elements, there is, indeed, a splendid simplicity about this installation. It is based on an unerring eye, a highly selective expertise."[32] For Murphy, beauty was important not only in the natural environment but also in the work environment. "Evil begets evil, and ugliness, like any other disease, is communicable," Murphy pointed out. Dorothy Chandler also believed that beauty was not frivolous and was worth what it cost.

In an address on the aesthetics of the environment that he had presented in Los Angeles almost a decade earlier, Murphy had warned of the unrelenting disfigurement of the community by urbanization: "Unless we begin to comprehend and deal with this monster that technology has thrown up to the twentieth century, urbanization will become not only the most pervasive phenomenon of our time, but the most brutalizing force in human history." He had reiterated the concerns of young activists who called for protection of the environment and added his protest against blighted neighborhoods left behind by laissez-faire private developers, the lack of parks and open space, the contamination of air and water by industrial pollution, and the affront to the senses of a countryside "desecrated by billboards."[33]

In Washington, D.C., Alexander Butterfield, former presidential appointments secretary, appeared before Congress and revealed that since 1971 President Nixon had secretly recorded his White House conversations and telephone calls. Any planning in the Oval Office for a cover-up would be found on the tapes. On July 23 President Nixon refused to turn over the audiotapes, claiming they were protected by executive privilege.

As Murphy and the nation grappled with the details of the scandal that summer, Murphy's son graduated from UCLA and prepared for his first year at the UCLA School of Medicine. Franklin Lee had had a bad start at Berkeley; like so many of his peers, he indulged in new experiences, including drugs. By his sophomore year his grades had declined, and his father managed to secure a midyear transfer for him to UCLA. After a fresh start in Los Angeles his grades improved, and in 1973 he graduated cum laude, with a major in anthropology. When he was accepted to medical school, his father was elated. He presented his son with a state-of-the-art microscope after writing letters to American Optical and Bausch and Lomb, meticulously researching prices and features. In summer 1971 young Franklin had worked in his uncle George Murphy's laboratory at Cornell Medical School, and he and his physician uncle became close. George was surprised and disappointed that Franklin selected UCLA over Cornell in order to stay close to his current girlfriend. The attractive twenty-one-year-old brunette was a humanities major at UCLA and a part-time model. Their relationship was intense, passionate, and turbulent, and when she abruptly left for New York and did not return Franklin was devastated. He grew increasingly depressed during the first few weeks of medical school.

Murphy received a frantic late-night phone call from the young woman in New York. Murphy immediately jumped in his car and drove to his son's apartment. He rushed inside and found Franklin semiconscious. Murphy grabbed his son in his arms and took him to the emergency room at UCLA, where he was treated for an overdose of narcotics, having attempted suicide. When Franklin was out of danger, Murphy returned home to Robert Lane and in a panic threw out his entire collection of antique medicine bottles for fear his son might try to ingest the contents, mostly nineteenth-century opium-based compounds. The bottles had passed from one generation of Murphy physicians to the next.

Murphy secured outstanding psychiatric counseling for Franklin as a result of a referral from his close friend, Sherman Mellinkoff, dean of UCLA's medical school. Franklin recovered quickly and was able to resume his studies. Murphy kept a close eye on his son and spoke frequently with his two roommates. Judy reacted to the incident with disbelief, followed by intense anxiety, which Murphy tried to alleviate with candid talk concerning Franklin's ongoing therapy. Franklin immersed himself in his studies, and despite the well-known pressures of the first year of medical school he received high marks, surprising both himself and his father. He later recalled the episode with regret and described it as a "stupid mistake."[34]

· · · · ·

On September 4 Murphy forced himself to put the frightening episode concerning his son out of his mind and muster the full attention needed to chair the fall meeting of the Times Mirror board of directors, at 280 Park Avenue, the company's New York office. On the conclusion of business, Murphy hosted an impressive Manhattan party for Times Mirror directors, wives, and special guests in the Hunt Room of the renowned 21 Club. Naturally, Murphy extended invitations to his brother and sister-in-law, George and Annette Murphy. The private party in the dimly lit former speakeasy was a smash. Murphy not only made his mark with the eastern power establishment but also introduced additional westerners into the East/West mix. As Murphy proudly said to Katharine Graham, in responding to her letter afterward, the event was proof that the "twain can meet."[35] Among those in attendance were New York's Governor Nelson A. Rockefeller and Senator Jacob K. Javits; David Rockefeller, chair of Chase Manhattan Bank; Joseph F. Cullman III, chair of Phillip Morris; Gustave L. Levy, chairman of Goldman, Sachs and Company; and William T. Seawell, chair of Pan American Airways. Major figures in media and communications also turned out: Robert W. Sarnoff, chair of RCA; Paul Miller, chair of Gannett Company; Gardner Cowles, chair of Cowles Communications; Katharine "Kay" Graham, chair of the Washington Post Company; Arthur O. "Punch" Sulzberger, president and publisher of the *New York Times;* Dorothy Schiff, president and publisher of the *New York Post;* Andrew Heiskell, chair of Time Inc.; and W. H. "Tex" James, president and publisher of the *New York News.* Academe was represented by William J. McGill, president of Columbia University, and James M. Hester, president of New York University.[36]

On September 6 Franklin and Judy left Manhattan and traveled to Paris to rendezvous with Charles and Carmela Speroni and bask in the old-world elegance of the Hotel Lotti, situated between the Tuileries Gardens and the

Place Vendôme. With Professor Speroni behind the wheel and Murphy riding shotgun, the couples enjoyed four weeks driving the country roads of France and Italy. For the moment Murphy was able to escape the troubles at Times Mirror, Watergate, and worries over his son as he soaked up a lively art history lesson from Speroni—"the best tutor a chancellor could ask for." The memorable excursion ended with a candlelight evening at Château Lafitte in the company of the illustrious French banker and wine connoisseur Baron Guy de Rothschild.[37]

Following his return home, on October 8, Murphy was faced with Norman Chandler's rapidly deteriorating health. He wrote Walter H. Annenberg later that afternoon, "I have spent the morning discussing Norman with Otis and it is not a happy situation."[38] The older Chandler's throat cancer had spread, and as a physician, Murphy expected the end would come soon.

THE PASSING OF NORMAN CHANDLER

On October 20, 1973, in the "Saturday Night Massacre," President Nixon fired Archibald Cox and abolished the Office of Special Prosecutor. The same night seventy-four-year-old Norman Chandler died at Good Samaritan Hospital in Los Angeles. His death marked the end of an era for Los Angeles and the Times Mirror Company. As news of his death spread, heartfelt words of condolence poured into Times Mirror Square from people around the world who had known the warmhearted, genteel publisher and corporate executive.

Without question Norman Chandler was the principal architect of the modern Times Mirror Company and had presided over its greatest expansion in its remarkable eight-decade history. As Murphy pointed out in his eulogy, delivered at a private memorial service: "The vital statistics of his long and productive life are known to most, for he was no ordinary citizen. He was the scion of a distinguished grandfather and father whose lives encompassed the growth of this city from sleepy sun-drenched village to bustling metropolis and whose efforts contributed mightily to this development." Murphy paid tribute to Norman's business acumen and, in a heart-warming touch, said that "the first and perhaps most important evidence of his innate good judgment was his success in convincing Dorothy Buffum that she should join him in what became a remarkable odyssey through life." He spoke of the affection in which Chandler was held by everyone in the Times Mirror organization: "And so Norman, I say to you—Thank you from all of us—for being you—and for having touched us as you passed our way."[39]

Norman Chandler's remains were taken to the Chapel of the Pines for cremation in accordance with his wishes. The ashes were carried by Otis Chandler to Dana Point, where he paddled his surfboard a hundred yards from the shoreline and released his father's remains into the ocean. Norman's daughter, Mia, swam near her brother and watched as her father's ashes drifted out to the open sea. "For all his having been born to great wealth, to the assurance of power," his *Times* obituary read, "Norman Chandler was a singularly gentle man. Yet he impelled Times Mirror, in his own calm fashion, into the nation's largest publishing corporation."[40]

The death of her husband after fifty-one years of marriage was a jolt to Dorothy Chandler, whose emotions ranged from despair to anger over Norman's lifetime habit of pipe smoking that hastened his death. Otis recalled that his mother went through various stages of numbness and tears. "She used to talk to Norman after death in a stern voice, 'Why did you leave me so early, so alone?'" he recalled.[41] Her grief was enormous, and for a time she slid into isolation. "When that chair is empty," she said later, "you just sit there by yourself night after night."[42]

One thing Dorothy Chandler could not forgive was Richard Nixon's behavior during the last painful year of Norman's life. In the months preceding Norman's death, President Nixon had telephoned and said he would come to visit. "Norman Chandler was delighted," wrote David Halberstam in *The Powers That Be.* "Watergate was a very distant thing to him, he knew he was dying and he was appreciative of this gesture." Norman, although very weak, mustered strength to dress and be ready for the visit, but Nixon did not arrive, nor did he call or explain. On a second occasion Nixon was expected to arrive at Los Tiempos, and again he did not arrive and did not call. Norman's disappointment was not forgotten by Dorothy Chandler, who told Halberstam that she wrote Nixon a "blistering letter which said that he was a dreadful man, which was proved by the fact that he would stand up Norman Chandler—who had been his friend and done so much for him—when he was terminally ill." As far as she was concerned, she told the author, Richard Nixon was "*a friend to no man.*"[43]

Murphy did what he could to bolster Dorothy Chandler's low spirits, and his calendars show that he visited her often after Norman's death. Concerned about her uncharacteristic retreat into isolation, he attempted to persuade her to return to some kind of social life. In June 1974 he succeeded in persuading her to join him on a trip to the magnificent Rockefeller home at Kykuit, where she could enjoy the serenity and pleasures of one of the loveliest private estates in the world. The trip proved a successful tonic for the ailing widow, and Murphy expressed his gratitude to Nelson and Happy Rockefeller. "This is really the first significant event that she has attended since Norman's death and I hope that it represents the beginning of her coming out," he wrote.[44]

. . . . .

January 1974 brought changes at Times Mirror. Albert Casey, who had worked closely with Norman Chandler to implement the company's far-reaching diversification program, resigned as president to become chair, chief executive, and president of American Airlines. During his eight years of service, Casey had reported first to Norman Chandler and then to Franklin Murphy. He was the company's chief operating officer developing specific plans for expansion and acquisitions and supervising the company's vast operating groups and subsidiaries. He had been stung by the surprise announcement of Murphy's appointment to the chairmanship in 1968. Although he was president of the company, he was still only number two and recognized he would never be named chief executive officer. "It wasn't a matter of ego," Casey wrote in his memoirs about his decision to depart. "It was simply that after twenty-five years in business I had a desire to run my own show."[45]

Robert F. Erburu, forty-three years old and a native of Southern California, was elected to succeed Casey in February 1974. A graduate of the University of Southern California and Harvard Law School, Erburu was an associate at the law firm of Gibson, Dunn and Crutcher when he was loaned to Times Mirror for six months in 1961 to help with the rash of acquisitions. Norman Chandler was soon impressed with the young man and brought him into the company as assistant general counsel. The great-grandson of Basque sheepherders who had settled in Ventura County, California, the soft-spoken, deeply religious executive settled quickly into the mode of operation at Times Mirror. (Interestingly, Erburu had majored in journalism and was editor of the student newspaper at USC. This early interest in journalism was a factor in his decision to leave private practice and accept the position at Times Mirror.)

At the time of his arrival the company had just obtained New American Library and was rapidly acquiring additional publishing companies as well as newspapers. In 1964 Erburu had worked closely with Casey in preparation for the company's listing on the New York Stock Exchange followed by its first public offering of Times Mirror stock, a $40 million 4.5 percent debenture issue, and a later secondary offering of common stock valued at more than $15 million. His final year as general counsel was consumed with the extraordinary legal work involved in acquiring Newsday, Inc., of Garden City, New York, and the Times Herald Printing Company of Dallas, Texas.

Erburu had joined the board of directors in 1968, and in 1969 he was appointed senior vice president. When Erburu was elected president of Times Mirror after Casey's departure, he began to work directly with Chairman Murphy. The new executive troika became Murphy, Chandler, and Erburu. Murphy was impressed by Erburu's ability to grasp a situation and find solutions. He preferred to delegate, and Erburu was one of those talented executives who liked to show what he could do. In addition to their working relationship, the men became close, comfortable friends. As their friendship grew, there was little they did not share with each other. Erburu admired the chairman's civic commitment and his aspirations for Los Angeles. Murphy took pleasure in introducing Erburu to the power establishment and guiding him to important roles in the life of the city. Their personal relationship was such that in 1975 Murphy named Erburu and the Bank of America as coexecutors of his estate. In a letter to his son-in-law, attorney Craig Crockwell, regarding his will, Murphy said that in all matters requiring a decision, "in the division of personal property or anything else, Robert Erburu's judgment would be final."[46]

· · · · ·

At the end of pressure-filled days at Times Mirror Murphy would leave the office and slide behind the wheel of his little Mustang Ghia. First introduced by Ford in 1974, the Ghia was an upscale luxury-edition Mustang with sporty vinyl top and a finely appointed interior with rich wood grain finishes. Turning right on Second Street to Broadway from Times Mirror Square, then one block to Third Street, Murphy would kick the Mustang into gear as he traveled west onto the Harbor 110 and merged onto the broad Santa Monica Freeway.

Murphy told Ford President Lee Iacocca that he had never enjoyed driving a car more. "It has attracted an enormous amount of attention wherever I go—whether at the Bel Air Country Club, parking lots in Beverly Hills, [or] down here at Times Mirror Square," he said. "The only thing I don't like, but it is no fault of ours, is the damn chest seat belt. I have discovered that women—including my wife—hate it even more. I think they all realize that it is the fault of Ralph Nader and not the fault of Ford."[47]

Murphy left his seatbelt unfastened, in just the same fatalistic manner in which he continued to chain-smoke several packs of cigarettes a day, a lifetime habit he began in medical school. He made sporadic efforts to quit but would not fully kick the habit until the end of the decade. Judy also continued to smoke heavily. Murphy stayed in command of his tightly packed work schedule while continuing to neglect his health; he never exercised, he drank heavily, he ate rich fatty foods, and he stayed up late. He scrupulously kept his commitments and rarely missed a board meeting or an important Times Mirror function, but at one directors' meeting at the Ford Motor Company offices in Dearborn, Michigan, he abruptly left the room during a critical report on Ford's steel facilities.

Worried, Henry Ford II ran behind him as he headed for the men's room. When Murphy told him he was in tremendous pain and must see a dentist, Ford picked up the telephone and arranged an emergency appointment. After his return to Los Angeles, Murphy, following his unshakable routine of sending follow-up notes, wrote thanking Ford for his thoughtfulness and also asked him for the name and address of the dentist. "I would like to write and thank him for his great courtesy," Murphy said.[48] He was not yet sixty years old, but health problems that included backaches, headaches, and sharp pains in his mouth and jaw plagued him. He took an analgesic or had a drink and carried on regardless of the pain.

"A CANCER ON THE PRESIDENCY"

Henry A. Kissinger replaced William P. Rogers as President Nixon's secretary of state as war yielded to an uncertain peace in Vietnam. The last U.S. troops had pulled out in March 1973. In the Middle East a volatile uneasiness existed between Israel and the Palestinians and neighboring Arab states, and in Indochina long-standing conflicts still remained unresolved by the Nixon Doctrine. Kissinger's "shuttle diplomacy" continued to be called upon.

Murphy sent Kissinger his hearty congratulations on his cabinet appointment in a letter dated August 22, 1973: "During the first four years the doors had been opened [to China and the Soviet Union], and during the second four years the task [will] be to walk through the doors. It seems to me that your enlarged role will make this important exercise even more likely. Good luck."[49] It is not known if Murphy changed his opinion about Kissinger's methods that prompted his resignation from the FIAB; however, he was a proponent of peaceful coexistence with the Communist world and therefore welcomed Kissinger's diplomatic efforts rather than a hard-line policy based on nuclear threats. When Kissinger was awarded the Nobel Peace Prize in 1973 for his efforts in Vietnam, Murphy wrote Kissinger again on October 17: "In re. the Nobel Peace Prize—well deserved and hearty congratulations."[50]

By October Egypt and Syria had attacked Israel on Yom Kippur, creating the Middle East crisis that Kissinger had feared. The corollary action of the OPEC nations was an oil embargo, felt in the United States by soaring inflation. In Washington an embattled Richard Nixon was fighting to withhold tapes from investigators, and in a scandal not related to the Watergate cover-up, Spiro Agnew resigned as vice president and Gerald Ford was appointed the first vice president to take office under provisions of the Twenty-fifth Amendment to the Constitution. With Senator Ervin's committee continuing hearings into November, the year was one long, mesmerizing civics lesson for the American public.

· · · · ·

In July 1974 Murphy dined at the White House with President Nixon and budget director Roy L. Ash. It would be the last time Murphy would see Nixon as president. Soon after his return to Los Angeles, the U.S. Supreme Court rejected the president's assertion of executive privilege and unanimously ruled that White House audiotapes must be turned over to prosecutors. By the end of the month the House Judiciary Committee passed the first of three articles of impeachment charging the president with obstruction of justice. Examination of the subpoenaed tapes had revealed that six days after the Watergate break-in the White House system recorded a pivotal conversation in which President Nixon instructed Haldeman to have the CIA warn the FBI to halt its investigation of the Watergate burglary because national security was involved. In a conversation among Nixon, Haldeman, and John Dean recorded in the Oval Office, Dean is heard discussing the cover-up with the president, telling him that it is a "cancer on the presidency" that must be excised.

When the revelations were made Murphy was in the hospital at UCLA undergoing painful surgery on his jaw. Confined to his bed, he watched the historic moments unfold on television as the Nixon presidency came to an end. Nixon resigned on Friday, August 9, 1974, and images of a broken politician waving from the steps of the presidential helicopter were flashed around the world. Vice President Gerald Ford assumed the nation's highest office and, after taking the oath, set the tone in his acceptance speech for his short presidency: "Our long national nightmare is over." No one knew what impact the president's resignation would have on the nation and its economy. Like other chief executives, Murphy watched anxiously as the Dow fell on twenty of the next twenty-five trading days. On September 8, Ford issued a full and unconditional pardon of Nixon.

Throughout the Watergate crisis, the public, looking for answers, had increasingly turned to newspaper coverage, and the *Los Angeles Times* and other Times Mirror newspapers experienced a dramatic surge in newsstand sales. (Virtually every copy of the *Times* edition containing the entire 1,308 pages of the Watergate tape transcripts sold almost immediately.) The public was gripped by the president's crude language and the plotting of illegal acts in the Oval Office. *Times* reporters and editors received kudos for their in-depth coverage; with the guidance of publisher Otis Chandler and editor Bill Thomas the *Times* delivered to its readers a clear-headed, first-rate analysis of a rapidly unfolding piece of American history. Reporters from the *Washington Post* were perceived as the primary journalists who uncovered the scandal, but during the first several weeks after the break-in at the Watergate complex, the Washington bureau of the *Los Angeles Times* had played a "nip-and-tuck game of one-upmanship" with the *Washington Post*'s Carl Bernstein and Bob Woodward.[51]

Times reporters Jack Nelson, Bob Jackson, and Ron Ostrow were "right at their heels, even pulling ahead of the intrepid *Post* a few times," remembered one longtime staff writer. At one point Watergate judge John Sirica jailed *Los Angeles Times* Washington bureau chief John F. Lawrence for contempt because he refused to release audiotapes of his interview with a key Watergate figure.[52] Murphy appreciated the performance of the Washington bureau, and the week after Nixon's resignation he wrote John Lawrence, "I know that the pressures of time and energy must have been enormous. However, your efforts have paid off on a superb coverage of an unprecedented and complicated situation. Hearty congratulations."[53]

On New Year's Day, 1975, after a lengthy trial, a Washington jury rendered guilty verdicts against White House Chief of Staff Haldeman, Domestic Adviser Ehrlichman, Assistant Attorney General Robert C. Mardian, and former Attorney General Mitchell, all of whom were sentenced to prison.

· · · · ·

The nation was moving forward. It was too soon to give the former president credit for his achievements in foreign policy, and it would be some time before he would sit down with David Frost for his first in-depth post-presidential interview, but dozens of journalists and authors embarked on projects to chronicle the Watergate saga.

In fall 1974 Murphy met several times in New York with Theodore White, author of the best-selling series *The Making of the President*. After obtaining White's agreement that their meetings were to be strictly confidential, Murphy shared his insights into plebiscitary politics and manipulated party campaigns; and he provided astute psychological portraits of key Watergate players. White found Murphy's comments "marvelous" and, with Murphy's approval, included the information, without attribution, to good effect in his landmark book *Breach of Faith: The Fall of Richard Nixon*.[54]

In a four-page, single-spaced typed letter to White dated November 25, 1974, Murphy speculated on how the Watergate cover-up came about:

> As I indicated to you, I think it comes down to a very specific reason— namely, that to Bob Haldeman—Richard Nixon was alpha and omega. In short . . . to him Nixon could do no wrong and represented the best good hope for this country and the solution of its myriad of problems as far as Haldeman was concerned. I guess you could almost say it was a clear-cut case of hero worship and an absolutely unswerving loyalty to the man and that for which he stood.
>
> After the break-in, it would be my view that Haldeman's reaction could have been one of anger as to the stupidity of the act and above everything else—alarm that such an act might interfere with what he regarded as the most important thing in the world, namely the reelection of Nixon.

Murphy thought that whatever illegal acts Haldeman participated in, "he did so with a recognition that they were illegal but that on balance, nearly everything was justified to guarantee the reelection of his friend and hero."

Murphy blamed the isolation of the president for much of the problem. He told White that early on he had suggested to Haldeman that Nixon hold periodic "stag dinners," like the ones Murphy had attended when Eisenhower was in office, as a way to engage in dialogue with leaders outside the White House. Haldeman dismissed the idea as unduly tiring for the president. Also noteworthy, in Murphy's view, was Haldeman's ego involvement and pleasure in exercising power and influence. "I suspect that is only human," Murphy wrote. He criticized the part played by CREEP, which was composed "almost entirely of political amateurs" who had usurped the work of the reliable and experienced Republican National Committee. "None of what I have said should be considered justification for perjury, obstruction of justice and attempts to manipulate departments of the government," Murphy emphasized. "In fact, I shake a little and am somewhat frightened in contemplating what might have happened had the cover up been successful. Perhaps then arrogance would have known no bounds and we might well have had some dark days."[55]

White's book appeared in bookstores in 1975 and was reprinted four times during that year. As the book climbed on the *New York Times* bestseller list, private citizen Nixon remained in seclusion inside the walled compound of his seaside San Clemente home.

PRESSURES AND PRESTIGE

The pressures on Franklin Murphy as chairman of the Times Mirror board were mounting. The year 1974 proved a difficult one with consequences that continued into 1975. A hostile work stoppage at the company's two newsprint mills in Oregon lasted nearly twelve weeks and generated heavy losses; a depressed economy lowered newspaper advertising revenue and circulation; most of the company's magazine properties suffered from the impact of higher paper costs and reduced demand; meeting requirements of revised federal fair trade laws required an expensive new distribution system for the *Times*. Although record profits of previous years were not achieved in 1975, the powerful troika of Franklin Murphy as chairman and CEO, Otis Chandler as vice-chairman and publisher of the *Times*, and Robert Erburu as *Times* Mirror president continued to deliver stability and an aura of strength to the company. The men held one another in high esteem and worked closely together.

It was apparent to Murphy that difficult days were ahead. Company revenues for 1975 exceeded $806 million, but profits remained weak. The nation was caught in the grip of seemingly intractable inflation, and there was no consensus among President Ford's advisers on how to deal with it. Murphy grew concerned about an unprecedented federal deficit that he felt would lead to a sharp rise in interest rates, which in turn would harm the housing and automobile industries, both essential to financial recovery. Alan Greenspan, who led President Ford's Council of Economic Advisers, initiated an innovative stimulus package and tax plan to counter the 1974–75 recession, but its effectiveness remained to be seen. "I guess we will somehow muddle through," Murphy said.[56]

. The multiple entities comprising the Times Mirror Company provided some welcome advantages during the recession. Newsprint was in short supply in California, but the *Times* was able to fill the bulk of its immense paper requirements from the Oregon-based Publishers Paper Company, a Times Mirror subsidiary. Murphy had implemented a reforestation program covering more than fourteen thousand acres of company-owned timberlands. His groundbreaking paper recycling facility opened in September 1975 in Oregon City, producing forty tons of pulp per day through an innovative de-inking system. Murphy's ultimate aim, far-sighted for the era, was to make recycled material an important part of the company's newsprint operations.[57]

In spite of rough times, record earnings were achieved by Times Mirror's publishing group, led by stellar sales from the paperback edition of *Joy of Cooking* and Erica Jong's *Fear of Flying*. Substantial revenues continued as well from the professional books division. The Information Services Group, which included mapping companies and engineering and educational suppliers, also reported respectable earnings to Murphy.

The year 1975 was a prosperous one for Murphy personally; his income at Times Mirror exceeded $500,000, and his directorships at Ford, Hallmark Cards, Bank of America, and Norton Simon, Inc., earned him an additional $71,521 in annual retainers and fees. He maintained his hectic travel pace, managing to juggle his extensive obligations.

· · · · ·

Murphy's appointment calendar rivaled Phileas Fogg's eighty-day dash around the world. The first six months of 1975 provide a good example not only of the pace of his daily life but also of his traveling style:

January 8: Murphy flew first class on American Airlines to Detroit, where a Ford Company car whisked him to the board of directors meeting at the Ford Motor Company followed by private visits with Henry Ford II.

February 10: Again in Detroit and Dearborn, he left for New York City on the Ford plane and stayed at Fifth Avenue's Pierre Hotel, attended board meetings of Norton Simon, Inc., and handled pressing business at the Kress Foundation.

April 27: He ventured to Miami to convene a meeting of the President's Biomedical Research Panel at the Royal Biscayne Beach and Racquet Club, followed by a flight to Baltimore, where he was met at the airport and driven to the home of Senator Edward Kennedy for a private dinner at the Kennedy home with Senator Jacob Javits.

April 30: After an evening at the Madison Hotel in Washington, Murphy attended breakfast meetings at the Brookings Institution think tank followed by lunch at the University Club. Later he met with members of the acquisitions committee of the National Gallery of Art, followed by dinner at the home of Paul Mellon.

May 1: After morning meetings with National Gallery director J. Carter Brown and a meeting of the board of trustees, Murphy left Washington on a nonstop United Airlines flight to Los Angeles, where he rushed home to change his clothes and emcee a candlelit black-tie dinner in honor of Dr. Jules Stein, chairman of MCA and a personal friend.

June 6: Murphy presented the financial outlook of Times Mirror to the New York Society of Security Analysts. After that exhausting session he chaired a meeting of the Kress Foundation board called to fill the vacancy left by the death of board member Governor Alfred E. Driscoll. (Murphy proposed John C. Fontaine, a New York lawyer active in a number of arts-related charitable organizations, who later succeeded him as chairman of the Kress Foundation.) That evening he boarded a TWA 747 bound for Madrid, where he was met by a Ford driver and taken to the Hotel Ritz.

June 7: He traveled via a Ford company plane to Jerez, where he joined a suntanned and straw-hatted Henry Ford II and other company directors to watch a bullfight followed by an outdoor barbecue at the Prado Farm.

June 8: Murphy (dressed in a dark business suit as suggested) accompanied Henry Ford II to the Madrid residence of Prince Juan Carlos, the Palacio la Quinta, for a private reception. That afternoon Murphy and Ford met with the Spanish prime minister Carlos Arias Navarro and afterward engaged in heated discussions with Claudio Boada, chairman of Ford of Spain, Inc., concerning problems at Ford's Valencia plant.

Murphy moved seamlessly from one venue to the next, offering his opinion, dispensing advice, and solving problems. Carter Brown remembered the multitasking Murphy on one Washington trip jumping up from the dinner table to conclude an acquisition for Times Mirror. Brown watched from a distance as Murphy, in the era before cellular telephones, spent fifteen minutes hunched over a hallway pay phone. Murphy refused to say what it was all about, and Brown recalled reading the details of the multimillion-dollar transaction on the front page of the next morning's *New York Times*.[58]

THE FORCED RETIREMENT OF DOROTHY CHANDLER

Dorothy Chandler had spent more than twenty-seven years as an employee and member of the Times Mirror board. In the atrium of the new executive building, the fountain sending jets of spray shimmering beneath the skylight bore a plaque reading:

DOROTHY BUFFUM CHANDLER
AN EXPRESSION OF APPRECIATION FROM HER ASSOCIATES
FOR HER VISION AND LEADERSHIP IN THE CONCEPTION AND
COMPLETION OF TIMES MIRROR SQUARE

What the plaque did not describe was her insistence that journalistic excellence and long-term profitability be part of the Times Mirror image as well as style.

After the death of Norman Chandler, Otis made it increasingly clear that a plan for the matriarch's retirement was needed. According to his biographer, Otis asked Murphy to "evict his mother from Times Mirror Square." In deference to Dorothy's grief, Otis said, he had tolerated his mother's meddling, but the time had come for her to leave—there was simply "no reason for her to take up corporate space."[59] He was exasperated by talk of his mother's influence and vigorously denied that she had any real control over him or over the editorial affairs of the *Times*. "You couldn't depend on her," Chandler told one journalist. "She didn't know anything about the business. I don't think she ever worked until she was appointed a vice president and really given responsibility for certain public relations functions of the corporation. She never worked as a reporter or a salesman. Never worked in production. There's no way she could help me."[60]

But there was substantial evidence to the contrary. The opinion expressed in a *Life* magazine feature in 1956—that she was a "force in journalism, politics and civic affairs"—is confirmed by her surviving personal papers, which reflect the depth of her involvement in the company's strategic business planning during a period of rapid change.[61] By 1961 she operated as a company vice president; with a staff of "two men and several secretaries," she supervised production of the company's annual report and quarterly shareholder reports and planned the company's annual shareholder meetings. She assumed responsibility for corporate relations with the public, making speeches and devising an effective public relations strategy. She took complete charge of the company's physical facilities, working with architects and builders, and in concert with Murphy she orchestrated plans for the new executive building.

Early in her career at Times Mirror Chandler had presided over the *Times* women's section, on salary as an assistant to the publisher. After World War II she recognized that women were taking up new interests, and she felt the "society section" should be revamped. "The idea of the traditional ladies club, the sewing circle and all [those] gossipy society things, I felt were of the past," she said. "Women had gone beyond that."[62] She instituted the women's section, where the civic work of Los Angeles women could be reported. She also for a time worked as a journalist, writing colorful features about the 1952 Republican National Convention in Chicago and the 1953 Eisenhower inaugural. Her punchy journalistic style was praised by the women's rights activist Margaret Sanger, who wrote Chandler to compliment the sparkling, amusing reports in her "Convention Chatter" column. "Give us more of it," Sanger wrote.[63]

Despite her obvious contributions, some executives insisted that Dorothy Chandler's influence over Norman and Otis Chandler had definite limits. "She had her opinions," recalled Robert Erburu, "but without question the real control was exercised by Norman Chandler alone." Erburu suggested that the idea that Dorothy Chandler held great sway behind the scenes at Times Mirror was an urban myth, perpetuated by journalists and authors because it made a better story. "Those with firsthand knowledge of the Chandler family dynamics take exception to the portrayal of Dorothy Chandler as the real power behind the throne," he said.[64] But Erburu conceded that she and Norman "certainly worked as a team." Genuine tribute could be paid, Erburu felt, to her spirit and civic reach.

Albert Casey was quick to praise Dorothy Chandler's business acumen. He told one journalist that some Times Mirror executives could be seduced by a shiny balance sheet, but Mrs. Chandler "stepped outside the economics and looked at the products. She questioned everything."[65]

Times Mirror senior executive Peter Fernald asserted: "I observed her for eighteen years. She was the brains of the family and the brightest of the Chandlers. . . . She was always probing and questioning. When she was removed from the board the company may have lost its most loyal asset. There was no one left to ask the hard, ugly questions."[66]

"What Otis Chandler failed to realize," Fernald observed, "was that Mrs. C worked through Norman to engineer what needed to be done. She single-handedly ensured the future growth of the company through her shrewd decision to remove Norman as publisher so he could focus his attention on the difficulties concerned with a massive and modern diversification program."[67]

Her instincts proved sound. The transfer of power was a critical moment in the history of Times Mirror and symbolized the peak of Dorothy Chandler's influence. Her son might owe his mother credit for his powerful position, but he more than repaid her by bringing the *Times* to journalistic excellence. David Halberstam recognized Dorothy Chandler as a woman of soaring ambition—ambition for her husband, for herself, and most of all for her son. "She became the Chandler incarnate," Halberstam wrote, "more Chandler than the real Chandlers. . . . Her arrival ensured that the dynasty survived and expanded during Norman's tenure, but, more important, the intensity of her will and the fierceness of her spirit profoundly affected her son Otis and thus perpetuated the dynasty for one more generation."[68]

Dorothy Chandler herself was never in doubt about the issue of her power. In the years after her retirement an intrepid interviewer asked her, "It's been said that you masterminded Otis into this role [of publisher]. Is this essentially correct or incorrect?" "Correct," she responded, without a moment's hesitation. "I wanted it to be a better paper, better writers, better paid people, a better Washington bureau and all the things that have happened." As she explained her influence: "I had to be Norman's motivation. He wasn't motivated for money or the *Times*. I felt he needed me for this motivation. And the Times wouldn't be where it's at today without this motivation."[69]

After the loss of her husband, however, Chandler found herself increasingly isolated from company operations by a new corporate regime and management experts. In Murphy's view there was no precise role for her and good reason for her to leave the board. "She had completed her tours and now it was time for her to go home," Murphy said later.[70] It was a sensitive and difficult assignment even for Murphy, widely appreciated by colleagues as a boardroom diplomat par excellence. It may have been the right thing to do, and as the first nonfamily leader of the Times Mirror conglomerate Murphy was the right man to do it. But there was no possible scenario in which he could win on behalf of both the company and his longtime friend and colleague.

Otis Chandler, at this time, was confronting difficult business decisions for the company and the newspaper while also facing continuing civil suits from the GeoTek scandal. He was working to restore his reputation for good judgment; what he did not need was his mother giving the impression that he was under her thumb. He was disparaged as a rich kid, a lucky heir, a jock—the shotput champion. Even several Pulitzer Prizes later, with the *Times* garnering plaudits as the flagship of a national newspaper empire, he still won only grudging acknowledgment from journalism's intellectual elite. He claimed it did not bother him; the challenges that invigorated him were not the ploys of cerebral one-upmanship but extreme sports and wild-game hunting.

Lack of respect did bother Dorothy Chandler. When Robert Towne won an Oscar for his screenplay for the film *Chinatown* (1974), featuring a Chandler-like patriarch ominously directing a scare campaign for a dam to make a fortune for himself and his cronies, her exasperation reached the boiling point. Although the Times Mirror Company had now gained the recognition it deserved in financial circles, the newspaper was not coming into the public consciousness the way she had hoped. It galled her that the hero reporters of the *Washington Post*—Woodward and Bernstein—had won America's respect and that Katharine Graham was now known to everyone as the courageous publisher who gave the green light to expose the Watergate cover-up. The *Los Angeles Times,* on the other hand, was the newspaper accused of "creating" Nixon. Dorothy Chandler felt the GeoTek episode had been blown out of proportion, and now Hollywood had seen fit to besmirch the newspaper and the family with a sex-driven tale of murder and fraud.

· · · · ·

Murphy understood the significance of Dorothy Chandler's role in the life of Los Angeles, indeed in California. He had seen her at work and had known her as an indomitable player and a shrewd one. Joan Didion, an astute observer of Los Angeles, wrote, "Even Mrs. Chandler's admirers have tended to marginalize her efforts, to speak of her defining influence on Los Angeles as an involvement with culture." Didion took issue with culture viewed as essentially an appropriate "feminine" interest: "What Dorothy Buffum Chandler did was no more about 'culture' than what Phoebe Apperson Hearst did [for the University of California] was about Beaux Arts architecture. What each of them did was will an idea of a place into being, and they did it because they shared an understanding that their personal and business fortunes would be inextricably linked to the fortunes of the places in which they lived, that their houses could prosper only to the extent that the places outside their houses prospered."[71]

Murphy sought opportunities to discuss with Dorothy Chandler her goals and the subject of her retirement. After her long period of mourning, she had returned to board meetings bewildered by all the change during her absence. She consumed board time with her many questions about decisions that had already been made. Otis was especially exasperated with her for asking for the kind of detailed information that she used to receive when she and Norman were initiating the company's expansion. The company was now managed by professionals who handled such details, but his mother was stuck in the old days before computerized research and advisers with specialized expertise.

In his affection for Dorothy and out of concern for her mental health and spirits after Norman's death, Murphy had arranged entertainment and outings for her, but he failed to tutor her in the new management approaches and changing ethos of the era. Yet after any number of meandering discussions, Murphy was not sure that she had agreed to give up her position on the board as a director emeritus. As a matter of clarification, and perhaps in some exasperation, on May 19, 1975, he dictated and sent to her the terms of her mandatory retirement:

1. You will continue as an employee of Times Mirror as the Assistant to the Chairman until May 19, 1976—at which time you will retire as an employee of Times Mirror.

2. You will serve as Emeritus Director of Times Mirror until the annual meeting of the company in May of 1976.

3. You will move your office from the atrium to an office off the west corridor on the sixth floor, which you will occupy until your retirement from the company in May 1976.

During her last year of service, she was to be evicted from the beautiful atrium court she had created with such care and concern for the comfort of the executives and the image of the company. After dispatching the letter by messenger, belatedly recognizing that the date was also Dorothy's birthday, Murphy instructed his secretary to rush a Western Union Mailgram of good wishes to the Chandler home. The telegram read simply: "Happy Birthday and many more of the same, Franklin."[72]

At the next annual meeting of the Times Mirror Company, Murphy stood to address the assembled shareholders and executives and revealed publicly for the first time the matriarch's official retirement: "Finally, I want to take special note of Mrs. Dorothy Buffum Chandler, who will not stand for her re-election by the board as a director emeritus." In his carefully composed praise of her, Murphy noted that "Mrs. Chandler has served this company since 1948 in a variety of important capacities" and that "side by side with her husband, Norman Chandler, she played an important role in the growth of the *Los Angeles Times*." He noted in particular the complex of buildings that would serve as an "enduring symbol" of her achievements. He then announced, "This annual meeting signals the end of [her] relationship [with Times Mirror]. This company will always be most deeply in her debt as, of course, is the city of Los Angeles as a result of [her] contributions to improving the quality of life for all its citizens."[73]

Following the announcement, Murphy telephoned Dorothy to make arrangements to see her, but to his surprise he learned that she had already departed Los Angeles on an extended vacation. "To my distress I learned that you . . . had left," Murphy wrote in a hasty letter to her. "I wanted to tell you personally—namely that I hope this trip will be exciting, interesting and everything you hope for."[74]

Chandler's removal from the Times Mirror organization closed the door on her deep and close association with Murphy. He had served her as Titan-chancellor, civic booster, and Times Mirror chairman of the board. Murphy had duked it out with county supervisors, mayors, and governors to promote her interests. He had made a success of the transition that enabled her husband's retirement, and he had helped to engineer her son's rescue during the GeoTek scandal. He had been one of her closest friends and allies, sharing with her, along with Ed Carter and Howard Ahmanson, a genuine desire to prepare Los Angeles for greatness with cultural pavilions built by philanthropy and civic partnerships. Now Murphy forced her compulsory removal from the organization that had for so long engaged her passionate interest. It was as though she were dismissed from the Chandler dynasty, as though, in essence, she were not, and never had been, a vital part of it. In this unhappy manner, Chandler moved from being an admirer of Murphy to being his antagonist. Later she became his quiet enemy.

Soon after Dorothy Chandler's official departure, Otis instructed editors to abolish the Woman of the Year award. "The dropping of the Woman of the Year is a sign that Otis is totally on his own," said Nick Williams. The award had symbolized her last remnant of power. Dorothy Chandler was not consulted, nor was she informed until she read about it in the *Times*.

Upset and tearful, Mrs. C felt the wound all the more for the new era it surely represented. As gender designations became banned, the classified section no longer took ads for Girl Fridays, and Woman of the Year, too, had become anachronistic.

Some months later company vice president and general counsel John E. Flick mailed Chandler a copy of Murphy's laudatory comments concerning her company career. The correspondence was found ripped in half among Mrs. Chandler's surviving personal papers.

Sadly, her removal from the Times Mirror board, the loss of Norman Chandler, advancing age, and poor health brought Dorothy Chandler's slow fading from the scene. For a few more years, she conducted her remaining civic affairs inside the small outbuilding by the swimming pool that she called her "Pub."

In an in-depth profile in *Esquire* magazine in November 1977, headlined "The Word from Mamma Buff," Lally Weymouth, daughter of Katharine Graham, revealed Dorothy Chandler's disparaging opinions about Franklin Murphy. Indeed, Murphy was astounded to learn from the article that Chandler bitterly regretted her decision to recruit him as the chairman of Times Mirror. "What I saw for the company he has not fulfilled the way I'd hoped," she said. "I think it was not the position for him. He should have been in politics." She said she resented Murphy leaving her out of important business decisions once he took the helm as chairman. "His feeling about women is certainly very chauvinistic—and that's surprising," she said. "Franklin always couldn't wait to get rid of me," Chandler confided to Weymouth. "I think he's very jealous of women. He was very jealous of me. He couldn't wait to get me out of there."

Murphy, who was also interviewed by Weymouth for the *Esquire* article, endeavored to explain that Mrs. Chandler's influence at the *Times* had peaked in 1960 when Norman named his son publisher. Yet his comments about the demise of Mrs. Chandler's power seemed crude when read on the page: "She made the transition from sleeping with the publisher to only talking with the publisher," he said. "And you know that's a big difference." As Murphy pictured the difference: "Oh, you're sitting down in your nightclothes with a martini, having a nightcap, and you talk freely and easily and it's unstructured," but that is not what happens when you call up your son. Murphy added that when Norman Chandler relinquished the publisher's role to Otis, he stepped out of the way and never interfered. "Mrs. C never really accepted that view. She had no hesitancy in talking to Otis whenever she felt that something was wrong."[75]

According to Peter Fernald, who often escorted Dorothy Chandler to civic events after her husband's death, Mrs. C, as he always called her, confided to him that backing Murphy as chairman for Times Mirror was "one of the three greatest disappointments of her life." It remains unknown what the other regrets might have been.[76]

In the end, Dorothy Chandler may have presented just the sort of personnel problem that she had admired Murphy for solving in other contexts; nevertheless, it was unfortunate that her dismissal was not handled more graciously. Later, when he was asked about her harsh accusations against him, Murphy replied with diplomacy, "She's a strong woman with strong opinions."[77]

SEVEN

Power and Philanthropy

UNLIKE THE EAST COAST WHERE power typically devolved from one generation to the next through private fortunes, power in the West rested with the owners and managers of the region's most powerful and successful corporations. As early as 1963 the *New York Times* detected a shift in the Pastel Empire: new names and new money were competing with old families for prominence. Active newcomers growing affluent in the retail business, industry, and finance were described as embarrassed by the city's cultural deficiencies and eager to do something about it. The old guard either retreated to suburban bastions or faded "into the palm trees."[1]

The network promoting corporate interests flourished in prestigious sanctuaries such as the Bohemian Grove, the California Club, or the somewhat mysterious Committee of 25. As board chairmen, foundation directors, and politicians came and went, the basis of power in California grew more fluid and more diverse. Murphy's experience confirmed this: in the West he moved steadily into positions of power that would have been denied him in the East.[2]

As chairman of the mammoth Times Mirror Company, Murphy was a key player among the state's power brokers. His membership in this rarefied group was confirmed when he was asked to join the state's most exclusive men's club. The Bohemian Club, founded in 1872 by a group of San Francisco journalists, evolved into a bastion of the rich and powerful, "the greatest men's party on Earth," President Herbert Hoover called it.

Membership in the club was so exclusive that it often took decades to be admitted, and its waiting list numbered in the thousands. Richard Nixon, one of the group's noted members, once said with more truth than humor, "Anyone can aspire to be President of the United States, but few have any hope of becoming president of the Bohemian Club."[3] At its 2,700-acre hideaway, the Bohemian Grove, among the redwoods along the Russian River, members and their guests slept in tents or cabins, hiked and socialized in the woods, or took part in the jesting of member-produced theatrical performances. The encampment was heavy on drinking, pranks, and gossip. It reportedly opened with the "Cremation of Care," an elaborate ritual in which the Bohemians assembled in a rustic amphitheater to witness an effigy of Dull Care set ablaze under the watchful eye of the club's symbol, a forty-foot sculpted owl. (According to club legend, once Care had turned to ashes, club members could forget their outside concerns and enjoy the good company.)[4]

The annual outing also featured background talks by highly placed government or business figures. According to one story, Dwight Eisenhower so impressed Republican members chatting among the redwoods that he was suddenly considered presidential material. Nixon was said to have begun his political comeback with a lakeside talk that struck a chord with powerful leaders. In a letter to Dorothy Chandler, found in her personal papers, Nixon made note of his "pleasant encounter with Norman" at the Grove for precisely such high-level camaraderie.

The exact year Murphy joined the Bohemian Club is unknown, as membership records are confidential, but Murphy mentions experiences from the summer 1969 encampment in his correspondence.[5] He made use of his membership to socialize and foster friendships with an array of luminaries, men who would be of value to him as he undertook philanthropic and cultural projects.

PUSHING THE *NEW YORK TIMES* OFF ITS PERCH

A pile of mail at Times Mirror awaited Murphy on his return from the Grove in 1975. His secretary, Imy Butterfield, a tall, slender brunette who wore classic suits, operated with great efficiency, and adored her boss, placed a note on top of the stack: "Dr. Murphy—You hit the jackpot! A letter from the President and Vice-President of the United States in one mail packet!"[6]

As chairman of the company, Murphy could boast that business was humming. As 1976 unfolded Times Mirror achieved its best year yet and stood on the threshold of becoming a billion-dollar enterprise. Murphy was able to announce record revenues of $976 million, up 21 percent over the previous year.[7] For the moment, if the nation's economic outlook continued to improve, Murphy had little to fear. Indeed, the year 1977 marked the first time revenues at Times Mirror exceeded $1 billion. It was also the year that the Franklin Murphy, Otis Chandler, and Robert Erburu troika was designated the Office of the Chief Executive. Murphy continued as chairman and chief executive officer, but the three-man team shared responsibility for the overall direction of Times Mirror.[8] "Murphy is the head coach," Chandler told reporters. "He leaves the running of the team to Bob and me. But he's there to monitor closely what we do. We don't have three managers. We have two managers and one senior person who presides and watches over the company." Acquisitions and major decisions for the company were a "mutual activity on a senior level," Chandler stressed, meaning that all three joined in the final decision.[9]

The Office of the Chief Executive ran a fast-paced operation. Chandler, now forty-nine, was featured on the cover of *Business Week* during a frenzied bidding war among newspaper publishers eager to snap up smaller independents before the best were gone. As the cost of acquisitions mounted, publishing enterprises such as Times Mirror, the Gannett Company, the New York Times Company, and the Washington Post Company scrambled to acquire metropolitan newspapers, chains, and independents to increase profits and promote growth. Times Mirror was running hard to stay in the game. Murphy had stumbled when he lost a $100 million bid to William W. Baker to acquire the Kansas City Star Company; it was acquired by Capital Cities Communications for $125 million. In another disappointment, Murphy, Chandler, and Erburu thought they had secured acquisition of the Booth newspaper chain after discussions with senior Booth family members; however, Times Mirror offered only $40 a share on Booth's outstanding stock while the shrewd, up-and-coming media mogul S. I. Newhouse bid $47 and quickly closed the deal.

Times Mirror may have lost several choice properties, but its conservative approach was applauded by industry observers who ranked it the country's most profitable publicly held publishing company. It was slightly behind in overall revenue, but Times Mirror now exceeded venerable Time, Inc., for the industry's number one slot in profits. "When you have cash flow of $100 million," Murphy said, "you have [real] assets you can make acquisitions with."[10]

One of Times Mirror's greatest success stories was its acquisition of *Newsday*, purchased in 1970 for $57.8 million—twenty-four times its earnings. At the time the price was considered too high, but Times Mirror was able to boost *Newsday* profits by a whopping 72 percent in the first year (in part by doubling the price of the paper to ten cents). Over the next few years the editorial staff was revitalized under the direction of David Laventhol, its advertising and marketing efforts were vastly expanded, circulation increased, advertising sales boomed, and total revenues more than doubled over time to nearly $100 million.

Times Mirror now owned four newspapers, the *Los Angeles Times, Newsday*, the *Dallas Times Herald*, the *Daily Pilot*, and four magazines, *Golf, Ski, Outdoor Life*, and *Popular Science*. Its book publishing group included such stellar properties as Matthew Bender and Company, C. V. Mosby Company, Year Book Medical Publishers, and Harry N. Abrams. It owned television stations in Austin and Dallas–Fort Worth and extensive cable-television operations centered in California and New York. The company also gained substantial revenues from its newsprint and forest-product enterprises, directory printing, and technical graphics products. "I think we are diversified more significantly than any other communications company," Murphy told reporters. The figures backed him up: when 1977 revenues reached $1.4 billion, the company's net income was 36 percent higher than the previous year's all-time record. Earnings rose to $2.77 per share from $2.03 the previous year. The *Los Angeles Times* alone generated revenues of $332.5 million, carrying 136 million lines of advertising and a circulation of one million.[11]

In a 1977 memo addressed to Chandler and Erburu, Murphy stated that his main management objectives were increased corporate profits, further large acquisitions in newspapers, book publishing, or television, and an intensive examination of the company's legal options regarding the question of television-newspaper cross-ownership.[12] He also wanted to continue the search for outstanding new directors to fill expected vacancies on the Times Mirror board. In December Roger Heyns, president of the William and Flora Hewlett Foundation, former president of the American Council on Education, and a longtime Murphy friend, was appointed the board's fifteenth member.

· · · · ·

During his summer safari, Otis Chandler tracked a rare Ethiopian antelope and mounted its head on the wall of his trophy room at his San Marino residence. Returning to work, the "crown prince of the press," the heir who transformed the *Times* into a newspaper of journalistic quality, was not to rest on this achievement. He had another goal in mind. The trophy he really wanted—the real success he sought—was to have the *Los Angeles Times* acknowledged as the nation's leading newspaper, leaving the *New York Times* in the dust. He felt he was well on his way when he was suddenly confronted with the revival of the *Herald-Examiner* following the appointment of former *Times* associate editor Jim Bellows as its new editor. The announcement was the opening salvo of a battle in which the Hearst Corporation pledged to make Los Angeles once again a competitive newspaper town.

Bellows had left Los Angeles for Washington to head the ill-fated *Washington Star.* When he returned as editor of the *Herald,* he immediately put together a "scrappy team" of talented reporters, as he called them, who managed to scoop the *Times* on important local news stories. Coming in second on local coverage was a deep embarrassment to editor Bill Thomas and threatened to undermine Chandler's objective.[13] Bellows used journalists such as Jimmy Breslin, Jane O'Reilly, Willie Morris, and Dick Schaap to write feature columns, and when the *Times* chose not to publish Gary Trudeau's controversial *Doonesbury* comic strip, Bellows ran it. "We didn't have a lot of people," remembered Bellows. "We didn't have a lot of money. But we were on a higher mission. We were going to save the *Herald!* We were going to raise the *Titanic!*"[14]

Sensing that the last lap in his race against the *New York Times* was imperiled by the feisty revived *Herald,* Chandler called on the talents of Tom Johnson, thirty-five-year-old publisher of the *Dallas Times Herald* and previously executive vice president of the Texas Broadcasting Corporation, who had served as President Johnson's deputy press secretary.[15] Another key consideration was that Chandler was expected to step into Murphy's shoes when the latter retired in 1981 at sixty-five. After conversations with Murphy and Erburu, Chandler decided to bring in Johnson, who would likely succeed him as the newspaper's fifth publisher.[16] The post would include day-to-day responsibility for the business affairs of the newspaper, supervision of the budget, and general administration.

Chandler's dual roles as publisher and vice-chairman of Times Mirror sapped his strength and energy, increasing his frustration in his obsession to outrank the *New York Times.* "My spastic colon was bothering me night and day," he remembered.[17] By the late 1970s he felt he was less and less publisher and more and more corporate executive: "I was frankly wearing out with all of the jobs I was doing for the company simultaneously." As his focus was increasingly fractured, Chandler urged Johnson not to hesitate to move the interests of the *Times* forward, but he also reassured newsroom staffers that Bill Thomas would continue to have full editorial control. Soon after his arrival, Chandler confided to Johnson the extent of his ambition: "As you get to know me better, you will find me to be a fighter, an uncompromising advocate of quality and excellence . . . and a *fierce competitor.*" He expected to find the same characteristics in Johnson: "I set about to make [the *Times*] the best there was. . . . Together, we are going to push the *New York Times* off its perch. Somehow, someday, in spite of geography, tradition, Eastern snobbery and the like, there will be recognized only one superior newspaper, and it will be located of all unlikely places way out West in Indian and smog country—LA!!!"[18]

By 1978, when Murphy marked his tenth year as chairman of Times Mirror, the company's future seemed full of promise. Sales were expected to reach $1.5 billion by year's end and top $2 billion in 1981, the centennial of the *Los Angeles Times* and Murphy's official retirement date. The company embarked on its largest expansion program to date, with planned expenditures of more than $500 million in plant modernization and technology, including hundreds of new Data General computer terminals. With the acquisition of cable and television broadcast communication properties, most notably five stations from Newhouse Broadcasting Corporation for $82.4 million, Times Mirror now owned five VHF and two UHF stations, the maximum allowed under federal law. The Times Mirror leadership had exceeded its goal of doubling the company's earnings every six years. Top executives were well paid and, under a series of incentive awards, could earn up to 40 percent of their income in bonuses each year.[19]

On August 30 Otis Chandler penned a personal note to Murphy to express his heartfelt appreciation for a decade of remarkable growth:

> It barely seems possible that some *ten* years ago this company came under the chairmanship of this "character" from Kansas via UCLA. As a participant in that decision to offer you the job, I regard my decision then as one of the best moves I have *ever* made! You have become a dear friend, a valuable associate and have made an enormous contribution to this enterprise and to our community, our nation and indeed the world at large. . . . I look forward to another ten years with you.[20]

Robert Erburu wrote Murphy that their business record over the past ten years had been spectacular: "What must be the most satisfying for you (as it is for Otis and me) is the knowledge that Times Mirror has grown in stature as well as size. Your leadership has been central to that accomplishment and you should be very proud." Erburu went on to express his admiration for Murphy, to whom he had become devoted as a friend and colleague. The billion-dollar troika had much to celebrate, but Chandler still had his eye on the trophy that he wanted most and that he hoped to obtain as publisher, or at the very least not later than his term as chairman—he was due to succeed Murphy in 1981.[21]

HENRY FORD II VERSUS LEE IACOCCA

Murphy had served as a director of the Ford Motor Company for twelve years through a period of profound transformation in the automobile industry. In the early 1970s Ford and its subsidiaries in Europe had enjoyed strong growth and profitability, enhanced by the introduction of the popular Mustang. However, by the mid-1970s the company faced its most difficult years as an unprecedented products-liability crisis gained national attention. The Pinto, a popular compact car manufactured between 1971 and 1976, was involved in horrific accidents in which the car's gas tank exploded in rear-end collisions. Publicity from widespread news reports had severely damaged Ford's public image, and the flood of wrongful death lawsuits consumed much of the energy of company management and the board of directors.

Tensions ran high between Lee A. Iacocca, the company's charismatic president, and Henry Ford II, its chairman, throughout much of this period. Sidney Weinberg, who had been an enormously constructive influence on Ford, virtually a surrogate father, had died in July 1969, at the age of seventy-seven—before the Pinto debacle—so Ford faced this difficult chapter without his trusted adviser. As a result, Ford turned increasingly for counsel to Franklin Murphy, who was considered the "conscience of the board."[22] The increasingly dysfunctional relationship between Ford and Iacocca exacerbated the crisis.

As Murphy remembered the events, after Iacocca introduced the highly successful Mustang and his picture appeared on the covers of *Time* and *Newsweek,* he became *the* face of the Ford Motor Company in the eyes of the public. "Iacocca was infused with a little of the ego-building blood that Henry had been infused with all of his life," Murphy recalled. That made for tension. "After all," Murphy noted, "you can't have been Henry Ford II—with all the privileges of being Henry Ford, and . . . described as the savior of one of the great American industrial companies—and not develop a little sense of ego and pride, especially about Ford Motor Company. It's *his* company; *his* name is on the building." "On the other hand," Murphy continued, "there's Lee Iacocca, son of an immigrant from Sicily, growing up in Allentown, Pennsylvania, and filled with ambition. He was probably driven by a father and a mother who had great ambition for this boy of theirs, who was bright, quick, and did extremely well at Lehigh University. He often told me [that] as a boy, he said to his father, 'One day I'm going to be the president of Ford Motor Company.'"[23]

Because he recognized that Iacocca had great skills and was a shrewd marketing man as well as a first-rate automobile man, Murphy, for the good of the company, visited Ford and attempted to convince him that some kind of rapport must be forged between the two men. Murphy recalled that Iacocca had reached the point of being tortured, "like an insect with its wings being taken off."[24] Right after his visit, Murphy summarized his advice in a lengthy letter:

> [Lee] really wants to please you and fully recognizes you are the leader. I therefore urge you with even greater fervor than during our last conversation to seize the opportunity to develop a closer personal relationship with Lee. . . . It will mean everything to him and I think it can only benefit the company. . . .
>
> Clearly, because of your position, you should initiate such a dialogue and I will be so bold as to further suggest that you should try to make it informal and casual. What I mean is that perhaps instead of calling him into your office, you might from time to time informally pop into his office for a cup of tea, a cigar or toward the end of the day—perhaps even a drink. I know your time is enormously limited, but in terms of priority at this particular juncture, I can think of nothing that would have higher priority than what I have suggested.

"Pardon me for being so long and perhaps too bold," Murphy wrote in closing, "but if I were not, I suspect I would not be earning my Director's fee and what I hope is your confidence."[25]

On his visit Murphy had also met with Iacocca and, in a candid and fatherlike manner, given him "tips" for dealing with Ford. Iacocca later wrote Murphy: "I have spent the whole weekend marveling at what you did for me in the short span of one hour on Thursday. First and foremost you took the time to talk to me because you genuinely *care* about me and the company. For this I am deeply grateful to you. Keep in mind yours is the first talk I've had with anybody during these past dismal, depressing 18 months." Iacocca continued, "But most of all, what you did for me, as usual, you went right to the heart of the problem—You can't have a good business or any other relationship without first having a good *human* relationship." Iacocca said that he had had an hour-long conversation with Ford. "It was the best and most relaxed talk I've had with him in five years. Enough said. Thank you again, Franklin."[26]

Two weeks later, when Ford was admitted to St. Joseph's Hospital in Ann Arbor for treatment of an undisclosed illness, Murphy quickly contacted him and expressed his wishes for a speedy recovery. "Now you can look forward to less food, less nicotine and more exercise," Murphy told Ford, "which in the end will make you more handsome than ever before."[27]

By June Ford demonstrated his gratitude to Murphy for his friendship, advice, and personal concern and for his efforts on behalf of the company. He sent an unsolicited donation of a prized 1938 Aristide Maillol bronze to the Murphy Sculpture Garden at UCLA. The surprise touched Murphy for the garden had been close to his heart. "I interpret it as a generous expression of our long-standing friendship," Murphy wrote Ford, "and I am sure you realize that I reciprocate your feelings very deeply indeed."[28]

· · · · ·

The fragile harmony between Iacocca and Ford was not destined to endure. When Ford abruptly fired the company president no one on the board of directors was surprised. Looking back, Murphy remembered the event in Dearborn as a Greek tragedy: "We all saw the tension rising. Hell, it was obvious."[29] But Iacocca's sudden dismissal was ill timed. Management was battling stockholder allegations of financial misconduct and struggling with a falling stock price. Worldwide headlines over the firing of Iacocca were the last thing the beleaguered company needed.

Before the ax fell, Murphy and another director, Bob Oelman, went to Iacocca and urged him to get off "his high horse and talk it out." They returned to the board and reported that Iacocca was willing to work out his differences with Ford. "All of us . . . as I look back on it," Murphy recalled, "hoped that some miracle would happen."

Ford, however, approached the board and said, "It's very simple. It's Lee Iacocca, or me. I'm going to leave the room, and you all decide whether you want me to stay or you want Iacocca." Murphy stood and faced his friend. "Henry, don't bother. You know perfectly well that there is not one person in this room who wants you to leave the company and if that is the choice, Mr. Iacocca will have to go." Murphy recalled that not a single board member objected. "Ford Motor Company was Henry's God," Murphy remembered. "His name was on the building; it was a nameplate all over the world. I honestly believed that Ford Motor Company was more important to him than anything in the world."[30]

Philip Caldwell replaced Iacocca as Ford Motor Company president. In March 1980 Ford retired and gave the chairmanship to Caldwell, but he retained his seat on the board of directors. The company faced a lengthy list of setbacks. Financial analysts criticized Henry Ford II for his cancellation of the development of a new small car intended to succeed the Pinto. As Japanese compacts became increasingly popular in the United States, the company found itself unable to compete. Adding to its troubles, U.S. car manufacturers were obligated by the Clean Air Act to develop automobiles with strict emission standards.

Despite the public attacks, Ford remained convinced of his company's prospects. "Now that the second shoe is dropped and you are no longer Chairman and Chief Executive Officer," Murphy wrote Ford on his retirement in 1980, "let me say simply that I agree with everything that has been said about your extraordinary performance over the years in that difficult and demanding job. I also agree that you have been, beyond doubt, the leading business statesman in this country in the post-war period." "However," Murphy continued, "even more important to me has been the warmth and depth of your friendship and the great personal joy I have had in being associated with you. It has been a rare experience."[31]

THE LEGACY OF HOWARD F. AHMANSON

From the moment Dorothy Sullivan had pressed Murphy to join the Ahmanson Foundation as trustee, there was rarely a day in which Murphy did not attend to its needs. The unexpected death of Howard Ahmanson in 1968 had triggered a complex set of legal and financial problems, and the decisions made during these crucial ten years, Murphy fully recognized, would have a profound and permanent impact on the foundation's future. Ahmanson's estate had been constructed so that the bulk of the company stock would pass to the foundation on the financier's death. In this manner the family could retain control of the funds, make dispersals to philanthropic endeavors as it wished, and also avoid the need to sell the company in order to pay the heavy estate taxes. However, passage of the 1969 Tax Reform Act disallowed this approach, and the Ahmanson Foundation was forced to begin plans for a significant divestiture. Foundation trustees anxiously met to consider their options for sale and transfer of stock needed to comply with Section 4941 of the act, which prohibited financial transactions between the foundation and family members. Known as the prohibition against self-dealing, the new rules were intended by Congress to address concerns about the use of foundations for personal gain.[32]

Murphy outlined recommendations for Sullivan to develop a long-range policy for grant-giving that would meet the new federal requirements. Under the Tax Reform Act the foundation was required to give away immense sums each year—a minimum of 5 percent of the market value of its foundation's assets. How could the foundation meet this requirement when its resources were in stock? Murphy devised a proposal to not only meet government requirements but also conform to Howard Ahmanson's goals. He recommended making a few large endowment grants to major institutions that could accept stock instead of cash and limiting the number of grants to projects needing immediate cash.

"I believe that since the money was made in California, especially Southern California," Murphy told Sullivan, "it should—to the largest extent—be spent in California." He also advised Sullivan: "I would very much like to see us build the strength of major institutions already in existence in which Howard played such an important support role during his lifetime. I have always been a great believer in building strength on strength."[33] He used the phrase to describe his fundamental preference for assisting institutions with a proven track record. His nominations for major grants reflected this philosophy as well as what he thought were Ahmanson's interests: endowed professorships in biology or medicine at USC ($800,000); an endowment fund for art acquisitions for the Ahmanson Building at the Los Angeles County Museum of Art ($2 million); an endowment fund for the Music Center Arts and Education Fund in support of the Ahmanson Theatre ($2 million); an endowment fund for research into neurological causes of deafness at UCLA ($1 million); a building for the History of Business and Economics at the California Museum of Science and Industry ($1 million); and doubling of the annual contribution to the Independent Colleges of Southern California.

The new pressures on the foundation were staggering. It was required to divest itself of the majority of H. F. Ahmanson and Company stock by 1984 to comply with the fifteen-year deadline specified in the new tax act. Sullivan had received a life interest in the income from that portion of her stock that was donated to the foundation, but attorneys were hard-pressed to devise ways to protect her interest, do the best thing for the foundation, and still conform to the tax law. Compounding the already complex situation, Caroline L. Ahmanson, Howard Ahmanson's widow, married to him for just three years before his death, filed suit against the estate. In October 1970 foundation trustees, fearing a protracted legal struggle, secured the services of Joseph A. Ball to represent the foundation. Fortunately, an amicable agreement with Caroline was secured relatively quickly; the exact figure remains confidential, but it is widely believed that the second Mrs. Ahmanson received a court-sanctioned settlement in the range of $5 million. Resolution of this aspect of the foundation's legal woes was a welcome achievement in the mounting uncertainty about its future.

In May 1972 Murphy had in hand an agreement for redistributing stock between the foundation trustees and Ahmanson family members, dealing most importantly with shares in which Dorothy Sullivan had an interest. Negotiations among family members had been acrimonious, and this proposal was what they could agree to, but Murphy worried that it might not pass muster with both the Internal Revenue Service and the California attorney general, as required. The IRS approved the exchange, but in August 1973 the trustees of the Ahmanson Foundation were taken aback to learn that the state was withholding approval. Attorney General Evelle J. Younger charged Sullivan with improperly diverting organization funds to enrich herself in the exchange agreement and filed suit against Sullivan and the foundation.[34]

Younger argued that Sullivan would unjustly profit from the agreement and that since substantial funds would be diverted from the foundation to the detriment of the public, the agreement was a breach of trust by the foundation's officers and directors, who were named as defendants in the lawsuit. In September 1974 the trustees hired Daniel N. Belin, an outstanding Harvard Law School–educated attorney, a member of the Los Angeles law firm McKenna, Fitting and Finch, to represent the foundation and H. F. Ahmanson and Company. At the same time Sullivan resigned as president and foundation trustee, leaving the question unsettled as to who in the Ahmanson family would take over leadership.

Murphy familiarized himself with the complexities of the litigation; a builder of consensus, he worked closely with Belin to devise a basis on which the litigation might be settled. The agreement ultimately drafted gave the Ahmanson Foundation approximately $100 million more in stock than it would have received under the original 1972 agreement. The California attorney general approved the revised agreement and arranged to settle with the foundation trustees. However, just as Murphy and the other trustees thought they could breathe a sigh of relief, they were slammed with further challenges from the IRS, which claimed that the new proposal violated federal tax law. The Ahmanson Foundation and its trustees were immobilized, caught in a dispute between their two principal regulators.

. . . . .

Howard Ahmanson Jr. was twenty-two years old in 1972 when the foundation became mired in the negotiations with state and federal agencies. Murphy realized the Ahmanson heir was ill equipped to manage the foundation his mother and father had established. He was a quixotic young man, unsure of his abilities and undetermined as to what he wanted to do with his life. His effectiveness was further limited by sudden mood swings and continued odd behavior. Murphy at this time learned of new research on the neurological disease known as Tourette's syndrome and called the family's attention to the possibility of having at last a proper diagnosis of Howard Jr.'s condition. The complex set of symptoms had not been defined up to that time, and his strange outbursts had been a mystery to the family.

Throughout the legal entanglements, the question of leadership remained unsettled. Murphy felt strongly that Howard Ahmanson's nephew, Robert Ahmanson, would be the best choice. After months of subtle prodding of fellow trustees, he engineered Robert's election as president of the foundation in October 1974. Simultaneously, Robert's brother, William H. Ahmanson, was reelected foundation vice president.

In the course of the family's disputes over leadership, Murphy had diplomatically and skillfully shifted the mantle from Ahmanson's son to his nephew. He persuaded Robert Ahmanson in a hallway conversation during a board meeting that he should accept the critical role of foundation president. Just as Sullivan's insight in securing Murphy's service as a board member proved invaluable to the foundation's interests, Murphy's installation of Robert Ahmanson as foundation president would turn out to be an early, crucial, right decision.

Though the full extent of the challenge was not known at the time, Robert Ahmanson faced fifteen years of grueling litigation to secure the foundation's future as well as hard work to shepherd the organization through economic recession and recovery in a rapidly changing cultural and socioeconomic landscape. Despite the endless, exhausting legal entanglements, he grew to relish the assignment that Murphy had maneuvered him into. Murphy had felt that Robert was far more suited to the foundation's work than William, his older brother, who did not share Robert's interest in philanthropy or the cultural arts. "Giving money away disturbs every fiber in my brother's body," Robert Ahmanson once said.[35] The role of foundation president was the perfect niche for Robert; William's business talents were put to best use in a sequence of executive positions in H. F. Ahmanson and Company. According to Robert DeKruif, both Howard Ahmanson and Murphy had firmly believed that an individual in the wrong niche in an organization damaged not only the organization but the person as well. Murphy, in the course of his multiple careers, proved to have uncanny skill at picking the right man for the right job at the right moment.

· · · · ·

Robert Ahmanson and Murphy spoke on the phone daily, addressing urgent problems as they arose. During the height of foundation litigation it was not unusual for Murphy to speak with Ahmanson fifteen to twenty times a week. The bond forged between the two men was so deep that Ahmanson considered Murphy the most important figure in his adult life. Murphy's devotion to the foundation and its problems and his close relationship with Ahmanson left little time for his own family; and during this period, the most brutal years of the foundation's battles, Murphy was largely absent from his own son's life, creating a void that distanced one from the other.

Murphy's mentorship meant that Robert Ahmanson was the beneficiary of sometimes unusual and practical perks. One instance, intended to surprise and benefit the foundation's young leader, occurred early one morning when Murphy telephoned Robert and asked for a favor. Murphy explained that he needed to drive a man from his hotel to the airport but was simply unable to do it. He asked Robert if he would go in his place. "I know you will enjoy meeting him," Murphy told him cryptically. When Robert Ahmanson arrived at the hotel, he was surprised to learn that his mystery passenger was David Rockefeller. The two had much in common—formidable families active in philanthropy, awesome foundation resources, and all the joys and troubles attendant on wealth and position. It was the start of a friendship that would last for the next thirty years and another example of Murphy's matchmaking skill.

Robert Ahmanson recalled that he had been hesitant when Murphy urged him to head the foundation. "I hadn't even considered it, and it has been the best thing that ever happened to me."[36]

· · · · ·

In the philanthropic world the extent to which a donor's family should exercise control over investment of a foundation's funds or decisions about its grant program is a recurring controversy, but Robert Ahmanson's performance could not be faulted. During the foundation's most turbulent period, he demonstrated character, flexibility, and efficiency. Once Murphy had managed to get a grip on the enormous legal conflicts pressing the foundation, his contribution as trustee took on another dimension. In concert with Robert Ahmanson, he worked to define a precise strategy for grant making. Murphy spent long, patient hours with board trustees in thoughtful discussions about the goals of the foundation, the needs of the community, and the best means to maximize the impact of each grant. Ahmanson said of Murphy's technique for chairing meetings that he liked "to dispose of problems in a hurry" and that he kept the board meetings moving. Yet he could be endlessly patient when the situation warranted or a philosophical issue was at stake.

None of the trustees, including Murphy, received compensation for their labor on behalf of the foundation. However, a program known as the Individual Trustee Responsibility Fund (ITRF) was initiated whereby each trustee could choose the recipients of certain funds each year; each trustee could designate $30,000 (the amount steadily increased to $300,000) each year for individual grants. Robert Ahmanson noted that the ITRF grant program was a favorite with Murphy; he had his grantees picked out each year and checks signed and in the mail before the end of the board meeting. His selections constituted a biography of his life's work and enthusiasms—the University of Kansas was frequently remembered; and UCLA's library, notably the Aldine Collection, and ethnic arts facilities received continued attention. It was with great personal pleasure that he sent $50,000 to expand the rare book collection at the Clark Library, a special interest of Robert Vosper. Murphy also made repeated contributions of $25,000 or more to the libraries at the University of Kansas, where he and Vosper had shared their bibliophilic mania so many years before. Nor did he overlook his original career goal: "Dr. Murphy" vindicated his training by making crucial grants for medical research at Kansas and UCLA.

Though firmly transplanted in Southern California, Murphy could not get Kansas entirely out of his mind. In nostalgic moments he and Judy would talk of having a second home—perhaps a retirement home—in Kansas. His regret at not having completed the work he had hoped to do in his eight years as chancellor of the University of Kansas probably motivated him to arrange for the Ahmanson Foundation to endow three professorships there in the fields of music, art history, and medicine (cardiology). When the appreciative chancellor at KU, Archie R. Dykes, wanted to name the endowed chairs for Franklin Murphy, Murphy refused. Later, with the connivance of the Kansas board of regents, Dykes named the professorship in music for Franklin's mother, Cordelia Brown Murphy; Franklin's father was honored in the naming of the chair in cardiology; and the professorship in art history was named for his wife, Judith Harris Murphy.

· · · · ·

As the foundation board's advocate and protector, Murphy was by all accounts "the heavy," able to snap trustees to attention and move the agenda quickly. When trustees disagreed on funds to be dispersed, Murphy often ended the group discussion for the time being but later made numerous telephone calls to forge a compromise. During the mid-1970s, the steep decline in the financial markets cut deeply into the nation's economic performance, drastically reducing the value of the Ahmanson Foundation's assets. Trustees worried that the foundation's then-current $125 million value would decline further, but Murphy pressed the board forward, urging them to keep in mind Howard Ahmanson's belief in the growth of Southern California and his goals for the region.

In January 1975 Robert Ahmanson called Murphy with alarming news. Dorothy Sullivan, whose current husband, Denis Sullivan, was a Princeton University alumnus, had announced she was making a donation to Princeton of her lifetime interest in the income from the 300,000 shares of H. F. Ahmanson and Company stock held by the Ahmanson Foundation that had been, and still were, the subject of so much controversy. The news came as a shock and a sharp disappointment to Murphy, who had hoped that Howard Ahmanson's wishes would be respected and that foundation funds would be used primarily to benefit Los Angeles. "As I have many times said," Murphy told Robert Ahmanson on learning of the Princeton gift, "we trustees of the Ahmanson Foundation inherited a very complicated and unprecedented problem not of our own making."[37]

The pressures were enormous to fix the situation before litigation was required. Murphy advised Ahmanson that, guided by the foundation's legal experts, the trustees should formulate a proposal for settlement with Dorothy Sullivan, a settlement that would have to be agreed to by all parties, including the state attorney general and the IRS. If the parties could not arrive at an agreement, Murphy acknowledged with resignation, the matter would have to be settled by the courts.[38]

Legal complications for the foundation seemed to have no end. In September, on the eve of his and Judy's departure to Europe for their annual four-week vacation with Professor Speroni and his wife, Carmela, Murphy wrote to William Ahmanson confiding his guarded hope that a negotiated conclusion with the IRS and the state of California was near: "I believe that everything I could humanly do has been done. We have the ball on the one yard line and I am counting on you and Dan [Belin] to call the play that makes the touchdown." Murphy thought that the solution at hand, if approved, would be equitable and would generate "no adverse publicity to the Foundation, the Company or to the Ahmanson family." He wished Robert and the legal team success in his absence; he knew that failure now would mean extensive litigation far into the future.[39]

For Murphy personally, much was riding on the outcome of the legal maneuvers. His ambition to share in making cultural experience widely available had set him on a quest for an entity that could serve art and culture. Now he felt he had a viable resource at hand if only he could free the Ahmanson Foundation from the snares that held it, like Gulliver enmeshed in a Lilliputian net. Through the years his belief in the importance of art to the human spirit had not diminished, and he was determined to see works of art available to the widest possible public. He had run headlong into political quagmires, thwarted by ambitious governors—in Kansas and in California—who capitalized on the hesitancy of voters to tax themselves for art and culture. Impatient with the compromises and delays inherent in the political process and exasperated by ego clashes in the academic world, he had turned with fresh optimism to private foundations as offering a steady reservoir of funds for the arts; in addition, foundations generally had a built-in belief in the value of promoting cultural achievement. Murphy saw the Ahmanson Foundation as a magnificent opportunity to realize his concept of civil society enriched by art. Howard Ahmanson had known that a vital, expanding metropolis must have an arts infrastructure. Murphy felt that if only he could get the foundation freed of the restraints that now immobilized it, he could move forward with sponsoring the cultural growth that he knew Ahmanson would have supported had he lived. The ambitious plans could fall by the wayside if litigation did not end soon and government regulations wiped out a major portion of the resources. Murphy's plans were on the tenuous edge of being realized or being destroyed.

. . . . .

By the end of the year, cautious but hopeful, Murphy wrote William Ahmanson: "I believe we are coming up with a solution that will be most protective of Dottie and will get both the government and the lawyers off our backs." He closed his letter by stating that once the legal issues were resolved, the foundation could become "one of the most important forces for good in Southern California."[40]

Murphy was unduly optimistic, for in 1977 the foundation trustees were charged by the IRS with underpayment of estate taxes. At issue was the fair market value at the time of Ahmanson's death of one voting share of stock retained through a trust that he controlled. The amount of estate taxes owed by the foundation was tied to the value of this single share in a "super-holding" company known as Ahmanco, Inc. Litigation concerning the one share would last for an excruciating ten years.

Howard Ahmanson had maintained control over Home Savings through an elaborate corporate structure involving voting and nonvoting stock. The holding company, H. F. Ahmanson and Company, owned most of the stock of Home Savings; H. F. Ahmanson and Company had tens of thousands of nonvoting shares outstanding but only one thousand shares of voting stock. The stock was not publicly traded, and all shares were held by Ahmanson-created trusts or the Ahmanson Foundation. Six hundred of the one thousand voting shares were the asset, the only asset, of the super-holding company. Ahmanco had one hundred shares of stock outstanding, ninety-nine of which were nonvoting and one of which was voting. Howard Ahmanson retained one voting share of Ahmanco through a trust that he controlled.[41]

The IRS took the position that ownership of that single Ahmanco voting share allowed Ahmanson to control a vast financial empire and that a significantly high value should therefore be ascribed to it for estate tax purposes. The Justice Department maintained that the value of the single share was not its $157,000 market value but a staggering $68 million. The foundation paid the additional taxes as assessed, but on behalf of the foundation, Daniel Belin protested the assessment and proceeded to represent the foundation at trial. The trial lasted three weeks. Robert Ahmanson was present in the courtroom to observe the proceedings in their entirety.

Expert witnesses for the government testified that the single share of voting stock carried tremendous prestige for its owner by giving majority control of H. F. Ahmanson and Company stock. U.S. District Court Judge Peirson M. Hall was not convinced by the government's argument and ruled in March 1979 that the foundation was entitled to a tax refund. He found that it was "utterly inconceivable in a world of reality" that anyone with $68 million to spend would pay such a figure for the one share of stock. "It defies all rationalization [that] someone who had that kind of money would spend it that way," Judge Hall told attorneys from the bench. He went on to state that the only reason anyone would be willing to pay

$68 million for the single share of stock would be to pursue a course of "adventurism or piracy" at the expense of the other stockholders.[42]

To Murphy's great relief the Ninth Circuit Court of Appeals upheld the foundation's position. On conclusion of the litigation, the foundation recovered $13 million, which represented more than 90 percent of the estate taxes that the IRS had assessed and collected. It was reported at the time to be the largest estate tax refund ever made by the U.S. government.[43]

But there was more to come. As Murphy feared, time was running out. It was becoming apparent that the foundation could not meet the 1984 deadline to divest sufficient stock to meet the requirements of the Tax Reform Act of 1969 without suffering a tremendous loss. Through official and unofficial channels, Murphy succeeded in spring 1982 in introducing a federal tax bill that would give the foundation a ten-year extension of its 1984 deadline to sell $70 million in stock in H. F. Ahmanson and Company. The extension of time was imperative for the survival of the foundation. The bill's sponsor, state representative Robert T. Matsui (D-Sacramento), told reporters that a forced sale of the Ahmanson Company stock between spring 1982 and 1984 could have a disastrous impact on the foundation and the troubled savings and loan industry. His proposed "Ahmanson Bill" would permit the Ahmanson Foundation to sell the securities at a rate of 10 percent a year over the next decade.

Calling on his longtime association with fellow Kansan, Senator Robert J. Dole, Murphy had persuasive briefing materials prepared and sent to Dole's staff for distribution. He expressed his urgent hope that Dole and his Senate colleagues could prevail in the upcoming committee sessions to ensure passage of the Ahmanson proposal. "You will recall that we are not asking for the elimination of our divestiture requirement," Murphy wrote Dole in July 1982, *but merely an extension in time to accomplish it.*" He assured the senator that Home Savings was strong and would weather the current recession: "The stock will inevitably come back to its proper level, but if we were to divest the very large number of shares right at this moment, it would be catastrophic for the Company, the Foundation, and perhaps the savings and loan industry itself." In closing his letter, Murphy stressed the ripple effect that a loss in Ahmanson stock value would have on educational and cultural institutions across the country: "The Ahmanson Foundation has in the past been very generous to the University of Kansas and will continue to be so into the future."[44]

Belin testified in support of the bill before the Senate Finance Committee, and Murphy called on influential friends and acquaintances to pressure needed members of Congress for their vote. In short order the trustee's front- and back-channel communications, official and unofficial, recorded and unrecorded, gave evidence of success. Through the efforts of Senator S. I. Hayakawa of California, the bill was voted on by the full U.S. Senate and passed. As the bill was on its way to the House of Representatives for approval, the IRS suddenly agreed to the settlement it had previously opposed, and the bill was dropped. The exchange of stock in the 1972 agreement between the foundation and Dorothy Sullivan could now be implemented. As a result, the foundation received more than $100 million in stock, which otherwise would have been lost to philanthropy.

Belin found Murphy an extraordinary person to work with during the legal morass. "One key was that he did not and would not get bogged down in detail or trivia. He saw the big picture and always moved forward with the big picture in mind," Belin said later. He also called Murphy a great communicator: "He spoke persuasively and compellingly and had an aura, a charisma, a stature, a credibility that made him enormously effective."[45]

THE IMPACT OF THE AHMANSON
FOUNDATION ON LOS ANGELES

In addition to protecting the enormous financial assets of the Ahmanson Foundation, Murphy guided the institution to a sense of purpose and humanistic goals. Robert Ahmanson claimed it was Murphy's vision that was expressed in the foundation's grant-making choices.[46] Murphy wanted each dollar of the millions bestowed on the community to serve as a catalyst, to activate constructive energies. A series of gifts in the arena of the arts, medicine, and education were developed based on Murphy's view of the cultural needs of what he liked to call a civil society.[47] These gifts included grants to every important museum, library, and educational and cultural institution in the city for buildings, galleries, endowments, scholarships, books, and art acquisitions. By the time the foundation celebrated its thirtieth anniversary in 1982, nearly $10 million had been distributed in Los Angeles.

Although Howard Ahmanson was gone, his foundation's strong-willed trustee worked with an eye to his intent. "I had talked to Howard enough," Murphy said, "to know that basically he wanted the money he had made in Southern California spent in Southern California, and spent in areas that Howard himself had indicated he was interested in."[48]

The impact of this interpretation of Ahmanson philanthropy was visible at the Los Angeles County Museum of Art, whose collection of European painting and sculpture was greatly enhanced by spectacular foundation gifts. Artists from the fifteenth to the early twentieth century were represented among the Ahmanson masterpieces, including Rembrandt's *Raising of Lazarus,* which had hung over the fireplace of Ahmanson's Hudson Avenue home; Georges de La Tour's *Magdalen with the Smoking Flame;* and important works by Canaletto, Goltzius, Bellini, and Champaigne. The foundation also gave significant sums to the museum's Departments of Far Eastern Art and Indian and Southwest Asian Art and its conservation center and library.

Murphy derived tremendous pleasure from participating in the foundation's selection of European masterworks for donation to the museum. His friendships with Terisio Pignatti, professor of art history at the University of Venice and regarded as one of the greatest living experts on Venetian art, and Mario Modestini, the highly skilled former curator and conservator of the Kress Collection, gave him access to their advice on recommendations to the trustees. Some of Ahmanson's purchases in the early days of his collecting had not been properly authenticated, some critics had claimed; consequently, foundation trustees were especially sensitive to matters of authenticity and provenance when considering works for purchase.

In one instance the board waited anxiously to hear Murphy's findings about a painting that might or might not be by Titian. "Pignatti confirmed it was unquestionably by the hand of Titian," Murphy reported. "In brief, he indicated that he did not think a Titian portrait of this quality was likely to be available again and he thought it would be a distinguished acquisition for the County Museum." The desirability of the purchase was further confirmed after Modestini examined the painting and informed Murphy he did not have the slightest doubt that the sixteenth-century portrait of a Venetian senator dressed in crimson velvet robes was in fact Titian's coveted *Portrait of Giacomo Dolfin.* Murphy immediately wrote Robert Ahmanson with the good news: "Modestini has cleaned more great Italian pictures than any living person and I would trust his judgment about authenticity quite as much as I would any art historian."[49]

Murphy urged the board to act before the masterpiece could be snapped up by a museum in another city. Once the painting was installed in the permanent collection in the Ahmanson Gallery, LACMA became home to the only work by the artist in a public collection in Southern California. The painting soon proved a favorite of museum visitors.

Murphy relished the acquisition side of his position as trustee and took a childlike joy in discovering details concerning the European masters. The chance to bid on millions of dollars' worth of rare works filled him with awe and reminded him of the passions awakened in him during his year abroad as a university student wandering through the great museums of Europe, emotionally transported to the Renaissance. Murphy now controlled the formidable resources of a highly important foundation and guided its selection of masterpieces; the boy from the midwestern plains now chose what paintings by which great European masters would hang on the museum walls of a great modern city.

· · · · ·

Ahmanson family dynamics continued to occupy the foundation as the Ahmansons and the trustees mourned the death of Dorothy Sullivan in 1979, after a lengthy and painful illness. Murphy attended the funeral services and brought consolation to Howard Ahmanson Jr., who was deeply grieved by his mother's death. "Doc Murphy" had continued to counsel and advise the young man over the years. Murphy supported young Ahmanson's marriage to Roberta Green, a native of Perry, Iowa, who had moved to California and worked as a religion reporter at the *Orange County Register*. The couple were wed on January 25, 1986. The following year, on November 29, the couple welcomed the birth of their only child, David, who arrived hale and hearty at nine pounds, five ounces.[50]

Murphy also advised the Ahmanson heir regarding his gifts of art to the Los Angeles County Museum. Murphy wrote to Howard Ahmanson Jr. expressing his personal appreciation for his contributions and telling him that his father would be pleased that his son's "generosity should be so evident in the building that will always bear the Ahmanson name."[51]

As the 1980s came to a close, the financial health of the foundation was sound. Once the majority of the legal issues were resolved, Murphy set his mind to ensuring future continuity by adding new talent to the board to help Robert Ahmanson lead the foundation forward. Murphy had hesitated to invite new trustees to serve on the board in the midst of the legal challenges, but by 1988 he was confident that the worst was over. On his recommendation, board membership was extended to Murphy's protégé Robert Erburu and later to the businessman Lloyd E. Cotsen.

The foundation also secured the services of a highly competent and dedicated new managing director, Leonard E. Walcott Jr. Murphy had great faith in Walcott's ability and considered him a "first rate catch for the foundation."[52] By the close of the decade, operating under the sage stewardship of Murphy, the assets of the Ahmanson Foundation were a healthy $437 million, and the trustees were in position to dispense nearly $20 million each year in grants to benefit Los Angeles. Although Murphy did not live to see it, the value of the foundation funds would approach the $1 billion mark by 2004.

The greatest gifts of friendship that Franklin Murphy gave Howard Ahmanson came to Ahmanson posthumously in two ways—Murphy's stewardship of the Ahmanson Foundation and the guidance Murphy gave Ahmanson's only son. Murphy served far beyond ordinary fiduciary duties in his concern and support for the Ahmanson family. Robert DeKruif claimed that of all Murphy's efforts, what would have meant the most to Ahmanson was that Murphy ensured that Howard Jr. received the support and direction he needed to create a productive and satisfying life for himself.

It was in his role as Ahmanson Foundation trustee that Murphy made his single greatest contribution to the public welfare of the city. As the dominant trustee on the board, Murphy managed to guide the besieged institution through its most precarious era, fifteen years of legal confrontations with the IRS, the state of California, and various members of the Ahmanson family. Robert Ahmanson is quick to give Murphy credit for making the foundation the entity it has become. Operating in a position largely hidden from the public, Murphy guaranteed a prodigious philanthropic fund for the benefit of Los Angeles. In spite of his fears during the interminable litigation that all his efforts could come to nothing, his service to the foundation ultimately served the community on a scale that could then scarcely be imagined.

THE CONFIRMATION OF NELSON ROCKEFELLER

While the Ahmanson Foundation was in the thick of its legal struggles, Washington focused on the difficulties facing Gerald Ford's new administration. Nelson Rockefeller had received the vice presidential nomination from President Ford on August 20, 1974, but securing confirmation proved enormously difficult. Murphy found himself bolstering the spirits of his anguished friend, who faced hours of brutal scrutiny in the confirmation hearings. Almost immediately after Nixon's resignation, Murphy had written to Ford, urging him to nominate Rockefeller as the best-qualified Republican to fill the vice presidential vacancy. Murphy advised the president that the first few days of his administration were critical, as a vast executive bureaucracy had been without the full attention of a chief executive for months, and that he must move decisively to generate early confidence in his leadership both at home and abroad. Rockefeller had expertise in specific areas in which the president had no equivalent experience. Murphy recited Rockefeller's significant background in foreign affairs and his service under four previous administrations.[53] Murphy also pointed to Rockefeller's domestic experience—four terms as governor of New York and service as undersecretary of the U.S. Department of Health, Education, and Welfare in the Eisenhower administration. As vice president, Murphy urged, Rockefeller would broaden the political base of the new president, "as he has long been identified on domestic matters with the more liberal part of the Republican party. No one else could bring such credentials to the office of Vice-President."[54]

Rockefeller had been the subject of intense congressional scrutiny at the time of his previous presidential appointments, and the FBI had investigated him thoroughly (in fact, Rockefeller's FBI file later released under the Freedom of Information Act totaled over 1,500 pages), but the congressional confirmation brought additional probing. The hearings quickly turned ugly, subjecting him to a heated inquisition on Rockefeller wealth and dominance.

"My temper is getting a little short as I watch these continued 'pot shots,'" Murphy told Rockefeller during the worst weeks. "I hope you realize that there are millions who feel just as I do and I hope that you will stay right in there." "If irresponsible sources can cut you down with your extraordinary record of public service and private philanthropy," Murphy said, "I begin to despair as to whether any truly gifted and active person may be permitted to give political leadership to this country."[55] Behind the scenes, Murphy worked the phones and made several trips to Washington to speak privately with influential senators.[56]

The hearings were widely watched, and in one dramatic moment the irrepressible and elegant politician leaned forward and in near-exasperation told the Senate committee, "This myth about the power which my family exercises needs to be brought out into the light. It just does not exist. I've got to tell you, I don't wield economic power."[57] By December Rockefeller's stormy confirmation was concluded and he was administered the oath of office on December 19, 1974. He was now restored to a political path, raising his hope that perhaps he could run successfully for the U.S. presidency, his lifelong ambition. Murphy sent hearty congratulations to his friend. "The country is now in good hands again," he wrote.[58]

The lengthy and grueling congressional inquiry into the Rockefeller fortune had taken its toll, however, and when Murphy accompanied his friend to quiet retreats at Kykuit, he observed Rockefeller growing increasingly bitter over the brutality of politics. Rockefeller still aspired to be president, but fate was not on his side. On Sunday, January 27, 1979, Murphy awoke to news bulletins that Nelson Rockefeller was dead. He was seventy years old. Over the next several weeks accounts surfaced that Rockefeller had died in the bedroom of his Manhattan townhome in the company of a female assistant who was twenty-six. The young woman's delay in calling for emergency paramedics generated widespread gossip. Murphy was grief-stricken.

"I was shocked to learn of Nelson's passing. He was a remarkable man and a wonderful friend," a shaken Murphy told Happy Rockefeller.

"Nelson enjoyed greatly his association with you and I know you feel his passing deeply as do I," she responded.[59]

Murphy would miss his association with Rockefeller, grandson of one of America's most legendary tycoons. He had understood the familial drive that set Rockefeller on a path toward political ambitions that could not always be reconciled with his personal temperament and desires, a drive that pushed him relentlessly in quest of a goal he was never to reach.

· · · · ·

The rigors of Murphy's responsibilities to the myriad interests he served began to take a physical toll. His face showed deep lines around his mouth and dark bags under the eyes, giving him a tired, unhappy look. He now wore pricey European-style reading glasses that he placed on the tip of his nose. In July 1979 he was stricken with a skin disorder that he was unable to diagnose. Alarmed, he visited Dr. Harvey A. Zarem at the UCLA Medical Center, who was able to prescribe a course of successful treatment. His skin problem vanished, but the damage done by years of smoking, poor diet, and little exercise was irreversible. Murphy was only sixty-three, but he looked ten years older, and he found it increasingly difficult to maintain the pace of constant travel, speech making, entertaining, and correspondence that his position demanded. His jowls now sagged beneath his jawbone, and his collar and tie bunched around his thickened double chin.

Still, his overall presence was more commanding than ever, with his steady blue-gray eyes, quick wit, and astounding memory for names and details that rarely failed him. Murphy's quick temper may have abated with maturity, but he was even more prone to say what was really on his mind, a prerogative of age and position. Despite the physical ailments, including severe backaches and a stiff neck, he refused to slow down.

After the arrival of grandchildren, Murphy got a second chance at the role of fatherhood. Martha, married to attorney Craig Crockwell, had given birth to their daughter, Erin, in 1971. The youngster soon became a favorite of her grandfather, who was especially pleased about her interest in art. Murphy wrote to tell her how happy he was to receive the still life she painted: "It is truly beautiful and shows that you have great talent. That being the case, I certainly hope you continue to practice your drawing and painting. You have a great future as an artist, even if you wish to have it only as a hobby."[60]

When he missed Erin's elementary school graduation he sent her a note congratulating her on receiving the highest award of the graduates. "I must say," Murphy wrote, "that this honor . . . does not surprise me in the least."[61] Murphy was so persistent—and so premature—with advice to Erin about her future that Martha, never reticent about speaking up to her father, told him to back off a bit and enjoy her childhood years while they lasted.[62]

Joyce and Chip Dickey welcomed a son, David, early in their marriage and a daughter, Judith, six years later. The Dickey marriage had been rocky, but the couple, after settling in Kansas City, managed to create a home together and were becoming a part of community life when Joyce was diagnosed with the early stages of multiple sclerosis. To the relief of the family, her condition was stable, but Murphy feared that the long-term prognosis could not be good.

With one year remaining at UCLA Medical School, Franklin Lee had found love and stability. He met Wendy Jones when she worked as a nurse at UCLA, and they were married one year later. Murphy was surprised by the unexpected event and worried that his son was too young for marriage, and ill prepared, with medical school still to finish; but he did what he could to be supportive. Through his contact with Ahmanson Company executive Robert DeKruif, he helped the couple to secure a loan from Home Savings to purchase a home for themselves.[63]

Murphy possibly overreached his fatherly prerogative when he included a stern message with his congratulations on Wendy's pregnancy: "Remember what I said—namely, that you should not in any way compromise your current educational program, for you will never be able to make it up in the future and, in the end, it would be a great disservice to you, to Wendy, and to your children." In the letter Murphy meddled a bit further, telling Franklin that he and Wendy's father had discussed the matter a few years earlier and had made a contingency plan if Wendy had to give up her job: "Mr. Jones said that should be no problem and that he had told Wendy he would be disposed to make up for the loss of income for a period of time. Therefore, between Mr. Jones and myself, there ought to be a way of solving that problem, if indeed it arises."[64] Murphy made pointed reference to the fact that three successive generations of Murphy doctors had managed to finish their medical education before starting a family, most notably Murphy's own father, who did not marry until he was in his forties and his career was well under way.

The birth of his grandson and namesake, Franklin Douglas Murphy, moved the senior Murphy to send Wendy and Franklin photographs from his own youth. One showed a slim, athletic young man on skis. "The second is a photograph taken of me at some uncertain age; you may wish to compare it with the way Franklin Douglas looks as he matures," he wrote his son.[65] Murphy sent yet more directions to the young couple when he read a newspaper account of coyotes in the hillside neighborhood of Woodland Hills, in northwestern Los Angeles, where they had purchased their home. Murphy sent the clipping along with worried instructions that they not leave the baby unattended—even in a playpen—in the yard.[66]

After Franklin Lee joined the faculty and staff of the UCLA School of Medicine as an assistant professor of cardiology, the relationship between father and son was warm, though they seldom saw each other. Murphy was extremely pleased with his son's decision and wrote him in June 1983: "Again, let me tell you how delighted I am concerning the good news in relation to UCLA. The more I think about it, the more I am convinced that this is the move to make at this particular point in your career."[67] Murphy may have had a hand in the UCLA job offer, for he had sent repeated directives to his son after he passed his medical board examination, urging him to take advantage of the advice of Dean Mellinkoff. "I urge you to call him and make an appointment to discuss your future," he said. "I really would not put this off too long."[68]

· · · · ·

With all four Murphy children married and out of the household, Willia and Ted Roberts remained, caring for Franklin and Judy despite their own advancing age. Willia continued to iron Murphy's boxer shorts and pajamas, just the way he wanted them, maintained the household, and did the family cooking. She was never able to master the intricacies of fine dining now required for entertaining at the level of the Murphys' new status, so caterers were called for such occasions and Willia reluctantly relinquished her kitchen. Ted continued to drive Murphy to the airport and pick him up on his return from his numerous domestic and international trips.

When Murphy learned that the couple who had performed household duties for the family for so many years were terrified about an audit by the IRS, he canceled two days of pressing appointments to attend each session with them and the IRS auditor until the $170 dispute had been resolved and the Roberts' honesty vindicated. According to Carolyn, Willia and Ted were a rare gift. "They gave their lives to serve Mom and Dad," she said.[69]

THE CHAIRMAN OF TIMES MIRROR RETIRES

At the corner of First and Spring Streets in downtown Los Angeles the executive offices of Times Mirror were awash in good spirits. The 1980s would prove the most prosperous decade in the lengthy history of the Times Mirror Company. Five of the company's operating groups, led by outstanding performances in newspaper and broadcast operations, posted increased profits. Revenues in 1980 totaled $1.87 billion, an increase of 13 percent from the previous year. The following year the *Los Angeles Times* was one hundred years old, and Times Mirror reached record revenues of $2.16 billion. A backward glance at the company's dividends reflected the meteoric rise of the media conglomerate even when adjusted for inflation: in 1971 the company's annual dividend was 25 cents; ten years later Franklin Murphy was able to announce a remarkable $4.40 per share.

After receiving a copy of the annual report showcasing the company's growth, U.S. Chief Justice Warren E. Burger wrote Murphy to offer his congratulations and tender a clever jibe at what he perceived to be the *Times*'s negative editorial attitude: "I am delighted that Times Mirror and its stockholders have done so well in the very decade when, editorially, it has proclaimed that the 'sky is falling' and 'disaster has overtaken America's free press.' Would that we could all survive 'relentless assaults' and 'disasters' so well!"[70]

The new streamlined design of the *Times* accompanied the newspaper's improving reputation. "The face lift will enhance years of change that run deep," wrote *Newsweek*. "Under the twenty-year stewardship of Otis Chandler, 53, whose family has been at its helm since 1886, the paper has matured from a parochial civic booster into one of the nation's three best metropolitan dailies, closing steadily on the *New York Times* and the *Washington Post*."[71] Otis Chandler had not reached his goal of supplanting the *New York Times*, but in the process of becoming one of the nation's preeminent newspapers the *Times* also became the richest. Gross revenues from the *Times* in

1980 reached $550 million. The newspaper's fleet of "propane-powered, smog-free trucks" painted with the newspaper's eagle logo delivered one million copies each day, giving it the second-largest daily metropolitan circulation in the nation, second only to the *New York Daily News*.[72]

On January 29, 1981, Franklin Murphy celebrated his sixty-fifth birthday and retired from his position as chairman of the board and chief executive officer of the Times Mirror Company. Murphy now became chairman of the executive committee of the board of directors, a position he would hold until the age of seventy. Robert Erburu succeeded Murphy as chief executive officer, and Otis Chandler became chairman of the board. The momentum built by Norman Chandler and carried forward by Albert Casey and other Times Mirror executives was still in place, and the sheer strength of that earlier "flawless strategy" would carry Times Mirror forward for the next several years. But later the once rock-solid media giant would face the first indications of a downward spiral.

As chairman of the executive committee, Murphy stepped into the position that Norman Chandler had occupied when Murphy came on board in 1968. However, unlike his predecessor, Murphy remained relatively active and continued to participate in corporate-level decisions, working with Erburu and Chandler. "The structure is a common one in American corporations," Murphy explained. "In short, I am what you might call 'the elder statesman of the company.'"[73]

The Times Mirror Company distributed a press release explaining that Otis Chandler now maintained the title of editor in chief of all Times Mirror media, having served as publisher of the *Los Angeles Times* for twenty years. The new publisher was Tom Johnson, who had been president of the newspaper since 1977. The executive changes coincided with the company's plan for a vigorous program of technological development as the looming information explosion soon became its most consuming task.

• • • • •

Franklin Murphy had guided the conglomerate as the Chandler family's influence waned after the death of Norman Chandler and the compulsory retirement of Dorothy Chandler, but throughout the transition he had protected the Chandlers' holdings and retained their respect. If Times Mirror's greatest asset was goodwill, as Dorothy so often said, Murphy deserved much credit for functioning as its leading corporate citizen. Tom Johnson, commenting on the occasion of Murphy's retirement, expressed the appreciation many felt for Murphy's tenure as chairman: "While the revenues, profits and acquisitions will be seen by many generations to follow, your imprint has been even more significant in your commitment to quality, your demand for excellence, and your dedication to the highest standards of integrity in all that we undertake."[74]

But there were those on the scene who did not hold the chairman in such high esteem; not everyone was a Franklin Murphy fan. Jim Bellows, once considered a potential successor to Nick Williams, had left the *Times* in 1974 to take over as editor of the financially strapped *Washington Star.* Bellows, a creative underdog who had nurtured the careers of an amazing roster of offbeat American journalists, considered Otis Chandler the best publisher he ever worked for. But he considered Murphy inconsequential, "all smoke and mirrors." Bellows said Murphy was like a vapor that entered and exited a room without leaving anything of real substance behind.[75] He also had sharp conflicts with the Chandler family. In his memoir he wrote that he and the *Los Angeles Times* were never a good fit. "I felt newspapering should be fun; the Chandlers thought it was work. Or duty," he said.[76]

Other senior Times Mirror executives criticized Murphy's short attention span and aversion to details. While they admired his far-reaching civic persona, they felt his list of board memberships and foundation duties reduced the time and attention he had for pressing business at Times Mirror Square. As chairman and chief executive officer, Murphy routinely left day-to-day functioning of the company to less senior executives. There were critics who believed God was in the details, which Murphy abandoned. Other executives on the scene appreciated his hands-off management style that focused on the bigger picture, permitting experienced managers to get their work done with little interference or crippling micromanagement. If criticism of his tenure as chairman of Times Mirror wounded Murphy, he apparently never showed it.

On New Year's Eve, hours before Murphy's official departure as CEO, Erburu penned a personal note to him: "You did far more than 'not get in the way of others' as you have often observed. Someday I think what you did will be clear to all."[77]

· · · · ·

Murphy's official role at Times Mirror was diminishing, but there was always room for improvement at the *Times,* and a nudge from the former company chairman was not uncommon. Murphy good-naturedly reprimanded Anthony Day, the *Times* editorial page editor, about misuse of the King's English:

This morning, I came to my breakfast table eager to start my day once again by reading the editorial pages of the Los Angeles Times while sipping my morning cup of decaffeinated coffee. . . . It took two readings for me to become convinced that the editorial did, in fact, contain the language . . . "we cannot see junking up the state Constitution . . ." "Junking up"!! With accelerated pulse, and more in sorrow and indignation than in anger, I promptly turned to my copy of Webster's New World Dictionary of the American Language which is to me what the Bible was to Saint Jerome. As I expected, nowhere could I find the phrase (or word) "junking up."

Murphy jocularly admitted to becoming mildly reactionary with age, but said he hoped for better from his "favorite newspaper."[78]

Murphy looked forward to staying on at Times Mirror in a less pressured capacity and allotting more time to his efforts on behalf of the cultural arts. He continued the professional relationships and associations that enabled him to operate behind the scenes with increasing clout as one of America's most effective trustees. Murphy particularly relished the time he spent at the scenic Bohemian Grove on the Russian River in Sonoma County, and each summer he borrowed his son's sleeping bag and set out for the retreat. Under club rules all conversations were off the record, but his letters mention fellow Bohemians and Reagan administration stalwarts George H. W. Bush, George Shultz, Edwin Meese, Caspar Weinberger, and William French Smith.

The goings-on at the Grove were shrouded in mystery. "Is it a tool of the rich right-wingers aiming to control the world?" asked one author. "Or merely some wacky millionaires fond of dressing in drag and engaging in odd rituals at an annual encampment in the woods?"[79] In reality, club members conceded, the Bohemians were much less ominous than their reputation as a "conspiracy-laden vehicle of the industrial complex." Deal making was "strongly discouraged" among members, who were said to be linked "by a love of the arts." The popular San Francisco columnist Herb Caen once said that the Bohemians may have been devoted to art, but it was the art of drinking a good martini.[80]

Murphy took special pleasure in arranging for the *Times* to be hand-delivered daily to the encampment. "I am sure you will be pleased to know that the *Los Angeles Times'* appearance at the Bohemian Grove has been an absolute smashing success," Murphy wrote in a memo to Phillip Williams, Tom Johnson, and Robert Erburu. He recommended that they continue to provide delivery of the paper to the Grove: "There are not many places where you can get America's leading political, business and professional leaders together in such quantity and quality."[81]

Men and women who composed the current cadre of educational leaders and art patrons saw to it that Murphy was suitably honored on his sixty-fifth birthday. Among the events, a new gallery in the expanded Ahmanson Building at the county museum funded by the Kress Foundation was named the Judith and Franklin Murphy Gallery. A surprise gift that greatly touched him was a handsome festschrift, compiled and published in his honor by his closest friends. Titled *The Shape of the Past,* the collection was the work of eighteen esteemed scholars in archaeology, anthropology, and art history. It was published by UCLA's Institute of Archaeology and the Office of Chancellor Charles Young and coedited by Giorgio Buccellati, the institute's director, and Charles Speroni, emeritus dean of the College of Fine Arts.

Letters of congratulations acknowledging Murphy's place in the world of serious art and the humanities were received in recognition of the festschrift. In a letter to Charles Young, Daniel Boorstin, Librarian of Congress, wrote: "I have long admired him and his work. He sets an example for all of us." And from Paul Mellon: "A fine tribute to Franklin Murphy whose interest in and contributions toward art and archeology have been far-reaching and profound."[82]

GOLDEN DONORS

Murphy's close ties to American family dynasties brought him invitations to enjoy the comforts of many of the great private residences of the century—Kykuit in New York's Hudson Valley, home to three generations of Rockefellers; Paul Mellon's Upper East Side Manhattan townhouse along "Millionaire's Row" at Seventieth Street between Park and Lexington; Brick House at Oak Spring, the serene Mellon family home in Upperville, Virginia; Sunnylands, the Walter Annenberg oasis in Palm Desert, California, with its vibrant impressionist collection; and the scenic eighty-seven-acre lakefront estate in Grosse Pointe, Michigan, where Henry Ford II had romped as a boy on the manicured lawns of the Cotswold-style mansion built by Edsel and Eleanor Ford. Murphy earned the reputation of being the perfect guest, a welcome addition to any party or social function. The very rich loved him, and he loved them back. Naturally, while he enjoyed invitations to these great homes and the company of their wealthy masters,

Murphy kept an eye out for philanthropic bequests that could follow in due course.

A good example of his technique was an event he planned in which he brought together a glittering array of personalities in the arts, government, and media for a black-tie dinner in honor of Howard H. Baker, U.S. Senate majority leader. The party was hosted by Franklin and Judy at the Corcoran Gallery in Washington, D.C., on behalf of the Times Mirror Company on January 5, 1981. In attendance were President-elect and Mrs. Ronald Reagan and Vice President–elect and Mrs. George H. W. Bush. The guest list also included Senator Strom Thurmond, Jack Kemp, Art Buchwald, Mr. and Mrs. Harry H. Wetzel, Mrs. Norman Chandler, Otis Chandler, Robert Erburu, Mr. and Mrs. Robert H. Adams Jr., Mr. and Mrs. Armand Deutsch, Mr. and Mrs. Earle Jorgensen, Mr. and Mrs. Henry Salvatori, and Mr. and Mrs. William French Smith. The *Washington Post* hailed the party as the most elegant and important occasion of the year. The event served as an appropriate kickoff for Murphy's new role as executive committee chair of Times Mirror, which he planned to use to great benefit in pursuing his overlapping duties as trustee, officer, or ex officio member of more than thirty regional and national educational, cultural, philanthropic, and corporate boards.

Following the affair, Murphy remained in Washington. He spent time with Daniel Boorstin and took pleasure in his role as trustee of the National Gallery. The Gallery had mounted a special exhibition in honor of the presidential inaugural, and Murphy's emotions very nearly got the best of him when he viewed the midwestern artist Thomas Hart Benton's epic mural *Trail Riders,* which occupied a prominent position. He had personally known Benton and, impressed by the spirit and values of the Great Plains that his work evoked, had endeavored to acquire some of his paintings for the University of Kansas.

On the freezing cold morning of January 20, Murphy watched Chief Justice Warren E. Burger administer the oath of office on the west front steps of the U.S. Capitol as Ronald Reagan was inaugurated as the nation's fortieth president. Reagan's political ascendancy had come as a surprise to Murphy, who had been convinced that Reagan would not receive the Republican Party nomination. "My problem with Reagan," Murphy told businessman Dortch Oldham, "is that he tends to surround himself with second-rate people. The office of Presidency has become so complicated that in my view the name of the game of a successful Presidency is to have really competent advisors."[83]

Murphy's dislike had begun during Reagan's heated clashes with the University of California regents over the state education budget. At the time Murphy believed Reagan's divisive actions would cost him his political future. But, in retrospect, Murphy had read the voting public wrong. He attended the inaugural with mixed feelings. He took solace in the fact that George H. W. Bush had been selected vice president. In 1980 Bush declined Murphy's offer to join the board of Times Mirror when it became apparent that he would become the vice presidential candidate on the Reagan ticket. Murphy told Bush that the outcome was to the benefit of the nation: "I guess I would have to say that Times Mirror lost a good potential director, but the nation got a superb Vice President!"[84]

Murphy and his brother, George, had great regard for Bush. Tempering his feelings about Reagan, Murphy wrote Bush after his smashing victory, "Many people feel as I do—namely that although we have great respect for President-elect Reagan and are sure that he is going to do a great job, we are delighted to know that you will be at his side and in the inner circle."[85]

· · · · ·

The year 1981 continued to be a whirlwind of obligations and entanglements in Murphy's concentric circles of politics and philanthropy. In Los Angeles on March 27 Murphy was pulled up short by an automobile accident. As Murphy drove his favorite Ford Mustang Ghia south on Coldwater Canyon he was struck by an approaching car at Cherokee Lane. After a few days of bedrest, a bruised and bandaged Murphy resumed his hectic schedule. In April he visited the Walter Annenbergs for a three-day weekend at Sunnylands with a handful of luminaries from the divergent worlds of politics, art, and science. In May he delivered a stirring commencement address at Johns Hopkins University and was awarded an honorary degree; he delivered a somber eulogy for Dr. Jules Stein before a tearful memorial assembly; he attended a tribute for Henry Mancini with Otis Chandler and his second wife, Bettina; and he took a tour of the UCLA Medical Center with its dean, Sherman Mellinkoff, and Robert Ahmanson to help secure for UCLA a pioneering $1 million grant for brain research.

In June he was appointed to the President's Task Force for the Arts and Humanities cochaired by Charlton Heston; in July he and Ed Carter hosted a small breakfast for Andrew Knight, editor of the London *Economist,* with leading Los Angeles figures at Pasadena's California Institute of Technology. In August he thanked James Baker II, Reagan's White House chief of staff, for the initiative he showed in undertaking to preserve the museum endowment program in the House reconciliation bill, which proved a tremendous boost to the future of museum operations. "It has cost the government nothing" Murphy told Baker, "yet if it had been eliminated, it would have been a grave blow to all major American art museums and would have reflected real discredit on our country."[86]

One exhilarating occasion followed another until late August when he was called on for the sad task of delivering the eulogy at the memorial service for Edwin Wendell Pauley, who had lent his name and funds to build UCLA's Pauley Pavilion, by now familiar to sports fans everywhere; the big bear of a man had been chair of the powerful University of California Board of Regents when Murphy came to Los Angeles as chancellor. Other events of the summer ranged from joining a handful of leading business executives for a private meeting in Los Angeles with President Reagan to consuming beer and hot dogs with Peter O'Malley, president of the Los Angeles Dodgers, as they watched the hometown team win the World Series.[87] In October Franklin and Judy took an extraordinary five-week trip, with stops in sixteen cities from Kansas City to New York, to Europe and entertained or were entertained by a striking list of prominent figures as Murphy furthered the far-flung interests of the Ford Motor Company, Hallmark Cards, the Kress Foundation, the National Gallery of Art, the Ahmanson Foundation, the Los Angeles County Museum of Art, and Times Mirror.

PART III

Trustee

EIGHT

The Los Angeles County Museum of Art

THE COUNTY MUSEUM IN HANCOCK PARK shares a site with the Rancho La Brea Tar Pits, the world-famous repository of Ice Age fossils in the heart of the city's Miracle Mile commercial district. The tar pits formed when crude oil seeped to the surface, leaving pools of sticky asphalt, which was used for waterproofing for thousands of years by Native Americans. The heavy, viscous asphalt had trapped unwary animals through the ages, creating a treasure trove of ancient animal remains. In contrast to the bubbling black pools and the odorous pits, the museum was designed as a group of pristine white pavilions on a raised plaza, surrounded by reflecting pools featuring the arching sprays of fountain jets.

Murphy had hoped that once the county art collection moved into a building of its own, away from the science museum in Exposition Park, with its taxidermy and dioramas, its kooky reputation could be overcome. He was disappointed that the grand architectural plan by William L. Pereira and Associates did not win acclaim. The style was described as ponderous in spite of the intended effect of handsome floating pavilions. As the months went by, sniping by critics was not the only architectural problem that faced the trustees. Gas from the petroleum-bearing sedimentary rock broke through the bottom of the reflecting pools, leaving them shimmering with oil slicks. Experts were called in, but, unable to fix the exasperating leaks, they recommended that the pools—the signature architectural feature of the museum—be drained and removed.

Since it was increasingly clear that because of scarcity and soaring prices, the museum might never achieve true distinction in European art, trustees planned to focus on creating a comprehensive historical survey, developing areas of specialization, and increasing the number of major pieces. The board faced considerable hurdles in its next phase of development, and in 1970 it persuaded Murphy to take on the difficult role of museum president. In Murphy's view the most pressing issue facing the museum was that it was an art museum without art—it owned little of real value to hang on its walls. Murphy had a remedy in mind, however: he planned to obtain the prized Norton Simon Collection. At the time the market value of Simon's objects was estimated at $150 million. "Were it to be acquired by the county museum," Murphy told the trustees, "we could properly claim to have one of the most important collections of art in this country." In addition, ownership of Simon's collection, he pointed out, would be a magnet for future important donations.[1]

THE PURSUIT OF NORTON SIMON AND ARMAND HAMMER

Norton Simon was a brilliant, agitated man who thrived on generating conflict. Murphy believed that Simon still hungered for recognition, despite the enormous wealth he had amassed building Hunt Foods into the extremely successful Norton Simon, Inc. In a stroke of good timing, Simon took up art collecting in the 1950s, an era of relatively low prices, and in an additional wise move, he seized the opportunity to work closely with Richard Brown, who at the time was the energetic young curator of art in the Exposition Park museum. Benefiting from Brown's tutoring, he assembled a collection that had quality and cohesion, elements often overlooked in the buying sprees of other wealthy collectors. Though most of the historic artworks worth having were owned by museums, Simon managed to acquire an extraordinary collection by buying French impressionists as well as old masters from private sales and turning up at auction houses to flummox other bidders (and sometimes auctioneers) with his erratic bidding. His collection included paintings by Raphael, Sandro Botticelli, Peter Paul Rubens, Jacopo Bassano, Lucas Cranach, Paul Cézanne, and Wassily Kandinsky; massive bronze sculptures by Auguste Rodin, Henry Moore, and Aristide Maillol; and prints by Rembrandt, Francisco Goya, and Pablo Picasso. (Later he became a major force in the Indian and Southeast Asian market.)

Although Simon's real intentions were unknown, he dangled before the LACMA board the possibility of the hoped-for gift of his collection, firing off a list of requirements to be met before negotiations could begin. The board and museum staff hustled to meet Simon's demands, but invariably he was never satisfied. When Simon saw museum visitors carrying umbrellas dangerously close to his artworks on loan, he flew into a rage, ordering pictures removed and demanding more guards. When valuable pieces housed in museum storage could not be located quickly, he terrorized the staff with his anger. He also complained vociferously that the museum's insurance was inadequate for a collection such as his. Murphy hurriedly approached county supervisor Ernest Debs and requested additional funds. "Unless we can provide both the insurance protection and physical protection by way of adequate guards," Murphy pleaded, "Mr. Simon quite naturally might be inclined to look to other museums where such protection can be provided."[2]

After he managed to get insurance in place to satisfy Simon, Murphy grew guardedly optimistic. But in spring 1971 Simon stunned museum trustees with the announcement that he planned to sell at auction more than seventy paintings and sculptures—most of which were already on loan to the museum. Valued works by Edgar Degas, Paul Gauguin, and Vincent van Gogh were tagged for sale. Murphy visited Simon at his Beverly Hills home in July to discuss the situation further, hoping Simon would make a commitment regarding at least a portion of his collection. However, he found the sixty-three-year-old tycoon quarrelsome and defensive. Simon's personal life was chaotic at the time: Lucille Simon had filed for divorce after thirty-seven years of marriage, and Norton Simon was disgruntled about his recent defeat in the Republican primary in his bid for the U.S. Senate. Simon felt he had been badly used by the press, especially the *Los Angeles Times,* in the ill-advised campaign. Murphy often found that his position with Times Mirror made him the recipient of misplaced outrage. Even if nothing was said, men accustomed to control held it against him that he could not or would not control what appeared in the newspaper. As Murphy prepared to leave the meeting, Simon told him that he would have something definitive to say next month—but Murphy had heard that line several times before.[3]

Months went by with no decision from Simon. Then, in November, he shocked the museum trustees even further by abruptly resigning from the board after fourteen years of active involvement. When called by reporters for comment, Murphy calmly stated that Simon's ties to the museum were strong: "Norton Simon continues to be a generous lender to this museum as he has been ever since its founding."[4]

Two weeks after Simon's resignation, the museum director, Kenneth Donahue, made a last-ditch effort to appease him with a conciliatory proposal for creation of a special "Norton Simon Collections Committee," with members selected by Simon to give direction to the museum regarding his collection. Simon found the proposal too little too late and declared that he was so unhappy he was thinking of selling his entire collection. Simon hired Robert S. McFarlane, the son of an old family friend, to manage his several foundations, a move that briefly encouraged both Murphy and Donahue. Murphy found McFarlane intelligent and able, and after their first meeting he was able to secure arrangements for an exhibition of objects on loan from Simon's collection. Murphy saw these developments as positive, possibly putting transactions with Simon on a new footing. He told one museum official that he believed LACMA was still the odds-on favorite to receive Simon's collection, "if we can maintain a businesslike, efficient and effective relationship."[5]

The planned exhibition opened on June 16, 1972, but not without problems right to the last minute. An exhausted Murphy wrote McFarlane after the opening, "I doubt if any museum could have done any better with the time allotted than we have done." He added in resignation, "If Norton finds this exercise not to his full satisfaction, I am convinced he will never find any exercise to his full satisfaction."[6]

· · · · ·

Simon's collection would go a long way toward satisfying the museum's quest for quality works, but it was not the only collection the museum desired. For nearly two decades, oil tycoon Armand Hammer had promised millions of dollars in donations to dozens of art institutions. In 1971 Hammer boldly announced his plan to bequeath to the Los Angeles County Museum more than $10 million in paintings, including a "world-famous" van Gogh.[7] Murphy was quick to praise the gift as "momentous." "It is a further guarantee that the people of this area will not be denied the opportunity to see great works of art so long given to the citizens of other great cities of the western world," he said.[8]

Since the quality of his collection was uneven, Hammer had been eager to enlarge his holdings and increase the number of paintings on loan to various museums and had indulged in frantic buying sprees. Many of his purchases gained him considerable press coverage at art auctions but did not necessarily result in the acquisition of fine-quality works. In fact, critics were becoming increasingly dismissive of his collection. Following one Hammer exhibit at the Smithsonian Institution, Paul Richard of the *Washington Post* said, "Never have so many major masters been represented in this city by canvasses so poor." The Toulouse-Lautrec was a "hack job," the Goya was "trivial," the van Gogh was "ugly."[9] "It was the kind of review that would have broken the will of some collectors," noted Robert A. Jones in the *Los Angeles Times*. "All that energy, all those millions, and the result was humiliation."[10]

With a vested interest in improving the quality of paintings that would later be donated, Murphy encouraged Hammer to hire John Walker, former director of the National Gallery, as his consultant. Walker was given control of the collection; under his guidance half of the paintings were sold, and new, more important pieces were acquired. Walker served as Hammer's consultant for two years (from 1970 to 1972), saying later that he found Hammer difficult but fascinating.[11] The collection grew in respectability but was still criticized as a poor mix. Critics found it failed to "reflect a passion for the art itself but [only] a desire to amass the correct group of names."[12]

At the time Hammer announced his generous gift, trustees felt confident that the museum could count on his pledge. The spectacular Hammer-inspired Soviet exhibition of impressionist and postimpressionist paintings (the same exhibition that President Nixon missed because of the escalating drama of Watergate in 1973) demonstrated Hammer's seeming commitment to a strong future relationship. The exhibition was the first time masterpieces on loan from the Soviet Union had toured the United States and included works by Henri Matisse, Paul Gauguin, Pablo Picasso, Paul Cézanne, and Vincent van Gogh. Hammer had conducted negotiations for the exhibition with Soviet cultural minister Yekaterina Furtseva. (The arrangements were reportedly made after Hammer donated a Goya portrait valued at $1 million to the Hermitage Museum in addition to several other paintings from his collection.)[13]

The historic cultural exchange with the Soviets had been vehemently opposed by conservative organizations, which protested to the County Board of Supervisors and bombarded museum officials with accusations of subversion. Murphy insisted on unprecedented security measures; he hired more guards, barred press photographers from entering the exhibition, and required museum staff to wear special badges. When the masterworks arrived, there was a flurry of excitement as the paintings were uncrated and placed behind bulletproof glass. Two bomb threats on the day of the opening forced a nerve-wracking evacuation of the museum, but with order restored by dusk, Murphy became the calm and amiable host leading museum donors, trustees, and distinguished guests through the Frances and Armand Hammer Gallery.

At the museum preview dinner in the Ahmanson atrium, dining tables were covered in black and gold cloth and guests were served "Beef and Noodles à la Russe." Before dessert was served Murphy stood to acknowledge the international guests. He also gave ample credit to the museum trustee who made it all possible. "You wouldn't have dined half so well if it hadn't been for the generosity of Dr. Hammer," he said. Murphy then introduced the four county supervisors present—Pete Schabarum, Ernest Debs, Kenneth Hahn, and James Hayes—who were given a loud round of applause for their support of the controversial undertaking. "This exhibition is not only an important artistic event," Murphy announced, "but it also signals the growing dialogue between the United States and the Soviet Union—a dialogue which means so much to the future peace and tranquility of the world."[14] Murphy's support of cultural exchanges with the Soviets began during his years in Kansas, and since then he had been confronted by one conservative faction after another over a policy that seemed to him not only appropriate but imperative as well. He was glad to facilitate Hammer's desire to be a player in international cultural exchange since Hammer brought resources to a cause he readily championed.

Not long after the success of the Soviet exhibition Hammer abruptly announced that he would give title to his pictures to the county museum only if they were permanently hung together in perpetuity inside the Hammer Gallery. According to Hammer, this condition was nonnegotiable and a prerequisite to any permanent gift.

Murphy was perplexed, then outraged. In a memo to Edward Carter, Murphy outlined the dilemma: "At no time in our negotiations with Armand Hammer was there ever any commitment to hang his pictures together or in any one place," he wrote. Even if Hammer were willing to put up the $4.5 million to $5 million for an addition to the Ahmanson Building to the north—about which there had been some discussion—Murphy was opposed to hanging Hammer's collection in one place in perpetuity. "It would set a precedent that would be impossible to follow, and even though I would love to have the entire collection, it certainly doesn't deserve [that] kind of exception." Murphy said that such an exception might be appropriate for a collection of unusual quality, such as that of Norton Simon, but not for Hammer's. It was doubtful, Murphy felt, that Hammer would offer to build an additional gallery since Occidental Petroleum stock was suffering a downturn. Murphy pointed out that LACMA already held title to five of Hammer's very best pictures and that important gifts from other local collectors would one day come to the museum. "In short," Murphy reminded Carter, "we are not desperate."[15]

· · · · ·

The museum with its marble-clad buildings adjacent to the ancient tar pits looked sadly derelict amid drained reflecting pools and exposed plumbing for nonfunctioning fountain jets. When the Los Angeles County Board of Supervisors approved $340,000 to relandscape the museum grounds and eliminate the troublesome pools, Murphy was jubilant. He told his fellow trustees that he had simply had it with the damn pools and would under no circumstances use a water feature as a design element, anywhere, ever again. Museum officials embarked on a plan in February 1974 to install a three-acre garden that would provide space for a notable gift of sculpture from B. Gerald Cantor, founder and chairman of the global securities firm Cantor Fitzgerald. Following Murphy's recommendation, the board selected the architectural firm of Cornell, Bridgers and Troller to design the proposed garden, the same firm that had conceived the berms and paths of the UCLA sculpture garden named in Murphy's honor.

It was soon apparent that the county appropriation was far too small for significant innovation. Even after the budget was increased to $510,000, the plan was more modest than Murphy had envisioned. In addition, the design phase was rushed to completion to accommodate administrative quirks of county contracts and the trustees' desire to have the garden completed in time for the museum's tenth anniversary. In reviewing the plan for the new sculpture garden, the *Times* architecture critic found it adequate but unadventurous.[16] The centerpiece sculpture was to be a heroic Rodin called *Monument to Balzac*. Sycamores and Canary Island pines were selected to enliven the vista otherwise dominated by the museum's stark, monochromatic marble facade after the reflecting pools and fountains had been removed.

The limitations of the new sculpture garden invited a rehash of criticism about the museum buildings. Some still wished a different architect had been chosen. Murphy played the diplomat and focused attention on the $6 million Cantor gift, which he heralded as one of the greatest and most significant contributions ever made to the museum: "All of the citizens of L.A. County will long be in the debt of Mr. Cantor."[17]

· · · · ·

The realist in Murphy recognized that hope of obtaining Norton Simon's collection was dwindling. He told Norman Barker Jr., chairman of the board of United California Bank, that his relationship with Simon had become "remote—even chilly." After it became known in spring 1974 that Simon had developed a new relationship with the Pasadena Museum of Art and that he would install most of his collection of old masters and Asian masterpieces there, Murphy took the high road and sent his personal good wishes.

"The Pasadena deal is one of those rare ones in which all parties benefit. HEARTY CONGRATULATIONS!" he wrote shortly before the Pasadena institution was renamed the Norton Simon Museum. Later, when Murphy heard that Simon was despondent over the criticism his museum had generated among members of the city's contentious art circles, Murphy repeatedly telephoned and wrote the sixty-seven-year-old collector to bolster his spirits. "What I do know, having run two public institutions and therefore having some experience with the press," Murphy wrote, "is that in the end, it is the reality, not the speculation, that has the ultimate impact on people, and I suspect that this will be the case when the Pasadena museum is reopened with the installation of significant portions of your collections."[18] (Ten years later, Simon would be increasingly disabled with Guillain-Barré syndrome, a crippling neurological disorder.)

Although his term as museum president was coming to an end, Murphy continued to promote his vision for the museum's future. He advised the incoming museum president, Richard E. Sherwood,[19] that the chief goal for his administration must be to increase and upgrade LACMA's permanent collection. Murphy was optimistic that other private collections would come to LACMA, such as those of Taft Schreiber and Charles Laughton. Murphy also hinted at the possibility that Lucille Simon might be induced to part with some of her renowned pieces, despite the museum's lack of success with her former husband. Walter Annenberg might well give LACMA paintings from his extraordinary collection of impressionist works. The museum was steadily gaining distinction for specializations in Islamic art and Peruvian textiles and now had one of the five major collections in the Western world of the art of India, Nepal, and Tibet.[20] Although the museum was not as well positioned in old masters as Murphy had hoped, Burton B. Fredericksen, curator of paintings for the J. Paul Getty Museum, complimented him at the end of his presidency: "At a time when it had become nearly prohibitive to attempt to acquire important pre-nineteenth century paintings, you have succeeded in getting some extremely fine ones."[21] Murphy continued to wish for a better representation of works from the European Renaissance—his special interest.

Murphy urged Kenneth Donahue to devise ways in which the exhibition space in the Hammer and Ahmanson Buildings could be better utilized. He warned Donahue to deal carefully with Hammer and his desire for an exhibition of his entire "upgraded" collection at LACMA; this should be with the proviso, Murphy insisted, that Hammer give title to the museum for the paintings he had promised. Murphy looked forward to the forthcoming tenth-anniversary exhibition and reminded Donahue that he must start planning it now: "It is your responsibility to give the leadership and to prevent unnecessary tension and confusion."[22] Murphy envisioned the anniversary as a time to call attention to the new, enhanced status of the collection and persuade the art world that LACMA had taken its place among world-class museums.

In the museum's first decade more than thirteen million people had visited the museum, more than $30 million worth of art had been donated, and there were pledges for millions more in future gifts. More than eighty-four major exhibitions had been staged, and loans of art had been made to thirty-five states and nineteen foreign countries.

The announcement of the tenth-anniversary celebration drew extensive press notice, with most commentators in agreement that the museum had much to celebrate. "Despite a good deal of controversy at LACMA in its brief history," wrote Henry Seldis, "it has become a national and international institution of note."[23] One accolade in *Apollo,* the distinguished British art monthly, informed European readers that "no other American museum ha[d] gone so far so fast."[24]

To mark the museum's milestone, two major events were planned. April 8, 1975, was to be the opening of *X, a Decade of Collecting,* displaying acquisitions from the past ten years. Then in June the official opening of the new B. Gerald Cantor Sculpture Garden would coincide with the seventieth annual meeting of the American Association of Museums, hosted by the museum. Noted museum personalities from around the world were expected to attend, including Thomas Hoving, director of the Metropolitan Museum in New York, Thomas M. Messer of the Guggenheim, and, from Europe, Pontus Hulten of the Centre Georges Pompidou in Paris, Michael Compton from London's Tate Gallery, and E. E. deWilde of the Stedelijk Museum in Amsterdam. LACMA was also mounting a symposium on modern art for the distinguished guests and was making every effort to demonstrate that it had become an institution worthy of respect.[25]

To celebrate the museum's ten-year mark, Franklin and Judy Murphy hosted one of the black-tie parties in their Robert Lane home. Franklin was fastidious about the guest list and about which VIP should be assigned to which party. In a note to longtime museum trustee Mrs. Freeman Gates, Murphy cautioned about the delicate matter of which county supervisor should be assigned to which party: "I understand that Carter will have Schabarum; I will have Hahn; Brody will have Hayes; Sherwood will have Edelman and you will have Ward . . . there remains the question of Ernie Debs. I cannot have him because I have Hahn and they mix like oil and water." Murphy reminded Gates that Debs, in spite of some problems, had been "a tremendous supporter."[26] An astute facilitator, Murphy knew the importance of seating arrangements. Using his wife's kitchen scissors, he cut out cardboard circles, tables for eight that underwent several critical revisions until harmony was assured. Placating the county supervisors and building their pride in LACMA was a time consuming but essential part of Murphy's service to the museum.

The evening of the exhibition preview was hailed by society columnist Jody Jacobs as one of the most important civic occasions of the year. Those in attendance, Jacobs noted, represented the "super strata of the big fund raisers (like past presidents Edward Carter and Sidney Brody) the big donors (like Anna Bing Arnold, the Hammers, members of the Ahmanson family, Joan Palevsky) and the big art collectors (like Norton Simon, the Walter Annenbergs, the Frederick Weismans, the Hal Wallises, [and] the Julian Ganzes)." Hannah Carter, known for her taste in fashion, provided a "touch of sentimentality," wearing the same dress that Balenciaga had designed for her to wear at the museum's opening ten years earlier.[27]

Murphy had labored to cover all the bases. He felt the exhibition demonstrated a tremendous accomplishment. But his euphoria abruptly crashed when he read an account of the museum's anniversary bash in *Newsweek*. Again the museum's past troubles were recounted and its architecture derided as an ugly, concrete neo-Fascist bunker. "Within one year [of its opening]," Sunde Smith of *Newsweek* wrote, "Director Rick Brown had resigned, fed up with trustees who had already countermanded his choice of an architect and insisted on naming wings and even entire buildings after themselves. Before long, the grand plan for building a first rate collection of old masterpieces floundered as art-market prices rose astronomically. It is no wonder that LACMA's friends are grateful to see the museum still alive." Smith offered little hope of success for the museum: "This *enfant terrible* of museums seems unlikely to discard its stormy past—or its internal problems overnight. Norton Simon has gone, the rich and powerful still thrive, wrangle and dominate the museum." One quotation attributed to veteran art dealer Paul Kantor claimed that Donahue had "no interest in art, organizes nothing, does nothing." The feminist artist Judy Chicago charged that "the museum is out of touch with the community."[28]

When he read the feature, Murphy flew into a rage and swore to Philippa Calnan, the museum's public relations director, that he would never permit himself to be interviewed by Smith or any member of the *Newsweek* staff again. Murphy was furious over the slur against Donahue, a recognized scholar of Baroque art, who had dedicated himself to the museum through difficult years.[29] "It becomes a little discouraging to trustees like myself who have worked without compensation tirelessly over a period of ten years to help build a museum of real quality," Murphy said in a letter to Calnan. "I suspect that the museum with its collections and its programs will continue to grow in visibility and service, while Sunde Smith . . . [will] slip into well-deserved oblivion."[30]

The stinging *Newsweek* critique was momentarily forgotten when six hundred invited guests attended the opening reception for the new Cantor Sculpture Garden. The garden was a special source of pride for Murphy and District Supervisor Edmund Edelman, who were seen strolling about the grounds, smiling like "fathers of newborn infants." Camila Snyder, arts reporter for the *Herald Examiner,* told readers that the new landscaped garden was "almost as monumental as the 27 sculptures set like jewels among the 47,000 square foot crown of land."[31] The garden functioned as B. Gerald Cantor had wanted, allowing each work to be viewed from many angles. Works by Calder, Maillol, and Moore dotted the grounds at every turn of the decorative paths.

· · · · ·

The pursuit of Armand Hammer's collection continued. But in the midst of Hammer's pledges and promises to LACMA, none of which had come to pass, Hammer found himself indicted in November 1975 for making $54,000 in illegal campaign contributions to the reelection campaign of President Richard Nixon and faced a possible term of three years in federal prison if convicted. Hammer turned to Murphy for help.

Murphy reluctantly wrote on Hammer's behalf seeking leniency. The text of this letter has been lost. However, the letter written by Hammer expressing his enormous gratitude to Murphy has survived: "Thank you for your heartwarming letter of Sept. 22 to Judge Jones. If anything can move the judge, your letter will do it! Needless to say, I am grateful to you beyond words."[32]

Hammer's lawyers argued that the oilman was too weak to travel and that the stress of the impending trial might kill him. The case was transferred to Los Angeles after Hammer was hospitalized with a "debilitating heart condition." When he finally appeared in federal court, Hammer was pushed to the defense table in a wheelchair. One lawyer described him as a sick old man who could not be expected to know what others in the company were doing. Hammer blamed Tim Babcock, a former Montana governor and a former Occidental Petroleum Corporation subsidiary official, for passing the money to the Nixon campaign. Owing largely to advanced age and poor health, the seventy-seven-year-old board chairman was eventually fined $3,000 and placed on probation. Babcock, who had previously pleaded guilty to making the illegal payments for Hammer, was sentenced to four months in prison.

Hammer was "blessed by a miraculous recovery" as soon as the trial ended. In May 1976 he officiated at Occidental's annual meeting and, according to the *Los Angeles Times,* "displayed his characteristic forceful personality," parrying with hecklers and dismissing his crimes as insignificant.[33] Later in the year he flew to Moscow, scene of his first business triumphs, to attend to the details of his traveling art exhibitions.

THE CHALLENGE FOR A NEW DIRECTOR

Kenneth Donahue, who had served as LACMA's director since 1966, planned to retire on his sixty-fifth birthday, but poor health forced him to unexpectedly announce his resignation in 1979. The museum began a prolonged search for a new director, which ended in January 1980 when the trustees appointed Earl Alexander Powell III. Murphy had urged the board to consider Powell, whose work as executive curator at the National Gallery of Art proved he had the energy, forcefulness, and personality needed at the troubled museum. The trustees had reviewed dozens of candidates for the position, and after Fred Cummings, director of the Detroit Institute of Arts, declined the position, Powell was selected.[34]

Murphy was elated with the appointment. Though Powell had not been the trustees' first choice, Murphy saw his appointment as an important step toward shaping the museum for the future, perfecting its collections, and securing once and for all the promised works from Armand Hammer. "I hope you are as pleased as I am with Rusty Powell," Murphy wrote Hammer shortly after the announcement. "We were extremely lucky to get him and I think he will develop into one of the best museum directors in the country."[35]

Unlike his predecessor, who resisted the meetings and ceremonial functions that threatened to consume the director's time, Powell was from the ranks of new-style museum directors who increasingly served as public figure and fund-raiser. Enthusiastic, capable, well trained, and self-confident, Powell epitomized the blend of scholar and social powerhouse that meshed with Murphy's game plan to build a museum of distinction. "A museum director is no longer a Procrustean object in a dusty room," Powell told the *Los Angeles Times*. "Today a museum director has to be a first class diplomat, administrator, manager, PR man and sociologist."[36]

Powell had earned his Ph.D. at Harvard's prestigious Fogg Art Museum, a traditional training ground for America's top museum officials, where he specialized in European and American art of the nineteenth and twentieth centuries. At the National Gallery Powell had managed sections of the professional staff and successfully served as curator in charge of many of the big international shows that had helped to reshape the public's perception of the museum. He had an engaging personality and upbeat style that were unusual in the rarefied world of fine art. "The National Gallery was my baptism of fire," Powell recalled. "I arrived on the loading dock the same day as [the blockbuster exhibition] 'Treasures of Tutankhamen.'"[37]

Powell's ruddy complexion and blond-red hair qualified him for the nickname "Rusty." The brash new museum director with a dynamic personality may not have realized fully what awaited him in Los Angeles. According to the *Times* arts critic William Wilson, the directorship at LACMA was not universally regarded as a plum assignment. The new director faced fiscal handicaps and entrenched administrative problems. The museum took a terrible blow under Proposition 13, making funds for its physical plant more problematic than ever. It was no secret that the director's realm was restricted by the micromanagement of the board of trustees, who were, according to the art world grapevine, persistently "intrusive and tyrannical."[38]

When Powell was officially named to the directorship, the news exhilarated and alarmed the art community. At thirty-six he seemed too young for such a weighty job, and it was noted that he had never before directed a museum. But Powell's former boss and mentor, National Gallery Director J. Carter Brown, "took a schoolmaster's pride" in his appointment and declared Powell well qualified. "We are not so joyful at losing him," Brown said. "I recruited Rusty in Texas when I spotted that rare combination of scholarly excellence and administrative sense. I knew he was directorial material."[39]

The "Whiz Kid of Wilshire Boulevard," as *ARTnews* magazine dubbed Powell, arrived in Los Angeles at a pivotal moment in the city's cultural history. In 1980 when he took up his duties Los Angeles had begun a yearlong bicentennial celebration of its founding in 1781. Current movers and shakers seized the opportunity to show that Los Angeles had grown into one of the great cities of the world. Much of the change had taken place in the previous two decades. The downtown skyline that Murphy saw in 1960 was limited to 13 stories, except for the City Hall tower; now office buildings of 50 and 60 stories, glass-sheathed towers bearing the logos of banks and international corporations, defined the financial district. Los Angeles was indisputably an important part of the global economy serving the financial and trade needs of the Pacific Rim; the harbor at San Pedro was the leading port on the West Coast in cargo shipping, poised to exceed the Port of New York in a few years.

The cultural and intellectual life of the city had grown as well. Caught up in the celebration of achievement, Murphy could look to notable accomplishments that he had witnessed. The Music Center was drawing crowds to outstanding productions; the *Los Angeles Times* had become a newspaper of journalistic quality with a solid base of devoted readers; UCLA and other area colleges rode out the ferment of the 1960s and were broadened and enhanced as a result. The UCLA library that had meant so much to Murphy had suffered from tight budgets, but his cherished Aldines, the elegant Renaissance volumes, had grown into a substantial collection. If he had a disappointment it was that the county museum had not become the prestigious institution he and the trustees had envisioned. The many meetings and discussions among trustees came to the same conclusion: success of the museum depended on enticing collectors with significant works. Given the short supply of great paintings and the tremendous cost in the current art market, LACMA had no other way to build a collection of note.

It was apparent to everyone that LACMA was too small and cramped to house and do justice to the kind of collection they wanted to assemble. In the many discussions about increasing gallery space, the expansion of the Ahmanson Building seemed an obvious choice. Murphy thought that the threat from regulatory requirements that had enmeshed the Ahmanson Foundation for so long would soon be resolved, and the foundation would be in a position to fund an expansion. He felt it would be very much in keeping with what Howard Ahmanson would have wanted.

Murphy also believed that Armand Hammer, who felt the Hammer Wing was isolated in the museum complex, might well support an expansion in which additional galleries could connect the second-story Hammer

Wing to the Ahmanson Building. A major consideration in all the discussion about expansion was how to construct another building that would be a part of the existing complex. Ultimately, the most satisfactory solution seemed to be to give up the front lawn that sloped up from Wilshire Boulevard to the courtyard and locate a new building at the Wilshire Boulevard sidewalk. A new approach to the museum, a grand portal of some kind, could lead visitors up to a piazza from which they could enter the various galleries. The new courtyard would need to be an inviting, bustling place with display and refreshment stands that would add to the pleasure of a museum visit. To Murphy's mind, a perfect patron for such a public square would be the Times Mirror Foundation.

With the architectural wish list in hand, estimates were drawn and refined. It appeared the undertaking would be in the neighborhood of $20 million. A campaign to raise the funds was approved by the Museum Associates, and Carter set out to test the waters, to see what they could expect from large donors. Powell had arrived just in time: the expansion plan would be his immediate assignment and challenge.

· · · · ·

In addition to the expansion at the county museum, a huge redevelopment project in the downtown Bunker Hill district was under way to create another museum, scheduled to open in 1983: the 100,000-square-foot, $16 million Museum of Contemporary Art (MOCA), which was poised to become a first-class contemporary art institution. Pontus Hulten, retiring director of the Centre Georges Pompidou in Paris, had been named its first director.

The establishment of the new MOCA was initially a sore subject for Murphy. In an early meeting with Eli Broad (real estate developer and philanthropist) and Max Palevsky (art collector and founder of Scientific Data Systems [SDS]), Murphy told Broad that he would host a Times Mirror luncheon for the downtown business leadership so that Broad could explain the museum. However, days later Murphy did an about-face. He informed Broad that he could not help launch the new project because of his longtime involvement with LACMA, which was about to embark on an expansion and a campaign to build a significant endowment for acquisitions:

> For me to pursue vigorously the LACMA programs and simultaneously to appear to be involved in the program of the downtown museum could only be confusing to my friends in the downtown area.

Having said all of the above, I must at the same time state that I hope the downtown museum succeeds. Los Angeles is large enough and important enough as a center of artistic activity to have a museum dedicated primarily to living artists and their works. . . . Indeed, if asked, I will indicate that I think it is an excellent idea as I have, in fact, done to date. It is just that I cannot ride two horses at the same time and I hope you and Max Palevsky will understand.[40]

Despite his initial reluctance, in December 1980 Murphy was instrumental in securing a $250,000 grant from the Times Mirror Foundation for the endowment drive of the Museum of Contemporary Art. "We are happy to participate in this very important addition to downtown Los Angeles," he wrote Broad shortly after the foundation's unanimous vote.[41] But Murphy and other LACMA officials remained anxious about the impact MOCA would have on anticipated LACMA modern art installations in the future.

· · · · ·

Murphy proved correct in his assessment of Powell's potential. During his first year as director, Powell invigorated the institution with a new spirit, embroiled as it had been in policy disagreements between staff and trustees, personality clashes, and public criticism. "He lit a fire under all of us," remarked one museum staff member.

Within his first few months as director, Powell oversaw the installation of the exhibition *The Armand Hammer Collection: Five Centuries of Masterpieces,* which opened to widespread attention in spring 1980. Hammer's collection, which featured 109 paintings and drawings from the Renaissance to the early twentieth century, arrived at the county museum following a tour of thirty cities around the world. The proud industrialist unveiled for the press his new acquisitions as well as such old Hammer favorites as Rembrandt's *Juno.* It was Rembrandt's *Portrait of a Man Holding a Black Hat* (ca. 1637), recently purchased by Hammer for $2 million, that promised to be the star attraction. The swagger portrait portrayed Frederick Henry Prince of Orange-Nassau dressed in a gold-braided, lace-collared taffeta jacket.

On the evening of April 23 museum trustees, supporters, and critics previewed the collection and dined at elegantly decorated tables in the atrium of the Ahmanson Gallery. Guests at the event were on the edge of their seats as Hammer rose to speak, anticipating the drama of an unexpected announcement. The businessman–art collector beamed at the expectant crowd and made a few general remarks; then, in keeping with his reputation for the grand gesture, he told them that he intended to donate $1.5 million to expand the second floor of the museum's Hammer Wing and join it to the Ahmanson Building. Then, with a sly grin, Hammer declared that he was donating his *entire* collection of Honoré Daumier lithographs to the Los Angeles County Museum of Art.[42]

The crowd burst into applause, but longtime museum trustees were stunned. The real drama of the Daumier collection was fully known to the museum's board members, and they found Hammer's grand gesture a fraud. Five years earlier the collector George Longstreet had offered several thousand Daumier prints to the county museum for $250,000. The collection had been painstakingly amassed by Longstreet over the course of fifty years.[43] Hammer, who had been a trustee for seven years and knew the museum intended to buy the prints, nevertheless moved to obtain the lithographs for himself. The LACMA board was infuriated but feared that a confrontation over the Daumier prints might end the institution's hope of acquiring Hammer's full collection. Under the guidance of LACMA president Richard Sherwood, the trustees decided not to take action against Hammer, who wrote Sherwood that after purchasing the collection in his own name, he would donate it to the museum in five years "when there was a reasonable expectation that the collection will have doubled in value"— maximizing the possible tax benefits.[44] Sherwood then asked Hammer to confirm his commitment by executing a legally binding gift and inserting a codicil to his will granting the collection to the museum. Murphy and Ed Carter, who had joined Sherwood in extensive, agonized discussion of the issue, concurred with this approach. The museum would forgo the opportunity to purchase the Daumier lithographs in anticipation that Hammer would donate them to the museum. Hammer promised to sign a formal document on his return from Europe.

For the next several years the parties and their lawyers exchanged unpleasant communications concerning Hammer's delay in signing the agreement. By September 1977 Hammer had still not confirmed his pledge to turn the collection over to the museum. Though he did execute a codicil to his will bequeathing the collection to the county museum should he die before the five-year date, that commitment had no real legal effect until after his death, and museum trustees knew that the codicil could be modified at any time.

A year before LACMA's exhibition of Hammer's touring collection, the museum mounted a centennial display of Daumier's work. At a banquet to kick off that event, Hammer, in his usual style, had announced that he would give the Daumiers to the museum upon his death. "I was dismayed by Hammer's speech," a disturbed Richard Sherwood wrote at the time in a memo to museum trustees Murphy, Ed Carter, and Camilla Chandler Frost. Hammer had promised to hand over the prints in five years but was now talking about a donation upon his death. Moreover, Sherwood was uneasy about Hammer's promises about his full collection and his demand that the objects be shown as a unit. Sherwood urged the trustees to settle the issue of the Daumiers now rather than have the prints caught up in a unitary display condition.[45] He gave serious thought to suing Hammer for immediate transfer of the Daumier collection, but he knew the waltz of seduction to obtain the other Hammer masterpieces would have been brought to a fruitless halt.[46]

After Hammer made his 1980 pledge amid the fanfare of the festivities celebrating the opening of *The Armand Hammer Collection,* the museum tried to affirm and document Hammer's intentions. On May 27, the Museum Associates, the private-sector support arm of the museum, executed an agreement with Hammer stipulating that funds from the Hammer Foundation would be used for the purposes of enlarging and refurbishing the Hammer Wing, relocating the conservation laboratory, and connecting the wing to the Ahmanson Gallery. The document stated that on or before his death Hammer intended to bequeath the "Armand Hammer Daumier Collection" and certain works of art known as the "Armand Hammer Foundation Collection" to the county museum for public display on a permanent basis. According to the document, the Museum Associates would retain ownership of the collection.[47] The agreement also addressed conditions for display, stipulating that following the donation, 50 percent of the paintings of the Hammer Foundation Collection were to be kept "prominently, permanently and continuously displayed on the third floor of the Hammer Wing," with no other works of art "intermixed therewith." Each artwork was to bear an appropriate plaque identifying it as part of the Armand Hammer Collection or the Armand Hammer Daumier Collection, and "as part of that gift to the museum by the Hammer Foundation or Armand Hammer." In an additional accommodation to Hammer's wishes, it was agreed that at least once every four years the entire Armand Hammer Collection would be displayed for a continuous period "of not less than three consecutive months" and that every fourth year a materially larger portion of the Daumier collection was to be displayed. Following the tedious concessions and stipulations, painstakingly worked out, the museum trustees believed they finally had Hammer legally bound to honor his word.

· · · · ·

Murphy did manage to persuade Hammer to make another large gift to the public during this period—by establishing the Armand Hammer Center for Leonardo Studies and Research at UCLA. Hammer agreed to permit scholars at the center to have special access to his newly acquired—and renamed—Codex Hammer, the last notebook of Leonardo da Vinci remaining in private hands. Previously owned by the family of the earl of Leicester and known as the Codex Leicester, the scientific notebook had been written and illustrated by Leonardo da Vinci in approximately 1508. It consisted of diagrams and sketches of scientific phenomena and the artist's renowned mirror-image writings.

Bidding from a front-row seat at a London auction house, Hammer paid $5.2 million to buy the manuscript. Hammer considered the price a bargain; some experts had predicted a sale price as high as $25 million.[48] Murphy had been amazed when he learned of Hammer's purchase. "BRAVO! Your acquisition of the Da Vinci is an absolutely extraordinary coup. I think only you could have pulled it off," Murphy wrote. "And, of course, one day it will be one of the stunning possessions of the Los Angeles County Museum."[49]

With the Hammer purchase, Los Angeles possessed the only original Leonardo codex in the United States, and Murphy advanced his goal of making UCLA the world center of studies relating to Leonardo. The university already housed the Elmer Belt Library of Vinciana, and the University Research Library's Department of Special Collections owned the important collection of original editions produced by the Aldine Press of Venice. "Everything is in place for the creation of an international center on Leonardo da Vinci and his times," Murphy told Hammer. He suggested an amount of $400,000 for the endowment of a professorship in Renaissance studies. The income from an additional endowment of $600,000 would support visiting scholars from all over the world who would come to UCLA and work with the Hammer codex and the library collections. The endowment would also sponsor seminars and scholarly publications. "In short," Murphy wrote Hammer, "an endowment of $1 million, plus the unique library and manuscript resources and the international visibility of [distinguished Leonardo scholar] Professor Pedretti, would bring instantly to life an internationally known center of focused scholarly activity concerned with Leonardo and the Renaissance now and into the future."[50]

Murphy understood Hammer's thinking and his desire for international attention. It was a perfect pairing by Murphy of patron and patron's interest. Hammer made the commitment, and in March 1985 the UCLA chancellor, Charles E. Young, announced the $1 million gift to establish the Leonardo Center. In publicizing the gift, Hammer called the center a very special environment "where worthy scholars can study the work of perhaps the greatest mind of all times." "This new Center," he added, fairly crowing with delight, "will undoubtedly make UCLA the pre-eminent center for Leonardo studies in the United States and perhaps throughout the world."[51] It took Murphy nearly three years (1982–85) of cajoling and socializing with Hammer to obtain this commitment. The gift, under the auspices of the Armand Hammer Foundation, included not only the new center but also the Armand Hammer Chair in Leonardo studies.

THE COUNTY MUSEUM IN PERIL

The museum had suffered a 10 percent cut in funds from the county after the passage of Proposition 13 in 1978. The cut represented a $284,000 loss to the museum's annual operating budget. Museum officials feared additional adverse effects as county supervisors discussed the possibility of reducing the museum's staff and even closing the institution. The trustees met in frantic sessions to determine how best to safeguard the collections should the county fail to provide critical maintenance costs. By spring 1980 a new crisis loomed when county engineers reported that the facility's aging air-conditioning and humidification system would soon be beyond repair. The situation was dangerous. Tens of millions of dollars of paintings and sculpture housed in the museum required temperature and humidity control. Of special concern to the trustees was the long-range impact on the museum if Hammer officially withdrew his pledge of future gifts, claiming inadequate facilities would put his works at risk.

Murphy took it upon himself to convince the County Board of Supervisors of the museum's dire need. True grit in tough situations had earned Murphy his reputation as LACMA's most influential trustee; this time he relied on his longtime relationship with Supervisor Kenneth Hahn to thwart a disaster in the making. In July 1980 Murphy wrote Hahn a detailed letter reciting the millions of dollars private donors had contributed to provide the museum buildings and acquire art, relying on the county's agreement to provide maintenance and staff.

As a result of this great private effort and the remarkable support of the county, in which you have been a central figure, we have created something that not only reflects great international credit on the county of Los Angeles, but also provides education and happiness for all of our citizens young and old alike. All of this has been accomplished as a result of that remarkable contract between the museum trustees and the county of Los Angeles, in the making of which you played such a key role.

The contract of course provides that the trustees will find funds for the building and to expand the collection but that the county will provide for the basic upkeep and continuing maintenance and replacement.

It is impossible to go back to the already generous and open handed donors (Ahmanson and Hammer) and ask for an additional million dollars to replace an existing mechanical facility, and yet if and when this facility breaks down, irreparable harm could be done to the objects of art—and it could be a signal to Armand Hammer and others that their collections could be better taken care of elsewhere.

Accordingly, I am wondering, if you could personally look into this and come through once again on behalf of the museum. I frankly do not know where else to turn and I have always been able to count on you.[52]

· · · · ·

Camilla Chandler Frost, daughter of Dorothy and Norman Chandler, was appointed president of the museum board in 1978. At the installation dinner for the museum's first woman president, retiring board chairman Richard Sherwood said that he felt as if he were passing Frost a flaming baton. Frost undertook rescuing and restructuring the beleaguered museum, now faced with financial problems that included a decline in museum attendance, a shrinking endowment, the impact of Proposition 13, and uncertainty over fund-raising for expansion. The private sector had stepped in to fill the county-created gaps in the operating budget, but the museum had almost exhausted its reserves and needed a substantial restitution of public funds.

Frost had served as a museum trustee for many years and had worked on nearly every museum committee. She took the helm as president as the landmark $20 million expansion campaign got under way. Ed Carter served as chairman of the campaign, the first major campaign since the museum's founding, when Murphy had served as chairman. It seemed inconceivable that the funds could be raised, but $10 million was pledged almost immediately. The campaign proposed $5 million for the museum's endowment and $5 million earmarked for acquisitions. The Ahmanson Foundation pledged $4.5 million for expansion of the Ahmanson Building;

$2 million for the connecting link between the new Ahmanson addition and the existing upper-level Armand Hammer wing was solicited from the Hammer Foundation; and $3.5 million came as a gift from the Atlantic Richfield Company (ARCO) for the construction of a new building on the Wilshire Boulevard frontage (later named the Robert O. Anderson Gallery for Modern Art).

Carter and Murphy also obtained significant pledges from the Times Mirror Foundation and the Irvine Foundation. A number of individuals, including museum trustee Anna Bing Arnold, each pledged $250,000 or more, as did many of the city's major banks and corporations. In one letter of appeal to R. Stanton Avery, founder and chairman of Avery International of Pasadena, Murphy promised Avery that a gift of $250,000 would entitle the donor to dictate the name of a new gallery in the expanded Ahmanson Building. "Whether you wish to commit to this level or not, I do hope you will consider making a substantial pledge toward this project," Murphy wrote. "We will certainly never have another major incentive of this type for the museum during our lifetimes."[53]

After more than $20 million had been pledged and received, Murphy was asked how the seemingly impossible figure had been realized. "Well, so far," Murphy replied, "it's just been me and Ed Carter on the telephone."[54]

. . . . .

In June 1981, when LACMA's trustees learned to their great consternation that the county budget had been slashed again and that the conservation department might have to be eliminated, Murphy again sought help from Supervisor Hahn. In his appeal Murphy warned about the potential impact of its demise.

"This is a real body blow!" Murphy told Hahn. "It could lead to deaccreditation of the museum, which would be a terrible black mark on the community, and I can assure you that it would cause Armand Hammer and other potential donors to reexamine their commitment. Objects of art are in constant need of evaluation and conservation. It is the obligation of all of us to protect these priceless objects." Furthermore, he argued that eliminating the department would bring a screeching halt to visiting exhibitions like the enormously popular Tutankhamen. No major museum in the world was without a first-rate department of conservation. "It is unthinkable," Murphy continued, "that at this point in the history of our museum, wherein so many individuals, corporations and foundations have invested tens of millions of dollars, that this body blow would be delivered. In all of my years of involvement in the museum, I have 'rolled with the punches' when it came to budget time, but this proposal leaves me literally speechless. Its implications are horrendous."[55]

But the erosion in county support continued, and the prospects for the future seemed truly desperate. By every measure the private sector had met both the spirit and the letter of its contract with the county, providing at no cost to taxpayers three museum buildings and an increasingly distinguished art collection. In addition, the museum had achieved one of the largest paid memberships of any American art museum. Yet the county failed to meet its commitment for maintenance and other costs. Murphy refused to let donated funds so essential for the expansion plan and a new image for the museum be eroded by picking up the costs the county was supposed to cover.

Murphy and Powell met with Supervisor Edmund D. Edelman to seek some kind of compromise. Murphy found Edelman lukewarm to the museum in general. "I have shot all of my rhetorical cannons," Murphy wearily told the trustees. His concern was not only this year's budget but also the fact that the museum would have to deal with Edelman over the next several years. "I would not trust him to do anything without continuing and significant pressure," Murphy warned.[56] Murphy articulated the frustration of the county museum in a letter to Supervisor Edelman in March 1982. The letter was an example of Murphy's masterful tailoring of an argument. He stressed not the cultural importance of the museum but its contribution to the economic life of the city. He had trouble, however, concealing his anger as he hinted broadly that some very big names in the city would never support Edelman again if county funding failed.

> We have created in Los Angeles County a world-class museum, one of several cultural facilities that have helped change the national and world image of this community, something that clearly assists in our economic development among other things. We have in prospect great collections that have been promised to us of a value of close to another $100 million and we are planning to showcase this and other cultural facilities to the whole world at the time of the Olympics in 1984. Yet this could come crashing down around us if the Board of Supervisors does not, or will not, stand up to their contractual obligation, at least in some reasonable fashion.
>
> As I told you at our meeting, we are seeking an *infinitesimal fraction* of the total county budget to deal with the image of this community around the world—as well as to provide creative and stimulating experiences for thousands of school children of all ethnic backgrounds in addition to more thousands of adults and young people.

If all of this collapses or if at best the Los Angeles County Museum of Art becomes a second-class provincial enterprise, it clearly will not be the fault of Edward Carter, Richard Sherwood, Howard Allen, Robert Anderson, Norman Barker, Eric Lidow, Camilla Chandler Frost, Anna Bing Arnold, Armand Hammer or Franklin Murphy, and many others, most of whom are your constituents and long time supporters. If this happens, I, for one, will work to make it clear to the public where the responsibility really lies, not with the trustees but with the board of supervisors.

I hope you will excuse me for speaking plainly but I have given more than 20 years of my life and my energies to this community in a variety of ways in an effort to make it a better place and to improve its image. I am too intellectually and emotionally involved in the cultural development of Southern California generally, and the Art Museum in particular, to face such a bleak prospect in a casual way. I know that my colleagues on the Board of the Art Museum who have devoted as much or more time, energy and money to the museum feel just as strongly.[57]

In a memo to the museum trustees, Murphy declared that he would support a high-visibility lawsuit with lots of publicity to explain how year after year, even before passage of Proposition 13, the supervisors had reneged on their contract.[58]

. . . . .

The private sector funds were preserved for the expansion program. The Ahmanson and Hammer projects were completed together, with the ARCO-funded building to come later. In March 1983 Frances and Armand Hammer and Rusty Powell gripped the handle of a pair of oversized scissors and cut the ceremonial ribbon to celebrate completion of the Hammer Bridge, consisting of three galleries housing the Hammer collection of old masters, impressionist paintings, and drawings. Smiling broadly for the cameras, Hammer proudly announced, "It's the happiest day of my life." "It feels wonderful," he said. "And I'm so happy my collection has found a permanent home." The newly appointed president of the county museum's board of trustees, Julian Ganz Jr., expressed appreciation to Carter and Murphy, who had launched the successful campaign.[59]

During its first opening week, William Wilson confirmed the renovation's success by calling it a virtually new museum. "The new LACMA is revivalist-traditional in spades. Visitors are going to feel as they do in great old-line museums from the Met to the Louvre, progressing at a stately pace from one imposing space to the next, never worried about getting lost because if you just enjoy the art, following your nose and sense of history, eventually you'll come out where you started." Wilson praised the skylights, the new quartz lighting, and the seamless blending of the old and new galleries. "But for anybody who's been visiting the museum since we were all kids in Exposition Park," Wilson continued, "the real revelation is the reappearance of half-forgotten old friends or objects so long in storage they were virtually unknown."[60]

As the week of events celebrating the "new LACMA" came to an end, Murphy expressed his heartfelt thanks to the museum's able director: "Now that the Ahmanson and the Hammer expansions have been opened, I am moved to write to tell you how enormously pleased I am with the result and how deeply grateful I am to you and your colleagues at the museum for having pulled this off with such skill and such taste. You are now the manager of what all must recognize as a truly world-class museum—and we still have wonderful things ahead of us."[61] Powell's abilities would soon be put to the test again, but he had a brief respite to enjoy praise and celebration.

Construction of the new Robert O. Anderson Gallery, which was intended to provide a badly needed physical focus for contemporary art and pull the meandering museum into a "coherent architectural whole," was not due to start for some months. The new structure was to hug the sidewalk for 300 feet along Wilshire Boulevard and feature a ceremonial portal and grand staircase leading to the museum's courtyard. It was to house 90,000 square feet of additional gallery space on three levels, all devoted to twentieth-century art.

LOS ANGELES IN "ART HEAVEN"

Some three years later, in winter 1986 world attention focused on Los Angeles, as the city celebrated the debut of two new monumental art venues. On November 23 LACMA opened the new Robert O. Anderson Building for modern and contemporary art. One week later festivities marked the completion of the $22 million Museum of Contemporary Art in Bunker Hill's California Plaza Development. The proliferation of gallery space for twentieth-century art in Los Angeles was accompanied by a media blitz with press conferences, tours, and parties. In its cover story "Artful L.A.," the *New York Times Magazine* announced that the city was on the verge of "attaining world-class status." The *Chicago Sun Times* acknowledged that "the City of the Angels, never one to hide its halo, has taken off into art heaven where [new] museums sprout like palm trees."[62]

Nine hundred VIPs including museum dignitaries, art collectors, donors, and artists braved a rare Los Angeles rainstorm to attend the opening party at LACMA's Anderson Building. Throughout the evening umbrella-carrying guests arrived to tour the four-story, 155,000-square-foot structure and preview the contemporary art exhibition that included David Hockney's *Mulholland Drive,* Andy Warhol's *Kellogg's Corn Flakes Boxes,* and Claes Oldenberg's *Giant Pool Balls.*

The Robert O. Anderson Building (named for the chairman of the executive committee of ARCO) and the adjacent Times Mirror Central Court had cost a total of $35.5 million. But not everyone was pleased with the result. A blistering critique of the Anderson Building, the work of principal architect Norman Pfeiffer of Hardy Holzman Pfeiffer and Associates, ran in the *New York Times* just in time for the public dedication. Ironically, it brought people out in the rain to see what all the fuss was about. LACMA director Powell reacted with restraint. "The fact that it is controversial makes it an exciting building," he told reporters.[63]

The architecture of the two new art venues challenged the descriptive powers of the local press. The Tokyo architect Arata Isozaki's MOCA and the county museum's Anderson Building shared, according to one optimistic commentator, an aura of subtly stylish postmodernist exoticism. "It is impossible to escape the feeling that the two sets of out-of-town architects have indulged in little wry architectural winks at the Southland's stereotype as a lush oasis of stylish hedonism," wrote the *Los Angeles Times* art critic William Wilson. The Anderson Building featured a massive facade of stone, tile, and horizontal glass blocks with a vaulted entrance leading to the newly completed Times Mirror Central Court. "Some wag will surely dub it 'Deco-Babylonian,'" Wilson said. In contrast, he said, "MOCA is a graceful chimera of glass pyramids, massive stone, a barrel vault on stilts and rather hip-looking green panels. Some irreverent upstart is bound to call it 'Egypto-Romanesque-Hot-Rod.' . . . Yet the buildings may well turn out to be architectural masterpieces that serve art."[64]

Powell was disheartened by continuing barbs about the imperial design of the Anderson Building, which was intended to give the museum a unified façade and a gracious entry. Despite the uproar Murphy believed the remodeled and enlarged museum was a triumph and would not have been possible without Powell's imagination, dedication, and determination. "From the day you arrived in Los Angeles," he wrote Powell, "you have brought a breath of fresh air not only to the Museum but to this community as well." He credited Powell with LACMA's growing visibility in international art circles and thanked him for his efforts in that regard.[65] Snipes at the Anderson Building notwithstanding, museum mania had infected

Los Angeles. In addition to the Anderson Building and MOCA, the city witnessed the completion of the Afro-American Museum of Cultural History in Exposition Park, the renovation of the Southwest Museum near the Arroyo Seco, and the opening of the new American Gallery at the Huntington Library in San Marino.

Since the mid-1960s almost a dozen new art museums or special exhibition galleries had been built or renovated, infusing new life into Los Angeles's often-noted cultural void.[66] If all that were not enough, the Getty Museum, housed in a replica of a Roman villa at Malibu, was fast acquiring a fine collection of its own after receiving a billion-dollar bequest from J. Paul Getty. Murphy would later be deeply involved in the planning of the new museum and cultural center that resulted from the bequest.

· · · · ·

Murphy was called to combat a brewing scandal at LACMA in November 1987, when a well-meaning financial gesture by museum officials for the benefit of its director erupted into an embarrassing investigation headlined for several weeks by local reporters.[67] The California state attorney general's office announced that it was reviewing a $972,135 low-interest loan made by the Museum Associates to Rusty Powell. Immediately, a front-page headline appeared in the Sunday *Daily News:*

MUSEUM HEAD'S LOAN PROBED
Director Powell Gets $972,135 from Art Charity to Buy Home

The handsome home in question was located at 355 June Street in Hancock Park near the Wilshire Boulevard museum, on one of the neighborhood's most beautiful and expensive blocks.

Deputy Attorney General James Schwartz told reporters at both the *Los Angeles Times* and the *Daily News* that an audit of the museum had begun after a computer program designed to detect suspicious cases "caught the Powell loan." Schwartz said that the state was attempting to determine if the low-interest loan should be considered part of Powell's gross income and, if so whether the director's compensation was excessive, in violation of state law. Supervisor Edelman added to the fracas when he commented that he viewed the loan as a supplement to Powell's pay and a decision within the purview of the museum trustees. His comments triggered more scrutiny, this time by the IRS as to exactly what the young museum director had listed as gross income. In addition to a total salary of $149,297 in county and charitable funds, Powell received reimbursement of $79,786 in expense money for 1986 according to federal records. "He's worth more than that," Daniel Belin, president of the museum trustees, told *Daily News* staff writer Beth Barrett.[68]

Naturally, Murphy was disturbed by the brouhaha. Though none of the funds in question were derived from public sources, it became apparent to Murphy that it was the *appearance* of impropriety that the board of trustees needed to overcome. After a few well-placed telephone calls, he determined that the key issue of the loan's legitimacy hinged on whether the residence was necessary to secure the director's continued employment. If that were established, such a mortgage loan to the museum's director was legally permissible. It was true that a survey of one hundred fifty museums had indicated that only a handful of directors received housing allowances, and none reported receiving home loans.

Yet the case for the loan was strengthened by the fact that Powell had used the residence extensively for more than two dozen important fund-raisers, which produced far more money than the cost of the loan. During this time more than $200 million of art had been acquired, the museum's gallery space had doubled, and many important facilities had been added. The museum now had more than eighty thousand members, the largest resident membership of any art museum in the United States. The previous year attendance exceeded one million.

Belin and Murphy incorporated these impressive statistics into the response they drafted. Their statement served not only as a legal analysis but also as a briefing for the media on Powell's accomplishments and his value to the museum. In the final statement the trustees indicated that there was nothing unusual or inappropriate in a nonprofit organization's furnishing its director with a residence to be used for institutional promotional purposes. Furthermore, when the home was purchased in 1984, the trustees were well aware that in Powell the museum had one of the most promising museum directors in the country and that a number of major museums were actively seeking directors. The trustees of the county museum, Belin argued, deemed the loan necessary to secure the officer's continued service. Murphy, at the time board chairman acting on behalf of the trustees, assured the public that Powell's compensation was in the midrange of compensation to directors of major museums in the United States.[69] The legal footwork served its purpose, and the purported scandal soon died.

Franklin Murphy had been enticed to Los Angeles by the city's promise of cultural growth and its apparent readiness and eagerness for a cultural explosion; he had perceived vitality, creativity, and willingness—all ingredients for a sophisticated, world-class cultural environment. By the end of the 1980s he was seeing much of what he had envisioned take shape. He took satisfaction in knowing that he had had much to do with making it happen. The museum, just a glint in Carter's eye when Murphy arrived in Los Angeles, was now a well-functioning facility growing in popularity with the public and in respect in the art world.

He continued to actively serve on the museum's Executive Committee as well as its Acquisitions and Exhibition Committee, but he did his best work outside any official role. He served as guardian and fierce watchdog over the museum's funding amid the continuous fiscal struggles with the county supervisors. Little escaped his attention, especially when it involved an important museum benefactor. When Murphy learned that Anna Bing Arnold, who had been exceedingly generous to the museum, was being neglected, he was moved to action. To that end he wrote museum president Richard Sherwood in February 1986:

> A few evenings ago, Judy and I took Anna Bing to a dinner. During the evening, I indicated that I was somewhat saddened not to see her at board meetings of the Art Museum. She asked me if I had not heard that she had resigned. I told her I was slightly confused about that issue. She then went on to say that her memory was failing and she found it somewhat uncomfortable to try to sit through a board meeting.
>
> I asked if she would object to our electing her an Honorary Life Trustee and explained that that meant no obligation to attend meetings but an opportunity to attend everything, including social and scholarly affairs at the museum. She was delighted at the prospect and said she would be honored.[70]

Murphy continued to shore up slips in the museum's patron outreach by helping Rusty Powell to draft a letter to Robert Ahmanson to counteract negative reports that had distressed trustees of the Ahmanson Foundation. Murphy recommended that Powell mention in his letter a compliment paid by Emmanuel de Margerie, French ambassador to the United States, about the museum's collection and, in particular, the Ahmanson gifts. As Murphy explained:

> [The ambassador's comments were the] kind of reaction that we get increasingly from very sophisticated and knowledgeable people from not only this country but all over the world.
>
> There is no way to really express the enormous gratitude that we have toward the Ahmanson Foundation. In turn, the trustees of the foundation can take great satisfaction in that the fruits of their generosity do not go unnoticed.[71]

Left to right: Robert Erburu, Otis Chandler, and Franklin Murphy in the atrium of the executive office building of the Times Mirror Company. The newspaper's climb to excellence peaked under the stewardship of publisher Otis Chandler. (Courtesy Franklin L. Murphy)

As chairman of the Times Mirror Company in 1968, Murphy was at the helm of a multinational publishing conglomerate during a historic period of social and political turmoil. (Courtesy Franklin L. Murphy)

Opposite top: Oil tycoon Armand Hammer, chairman of the Occidental Corporation, with Franklin Murphy. For nearly twenty years Murphy had sought to obtain Hammer's art collection for the Los Angeles County Museum of Art. In 1988 Hammer announced plans to build his own vanity museum, the Armand Hammer Museum of Art and Cultural Center. (Courtesy Special Collections, UCLA)

Opposite bottom: The unexpected pardon granted to Armand Hammer by President Nixon, striking the oil magnate's conviction for illegal election contributions, prompted Paul Conrad to draw one of his insightful cartoons. (Courtesy Paul Conrad)

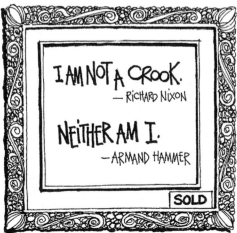

I AM NOT A CROOK.
— RICHARD NIXON

NEITHER AM I.
— ARMAND HAMMER

SOLD

Franklin Murphy had been chancellor at UCLA for one year when he traveled to Washington, D.C., in December 1961 for the Kress Foundation's long-planned celebration at the National Gallery of Art. *Life* magazine called it "the Great Kress Giveaway," the distribution of a fortune in European art amassed "from the nation's nickels and dimes." Here Murphy (at right) congratulates Lawrence Sickman of the William Rockhill Nelson Gallery (now the Nelson-Atkins Museum of Art) in Kansas City, Missouri. (National Gallery of Art photo; courtesy Franklin L. Murphy)

Opposite top, left to right: President John F. Kennedy, Franklin Murphy, and National Gallery Director John Walker. (National Gallery of Art photo; courtesy Franklin L. Murphy)

Opposite bottom: Paul Mellon, philanthropist, major benefactor, and trustee of the National Gallery of Art. Paul Mellon's father, the financier Andrew Mellon, had conceived the idea for a national gallery and funded its construction but did not live to see his dream brought to fruition by the dedicated and concerted effort of his son. (National Gallery of Art photo; courtesy The Ahmanson Foundation)

Franklin Murphy with First Lady Nancy Reagan in the receiving line at the National Gallery. (Courtesy The Ahmanson Foundation)

Opposite top: The National Gallery of Art, Washington, D.C. Franklin Murphy succeeded Paul Mellon as chairman of the National Gallery in 1985. (National Gallery of Art photo; courtesy The Ahmanson Foundation)

Opposite bottom: The talented J. Carter Brown served as director of the National Gallery of Art from 1969 to 1992. (National Gallery of Art photo; courtesy The Ahmanson Foundation)

Franklin Murphy escorting Diana, Princess of Wales, through the National Gallery on the evening of November 11, 1985. Photographs of the princess inspecting British treasures on display with Murphy as her guide appeared on society pages around the world. (National Gallery of Art photo; courtesy The Ahmanson Foundation)

Opposite top: J. Paul Getty as a young American industrialist and head of the Getty Oil Company. He bequeathed the bulk of his vast estate to the J. Paul Getty Museum. With this unexpected endowment, the small museum, operating at the time in a replica of a Roman villa in Malibu, became the richest museum in the world. (Research Library, The Getty Research Institute, Los Angeles)

Opposite bottom: Franklin Murphy played an early role in the conception of the Getty Center, created after the death of J. Paul Getty. Murphy did not live to see the public opening of the massive art complex, hailed as the new "Acropolis of Los Angeles." (Courtesy The Getty Center)

Franklin Murphy's farewell to the National Gallery on the evening of September 29, 1993. The year 1993 also marked the fortieth anniversary of Murphy's service to the Samuel H. Kress Foundation. (Courtesy The Ahmanson Foundation)

Left to right: Judy Murphy, Franklin Murphy, Michael Eisner, Jane Eisner, and Uri Herscher. The vision for what would one day become the Skirball Cultural Center was introduced to Los Angeles in 1985 by Uri Herscher. Franklin Murphy played a pivotal role in the founding of the institution. (Courtesy the Skirball Cultural Center)

A model depicting the fully realized Skirball Cultural Center, designed by renowned architect Moshe Safdie. Hailed by the *New York Times* as "a lesson on how to connect the eye to heart and mind," the Skirball Cultural Center, which opened to the public in April 1996, has established itself as one of the world's most dynamic Jewish cultural institutions and a prominent cultural venue in Los Angeles. (Courtesy the Skirball Cultural Center)

NINE

The National Gallery of Art

BY 1985 FRANKLIN MURPHY HAD SERVED for twenty-one years as a trustee of the National Gallery, the renowned institution founded by the financier Andrew Mellon. He had worked closely with Paul Mellon, who was determined to bring to fruition his father's dream: a national gallery that would be enthusiastically patronized and claimed by Americans as their own sanctuary for great works of art.[1] Murphy not only understood Andrew Mellon's concept for the Gallery, but he perceived the psychological underpinning that drew Paul to devote himself to his father's plan. "This Gallery is a reflection of the love of one man for his country and the love of another man for his father," he said.[2]

When Paul Mellon retired as chairman of the National Gallery, he was confident that Franklin Murphy, who was succeeding him, would continue the work of the Gallery. The evening Mellon invested Murphy with his duties was a stirring occasion. The elegant event and the prestigious guest list would have awed the most jaded socialite; for Murphy, the gathering affirmed that Americans of prominence were increasingly inclined to place value on the protection and promotion of art and culture. The United States had succeeded in creating an economic structure that promoted philanthropy and stewardship. Americans who had risen to success saw merit in preserving ties to European cultural roots and artistic traditions. Murphy's quest, dating from his efforts in Kansas, to bring the enrichment of art into the lives of all Americans had led him to this evening.

The invitation for the May 3, 1985, gala farewell to Paul Mellon read "White Tie and Decorations." The *Washington Post* reporter covering the event described the yellow sashes, red ribbons, and gleaming gold and silver medallions that glittered on the chests of giants of American business, politics, and philanthropy, "names as weighty and shimmering as medals—Mellon, Whitney, Annenberg, Bruce, Bass, Heinz, and Bush."[3] More than four hundred guests took part in the occasion, strolling through the galleries in evening gowns and swallowtail coats, enjoying the music and fresh flowers, visiting and chatting—a community of the powerful and important. Especially for the event and in acknowledgment of Mellon's interest in fine horses and horse racing, the curators had mounted an exhibition of paintings, some from Mellon's own collection, by the British painter George Stubbs.

"Paul's retirement ends one of the most remarkable episodes of American history," Murphy told the *Washington Post.* "There are good young collectors, yes, and there will be collectors who will make the effort, but there will never be another Paul Mellon. He is unique." Murphy noted another handicap the museum would face: "The times have changed. Money is more difficult to come by, and so is art." "It's the end of an era in the history of American philanthropy," the National Gallery's director, J. Carter Brown, acknowledged.[4]

Mellon, who would turn seventy-eight in June, first became a trustee in 1938. He resigned the following year for military service during World War II and was reelected to the board in 1945. He accepted the presidency of the National Gallery in 1963 and became chairman in 1979. During his term, Mellon had guided the Gallery's officers and the noted architect I. M. Pei through the difficult design period and the successful construction of the Gallery's East Building.

As the gala got under way, Vice President George H. W. Bush and Barbara Bush stood in the receiving line with Paul and Bunny Mellon, flanked by Chairman-elect Murphy and Director Brown, to greet notable guests, including Supreme Court Justices Warren Burger and Sandra Day O'Connor and Secretary of Defense Caspar Weinberger. In addition to ambassadors and members of Congress, celebrated American artists moved down the reception line. Murphy stood beside Barbara Bush, who was wearing a vibrant blue gown with her familiar pearls; Murphy was resplendent with a yellow sash fastened diagonally across his white shirtfront and a medal-adorned emerald green ribbon at his neck. The left side of his formal tailcoat displayed additional ribbons and decorations. Judy Murphy, standing near her husband, was attired in a floor-length black silk gown. Her figure had grown matronly, but she still had the beauty and erect bearing of the statuesque young woman who had married Franklin Murphy forty-three years earlier.

The banquet was held in the rotunda of the West Building, set up with tables decorated with tendrils of clematis vines winding through the branches of the candelabra centerpieces. During the candlelit evening, scores of waiters moved across the marble floors carrying huge silver platters of shad roe mousse and rack of lamb. For dessert, guests were served exotic fruits with orange raspberry sorbet smothered in white clouds of spun sugar.

President Reagan made an appearance by way of videotape projected on a large screen (he was without white tie or decorations, attired instead in a business suit). "The generosity of so many of you sitting in the rotunda tonight," he said, "is a glowing example of what the private sector in this land of ours can accomplish." Brown, dashing in his full-dress tailcoat, white tie, neck ribbon, and medal, then stood to share his thoughts about the billionaire philanthropist and the extraordinary experience it was to know him. "I came to realize," Brown told the gathering, "that this man's passionate devotion to beauty, to the poetry of the visual world, and to the humanities surpassed that of anyone I knew, of any professional in the business." Afterward Paul Mellon walked slowly to the microphone as a quiet hush filled the room. In his familiar soft voice he offered reminiscences of Andrew Mellon: "Thoughts of my father always bring me mixed emotions. He had a very contradictory nature. . . . It is not for me to praise his accomplishments or assess his failings. I do know that this country owes him its gratitude for his foresight and generosity in founding the gallery." Mellon expressed his satisfaction in seeing his father's vision of a national gallery become a reality and "to have been part of it as it evolved into what is now a great national asset, with a national constituency and programs harmonious with its national mission." He then told the assembled guests: "Nothing has given me greater pleasure than to be succeeded as Chairman of the Board by Franklin Murphy."[5]

Enthusiastic applause, amplified by the rotunda's dome, followed Mellon as he returned to his seat. John R. Stevenson, president of the Gallery, came to the podium to announce that the campaign to raise a permanent fund for acquisitions, the Patrons' Permanent Fund, had reached the ambitious goal of $50 million as a retirement tribute to Mellon.[6]

The evening drew to a close as guests lingered in the colonnaded portico savoring the experience they had shared. The sound of the Gallery's fountains filled the night air as chauffeurs brought the line of sleek dark limousines to the building's front steps. Franklin and Judy returned to their suite at the historic Willard Hotel. Their rooms were filled with flowers and congratulatory messages. The night confirmed Murphy's prominent status and the validity of his sense of achievement; he felt united with the talented and privileged leaders on whose shoulders rested responsibility for the cultural welfare of the nation.

JOINING FORCES WITH J. CARTER BROWN

As chairman of the National Gallery, Murphy's best asset was its director, J. Carter Brown. Born in 1934 into Rhode Island's leading family, Brown had been prepared from birth for a role of cultural importance. Roger Williams, who founded Rhode Island as a colony pledged to religious toleration, was an ancestor, and generations of successful merchants and traders had accepted civic and cultural duty as a matter of course. Brown University carried the family name.

Brown grew up in the cultured atmosphere of a home where old masters hung on the walls. Music and art were essential joys of his family, and their summer estate at Newport had been landscaped by Frederick Law Olmsted. When he left for Harvard, Brown took from home a Matisse drawing and a Cézanne watercolor to decorate his room. He graduated summa cum laude in 1956, took a master's degree at Harvard Business School, and plunged into the rarefied world of art connoisseurs as a Bernard Berenson protégé. With his career path in mind he obtained an MA from New York University's Institute of Fine Arts, renowned for curatorial training. Director John Walker brought him to the National Gallery in 1961.[7] On Walker's retirement in 1969, Brown was named to succeed him.

Brown, the Yankee aristocrat and aesthete—learned and thoroughly conversant with the protocol of the institution—brought a new exuberance and a fresh democratic approach to his duties as director. Colleagues found themselves surprised but not unappreciative when with elegant showmanship he took over in a burst of energy as a "kind of ringmaster."

The pairing of this spirited, youthful director with Murphy as chairman produced an exceptional period in the Gallery's history. They were responsible for garnering unprecedented private donations and public support for the Gallery. Even before assuming the chairmanship, Murphy had delivered

significant contributions from donors he had carefully cultivated, donations that left Brown impressed with Murphy's matchmaking and net-
working ability. In the early 1970s Murphy had been instrumental in obtaining grants of $100,000 per year from the Kress Foundation to fund the
Gallery's photo archive, eventually providing more than $1 million in sup-
port. Murphy had managed to induce Donald Hall of the Hallmark Foundation to pledge $500,000 to the Gallery's acquisition fund, an exception
to the Hall family's rule to give only in the Kansas region. Murphy had also
engineered a gift to the Patrons' Permanent Fund from the Ahmanson
Foundation, where he served as trustee, making the Los Angeles foundation part of the nationwide support sought for the National Gallery.

John Stevenson had responded to Paul Mellon's often-expressed anxiety
that rising prices would limit future acquisitions by proposing the Patrons'
Permanent Fund as an ongoing resource for purchases. Very much behind
the scenes Murphy had obtained a significant gift to the fund from Walter
Annenberg, the publisher and art collector whom Murphy had known for
many years. With Stevenson's fund-raising drive under way, Murphy
demonstrated his well-known ability with the telephone: a call from Murphy produced a $2 million pledge from Annenberg that speeded the
Gallery to its $50 million goal in time for Mellon's retirement celebration.
Murphy acknowledged Annenberg's pledge as "further evidence of your extraordinary commitment to improving the quality of life in this country."[8]
Annenberg in turn replied: "I think it only fitting that other citizens in our
country begin to recognize a responsibility to shoulder some of the financial burdens in the further development of this great institution."[9] The Annenberg donation was an example of the Murphy technique at work: the
gift came to the Gallery as a direct result of Murphy's skill at detecting un-
spoken desires. Because he knew the Annenberg family story he knew to
pitch his request to Annenberg as an opportunity to serve as a respected national patron.

· · · · ·

It took some time for Gallery officials and staff to adjust to the departure
of Paul Mellon. Each time Murphy faced a difficult decision as chairman,
he would take a deep breath and ask himself, "What would Paul Mellon
have done?" One year into his new role, Murphy wrote Stevenson, "It won't
be exactly the same without Paul but we have a wonderful instrument, and
I believe we know how to play it." "Paul, I think, really wants or would
want exactly the same thing we want," he added. "The highest quality of
everything."[10]

Murphy greatly admired Mellon. There were those at the National Gallery who said he would have liked to be Mellon, and, indeed, Mellon embodied traits that Murphy would have enjoyed finding in himself. Mellon had successfully arranged his life to accommodate dedication to social responsibility as well as freedom to indulge his personal appetites. His beautifully appointed homes, his stables and racehorses, his travels and his collecting, all were the pastimes of a vibrant, educated man of wide interests. He conducted his work with the Mellon Foundation and the National Gallery of Art with the temperate acceptance of a duty that came with his inheritance, a mind-set different from the exhausting zeal and sense of mission that had fueled Murphy from the time of his early aspirations in Kansas.

Asked by Tom Christie of *California* magazine to fantasize a perfect day with an honored guest from outside the state, Murphy offered a companionable outing with Paul Mellon. (In previous issues the magazine feature had described where the author Norman Cousins would take the *New Yorker* editor William Shawn and what the filmmaker Tony Bill would show the art critic Hilton Kramer.) Murphy wanted his ideal day with Mellon to begin at Santa Anita Racetrack, followed by visits to the Huntington and Clark Libraries. At the end of the day, on the way to the airport for Mellon's return flight, they would stop at UCLA, where Murphy could give him a tour of the Rodin, Maillol, and Calder works displayed at the Franklin Murphy Sculpture Garden. "All in all," Murphy wrote, "it would be a brief visit packed with horses, art and rare books as well as with gifted people of like interests."[11] Although Murphy had reached a level of prestige in which he worked and socialized with the wealthy elite, he was still the outsider; charismatic, talented, persuasive, and goal driven, he was welcomed, but he was also held at a subtle distance.

· · · · ·

In Murphy's opinion the National Gallery was America's finest example of the mix of public and private resources. It was a partnership between the federal government and the American people. Andrew Mellon had asked that the government provide only the land on which to build the museum and funds to operate and maintain it to serve the nation. Congress was not to appropriate funds for art. Mellon believed that the private sector would join him in donating works to the nation and its gallery. To this end he insisted that the museum not bear the Mellon name.

Andrew Mellon did not live to see the fulfillment of his vision, but in the decades after its dedication the National Gallery received important collections from such donors as Samuel H. Kress, the Widener family, Lessing

Rosenwald, and Chester Dale. These magnificent early gifts were followed by donations of artworks of great beauty from other private collections. Notable works also arrived from Paul Mellon and his sister, Ailsa Mellon Bruce, both of whom had inherited their father's fascination with art and had become astute collectors. From the inception of his father's plan, Paul had been involved with the creation of the gallery, though both he and his sister had been surprised by their father's revelation. The declaration of a full-blown resolution was typical of their uncommunicative father. Paul adjusted easily and saw the plan to completion after his father's health failed. Ailsa Mellon, however, was slower in warming to the idea of the National Gallery. Her affection finally grew through the ministrations not of her brother but of Gallery Director John Walker.

Ailsa had married David Bruce, a dashing young businessman and future diplomat, but the marriage between the outgoing, energetic Bruce and the reclusive, hypochondriacal Ailsa was not destined to endure. Andrew Mellon had thought well of David Bruce and had selected him to be one of the original trustees of the National Gallery. But after Mellon's death David asked Ailsa for a divorce. During the war years, the couple had been separated by David's duties in the intelligence service. He returned home from Europe deeply in love with a colleague serving with him abroad. The shattered, unhappy heiress then retreated even more into herself until the urbane Walker enticed her back into some degree of activity. She enjoyed his sophisticated, erudite company. Under his guidance and that of J. Carter Brown she took an interest in the Gallery and became involved with its needs.

· · · · ·

Several days after the memorable white-tie gala Brown wrote Murphy to say how enormously pleased he was that Murphy—from the West Coast, not the East—had agreed to assume the chairmanship of the board: "You and I have often talked about our mutual passion for making this national gallery *truly* national. On the symbolic level alone, your ascendancy does us a tremendous service. But beyond that, to have our top person to be one of such extraordinary gifts, and one with such an extraordinary record of service already to this institution, fills my heart with joy."[12]

Both Murphy and Brown were dedicated to making art accessible to a wide audience. To the head-shaking displeasure of staid connoisseurs, Brown mounted popular exhibitions, referred to as "blockbusters," that drew enthusiastic crowds, and this approach was soon adopted by museums across the country. Working together and ignoring the critics, Murphy and

Brown threw open the doors of art to an ever larger audience. Brown was far-ranging in selecting works for his big exhibits; he felt no need to confine the Gallery's space to old masters and familiar American works. He presented his blockbusters with promotional skill, enticing crowds to *The Treasures of Tutankhamen* (1976), *The Splendour of Dresden: Five Centuries of Art Collecting* (1978), *Rodin Rediscovered* (1981), *El Greco of Toledo* (1982), *The Art of Paul Gauguin* (1989), and *Titian: Prince of Painters* (1990). The shows were so popular that the *New York Times* noted that Brown, an aristocrat from birth, was a surprising champion of culture for mass consumption.

Brown also had poured his energy into working with Paul Mellon to complete the Gallery's new East Building, which opened in 1978. The I. M. Pei design was to become an architectural symbol of the era, an attraction in itself, drawing visitors from around the world to view the handsome angular structure with its imaginative use of glass and natural light. The addition of another building had been contemplated from the very beginning, when in the 1930s Andrew Mellon stipulated that the government preserve land contiguous to the museum for future growth. The new East Building was, in fact, another Mellon family gift to the nation as funds to build it came from Paul and Ailsa Mellon, and from their joint foundation, the Andrew W. Mellon Foundation.

Murphy heralded the East Building as "a classic example of that great American invention, the commingling of public and private funds to enhance the cultural life of our people."[13] He had been actively involved in museums whose funding was of three types: private, public, and a combination of public and private. In his view the latter was the ideal situation. "Cultural activities do require the financial involvement of the state," Murphy said. "On the other hand, we all know what happens to an over-involvement with the state in any enterprise: something called bureaucracy." For Murphy, this led to mediocrity and a lack of courage.[14]

In his contract with the U.S. Congress, Andrew Mellon had stipulated what he thought would be an effective governing board for the National Gallery. There would be nine trustees: five would be private citizens; four would be government officials, ex officio members of the board, namely, the secretary of the Smithsonian Institution, the chief justice of the United States, the secretary of state, and the secretary of the treasury. For the first four decades the chairmanship was held by a succession of five chief justices, but in 1979 Paul Mellon took over, followed by Murphy in 1985.[15]

In Murphy's view the board's makeup assured that the private sector would determine what the National Gallery of Art should be for the nation:

"There were five of us and four of them," he said, "so if push ever came to shove, the private sector would prevail, assuming the private sector had unanimity."[16] Trustee meetings generally proceeded smoothly as members were well versed in the duties of stewardship from their corporate and financial experience. Yet, as could be expected, by attracting powerful, successful people as trustees, the board brought together strong, forceful, and willful personalities as well.

THE VISIT OF PRINCESS DIANA

In the world of trusteeship Murphy was evolving into a virtuoso performer. Murphy, a Ford Motor Company board member, managed to coax Ford chairman Donald E. Peterson to come to the rescue of an unprecedented international exhibition, *The Treasure Houses of Great Britain—Five Hundred Years of Private Patronage and Art Collecting,* scheduled to open in 1985. An enormous undertaking, involving more than two hundred major private collections from Great Britain, the exhibition was to be mounted on the top two floors of the East Building with over seven hundred fine objects, including paintings, furniture, sculpture, textiles, silver, and porcelain. Brown traveled through the English countryside, once arriving by helicopter, visiting various country estates to cajole owners into lending works of art for the show. He knew exactly which objects he wanted and where to find them. Impressed by the beguiling, knowledgeable museum director, most collectors agreed to loan their treasures.

The exhibition, which was fully supported by the British government, was to display objects exceeding a quarter of a billion dollars in value.[17] Several U.S. sponsors, however, failed to deliver funds as promised. Murphy and Brown became worried. Adding to their concern, they were informed as the opening date neared that the Prince and Princess of Wales would be attending the gala dinner and exhibition preview. Also expected were such luminaries as Armand Hammer, Pamela Harriman, Henry Ford II, and the cellist Yo Yo Ma, as well as Chief Justice Warren E. Burger, Justices William H. Rehnquist, Harry A. Blackmun, and Byron R. White, and White House Chief of Staff Donald T. Regan. It was imperative that they find additional funding—fast.

Murphy's appeal to Peterson resulted in the Ford Motor Company's pledge of $1.5 million, the largest grant in its history. This was matched by a special vote of Congress appropriating $2 million after intensive lobbying by both Murphy and Brown. The exhibition was back on schedule.

"With the visit of Prince Charles and Princess Diana only days away," gushed one reporter in Washington, "the capital of the United States has gone gaga!"[18]

The evening the royals arrived at the National Gallery, November 11, 1985, was cool, but the chill in the air did not deter the crowds that flocked to the entrance to catch a glimpse of the Prince and Princess of Wales. The visit by the royals had garnered widespread interest from the media, especially as it was the first visit to the United States by Princess Diana. The *Daily Telegraph* reported that Washington had succumbed to an "orgy of monarchist hysteria." It was noted that at one point during a windy tour of the city Princess Diana grabbed her hat, catching it just before it was blown away. The video coverage of the quick-acting princess was played and replayed on American television, the English paper reported, "as if it were somehow miraculous."

Wearing formal attire, Murphy escorted the princess for a tour of the exhibition. The young princess, dressed in an off-the-shoulder, white-beaded gown by LaVetta, listened attentively as Murphy singled out works in the collection. Photographs of the tall, slender princess with her beaming smile and artfully coiffed hair gazing at the British objects alongside the Gallery's short, portly chairman, who was obviously charmed by Her Highness, appeared on the society pages of newspapers around the world. For Franklin and Judy, the evening was another high point in Franklin's career. Judy was dressed in a shimmering black-beaded gown—by coincidence, also designed by LaVetta. In the photographs Judy is an attractive, poised matron, smiling, bemused, as her husband guides the glamorous princess through the gallery.[19]

In his opening remarks Murphy welcomed not only the royals but also the chief justice, the secretary of state, members of the British parliament, and members of the U.S. Congress. He acknowledged the attendance of the two leaders of the Appropriations Committees—Senator James A. McClure of Idaho and Congressman Sidney Yates of Illinois—who had helped to ensure the commitment of federal support, and he made a point of mentioning the hefty Ford contribution that saved the day. "I hope I may be excused for taking special note this evening of the Ford Motor Company," Murphy told the invited guests. "I do so with some pride for, in addition to serving as a trustee of the National Gallery, I also serve the Ford Motor Company as Director. You should know that without a most handsome subvention from Ford, this exhibition could not have been mounted."[20] Murphy made the announcement with no feeling of conflict for having arranged the donation. His uprightness in such matters meant that in his eyes his future vote on the Ford board of directors would not be affected. As for the possibility of conflict, he lived in an era when less attention was given to apparent conflicts and trustees relied instead on individual integrity.

Murphy directed well-deserved praise for the exhibition to Brown. "As for the National Gallery," Murphy said, "the *sine qua non* to our involvement has been our imaginative and gifted director, Carter Brown. He and his talented staff have made what seemed to be an impossibility come to the wonderful reality which you have seen tonight."[21]

· · · · ·

Murphy's reputation for clear thinking in a storm was repeatedly tested in his performance on the various fractious boards on which he served. The relationship between a museum's board of trustees and the museum's director, he had learned, was invariably and inherently problematic—more problematic, it seemed, than a business board's relationship with a CEO. The director and the curatorial staff rightly considered themselves experts in their respective fields, but it often happened that trustees were collectors with their own opinions, in addition to persons of means. Indeed, a collector who owned extraordinary works was often appointed a trustee because the board hoped his or her collection would be bequeathed some day to the museum, as had been the case at the National Gallery with Samuel H. Kress and Chester Dale. Yet, despite the potential windfalls, museums often ran into difficulty with such collector-trustees.

"The danger here," Murphy pointed out, "is that the collector who is a businessman, who has a good eye, but who is not really trained and has had experts guide him in his collection, suddenly fancies himself 'the expert,' and he starts telling the curator, 'I don't think you should buy this; I don't think you should de-access that; I think you hung these in the wrong juxtaposition.' . . . In all the museums that I have been involved with, one thing that I have always fought for is that the final decision be with the professional." Although mistakes might be made, Murphy acknowledged, at least they would be made by experts, not by wealthy, opinionated autodidacts. At the same time, Murphy felt the board had every right to quiz the professionals. "The professional has got to understand that the board has a fiduciary responsibility. They are either representing the public, or they are representing the private donors."[22] Murphy was known for badgering museum administrators with detailed questions for which he wanted accurate and immediate answers, but nitpicking as his concerns might appear, he consistently relied on the judgment of the art professional in the end, a policy that gained him high marks with institution staff members.

He never hesitated to take a firm stance in controversial incidents; he did his homework, was confident about his facts, and suffered no anxiety about possible personal attacks. He lived his life with his own brand of integrity, and as a result he did not fear the threat of scandal. As one colleague observed, nearly every aspect of Murphy's public life could be printed on the front page of the *New York Times* without embarrassment. In all likelihood, the colleague had in view Murphy's fiscal probity and fair dealing rather than anything approaching picture-perfect family life or marital fidelity. A later era might have found more to criticize in Murphy's private life. Yet in his own day his reputation enabled him to step into a nasty fracas with no fear of retaliation, no business sins to atone for, and nothing otherwise to hide in his professional dealings. Personal peccadilloes and shortcomings were excused or rarely discussed in the sophisticated world of art connoisseurship, and such matters were of little interest to the political and cultural decision makers with whom he collaborated. Murphy had conducted himself with such consistency that he had little to fear from tale-telling enemies. The expense accounts he submitted were impeccably and appropriately prepared; and if his travel accommodated the womanizing that was rumored about him, it was not reflected on his reimbursement requests. Gossip about him might have made a difference had he aspired to elective office, but he had long since decided against that option.

COURTING COLLECTORS ARMAND HAMMER AND WALTER ANNENBERG

On October 10, 1986, after weeks of arguing with his lawyers, a reluctant Armand Hammer put pen to paper and formally bequeathed to the National Gallery of Art a collection of drawings that met the museum's high standards. Murphy and the trustees were relieved to have Hammer's signature on record and the artworks in hand. Hammer's gift to the National Gallery included drawings by Leonardo da Vinci, Michelangelo, and Raphael—the "triple crown," Brown called them. The gift also included works by Albrecht Dürer, Paolo Veronese, Rembrandt, Antoine Watteau, Giovanni Battista Tiepolo, François Boucher, and Jean-Honoré Fragonard in addition to Camille Pissarro, Edouard Manet, Edgar Degas, Paul Gauguin, and Paul Cézanne.[23] Moreover, Hammer gave the Gallery $1,101,681 for the purchase of Raphael's black-chalk drawing, *The Madonna and Child with Saint John the Baptist* (ca. 1507).[24] This full-scale cartoon study for *La Belle Jardinière,* the famous Raphael Madonna in the Louvre, was pricked with tiny holes for chalk transfer of the image to the wood panel for the painting. Such cartoons are extremely rare, and the National Gallery felt fortunate to have the Hammer funds to acquire it.

Hammer's superb collection of drawings had been enhanced by ten years of disciplined adherence to the advice of his consultant, the former Gallery director John Walker, as well as by the patience and recommendations of J. Carter Brown. Unlike his pledges to the Los Angeles County Museum of Art, his transfer to the National Gallery had been stipulated in writing. He wanted his name prominently displayed in some grand style, but Murphy and Brown promised only an "appropriate sign at eye level" designating the gallery space as the Armand Hammer Collection. Hammer was also promised a marble plaque in the foyer of the Seventh Street entrance to the Gallery that would express the appreciation of the institution to the Hammer Foundation. Finally, an appropriately sized plaque would be mounted beneath the Raphael ("in accordance with the customary practices of the National Gallery"), which would read "Purchased with Funds from the Armand Hammer Foundation." The eighty-eight-year-old Hammer had hoped for a greater tribute, but National Gallery policy did not permit naming sections of its buildings for its donor patrons, a condition that had been firmly established by Andrew Mellon and benefactors such as Samuel Kress and Joseph Widener. The well-established precedent made Hammer's demands moot and saved considerable argument, much to the relief of National Gallery trustees and curators.

Right up to the last, the courtship of Hammer proceeded one step forward, two steps back, but Murphy and Brown finally brought Hammer to the table and forced him to sign. After the commitment was duly memorialized in a legally binding contract, Brown wrote Murphy, "This is quite simply a fan letter. As a New Englander, I'm not given to such effusions. However, I did want you to know how enormously I admired and appreciated your performance as a Trustee over the last meetings."[25]

A small gallery in the West Building was designated for the Hammer collection. At the far end, a chapel-like alcove was created to display the Raphael cartoon. The *Washington Post* praised the setting and informed readers that the Hammer collection, "if placed on the market right now, might fetch as much as $40 million."[26] "Don't congratulate me," Hammer told one museum patron who complimented him on the magnificent drawings. "Congratulate Carter. Now they are his. They are no longer promised. The promise is fulfilled. They are in Washington to stay."[27]

• • • • •

In his ongoing courtship of the high-handed, exasperating art patron, Murphy found it necessary to attend numerous over-the-top social events put on by Hammer. Following Hammer's gift to the National Gallery, for instance, Murphy felt obligated to accept his invitation to attend his eighty-ninth birthday party at the Beverly Wilshire Hotel. Judy selected an appropriate gown and accompanied her husband, despite her disdain for Hammer's self-aggrandizing productions. Merv Griffin, serving as master of ceremonies, introduced the musical presentation of maestro Mstislav Rostropovich, who performed the *Andante* from Rachmaninoff's Cello Sonata, Opus 19. This was followed by a pas de deux from *Flower Festival in Genzano,* performed by Ludmila Lopukhova and Simon Dow of the San Francisco Ballet. Placido Domingo then sang the torch song "Besame Mucho," followed by a birthday salute delivered by Dinah Shore accompanied by the Coconut Grove Ballroom Orchestra under the baton of Mort Lindsey. For the finale, Dom Perignon was poured into hundreds of crystal flutes and huge slices of Hammer's ten-tier, white-frosted birthday cake were delivered to each table.

Behind the scenes, Murphy had worked for several years to secure for Hammer some kind of national recognition for his cultural philanthropy. Murphy's efforts came to fruition several months later when in June 1987 Hammer was awarded the Presidential National Medal of Arts. Recipients of the award were selected by the president based on nominations reviewed by the National Endowment for the Arts. The medal was intended to honor individuals who encouraged the arts in America and offered inspiration to others through distinguished achievement, support, or patronage. "Armand's generosity is really legendary," Murphy wrote Francis S. Hodsoll, chairman of the National Endowment, in support of Hammer's nomination. "He has, as you may recall, made major commitments to the National Gallery, to the Corcoran, to the Los Angeles County Museum, to UCLA— all of these relating to gifts of art and/or money—and a substantial contribution to the creation of a Center for Studies relating to Leonardo da Vinci. I do believe that he should receive serious consideration for the award."[28]

According to one knowledgeable source, there was considerable commotion when Hammer's name was submitted. The nomination was reportedly turned down and later revived only by a personal visit from the "noble doctor to the White House," as the insider confided.[29] (In addition to Hammer, other recipients of the award that year were Ella Fitzgerald, Isamu Noguchi, William Schuman, and Robert Penn Warren.)

· · · · ·

Murphy was the measured diplomat when it came to dealing with rich and powerful donors. His skill lay in determining the emotional triggers that moved them—not the same in all cases and not always readily apparent. Hammer's tremendous need for ego stroking was visible enough, but it was not in Murphy to stoop to sycophancy. Appropriate congratulations and carefully phrased compliments were enough. Though Murphy might jump to take their phone calls and abandon a family dinner for philanthropic purposes, Robert DeKruif remembered that Murphy never kowtowed to rich donors, never acted as a flatterer or a toady. "He loved to be in the company of the rich and powerful," DeKruif said, "and they loved to be around him, but he more than held his own."[30]

Murphy's position as chairman of the National Gallery while at the same time heading a major media enterprise was unique until one other publishing executive, a native New Yorker, was called to a comparable role. Arthur O. "Punch" Sulzberger, publisher of the venerable *New York Times,* was appointed chairman of the Metropolitan Museum of Art in 1987. Murphy wrote to congratulate him on his well-deserved appointment. Sulzberger and Murphy were now like two peas in a pod, happy rivals with lofty agendas, aware that they shared a sacred trust. "I love friendly competition," wrote Sulzberger, "and I look forward to stealing a great many ideas from the National Gallery and implementing them in New York."[31]

The art of Murphy's Washington trusteeship was severely tested in 1991, seven years into his service as chairman, when he was confronted with the highly sensitive problem of two members of the elite board who had fallen in love and married during their tenure as trustees. John Stevenson had been a senior partner in the powerful law firm of Sullivan and Cromwell and once served as a Mellon family attorney. He enjoyed a long and distinguished career, including service as assistant secretary of state.[32] Paul Mellon had asked Stevenson to join the board of trustees in 1975. He became Gallery president in 1978 and was a driving force behind the success of the Patrons' Permanent Fund. He began courting his trustee colleague Ruth Carter, daughter of the publisher and oilman Amon Carter.[33] She had been active in the American art world through her highly visible role at the Amon Carter Museum in Fort Worth. Since 1975 she had served as chair of the Gallery's Collectors Committee, which established an annual gifts program to enhance the Twentieth-Century Collection.[34] Then, starting in 1979, the talented and charismatic Carter served as a Gallery trustee.

When Stevenson and Carter married in 1983, they remained devoted to the Gallery and continued to make considerable contributions in time and effort. At first Mellon did not feel the issue of the marriage was adverse to the interests of the Gallery's board. At one point Mellon discussed the matter with Stevenson. Stevenson felt keenly that it would not be fair if either he or his wife were dropped from the prestigious museum board. But by spring 1991 Mellon had become deeply troubled about the union, which resulted in a large measure of the board's power belonging to one family. "Under the current circumstances," Mellon wrote Murphy, "Ruth should retire from the board."[35]

Based on his family's long history with the Gallery and his deep concern for its welfare, Mellon insisted that in the future no two immediate members of the same family should serve on the board at the same time, and no general trustee, regardless of the length of his service, should serve beyond the age of seventy-two. He added that he wished the board to make a one-time exception in the case of Murphy (then seventy-five) and Stevenson (then seventy). He asked that both men serve for three more years, regardless of age. Further, Mellon insisted that a member of the Mellon family be named to the board. "I am sure you recognize my interest and affection for the Gallery is related to the fact that the Gallery was founded by my father, and, as you know, my late sister, Ailsa, and I have tried to maintain and expand the ideal of my father's gift to the nation. I think it is not inappropriate, therefore, to make every reasonable effort to have an immediate member of the Mellon family serve on the board."[36]

Murphy was thrust into the center of the fracas, faced with the dilemma of removing a loyal member of the board and providing a trusteeship for a member of the Mellon family while at the same time protecting the best interests of the institution. It was the kind of crisis that tested Murphy's skill. It would take him several more years to fashion a fair solution that would maintain both the solidarity and the morale of the board.

· · · · ·

In his role as a trustee of both the Los Angeles County Museum of Art and the National Gallery, Murphy was obligated to put the best interests of these institutions first. This was true even when conflicts arose among competing museum directors, or when the interests of wealthy patrons collided with the needs of the institutions. Murphy encountered one such conflict with Walter Annenberg in 1976 after he announced his intention to install a $20 million communications center at New York's Metropolitan Museum of Art, where he served as trustee. The center was to use advanced techniques of modern communications—films, television, tapes, slides, reproductions, and other devices—to disseminate information about art in an effort to reach the widest possible audience.

The idea for the center had been sparked by the television series *Civilisation* hosted by the art historian Sir Kenneth Clark. Annenberg nourished the hope that Clark's award-winning survey of the world's artistic heritage could serve as a prototype for other efforts. However, the project brought instant criticism when it was learned that the center was to be headed by the "brilliant and arrogant" Thomas P. F. Hoving, who one week earlier had announced his retirement from his post as director of the Metropolitan.[37] Hoving had failed to inform the Metropolitan's board of trustees of his plan to join Annenberg in creating a division of the Annenberg School of Communications at the Metropolitan (branches already existed at the University of Pennsylvania and the University of Southern California).

The merger of a school of communications with the renowned museum could have far-reaching implications for the educational role of museums in the future. As one example of what the new center might do, Hoving cited the filming of art collections in museums throughout the world. He told the *New York Times* that he had already held preliminary discussions with the Louvre and the Russian Ministry of Culture about the possibility. Hoving mentioned plans for completing a film series on the ancient cities of Pompeii and Herculaneum or a film about the conservation of paintings.[38]

The entire project raised provocative questions in the art world. The potential "commercialism" that the center might bring to the esteemed Metropolitan was a touchy issue and brought the proposal under attack. Eugene V. Thaw, a noted international art dealer writing in the British weekly journal *The Spectator*, summed up the controversy: "Should anyone—in this case, Annenberg, a newspaper publisher with vast wealth, the close friend of Nixon—be permitted to 'buy' space in the Metropolitan? Will the manipulation of works of art in the variety of media techniques proposed bring the public closer to art or keep them further removed?"[39] To his astonishment, instead of receiving the gratitude of New Yorkers, Annenberg was attacked for his "self-serving gesture." Criticized as a defender of Richard Nixon and said to have been appointed ambassador to the United Kingdom (1969–75) only because of his great wealth, Annenberg felt assaulted. His proposal, in spite of the magnitude of the gift, was considered an "outrage." Barbara Goldsmith, writing in *New York* magazine, called the idea the "Watergate of the art world." In a column bearing the headline "Heir to a Soiled Fortune Buys a Museum's Soul," Pete Hamill claimed that the proposed fine arts center was a scam. "If Hoving has his way, the museum could change its name to Metropolitan-Goldwyn-Mayer," he wrote.[40] Reporters and commentators used the occasion to remind the public of the troubles of Walter's father, Morris Louis Annenberg, who had participated in the unsavory Chicago newspaper wars and purportedly earned most of his fortune wiring race results to bookmakers.[41] Morris Annenberg purchased the *Philadelphia Inquirer* in 1936, but he was convicted of tax evasion in 1940 and died soon after his release from prison. He pleaded guilty to avoid the ignominy of a trial and to prevent his son, who had also been indicted, from having to stand trial.

Murphy followed the controversy with interest; it was much discussed among trustees of the various institutions he served. Though Walter Annenberg had pledged $20 million to the Metropolitan for the new media center, it was still very much undecided which museum would win his staggering art collection, probably the finest collection of impressionist and postimpressionist paintings in private hands. As a rule, Annenberg and his wife, Lee, never lent the paintings for exhibition, and only fortunate guests at the Annenbergs' desert estate had the privilege of seeing the masterworks firsthand. Franklin and Judy Murphy had been invited on many occasions to Sunnylands, a 208-acre estate nestled in the desert east of Los Angeles in a semiprivate enclave known as Rancho Mirage. The 32,000-square-foot mansion, which Murphy declared "one of the most beautiful houses in the world," had every amenity that could be desired. But the real draw was the staggering collection. Museum curators with humor and truth called Annenberg's desert retreat "Art Camp." "Walter Annenberg doesn't have to be jealous of museums," observed Gerald van der Kemp, curator of the Monet Museum at Giverny.[42]

Murphy spent hours viewing such remarkable works at Sunnylands as van Gogh's *Roses,* which hung above the black marble fireplace. Edouard Vuillard's *The Album* was particularly cherished by Annenberg not only because of its rich colors but also because it pictured the seven Nathanson sisters; Annenberg had seven sisters himself. Among his other works were Berthe Morisot's *The Pink Dress,* Auguste Renoir's *The Children of Catulle Mendes,* Paul Cézanne's *Seated Peasant,* Paul Gauguin's *Three Tahitian Women,* and Henri de Toulouse-Lautrec's *Streetwalker.*

The hallways in Annenberg's home were filled with drawings from Cézanne's sketchbooks, a display that Murphy especially enjoyed. Like the gardens depicted on the Monet canvases, the lush Sunnylands oasis was brimming with blooming flowers along paths that wound around inviting streams and ponds. But the beauty of the landscape paled in comparison to the paintings inside. Murphy not only appreciated the art but also genuinely enjoyed the company of the lively publisher. Their conversations ranged from the history of the Roman Empire to the intriguing gossip of big business and high-end art. Murphy was pleased to be an amiable and entertaining guest, but as a trustee, he was always mindful of the hope that Annenberg's collection would someday find a permanent home at the National Gallery or perhaps the Los Angeles County Museum. Murphy acknowledged that it was a challenge to maintain a hearty friendship with a collector when the goal was acquiring his collection. Suspicion and mistrust were bound to result. It was a delicate matter, Murphy found, to befriend a great collector and value the prospect of a meaningful association while simultaneously working for the interests of institutions he served. After Annenberg was told by a mutual friend that Murphy had made disparaging remarks about him and about the proposed communications center at the Metropolitan, Murphy was quick to apologize and explain. He wrote Annenberg in November 1976:

> Yesterday evening at the opening of the New York City Opera a mutual friend of ours told me about a purported comment of mine which had been told to you and which had understandably irritated you. Apparently you had been told in connection with your recent gift of $20 million to the Metropolitan Museum that I had remarked that Tom Hoving had "conned" you into financing a building to [enable Hoving to] escape from John Pope-Hennessy. If that in fact were true and in proper context, I would not blame you for being irritated. I thought therefore that you might like to know the full extent of what was in fact said.

Murphy then explained that in the midst of conversations about Annenberg's much-discussed proposal, he predicted that there would be gossips in the museum world who would credit Hoving with having "conned" Annenberg. Murphy said his response in those conversations had been to say that he thought Annenberg's proposal was a "bold and imaginative initiative," one that he applauded. Murphy closed his letter by saying, "I cannot imagine any person who knows you and your extraordinary track record believes that you could be 'conned' by anybody for anything!"[43]

In the end the controversy connected with the proposed Annenberg communications center proved too much, and in March 1977 the benefactor rescinded his multimillion-dollar offer to the Metropolitan. Years later Annenberg was still disappointed, and somewhat bitter, about the episode. "I had a tremendous desire to make art available to people," he told William Wilson of the *Los Angeles Times,* "but the idea was attacked by the politicians. I withdrew the offer. Why put up with such abuse from political figures?"[44]

The misunderstanding with Murphy was forgotten, and Annenberg renewed his invitations to Sunnylands. There Murphy met prominent and celebrated individuals who were added to his widening circle of important associations. At one memorable weekend at the desert oasis, for example, Franklin and Judy joined the company of the publisher and collector Malcolm Forbes, the politician Clare Booth Luce, and the diplomat Walter J. Stoessel Jr.

When Murphy left behind some of his monogrammed shirts, Annenberg's butler had them washed, starched, and sent by messenger to Times Mirror Square the following day. Never one to skimp on gratitude, no matter how big or small the gesture, Murphy sent a letter of appreciation to Annenberg's butler for his thoughtfulness in dispatching the forgotten items.

TRUSTEESHIP AND SUCCESSORSHIP

Murphy candidly admitted that he was only able to sustain and realize his vision for the National Gallery through the day-to-day dedication of Carter Brown. Murphy recognized Brown as the public face of the Gallery who had created a global impact on the museum world. Once asked by an executive at Times Mirror how he could possibly manage the enormous enterprise along with his other duties, Murphy replied that the Gallery practically ran itself as long as Brown was in charge.[45] "Carter brought this museum into the twentieth century, in terms of programs, in terms of exhibitions, in terms of collecting," Murphy said. "Carter has a genius for public relations in the best sense of the word. The *best* sense of the word, not the flack sense. Promoting the Gallery, promoting the national character of the Gallery, influencing the Congress, utilizing the Gallery to influence the Congress, and in pushing—and he is a strong, strong advocate— the educational and outreach programs of the Gallery."[46]

At ease in the world of Washington, Brown had managed to increase federal funding to the National Gallery from $3.2 million to more than $50 million and in concert with Murphy had prompted congressional action to indemnify art on loan from abroad, saving museums around the country from prohibitive insurance costs. By mounting extravaganzas that had made art popular with the public, Brown had continually surprised art-world observers with his ability to put his elegant finger on exactly what was needed to bring art to a broader audience. In addition, he had astutely included opportunities for exclusivity for collectors and potential donors by offering glittering black-tie dinners and receptions. He honored the important and powerful at such events, but those receiving the greatest acknowledgment from him were visiting artists, among them Georgia O'Keeffe, Andrew Wyeth, Robert Rauschenberg, and Roy Lichtenstein. Brown was readily credited both for his erudition in art and for his instincts in judging artistic merit.[47]

In spring 1992 the National Gallery came to the end of its year-long fiftieth anniversary celebration and to the conclusion of the immensely popular show *Circa 1492: Art in the Age of Exploration.* This exhibition—one of the most ambitious, lavish, and well received of Brown's tenure—brought together more than six hundred paintings, sculptures, prints, drawings, maps, scientific instruments, and decorative arts from five continents. After seeing the Gallery through its anniversary year, Brown felt satisfied with his twenty-two years as director. Although he was only fifty-seven, he felt it was time for him to retire.

Brown made his announcement in January 1992. Brown's decision caught the tight-knit board of trustees by surprise. Murphy was told the news only one day before the public announcement. "We're in a quasi state of shock," Murphy told Carol Vogel of the *New York Times,* when asked for names of a possible replacement. "We've only known about this for 24 hours, so we haven't had time to think about a successor."[48]

"I only started thinking about retirement a month ago," Brown explained. "The time just seemed right." In his resignation letter Brown told the board he was leaving to devote more time to parenting and additional family responsibilities. For reasons of his own, Brown did not share additional information about his decision with Murphy. He was willing to stay on until his successor was installed, but he planned to depart no later than December 31.

Finding another director with the skills, panache, and charisma to take the National Gallery into the twenty-first century would be a difficult task.

The surprising announcement set off speculation in the art world as the names of prestigious museum officials were tossed about by an anxious board, keenly aware that an appointment was needed by year's end. Edmund Pillsbury, director of the Kimbell Art Museum in Fort Worth and founding director of the British Art Center at Yale University, was considered a leading candidate (he had recently declined an invitation to become director of the National Gallery in London). Among the others discussed for the position were James N. Wood, director of the Art Institute of Chicago; John Wilmerding, former deputy director at the National Gallery and a professor of American art at Princeton University; and Murphy protégé Earl "Rusty" Powell III, director of the Los Angeles County Museum of Art. John Walsh, the talented director of the J. Paul Getty Museum, was also considered. Because of his connections with the various institutions involved, Murphy recused himself from the official recruitment process. Once Walsh withdrew his name from the running, Powell seemed to many the obvious choice. Murphy resolved to let the process take its course, expecting that by spring his personal choice—Rusty Powell—would be the front-runner.

TEN

The Samuel H. Kress Foundation

IT WAS FRANKLIN MURPHY'S ROLE as a trustee for the Kress Foundation that had brought him to the attention of Paul Mellon and resulted in the invitation to join the National Gallery's board. Through his association with both institutions Murphy became a "living link" between the legacy of Samuel Kress, the Kress Foundation, and the National Gallery.

Indeed, Murphy's long career as a trustee for the arts had begun when, as chancellor of the University of Kansas, he forged relationships with two wealthy families, the Hall family of Kansas City and the Kress brothers of New York. His close ties to Joyce Hall, founder of the Hallmark greeting card company based in Kansas City, Missouri, brought not only financial contributions to the University of Kansas but also an invitation in 1951 for Murphy to join the company's board of directors. Hall became an adviser and counselor to Murphy, and the two men embarked on a lifelong friendship, despite their twenty-five-year difference in age.

Hall's story was an old-fashioned bootstrap account of success; he was a picture-postcard peddler who created a multimillion-dollar international greeting card enterprise. Through Hall, Murphy gained his first glimpse inside the world of big business; of even more significance, he observed Hall's unusual commitment to the cultural arts. The company's generous support of the Kansas City Symphony and the Nelson-Atkins Museum of Art offered a pattern for "enlightened capitalism" that Murphy believed could be copied by others.[1]

Murphy's close association with Joyce Hall prepared him for his future relationship with Samuel H. and Rush Kress. Murphy did not know it at the time, but the brothers would inaugurate for him his lifelong study of the family dynamics of wealthy donors and their heirs; the Kress Foundation was the training ground for his subsequent role as culture broker and as trustee of important regional and national institutions.

THE KRESS BROTHERS

Murphy first met Rush Kress after World War II when, as the young dean of the KU medical school, he went to New York City in search of funds to expand the university's medical center. "I learned by the grapevine," he said, "that the Kress Foundation was interested in supporting medical activities." Murphy knew very little about the foundation; in fact, at the time he did not realize that its primary support went to the arts.[2] Rush Kress was sufficiently impressed by Murphy to authorize a $150,000 grant—conditioned, however, on Murphy's ability to raise a matching amount from local sources. If Kress thought that the youthful dean of a minor midwestern college would be unable to solicit the balance in his hometown, he did not know Murphy. Murphy claimed he returned from his New York trip, explained the situation to Joyce Hall and other local businessmen, and obtained the matching funds in "twenty minutes over dinner."

In 1953, two years after he became chancellor at KU, Murphy was surprised by a telephone call from Rush Kress inviting him to join the foundation as a member of the board of trustees. "They wanted somebody on the board that knew something about medicine," Murphy said.[3]

Only after he joined the board did he learn the full story behind the Kress fortune and the dynamics of the Kress brothers' relationship. The elder brother, Samuel, had opened the first S. H. Kress and Company Five and Ten Cent store in Memphis, Tennessee, in 1896. Over the next two decades the chain steadily expanded, bringing Kress into the league of America's wealthiest tycoons. Especially intriguing to Murphy was the discovery that Samuel Kress indulged a passion for the Renaissance and had turned his Fifth Avenue apartment into an Italian palazzo where he sought to live in the style of a sixteenth-century merchant prince among the paintings, sculpture, and fine furnishings of that creative and imaginative era.[4] One art authority who visited the apartment, bemused by Kress's vision of himself, recalled that Kress displayed his Renaissance paintings in the odd manner of a retail merchant showing his wares.[5] With the help of Bernard Berenson ("B.B."), the renowned authority on Italian paintings based in Florence, Kress culled his collection and concentrated on acquiring only the finest Italian works.

Following his amazing commercial success, he established the Samuel H. Kress Foundation in 1929 "to promote the welfare and progress of the human race." Throughout the years of the Great Depression Kress distributed paintings from his collection to regional galleries in cities where Kress stores were located. The gifts affirmed his concept of himself as a paternalistic prince, returning the fruits of his fortune to the people "for their education and personal enrichment."[6] It was the European tradition that he sought to disseminate, wanting Americans to be steeped in the art and values of Western culture. He even gave each Kress store a distinctive architectural design, referencing a historical style, while serving a utilitarian and instructive purpose.

After a debilitating stroke in 1945 rendered him unable to speak, he depended on his brother, Rush H. Kress, fifteen years younger, to act on his behalf. Rush became president of the Kress Foundation and vice-chairman of the S. H. Kress and Company board (Samuel Kress continued to hold the title of chairman).[7] Murphy said that his work with Rush Kress called on all his diplomatic skill. "Rush was a strong-willed, difficult human being, I'll tell you," he confided years later.[8] John Walker, who was a curator at the National Gallery in those years, wrote in his memoirs that he came to understand why Rush was so demanding. "He wanted to make the Samuel H. Kress Collection an enduring monument to his brother and wanted his brother's collection to be the greatest in America."[9] It was a single-minded goal that would later threaten disaster for the Kress business and the foundation.

· · · · ·

Murphy's involvement with the Kress Foundation during the 1950s coincided with a shift in his own philosophy. The foundation brought him on as a physician and scientist, but his contribution as a trustee shifted to the foundation's cultural pursuits. In his personal philosophy at the time, he was becoming less enamored of the rationalist, scientific approach to the problems of humankind. During the cold war leading scientists debated the purpose of increasingly deadly nuclear weapons, and many thinking people questioned the results of a value-free science that had brought humanity to the point of universal destruction. (Later, in the 1960s, as chancellor of UCLA, Murphy would witness a different attack on science, not the complaint that science was value-free, but that it was not value-free—that it reflected the interests of governments, industrial sponsors, and the prescribed social order.)[10] As dean of the KU medical school, he urged young doctors to nurture the spiritual and aesthetic components of their lives. More and more, Murphy was making time in his own life for art, music, and books.

By the time Murphy joined the Kress board the Kress Collection had grown to distinction under the stewardship of director Guy Emerson. The collection included works by many of the greatest European artists: Giotto, Sandro Botticelli, Fra Angelico, Filippo Lippi, Raphael, Titian, Giovanni Battista Tiepolo, Franceso Guardi, and Canaletto. The best of these were destined for the National Gallery, for Kress had been the first to answer Mellon's call for men of means with great collections to supply the museum with art worthy of a national gallery. The Kress experts worked closely with the National Gallery's first director, David Finley, and John Walker to implement the Kress goal—"to create the most complete collection of Italian art existing in the world," and to have it ready for the grand opening of the museum.[11] In March 1941 when President Franklin D. Roosevelt dedicated the National Gallery of Art, accepting the magnificent building on behalf of the nation, the public stepped through the great bronze doors and found a breathtaking display of paintings from the Samuel H. Kress Collection.

In 1953 when Murphy joined the Kress Foundation board thousands of valuable objects still remained in the foundation's possession even after the official gift to the National Gallery. These constituted the later "Great Kress Giveaway," over which Murphy presided but which Samuel Kress did not live to see. He died at his home on September 22, 1955, surrounded by the art he loved. He was ninety-two. Rush had carried the heavy burden of running his bedridden brother's company and directing the foundation. "But the power he grasped so tenaciously he looked upon as an inherited duty," wrote Walker in recollection. "He was always, as he would have been the first to say, the surrogate of a ghost."[12]

· · · · ·

As the least experienced of the ten trustees when he joined the Kress Foundation board, Murphy had anticipated that the experience would afford him skills for stewardship in the nonprofit sector and entrée to higher echelons of corporate life that would benefit the University of Kansas. What Murphy had not anticipated was that he would cut his teeth as a young trustee during one of the fiercest battles in U.S. history involving a philanthropic foundation.

His nine fellow trustees were men with distinguished reputations in business and finance, including Frank M. Folsom, chairman of the executive committee of the Radio Corporation of America (RCA); Harold Helm, chairman of the Chemical Corn Exchange Bank; Paul L. Troast, former head of the New Jersey Turnpike Authority and president of the Mahony-Troast Construction Company; and G. Keith Funston, president of the New York Stock Exchange. This group of high-powered executives watched with grave concern as Rush Kress grew increasingly incapable of making critical decisions. Because he devoted most of his time after Samuel Kress's death to the foundation, he failed to give attention to the company's operations, which suffered a steady drop in sales and earnings.[13] Unlike its competitors, the Kress Company did not expand into the high-traffic suburban shopping centers but remained in downtown areas. In 1957 Kress fell to third in sales, behind F. W. Woolworth and S. S. Kresge and Company.[14]

The prospects of the five-and-dime empire determined the future of the Kress Foundation, which held roughly 40 percent of the outstanding stock in the company.[15] Many charitable foundations owned working control of large business enterprises, but in the notable instance of the Ford Foundation, the possibility of foundation control of the business entity had been vigilantly avoided when the Ford Motor Company went public. Investment adviser Sidney Weinberg, a partner in Goldman, Sachs and Company, had devised a solution that was widely admired in financial circles, for it was no easy task to satisfy the Ford Motor Company, the Ford family, the foundation trustees, and government regulatory agencies. It was to Weinberg that the Kress trustees turned for his view of their options. Weinberg, known as "Mr. Wall Street," had served five presidents and at one time sat on thirty-one boards.

Murphy's learning curve as a trustee accelerated as he watched Weinberg at work and found his own role in what was to be a seismic event in the philanthropic world. Murphy cultivated a close personal association with Weinberg and through him met other giants of American capitalism, including Henry Ford II. Kress, however, was infuriated that the trustees were consulting Weinberg; and on May 22, 1957, perhaps sensing what they had in mind, he shocked them all by asking for the resignation of Franklin Murphy, Keith Funston, and H. H. Helm. Funston and Helm refused to resign, but Murphy, still learning the corporate and institutional ropes, sent his resignation letter as requested. The other trustees, however, urged him to reconsider, as they needed to stand together to elect new members for the company board. As a result Murphy wrote Kress withdrawing his resignation.[16]

By February 1958 the Kress boardroom struggles had moved to the front pages. The *Wall Street Journal* reported on Valentine's Day that Kress, in a far from loving mood, had charged certain trustees of the foundation with plans to take unlawful control of the Kress Company. Murphy was among those accused.[17] By the end of the month the trustees countered by announcing they would try to win control of S. H. Kress and Company's 261-store chain in a proxy fight, which the *New York Herald Tribune* promised would set new precedents in the world of finance. The contest marked the first time since the Securities and Exchange Commission was formed that a foundation had acted to protect earnings by seizing control of the company that founded it.[18] "As far as I am concerned, right, both moral and legal, is on our side and I hope we stand firm," Murphy wrote his fellow trustees.[19] The *New York Times* predicted that the outcome of the Kress action would ultimately affect the status of six thousand other nonprofit foundations and trusts with some $7.5 billion in assets.[20]

March opened with the foundation trustees meeting in an emergency session that continued throughout that week. On March 7, after days of angry, fruitless debate with Rush Kress, the trustees were startled by an unexpected change of heart. Kress suddenly seemed softened and subdued. In an emotional statement to the trustees he surrendered control of the company. The men present in the room were deeply moved by the anguish of the confused and elderly Kress heir. "When I requested your resignation," Kress told them, "I was acting in good faith and on the basis of belief that you were working against my interests." Kress told them that he had "now learned beyond question" that he was entirely misled. Kress spoke of the esteem in which he held the trustees and reiterated his affection for them, calling them his closest and most loyal friends. "Many of you I have known for 20 years or more and all of you are on the Board at my personal invitation. I now realize that you have no possible motive for doing anything which would be against my interest or that of the foundation or the company."[21]

The stunned trustees, grateful for the sudden and complete reversal of Kress's position, set to work to restructure the company's board with experienced executives. Murphy had been more than a front-seat witness to a major corporate upheaval; he had been a participant in the revolution. He had acquired a rare education in the intricacies of business and the options available to a foundation to protect its endowment. The techniques he learned came into play later in his work with other foundations, notably his fifteen-year struggle to preserve the assets of the Ahmanson Foundation.

GIVEAWAYS AND PRESERVATION

After Kress's concession Murphy and the other trustees turned their attention to distributing the remaining art in the Kress Collection to regional galleries and museums. In December 1961, Murphy, now chancellor at UCLA and chairman of the foundation's executive committee, traveled to Washington, D.C., for the foundation's long-planned celebration of what *Life* magazine called "The Great Kress Giveaway"—the distribution of a fortune in European art amassed "from the nation's nickels and dimes" spent at the Kress variety stores. Murphy took immense pride in the project; and the ceremony at the National Gallery of Art, at which he officiated for the Kress Foundation, was a high point in his life. President John F. Kennedy and leading figures in the American arts were on hand to see more than three thousand works valued at over $100 million given to U.S. museums.[22] Dressed in black tie and tuxedo, a beaming Franklin Murphy greeted Chief Justice Earl Warren, the National Gallery's chairman. Photographs taken at the event show Murphy in his prime, grinning from ear to ear, shaking hands with President Kennedy, and stooping to embrace eighty-four-year-old Rush Kress, confined to his wheelchair.

As Murphy handed over the masterpieces, he described them as a "great and glowing treasure of man's reaction to his own history and own environment by way of brush and chisel." He announced that some twenty museums were to receive fine European paintings as part of the Kress Regional Galleries Program; additional gifts of Kress study collections went to colleges and universities. The Metropolitan Museum of Art received French porcelains, furniture, and Gobelin tapestries; rare illuminated manuscripts went to the Pierpont Morgan Library; the Philadelphia Museum of Art received tapestries designed by Rubens and Pietro da Cortona. By the end of the evening the Kress Collection had been dispersed to forty-five institutions in twenty-nine states, Puerto Rico, and the District of Columbia.[23] It was especially meaningful to Murphy that the works would become part of the cultural experience of communities across the country, enriching, in particular, cities and towns distant from the great cosmopolitan centers.

· · · · ·

Following the death of Rush Kress in 1963, Murphy was named president of the foundation.[24] He guided the New York–based institution in a change of direction: it would now focus on the conservation and restoration of works of art and architecture. In addition, he created a distinguished program for educational fellowships.

In his new role, Murphy was ably served by Mary Davis, who acted as assistant to the president and carried out the institution's day-to-day functions from the foundation's offices in New York. Davis, previously secretary to Guy Emerson, director of the Kress art collection, was a self-taught art expert, having gleaned much of her knowledge when she served as liaison between the foundation and the conservator, Mario Modestini.[25] Although devoted to the foundation and its work, the formidable Miss Davis, a spinster, could be tenacious and difficult. After a time Murphy offered Davis the chance to become executive vice president of the foundation, on condition that she obtain a master's degree in art history. "And by golly, she did!" Murphy said.[26] She served as the foundation's driving, although sometimes frictional, force under Murphy's watchful guidance for the next nineteen years.

By 1981, however, Murphy was confronted with the sad responsibility of easing Davis into mandatory retirement. Murphy anticipated the appointment of arts scholar Marilyn Perry as the institution's new executive vice president. Perry's background was ideal. A former Kress Fellow, she had earned an M.A. from the University of North Carolina at Chapel Hill and M. Phil. and D. Phil. degrees from the Warburg Institute at the University of London. During her years in Italy, she had received fellowships from the University of London, Harvard University (the Villa I Tatti), and the Gladys K. Delmas Foundation. She was a trained historian of Italian Renaissance art and a solid administrator.

But Davis's departure did not proceed smoothly. As the date neared, she became increasingly tearful and angry. "I am saddened, but not entirely surprised by Mary's behavior," Murphy told Perry. "As the retirement day comes inexorably closer, she clearly is going to have emotional problems and they will be reflected both in her relationship with you and with me. . . . I hate to be trite but the key word is patience."[27] Murphy insisted that Perry stay outside the fracas and let the brunt of the problem fall on his shoulders.

Two weeks before Christmas 1981 the foundation hosted a dinner in Davis's honor at the St. Regis Hotel. Following the tribute, Murphy wrote Davis, "Together we brought the Kress Foundation out of utter chaos and made it into a respectable entity. By your totally dedicated activity, the Foundation has become internationally known and indispensable to the health of art historical activities in the country and abroad."[28] But Davis responded in a torrent of rage in letters addressed to Murphy at his Times Mirror office. Murphy, who diagnosed her condition as "paranoid," was deeply saddened.[29] After weeks of turmoil Murphy was forced to ask Davis to leave the foundation and never return.

Several months later he saw to it that the Kress Foundation formally recognized Davis's work by way of a plaque on the Byzantine Palace in Tel Lachish, Israel, which had been excavated with funds provided by the foundation. The inscription chiseled on the plaque read:

THIS BYZANTINE PALACE WAS RESTORED THROUGH THE
GENEROSITY OF THE SAMUEL H. KRESS FOUNDATION
IN HONOR OF MARY M. DAVIS

Murphy frequently said that the mark of a good administrator is the ability to identify and recruit good people. On the other side of that coin is the fortitude required to fire people when they are not performing, no matter how fond you are of them personally. "Once having identified and recruited people of quality," Murphy explained, "the second job is to convince them to share your vision of whatever it is you want to do. That's critical, in that they'll work their tail off if they believe subconsciously that they participated in the decision. They'll work very hard then to make it come true." A system of "psychic rewards" was also important. There is, Murphy explained, "[the] reward and satisfaction of seeing a job well done, and the leader has got to be shrewd enough and self confident enough to share credit. Pour credit on. If it's 'we,'—I couldn't have done it without him, I couldn't have done it without her, why, then you've got loyalty. So you've got loyalty now, you've got people willing to go beyond the call of duty and you've chosen them well and they're motivated and rewarded and then you can just sit back and they'll do the work. They're the ones that make the hero of you."[30]

· · · · ·

Murphy considered Marilyn Perry a tremendous asset, and he was able to turn over to her the majority of the foundation's business. But his active involvement did not lessen even after Perry succeeded him as president in 1984 (he assumed the role of chairman). Together they forged many international projects: completing the small museum for cathedral treasures in Toledo, Spain; creating a conservation laboratory for the Soprintendenza of the Belle Arti in Venice, Italy; conducting excavations at Tel Lachish,

Israel; and depositing a photographic archive of drawings from the Biblioteca Ambrosiana in Milan at the University of Notre Dame. Murphy could not use enough superlatives to describe Perry's stewardship of the foundation.

As chairman, Murphy continued to further the foundation's goals through his personal network. Prominent leaders in the humanities with whom Murphy stayed in close touch received invitations to attend special sessions during the foundation's annual board meetings. In 1987 the foundation's reception included such cultural and educational heavyweights as Vartan Gregorian, director of the New York Public Library; John Sawyer, president of the Andrew W. Mellon Foundation; Franklin Thomas, president of the Ford Foundation; and John Brademas, president of New York University. These Murphy mixers linked the players who were the backbone of support for culture, art, and humanism, and they helped solidify Murphy's status as one of the nation's most respected brokers of culture.

In addition, Murphy funded compelling projects worldwide through the Kress Foundation European Preservation Program and the foundation's close alliance with the World Monuments Fund (WMF), founded by the dynamic Colonel James A. Gray. (Gray was widely respected for his early work in the campaign to save Venice.) The Kress Foundation and the WMF (previously known as the International Fund for Monuments, or IFM) collaborated on dozens of conservation projects. For nearly twenty years Colonel Gray maintained a close working association with Murphy as the Kress Foundation provided critical financial support while the WMF supervised various projects. Perry was later named chairman of the WMF, which strengthened the close ties between the two groups. Over the years the pairing resulted in the preservation and conservation of great monuments throughout the world, ranging from ancient Roman ruins in Asia Minor to the jungle temples of Cambodia.

• • • • •

Public attention rarely focused on the maintenance and cleaning of important artistic treasures. But in March 1987 worldwide controversy erupted over the most daring art restoration and conservation project of the twentieth century—the cleaning of Michelangelo's renowned frescoes in the Sistine Chapel.[31] As the work progressed, surprising rich hues of mauve, yellow, pale blue, and ice green emerged. "The cleaning," wrote the *Wall Street Journal*, "has lightened Adam's yellow mop of hair and returned to the serpent the golden-green glimmer of meaty coils."[32] The unexpected bright colors startled experts. The debate became so fierce that prominent artists petitioned Pope John Paul II to immediately halt further restoration.[33] In an attempt to calm the uproar, Walter Persegati, secretary of the Vatican Museum, told the *New York Times* that Michelangelo painted the frescoes in bright colors to be seen with limited light from small windows or from ancient oil lamps. One art authority, however, claimed that further cleaning would remove a final layer of sizing that Michelangelo had used to unify the colors. James Beck, professor of art history at Columbia University, warned that the workers were cleaning the ceiling with a product similar to Easy-Off oven cleaner.[34] Other scholars feared that the project, now half-completed, would expose the frescoes to further damage from pollution, bright light, or humidity.

In response to these claims, the Kress Foundation assembled and dispatched an international group of leading conservators to inspect the work on the chapel ceiling and issue its findings. Along with Andrea Rothe, conservator of paintings at the J. Paul Getty Museum, the Kress Foundation invited David Bull, head of painting conservation for the National Gallery of Art, and John Brealey, chairman of the Department of Paintings Conservation at the Metropolitan Museum of Art.[35]

After close inspection the panel ruled that the Italian conservators were not overcleaning the masterpiece and reported that the freshness of the colors and clarity of the forms on the ceiling "affirmed the full majesty and splendor" of Michelangelo's creation. The team reported that the original colors were obscured by layers of soot, glue, salt deposits, and residue from previous restorations. In some areas they found that water seepage, condensation, and the efflorescence of salts had created mottling and hazing. "All these conditions," their report pointed out, "combine to falsify the grandeur of Michelangelo's intention by flattening the forms and reducing the colors to a monochrome that has misled generations."[36] "Once they turned off the lights, we were all amazed," Andrea Rothe recalled. "It looked so rich and so beautiful."[37]

Murphy took satisfaction in the widespread international coverage of the Kress expedition. In the United States the report filed by the conservators filled colorful pages in *Time* and *Newsweek* magazines and was thoughtfully covered in the *Wall Street Journal,* the *New York Times,* and the *Washington Post.* The foundation was enthusiastically applauded for its attention to global cultural conservation.

When questioned about the need for the Kress Foundation to spend precious funds for restoration projects outside the United States, Murphy answered without hesitation:

We're a global village . . . more than that we are a global culture. I will not ever admit that the Renaissance helped only the Italians. I am an inheritor of the Renaissance. All of us are. We are the inheritors of a single strain of cultural development and creativity. We owe much to Greece. We owe much to Rome. We owe much to China. We owe much to each other. And I think, therefore, we have an obligation to pay something back. I have never felt guilty about spending American dollars in Italy or Germany or in Britain or in Egypt or in China.[38]

ELEVEN

The J. Paul Getty Trust

OF THE MANY TALENTED EXECUTIVES he came to know, Franklin Murphy had particular admiration—and affection—for George F. Getty II, executive vice president of the Getty Oil Company and eldest son of the oil tycoon J. Paul Getty. Both Murphy and George Getty joined the board of directors of the Bank of America in 1968 and frequently traveled together to San Francisco for board meetings. Nineteen sixty-eight was also the year *Fortune* magazine put J. Paul Getty at the top of their list of America's richest men, estimating his assets at $2 billion.[1]

On one of their trips to San Francisco, Murphy and George Getty, with cocktails at hand, relaxed in the leather seats of the Getty corporate jet, and as a respite from their responsibilities indulged in the pleasure of lighthearted conversation. George, forty-four, was an amiable, handsome man; his reticent nature contrasted with Murphy's outgoing, talkative style. Murphy learned that George directed company operations of Getty Oil in Los Angeles while his father remained in seclusion at his home near London. Despite the distance, the elder Getty asserted a daily presence by telephone, always ready to second-guess his son. Murphy was familiar with the tenacious hold that fathers can have on adult sons; he had observed successful men who, in one way or another, were driven to achievement because of failed relationships with their fathers. But of the various kinds of family interactions that had come to his attention, none were as bizarre as those of the Getty family.

FAMILY DYNAMICS

George F. Getty II, named for his grandfather, was J. Paul Getty's son from his first marriage. Getty had married and divorced five times and produced five sons: George, Ronald, J. Paul Jr., Gordon, and Timothy, who died at the age of twelve. Getty fantasized a dynasty in which each of his four surviving sons would be assigned a piece of his far-flung oil empire, but by the time the boys reached adulthood, he considered them all a disappointment. George was the natural choice to head the family business, but Getty did not intend to let his firstborn feel secure. By various devices he kept George's half brothers nipping at his heels. It exasperated Getty that George was overly cautious—deficient, his father felt, in the kind of drive that fueled a powerful executive. George's eldest half brother, Ronald, had more or less removed himself from the race and renounced any desire to be his father's favorite. He was a large, stolid man with a disciplined, stubborn mind. He took a salaried position as a marketing manager in the oil company, serving out his time until he came into his inheritance. George's second half brother, J. Paul Jr., had been a threat to George's position when they were younger. Paul was considered the most intelligent of the boys, as well as the best-looking and most charming. Getty had great expectations for him and sent him to Italy as director of oil operations after a short apprenticeship in California. His Italian assignment was such a disaster, however, that his father fired him—a turn of events that left the flamboyant young Getty free to indulge in Rome's enticing *dolce vita*. He joined a glamorous circle of young, wealthy devotees of the counterculture who roamed from Italy to Morocco, with opium a major feature of their lifestyle. When his wife died of an overdose Paul's glittering life collapsed, and he succumbed to an overpowering depression. He left Italy and retreated to a hotel room in London where he lived for many years as a drug-addicted recluse watching endless hours of television on banks of TV sets, surviving on drugs and ice cream.[2]

George discounted any threat from his youngest half brother, Gordon, who was Paul's full brother and seemed the least competitive of the group. Gordon was a talented musician and composer; if he had aims of great achievement, it was in opera, not oil. To everyone's surprise, the dreamy but obstinate Gordon suddenly spoke up, insisting that irrespective of their participation, or lack of participation, in the oil business the sons were enti-tled to a larger distribution of income from the family trust that their grandmother had set up for them.

The Sarah C. Getty Trust had come into being in 1934 when Getty's wid-owed mother, furious over her forty-year-old son's irresponsible lifestyle, put the family oil holdings in trust, limiting her son's access to his legacy and preserving an inheritance for Getty descendants. As a young man in California, J. Paul Getty had cultivated a reputation as a rich playboy, much to his parents' displeasure. He was said to have been a grave disappointment to his father, George F. Getty, founder of the oil company, and to have for-feited any confidence his mother might have had in him after his father's death. Resentful that his mother had established the trust, Getty took on a fierce, all-consuming desire to amass a fortune—one that would be greater than his father's.

Getty achieved his goal by increasing the value of the Getty Oil Com-pany and steadily extending his reach in the oil world. He had pursued a strict policy of cash retention through the 1960s, limiting Getty Oil divi-dends and reducing trust income available for distribution. (The trust owned approximately 40 percent of the shares of Getty Oil.) Gordon's pres-sure on his father to start paying significant dividends was an alarming de-velopment, but Getty thought he could resolve the matter by sending George to reason with Gordon and offer him a job. However, the job offer authorized by his father offended Gordon even more; Gordon said he could make better money as a ski bum in Squaw Valley.

After instructing George to hold firm against Gordon, Getty suddenly re-lented, all the while blaming George for Gordon's spiraling out of control. Afraid of disclosures in which "the world press would have a field day,"[3] he declared a cash dividend. However, the angry tycoon followed this concil-iatory gesture by removing Gordon as a successor trustee empowered to di-rect the Sarah C. Getty Trust after his death. He told George that he re-sented being blackmailed by Gordon and ordered him to inform Gordon that he never wanted to see him again. Gordon retaliated by attacking the trust in court. The value of the trust, composed of Getty Oil shares, stood at $293 million, having increased 16 percent compounded annually since 1934. Getty Oil had limited dividends, and the funds were used to build the company and J. Paul Getty's private wealth. If Gordon succeeded in his suit, distribution to the trust beneficiaries would expose Getty to an income tax levy on $72 million in stock. To Getty's horror, he realized that to pay the taxes he would have to liquidate the Getty Oil holdings that he owned personally, thus severely affecting the fortune that had put him in the top rank of American billionaires.[4]

As vice president of Getty Oil, George faced the challenge of operating the company and keeping the stock price stable in the face of family litigation. No matter what action he took, he could expect ridicule and criticism from his father. In tension-relieving self-deprecation, George took to describing himself to Murphy as the vice president in charge of failure; his father, he said, had the exclusive claim on success.[5]

· · · · ·

In addition to his duties at Getty Oil, George Getty was assigned responsibility for his father's museum on the Pacific Coast at Malibu, actually a Spanish-style ranch house on sixty-four acres that Getty bought soon after World War II. George headed a board of trustees, largely his father's oil colleagues, who oversaw Getty's art collection. The collection was open to the public several times a week to comply with federal tax laws and consisted of several rooms of eighteenth-century French furniture, galleries with an assortment of European paintings, and a room displaying marble Roman portrait busts; other noble Romans were stored in the basement. The ranch house had been a weekend home for Getty and his fifth wife until Getty left for England in 1959. He had not anticipated staying abroad permanently, so the home was kept ready for his return. Getty opened the museum to the public with a professional staff in charge; W. R. Valentiner, who formerly directed the Detroit Institute of Arts, and the art historian Paul Wescher provided leadership in the early years.

The museum was a sleepy operation largely hidden among avocado, eucalyptus, and coastal cedar trees. Scholars and visitors who made their way up the gravel road found rooms and corridors of the original house crammed with art. A favorite acquisition of Getty's, the *Lansdowne Herakles,* occupied one end of a new gallery built in 1957. The larger-than-life-size marble statue stood in front of a bank of windows so that the bright sunlight illuminated the musculature of its chest and torso. Getty had acquired the sculpture, a Roman copy in marble of a Greek original, from the Lansdowne family for the bargain price of $30,000 in the early years of World War II when panic selling pervaded the art market. The statue had been unearthed in 1790 from the ruins of Hadrian's villa near Tivoli, a provenance that had special significance for Getty; he often identified his goals with those of the emperor Hadrian as art patron and monument builder.[6]

The art operations up to now had not been difficult or demanding for George, but in 1968 Getty announced his intention to build a new museum. What he said he had in mind was a full-scale, near-replica of a first-century Roman villa in a canyon on the Malibu property. He wanted the public to have the experience of arriving at the home of a wealthy Roman; museum visitors would enter the garden of the enclosed peristyle, walk the length of the colonnaded portico, and then step into a grand marble-floored vestibule that would open to the galleries. Getty's villa was to be patterned on one buried in the ancient seaside town of Herculaneum under the solidified ash and mud of the Mount Vesuvius eruption that had destroyed Pompeii and wiped Herculaneum from memory.

Murphy was very interested in hearing George's description of his father's plans. In the past the Los Angeles County Museum of Art had enjoyed a good relationship with Getty, who had contributed several remarkable pieces, including the Rembrandt *Portrait of Marten Looten* and the extraordinary Ardabil Carpet, created in Iran in 1540.[7] Murphy hoped to have LACMA come to mind when the billionaire collector distributed works in the future. Looking ahead, Murphy doubted that Getty's Roman villa would have adequate space for his expanding collection or be suitable for some of his prized objects. Murphy offered George his assistance and told him he would like to meet his father to discuss their mutual interests in the Los Angeles art environment.

George secured an invitation for Murphy to visit his father at Sutton Place, the Tudor mansion near London where Getty lived in seclusion. The Murphys were to join George and his wife to lunch with Getty in the history-filled house where love-obsessed Henry VIII pursued Anne Boleyn.[8]

AN AFTERNOON WITH J. PAUL GETTY

Franklin and Judy Murphy arrived as scheduled at Sutton Place on the afternoon of September 30, 1971. After passing through a few checkpoints where telephone messages were relayed, the Murphys' car was waved to a circular drive in front of the house. Immediately, several of the fiercest-looking dogs that Murphy said he had ever seen surrounded the car. "I knew darn well I was not going to get out of that car as long as the dogs were there," Murphy said, telling the story years later. The apprehensive chauffeur asked what he should do. "Just stay here," Murphy told him. "I suspect somebody will appear."[9]

A butler emerged from the great stone entry, a sharp whistle pierced the air, and the dogs disappeared. The enormous mansion (55,000 square feet) was surrounded by terraces, yew hedges, pools, and vast green lawns that, as Murphy observed, "stretched into the horizon." Getty had purchased the Tudor showplace with its 775 acres from the land-rich, cash-poor, fifth duke of Sutherland for only 50,000 pounds (roughly $140,000) in the late 1950s. Getty liked to boast that he closed the deal for less than one-twentieth of the property's value, making it an even shrewder investment than his purchase of the Pierre Hotel in Manhattan. "It was a beautiful, beautiful place," Murphy recalled of Sutton Place. "He obviously loved it."[10]

Getty's reputation for demanding bargains was well known in the art world during his forty-five-year on-again, off-again passion for collecting. He spent millions of dollars on acquisitions, but in the opinion of experts his fixation on price had kept him from assembling the magnificent, unified, world-acknowledged collection that he could have afforded. When he began collecting art in the years preceding World War II, he decided to concentrate on works that were of fine quality or of historical significance but were not in great demand by other collectors. He was drawn to the decorative arts of eighteenth-century France, especially the possessions of the Bourbon kings and their queens and mistresses, works that he found of impeccable craftsmanship. To his pleasure, in June 1938, early on in his collecting, he acquired at auction several items of furniture that had belonged to Louis XIV and Louis XV.

In the 1950s, when the craze among collectors was French impressionist paintings, Getty slipped into auction houses to claim furniture, carpets, and decorative pieces that were drawing little attention. Claude Sere, a Paris antiques dealer, noted Getty's objective: "He could purchase a fine Louis XV piece for $30,000 when a Cézanne was going for $600,000."[11] There were also good buys to be had in antiquities. Getty previously had sent his finds directly to California to be displayed in the house at Malibu, but after his purchase of Sutton Place he hung his favorites in the immense rooms of the great house where he could enjoy them.

With a showman's relish, Getty led the Murphys into the manor's Great Hall. The room was in total darkness. Their host opened a hidden panel and turned a switch; lights illuminated a huge painting, *Diana and Her Nymphs Departing for the Chase*. The painting, attributed to Rubens, depicted a bare-breasted Diana with similarly exposed attendants, one of whom is determinedly resisting the attentions of a satyr. The painting, for which Getty had paid $400,000, was obviously of great significance to him, and Franklin and Judy gave it effusive praise. The Murphys were then guided to Getty's Van Dyck portrait of Agostino Pallavincini and his prized Rembrandt, *A Portrait of Saint Bartholomew*.

Getty had managed to acquire a few excellent works, but his total collection, which numbered hundreds of paintings, was not highly regarded. "All but 10 paintings should be sent back to their original owners for free," one authority groused.[12] Unfortunately, Getty's beguiling Diana and nymphs, it later would turn out, was not by Rubens's hand, after all.[13] After deciding to build a new museum on his Malibu property, Getty began to make his art purchases with greater discernment, engaging experts to advise him. In June, a few months before the Murphys' arrival, he had spent $6 million at Christie's auction house for paintings by Titian, Van Dyck, and Boucher.

George Getty and his wife arrived and joined the luncheon group. The meal was served in the vast dining hall. A long, narrow refectory table with gold candelabra positioned every few feet down the center was to be their dining board. Getty sat at the head of the table, his back to the intricately patterned leaded-glass windows that sent shafts of autumn sunshine onto the gleaming oak surface. The four guests took seats at their host's end where the courses of the lunch were served, the rest of the table abandoned to empty chairs.

Over lunch Getty and Murphy discussed conservation work needed on the Ardabil Carpet. The Persian masterpiece, 23½ feet long and 13 feet wide, containing more than thirty-five million knots, had been acquired by Getty for the bargain price of $68,000 from the art dealer Joseph Duveen when he was dying from cancer. After Murphy's description of LACMA's concern about the carpet, Getty offered financial assistance to complete the restoration and cleaning but was not specific as to any dollar amount.

The party retired to another immense, beautifully furnished room. Getty asked an initially puzzled Murphy if he would like to see his museum. The mystery was dispelled when a butler arrived with a scale model of the Roman villa planned for Malibu. The butler put the model on the floor, and the seventy-nine-year-old Getty got down on his hands and knees to point out the museum's features. Franklin and Judy exchanged a quick glance, then dropped to their knees as well. They crawled around the floor like children as the billionaire collector pointed out features of the miniature museum patterned on the Villa dei Papiri of Herculaneum. The intricate model had been constructed so that Getty could lift its Roman tile roof to peer into the floors below. "What astonished me," Murphy recalled, was that Getty actually had "little scale models of the paintings that he owned, and sculptures in place on the tiny walls." Getty, in the role of curator, placed the miniature art objects precisely as he chose. "I don't want any so-called art historian coming around playing games with what I put together," he said.[14]

The bricks-and-mortar version of Getty's model was already under construction in the scenic, windswept canyon at Malibu. Ground had been broken in 1970 for the re-created villa. The ancient Roman town of Herculaneum had fascinated Getty from the first time he visited the site as a young man. The buried town and the remarkable villa had been the setting for a novella he wrote and published in the mid-1950s titled *A Journey from Corinth.* Getty attributed special meaning to the legend that the seaside town had been founded by Hercules on his return from Iberia.

Exploration of Herculaneum had begun in 1750 under the auspices of the king of Naples. Miners and quarrymen dug shafts and tunnels through the rock-hard volcanic mud to reach the buried villa. They hauled out a wealth of bronze and marble sculpture and rolls of papyri (earning the villa its Italian name, Villa dei Papiri). The treasure hunt had been set off when well diggers outside a monastery hit a hard underground surface that turned out to be a marble floor of amazing beauty and intricacy. The mosaic design of concentric circles was the floor of a gazebo in the garden of a large private home, suggesting that even more valuable items would be found in the villa itself. The artifacts hauled from the excavation caught the imagination of the world; the discovery became the momentous art and archaeological event that launched the eighteenth-century classical revival, offering an aesthetic to accompany the scientific-minded European Enlightenment.

As the tunneling progressed room by room into the villa, a Swiss explorer and engineer drew the floor plan, delineating the various chambers, the central atrium, and the 350-foot-long peristyle around a courtyard with a deep fishpond. Getty had used his knowledge of the floor plan to write his fictional account of Roman life, and he turned to the floor plan again to plan his new museum. As author, he had visualized his protagonist strolling through the peristyle and entering the rooms of the villa; with the model of his museum in hand he had a more concrete way in which to wander the villa in his imagination. The luxurious life of Rome's early imperial period embodied many of Getty's views on art, culture, sexual mores, and power. With his villa he would re-create a unique historical moment, one that he thought had much to teach the present, and offer it to the public in a museum on the scenic coast of California.[15]

· · · · ·

During lunch, Murphy engaged Getty's attention and his warm response with the suggestion that the Getty Museum use the Los Angeles County

Museum's conservation laboratory, as it could mean considerable savings. Later Getty instructed his curator of paintings, Burton B. Fredericksen, to take full advantage of Murphy's offer.[16] After lunch the group strolled through the rooms of the historic house with Getty pointing out the artworks that were to go to the new museum. Murphy felt that since Getty had recently made a $6 million purchase, he was now willing to spend large sums to build a significant collection, one destined for Los Angeles. Murphy hoped that Getty would feel comfortable calling on his services in the future and would have confidence in him as an adviser to his son on museum matters. He felt he could assist George in much the same way that he had assisted Robert Ahmanson, Paul Mellon, and Rush Kress, all of whom had faced the challenge of implementing a patriarch's dream.

Though J. Paul Getty had been cordial and seemed to have enjoyed his guests, Murphy felt that Getty held himself back. According to Murphy, "He had a mask-like face that even when something was said that was really very humorous he was barely able to smile." Murphy said he chalked up Getty's lack of reaction to the solitary man's "ability to maintain a sense of quietude or whatever." Later, however, he learned that the real reason for Getty's stoic appearance was lack of elasticity in his facial muscles from numerous face-lifts. "I should have realized that, looking at him," Murphy said; "given his age, there were very few wrinkles in his face."[17]

Getty's beak-nosed, stern face may have made an inviting target for cartoonists, who depicted him as a Scrooge, but beneath the clenched expression there was an appealing side as well, according to his longtime secretary, Barbara Wallace. "He was incredibly vulnerable and soft," she said. "Yet the magnetism got you. You just felt you had to do things for him." Somehow, the tycoon could convey a neediness that won people's hearts even as he barreled over them.[18]

· · · · ·

Both George Getty II and Franklin Murphy expected more to follow from the Sutton Place visit. Murphy sent a note of appreciation to George after the trip expressing his belief that "constructive things" would certainly result. By using his technique of zeroing in on the other person's needs, Murphy had brought LACMA's conservation service to the attention of the billionaire collector who was widely known for his thriftiness. However, Murphy's effort to capture Getty's goodwill hit a brick wall when Fredericksen responded to Murphy's conservation proposal with a lengthy letter detailing past unsatisfactory efforts to work with LACMA's conservators. Murphy was disappointed, but he supported the prerogatives of LACMA's professional staff.

The more George came to know Murphy, the more he appreciated his skills, especially his administrative talent. When a vacant seat needed to be filled on the board of directors of Getty Oil, George sought Murphy's advice. He paid tribute to Murphy's reputation for integrity, writing that he needed a man who could act as the "conscience of the corporation, much as [Murphy did] on the Ford Motor Company Board."[19] Murphy in turn anticipated that his warm relationship with George Getty would be productive in many ways, especially in seeing a new museum added to Los Angeles's cultural venues, one that promised a fine collection. Murphy's hope was not to be fulfilled, however, for within two years, at the age of forty-eight, George would be dead.

THE GETTY CURSE

In the early hours of June 6, 1973, George Getty II, barely conscious, was rushed to the emergency room at Queen of Angels Hospital in Hollywood, where he was admitted under the false name "George S. Davis." The UCLA Medical Center was closer to the Getty home on Chalon Road, but Stuart Evey, George's friend and executive assistant, who had been called to the home by George's wife, hoped to conceal the oil executive's identity to keep his father from learning about the incident. George, admitted in a stupor from ingestion of alcohol and drugs, was bleeding from stab wounds to his stomach and thigh. The hospital's emergency staff treated the wounds, stabilized him, and admitted him in the expectation that he would sleep off the binge, but during the night a full-scale medical emergency arose. George fell into a coma, and the doctors were unable to revive him.

The *Los Angeles Times* reported the death, quoting a Getty Oil Company spokesperson at the hospital who attributed it to a cerebral hemorrhage; the later edition of the paper stated that police were investigating "suspicious circumstances" involving knife wounds. Family members informed police that Getty had been injured accidentally during a barbecue at his Bel Air home. Wounds to his stomach and left thigh seemed slight at first, but later the family decided he should be taken to the hospital. Teams of detectives dispatched to the Getty home questioned family members and friends, and though the detectives doubted the barbecue accident story, they found no evidence of an assault.

It was not until Tuesday, August 28, that Los Angeles County Coroner Thomas Noguchi, famous later for his best-selling books on forensic medicine, listed the cause of George's death as suicide. In a statement before a throng of reporters outside his office, Noguchi announced that after a thorough investigation he concluded that Getty had died of a combination of alcohol and drugs roughly fifteen hours after he told his family he was going to kill himself and locked the door to his bedroom. The *Times* reported that the coroner and his special investigator had found "no reason for Getty's apparently self-destructive mood" and that there was no evidence of marital, physical, or financial problems.[20]

Speculation raged about why the seemingly capable heir to the Getty Oil fortune would meet such a strange fate. The autopsy report contained a description of numerous scars and "small reddish-blue and purple bruises" found on the back of Getty's hands and forearms and inside his upper arms, leading the coroner to believe that Getty had been cutting his own skin, inflicting injury on himself for some time.[21] Thomas Petzinger Jr. of the *Wall Street Journal* offered a compelling explanation for the oil executive's self-mutilation: "He was suffering constant humiliation from his father. The old man refused to make him president of a newly reconstituted Getty Oil, keeping the title for himself; George was relegated to executive vice president. In abusive hour-long calls and in letters, he was barraged with criticism and cutting sarcasm from Sutton Place. Year after year, the attacks grew more mean spirited, more demeaning. . . . In the office, George would sometimes drive a letter opener in the back of his hand."[22]

Interestingly, in his autobiography J. Paul Getty wrote that the alcohol and barbiturates that his son turned to may have resulted from the fact that "he strove too hard to live up to the images of his grandfather and me."[23] Initially, when Getty was informed of his son's death, he "stared dumbly into space" for half an hour, according to his biographer Robert Lenzner. Then Getty "collected himself, and coolly began figuring out who was to replace George and the management changes that were needed."[24]

Murphy was stunned by the news. "Nobody was more shocked and amazed and puzzled at his death than I," Murphy said, calling George Getty a splendid human being and his death inexplicable.[25] "I had always thought of George as a stable, rational and well-organized individual," Murphy said sadly. "I believe his father fully intended to turn the company over to George. I'm told by others that George's death was an absolute blow from which Mr. Getty really in a way never recovered."[26] Soon after George's death Murphy sent his condolences to Getty: "I am sure you realize that he had become much respected in the California business community and his passing is really a great loss. It is difficult to say anything useful under these circumstances, but I did want you to know that I shall miss him and I share in your sense of loss." In a postscript Murphy added, "If, now that George is gone, I can assist you in any way in connection with your new museum, please do not hesitate to call upon me and I shall try within my limits to be helpful."[27]

After the death of his firstborn Getty reconciled with his fourth son, Gordon, the only one remaining whom he thought capable of directing the family business. He revoked his earlier directive and made Gordon a successor trustee of the Sarah C. Getty Trust. This action would create havoc later for the Getty heirs and, astoundingly, end one of America's great financial empires.

· · · · ·

The mysterious death of J. Paul Getty's eldest son proved only one incident in a grim series that would lead the media to speak of the Getty family curse. Five weeks after George's death the entire world watched in horror as news spread of the kidnapping of Getty's free-spirited grandson, sixteen-year-old Paul, son of Getty's third son, J. Paul Getty Jr. Getty had reports from a private investigator that the kidnapping had been faked by young Getty and his friends, but after a package was received at the offices of an Italian newspaper containing the boy's ear, a lock of red hair, and a note demanding 1.7 billion lira ($3.2 million), Getty could see no recourse but to pay the ransom. The kidnapped teenager's agony was prolonged by a postal strike that delayed delivery of the package for nearly three weeks. The kidnappers refused to negotiate and threatened to sever additional parts from the boy's body. Of the $3.2 million demanded, Getty put up $2.2 million and loaned the remaining $1 million to the boy's father, to be repaid from his share of the income from the trust. Paul was released by his kidnappers and picked up by local police as he staggered down a highway south of Naples.[28] Much later, reports surfaced that the teenager and his "hippie friends" had indeed staged the kidnapping, but it went terribly wrong when the young heir was captured by the local mafia. Only $17,000 of the ransom money was recovered, but evidence of the remainder turned up in the economy of various Sicilian towns where business ventures sprouted and a block of apartments appeared along a road known as "Strada Paul Getty."[29]

Murphy's sympathy went out to the oil tycoon who so soon after suffering the devastating news of his son's unexpected death had to endure agonizing weeks with his grandson in peril. Getty's dynastic plans were eroding, slipping from him. As the Roman villa for art neared completion at Malibu, Murphy hoped that the unusual museum project that had so much engaged Getty was providing some solace.

J. Paul Getty spent $18 million to build the Roman replica in the Malibu foothills facing the Pacific Ocean. But he was not on site; he knew the villa museum only through photographs and the firsthand accounts of museum officials. Getty had a lifelong fear of flying, and in his later years his anxiety extended to travel of any kind; what he needed of the world could come to him at Sutton Place. Arriving to consult with him were Norman Neuerburg, an authority on Roman antiquitics, and consulting architect Stephen Garrett, who had worked on other projects for Getty. Curators, too, were summoned to Sutton Place to receive their instructions and give their reports: Jiri Frel, heading the antiquities department; David Rinne, responsible for antiquities conservation; Gillian Wilson, curator of decorative arts; and Burton Fredericksen, chief curator.

Instead of an exact replica, the Malibu Villa dei Papiri was a "reconstruction based partly on fact and partly on scholarly imagination," according to museum officials.[30] Various adjustments in design were made to accommodate the Los Angeles building code. The peristyle was laid out with historical accuracy except that the 220-foot-long pool was only 18 inches deep, much shallower than the fishponds of Roman households; otherwise it would have required a full-time lifeguard. The ground-floor galleries exhibited Getty's classical collection, which was also displayed in the courtyard gardens, arbors, and atriums. The *Lansdowne Herakles* now had a gallery befitting its status—a circular sanctuary modeled after the domed underground temples to Hercules found in the countryside outside Tivoli. (The Hercules statue pervaded Getty's thoughts: the provenance of the famous sculpture figured in the plot of his novella of Roman life.) The marble floor of the Hercules gallery re-created exactly the swirling concentric circles of the magnificent gazebo floor that led to detection of the buried villa in 1750. The second-floor galleries were given over to Getty's collection of European paintings, eighteenth-century furniture, and decorative arts.[31]

On January 15, 1974, the J. Paul Getty Museum opened without the founder present, though everyone else involved in the Los Angeles art scene and art elite from across the country were in attendance. Franklin and Judy Murphy walked through the galleries they had previously visited in miniature, crouched on the floor at Sutton Place. Murphy diplomatically described his impressions after the grand opening: he found the eighteenth-century French collection dazzling, he said, and he thought the decorative arts pieces constituted one of the great collections outside France. However, he found the picture collection "disappointing" and the classical sculpture good, but nothing to match the collection at the Metropolitan Museum of Art. Less kind critics labeled the imitation Roman villa "Pompeii on the Pacific," calling it an inconveniently located, kitschy tourist attraction with only a handful of first-rate objects. But the museum quickly won the affection of the general public, who flocked to it in unexpected numbers, causing traffic and parking problems along the picturesque coastal highway.

· · · · ·

On June 6, 1976, three years to the day after the apparent suicide of his son, J. Paul Getty himself died. The London *Daily Telegraph* reported that the eighty-three-year-old tycoon lay in state in the Great Hall at Sutton Place. The open coffin was flanked by tall candleholders with beeswax candles, the bier guarded by security men. After his twenty-five-year absence Getty's last wish was to return in death to the California coast and to the Roman villa he had created but never seen. Unfortunately, Getty's wishes could not be immediately fulfilled; in fact, it would be three years before executors could obtain zoning permits to construct a modest mausoleum overlooking the Pacific Ocean. The deceased billionaire was stored ignominiously at the Forest Lawn Mortuary in Los Angeles awaiting completion of the burial site.

Not wanting any delay in settling the estate, lawyers immediately submitted Getty's will for probate in the courts of Los Angeles. Getty curator Gillian Wilson, who was in London at the time, learned of the will from the *Daily Express* headline:

THANKS FOR THE MEMORY
Getty's Girls Showered with Dollars.[32]

The front page featured photographs of the women mentioned in the will. There were twelve in all, including one former wife. Because the three remaining Getty sons and their children were provided for in the Sarah C. Getty Trust, Getty made few additional bequests to family members.[33] Some of the sums to his lady friends were substantial, but the total of the gifts was minor compared to the value of the estate.

In the last paragraph of the news item, Wilson remembered, she read that the residue of the estate would go to Getty's museum in Malibu. "I rang the museum and asked, 'What does this mean?' All I could hear was the clink of champagne glasses; they said, 'We don't know, we're still counting.'" Wilson recalled that amazement reigned. "We were all staggered, we could not believe it."[34] Getty had told curators to anticipate nothing from him other than his private collection at Sutton Place. There would be an endowment "to keep the lights on," he told them, but little if anything more.

Getty's original will, drafted in 1958, four years after the establishment of the galleries at the Malibu ranch house, bequeathed the bulk of his estate to the museum. This was not public knowledge, however, and museum officials were astounded when they discovered that the long-ago provision now endowed the museum with four million shares of Getty Oil stock, worth more than $750 million. The much-mocked replica of a Roman villa, according to museum officials, now had "an endowment vastly larger than that of the Metropolitan Museum's $130 million—larger even than the combined endowments of all the other major museums in America—and was sufficient to support an annual acquisitions budget of at least $50 million, maybe $100 million."[35]

The Getty will was repeatedly contested, however. Ronald Getty touched off a series of claims that took time to settle, and in an especially threatening development, the Getty family challenged the last codicil of the will, which put the assets of the museum under the direct control of museum trustees, not the family. After several grinding years in the courts the codicil was upheld. The museum was initially granted a large advance representing interest and dividends against the presumed inheritance, but disbursements were halted in 1979 as the museum faced more litigation and the IRS, challenging the museum's tax-exempt status, moved to collect $628 million in taxes.[36] The flurry of complicated legal issues forced the board of trustees to hold off on any art purchases until the bequest was actually in hand.

· · · · ·

After the various legal entanglements were more or less resolved, the trustees set about devising a future role for the now heavily endowed J. Paul Getty Museum. In September 1980, as museum trustee Otto Wittmann remembered, no one was quite sure how to run the museum in its new financial circumstances or what goals the institution could pursue legally. The trustees, Getty business associates or oil company executives, had served chiefly as fiscal advisers and had simply ratified the decisions made by Getty. Harold Berg, chairman of the museum's board, was the former CEO of the Getty Oil Company.

Otto Wittmann, who was invited to join the board in 1977, was the only trustee with any significant art background. He had served as director of the Toledo Museum of Art and had an insider's knowledge of the museum world.[37] He recognized that the enormous bequest was an amount greater than could be spent for art purchases without severely affecting the world art market. Wittmann tried to convince his fellow trustees to devise additional programs for the museum—art education, conservation services, and perhaps a library for art history and research—that could absorb some of the funds. He recommended setting up a foundation, if that was a legal option. Wittmann made no headway with the trustees, who argued that Getty left the money to the J. Paul Getty Museum and not to a Getty school or Getty library. Furthermore, they observed, Getty had never created a philanthropic foundation and was not known for dispensing funds. His museum was what Getty wanted to support, and that was how they felt the money should be spent. Wittmann said the trustees were not at all alarmed by the amount of money. "It was not much to them," he related later. "After all, they were oil men."[38]

Chairman Berg came to realize that the trustees were out of their depth when it came to making plans for a museum and conceded that they needed professional help. He urged the trustees to find a capable new leader to plan solutions for the problems they would face once the bequest was in hand. The trustees had no idea where to look. One of them knew Derek C. Bok, president of Harvard University, and suggested soliciting him for aid in finding a suitable candidate. Bok indicated that he was not familiar enough with the personalities on the West Coast to make a recommendation, but he offered the name of one man who had the experience and contacts to assist the trustees in their search. What they needed was someone who could help them "invent" what could become a great institution, he told them. The man he named was Franklin D. Murphy.

Sometime during summer 1980, Murphy was contacted by museum trustees Berg and John Connell. After an initial meeting in the Steinberg Room at Times Mirror, where he still served as chairman, Murphy agreed to come up with suggestions for the trustees on how to approach their task and to give them names of potential candidates to head the undertaking.

Both Murphy and Wittmann had grown up in Kansas City, and though Murphy was slightly younger, their families had known one another and Wittmann had followed Murphy's career. Murphy soon told the trustees that, as Wittmann had realized, the expected endowment was far in excess of what could be spent intelligently and responsibly on the museum alone, and he advised them to envision instead a multifaceted institution of which the museum would be but one part. The total institution could still be limited to art and art history, which were Getty's special interests.

In August, at the request of the museum's board, Murphy drafted a memorandum outlining an audacious cultural venture. It served as a manifesto for the museum's emerging identity. At the head of his memo Murphy inscribed, "It is far easier to accumulate wealth than to give it away wisely and with effect." The quotation, attributed to Andrew Carnegie, reflected the focused responsibility that Murphy urged on the trustees. Getty had created an operating trust most of whose revenue was to be spent on its own activities rather than funding the activities of others. But what activities were to be pursued? Getty had simply specified "education," which was required for tax exemption. "In my view," Murphy wrote, "trustees have an obligation to take into account the primary interests of the individual who created the trust or foundation which they serve. Mr. Getty clearly was fascinated not only with art per se, but history and archaeology as well. The structure and the contents of the museum that bears his name and his remarkable home in England, Sutton Place, are clear witness to these interests."[39]

Murphy pointed out that few foundations emphasized the humanities in their programs, the two notable exceptions being the Mellon Foundation, with assets of $800 million, and the Kress Foundation, with assets of $40 million. He felt that the National Endowment for the Humanities and the National Endowment for the Arts could not fill the void because they were subject to politicization, local pressures, and fragmentation. As a result there was a compelling need for research programs of high quality in the humanities.

Murphy's recommendations to the Getty trustees reflected the cultural priorities that he had been promoting since his days as chancellor at the University of Kansas. But he had long since come to the disillusioned conclusion that public universities cannot, or will not, adequately support the arts, and he had even less faith in government-supported efforts. Now he was informed that there was a treasure house of funds available. How should it be spent? As Murphy later wrote Bok, "The Getty Trust could have an enormous impact for the good."[40]

Art establishment leaders appreciated that Murphy had something much more nuanced and far-sighted than a shopping spree in mind. Significantly, Murphy, who had previously pushed hard to have the Ahmanson Foundation support existing institutions, among them the Los Angeles County Museum of Art, did not recommend that course to the Getty trustees. What he proposed would be something sui generis.

· · · · ·

Who did Murphy envision running the complex of activities he proposed? He told the trustees that they needed a chief executive with a proven track record of administrative competence and integrity, knowledge about the arts and humanities, and a personal commitment to the humanities in general. In addition, this person should understand the appropriate relationship between a chief executive and a board of trustees in the nonprofit setting. In other words, this was no ordinary CEO but someone who could deal well with the public and command the staff's loyalty and respect while fashioning new programs. The new Getty leader arguably would become the most powerful individual in the international art establishment.

Two candidates had been considered by the board and rejected.[41] After entreating Murphy to serve as a search committee of one, the board followed his strong recommendation and selected Harold Williams in February 1981. Murphy, who served on the board of directors of Norton Simon, Inc., had come to appreciate Williams's talent as chief executive during a period of consolidation of Simon companies.[42] Murphy had watched Williams manage a billion-dollar global business and effectively handle the peculiar and eccentric demands of Norton Simon. When Williams was preparing to leave his long association with Simon in 1970, he was persuaded to undertake a reorganization of the business school at UCLA. The university could offer him only a dean's salary, but Williams said he had made enough already in the corporate world and would like a hands-on creative challenge. The renamed Graduate School of Management that resulted under Williams's guidance brought distinction to UCLA and increased Murphy's admiration for Williams.[43]

The soft-spoken man with thick silver hair and owlish eyes behind large black-rimmed glasses was known for his warm, relaxed, congenial style. Born in Philadelphia to Russian immigrants, Williams had moved with his family to Los Angeles in 1934. He attended Roosevelt High School and worked his way through UCLA. He then trained at Harvard Law School, graduating at the age of twenty-one. On his return to Los Angeles to practice law, Williams went to work for Simon.[44] Williams said that "growing up in relationship to Norton Simon" was an "annealing" experience, the term used in industry for the process by which steel is hardened. "We survived each other," he said of his ordeals with the hard-driving, self-made Simon. In his work for Simon, he had the opportunity to watch how one of the world's great art collections was assembled. Over the years he and Simon visited galleries and museums, attended auctions, and talked a lot about art. Spectacular pieces from Simon's collection hung on the walls of Simon's company, and Williams recalled that art became very much "a part of the culture of the company itself."[45] This exposure to Simon's world led Williams to an abiding interest in art.

Following his seven years as dean of the Graduate School of Management at UCLA, Williams accepted an appointment by President Jimmy Carter to serve as chairman of the Securities and Exchange Commission, where he won praise for his early hard-line stance on corporate accountability. Some of Williams's recommendations that were resisted during his tenure came to be implemented later as the financial scandals—Enron, WorldCom, Tyco, and others—of the early twenty-first century unfolded. Williams recalled one early moment at the SEC when a long-term member of Congress called in a rage about the commission's vigorous investigation of one of his important constituents. Williams firmly and calmly informed the congressman of the commission's independent mandate, but after he hung up the phone, he took a deep breath and said to himself, "Harold, if ever there was any question about who the hell you are, you're going to find out in this job."[46]

Murphy was certain that with his varied background Williams was ideal for the mammoth Getty undertaking and that he would embrace the challenge. "There was an empty blackboard with a good deal of chalk and he could write his own ticket more or less," Murphy said.[47] The museum trustees met with Williams and offered him the position. Williams asked for a few days to think it over. He had left government service when President Reagan took office and was returning to the practice of law; he would have to give up a lucrative private practice to operate the Getty behemoth at much less pay. Williams decided to accept the offer provided the trustees would permit him to spend his first year researching and interviewing international experts to search out the role that the Getty Museum and its related institutions should play.

Soon after Williams's appointment as president and chief executive, the trustees asked Murphy to join the museum's board officially. Murphy hesitated, concerned about a conflict of interest with his involvement at both the National Gallery and the Los Angeles County Museum of Art. But the trustees urged him further, and Murphy reasoned that he could discipline himself to avoid any conflicts or the appearance of any impropriety. He was elected to the board on February 27, 1981.

Williams's legal and financial background would be invaluable in leading an arts institution that was deeply involved with an oil company—one entwined in hostile and unpredictable family relationships. Williams saw his charge as that of creating an institution that would be far more than a museum and that could responsibly use the Getty bequest; to that end he brought about a name change from the J. Paul Getty Museum to the J. Paul

Getty Trust, a name better suited to the multifaceted institution he was to develop.[48]

. . . . .

Williams set out on his self-described "year of exploration" to assess the collective needs of the art world and devise a range of new programs for the Getty, in addition to operating the museum. Williams explained to the board of trustees that the driving question during this year of exploration would be: "Where can we make a significant difference?"[49] Where could the Getty, an unusual institution with unusual resources, make the most striking contribution to the world of museums and art history?[50] The arts and humanities were to be the focus—but that mandate was broadly defined.

Williams began by consulting museum directors all over the country about what a museum ought to be. Wittmann put him in touch with directors of his acquaintance. "He then went to New York," Wittman related, "and came back and told me, 'I've hired the two most intelligent women I've ever met in my life.'"[51] One was Nancy Englander, at the time the director of New Hampshire's MacDowell Colony and previously the director of museum programs at the National Endowment for the Humanities. A self-confident, energetic woman with dark shoulder-length hair and striking blue eyes, Englander was poised and elegant in her demeanor but operated at high intensity, extremely passionate about her work and goals. The other woman chosen by Williams was Leilani Lattin Duke, a lively young educational professional who had a knack for persuading her fellow educators to think creatively and critically about art education and its role. Duke had served with the NEA and then directed the California Confederation of the Arts.

Englander and Duke joined Williams for the exploratory year. The team spent the next few months meeting with museum curators and directors, art historians, conservators, and educators, as well as experts in the emerging field of electronic technology. During the last half of 1981 and into 1982, Williams and Englander traveled throughout the United States and to Canada and Europe, including England, the Netherlands, France, Germany, Italy, Greece, and Switzerland. Their intent was to find out what needs were not being met and not likely to be met by existing institutions. It was a heady, exhilarating experience for the Getty envoys; they were welcomed by dedicated art world leaders who laid out half-abandoned aspirations that might now come to fruition. Amid the tedium of train stations and airline terminals the team spent hours together in excited conversation evaluating the direction the Getty Trust could take.

Gradually a master plan emerged that Williams could take to the board of trustees for approval.[52] In a series of presentations during early 1982, he described a conservation center addressing worldwide problems of aging art and architecture, an education component designed to change the way art is taught in the United States, and—as it turned out—an overly ambitious goal of building the world's largest computerized inventory of artworks. In a February presentation Englander outlined the scholarship component: the Getty Center for the History of Art and Humanities would include a residence program for scholars, a major expansion of the library, and new reference tools using pioneering information technology. The center was to take an interdisciplinary approach that Englander described as "unique in its philosophical underpinnings, in the concept of looking at the history of art in the context of the humanities."[53]

· · · · ·

Murphy's support as the most articulate, art-savvy member of the board was invaluable to Williams during this watershed phase of the institution's development. Except for Otto Wittmann, the board consisted of older men who knew petroleum but had no experience with a cultural institution. Williams and his team found themselves reporting their findings to a board that responded with blank stares and a lack of enthusiasm.[54] In Murphy's view most of the trustees were not truly qualified to make decisions that would affect the global art market and art institutions everywhere.[55] He became their interpreter, translating the sometimes esoteric language of art professionals. His Kansas background allowed him to talk the down-to-earth language of men more attuned to drilling rigs than to galleries and art auctions. It was rough going, but often the trustees relied on Murphy's judgment and voted the funds needed for some new proposal. "Franklin Murphy provided cover," Harold Williams recalled, "while I ran for daylight."[56]

At times, however, it seemed as if the trustees just went with their instincts or their sense of humor—well-honed attributes of men long able to indulge their personal whims. In a series of meetings Wittmann told his fellow trustees of curator George Goldner's enthusiasm for a Rembrandt drawing, a female nude with a snake clutched in her hand, thought to represent Cleopatra (in spite of her ample Dutch figure). Wittmann recommended that the Getty bid on the drawing in an upcoming auction; it would be a rare opportunity to add a superb work to the collection as the Getty, coming late on the scene, was unlikely to acquire premium Rembrandt paintings. The trustees protested that "Mr. Getty didn't collect drawings," and they did not want to get into something new. Wittmann persevered, telling them about the research Goldner had done and the undeniable importance of the Rembrandt. When the trustees finally agreed to the purchase, Wittmann felt they did so not because they understood the point he was making but because they liked the young curator's enthusiasm. They yielded in the spirit of "Oh, give the lad his drawing."[57]

It was in this surrealistic mode of operation, amid whimsy and puzzled incomprehension, that much of the early business of the Getty Trust was conducted. Not long after becoming a member of the board, Murphy realized that it would be essential to retire some of the older members and attract new trustees more knowledgeable about art institutions, trustees who could add vigor and diversity to the board.[58]

· · · · ·

Nancy Englander was appointed director of program planning and analysis in December 1982, thereby becoming Williams's chief deputy during the early institutional development. Lani Duke became the education specialist as director of the Getty Center for Education in the Arts.[59] Englander was Williams's eyes and ears. Her task was formidable: it fell to her to analyze needs and commitment of funds while keeping in mind the relationship of trust programs to one another and to the field at large. It was a large pie that she was to slice, but competition for the slices was intense and vociferous.

Williams won approval from the board of trustees in spring 1982 for an expanded institution, one with separate but interlocking centers. In addition to the museum, there would be seven operating programs: the Getty Center for the History of Art and the Humanities, the Getty Conservation Institute, the Getty Art History Information Program, the Getty Center for Education in the Arts, the Program for Art on Film, the Museum Management Institute, and the Getty Publication Program (later a part of the Grant Program developed in 1984). Adjustments would be made as the years went by, but as Williams saw it, the ultimate mission of the J. Paul Getty Trust was nothing less than a contribution to art as grand as its endowment.[60]

In spite of the forward momentum for a multifaceted institution, puzzlement continued as to why Getty had left such a staggering sum to his museum. The villa and his art collection obviously had great significance for him, but without more detailed instructions his trustees were left the burden of divining what it was he had in mind. The suggestion was raised that perhaps Getty did not realize the amount of money he was leaving to the museum—the implementing clause of his will had been written many years before, when the residue of his estate would have been much less—but that explanation seemed unlikely for a man who counted every cent and knew his net worth at any moment. Why did a museum he had never seen have such a pull on his emotions and resources? Some of those who had worked with Getty on the design of the villa had the impression that he always meant to visit it, to stroll through the peristyle, visit the galleries, view his great Herakles sculpture in its domed temple—but perhaps not in this life. One fact seemed certain: he had endowed it for eons.

· · · · ·

Throughout 1982 and 1983 Williams and Englander launched the components of the Getty's plan. Englander's work during this period was crucial: she acted as an interim director for the programs while simultaneously searching for permanent program leaders. By the time directors were recruited, many of the new programs had already taken shape. "She was able to identify the key players, the interesting issues, and where to put the money," recalled Deborah Marrow, who worked as a program officer under Englander. "She was really brilliant at that." Englander was unstoppable—intuitive and effective; she also expected people around her to be perceptive and quick as well. She demanded much of her staff and received much from them.[61]

Williams and Englander sought program directors with a record of accomplishment in their fields who could be entrepreneurial and creative in their thinking while at the same time working in an interdisciplinary fashion. It was asking a lot to expect creative people to avoid becoming overly invested in and protective of their newly hatched programs, but Williams felt there was great potential for intellectual synergy in the new Getty Center concept. For example, he felt that museums fail to present art in the broader context of social history, and he hoped the more holistic approach of the Getty programs would remedy that.

In spring 1982, six years after the death of J. Paul Getty, the legal issues connected with settling the estate were more or less resolved. Williams had masterfully stewarded the trust through years of tangled family lawsuits and tax disputes. The endowment, valued at $750 million when Getty died, was now worth a staggering $1.1 billion. Moreover, Williams and the trustees were ready with a plan that would relieve art world anxiety about this "embarrassment of riches," as a British journalist described it,[62] and provide responsible disbursement of the bequest.

The entire future of the Getty endowment was tied to the price of Getty Oil stock, a highly volatile and potentially erratic asset. Harold Williams, as president of the J. Paul Getty Trust, sought the golden moment when he could get rid of the vulnerable stock and diversify the trust's holdings. Even more perilous to the endowment, Williams feared, were the unpredictable actions of Gordon Getty, now sole trustee of the Sarah C. Getty Trust, which held roughly 40 percent of the total ownership of the Getty Oil Company. The Getty Oil Company had been shrewdly controlled by J. Paul Getty, who personally owned only 12 percent of the stock, but also controlled the 40 percent share held by the Sarah C. Getty Trust established by his mother. It was Getty's personal fortune, largely the 12 percent interest in Getty Oil, that he left to the museum. But the other 40 percent, under the Sarah C. Getty Trust, was now mostly under the control of Getty's younger son, Gordon. In addition to serving as trustee of the Sarah C. Getty Trust, Gordon Getty held a seat on the board of directors of Getty Oil.

Getty Oil stock declined from $110 a share in 1980 to $50 a share in 1982. Williams, aware that the price did not reflect the underlying value of the company's oil reserves, worried that Getty Oil would become attractive to raiders. Merger fever had overtaken Wall Street investment bankers, encouraged by lax antitrust enforcement and the free-market economic policies of the Reagan administration. A series of industries had been swept up in the rush to merge: food companies, the entertainment industry, and others, from paper products to technology. Williams's concern was right on target, for the market would soon see a rash of giant oil mergers that would be the largest in American business history.

Getty Oil Company executives tended to treat Gordon in a dismissive manner as a strange presence in their midst. He was six feet five inches tall and had a mop of black curly hair. His clothes and mannerisms suggested the absent-minded professor or the eccentric musician. However, the Getty scion, as unfit as he appeared for the responsibility, wanted nothing less than control of Getty Oil and the removal of Chief Executive Officer Sidney R. Peterson and other Getty executives. Gordon had long been dominated by his father and overshadowed by his half brother George. An intelligent man with a deep interest in the humanities, he had been a dismal failure in Getty business affairs. When he was a young man Gordon had been sent by his father to manage a key oil concession in the Middle East, but after a series of inept initiatives he wound up in jail. He was then subjected to repeated humiliation from his father, who sent him scathing letters and wired degrading assignments for him to carry out. He endured the contempt of his half brother George, who reportedly ridiculed the "dreamy" Gordon to their father. When Gordon brought his suit to force his father to pay out increased dividends to beneficiaries of the family trust, the senior Getty fought him ferociously in court for six years and allowed attorneys to picture Gordon as "an inept, gold-digging ingrate."[63]

If the name Getty was synonymous with family dysfunction, as one reporter observed, nowhere was it more exemplified than in Gordon's systematic attack on the Getty Oil Company. Psychologists could well speculate on Gordon's motivation. It was true the stock was undervalued, but additional profit could not have meant that much to Gordon. He was receiving $28 million a year from Getty earnings paid through the Sarah C. Getty Trust. His personal pleasures, which centered on music, were not expensive pursuits, and his lifestyle as managed by his socially involved wife was elaborate but well within the family means. As events unfolded Getty Oil officials who knew the emphasis J. Paul Getty had put on the company as a family enterprise came to believe that Gordon had launched a campaign of passionate revenge against his father.

Inside the executive boardroom of Getty Oil tensions ran deep as it became increasingly apparent that Gordon could no longer be controlled. J Paul Getty, as sole trustee of the Sarah C. Getty Trust, had named three equal co-trustees to serve after his death: his son Gordon Getty; his attorney, Cornelius Lansing Hays, whose brash and forceful representation of Getty interests had made him an intimate Getty associate for many years; and the trust officers of Security Pacific National Bank. Security Pacific, fearing more liability than they cared to take on, declined to serve, and for six years after Getty's death, Gordon Getty and Hays operated as co-trustees, with the authoritarian Hayes making the decisions. When Hayes died of cancer in 1982 Getty Oil Company insiders feared that Gordon would feel emboldened to make his move. Just what that move would be and when it would occur worried Getty executives, who debated among themselves possible options to thwart actions by Gordon.

Getty CEO and chairman Sidney Peterson maintained a coolly cordial relationship with Gordon at first; but friction between Gordon and the board intensified, and it became apparent that Gordon was determined to seize control of the company. He could easily do so by purchasing more Getty stock to add to the 40 percent stake he controlled as trustee of the family trust. More worrisome still, he could potentially dismantle the corporate giant by selling to a third party. Another route could be for Gordon to form an alliance with the J. Paul Getty Trust, which owned 12 percent of the stock. Such an alliance would constitute 52 percent of the stock and majority control of the Getty Oil Company. With that kind of control, as one observer noted, Gordon Getty could readily use an outside corporate raider to seize the company and name himself chairman. It was not long before Gordon announced that that was exactly what he planned to do.

Williams held a seat on the board of Getty Oil and witnessed much of the heated friction among Gordon, Peterson, and other members of board, but he remained focused on protecting the museum trust. The combined holdings of the family trust controlled by Gordon and the museum's stock controlled by Williams constituted unprecedented leverage over a billion-dollar global enterprise. As one fascinated business reporter noted, "Majority control of a public corporation by two shareholders was an anomaly in American business, and would prove a key factor as the Gordon Getty vs. Getty Oil story unfolded."[64]

Gordon was approached by Hugh Liedtke, chief executive of the oil giant Pennzoil, with an attractive offer in which Getty Oil would be reorganized: Pennzoil would own three-sevenths of the reconstituted company, and Gordon and the museum trust would own four-sevenths. Gordon would have the title of chairman, and Liedtke would be named chief executive. After days of bickering over price and terms, Gordon assured Liedtke that he would accept Pennzoil's offer. An emotional meeting of Getty Oil directors followed at which the terms were set for Pennzoil to purchase Getty stock at a price of $112.50 a share. But before the final paperwork was signed, John McKinley, chief executive at Texaco, made Gordon another offer—$125 per share. Gordon accepted. Williams joined Gordon in the agreement with Texaco, as his obligation was to obtain the best price for the museum's stock. When word reached Pennzoil that Texaco had managed to outbid them for control of Getty Oil, despite Gordon's prior assurances, Liedtke, a determined man long tagged with the nickname "Chairman Mao," erupted in rage. "We're going to sue everybody in sight," he said.[65]

The sale of Getty Oil to Texaco was the largest corporate acquisition in U.S. history up to that time. However, true to his threat, Liedtke instituted a lawsuit of gargantuan proportions, accusing Texaco of unlawful intervention in the proposed Pennzoil merger. The issue was whether Getty Oil already had a binding contract with Houston-based Pennzoil at the time it agreed to accept Texaco's higher offer.

Tremendous tension emerged among museum board members as the litigation grew; some trustees believed Williams acted beyond the scope of his authority during negotiations with Texaco. At one memorable meeting Harold Berg, board chairman and a former president of the Getty Oil Company, reprimanded Williams severely for acting without authority from the board. He expressed his indignation in front of the assembled trustees, attacking Williams for what he called duplicitous actions. With great effort, Williams managed to stay calm. He felt he had accomplished a major coup. He had delivered the trust's future from dependence on the Getty Oil stock price and, in the process, had earned an enormous billion-dollar premium for the museum. The windfall was so large, Williams said later, that if he had turned the Texaco offer down, he would have been in breach of his fiduciary duties.[66]

Following the sale of the trust's Getty stock to Texaco in 1984, the museum's endowment jumped to $2.27 billion, meaning the vexing problem of how to spend $65 million a year had just doubled. There were more hurdles, however, before the spending could commence. Pennzoil's suit sought $7.5 billion in actual damages and billions more in punitive damages. As a result, the officers of Texaco, Williams, and the museum's board of trustees, including Murphy, were entangled in complex litigation that brought a cloud of uncertainty for several years. It seemed possible that the museum trust could lose some or all of its fortune if Pennzoil prevailed in the suit. In a grave turn of events, after a seventeen-week trial, a Houston jury in November 1985 ruled against Texaco and awarded Pennzoil $11.1 billion in damages. Although the immediate fear was that the Getty Trust would be responsible for a significant portion of the damages, it was soon revealed that Williams had shrewdly demanded that the merger contract include an indemnification of the Getty Trust by Texaco in the event of litigation concerning the merger. Stung by the record-setting award to Pennzoil, the once-giant Texaco Corporation filed for bankruptcy protection. It was the largest American corporation ever to seek such protection. Ultimately the J. Paul Getty Trust was not liable for any portion of the eventual $3 billion settlement that Texaco paid Pennzoil in 1988.

"Gordon was no businessman," wrote *Wall Street Journal* reporter Thomas Petzinger Jr. "Everybody agreed on that. But his decision to sell out was perfectly timed, coming near the peak of oil prices, just before the Organization of Petroleum Exporting Countries (OPEC) lost its cohesion and world oil quotes dived into the basement. 'I picked up my marbles,' Gordon would say, 'and I took them home.'" The strange twisted saga that wiped the Getty name from the oil business and wrecked Texaco's fortunes prompted Petzinger to ask, "Would Texaco be seeking protection from creditors in bankruptcy court if J. Paul Getty had been a better father?"[67] Getty Oil was the creation of Gordon's grandfather, but it was J. Paul Getty, the second-generation patriarch, who planned a far-flung empire, its divisions headed by his sons. Gordon seemed out to bury once and for all the dream that had obsessed Getty and had overtaken and displaced any other instincts of fatherhood. Had Gordon at last proved himself a more astute and powerful business operator than his father gave him credit for, possibly outshining the old man?

Gordon Getty was not the only astute operator in this deal. In hindsight, the indemnification clause in the contract with Texaco may have been Williams's finest moment as steward of the Getty Trust resources, demonstrating his intellect, legal finesse, courage, and plain guts. Williams later acknowledged that he may have broken the rules in not addressing the board of trustees as events unfolded and in unilaterally making fundamental and, more often than not, irreversible decisions, but he defended his actions, stating that time was of the essence and that he could not allow the value of the trust to remain vulnerable to the price of Getty Oil stock. Furthermore, he was not confident that if he had consulted the board of trustees they would have approached the issue objectively, as many of them had long-standing relationships with the Getty Oil Company and would balk at its dismantling in the sale to Texaco. Williams was familiar with the treacherous world of the corporate takeover; he had experienced it from the vantage point of the boardroom with Norton Simon as well as from the hallowed halls of the SEC. As a result he was able to survive the crisis with little loss of sleep, confident that the endowment would be safe. Looking back at what has been widely called the bitterest and most controversial takeover in American business history, Williams said he failed to predict that Texaco would ultimately lose the court battle with Pennzoil. "Had I known that," Williams said years later, "I might have had more sleepless nights."[68] The man Franklin Murphy selected to lead the trust performed exactly as Murphy expected, and the trust was the beneficiary of his skill and nerve. "More dollars than J. Paul Getty had dreamed of came our way," Murphy said, thinking what a surprise the turn of events would have been to the parsimonious founder.[69]

AN ACROPOLIS FOR LOS ANGELES

As a private operating foundation, the Getty Trust is one of a relatively small group of U.S. foundations that create and run their own programs, in contrast to grant-making foundations, such as the Rockefeller and Ford Foundations, that fund the work of others. Tax law requires that an operating foundation spend 4.25 percent of the average market value of its endowment three out of every four years on programs it creates and operates. Grants and gifts to others were limited to no more than 0.75 percent of the endowment, but considering the size of the Getty endowment, the small percentage available for grants is still a significant dollar amount.

J. Paul Getty had left it up to the museum's trustees to implement his unspecified wishes, and they in turn had sought Murphy's guidance in shaping the institution's mandate. Murphy's most significant contribution here was to insist on narrowing the scope of the museum's programs and to promote the idea that the museum remain focused on European art before 1900. Murphy and Williams were adamant that the guidelines be clear and that the museum stay out of the business of modern and contemporary art and avoid, as well, expanding into art of non-Western cultures; the focus should be on increasing the breadth and depth of its existing collections. "We decided to concentrate on small, high quality objects for the museum," Williams says. "It was too late to be a comprehensive museum. It would have been too costly."[70]

John Walsh, the respected curator of paintings at Boston's Museum of Fine Arts and a former curator of European paintings at the Metropolitan Museum of Art in New York, became director of the Getty Museum in 1983 and, in the words of one art critic, brought with him "an imprimatur of East Coast prestige to the renegade institution." "He was a brilliant choice," Edmund P. Pillsbury, director of the Kimbell Art Museum in Fort Worth, said. "I don't know if he's liked, but he is certainly respected. And in this field it is more important to be respected than to be liked."[71] Deborah Gribbon, seizing the rare chance to build an important collection and work with the highly respected Walsh, left the Isabella Gardner Museum in Boston to serve as assistant director for curatorial affairs in 1984 and was later named deputy director and chief curator.[72]

When Walsh arrived, he was aware of the challenge and responsibility of the immense bequest, but he could not know that one year later, when the Getty Oil Company was sold to Texaco, the endowment would double—and then be cast in doubt as litigation ensued. In addition to the difficulty of planning acquisitions with an unknown amount to spend, Walsh faced the problem of overcoming the art world's notion of the J. Paul Getty Museum as an oddity, a replica of a first-century villa with an uneven collection of paintings and decorative arts, as well as suspect antiquities. "They'll never get the picture galleries right," Kenneth Clark, the British art historian, was quoted as saying after a visit in 1978 to the museum in Malibu, where he found paintings crammed in airless galleries on the second floor. Another critic had called the paintings "striking monuments to the second rate."[73] Gribbon herself observed: "It was going to cost a fortune simply to buy great paintings, since Getty had left behind a very uneven and generally disappointing collection much inferior to that of the Norton Simon Museum."[74] Although she felt that Getty had made a strong start in acquiring Greek and Roman antiquities, she believed purchasing additional works to make a truly worthy collection would be "an expensive and uncertain business."[75] Nevertheless, Gribbon thought that by focusing the collection on a few areas of European art, it could be distinctive: "The expanding Los Angeles County Museum of Art was providing the city with works representing the whole world, from the earliest times to the present. Why try to create another large general art museum?"[76]

Murphy agreed with this view. He visualized the Getty as concentrating on peak artistic achievement in Western culture. He saw no reason to broaden the geography to include the art of Asia, Africa, and the Americas, or any need to extend the chronology to include the twentieth century. Other Los Angeles museums were covering fields not included in the Getty's goals: Asian art at the Pacific Asia Museum, cutting-edge art at the new Museum of Contemporary Art, ethnic and folk art at UCLA's forthcoming Fowler Museum, and a specialized focus on English art at the Huntington.

The board wrestled with defining the kind of creative expression that met their mandate. In 1983 the museum had an opportunity to acquire the most remarkable collection of illuminated manuscripts in the world. The German chocolate manufacturer Peter Ludwig and his wife, Irene, had assembled 144 examples of medieval and early Renaissance illuminated manuscripts. Murphy was exhilarated by this opportunity to expand the museum's holdings in material related to the Renaissance; much to his surprise and disappointment, however, the board of trustees rejected the purchase, asserting that the museum was not in the business of books. "This is not the Morgan Library," one trustee curtly insisted. Murphy patiently pointed out that they would not be buying books but "illuminations." He called the art "medieval paintings," hoping to convince the trustees of the significance and value of the Ludwig Collection. After lengthy debate in heated meetings, Murphy managed to persuade the board that acquisition of the works was a rare and significant opportunity for the museum.

The arrival from Germany of the Ludwig Collection was an event celebrated by the museum and widely acknowledged as important to collecting in America. Murphy's longtime associate in the book trade, the rare-book dealer Jake Zeitlin, had participated in bringing the sale about. He professed himself amazed at Murphy's finesse in moving a stodgy, uninformed, unwilling board toward a good decision for the right reasons. "You are the greatest generative force that has emerged in this community," he wrote Murphy, "and I am very proud to have participated in a very small way in some of your activities."[77] The museum curators were also in awe of Murphy's achievement with the board. "He is the person on the board most aware of art," one curator said. "He always gets the point of why something is important."[78]

Over the next several years Walsh enhanced the painting collection with some superb masterworks, but he had to delve deeply into Getty funds to acquire them: for Jacopo da Pontormo's sublime *Portrait of Cosimo I de' Medici,* the museum paid $35 million in 1989; for Andrea Mantegna's *Adoration of the Magi,* $11 million; for Rembrandt's *Abduction of Europa,* $27 million; and for *Aphrodite,* a large Greek sculpture, $18 million, the highest price ever paid for an antiquity. Other notable acquisitions were Titian's *Venus and Adonis,* Vincent van Gogh's *Irises,* Pierre-Auguste Renoir's *La Promenade,* and James Ensor's *Entry of Christ into Brussels.* Praising Walsh's eye and commenting on the transformation of the collection, one writer said that what had been a rich man's folly was becoming a connoisseur's jewel box. "John started with odds and ends," said one expert. "Now he has high points he can build around. His acquisitions are quite extraordinary. He goes for quality . . . and the example has certainly resonated throughout the community and the art world."[79] This was the kind of praise that Murphy had hoped the museum's collection would merit.

The museum was frequently in the news in articles that described the quality and importance of works acquired and noted, in particular, record prices paid for some of them. In fact, Walsh put great effort into assuring the art world that the Getty was not embarking on a buying spree that would cause havoc in the international art market. The Getty acted with restraint in the auctions and declined to acquire works that were claimed as national patrimonies or that came on the market in dubious circumstances. "John has to tread a very fine line between being responsible and careful but sufficiently bold to justify good use of the Getty's resources," Kimbell Museum director Pillsbury noted. "We can't be the museum with the best collection in the world. It's too late for that," Walsh told audiences.

"But we can be the museum that does the most with its collection. That's our goal."[80]

. . . . .

The need for more museum space and the mandate to spend extraordinary sums to meet tax requirements inclined thinking toward a grand museum facility and a compound for the trust programs. The trustees unanimously voted to search for a site.[81] A hilltop plateau in the Santa Monica Mountains overlooking the neighborhoods of Brentwood and Bel Air caught their attention. Rising 400 feet above the surrounding plain, this site afforded a spectacular panoramic view of the city, the chaparral-covered hills, and the ocean to the west. The trustees purchased a total of 742 acres (including 500 acres owned by the University of California) before announcing plans to build a 940,000-square-foot art center.

"Once we found the Brentwood site, the search was over," Williams said. "It had so much to offer—great natural beauty, an elevated lookout point offering a unique perspective on the city and proximity to the freeway that allows the center to be an integral part of the fabric of Los Angeles." Williams insisted: "The Getty Center is for everyone. We would like everyone to feel a kind of ownership, to feel that it's theirs."[82] In the public commentary that followed, however, not everyone agreed with Williams. The symbolism of a castle on a hill was not lost on critics, who bemoaned the center's distance from the heart of the city. Murphy had wanted the planned complex to be more centrally located, but after consulting with leading land developers, he realized all the available sites would involve tremendous expense and a multitude of complications. After the hilltop site was selected he turned his attention to picturing ways in which the mountainous terrain could be made inviting for the public. He remembered the appeal of Italian villages that cascaded down hillsides and asked his brother-in-law, Lyman Ennis, an architect, to round up pictures and drawings for him of such settings.

In October 1984 the announcement was made that Richard Meier, known for his impressive, clean-line, stark white buildings in a contemporary international style, had been selected to create the buildings for the Getty Center.[83] Completion of the design was set for 1991. Williams was pleased with Meier's grasp of the center concept, and he felt that Meier understood the need to have buildings that fostered easy interaction among the denizens of the different programs. However, Murphy was said to have reacted with dread, complaining of the "damned white-refrigerator buildings" of Meier's usual style. The press called it the architectural commission of the century, the best since Rockefeller Center, and certainly the most attention grabbing. "This is put up or shut up time for me," Meier told reporters in acknowledging the awesome nature of the assignment.[84] In the excitement over the planned museum complex and the selection of Meier as architect, euphoria swept over the Getty, a feeling of elation and relief that would soon prove premature.

Murphy, who had come to know the neighbors of the nearby affluent communities during his years as chancellor of UCLA, predicted a battle royal over the giant construction project. Protests against the master plan were quickly mounted in a series of volatile community meetings. The trustees knew the project would be complicated, but they were unprepared for the difficulties they were to encounter. The *Los Angeles Times* arts reporter, Suzanne Muchnic, summarized the pitfalls: "The combination of constructing a six-building complex on a highly visible hill, appeasing neighbors, satisfying legal requirements, resolving geologic problems, dealing with environmental issues and accommodating exacting architectural plans—while building a public image for a wealthy upstart institution— was a daunting experience."[85] Before the work was finished more than one hundred restrictions would be added to the Getty Center's construction permit, the largest number of design-limiting conditions ever imposed by City Hall. An especially bizarre and onerous stipulation required that not a single load of soil could be hauled off the site before, during, or after construction. When Murphy, who had listened to condition after condition, learned of this latest neighborhood tactic, he simply threw back his head and snorted with laughter.

Williams was eager to get the Getty's seven operating programs, scattered in offices all over town, housed on one campus. The Getty Museum in Malibu would continue to house the Greek and Roman antiquities, but the other collections—paintings, furniture, and decorative arts—would come to the new museum building at the hilltop center. With the Getty Trust programs temporarily operating from different locations, Williams found that the interdisciplinary synergy he had hoped to see was not materializing. The Center for the History of Art and the Humanities, headed by Kurt W. Forster, was quartered in a Santa Monica office building where its staff was already in conflict with the staff at the museum in Malibu over library resources. The Getty Conservation Institute was working out of offices and laboratories in Marina del Rey as well as crowded museum facilities in Malibu. The Getty Art History Information Program was using temporary quarters at the same location in Santa Monica as the Center for the History of Art and the Humanities and was trying to stay in touch with its editors, who were scattered worldwide. The Program for Art on Film, a joint project with the Metropolitan Museum of Art, was housed in New York, and the Museum Management Institute was working from San Francisco. The Getty Center for Education in the Arts and the Grant Program were sharing space with the trust's administrative offices in Century City. Synergy was not happening; in fact, the various programs were growing increasingly jealous and protective of their particular areas of interest.

· · · · ·

The trustees continued to struggle with their ongoing, difficult but enviable problem—how to spend annually the large amounts of cash required by IRS regulations. The seven operating programs initially could not absorb all the funds the trust needed to disburse, so the Getty Trust took advantage of the tax code provision that allowed it to make grants to a specified extent, even though it was an operating rather than a grant-giving foundation. In October 1984 the *Los Angeles Times* ran a surprise announcement saying that the J. Paul Getty Trust was ready to distribute millions of dollars in grants and gifts to art institutions and individuals. The article described the establishment of an international grant program as an ongoing project to support the visual arts and art-related humanities worldwide. In addition to the international program, the Getty Trust would be awarding millions of dollars as onetime gifts to Los Angeles art institutions.[86]

Murphy served as chairman of the trustees' first grant committee, and Nancy Englander, in addition to her role as director of program planning and analysis, acted as the first director of the grant program. Murphy felt that local grants would enhance public relations for the Getty Trust as well as fund desirable work that the understaffed, inadequately housed Getty organization could not perform. All his professional life Murphy had sought ways to assure the preservation of cultural artifacts and expand the audience for art; he had studied means to educate the public to the importance of art, had beseeched legislators to support the arts, and had begged and cajoled donors to participate in his vision. Now he found himself at his desk with resources that exceeded all his dreams; it was up to him as chairman of the grants committee to direct the final decisions. He took out his ruler and lined six columns across a page representing the years 1985–90. At the left-hand edge he penned the names of Los Angeles institutions and organizations, each name allotted its line. Like a master gamesman who knew the competing interests of the pieces on the board and precisely how they interacted, he manipulated a chart in which millions of dollars would be spent to enhance the city's cultural life. There was no computer spreadsheet or calculator at hand, only a man with a blank sheet of paper, a pencil, and a ruler—but a man who had long been preparing for this moment and who possessed the in-depth understanding of the city and its needs. He then fine-tuned some of the dates and amounts with Englander, who added her revisions in blue ink to his penciled columns. The onetime Local Grant Program injected dollars directly into the bloodstream of cash-starved educational and cultural institutions: the Los Angeles County Museum of Art ($3 million over three years); the Museum of Contemporary Art ($3 million over three years); UCLA's Museum of Cultural History ($2 million over two years); and Plaza de la Raza ($500,000 in one year). Additional grants went to the Japanese American Cultural Center ($500,000), the Huntington Library ($1.5 million), the Clark Library ($1 million), the California Institute of the Arts ($1 million), the Southwest Museum ($1 million), Hebrew Union College ($1 million), Honnold Library at Claremont University ($1 million), Whittier College ($500,000), the Museum of Natural History Library ($500,000), UCLA's Library Program ($1 million), the California Community Foundation ($2 million); Otis-Parsons ($500,000), the Craft and Folk Art Museum ($500,000), and the Pacific Asia Museum ($500,000).[87]

The recommendations on Murphy's chart were approved by the board of trustees, who later included a multimillion-dollar grant for library development at the University of Southern California in memory of J. Paul Getty. "In total then, we will have spent $21 million on our local neighbors and will have touched all of the visible and not-so-visible cultural institutions and research libraries," Murphy wrote Williams.[88] As many of the city's leading cultural institutions suddenly received significant sums of money without asking, "overnight, *envy* became *gratitude*," Murphy observed.[89]

Doling out Getty grant money was a high point for Murphy. He knew that in the long run, as an operating foundation, the Getty would not continue to make large gifts; however, it did so for a brief time and, in fact, had no alternative. He made the most of the moment. He was able to live his improbable dream and dispense huge amounts of money without having wealth; he was a vicarious philanthropist, a fantasy billionaire.

Murphy continued to serve on the board of trustees grant committee supervising the more modest ongoing grant program that evolved. Deborah Marrow—who worked on grant proposals under the direction of Englander and later became director of the grant program (subsequently renamed the Getty Foundation)—remembered Murphy as the ideal chairman for the grant committee. "He was unbelievably knowledgeable about cultural institutions all over the world," said Marrow. "There isn't a person in an arts leadership position in Los Angeles that Franklin Murphy did not know and support in some fundamental way. . . . The grants—even small ones—really got him jazzed."[90]

. . . . .

Unexpected delays in the design phase of the mountaintop Getty Center frustrated Williams. Some six hundred Getty employees continued to be housed in "temporary" quarters from downtown to Malibu. Few felt they really knew Williams, the much talked of but infrequently seen leader, who was operating from an office tower in Century City. The museum at Malibu was virtually out of the loop and struggling with responsibility for a growing and evolving collection. Some staffers felt that with so much attention given to the design and construction of the new Getty Center, the Getty Trust programs were being neglected, and they complained that the trust's priorities had become confused.

As director of program planning and analysis, Englander moved from one program to another, solving logistical problems and keeping alive the concept of program interconnectedness. Murphy acknowledged Englander's skill and resourcefulness in getting the programs under way. "Nancy was very savvy, a very tough lady, single-minded lady, strong and knowledgeable," he said. "[She] knew a great deal about art and art institutions, . . . knew museums inside and out, and knew how they ran and who the people were." Murphy gave Englander credit for much of the Getty's program structure and the key people who were recruited.[91]

Englander and Williams had a close, effective working relationship that dated to the earliest days of the Getty Trust—before there was a firm concept of what the trust was to be. Eventually the two became romantically involved, and their relationship became generally known when they decided to live together awaiting termination of their marriages. Some staff members were upset and felt Englander's effectiveness in coordinating the programs was greatly diminished and her objectivity compromised. Some of the older trustees, uncomfortable with contemporary mores, found Williams and Englander's personal living arrangements unacceptable and insisted that Englander resign. Williams protested any suggestion that Englander should leave her post. "She was really the creative genius who defined what the Getty was beyond the museum," Williams pointed out, saying that her presence was needed to continue the work she had inaugurated.[92]

Englander felt the trustees should base their judgment on the work she accomplished for the Getty Center and not on their opinion of her personal life. "I had demonstrated enough of my professionalism that they didn't have to be concerned," she said.[93]

Murphy described the conflict as a tension-filled drama: "Certain members of the board were very, very upset about this, very. Very concerned. Quite honestly, I was not all that concerned. And there were several of us, Pat Whaley and I and a few others. We were uncomfortable with it. But we thought it was tolerable. There were some who were absolutely adamant and strongly angry about this. . . . Harold was standing firm that he's not going to change his personal life, he was very much in love with this lady, highly respected her and so on." When the matter became a standoff between Williams and the trustees, John Connell resigned from the board. "John's resignation was a direct result of the fact that Harold and Nancy remained together," Murphy said. "They did get married, of course, when his divorce and her divorce became final. But then there were others on the Board who were very, very vocal about this, [who] became highly unpleasant." Murphy said the controversy also took a toll on the already fractious staff, and he regretted that the matter was not resolved more readily. "Finally Harold agreed that Nancy had to retire. And we tried to make it a graceful retirement and we did the best we could but I suspect that there's a sense of real bitterness in both parties as a result of that It's the one unhappy episode in what is otherwise an enormously successful and happy business."[94]

Murphy had seen instances before of romance overtaking events. Murphy's friend Nelson Rockefeller had forfeited his chance for the presidency, the goal of his entire adult life, by divorcing his wife and marrying Margaretta Fitler Murphy ("Happy") in 1963. Romance had created a tense situation at the National Gallery, when Ruth Carter and John R. Stevenson, two mature trustees who had worked closely together on the board, decided to marry. Murphy understood how Williams and Englander had grown close amid the excitement of travel as envoys for the Getty Trust. For them, those early years of designing plans for the Getty Center were surely a never-to-be-forgotten time. Murphy himself had known the delight, more than once, of traveling with an attractive and knowledgeable female companion and coenthusiast for the work he was pursuing. However, he could not imagine himself throwing over his marriage and disrupting his family to make an extramarital relationship permanent, and he was puzzled by the sway of the heart that could make powerful men do so.

Englander left the Getty's professional staff but remained as a consultant for the next several years. Since there was no permanent director for the grant program, Englander acted as part-time director during her consultancy. In 1987 Deborah Marrow was appointed assistant director of the program and continued the work with Murphy on the local grants benefiting Los Angeles institutions. The sudden loss of Englander added confusion during a difficult early period and undoubtedly did damage to the longed-for synergy among the embryonic center programs. "After she left, there was a very real void," Marrow said.[95]

Englander's forced departure and Murphy's unwillingness to stand up for her in front of the board of trustees was a source of tremendous disappointment to Williams. He felt Murphy could have turned the board around had he put his mind to it. The staunchly conservative group of aging trustees had their own view of the matter, and Murphy refused to try to alter their mind-set. Williams recalled the sad episode as his greatest disappointment in Murphy as both friend and trustee. When asked why he thought Murphy refused to lend his considerable clout to resolve the fracas, Williams sadly recalled that despite all his strengths, "Murphy doesn't like to risk being on the losing side of anything."[96]

. . . . .

The controversy about Englander renewed Murphy's desire to see new membership on the board of trustees. Williams and Murphy were struggling with trustees who had spent their lives in the bitterly competitive oil industry and had little appreciation of the center's pioneering role; nor did they understand the need to nurture the spirit of the creative and talented officials who were dedicating themselves to bringing the center into existence. Murphy had deep reservations about the advisability of such a board of longtime wealthy comrades in arms running an operation like the Getty Center. Early on he warned Williams that "benign cronyism on the board could become the Getty's Achilles' heel."[97] Williams and Murphy worked together on a plan whereby board membership would have strict term limits and end with mandatory retirement. Plans were also adopted for increasing the number of members and rotating the chairmanship. They were hopeful that the revised membership terms would open the way for new trustees from different backgrounds who would energize the directorate.

Frank Wells and John Whitehead joined the board in 1989. As president and chief operating officer of the Walt Disney Company, Wells had had a central role in the company's revitalization. Whitehead had enjoyed a distinguished career as a senior partner at Goldman Sachs and Company and served as deputy secretary of state from 1985 to 1989. Harold Berg, who had served on the board of trustees for fifteen years, including twelve years as chairman, retired in 1990 after quiet maneuvers on the part of Murphy and other concerned board members to give him a graceful departure. The composition of the board following the term-limit changes brought broader cultural experience to the board but little ethnic or gender diversity. "The Getty is hardly alone among powerful cultural institutions in this regard," noted Christopher Knight in the *Times,* "but it's a serious liability for the achievement of its stated aspirations for the life of democratic culture."[98]

Williams continued to search out candidates for board positions who had a breadth of financial and cultural experience and were of an innovative bent. Jon Lovelace, Rocco C. Siciliano, and Herbert Lucas, Southern California corporate executives with proven interest in the arts, became trustees. Murphy friend and colleague Robert Erburu was also named to the board. Jennifer Jones Simon (Norton Simon's second wife and widow) joined the board, becoming its only female trustee and fueling optimism on the part of those who, like Williams, hoped that the Getty and Simon museums might merge their interests in some meaningful way. Kenneth Dayton, Vartan Gregorian, John Whitehead, and John Fey were recruited as trustees from outside the region in answer to Williams's desire for geographic diversity.

· · · · ·

Murphy served as chairman of the building committee for the trust from May 12, 1989, until the design phase came to a close in 1991. The immense cost of building the Getty Center on the challenging site became increasingly clear as plans were drawn and redrawn. In the face of repeated upward budget revisions, the trustees began to consider scaling back the project, or even turning to a different architect. But design was too far along for such drastic measures.

As construction estimates surged, a new accounting term was invented, "Getty Creep." The telling phrase would have embarrassed J. Paul Getty, a man notorious for tight control of the dollar. Williams wanted the Getty Center to be a masterpiece of architecture and believed that an enduring architectural achievement was envisioned, if not mandated, by the trust.[99] He had strong support from Murphy in this regard. Thanks to favorable financial markets, the endowment was continuing to grow, and the Getty could afford the ambitious project but not without a check on unlimited creep. Under Williams's astute financial system the assets of the J. Paul Getty Trust were carefully managed by highly specialized outside investment experts. Six years after the transfer of assets from J. Paul Getty's estate the trust's endowment—under Williams's watch—had increased by more than 270 percent.

During this period Murphy worked closely with Stephen D. Rountree, the energetic administrator who had served as deputy director of the museum until 1984, when Williams asked him to oversee the building program. (Later Rountree would be named executive vice president and chief operating officer.) Rountree met regularly with Murphy at the Times Mirror building, where he spread out charts and diagrams on a corner table in the cafeteria. The easygoing Rountree, a fifth-generation Californian who had grown up in the San Gabriel Valley, was a welcome relief in the high-stress, conflict-ridden process of building a billion-dollar arts metropolis. During the design phase, Rountree was expected to accommodate the needs of six or seven programs while keeping the trustees assured that what was on the drawing board was what had been promised. Despite his relative youth (forty years old in 1989) and his midlevel rank at the Getty, Rountree took on the role of go-between, a "translator," as he said, one who put out fires, mended fences, and "stopped high-powered people from killing one another."[100] Concerted effort was needed to placate the Getty's neighbors, and Rountree attended more than one hundred fifty meetings to address their concerns. Rocco Siciliano, who helped find the Getty Center site and chaired the board's building committee prior to Murphy, praised Rountree's skill, describing him as "an astute, balanced, imperturbable person" who deserved "the principal credit" for getting the project built.[101]

By fall 1989 the Los Angeles Planning Commission had approved the site master plan, and the board of trustees had accepted the schematic design. A futuristic automated tram for transporting visitors between the parking structure and center buildings had been accepted. The project's general contractor, Dinwiddie Construction Company, had been selected, and in November 1990, in the midst of widespread protests by residents, work had commenced at the north entry parking facility to create a construction staging area. The parking facility was scheduled to be the first element built. The design of the hilltop buildings was not yet settled, however. In crucial meetings of the design advisory committee, Murphy attended ex officio as trustee representative to offer reassurance and to hear the recommendations of the group of distinguished architects and design professionals who had been engaged by the board to provide what Williams called "loving criticism."

About this time the board became distraught to the point of panic about the mounting costs. In his role as chairman of the building committee, Murphy asked the trustees to recognize the complexity and ambition of the project, and he urged them to take enough pride in the goal to commit the necessary funds. In one memorable board meeting, Rountree recalled, Murphy listened impatiently to protests that mushrooming costs were being "criminally ignored." Finally, Murphy leaned forward, looked over his half-rim reading glasses, and asked with chilling patience, "Look. Does anyone remember what it cost to build the Taj Mahal?" The board members grew silent. "That's my point," he said.[102] The board ultimately agreed to expend the necessary amount.

Community leaders had been insistent that architect Meier's trademark design element of white panels not be used to clad the buildings. The afternoon sun would reflect intolerable glare, they claimed. In a meeting held early in 1990, Meier presented a scheme for using different types of stone with colors ranging from gray to green to red. Meier had put a good deal of work into this concept, but the multiple colors did not seem true to Meier's own aesthetic instincts. Rountree recalled that Murphy stood at the rear of the group while they examined a large drawing posted to the wall. Characteristically, Murphy's hands were in his pants pockets, his jacket pushed back, his tie slightly askew as he waited for the appropriate moment. Finally, as the group was hemming and hawing, further confusing Meier, Murphy said in a forthright, honest tone, "Richard, it's not you. It's too fussy. Keep it simple." Murphy's statement opened up the conversation and led to the widely admired choice of Italian travertine stone whose soft, beige, "classical" color would ultimately define the image of the center.

Meier's vision of the museum building as thoroughly modern in every detail was thrown into disarray by museum director Walsh's demand to have European-style galleries with deep-hued, luxurious fabric walls and carved, crown molding as a setting for the nineteenth-century paintings. Thierry Despont, a New York–based French designer, was brought in to work out a solution. Rountree gave Despont credit for taking on a difficult job and negotiating compromises between Walsh and Meier.

As strained as relations were between Meier and Walsh, they paled in comparison to the friction generated by the visionary landscape design of Robert Irwin, who rejected Meier's formal topiaries and classic walkways for a rambling, exuberant planting scheme. Rountree was a pivotal figure in assuaging egos and dealing with the conflicting visions of program directors. His job, he said, was "to help them articulate their needs and, at the same time, not lose sight of unity, coherence and synergy on the campus"—

a tall order but basic to Williams's and Englander's original concept for the center.[103] As the design issues became settled, the immense project drew closer to the date, now considerably delayed, when the final design could be unveiled and the art world invited to pronounce judgment.

· · · · ·

While the new museum for the center was still in the planning and design stage, Walsh was actively searching for outstanding works for its galleries. The J. Paul Getty Museum may have been the envy of the art world because of its huge endowment, but some in that world dismissed its billion-dollar status as inconsequential because it came too late in the art-buying game. "The sad thing is, they have all this money and there's nothing to buy," said Thomas P. F. Hoving, former director of New York's Metropolitan Museum of Art and later editor of *Connoisseur* magazine.[104]

Art authorities talked of "the Getty Factor" and feared that the Getty Museum would ravage the world's art market by driving up prices and carrying off the artistic heritage of Europe. But such a dramatic impact on the art market was not likely; the museum would be buying in only a few sectors of a market that was thought to be a $5 billion to $10 billion enterprise. The Getty Museum was not interested in twentieth-century paintings, the area of most volatility in the 1980s. The soaring prices that the art world saw in that decade were more a result of the excessive exuberance of private collectors than the acquisitiveness of museums. Collectors, especially those new to art, enjoyed the publicity promoted by auction houses eager to give the press yet another story about astronomical prices. Museums found it difficult to compete with such buyers. The Getty was outbid on several occasions.

Murphy insisted that the Getty never become identified as a "monster sopping up all in sight." He stressed careful attention to the subtleties of the ever-changing art market and was adamant about using a disciplined approach at unwieldy international auctions, avoiding impetuous or incautious bidding. The institution's officials, urged to be sensitive to the national patrimony of other countries, adopted a policy of cultural awareness and restraint. Murphy supported a grants program for selected European arts institutions, feeling that such grants would serve as an act of goodwill to alleviate some of the envy provoked by the rich endowment.[105]

In spite of the desire to participate responsibly, worldwide publicity cast a shadow on the trust's intentions when the Getty purchased a fourth-century Greek bronze of a young athlete. The sculpture had been discovered and lifted from the bottom of the Adriatic Sea off Fano in 1964 and sold to dealers. After careful cleaning the sculpture turned out to be one of the most beautiful Greek bronzes ever found. The statue had been offered to J. Paul Getty, who was tempted but said the price was too high; however, after Getty's death, the museum was able to buy the work at a more reasonable figure. Museum officials were taken aback when they were accused of working with a smuggling ring to remove the splendid bronze from Italy. After legal turmoil and the kind of adverse publicity that the Getty strove so hard to avoid, the Italian courts ruled that the sculpture had been found in international waters and was not subject to Italian patrimony laws. The splendid bronze was given, in good faith, an honored place in Getty's Roman villa on the Pacific coast.

But the question of ethics was raised again. In 1987 Thomas Hoving, in *Connoisseur,* charged Walsh and the Getty Museum with "overweening opportunism, shoddy management, duplicity, fear, stupidity and warped values."[106] This was not the first time Hoving and Walsh had clashed. Their personal and philosophic differences dated from fourteen years earlier when Walsh was a curator under Hoving at the Metropolitan Museum. Hoving had since become a roving critic of American museums, critiquing the politics, policies, and aesthetic judgment of museum officials nationwide; his comments were greatly disconcerting to image-conscious Getty officials.

Murphy became alarmed when a spate of bad publicity descended on the Malibu museum concerning policies about antiquities. After the disclosure in spring 1987 that the Getty's veteran curator of antiquities, Jiri Frel, may have engaged in misconduct by allegedly accepting donated artworks and recording them at unusually high prices, Murphy felt that Hoving not only fanned the media flame but also added fuel. Murphy was further concerned in 1988 during an incident in which the Getty Museum was charged with the illegal acquisition of an important antiquity, a large limestone and marble statue believed to date from 420 B.C. and thought to represent Aphrodite. Revelation of the Getty's acquisition of the statue had created quite a stir in the art world. Hoving stepped forward to claim that the Aphrodite had been found at an Italian archaeological site and smuggled out of the country. The *International Herald Tribune* reported that Hoving had tipped off Interpol and the Italian government.

A lengthy investigation revealed no foul play on the part of the Getty Museum, and Hoving's charges of illegal activities were deemed unfounded. Nevertheless, some of Hoving's scathing attacks concerning the authenticity of other museum objects proved legitimate. In November 1988 the museum revealed that a marble "Head of Achilles," thought to be a fourth century B.C. work by the Greek sculptor Skopas, was indeed a fake. The sculpture had arrived at the museum during Frel's tenure as curator. It was also at Frel's urging that the Getty bought another Greek sculpture surrounded in controversy, a kouros. The authenticity of the kouros remained a subject of debate, and the marble male figure was displayed subsequently with a museum card describing it as "Greek, about 530 B.C., or modern forgery." Murphy was sure that there were no irregularities in the acquisition of the Aphrodite; however, years later it would turn out that there were serious questions about the Getty's acquisition of the statue, as well as other antiquities.[107]

. . . . .

In October 1991 Murphy and the trustees of the J. Paul Getty Trust were at last ready to unveil the plan for their bold museum complex, seven years in the design phase. Models and drawings that revealed how the twenty-four-acre, one-million-square-foot Getty Center was to function "put a unified face on a far-flung and sometimes confusing art empire," Christopher Knight wrote in the *Times*.[108] Already a popular metaphor was emerging as news accounts referred to the forthcoming collection of buildings as "an Acropolis for Los Angeles." Richard Meier called it "without question the most complex project imaginable." Ada Louise Huxtable expressed her belief that the mountaintop compound would "establish Los Angeles as a major world center in artistic research and scholarship."[109]

The $360 million interdisciplinary arts campus was now slated to open in 1996. When finished it would house under different roofs the Trust offices, the Center for the History of Art and the Humanities,[110] the Conservation Institute, the Art History Information Program, the Center for Education in the Arts, the Grant Program; and, in several buildings, the Getty Museum. Wanting to encourage the public's interest in the museum, Director Walsh described for the press the planned access to the hilltop by a scenic tram ride from a six-level underground garage. He promised a treat at the top of the hill: "This will be a sanctuary for the mind, both stirring curiosity and satisfying it." The museum would consist of five two-story pavilions grouped around a garden courtyard. A guiding principle in planning display space had to do with the element of light. Paintings were to be displayed on second levels with natural light; decorative arts, manuscripts, drawings, and sculpture were destined for the first floor under low electric light. "This architecture forces you to see the uniqueness of California light," Meier said. He described movable louvers that would respond to the sun's movement during the day, bringing sunlight into the galleries but keeping direct rays off paintings.[111]

Writers on the art scene compared the Getty's proposed complex to New York's esteemed Metropolitan, built in the 1870s in an era when Los Angeles was still shaking off the dust of the frontier. "It's a significant part of a continental shift, if you will," Williams liked to say, pointing out that the population was moving west, the economy was moving west, and so, of course, the best of the culture would follow.[112] Early reviews of the design were favorable. *Vanity Fair* and the *New Yorker* were generous with laudatory remarks, as was London's *Telegraph* magazine. Los Angeles mayor Richard Riordan declared with considerable pride that the new Getty Center "captures the spirit of our city's [cultural] renaissance."[113]

Some thought the center fell short by failing to embrace the diversity that would define the multiethnic, Pacific Rim city in the next century. Social critics found the Getty Center on its promontory in the affluent West Side an elitist institution disconnected from the polyglot population of the wider area. Murphy had long been a staunch supporter of diversity, but to him diversity did not mean a little of this and a little of that. When he talked of valuing pluralism, he meant providing opportunities for in-depth cultural experiences. At the same time that he was guiding the direction of the Getty, Murphy was meeting with Uri Herscher to offer advice for a cultural center to present Jewish heritage in the context of the American experience. Land for the Skirball Cultural Center was purchased six months before the Getty trustees' purchase of their mountaintop site, and the two nearby institutions were under construction at the same time. Murphy had similarly taken an early interest in the Japanese American Cultural Center, making civic leaders aware of its value to the city. A special area of interest to Murphy was the culture of non-Western and nonindustrialized societies, and he was elated by the recent completion of the Fowler Museum of Cultural History at UCLA, which would house the ethnic art assembled thirty years earlier when he was chancellor. Murphy saw the Getty Museum's role in devoting its collection exclusively to European art as contributing to and carrying forward the idea of pluralism in a dynamic multicultural city by being a resource for truly fine expressions of the Western heritage: "If the museum tries to be all things to all people it will fail. The museum must continue to do what it set out to do and do it absolutely the best possible way."[114]

"The momentum is here," Williams announced. "The future is now."[115] The proposed cluster of marble-faced buildings rising in grandeur on a height visible from all directions announced the center as a cultural powerhouse, the most anticipated and expensive undertaking in recent memory. But it remained to be seen whether the colossal endeavor would open to the public on time and whether the bold vision would be embraced by the art world. Murphy, now seventy-five and coming to the end of his service to the Getty Trust, had every confidence that the center would be acclaimed a success.

TWELVE

Three That Got Away

BY THE AGE OF SEVENTY Franklin Murphy had reached icon status among the culture shapers of Southern California through his powerful overlapping roles as trustee for the Los Angeles County Museum of Art, the Ahmanson Foundation, and the J. Paul Getty Trust. While other men his age were withdrawing from the scene, Murphy continued his frenetic pace. The flow of phone calls, invitations, and urgent appeals never slowed. He neglected his health and counted on his Irish yeoman genes to see him through. He was troubled with gout and hypertension, neither condition helped by the rich fare served in the fine restaurants where he socialized with the city's power brokers. His face grew sallow and puffy. The deep bags under his eyes and his distinct jowls gave him a sad, bloodhound look. Yet he was still attractive to women, a subject of marvel to some of his male colleagues.

Murphy fashioned a unique role for himself in the course of channeling tens of millions of dollars of private funds and foundation grants, as well as taxpayer dollars, into support of the arts. The California historian Kevin Starr described him as a leader without peer, a sort of unofficial magistrate whose blessing was sought for every significant civic endeavor.[1] He may have done more to shape the cosmopolitan, cultural image of Los Angeles than any other person of his generation, but despite his considerable achievements he took his disappointments hard. The greatest of these setbacks came when three wealthy Los Angeles tycoons denied his institutions their prized art collections.

For nearly twenty years, Murphy had courted Armand Hammer, chairman of the Occidental Petroleum Corporation, in the hope of gaining his collection for the Los Angeles County Museum of Art. Murphy had held banquets in Hammer's honor and named him to the LACMA board of trustees. In turn Hammer had publicly affirmed his intention to give his artworks to LACMA, not only telling local officials but making announcements to the international art world as well.[2] Hammer had also signed a nonbinding agreement in 1980 stating his intention to transfer title to his collection upon his death.

By 1987 Murphy and other LACMA trustees felt that in view of Hammer's advancing years—he was eighty-nine—it was imperative to get him to back up his declared intentions with a formal, binding agreement. Murphy had been caught unprepared for two deaths that year, those of his brother George and Henry Ford II; with his grief still fresh, it was very much on his mind how suddenly death can come. In July Daniel Belin, then president of LACMA's board of trustees, went to visit Hammer at Occidental Petroleum headquarters, hoping to finalize his commitments to the museum.

In the course of their summer-long negotiations Hammer informed Belin that the 1980 agreement with the county museum was no longer satisfactory, and he presented a twenty-nine-page proposal prepared by his lawyers detailing new stipulations. Hammer's latest demands were reminiscent of the tactics he had employed in the early 1970s, when he demanded that his paintings be displayed together in perpetuity in the Frances and Armand Hammer Wing. Hammer insisted that his collection could not be dispersed throughout the museum to "mingle with other artworks." He demanded an entire floor of his own, one that would contain several galleries that would be called the Armand Hammer Collection. In addition, the names of any other donors had to be removed. Most troubling was Hammer's insistence that the museum never sell any work from the collection. The Hammer Collection was to "remain as it was presently constituted, forever."[3] Each of Hammer's demands violated established museum policy and was a source of outrage to LACMA officials. Trustees bickered among themselves over tactics and just how far the board should go in yielding to Hammer.

As discussions continued the demands escalated. Further proposals required that in addition to the designation for the Armand Hammer collection, the main entrance must be outfitted with a full-length portrait of the oil tycoon. Inside the galleries the Hammer name was to be conspicuously displayed. A new research area in the Daumier section would be named the "Armand Hammer Daumier Study Center with funds provided by the Armand Hammer Daumier Fund." The Leonardo drawings (formerly known as the Codex Leicester) were to be called the "Codex Hammer" with the gallery named the "Codex Hammer Gallery." The new galleries were to have their own curatorial staff selected entirely by Hammer. The proposal even stipulated that in the event of a breach of any provision, the collection would immediately revert to the Armand Hammer Foundation.

The trustees reviewed the documents with growing bewilderment. Belin calmly pointed out that what Hammer proposed was nothing short of a "museum within a museum." Trustees worried that he wanted an arrangement on a par with the controversial deal struck between the investment banker Robert Lehman and the Metropolitan Museum of Art. Lehman had demanded a separate wing to house his collection of European masterpieces, plus a staff that was answerable to the Lehman Foundation. But Lehman arguably owned the greatest private art collection of his era and was in a sound position to make demands. In art circles Hammer's paintings were not deemed comparable in quality or value to works in the finest collections; among Los Angeles collections, Hammer's collection was less well regarded than that of Norton Simon. Nevertheless, the museum trustees were keenly aware of the value of Hammer's major paintings. For example, van Gogh's *Irises* had recently brought $54 million at auction, though it was not considered the artist's finest work. Some of the paintings in the Hammer Collection were valued at millions of dollars more than the museum could hope to raise in decades. To the museum trustees, the Hammer Collection was significant; and Murphy and Belin steeled themselves to continue their frustrating and arduous courtship.

After his meeting with Hammer at the Oxy Building in July, Belin met with trustees Murphy, Ed Carter, Camilla Chandler Frost, and Julian Ganz in the office of the museum director, Rusty Powell. The group were determined that the museum would not permit an independent staff for the collection, nor would they approve the removal of the names of other donors. The museum was willing, however, to discuss the possibility of giving Hammer his own galleries and exhibiting the collection as a self-contained unit. Yet speculation about Hammer's intentions worried Murphy enough that he alerted Powell in September to the need to document the museum's title to paintings already donated in case Hammer should demand their return. "I still remain puzzled as to the temerity of any kind of a suggestion that we would put ourselves in a position to return these pictures to Hammer come what may," Murphy told Powell.[4]

After a series of letters between Belin and Hammer, another effort was made to reach an accord. On October 8, 1987, the principal museum trustees drove to Westwood and gathered around Hammer's desk in the Occidental tower in the hope of creating a workable compromise. Hammer denied that he was trying to establish a "museum within a museum," claiming he only wanted a suitable curator. Belin hoped to pin down exactly what Hammer wanted in preparation for a specific final binding agreement. In one last effort at diplomacy, Powell invited Arthur Groman, Hammer's longtime attorney, to walk through LACMA's existing Frances and Armand Hammer Gallery to discuss exhibition options. (A well-known attorney with Mitchell, Silberberg and Knupp, Groman had included among his clients Howard Hughes and Judy Garland.) To accommodate Hammer's desires further, the trustees entertained the possibility that some donors might be persuaded to display their names in other locations.

In the end all these gestures failed. In January 1988 Hammer called a press conference to announce his plans to build his own museum. Surrounded by television cameras and news reporters on the sixteenth floor of Occidental's world headquarters in Los Angeles, Hammer played out the drama with the showmanship he relished. Standing beneath his prized Rembrandt painting, *Juno,* he yanked a blue velvet drape off the pedestal at center stage, which had drawn all eyes, and revealed a detailed model of the Armand Hammer Museum of Art and Cultural Center to be constructed adjacent to the Occidental tower. Designed by the noted New York architect Edward Larrabee Barnes, it was to be a two-story, 79,000-square-foot building.[5]

The new museum would be the future home of five centuries of art that included more than one hundred paintings from the Renaissance to the twentieth century. Hammer's announcement deprived LACMA of paintings by such European masters as Raphael, Correggio, Ingres, Rubens, Rembrandt, Watteau, Fragonard, Tiepolo, Boucher, Cézanne, Gauguin, Renoir, and van Gogh. The Leonardo da Vinci manuscript and drawings and the complete Hammer collection of the work of Honoré Daumier would now go to Hammer's own museum. The *Los Angeles Times* art critic, William Wilson, reciting Hammer's many pronouncements about his plans, deplored the loss to the county museum. Dumbfounded reporters pressed Hammer as to why he had broken his long-standing pledge, but Hammer responded only vaguely, "It's impossible for LACMA to do justice to the collection," and offered one explanation and then another for his stunning about-face. At first he claimed there would not be adequate space for his sizable collection, but later he told the *Times* he lost faith in the integrity of the museum after curators proposed displaying his paintings in galleries named for other donors. "If this could happen while I was alive, what could happen when I was gone?"[6]

In the opinion of the journalist Robert A. Jones, the trustees missed their mark with their resort to firm tactics to achieve a businesslike arrangement. "To Hammer, giving his art collection away was not business. It was everything that business wasn't. It was the thing that won him love in Beijing and Moultrie, Georgia. Chinese boys sold their bicycles to buy tickets, and they were grateful for the chance. Hammer might bargain over the details of his gift, just as he had bargained with the National Gallery, but the bargainers could damn well be grateful for the chance." What Hammer wanted, Jones wrote, was gratitude and recognition. "Hammer had been told that the paintings, the Codex and the Daumier Collection would bring $250 million if sold off at auction. Hammer thought he had been treated shabbily."[7]

At the unveiling of the architectural model for Hammer's new museum, Murphy had watched Barnes posing for photographs and describing plans for the interior courtyard, research center, library, and two-hundred-fifty-seat auditorium; it was chillingly obvious to him that the plan had been in the works for some time. While Hammer was arguing with Belin over the terms of an agreement for his gift to LACMA, he was secretly working with Barnes to create his own museum. It was hard, however, to know the mind of a difficult man like Hammer, who operated by some system of his own for granting rewards and punishment. It was likely that he set the museum up by escalating his demands so that he could later blame its officials for his decision to build his own museum. As Hammer offered various explanations for his decision, museum officials came to agree with Murphy that the architect was already at work on Hammer's museum while Hammer was delivering his blitz of requirements to the trustees.

Murphy himself was livid about the Hammer museum and called Hammer a "lying, cheating, no-good-son-of-a-bitch."[8] "Franklin would simply go VESUVIUS!" remembered Charles E. Young, "at the mere mention of Armand Hammer's name."[9] Any time the topic was brought up Murphy snapped angrily that he could not bear to discuss it. He was so outraged at

Hammer's announcement that he packed up several boxes of legal documents, memos, and personal letters and handed them over to William F. Thomas, *Times* editor and executive vice president. The package of February 4, 1988, was accompanied by Murphy's note:

> This is but a fraction of the written and contractual materials which the county museum has in its files. There are many more files which make it clear that he has broken promises, denied oral agreements, etc. He has either lost his marbles, or, as one of his friends confidentially told me, his egomania has now reached the level of a sickness.[10]

The boxes of Hammer documents weighed nearly twenty pounds and included many privileged attorney-client communications and minute details of Hammer's long, twisted history with the county museum.

Alarmed that Hammer might also withdraw his promises to the National Gallery, Murphy contacted Carter Brown and ordered a swift examination of Hammer's contract with the Gallery executed in 1986. "ZOWEE!" was the spirited response from Brown. "We asked [the law firm of] Sullivan & Cromwell to study our contract, and their lawyers in New York and California told us it is airtight. There is a major difference between his expressing an intention to bequeath to LACMA and the specific contract that we worked out, signed by him and the Foundation, to transfer title to us within a year of death. But I will believe it all when I see it. . . . Keep the faith!"[11]

What infuriated Murphy was that Hammer's actions constituted a breach of fiduciary duty. Hammer had used his knowledge as a trustee to bid successfully against the museum to acquire the Daumier lithographs in the mid-1970s. At the time museum officials did not take him to task for such underhandedness; it was the museum's understanding that the Daumiers would eventually be donated to LACMA along with the rest of the Hammer Collection.

Murphy may have blamed himself for not having been more perceptive, but the fact could not be denied that Hammer, as a trustee, not only was morally obligated to hold the welfare of the museum in the highest regard but also was legally required to do so. It was Hammer's failure to abide by this duty that so deeply offended Murphy. "He became our competitor and yet he was still on the board," Murphy told the *New York Times,* calling Hammer duplicitous in enticing the museum to hold back on acquiring works that he wanted.[12]

This final struggle with Hammer was an excruciating period for Murphy, a heartbreaking disappointment after years of dedicated effort to build for Los Angeles a museum of distinction. In Murphy's view what made a museum great was the support of the community that saw it as theirs. The ideal was to escape the art donor's mentality of "mine" and aspire to something closer to "our" great museum in "our" great community.

Hammer and his wife, Frances, had contributed significantly to the museum in its early years. They had provided substantial funds to enlarge and define the Frances and Armand Hammer Wing, and over the years Hammer had been instrumental in bringing great exhibitions, including the successful shows of impressionist and early modern paintings on loan from the Soviet Union. He had enabled LACMA to make a significant contribution to international cultural goodwill, which was in line with Murphy's view that art could play a role in foreign affairs. But Hammer's good deeds in the past could not overcome the damage that his broken promise inflicted on the Los Angeles County Museum. Critical time had passed; skyrocketing prices and a dwindling supply meant the museum could no longer hope to attain a world-class collection. Hammer's withdrawal of his collection from the same museum where he had been a trustee since 1968 was described by art critic Christopher Knight as a sad burlesque of public trust. "The damage done to a museum of which Hammer was a public trustee is lamentably real," wrote Knight.[13] The museum now faced the long and costly process of adjusting its collection.

. . . . .

The betrayal by Hammer, however, did not end the county museum's ambitious plans to build for the future. Murphy worked behind the scenes appealing for pledges from prominent individuals and institutions throughout Southern California. By the close of the ongoing campaign Murphy and other trustees awarded the title "Distinguished Benefactor" to thirteen donors who had each contributed between $1 million and $5 million to the Capital Campaign, including Mr. and Mrs. Joe D. Price, the Japanese Federation of Economic Organizations, the Atlantic Richfield Company, and the J. Paul Getty Trust. The museum's master plan called for weaving together new and old parts of the complex. The $13 million permanent pavilion for Japanese art that housed the Price Collection opened in 1988. In a last-minute appeal for a major contribution, Murphy approached Robert O. Anderson—a bold gesture in light of the significant funds already contributed by Atlantic Richfield and the fact that the Anderson Building, completed two years earlier, had not been well received (one review in the

New York Times had called the architecture shabby and inferior).[14] Murphy valiantly wrote Anderson:

> The Anderson Building has been a triumph; and although there has been some argument about its exterior (and this argument is rapidly disappearing), all the experts applaud to the skies the character and quality of the spaces within. And, of course, because of the building, we have been able to bring some really remarkable exhibitions to Southern California.
>
> The trustees have worked very hard indeed, especially Ed Carter and Mia Frost aided by the rest of us, to raise the adequate funds. We have, in fact, raised approximately $77 million, but the deficiency of $3 million is very troublesome; and I do make bold to suggest that it would not only be enormously helpful, but entirely appropriate if you could now make a substantial personal commitment to help us close out the campaign.[15]

Museum officials doubted there would be a favorable response, but eighteen days after sending his letter, Murphy received a call from Daniel Belin to report that Anderson had called from London to announce his pledge to satisfy the fund drive. Murphy was stunned. "This is wonderful news," he told Anderson. "The announcement of your gift will be a fitting climax to what had been a wonderful outpouring for the Los Angeles County Museum of Art."[16]

Against impossible odds LACMA's eight-year drive to raise $80 million for renovation and expansion came to a successful conclusion through the contributions of some thirteen thousand donors. The infusion of funds, according to Rusty Powell, "elevated the museum to a new level of prominence and quality."[17]

· · · · ·

In contrast to the swell of support for LACMA, the ambitious plans for Armand Hammer's new vanity museum did not go so well. Although Barnes had been lauded for his daring design of the Dallas Museum of Art, his blueprint for the new Hammer institution failed to win enthusiasm in art and architectural circles. By spring 1989 grading and excavation had stripped the land bare up to the back of the Occidental tower. Under the watchful eye of hazardous materials inspectors the contractors had laboriously removed the underground tanks of a former gas station and parking garage only to discover the concrete foundation of a previous structure, which had to be removed before footings could be poured. The construction budget for the new museum suddenly mushroomed from $30 million to $50 million. Renovation of the first four floors of the Occidental building, which were to be incorporated into the museum, also proved difficult and expensive.

As cost overruns mounted, Hammer, now ninety years old, put on a good face, and he declared to the *Los Angeles Times,* "At first I was upset that I couldn't go ahead with my original intent to give my collection to the County Museum of Art. But now I'm so happy to have a free hand while I'm alive." He claimed to be directly involved in all aspects of creating the museum and pleased with its progress. When asked about the museum's opening, he gave no exact date but promised reporters, "It will be a blockbuster."[18]

As the months rolled on, Murphy found he could read accounts of Hammer's museum and the tycoon's self-serving statements with less indignation. But his feelings changed in July 1989 when he learned of Hammer's presidential pardon. In his first exercise of the rare presidential prerogative, President George H. W. Bush granted a full and unconditional pardon to the ninety-one-year-old Hammer for his conviction stemming from illegal contributions to the Nixon campaign. Hammer immediately held a news conference to express his appreciation for what he called his long-awaited and anticipated exoneration. Murphy was thrown into another episode of anger and contempt.

The unexpected pardon prompted Paul Conrad of the *Los Angeles Times* to draw one of his scathing cartoons, which brought a guffaw from Murphy when he opened his morning newspaper. Two portraits were depicted, each framed in the ornate style of old master paintings. The inscriptions below the two read:

"I am not a crook"—Richard Nixon
"Neither am I"—Armand Hammer[19]

. . . . .

In December 1989 Murphy was saddened to read of the death of Frances Hammer. He had enjoyed a warm, cordial relationship with her during the planning stages for the Frances and Armand Hammer Wing. Frances was living apart from Armand at the time of her death, disturbed by his high-handed manipulation of Occidental Petroleum, in which much of her funds had been invested, and by his notorious and bizarre relationships with other women. In one strange instance Armand had employed a former airline attendant, Martha Kaufman, to act as an "art consultant" until Frances grew suspicious and objected. Armand then had Kaufman bleach her hair, change her appearance, and work with a speech coach to alter her voice, after which he introduced her to Occidental employees as Hilary Gibson, the woman who would be replacing Martha Kaufman. Frances was not fooled, nor were many Occidental people assigned to work with Kaufman/Gibson, though they kept quiet about it.[20]

Just before Frances's death, Armand Hammer traveled to the Soviet Union and held a much-publicized meeting at the Kremlin with Mikhail Gorbachev. The Hammer name was repeatedly in the news during 1990 as he toured on a "mission of peace," again to the Soviet Union, as well as Europe, China, and Japan. He dined with Mexico's president in Mexico City and with President Bush at the White House. Murphy became incensed as he read news coverage of Hammer that depicted him as a generous philanthropist and a dedicated goodwill ambassador.

Murphy shared his opinion of Hammer in private with his friends Charles E. Young, Robert Erburu, and Walter Annenberg, but he also recorded his feelings in a more specific and formal way in materials he assembled about Hammer and filed with his personal papers. "Anyone who for whatever reason would seek the truth about this man may find the materials in this file of some use," Murphy wrote in a memo dated September 9, 1990, to which he attached the following instructions: THIS BOX AND THIS MEMO SHOULD BE FORWARDED TO THE SPECIAL COLLECTIONS DEPARTMENT OF THE UCLA RESEARCH LIBRARY. The "file" consisted of four legal drawers of documents and ephemera spanning the years 1965 to 1988, some five thousand documents.[21] The twenty-three years of entanglements had been aptly described by Jonathan Kirsch as the ultimate drama of "Art, Law and Ego,"[22] and Murphy wanted the details readily accessible to future researchers.

The trove of material contains a series of letters between Murphy and Walter Annenberg in which their code name for Hammer was "LUCIFER." Every few months Murphy had mailed out a packet to Annenberg at Sunnylands with new revelations about Hammer. In one colorful exchange concerning Hammer, Annenberg wrote Murphy that the materials underscored the "carpet bombing that his life represents."[23]

Murphy clearly found a degree of satisfaction in putting together a thorough archive on Hammer. Honesty and loyalty were qualities that he demanded, and because he could not trust Hammer, he could not tolerate him. Murphy's abhorrence of Hammer permeated the memo accompanying the archival collection:

Without question the fact is that this man was a duplicitous, egocentric megalomaniac, and a crook besides. His dishonesty is manifest in a variety of words and actions, and his brutality toward members of his family and others is amply documented.

Hammer has denied that he is a crook in the sense that even though he broke federal election laws and was convicted, in spite of an almost obscene court performance amply documented in these materials, he was recently pardoned by President Bush. The facts are he has publicly misrepresented the meaning of this pardon.

Because he spread his personal as well as Occidental Petroleum's money around so lavishly and because he had a personal, large high-powered public relations staff and because he misrepresented with the greatest of ease, the real truth about this man (who is as close to being a scoundrel as anyone I have ever known) has been difficult to come by.[24]

Hammer's pardon especially galled Murphy, despite his high esteem for President Bush. Stories about Hammer's bribery of foreign government officials to gain concessions for Occidental Petroleum had circulated for years, as had rumors of Hammer's ready use of cash to entice cooperation for his personal projects. His reputation for going after journalists who delved into such matters was also well known. Murphy saw Hammer's illegal campaign contribution as part and parcel of his general attitude toward buying influence.[25]

Rusty Powell recalled that Murphy experienced a sense of personal failure in the unexpected outcome of his dealings with Hammer, especially in light of the commitments he had extracted: "He felt promises that had been made were broken, and he felt he had delivered Hammer but somehow was outmaneuvered."[26]

Nevertheless, Murphy did take some satisfaction in the fact that the National Gallery of Art was able to secure a binding commitment from Hammer with regard to his gifts. Brown and Murphy somehow had successfully *managed* Hammer's expectations from the very beginning and restrained his demands. Indeed, after Brown read the Hammer coverage in the *Los Angeles Times Magazine,* he wrote Murphy: "I am sorry if in any way the Gallery was cited as a justification for all this hardening of the arteries [of Hammer]. As you know, we have a strict policy of not naming the galleries after donors, and Armand understands that, as the issue was very carefully dealt with in our agreement."[27]

Hammer became part of a new trend that worried Murphy and others in the art world who saw wealthy collectors building private museums. In Europe the advertising icons Charles and Doris Saatchi endowed a private museum in London, and the German businessman Peter Ludwig had established the Ludwig Museum in Cologne. In the United States Dominique de Menil launched the Menil Collection in Houston, Wilhelmina and Wallace Holladay established the National Museum of Women in the Arts in Washington, D.C., and the Illinois manufacturer Daniel Terra opened the Terra Museum of American Art in Chicago. In Los Angeles Hammer joined the ranks of J. Paul Getty, Norton Simon, and others who were putting their names on the marquee by building vanity museums. "The rise of the boutique museum," observed William Wilson, "feels like the Middle Ages, with each aristocrat walled inside his own castle, isolated, jealously guarding his treasures. It feels like the neo-feudalism of the last three decades with people bottled up in their own fiefdom of race, gender, politics of corporate duchy. Maybe they should be called bunker museums."[28] Wilson noted that enlightened wisdom dictated that the proper place for private art collections was in large public institutions where they would have the best combination of aesthetic and historical meaning. In general, this was an opinion Murphy shared. He believed in the value of art as a means of opening minds and expanding human emotions. To this end art must be available to a wide audience.

· · · · ·

The long-drawn-out Hammer saga was close to its final curtain, but the aging oilman still had a few more shocks in store for the art world. Hammer's boutique museum faced more problems than unadorned walls. Two shareholder lawsuits sought to block Occidental Petroleum Corporation from underwriting the museum. The suits charged that museum expenditures were a waste of corporate assets and that Occidental directors and Hammer had breached their responsibilities to shareholders. The California Public Employees Retirement System, which owned more than two million shares of Occidental stock, sought to join the litigation and demanded that construction of the museum be halted and the Hammer art collection turned over to Occidental. Officials at Occidental objected to cost overruns that had pushed the estimated price of the building to nearly $80 million. In an effort to drastically reduce costs and quell further litigation, company officials, against Hammer's wishes, canceled many of the museum's planned luxurious appointments; the museum would have to open without its auditorium, restaurant, or library.

In June 1989 construction resumed when Occidental reached a tentative pact in the shareholder suits. A final settlement was later reached in which Occidental's expenditures for construction costs were limited to $60 million, plus a $36 million annuity. The company was required to be treated as a corporate sponsor and to publicly disclose all contributions. According to *ARTnews*, following the settlement, Hammer emerged as a "slightly chastened victor in litigation that challenged his right to spend company funds on a new museum for his private collection."[29] Murphy doubted that Hammer was much chastened.

· · · · ·

Hammer's last public appearance came at the opening-night ceremony for the Armand Hammer Museum of Art and Cultural Center on November 25, 1990. Hammer suffered from an irregular heartbeat, anemia, bronchitis, kidney trouble, and advanced bone marrow cancer. Medical measures to enable Hammer to attend the opening of the museum included a blood transfusion and large doses of painkillers. The arrival of the enfeebled, though still persevering, founder, who was determined to inaugurate his museum, was later recounted by Edward Jay Epstein in the *New Yorker:* "He had his hair trimmed and was dressed in a new tuxedo that had been designed to conceal his weight loss. Attendants strapped him into a wheelchair and he was carried, barely conscious, down the steps of his house to a waiting limousine."[30] The ill will that Hammer spawned spilled over into sneers at his "second-rate collection," which critics claimed couldn't even "measure up to Henry Frick's guest house."[31] Barnes's architecture was also vilified. Allan Parachini described the monument to Hammer as looking like a "shoe box wearing prison stripes."[32] *Vanity Fair* described it as a "squat cube horizontally striped like a Carvel ice cream cake."[33] Art critic Robert Hughes summed up the prevailing feelings of embarrassment and distaste when he wrote in *Time,* "Nobody can say for sure which museum [in America] is the worst. But we now know which is the vainest . . . the Armand Hammer Museum of Art and Cultural Center."[34]

Three months after Murphy wrote his memorandum on Hammer's character and began preparing his archival boxes for the UCLA Department of Special Collections, the billionaire art collector was dead. His death in Los Angeles on December 10, 1990, came just weeks after he had met with Rabbi Daniel Lupin of the Pacific Jewish Center to plan one final event—a belated bar mitzvah ceremony, even though Hammer had denied his Jewish heritage throughout his long life. The ceremony is traditionally held on a Saturday morning at a synagogue, but Hammer's bar mitzvah was scheduled for Tuesday, December 11, the first night of Hanukkah, at the Beverly Hilton Hotel. Ted Turner was listed as the honorary chairman, and Elliot Gould was to be the event's emcee. But as one journalist put it, "God withheld His blessing,"[35] and the night before the ceremony the ninety-two-year-old bar mitzvah boy slipped from the mortal world.

The board of directors of Occidental Petroleum quickly reorganized with a different power structure, and portraits and statues of Hammer disappeared from the Occidental premises. Hammer's estate was revealed to be smaller than believed. Family members and women friends were not remembered as promised, and a flurry of suits contested the will. The estate was encumbered by unpaid pledges Hammer had made to various institutions and charities, and litigation over the estate continued for years.

The executors of Hammer's estate and the board of directors of Occidental Oil transferred the Armand Hammer Museum of Art and Cultural Center to UCLA in 1994; the huge portrait of Hammer in the entry was removed. In one last symbolic turn of events the Codex Hammer was sold at auction for $32 million to the technology pioneer Bill Gates. Gates restored the name Codex Leicester.[36]

THE LOST TREASURES OF NORTON SIMON

Unlike his permanently broken relationship with Hammer, Murphy managed to continue a cordial association with Norton Simon even after Simon decided to establish his own museum. Murphy was satisfied by an arrangement in August 1988 in which the Norton Simon Museum agreed to loan twenty-one major works of American twentieth-century art to LACMA and more than a dozen other important pieces to Los Angeles's new Museum of Contemporary Art. The announcement marked a sudden change in policy for Simon's museum, previously reluctant to make loans.

The Simon pieces were to be displayed on the second floor of the Robert O. Anderson Building along with recently acquired additions to the county museum's collection. Among the objects to be displayed were Roy Lichtenstein's *Big Modern Painting* and Claes Oldenburg's controversial *Giant Soft Ketchup Bottle.*

The change of policy kindled speculation about whether Simon was rethinking the final destination for his celebrated collection. Negotiations to give his collection to UCLA had ended abruptly after an agreement in principle between Simon and UCLA had been reached in February 1987. If the arrangement had been consummated, the university would have taken over responsibility for the Norton Simon Museum in Pasadena, making it home to the greatest university-based art collection in the world.

The proposal to turn his museum over to UCLA initially seemed to have special appeal to Simon. But despite the considerable efforts by Chancellor Charles Young, negotiations with UCLA began to break down as the tycoon questioned whether the university could assure the care and security of the collection. Murphy developed doubts that Simon's collection would ever go to UCLA. As a trustee of the Getty Trust, Murphy had witnessed a similar fruitless struggle to achieve a legally binding relationship between Simon and the Getty Museum. However, Murphy kept the door slightly ajar, just in case Simon might surprise him.

Indeed, during this same time Simon purchased important works by Edgar Degas and Nicolas Poussin in joint ownership with the J. Paul Getty Museum, fueling speculation that the Getty was favored. Thomas Hoving, former director of the Metropolitan Museum of Art, claimed, according to an article in the *Chicago Tribune,* that Simon had indicated he would give his holdings to the Getty Museum if Hoving were to replace John Walsh, its present director. When contacted by reporters, Simon rolled his eyes and said, "The only response I can make is that Hoving is dealing in either fiction or fantasy."[37]

The fate of Simon's art collection had drawn fascinated interest throughout the Southern California art scene. Suzanne Muchnic articulated the intriguing questions in her article for the *Times:* "Will his $750 million collection of European and Asian art stay in Pasadena in the building that bears his name? Will the museum merge with the J. Paul Getty Museum? Will Simon donate the collection to other museums? Or will he sell the whole thing in the art auction of the century?"[38]

The Simon Collection, one art expert noted, could conceivably bring close to $1 billion at auction given wildly escalating world art prices. The value of the collection also rested in the fact that it remained intact. Even bitter critics of Simon's boutique museum grudgingly admitted that his stellar collection added real luster to the cultural life of Los Angeles and that to dismantle it would be a great loss.

Apparently the ugly saga with Hammer softened Murphy's feelings toward Simon. Simon had never made any commitments to the county museum in writing, nor had he made any false promises officially or unofficially with regard to the disposition of his collection. Despite Simon's exasperating characteristics—his unwillingness to make a decision, his propensity for secrecy, and his need for conflict—he had always treated Murphy with respect. In Murphy's view Simon was an unparalleled connoisseur of the arts who, having built a great fortune from humble beginnings, built from scratch one of the greatest private collections of art ever assembled.[39] John Walsh called Norton Simon "the best collector of our time."[40]

Simon's unusual style and bravado had appalled Murphy on more than one occasion, but now Murphy felt great sympathy for the aging collector, who was suffering the ravages of the paralyzing Guillain-Barré syndrome. After visiting LACMA during the Simon exhibition, Murphy complimented Simon and sent him favorable reviews of the show. In September 1988 he wrote Simon:

> I have today had an opportunity in a leisurely way to walk through the installation of the Norton Simon Museum pictures at the Los Angeles County Museum of Art. Although modern art is not necessarily my favorite in the field of art, I must say that these objects look perfectly stunning.
>
> I thought you might find the enclosed article, which appeared in the Sunday *Herald Examiner,* of some interest. It is by the art critic of the *Herald Examiner* which, as you know, is a Hearst paper; and as you also know, *Connoisseur* Magazine, Mr. Hoving's "bully pulpit," is also owned by Hearst. So Hoving cannot claim any undue influence by me or [Times Mirror CEO] Bob Erburu.[41]

Simon was pleased to read that the feature in fact was a rave. The Norton Simon show at LACMA could not fail to kindle renewed dreams of a merger. It was known—or suspected—that Simon's endowment was inadequate to maintain his collection and museum in perpetuity. But, having seen the Getty and UCLA courtships broken off short of marriage, Murphy was no longer among the dreamers. He went through the motions, but privately he was resigned—regretful but without rancor.

THE FATEFUL WOUNDING OF WALTER ANNENBERG

Murphy watched Walter Annenberg's private fortune zoom into the stratosphere when he sold his lucrative Triangle Publications to Rupert Murdoch for $3 billion. Annenberg had founded *TV Guide* in 1953 and pushed it to a circulation of 17 million before he sold it to Murdoch's News Corporation in 1988.[42] Annenberg had made enormous philanthropic, educational, and medical contributions through his pledge of $150 million to the Corporation for Public Broadcasting, the creation of the Schools of Communication at the University of Pennsylvania and the University of Southern California, and significant financial gifts to the National Gallery of Art, the Metropolitan Museum of Art, and the Mount Sinai School of Medicine and Medical Center in New York City, as well as the Eisenhower Medical Center in Palm Springs. President Reagan had named him recipient of the Medal of Freedom, the nation's highest civilian honor, in 1986.

Beyond his philanthropies Annenberg had gained prestige and honor with his art collection. The impeccable pictures were the envy of curators and made Annenberg the target of competing blandishments devised by eager directors of the world's great museums. When a *Washington Post* reporter asked Annenberg to reveal who was in line to receive his pictures, Annenberg gave a studied answer: "There is no diplomatic way to put it. Let's just say that I have an obligation to my paintings. And to the United States."[43]

It was no secret that Brown and Murphy aspired to gain the Annenberg collection for the National Gallery. They genuinely considered the Gallery the best repository, meeting both the interests of the collector and the requirements of the collection. Furthermore, Annenberg had indicated that he was disinclined to build a vanity museum as Hammer and Simon had done. Murphy appealed to Annenberg's strong sense of social responsibility, knowing that no amount of ostentatious tribute or lavish entertaining could be effective. Murphy's method was to tailor his tactics to the specific personality; and because of his long acquaintance, Murphy thought he understood Annenberg's goals. On January 25, 1988, Murphy wrote his longtime friend:

> When I learned that in March of this year you are to have your eightieth birthday, I reacted with a sense of incredulity. I use the word incredulity because your appearance and vitality so belies what I suppose is a valid vital statistic.
>
> On this occasion, I do want to tell you my sense of privilege to have known you over these past years, and I would assume that as you look back on your life to date, you can and will take proper pride in your extraordinary achievements.
>
> You took over a sound publishing company at an early age and made it into one of the most distinguished and profitable enterprises of its kind in this country.
>
> Then you took on the responsibility of representing the United States in perhaps the most important ambassadorial post in the world. You, with the able assistance of your wife, handled this responsibility with skill, dignity

and enormous success, freely and sincerely attested to by the leaders of all aspects of the British society.

You recognized early the obligation to return to your country a substantial portion of the fortune which you created by dint of skill, hard work and the basic American system. As a result your philanthropies have become nothing short of legendary and the good that they will generate will live on down through the years.

You have truly become one of America's most distinguished citizens, and on your eightieth birthday I want to tell you what a privilege it has been to be able to call you my friend.[44]

On another occasion Brown alerted Murphy that Annenberg had stopped by the National Gallery to stroll through the Gauguin retrospective, which featured several of his loaned paintings. The collector had been pleased with the public response to the exhibition and delighted by the long lines of visitors. During their candid conversation Brown took advantage of the moment to begin delicate discussions with Annenberg about the ultimate disposition of his pictures. Annenberg indicated that what appealed to him about the National Gallery was the composition of its small board that more or less guaranteed against getting "clowns," as he said. He expressed frustration with typical museum boards of fifty people or more.

In gently nudging the issue and promoting the National Gallery over the Metropolitan, Brown indicated that he had never thought of Annenberg as a New Yorker, particularly, but always as a resident of the country at large. Annenberg seemed to take the point, but he was not ready to make a commitment. He told Brown that he still looked forward to a long life. Brown reminded him that sometimes the arrival at a decision could bring peace of mind. Annenberg later followed up on the conversation in a letter to Brown:

I have not done much thinking about the ultimate solution of my pictures, but I must tell you in all frankness my thoughts evolve around four permanent sites—three museums and "Sunnylands" and, of course, the National Gallery of Art is one of the three museums.

As you may know, my last birthday was on the 13th of March when I became an octogenarian and now that I am four score I am preparing to plead the fifth and however presumptuous this might be, I expect to have several years in which to contemplate a permanent solution and I trust you will not only be understanding, but sympathetic as well.[45]

The Los Angeles County Museum of Art enjoyed favor with the Annenbergs; and though the Annenberg Collection as a whole was more likely to go to the more prestigious National Gallery, Murphy and the other trustees had reason to hope that a few choice items would be designated for LACMA. A great deal of effort went into mounting a splendid exhibition of French impressionist and postimpressionist paintings from the Annenberg Collection in August 1990, in the hope of impressing the Annenbergs with LACMA's skillful presentation and outreach into the community. Walter and Leonore Annenberg were honored by a weeklong celebration at the opening of this eagerly awaited show, which included van Gogh's *La Berceuse* and Gauguin's *The Siesta,* considered the last prime Tahitian-period picture in private hands. The exhibition was so popular that even though visitors were required to buy advance tickets marked for a designated day and hour, long lines snaked along Wilshire Boulevard.

Los Angeles was the third stop in the exhibition's tour. It had opened in Philadelphia, Annenberg's hometown, where a gala welcoming event was held at the Philadelphia Museum of Art. The show then traveled to the National Gallery of Art, where Brown had made sure it was handsomely presented. Reporters in Philadelphia and Washington, D.C., had badgered Annenberg to tell them his plans for his remarkable collection. "I have a personal desire to see the paintings stay together," Annenberg told them. Offering them no clue as to the ultimate destination of the collection, he added, "In the last six months, I've twice been offered immense sums to sell the whole collection. My response was, 'You are asking me to sell members of my family.'"[46]

In one interview, Annenberg was lighthearted about the prices he paid for his favorites, such as the $40.7 million laid out the previous year for Picasso's *Au Lapin Agile,* depicting a harlequin and a female companion in a bar. "I love a work of art that appeals to me on sight," he said. "It has to move me. . . . I found increasingly I am attracted to a work that tells something of a story." Picasso's *Au Lapin Agile* was painted while the artist was grieving for a friend who had killed himself over a love affair. Picasso put the vehemence of his feeling into depicting the girl in the picture, the person he held responsible for the tragedy. "But years later," Annenberg said in relating the story, "when she was old and sick, he visited her, laid a bundle of francs on her table and said, 'Now I forgive you.'" He wanted his paintings to be the kind that would continue to engage him. However, he admitted that he had made some wrong guesses. Once when he was offered two paintings, a Picasso and a Braque, he chose the Picasso—*Woman with a Mandolin*—but after a time found the female figure and her mandolin "rather insipid." He sold the painting and belatedly bought the Braque (*The Studio,* included in the LACMA exhibition). Noting that the Picasso was subsequently purchased by Norton Simon, Annenberg added with a grin, "I don't mean that as a criticism of Simon, of course. It's all a matter of taste."[47]

To highlight the Annenberg exhibition's presence in Los Angeles, Murphy arranged for William Wilson to interview Annenberg for a front-page *Calendar* feature for the August 12 edition of the *Los Angeles Times.* Murphy knew that both the quality of the works and their significance as a collection were unquestioned, so he believed that Wilson could not fail to give the exhibition praise, which Wilson did. Nonetheless, Wilson's article lauding Annenberg's extraordinary collection managed to offend the collector. Annenberg telephoned Murphy at his Robert Lane home in a rage, claiming the Sunday morning feature was a "vicious and personal attack." Quite unnecessarily, Annenberg protested, Wilson had included in his review unpleasant details of the Annenberg family's past. Annenberg claimed he had been sabotaged and defamed by the article, which included information about his father's imprisonment on charges of tax evasion and bribery.[48] Annenberg asserted that at no point in his interview had he made any remarks about his family's history. He was furious that, as he saw it, Wilson had contrived to make material "picked up from the *Washington Post*" seem part of his recent interview for no other reason than to embarrass him.[49]

Robert Erburu, by then chairman of the board and chief executive officer of Times Mirror, alerted by Murphy, read the Wilson feature with dread and immediately sent a letter to Annenberg at Cottage 5 at the Beverly Hills Hotel early on Monday morning, August 13:

> I am very sorry that the story in Calendar—which had been conceived of and intended as a positive piece on your collecting and your desire to share great art with the public—contained extraneous material that was hurtful to you personally. The sad thing is I suspect that Bill Wilson intended it to be positive in the sense he was putting certain events in a context not known which "explained them." That is not said by me as a justification—I think the inclusion was off the mark.
>
> Alas, our problem in this case was that the story was not reviewed by Shelby [Shelby Coffey, *Los Angeles Times* editor]. What wasn't done can't be done after the fact. I can only wish that it were different and express my regrets to you and Lee. . . .

[We] were looking forward to our luncheon with Lee and you. We will be very disappointed if you prefer not to come, but want you to know that our respect and affection for you both is undiminished. Life often takes turns that are painful, as you well know, and for us to cause you embarrassment is painful for us and something we very, very much regret.[50]

Erburu's letter did not pacify Annenberg, who could see no possible interpretation that would make Wilson's motives supportive of him. "Frankly," a still-outraged Annenberg wrote in reply, "I feel sorry for Franklin Murphy, who sincerely sought this interview for Wilson because he felt it would be an objective story on my art collection. May I add that I continue to be suspicious of who engaged Wilson to do his best to injure me in the columns of the L.A. Times."[51]

The Wilson piece put a damper on the opening for the Annenbergs and left museum officials and Murphy nervously doing their best to make the event festive and a tribute to the collectors. Murphy was distressed to see his friend pained, although the revelations about the Annenberg family's past were not new: the story had been known publicly for years. But he was concerned as well about the effect the article might have on decisions the aging philanthropist would make soon. Murphy was all too aware that Annenberg had found in his art collection a way to redeem his family name and achieve recognition and honor; Wilson's feature article could have a chilling effect on the billionaire's future generosity to Murphy's cherished institutions.

On Tuesday, August 14, Murphy penned his own letter of apology:

I think you must know how saddened I am at the recent turn of events. I had hoped and indeed I thought that a background story prior to the coverage of the exhibition would be of service to the people of this community as well as to the two of you. I never dreamed that such a background story would involve extraneous material. I am still shocked and am trying to find out how this could have happened. I hope you understand that my involvement in this whole thing came with absolutely the best of intentions.

I hope the bizarre outcome will not do violence to our long standing friendship which has meant so much to Judy and to me.[52]

. . . . .

Despite the repercussions from the *Times* feature, Murphy still held the hope of obtaining the coveted impressionist and postimpressionist masterpieces for the National Gallery. Although Annenberg told reporters that he did not plan to pass his paintings to family members after his death or sell them at auction, he still refused to say which institution would receive them. Annenberg had hinted at which museums he favored by several substantial gifts. London's National Gallery, for example, received $5 million in 1988 for renovation and air-conditioning in its French impressionist and postimpressionist galleries (perhaps, some speculated, in preparation for the Annenberg collection). The Metropolitan Museum of Art, the National Gallery, and the Philadelphia Museum of Art, leading American contenders in the competition, also received generous contributions.

Although the successful Gauguin exhibition at the National Gallery fueled speculation that the Gallery had won Annenberg's favor, the Metropolitan Museum had reason to anticipate the collection coming to New York. Annenberg had served as a trustee at the Metropolitan from 1974 to 1981, and his wife, Leonore, currently served as a member of the board. The Philadelphia Museum of Art was also a favorite, as it was near his boyhood home in Pennsylvania. The Los Angeles County Museum was mentioned as a possible dark horse candidate because Annenberg's estate in Rancho Mirage had been the home of the collection.

Murphy hoped that Annenberg's patriotism would persuade him to choose the National Gallery over the Met; and during their twenty-year acquaintance Murphy had subtly steered his attention to Washington, D.C. Annenberg had been pleased with the triumphant Gauguin exhibition, and Murphy thought the upcoming fiftieth anniversary of the National Gallery would surely impress him with its prospects and prestige. The moment seemed to be approaching for Annenberg to reveal his choice; he was nearing eighty-three years of age.

The anniversary gala would be the culmination of Carter Brown's ten-year effort to broaden the museum's donor constituency, greatly aided by a onetime tax bonanza for wealthy supporters. Tax laws since 1986 had limited the deduction amount that could be claimed, causing large donors to resort to making "partial gifts," so that a percentage of a work of art could be given and deducted each year. Congress had voted a onetime change in the tax law during 1991 that permitted deduction of the fully appreciated value of artworks in the year of the gift. As a result scores of wonderful objects came to the National Gallery: an incomparable 1877 American masterpiece by Winslow Homer, the jewel of the collection of Jo Ann and Julian Ganz Jr., arrived from Los Angeles; a painting of sumptuous white roses by van Gogh was a gift from Pamela Harriman; a glorious Toulouse-Lautrec portrait was donated by Betsey Cushing Whitney; and Cézanne's famous *Boy in a Red Waistcoat* was a birthday present from Paul Mellon. Altogether, the Anniversary Gift Committee successfully raised $25 million in cash gifts and pledges of prized works of art for the National Gallery's fiftieth anniversary celebration.

After a series of splashy Washington parties and press events to announce the new gifts, the treasures were to be featured in the exhibition *Art for the Nation: Gifts in Honor of the 50th Anniversary of the National Gallery of Art.* Jo Ann Lewis of the *Washington Post* wrote enthusiastically, "Together with works dating from Jacopo Bellini's 1459 Venetian panel painting of two saints to Wayne Thiebaud's 1963 painting 'Cakes,' from a portrait drawing by Jacques-Louis David (from Walter H. and Leonore Annenberg) to a portrait painting by Thomas Eakins (from Sen. and Mrs. H. John Heinz III), the upcoming show of 320 of these gifts may well represent the greatest birthday haul of the century."[53] Murphy was exhilarated by the gifts and by the outpouring of interest. The museum was becoming what it was intended to be—the people's gallery.

On March 11, 1991, just prior to his departure for Washington, D.C., to officiate in the festivities as chairman of the Gallery's board of directors, Murphy received a telephone call from Suzanne Muchnic in which she asked for his reaction to Annenberg's just-announced decision. The highly respected reporter was frantically compiling a feature for the morning edition that would inform Los Angeles readers of the surprise gift of Walter and Leonore Annenberg's $1 billion collection to New York's Metropolitan Museum. Murphy laughed out loud when he heard the story and told Muchnic that her information was wrong and it would be ludicrous to print it. Murphy said in unequivocal terms that Annenberg would never bequeath his collection to the Metropolitan without informing him first and that under no circumstances would Annenberg divert attention from the National Gallery during its fiftieth anniversary celebration. Despite Murphy's insistent denial, Muchnic's fast-breaking news story was featured on the front page of the *Los Angeles Times* the next morning.[54]

Annenberg had indeed announced that his entire celebrated art collection would go to the Metropolitan Museum of Art. "It's a stupendous event. We are overwhelmed by the gesture," said William H. Luers, president of the Metropolitan Museum. Luers told reporters that the museum would prepare galleries for the paintings, explaining that Annenberg "wants his collection to stay together as a whole, and that is how we will show it."[55]

On Wednesday, March 13, Murphy, in Washington, received a second jolt, this time an urgent phone call from Rusty Powell, who told him that he had just learned that Annenberg was giving the Los Angeles County Museum $10 million, the largest single monetary commitment the museum had ever received. In a prepared statement that he gave to LACMA's public relations office for release, Annenberg stated, "Leonore and I are extremely pleased to make this gift to . . . an institution whose leadership I deeply respect. We are hopeful that it will have a constructive impact on the museum." In his comments to the press Powell was effusive in expressing the museum's appreciation for the Annenberg donation, but a note of wistfulness underlay his mention of LACMA's shortage of impressionists now that Annenberg's fine examples were all going to the Met. "The importance of the gift cannot be underestimated," Powell said. "In the present context of philanthropy, the museum is very lucky. This would be a generous gift at any time, but the fact that it was made in a recessionary period, when gifts of artworks and money to cultural institutions have slowed down tremendously, makes it very special. We would be appreciative at any time, but the gift is particularly meaningful now."[56]

As Murphy arrived at the long-planned National Gallery gala, he experienced deeply mixed emotions. He knew that he and Carter Brown would have to endure press queries, not about the National Gallery's planned spectacular, but about the Annenberg gift that got away. As guests wandered from room to room at the grand black-tie event to preview the exhibition of paintings, sculpture, and drawings, the loss of the valuable Annenberg collection was like the elephant in the room that no one dared to acknowledge. All eyes turned to the receiving line in the atrium of the East Building when Walter and Leonore Annenberg shook hands with Director Brown and Chairman Murphy and posed for photographs. Earlier in the evening, when asked by the *Washington Post* if he considered Annenberg's announcement of his gift to the Met to be a party pooper, Brown had said, "It seems like a fine party to me." With the cool diplomacy for which he was known, Brown cited the 550 new gifts of art, "given by 164 donors, 116 of them new donors to the Gallery, from 21 states and five foreign countries."[57]

The fiftieth anniversary of the National Gallery was a joyous occasion for Paul Mellon, whose father had conceived the idea for a national gallery and had funded its construction but had not lived to see it in operation. Mellon added delight to the formal remarks of the evening by beginning his speech in mock solemnity: "Two score and 10 years ago, my father brought forth on Constitution Avenue a museum conceived in beauty by John Russell Pope that its treasures might belong in perpetuity to the people of the United States." His father's dream had become a public reality. "[What] touches me most is how broad the support of the Gallery has become."[58]

During the banquet ceremonies Mellon presented Murphy with the Andrew W. Mellon Medal for his twenty-seven years of service. It was the highest honor the Gallery could bestow. Murphy lowered his head as Mellon placed the gold medal around his neck; the guests then burst into applause. "I have served this gallery for half its life, which emphasizes its relative youth," Murphy said during the heart-tugging ceremony, made all the more moving for those in attendance who knew the chairman's cruel disappointment over the collection that had slipped from his grasp just forty-eight hours earlier.[59]

The evening came to a pleasant enough close, despite Annenberg's transparent attempt to deliver a cold hard rain on the National Gallery's parade. Even supporters of Annenberg's decision to favor the Met had to concede that breaking the news suffered from "poor form" or "bad timing." But according to one observer, the very fact that Walter Annenberg chose the most important occasion in the Gallery's fifty-year history to announce his gift, picking the same week that Franklin Murphy was to receive the Mellon Medal, made it a deliberate act of cruelty. "There was simply no earthly reason to choose that moment to announce it," recalled one observer. "It makes one wonder what bad blood really existed between the collector, the museum director and the chairman of the museum's board of trustees."[60]

Annenberg's $10 million gift to LACMA somewhat ameliorated the shock of his surprise announcement, but for Annenberg to have selected the Met and not the National Gallery inflicted an unexpected wound. Murphy thought his relationship with Annenberg had reached a stage of mutual respect and affection. It came as a wrenching realization that the truth was otherwise and that Annenberg had made his decision and issued his announcement without confiding his intention to him beforehand.

· · · · ·

Murphy's courtship of Armand Hammer, Norton Simon, and Walter Annenberg consumed prime years of his life but left him without the prizes he sought. Friendship with a targeted collector was a touch-and-go relationship at best. Nevertheless, Murphy approached each situation expecting respect, cordiality, and loyalty, and he was taken aback when he was not at least privy to the intentions of men he thought he knew so well.

PART IV

Steward

THIRTEEN

Changing of the Guard

THE VENERABLE *TIMES* EAGLE HAD SERVED since the founding as the familiar icon of the Times Mirror Company. In 1981 the company celebrated one hundred years as a Los Angeles institution and flaunted—deservedly—its success. In keeping with the fast-moving era, the intrepid raptor was given a new streamlined, semiabstract incarnation. Murphy retired from his position as chairman of the board at his sixty-fifth birthday and became chairman of the board's executive committee, where he functioned as an elder statesman, involved enough to take pride in the company and participate in the revelries of the centennial party.

In 1984 the company's annual report, sporting the updated eagle, offered much to brag about: Times Mirror set new highs with thirty thousand employees and revenues of $2.8 billion.[1] That same year, Los Angeles hosted the 1984 summer Olympics to great acclaim and mounted an arts festival that drew international attention to its growing status in the arts.

The next Times Mirror milestone for Murphy came in 1986 when he officially retired from the board at age seventy and assumed the title of director emeritus. At the same time Otis Chandler, only fifty-seven, relinquished the title of chairman of the board and took Murphy's place as chairman of the executive committee. Robert Erburu was named to succeed Chandler as chairman, combining his chairmanship with his current role as chief executive. For the first time in more than a century, Times Mirror was without a member of the Otis or Chandler family at its helm, a turn of events that puzzled many close to the scene, since Chandler had been considered the logical successor to lead the company and was certainly the preferred choice of Dorothy Chandler. Some observers claim, though not for quotation, that Chandler was ousted against his will and only reluctantly passed the torch to Erburu. Others, also unwilling to be quoted, maintain he voluntarily relinquished the title for his own reasons. As chairman of the executive committee, unlike Murphy in that role, Chandler became increasingly distant from company operations and occupied himself with a private museum he established in Oxnard, California, to display his collection of vintage cars and motorcycles, as well as big-game trophies from his hunting expeditions.

Insiders who were privy to the closed-door drama at the time recall Erburu's rise to the chairmanship and Chandler's unexpected side-step to the executive committee as a turning point for the company. Taking note of Murphy's largely custodial but hugely successful management, longtime employees referred to the Murphy-Chandler era as the "glory years." Chandler believed Murphy's greatest contribution lay in the way he recognized and developed the talents of the people who operated the company and its major divisions. Murphy's technique was "to encourage them, to provide counsel to them, but not interfere with their day-to-day operations," Chandler said. "That I define as superb wisdom."[2] It was a feather in Murphy's cap that his hands-off leadership proved so successful, although some critics say he failed to properly manage the company's long-term succession.

Murphy continued to offer some degree of advice on the company's direction and management even after his retirement. He maintained his office at Times Mirror and went there daily when he was in Los Angeles. He was always at important company events and did not hesitate to remind executives of the company's civic responsibilities in the new era of media frenzy. Erburu recalled that on occasion Murphy would charge into his office and announce that something needed to be done. "I would try and get the job done fast," Erburu said, "because I knew he would be back in thirty minutes to check on my progress."[3]

Times Mirror seemed so entrenched as an institution, so important to the life of Los Angeles, that no one could imagine its demise, but the retirements of Chandler and Murphy were early indications that an era was ending. It was not yet apparent, but new Times Mirror chairman Erburu would not preside over the invincible institution of earlier times. Over the next several years the company commenced a precipitous decline that led to break-even operations and, later, a significant loss. Watching all this closely was the Chandler family, whose members, through two trusts, owned more than 50 percent of the voting stock and maintained several seats on the board. It did not escape the attention of insiders that some dissatisfied Chandlers were contemplating changes in the company. Media companies across the nation were uneasy, not knowing what new technologies would rule the bottom line in the future. In the face of accelerating globalization, the earlier Chandler principle of absolute loyalty to the *Times* and its century-long connection to the community began to take a backseat to profits. For the new breed of executives who joined Times Mirror in the 1990s, journalistic excellence and civic attachments were secondary to the strength of the stock price.[4]

Erburu was hard pressed to satisfy the demands of the current generation of Chandlers for immediate results. The shift in emphasis was disappointing and "terribly frightening for Franklin," observed Erburu, who knew Murphy's regard for the long civic history of the company. Given the state of the economy and the Chandler family's attitude, Erburu doubted that Murphy himself could have rallied the support necessary to steer the company in the years ahead.[5] The *Times* would suffer the indignity of cost-cutting tinkering: employees would be offered buyouts, and the eagle would disappear from the daily masthead.

A TIME OF LOSS

Erburu had been mentored by Murphy, who had total confidence in him. The two men were very close; Murphy had become a surrogate father to Erburu, an emotional connection much like Murphy's relationship with Robert Ahmanson. The responsibility that Murphy took with these younger men was the same role of strength and authority he had taken with his brother, George. Throughout his life he had been protective of and encouraging to George, the quieter, more sensitive brother, who grew up in his shadow.

In addition to their genetic makeup, George and Franklin had inherited from their parents, as had their sister Cordie, the same value system and outlook. Their doctor father had approached life with the open, tolerant, information-seeking mind of the scientist: their home in Kansas City, Missouri, was exempt from the bigotry and religious extremism of the region.

There was no talk of Armageddon at the dinner table; Dr. Franklin Edward Murphy, rational and problem-solving, believed that men and women of talent and resources had a duty to the common good. He felt that civic life could be better, and he optimistically believed that conscientious effort could make it so.

The Murphy sons were teenagers when their father died, not yet beyond the self-absorbed, rebellious stage of adolescence. They took scant interest in their father's activities and were little aware of his civic work. In adulthood, as their successes came to them, the brothers thought often of their father, who, they knew, had expected them to do something important with their lives. It seemed preordained that their careers would involve medicine, but it was equally embedded in their makeup that art and music would be central in their lives. Young Franklin realized early that cultural interests could unite people across class lines, for he observed that cultural pursuits had been the means of his parents' acceptance into groups above their economic status.[6]

After George had completed his medical education at the University of Pennsylvania and his residency at Johns Hopkins Hospital, he and his wife, Annette, had moved to New York City, where George became associated with the Rockefeller Institute for Medical Research and in 1954 became an associate professor of pathology at Cornell University Medical Center.[7] Franklin frequently visited George during his business trips to New York, and it was not uncommon for the brothers to see each other several times a month. George and Annette lived in a magnificent two-story penthouse apartment, previously owned by Irving Berlin, at 103 East End Avenue, overlooking Gracie Mansion. The couple had been the leading force in a fifteen-year project that transformed an abandoned city asphalt plant into a park complex with a theater, athletic field, track, basketball court, and graphic arts studio. This remarkable facility, located at East 90th Street and York Avenue on the city's Upper East Side, was later named the George and Annette Murphy Arts and Sports Center.

Although he had suffered from leukemia for several years, George was only minimally incapacitated until the final months of his life. He died on Wednesday, July 15, 1987, in New York City at the age of sixty-eight. His last ten days were very painful. "The fact that the end was quick, was a blessing," the grieving Franklin conceded.[8] The funeral was held in New York City on Saturday afternoon, July 18. Norman Cousins, friend to both Franklin and George, delivered the tribute, saying that George would have delighted the ancient Greek philosophers with his fusion of art and science.

He praised George as a "gentle and meticulous listener" to those in his wide circle of friends who came to him for his good humor and wisdom.[9] Franklin and Cordie and their families traveled to Kansas City, Missouri, where the interment took place four days later. Franklin was distraught to have lost his brother; to come to terms with the death of his father, he had dedicated himself to the role of big brother to George. The pattern set by nurturing and advising his brother had then been repeated in his mentoring of younger men, some of them second-generation descendants of formidable business figures or scions of renowned dynasties. He understood what it meant to be haunted by obligation to familial goals.

In September Henry Ford II, a man Murphy considered his second brother,[10] suddenly died. The loss of two men whom he loved deeply in such a short span of time was excruciating. Murphy wrote Henry Ford's brother, William Clay Ford, expressing the pain he felt over the loss: "Although I had known for some days that Henry was critically ill, the reality of his actual passing hit me as though it were a body blow. . . . I loved him as a person. I know that the loss to you is very great but I can tell you that the loss to me and many others is also very great."[11]

Having served as a director of Ford Motor Company for over two decades, until his retirement in 1986, Murphy had known Henry Ford II better than most, and he had witnessed many of the highs and lows in Ford's celebrated career. Murphy recalled that Ford was, "in a way, a kind of Dr. Jekyll and Mr. Hyde. He was a loveable guy who would do anything he could for a friend, but woe betide you if you had crossed him." Murphy said that Ford could be mean, dressing down colleagues in an inexcusable way, but "he could be just as sweet and as lovely and as friendly and as generous as he could be. His Christmas presents to people were legendary." Two years after Ford's death, Murphy confessed that he still missed him. "He had become like a brother to me. I'd go into his office and visit for an hour or two about one thing or another, sometimes including his family problems, which he would share with me." Murphy noted that Ford had great respect for his grandfather, but he never talked much about his father. As Henry Ford II, he "had to bear the burden of the name—that's a hell of a burden. It's not easy having the name Ford."[12]

· · · · ·

Murphy, still reeling from the deaths of George and Henry Ford II, faced yet more heartache with the progressing illness of his daughter Joyce, who suffered from multiple sclerosis and by 1987 had become paraplegic. Few in Murphy's inner circle were aware of the extent of his daughter's devastating condition and the physical and emotional toll it was taking on the family. Murphy confided to one friend that Joyce's rapidly deteriorating health was one of the most complex and emotionally trying periods he and Judy had ever endured.[13]

Joyce's condition became more complicated when doctors discovered an unrelated lesion of the brain. Joyce was now forty-five years old and had two children, eighteen-year-old David and twelve-year-old Judith. Joyce's husband, Chip, had recently moved out of the family home in Leawood, Kansas (a suburb of Kansas City, Missouri), and a divorce seemed probable. The diagnosis of the brain condition was an additional blow, but it helped to explain to Franklin and Judy their daughter's disordered thinking as she piled up bills in a manic quest for something to bring her happiness. Joyce had competed all her life with her sister, Martha, for their father's affection, and though she had not helped her case by hastening into marriage in spite of her father's reservations, she felt Martha had received more than a fair share of their father's attention. After seeing a college application for Martha in which her father had written that Martha was the brightest of his four children, Joyce had come to feel the decks were stacked against her. In the illogical, emotional way in which family dynamics can evolve, Joyce turned against her father even as she longed for his love and attention.

In December Joyce's live-in help abruptly quit, which required Judy to leave immediately for Missouri and act as nurse and housekeeper while she searched for full-time help. Judy telephoned her husband nightly to discuss the disturbing details as it became increasingly clear that their daughter could no longer stay alone in the house where she had lived for the past fifteen years. Judy located a one-story house for lease where Joyce could function better and undertook the difficult task of moving Joyce and installing special equipment for her. She commuted back and forth between Kansas City and Los Angeles over the next few months while she and Franklin attempted to sort out the legal and financial issues of Joyce's care, in addition to the problems connected with custody of Joyce's youngest child, Judith. David was graduating from high school and would soon be leaving for college.

Judy pulled together all her management skills to set up a comfortable household. In the course of her marriage she had created various homes for her family, sometimes in trying circumstances but always with optimism; now she was readying a house to serve the saddest of situations. In addition to the real difficulties facing the family, Judy's fear about finances was exacerbated by witnessing her daughter's desperation. The Murphys faced the reality that Joyce would require round-the-clock attendants as she became increasingly unable to care for herself. They realized the tremendous expense that would fall on their shoulders. Franklin had come late to addressing the need to create financial security for his family, especially for his and Judy's later years. He had welcomed the position at Times Mirror as a source of the income he had not sought before. He now feared that the reserve he had accumulated would drain completely away as he paid for Joyce's care.

Fortunately, greatly needed help came from an unexpected source. In 1987 Murphy wrote Irvine O. Hockaday Jr., president and chief executive officer of Hallmark Cards in Kansas City, expressing his appreciation and relief that Hallmark had determined that Joyce would be entitled to company health insurance as a dependent of a director. "I cannot tell you what a burden you have taken off the heads of both Judy and me," Murphy said. "It is now quite clear from her hospital stay that Joyce is in for a very difficult time, and without health coverage, the expenses would literally be horrendous."[14]

Of special concern to Murphy was the welfare of his grandson David Dickey, who was applying for admission to Stanford University. Murphy had seen to it that David attended Pembroke in Kansas City. Wanting his grandson to have the same experience he and George had shared, Murphy had sent Joyce regular checks for his tuition. Eager for David's admission to Stanford, Murphy wrote its president, Donald Kennedy. He also spoke with Times Mirror director and longtime Stanford trustee Dr. Peter S. Bing about his grandson's application.

David had points in his favor for a college application; he had been an excellent student, had been active in soccer and basketball, and had served as editor of the school's yearbook. "My main reason for writing," Murphy told Kennedy, "is to tell you something of the difficulties under which this young man has performed and in spite of which he has done so well." Murphy explained that David had cared for his mother and twelve-year-old sister: "He has carried out these responsibilities with extraordinary skill and grace—all of which has led to a maturity well beyond his years. As a result he is tremendously respected by his peers and their parents and by his teachers, in short by all who know him." Murphy concluded, "I make bold to write you this letter for this is the kind of information that is not likely to appear in a regular college application."[15] Under no circumstances would Murphy permit his grandson's future to be sacrificed in the maelstrom of family hardship.

When Murphy resigned the chancellorship at UCLA he withdrew from the major battleground of the 1960s revolution but continued to find himself on the leading edge of change. As CEO of the Times Mirror Company, heading a giant media conglomerate, he was in the forefront of one of the greatest and most far-reaching aspects of postmodernity: instant worldwide communication. Similarly, as a director of the Ford Motor Company he helped steer the industrial giant through the throes of national deindustrialization, as *Post-Fordism* became the term to characterize the flexible modes of production needed in the global economy. Added to these momentous changes in the economic sector, retrenchment of the defense industry as the cold war came to an end resulted in displacement of large numbers of workers and a general anxiety about the future. The economy of Southern California, which had relied heavily on aerospace contracts, was particularly hard hit in the 1990s recession.

Expecting the economic downturn to worsen, Times Mirror executives turned to aggressive management. But analysts were critical of Erburu's business strategies; a list of costly miscalculations was printed in *Business Week, Forbes,* and the *Wall Street Journal.* Insiders were critical also of Erburu's heavy civic load, which included his membership on nearly a dozen philanthropic boards. Although Murphy had been lauded in his heyday for his community involvement, Erburu was pilloried for continual absences at Times Mirror because of civic obligations, another indication of changing corporate priorities. Operating losses of more than $150 million at *Newsday,* restructuring woes at the legal publisher Matthew Bender, failures in attempts to build profitable cable television properties, lackluster revenues from the $400 million acquisition of the *Baltimore Sun,* and the cost of employee buyouts at the *Times* were just some of the troubles laid at Erburu's door. But he was not alone: across the industry, advertising revenues were shrinking, and publishers and broadcasters were scrambling. With Erburu's retirement approaching amid a difficult economic climate, the question of succession was on the minds of the company's board and its executive team. Speculation swirled as to who would follow Erburu and what the succession would mean in the long run for the company and the fabled role of the *Los Angeles Times.*[16]

. . . . .

Franklin Murphy, Ed Carter, and Dorothy Chandler had formed an effective team as culture builders, and though observers might debate the merits and shortcomings of the institutions they conceived and built, at the end of the day the powerful triumvirate had delivered a great public university, a nationally recognized art museum, and a celebrated performing arts center. As Murphy liked to point out, Los Angeles, although a big city, could never become a *great* city without such civic landmarks. As the decade closed the old triumvirate exited the stage: Dorothy Chandler's health had significantly declined, and Edward Carter was less visible, though he was still on LACMA's executive committee and continued to take an interest in museum affairs. LACMA and the Music Center had both become so big that the amounts of money needed to keep them afloat could not be achieved through the old art of fund-raising as practiced by the pioneers. Murphy recognized this fact early and had begun to adopt new methods, moving away from reliance on individual wealthy donors toward a call on foundation resources and corporate benevolence.[17]

The old guard was now replaced by forceful corporate leaders, the likes of Eli Broad, David Geffen, and Michael Milken. These newcomers came from the new economy; their fortunes were not from traditional sources like oil or land sales but financial services, entertainment, technology, and global trade. Murphy, yielding to a new generation of culture brokers with new fund-raising techniques, assumed his elder statesman role with dignity. A few more years were left him. As he looked back, he knew his most productive years had spanned a remarkably individualistic, vibrant era, one less hard-nosed about the bottom line.

Painful osteoporosis kept Dorothy Chandler from tranquil weekends at Dana Point, where she had watched the surf in the distance as she worked on speeches and composed her handwritten thank-you notes. Marion Burke, her longtime secretary, still assisted with correspondence, but her incoming letters were few and visitors came less frequently. On those occasions when Robert and Lois Erburu arrived and were told she was too ill to receive guests, they left gifts and notes to let her know she was remembered. Entries in Murphy's date book show no visits with Mrs. Chandler during this period. By this time the deep admiration and affection the two once held for each other had turned into the chill of adversaries. They had shared triumphs and disappointments, but the sad ending of their relationship demonstrated that each was capable of inflicting wounds as well as enduring hurt and pain.

Murphy's authority in Los Angeles was still extensive, and though his influence rarely came to the attention of the general public, it was known well to those who needed to know it. Los Angeles mayor Richard Riordan called

Murphy the city's beloved "broker of culture,"[18] but William Wilson, who had covered Murphy for years, put little emphasis on lovability: "He was brave, constructive, admirable and not to be messed with." Others on the scene recalled that as Murphy grew older he was less patient, less agreeable, and prone to wounding outbursts.[19] Murphy tried to maintain his familiar fast pace, though there were now times when illness caused him to cancel an engagement or postpone a plane trip.

Despite his demanding and overlapping roles in foundation work, Murphy was a talented juggler who could keep a dizzying array of plates spinning. Asked if he ever found himself faced with conflicts of interest, Murphy acknowledged as much. "There's nobody, I suppose, in America before or since who has as many presumed conflicts," he said. But he noted that there was nothing he took more seriously than his fiduciary responsibility as a trustee. If one institution's needs collided with another's, Murphy said he simply "got the hell out of the way."[20]

· · · · ·

Murphy continued to make a notable difference in Los Angeles through the auspices of the Ahmanson Foundation. His lengthy battle to protect its endowment had paid off handsomely. By the 1990s the foundation was dispersing nearly $20 million each year in local grants. City museums receiving Ahmanson grants included the Museum of Contemporary Art, the Craft and Folk Art Museum, Pacific Asia Museum, and the Southwest Museum (one of the world's leading museums of Native American culture). Grants also helped to support the George C. Page Museum, the Los Angeles County Museum of Natural History, and the Cultural Heritage Museum. Contributions to the California Museum of Science and Industry led to designation of the museum's central building as the Howard F. Ahmanson Building.

Murphy urged Ahmanson trustees to consider the diverse needs of the city's people and cultures and to ratify grants for the Japanese American Cultural and Community Center, Plaza de la Raza, and the California Afro-American Museum. Murphy was not interested in a mishmash of cultural displays—a little of this one, a little of that one. What he wanted to see were cultural centers in which each group could display the best of its culture and take pride in its roots and its connection to Los Angeles.

In Murphy-directed programs of international outreach, grants were provided by the foundation to the Historic Churches Preservation Fund, the World Monuments Fund, and the Venice Committee for Monuments. His recommendations for foundation gifts also extended to institutions on the leading edge of medical research. On one occasion Murphy ushered Ahmanson trustees into his car for a short drive to UCLA, where Sherman Mellinkoff, dean of the medical school, gave them a tour of the extraordinary work under way. After visiting the school's vanguard Brain Institute, the trustees unanimously voted to provide $1 million for its pioneering research in positron emission tomography (PET), an imaging system for viewing the body's organs. Mellinkoff awed the trustees, as Murphy knew he would, by telling them that PET's impact on modern medicine would be comparable to that of the microscope on nineteenth-century science. Numerous gifts from the Ahmanson Foundation followed: the Ahmanson Biochemical Imaging Center, the first facility in the world devoted to the clinical use of PET; the Center of Health Enhancement Education and Research; and the Ahmanson-UCLA Cardiomyopathy Center.

In spite of his often-stated goal to adhere to Howard Ahmanson's desires, and even though he knew Ahmanson had not favored grants to publicly supported institutions, Murphy gradually moved the trustees to support UCLA projects, first at the medical school and then at other areas of campus need. The foundation contributed to the university's Museum of Cultural History (later known as the Fowler Museum) and donated $500,000 toward restoration of the beloved Royce Hall. The outdoor court of the newly refurbished auditorium was named the Ahmanson Terrace in recognition of foundation gifts. By the 1990s more than $23 million in grants from the Ahmanson Foundation had been directed to programs and projects in nearly forty university departments at UCLA. Most of these gifts were directed to areas of Murphy's special interest: humanistic studies, cultural history, and medical research and teaching.

Murphy took pleasure in the times he arrived on the scene to save an endangered city institution. One such midnight rescue came when KCET, channel 28, the city's only public television station, could not meet its monthly payroll and was forced to put its Hollywood studio up for sale; Murphy and Robert Ahmanson stepped forward with an eleventh-hour check for $500,000.[21] Vital Ahmanson Foundation support of KCET continued for many years.

Believing he understood Ahmanson's mind-set, Murphy led the foundation to devote major resources to strengthening undergraduate and graduate programs at a variety of Los Angeles institutions: California Institute of Technology; California State University, Los Angeles; Claremont Graduate University; Occidental College; Pepperdine University; and Scripps College. Funding was also directed to the region's arts education institutions, including the Otis Art Institute, the California Institute of the Arts, and the Art Center College for Design. Murphy acknowledged Ahmanson's concern for his alma mater with grants of millions of dollars to the University of Southern California designated for the Ahmanson Center for Biological Sciences, the Norris Cancer Center, and expansion of the Helen Topping Architecture and Fine Arts Library.

BUILDING A MULTICULTURAL CITY

When Murphy was approached by Rabbi Uri Herscher, executive vice president and dean of faculty of the four-campus Hebrew Union College–Jewish Institute of Religion, about his vision to build a cultural center dedicated to exploring the intersect between four thousand years of Jewish heritage and American democratic ideals, Murphy listened with interest. It was Herscher's hope that his idea for a new cultural center would demonstrate the creative spirit of Jews in every field of social, intellectual, and artistic effort and that such a center could reveal to Jews and non-Jews alike the connection to American freedom and opportunity of an ancient people with a rich and vibrant heritage.[22] Murphy's "interest was stimulated," Herscher recalled, "because Franklin understood the relationship between the Jewish people and American democratic values." He saw American Jews as playing an essential role in supporting and building democracy. "Your people take their values into the voting booth," Murphy told Herscher. Since the late 1970s Murphy had been involved with theologians, architects, and city planners who had joined forces to preserve the heritage of Jerusalem. Teddy Kollek, mayor of Jerusalem (1965–93), and his associates set themselves a daunting task to maintain a living city that did not betray Jerusalem's role as an ancient symbol of humanity's aspirations. As divisiveness and economic uncertainty gripped the historic city, deep-rooted challenges continued to confront Kollek and the Jerusalem Committee.

Murphy had first been exposed to fundamental Jewish concepts through his family's relationship with Rabbi Samuel Mayerberg of Kansas City, and he was intrigued that the center Herscher was proposing, based in Jewish values but reaching out but welcoming all, would thank America for the opportunities it has provided to Jewish and other immigrants. It was imperative to Murphy that the proposed center focus on education, grassroots outreach, and comparative cultures. Murphy furthermore insisted that the institution exist independent of a theological seminary. This was an important precondition for gaining his support.

The immigrant experience had shaped Herscher's own life. A child of refugees, his German Jewish parents fled Hitler's rise to power and made their way to British Palestine in 1935. Herscher's grandparents and most of his other family members were murdered in the concentration camps. In the mid-1950s Herscher's parents, along with Uri and his brother Eli, immigrated to the United States and settled in San Jose, California. He graduated from the University of California, Berkeley, and was ordained a rabbi at Hebrew Union College in Cincinnati, Ohio, in 1970; he later received a doctoral degree in American Jewish history. He embarked on an academic career and wrote several books on Jewish immigration to the United States and the sociology of American Jewish life, including communal utopias.

The concept for what would become the handsome "joyful forum" for Jewish tradition that invites the whole community—the grand Skirball Cultural Center—began in June 1981. That year Herscher solicited the vote of Hebrew Union College's Board of Governors to relocate the college's museum collection to the proposed cultural center. In 1983 critical seed money for the project came from Jack and Audrey Skirball through their Skirball Foundation. Born in the steel-mill town of Homestead, Pennsylvania, in 1896, Jack Skirball was ordained a rabbi at Hebrew Union College in 1921. He went on to enjoy a second career in motion pictures followed by great success in real estate development. His friendship with Herscher dated to 1964, when Herscher began his rabbinical studies. As Herscher was developing his idea for the center, Skirball helped him select and secure a scenic site in the Santa Monica Mountains adjacent to the San Diego Freeway, not far from the proposed site for the Getty Center. Two years later the celebrated architect Moshe Safdie agreed to plan the center's design.

Murphy came to Herscher's attention in an unusual way. Unknown to Herscher, Murphy had already enjoyed a rich history with the charismatic Jack Skirball. Herscher recalled that one time as he was preparing for a trip to Los Angeles while still based at the Hebrew Union College campus in Cincinnati, he was surprised when Skirball called him from Los Angeles to ask him to bring a crate of special Kentucky bibb lettuce for a man named Franklin Murphy. Herscher delivered the lettuce to Murphy's downtown office at Times Mirror Square. Later, when Herscher revealed his concept for a new cultural center, Murphy provided him sage advice and a critical list of people he should meet (and people he should avoid).

By 1985 Herscher was ready to present his fledgling idea for the cultural center to the people of Southern California at a gala event planned for 1,800 persons in the ballroom of the Century Plaza Hotel. This grand kickoff occasion needed a prominent figure to serve as honoree and as a recognizable name to draw people to the event—people involved in and concerned about Los Angeles's multicultural development. When Herscher urged the role on Murphy, he resisted but agreed if certain conditions could be met. He stipulated that he not be given any kind of award; he had medals and plaques enough. In addition, what he especially desired was that he be given the opportunity to pay tribute to Rabbi Mayerberg, who had been his father's closest friend and fellow activist in Kansas City and a longtime counselor and adviser to the Murphy family.

Mayerberg (1892–1964), ordained at Hebrew Union College, Cincinnati, in 1917, served the families of his Kansas City rabbinate tirelessly for thirty-two years. In addition, he was a powerful civic presence in Kansas City alongside Murphy's father during the 1930s fighting the corruption, patronage, and graft of political boss Tom Pendergast and his machine.[23] Mayerberg had comforted and counseled young Franklin and his brother, George, when their father died. Seventeen-year-old Franklin had asked Rabbi Mayerberg to deliver the eulogy for his father. The year was 1933, a time when such an ecumenical tribute was rare, but Dr. Murphy's activities had bridged many communities. Cordie Murphy, eleven years old, remembered a long cortege of cars winding up the road to the cemetery and people in attendance from every walk of life. Murphy returned to Kansas City to speak on the occasion of Mayerberg's retirement. Murphy now wanted to reciprocate Rabbi Mayerberg's tribute to Murphy's father by memorializing the role the rabbi had played in the life of the Murphys.

Herscher needed an underwriter to make the occasion memorable. Murphy suggested that Herscher contact Murphy's friend Frank Wells, president and chief operating officer of Walt Disney Productions. Wells agreed to cochair the event with Michael Eisner, chairman and CEO of the Disney Company, which would provide the evening's entertainment as well as generous funding.[24]

Herscher knew of Murphy's long friendship with Teddy Kollek and his love and concern for Jerusalem, which had influenced his championing the Jewish community, but Herscher thought that the more important source of Murphy's interest was his earlier relationship with Mayerberg.[25] The rabbi had helped him through difficult days of grief and indecision when he had to quickly leave adolescence and take up adult duties. Later, when Murphy returned from a student year abroad in Germany, it was the perspective learned from Mayerberg that helped him sort out the array of baffling impressions and experiences he brought back. Murphy's family had been enamored of German culture; his father and mother studied in Germany. Young Murphy had glimpsed a different Germany, one in which German culture and values were being subverted by the Nazis. In traveling on his own through Italy, his emotions had been captured by the art of the Renaissance. He considered himself a young scientist, and as a scientist he looked to his data, his facts, and his experience for answers and analyses; but the ideas he was wrestling with could not be readily quantified. It was Mayerberg's influence that helped him refine his thoughts on art, culture, and heritage. He and Mayerberg continued their dialogue through Murphy's years as chancellor first at the University of Kansas and then at UCLA.

Murphy paid tribute to Rabbi Mayerberg in his moving remarks to the 1,800 people gathered in the ballroom to honor Murphy and hear plans for the Skirball Cultural Center. He spoke of the historical Jewish commitment to the cultivation of intellect and talent by which the world's people, Jewish and non-Jewish, had been enriched. As Murphy concluded his remarks, Herscher stepped forward to present him with a gift sent from Kansas City by congregants of the temple Mayerberg had served. The small box contained Rabbi Mayerberg's gold pocket watch. Murphy, with tears rolling down his face, told the assembled crowd that he would treasure the timepiece and wear it as his own until the day he died.

Herscher had established a close bond with Murphy, and their conversations on a weekly basis covered a wide range of topics. They usually met at Times Mirror Square. Murphy was near the end of his tenure with the company and could look forward to the ease of retirement. Herscher observed that he was still vigorously pursuing plans for a cultural infrastructure to serve the special needs of Los Angeles. The cultural diversity of the city had to be accommodated in a manner to capture the advantage of pluralism without eroding into an uneasy, contentious polyglotism. "He was becoming even more of an idea broker," Herscher observed, "not only a cultural broker." He was especially concerned about the need for people to maintain a sense of their roots, their cultural identity, while at the same time fully participating in the larger social order.

Murphy, the matchmaker, led Herscher to relationships with foundation leaders that continued through the years. The Getty Trust and the Skirball Center became more than neighbors; their officials shared information through the building process and continued to support each other's vision as their institutions began to function in their new facilities. Through Murphy, Herscher met and continued close relationships with Robert Ahmanson, Harry Volk, Harold Williams, Rocco Siciliano,

Robert Erburu, and other early leaders embarked on the mammoth undertaking at the Getty hilltop.

Herscher enjoyed a close relationship with the prominent Haas family of San Francisco through his friendship with Robert Haas, his roommate when both were undergraduate students at UC Berkeley. Murphy maintained close ties to Walter Haas Jr., Robert's father and Murphy's contemporary; Murphy and Haas had weathered tough times together as board members of the Bank of America and had socialized often during the summer encampments at the Bohemian Grove. Murphy let Haas know that he fully supported Herscher's efforts. Once Safdie completed the architectural plans for the center, Murphy offered special praise. "The model of the Cultural Center is breathtaking in its beauty," he wrote Herscher in February 1988. "It will be an enormous addition not only to the cultural life but the architectural landscape of Southern California."[26] When more funds were needed to see the project fully realized, Murphy contacted Walter Haas again. "My enthusiasm for this project has not diminished," he wrote, "but has substantially increased. I hope that you and the other trustees of the Foundation can see fit to respond positively to Uri's proposal."[27]

Later Herscher would say the cultural center was "scarcely more than an inchoate aspiration" until Murphy breathed life into the idea. In acknowledging his gratitude to the master of master fund-raisers, Herscher told Murphy, "From you I have learned the meaning of vision and statesmanship."[28] Murphy's lifetime of relationships and experiences culminated in his being able to elicit checks for millions of dollars for projects of his choosing.

Murphy was asked by Herscher to join the Skirball Center's board of trustees, and he agreed. At the same time he suggested Erburu to Herscher, who invited him to serve on the board as well, fostering further the center's relationship with the Getty Center and numerous foundations. Today, a bust honoring Franklin Murphy sits atop a pedestal of Jerusalem marble welcoming Skirball Cultural Center guests to the Murphy Foyer of Ahmanson Hall on the Skirball campus with a Franklin Murphy quote inscribed: "The flourishing of the arts can only take place in a free society."

· · · · ·

As early as 1967, in an address to the popular lecture forum Town Hall, Murphy had pointed out that a society that is workable must bring minority groups and new immigrants into full participation. "We must become less mean-spirited," he said, warning about pressures building up in the face of intolerance and inequity.[29] In the course of his long career as a culture broker for Los Angeles, he seized opportunities to work on projects that directly reached out to different populations in the city.

City leaders in the Japanese community had approached Murphy in the early 1970s for aid in the construction of an $8.2 million cultural center in Little Tokyo, a West Coast counterpart of the highly successful Japanese American Cultural Center in New York City. Murphy embraced the project and sought funds from the Irvine and Kresge Foundations and various downtown business leaders, including Ed Carter and Eli Broad. Murphy managed to raise more than $1 million for the project, including significant contributions from the Ahmanson and Times Mirror Foundations. He served on the institution's board of directors helping to obtain multimillion-dollar loans from area banks for final construction, and he guided architectural decisions with the goal of creating a handsome addition to a revitalized downtown. He also extended valuable help for the center's comprehensive library of Japanese and Japanese American history and literature by promoting a close relationship with the UCLA library's Japanese American Research Project, a rich depository of material.[30]

The Japanese American Cultural and Community Center, at 244 South San Pedro Street, which included an art gallery and library, was completed in 1980; construction of the James Irvine Garden and the Japan America Theatre and Plaza followed. The complex became the largest ethnic cultural center in the United States. The center's one-acre open air plaza featured a major sculpture by Isamu Noguchi. In an appeal to the chairman of the board of Atlantic Richfield, Robert O. Anderson, for $250,000 to commission the Noguchi sculpture, Murphy said it was especially appropriate to have Noguchi involved. "He is not only half-Japanese and one of the world's most distinguished sculptors, but he was, in fact, born in Los Angeles."[31] Murphy's efforts were appreciated by the Japanese American community and handsomely acknowledged. In October 1982 the award of First Class of the Order of the Sacred Treasure was conferred on him by the Japanese government.[32] In November the cultural center's library was named the Franklin D. Murphy Library.

LINKING LOS ANGELES'S LIBRARIES

Murphy believed that great cities required a great library system, and no city that neglected its libraries could hope to attain greatness.[33] He set out to link the library resources of UCLA (the University Research Library, its Department of Special Collections, and the Clark Library) with those of the Huntington Library and the forthcoming library of the Getty Center. Through these combined resources he envisioned no less than a major center in Los Angeles for study and research in the humanities. UCLA's William Andrews Clark Memorial Library, housed in a classical revival building in an older, nineteenth-century pocket of Los Angeles, was a marble-floored archive known as heaven on earth for book lovers. The elegant library possessed one of the world's great collections of seventeenth- and eighteenth-century rare books and manuscripts. Murphy wanted to establish, in connection with the Clark, an interdisciplinary center with UCLA's Center for Seventeenth- and Eighteenth-Century Studies (funded in part by the commitment Murphy had extracted from Armand Hammer). Funding from the Ahmanson Foundation made his idea a reality; the library received a $225,000 grant on the occasion of its fiftieth anniversary.[34] The gift was the largest single contribution to the library from private sources since the original bequest by founder William Andrews Clark Jr. (who had named the library for his father, a turn-of-the-century U.S. senator from Montana who made his fortune in copper).[35]

In the 1970s Murphy took the lead in creating an endowment of $500,000 to acquire medical history books for the UCLA Biomedical Library in the Center for Health Sciences, making the collection one of the most distinguished in the United States. Earlier he had donated his father's collection of nineteenth-century medical books. Dean Sherman Mellinkoff named the endowment the Franklin E. Murphy Acquisitions Fund in tribute to Murphy's father. When told of the gesture, Murphy became tearful and told Mellinkoff that he saw the medical history project as a place where he and his father symbolically touched hands.

Murphy was methodical in his support of libraries and knowledgeable about the book trade, but his emotions took over when it came to books produced by the great Renaissance printer Aldus Manutius. The collection of rare Aldine volumes housed in the special collections department of UCLA's University Research Library was truly Murphy's passion. Murphy and Robert Vosper began the collection in 1961, and Murphy continued to foster its expansion with consistent support from the Ahmanson Foundation until it became the foremost repository for Aldines in the world. He loved to hold the small volumes in his hands and marvel at the printer's craft that had speeded the expansion of knowledge in such an artful and significant way. Nicolas Barker, an Aldine authority, has pointed to Manutius's popularizing of handheld books as a Renaissance phenomenon similar to the paperback revolution of the past half century. Manutius inaugurated his "portable library" of Greek and Latin classics in 1501 with the publication of Virgil's *Opera*. The books revolutionized scholarship by offering uniform texts that could be made widely available. Books from the Aldine Press were sought by collectors from the time they first appeared.[36]

The Aldine collection at UCLA, which came to be called the Ahmanson-Murphy Aldine Collection, eventually held 80 percent of the books printed by Aldus Manutius. "Franklin was not one who often wore his heart on his sleeve," remembered his colleague Daniel Belin. "[But] there was no mistaking his enthusiasm when he would bring his friends and scholars to see the Aldine Collection."[37] The small books lined up on glass-enclosed shelves with the dolphin and anchor colophon of the Aldine Press were a bibliographic display that encompassed both Murphy's passion for books and his most acquisitive ambition. Robert Vosper testified to the strength of Murphy's love of books, saying Murphy's enthusiasm was infectious and had persuaded him as a young, ambitious library professional to go, of all places, to Kansas. "I knew I would be working with a bibliophile chancellor," he said.[38]

Murphy defended the "jealous care of the bibliophile," but at the same time he sought full access for the qualified scholar. When a cache of rare books valued at $2 million was stolen in London and an American graduate student was arrested in New York City, Murphy was outraged. He wrote a series of letters to librarians and university chancellors about the need for heightened security. When it was discovered that UCLA's distinguished numismatic collection, mistakenly shelved in the open stacks, was stolen in broad daylight from the University Research Library, he hit the roof. He immediately ordered Brooke Whiting, then assistant head of Special Collections, to go into the stacks to see if he could find any Aldine imprints. To Murphy's horror, Whiting found several sixteenth-century Aldines sitting on the open shelves. Murphy jumped in his car and drove straight to UCLA, where he engaged in heated conversation with the university librarian, Russell Shank. He pleaded for better security and demanded the requirement of an identification card for entry to the library.[39] "How is this possible?" he wrote Vosper, now retired. "If this kind of thing can go on, it will certainly discourage people from giving rare and important books to the UCLA libraries."[40] "At the present time," Murphy groused to Chancellor Young, "any Tom, Dick or Harry may come in off the street and use our libraries. Maybe this was a good idea when people were honest, books less expensive and we had relatively unlimited funds to provide services to the 'broad community.'"[41]

Murphy was a voracious reader who read widely in the classics, literature, and medical history. He maintained relationships over the decades with others who loved books—Daniel J. Boorstin, Josephine Ver Brugge, and Robert L. Nikirk, as well as Loraine and Robert Vosper. He hosted members of the International Association of Bibliophiles at candlelit dinners at Robert Lane and engaged in a flurry of correspondence with authors and experts concerning books, often enclosing clippings or a loaned volume.

Murphy also maintained a steady dialogue with the noted Los Angeles book dealer Jake Zeitlin and with Stephen S. Lash of Park Avenue's auction house, Christie, Manson and Woods International; little escaped his attention in the area of his special interests. When the George Abrams collection, which consisted of European books printed in the fifteenth and sixteenth centuries—including Aldine imprints—came up for sale, Murphy acted immediately. His enthusiasm persuaded Robert Ahmanson and Lee Walcott to support the acquisition in an amount of $500,000.[42]

Murphy himself collected the books of the Irish writer Sean O'Casey, as well as pamphlets, pictures, and any ephemera he could find. Among the O'Casey manuscripts that Murphy collected were the original versions of the plays *Nannie's Night Out, Kathleen Listens In,* and *The Bishop's Bonfire* and holograph manuscripts of early poems, such as "The Sweet Little Town of Kilwirra" and "The Soul of Man." Murphy began a correspondence with O'Casey in 1956 that lasted until the author's death. He also engaged in lively discussion (107 letters) with literary experts around the world concerning the author. O'Casey's works appealed to Murphy both for their fierce social conscience and their lyricism, a quality that resonated with Murphy's own love of a way with words. The intriguing personal correspondence between Murphy and O'Casey touched on social themes as well as on personal details of their lives.[43] On O'Casey's death, Murphy wrote his wife:

I am sure you must have sensed how really close I felt to your husband, not merely through the music, song and poetry of his genius, but perhaps most importantly, by way of his great humanity. A more gentle, sweeter and compassionate man never lived.

Two nights ago I read to my two oldest daughters excerpts from some of his letters to me, and, not unexpectedly, their eyes, as well as mine, were moist, indeed full. There is no doubt that I shall be reading them over in moments and years ahead. They are a better tonic than any medicine I have yet discovered.[44]

Murphy also told O'Casey's widow that he had been convinced of O'Casey's genius very early and that his reputation would grow over time. In 1970, when the UCLA University Research Library celebrated the acquisition of its three-millionth volume, Murphy presented his treasured O'Casey items to the Department of Special Collections for the benefit of future readers and scholars.

· · · · ·

Murphy was devastated when the city's downtown central library was ravaged by arson in 1986. More than 375,000 volumes were destroyed and another 750,000 damaged by smoke and water. The old central library had held the affection of Angelenos; though they complained of its general inefficiency, they delighted in its 1920s protomodern architecture with Egyptian, Mayan, and Assyrian touches and even a nod to the futuristic. The design was the work of Bertram Goodhue, a master of exotic idioms for monumental buildings. It was the third-largest library in the nation, with 2.25 million volumes. Volunteers from all parts of Los Angeles came to the site to work in the charred, smoky building, rescuing what they could of the scorched and soaked volumes. Many of the saturated books were flash-frozen to await restoration.[45]

At the request of Mayor Tom Bradley, Murphy became a prime mover in assembling a committee headed by Lodwrick Cook, ARCO chairman and CEO, to raise millions of dollars for restoration and book replacement. A public campaign was to begin in the fall, but ahead of time Murphy and the Cook committee embarked on a strategy to obtain early "gifts of five to six figures" from the downtown business elite. It was hoped that this would jump-start a frenzy of check writing. Among the committee members were Phillip M. Hawley of Carter Hawley Hale Stores; Roy Anderson, chairman of the executive committee of Lockheed; David Burgitt, vice president at Coopers and Lybrand; Robert M. McIntryre, chairman of Southern California Gas Company; Simon Ramo of TRW; Lew Wasserman, chairman of the board of MCA; and Richard Riordan of Riordan, Caps, Carbone and McKinzie.

Murphy almost immediately secured a $2 million grant from Harold Williams of the J. Paul Getty Trust. With this gift in hand, he solicited checks from Eli Broad, chairman of Kaufman and Broad; Howard B. Keck, chairman and president of the W. M. Keck Foundation; Roger Heyns, president of the William and Flora Hewlett Foundation; Harry J. Volk, chairman of the Weingart Foundation; Edward F. Truschke of the BankAmerica Foundation; and Gerald Oppenheimer, president of the Jules and Doris Stein Foundation. The strategy paid off and triggered an unprecedented citywide response from civic groups and private citizens. But as the fundraising campaign neared victory, the final plans for reconstruction of the library remained problematic, and a fight ensued over how best to save the landmark building. It would be some years in the future, but the library would in the end receive a splendid renovation.

CIVIC PRIDE AND CIVIL UNREST

The tactic that Los Angeles undertook to wean itself from dependence on the war industry at the end of the cold war was a distinctive mix of new high-tech enterprises and financial services for the Pacific Rim, a route to recovery not available to other parts of the country. But the city's new economy and new global relationships resulted in great wage inequality, with no jobs or only low-paying service jobs for many of the dislocated factory workers. In fact, by the advent of the 1990s Los Angeles had the dubious distinction of having the fastest-growing wage inequality of any U.S. city, with increasing numbers of families falling below the poverty line.[46] In addition, low-income communities were hard hit by cutbacks in public services; the public schools had deteriorated, and rental housing was becoming more and more expensive and inadequate.

Murphy was adamant about the need to fully integrate the city's public schools. "Whatever dollars are required and whatever tolerance in our society is necessary," he said, "it must be done if you want your children to live in a society that has some peace, some quietude, and some relationship to the Constitution and to the Judeo-Christian ethic."[47] Resistance to school integration continued as white families moved away or turned to private schools or home schooling. Fair housing and fair employment laws failed to achieve racial integration when the post–cold war economy faltered and good jobs became scarce.

In spring 1992 one of the worst urban riots in contemporary American history exacted a heavy toll in Los Angeles's inner city. The violence of April and May left forty-five people dead and two thousand injured and caused more than $550 million in property damage. Widespread unrest erupted following the not-guilty verdicts in the trial of four police officers charged in the beating of an African American motorist, Rodney G. King. The battering of King was caught on videotape by a nearby resident. The incident occurred late at night, but the powerful beam of a police helicopter afforded ample light. Broadcast widely, the scene caused an outcry against the police, and replays of the tape fueled the enraged response when the officers were acquitted. Searing images, seen around the world, became a vision of Los Angeles torn by racial strife.

Demonstrators raging against the police and the justice system gathered on the steps of Parker Center, the city's Police Department headquarters, located in the Civic Center. At Times Mirror Square *Times* employees were locked inside for safety as they frantically compiled reports for the morning edition. Fires, violence, and looting spread throughout the central city and adjacent neighborhoods. Korean merchants were heavily targeted. Most of the city's cultural landmarks and museums were spared. The Los Angeles County Museum of Art and the Music Center remained intact.

Murphy was deeply disturbed. From his experience serving on civic committees that formed after the Watts uprising in 1965, he knew how complex the problem was. He had little faith in yet more studies and yet more government funds bringing long-range solutions. Tom Bradley, now serving his fifth term as mayor, appointed attorney Warren Christopher to investigate police policies and make recommendations to the city council. The beleaguered mayor reached out for help from all quarters to relieve the racial tension that had seized the city. Since chronic unemployment in the inner city was a contributing factor, he called on Peter Ueberroth to head a job-creating project called "Rebuild L.A." Ueberroth had been widely praised for his management of the successful 1984 Los Angeles Olympics; however, the problems of this latest assignment would prove overwhelming, and he would soon resign the post.

Murphy watched as the talents of politicians, city planners, and business leaders were brought together to solve the crisis in the fragmented and divisive city. Granted, the geography of Los Angeles contributed to fragmentation: the city encompassed a vast area, 470 square miles, divided by the Santa Monica Mountains into a wide coastal plain on one side and a broad valley on the other. But compounding the situation was the history of city planning—or nonplanning—that left population decisions to land developers who, with the enthusiastic support of the oil and automotive industries, built tracts ever farther out into the fringes, remote from the center of town. The city's history of deed restrictions in private property that excluded racial and religious groups and redlining practiced by banks and savings and loans also compounded segregation and fragmentation.

While other leaders turned their attention to studies of poverty, unemployment, and entrenched racial prejudice, Murphy took a different tack. He felt that Los Angeles, of all cities, needed the cohesive power of cultural facilities and civic tradition, and that was where he invested his energy. He may have been early in putting forward this aspect of city life as essential to the commonweal, but he was not alone. Economists, as well as social planners, were coming increasingly to value art and culture as one of the glues that hold society together. Even the World Bank, fearful that alienation of traditional societies would result in chaos, characterized culture as "social capital," recognizing it as a component of economic stability comparable in importance to education, water, sanitation, infrastructure, and an effective justice system.[48] Experts on the global economy were rejecting the idea that economic growth can solve everything and were coming around to recognizing that culture is one of the great, too often ignored assets in the world economy—confirming Murphy's perception and validating the emphasis he put on developing institutions to foster cultural pride and build healthy pluralism. As Murphy pointed out in his many public addresses, irrespective of differences, in accounts of their cultural memory and in their monuments and art all groups seek the same thing, to comprehend the essence and meaning of life.

RESCUE FOR THE HUNTINGTON LIBRARY

The burned-out storefronts of the inner city were a long way from the verdant gardens of one of the oldest and most revered libraries in the region— the historic Huntington Library situated in a wealthy San Marino neighborhood. Though it had escaped the fires and looting, it was imperiled by financial collapse.[49] Founded in 1919 by railroad and real estate developer Henry Edwards Huntington, the 207-acre estate housed a renowned research library and a premier collection of eighteenth- and early-nineteenth-century British art as well as western Americana, with 130 acres devoted to gardens brimming with more than ten thousand varieties of plant life.

In June 1992 Murphy was influential in securing financial aid for the venerated institution through $4.5 million in grants to kick off a campaign to create an adequate endowment. Three million dollars from the Ahmanson Foundation and $1.5 million from the Andrew W. Mellon Foundation were earmarked to begin a $15 million Library Initiative to increase the endowment for library services. Robert Erburu, newly elected chairman of the Huntington's board of trustees, announced the gifts.

Indeed, as a team, Murphy and Erburu, with Robert Ahmanson, nourished the city's important cultural venues during a period of profound economic uncertainty as they, in effect, became the self-appointed overseers of an amazing grid of grants and resources. (Erburu had joined the board of the J. Paul Getty Trust in 1987 and the Ahmanson Foundation in 1988.) Through their long association with the Times Mirror Company, Erburu and Murphy influenced grants provided by the Times Mirror Foundation. Their impact as culture brokers is exhibited in the way they pulled the Huntington from the brink of disaster: $1.5 million from the J. Paul Getty Trust for programs in research and education; $800,000 from the Times Mirror Foundation to endow a chair for a distinguished scholar of American civilization; another $1.5 million from the Getty Trust for programs in research and education; and a $100,000 grant in 1981 from the Ahmanson Foundation for renovation of the library's rare book reading room, followed in 1985 by a contribution of $800,000 to the library endowment fund.[50]

Murphy felt the diverse charitable foundations of America were a fundamental hallmark of American society. "There is no other country in the world in which the principle of private giving [for] the support of all kinds of institutions is so deeply ingrained," he said. Because private giving comes from diverse sources with varying goals and priorities, pluralism was to Murphy's mind as vital to cultural and political freedom as any part of the Bill of Rights. He was alert to any attack on private giving and spoke against hastily formulated, ill-considered tax reform that might limit incentive for philanthropy. The Tax Reform Act of 1969 had embroiled him in years of diligent work on behalf of the Ahmanson Foundation to preserve Howard Ahmanson's bequest, which was to have such importance for Los Angeles. Murphy felt the 1969 reforms had been mainly constructive, but during congressional debates on reform he was alarmed to detect "an ideological attack on voluntarism and, therefore, on pluralism . . . a significant push towards statism." In an address in 1978 to University of Kansas alumni and donors to the endowment fund, he urged his audience to prevail on Congress to promote private giving; otherwise, he said, educational and cultural institutions "become mere arms of an ever-expanding, anonymous, non-accountable government bureaucracy."[51]

The Huntington found a dedicated mainstay in Erburu, who assumed the chairmanship in 1991 after the retirement of R. Stanton Avery, founder and chairman emeritus of the Avery Dennison Company, who served as chairman for nineteen years. On the eve of his installation, at an afternoon Friends' Day lawn party, Erburu and two hundred guests paid tribute to Robert Ahmanson of the Ahmanson Foundation and Richard Ekman of the Mellon Foundation in festive toasts with pink lemonade and strawberries on the clipped green lawns of the Huntington grounds. The occasion supported two of Murphy's often-pronounced beliefs. It affirmed the willingness of the private sector to support cultural undertakings, and, in this instance, the support was for an institution with a significant role in Murphy's theory that centers devoted to the very best of a culture's art promote cultural pride and assure respect. In his role as trustee and culture broker he directed generous grants to non-Western cultural centers to enable them to offer their best for display, and he wanted the same prerogative for art of the Western tradition. The Huntington was outstandingly prepared to preserve and display—in elegant fashion—the intellectual and artistic products of the Western mind.

On a perfect Southern California afternoon with a light breeze and sparkling sunshine showing off to glorious effect the disciplined world of nineteenth-century landscaping, it was no stretch of the imagination for donors assembled on the flawless lawn to concur with Erburu's pronouncement that as a sanctuary for art "the Huntington represents the bright, the beautiful and the hopeful side of life."[52]

Gracious nineteenth-century-style lawn parties could not turn back the clock. Dire financial issues concerning the Huntington's future would plague Erburu's tenure as chairman. He managed to inject the institution with renewed vigor and, much in the manner of his mentor, worked behind the scenes garnering more than $20 million in gifts from foundations and individuals. Erburu came to love working with the rare and important collections, guided by a favorite Murphy aphorism holding art to be "a glowing treasure of man's reaction to his own history and own environment."[53]

FOURTEEN

The Doge of Los Angeles

FRANKLIN MURPHY REACHED THE MANDATORY retirement age of seventy-five in 1991 and gave up his seat on the corporate boards of Times Mirror, Bank of America, Hallmark, and Ford Motor Company, but he continued as a forceful trustee of the foundations and museums he served. He had mastered the art of trusteeship during an exceptional period in Los Angeles—a window of a few decades—when enthusiasm for cultural development made it possible for him to apply his talents to good effect. As newly built office towers attracted business in a surge to the West Coast, he was able to rally corporate chiefs to his cause. Later, as mergers, restructuring, and global competitiveness reduced available funds and the sleek office towers—the "trophy buildings," in real estate parlance—were purchased by international conglomerates, interest in local cultural venues declined and the bounty of corporate resources disappeared. In addition, the political climate made it increasingly difficult to bring government and private capital into partnership for the arts. Murphy remained visible, active, and highly respected. He was the person to go to when ideas for the arts needed refining—or funding.

With Murphy's seventy-fifth birthday at hand, friends and associates found it difficult to think of a way to honor him. He was frank in saying that he had been given enough plaques and trophies. His friends devised a plan for a commemoration in which institutions he had fostered would mount an exhibition or event of special interest. They succeeded only too well, for Murphy was often brought to tears by the diversity of events and the memories they evoked.

The birthday committee members were from the generation Murphy had mentored: Robert Ahmanson, Robert Erburu, Rusty Powell, Andrea Rich, Harold Williams, and Chuck Young. All knew Murphy well and had great affection for him, and they knew he would not put up with any ceremonial folderol. So many proposals were received that the committee extended the celebration to eighteen months. A handsome brochure was devised featuring the dolphin and anchor emblem of the Aldine Press, a touch sure to amuse and delight Murphy.

The kickoff celebration, on September 29, was a reception given by the UCLA Art Council for Murphy and his friends and guests for the opening of *Thirty-five Years of Acquisitions: An Exhibition of Works of Art on Paper.* During his chancellorship Murphy had taken a particular interest in the Grunwald Center Collection, prints dating from the Renaissance to the present. For him, the works on display were like old friends. The Art Council arranged for a presentation by June Wayne, founder of the Tamarind workshops, which were dedicated to preserving and teaching the art of lithography. Prints in a more utilitarian vein—though still art—were on display at the UCLA School of Medicine's Louis Darling Biomedical Library. An exhibit of rare medical works and illustrations, recently acquired through the Franklin E. Murphy, M.D., Fund, was especially arranged for Murphy. The expanding collection grew from his father's collection and was now funded in his memory, so the exhibit had a special pull on his heart.

At the UCLA University Research Library material was assembled for exhibits by the Asian American Studies Center and the Armenian Study Center, which had been inaugurated during Murphy's chancellorship. UCLA's fine Judaica collection was also on display. Much of its acquisition had been made possible by the prompt response of Mr. and Mrs. Theodore Cummings to Murphy's urgent funding request. As he mingled with friends in the library, Murphy related how the collection came to UCLA through a mysterious Swiss bank account and late-night international phone calls.

Perhaps the most emotional event for Murphy—the realization of twenty-nine years of promise and planning—was the long-awaited opening of the UCLA Fowler Museum of Cultural History in September 1992. The inaugural gala reception took place in the three-story, $22 million building handsomely designed and built into a hillside on the west side of Royce Hall. The architect, Arnold C. Savrann, had used red brick in the construction to blend with the university's original Romanesque buildings on the central quadrangle.[1]

In 1965 Murphy had secured the donation to UCLA of an amazing gift from the trust of Sir Henry Wellcome, an American-born entrepreneur who built a pharmaceuticals empire in Great Britain. The Wellcome trustees sent a staggering thirty thousand pieces of ethnic art to UCLA, which formed the core of the museum's collection. Until a museum could be built the objects were stored in UCLA's Haines Hall. When new objects arrived, Murphy would leave the chancellor's office to race to the basement for the thrill of seeing the crates opened to reveal fabulous objects of nonindustrial societies. He insisted that the art not be called "primitive" or even "preindustrial"; the art of nonindustrial societies was the description he preferred. From time to time makeshift exhibits would be mounted, but most of the objects remained crated, unavailable and unseen over the nearly three decades it took to bring the museum to fruition. For Murphy, it was exasperating that a collection that offered such a unique opportunity for UCLA, and for the growing cultural reputation of the city at large, was not given the priority it deserved.[2] Twenty years lapsed before the regents approved the museum facility and the lead gift for construction was received from Francis E. Fowler II, Phillip F. Fowler, and the Francis E. Fowler Jr. Foundation. When the museum's cost exceeded the allotment of state funds and the Fowler gift, Murphy set to work to obtain grants from the Getty Trust and the Ahmanson Foundation.

As chancellor in the 1960s, when sensitivity to world cultures was drawing the attention of scholars and activist students, Murphy conceived the launch of the museum to fill an obvious gap in the study of cultural history in non-Western traditions, though he never imagined it would take so long to bring the museum into existence. He thought UCLA's holdings combined with collections at the Southwest Museum and the Natural History Museum would make Los Angeles an important center for the study of ethnic art and would attract future collections. Among Murphy's disappointments about tasks left unfinished when he left UCLA, the unbuilt museum weighed heavily on him, and it was with great relief that he witnessed the opening as a part of his birthday celebration.[3] The new Fowler Museum was to become one of the nation's top four university-based anthropological museums, along with the University Museum of Archaeology and Anthropology at the University of Pennsylvania (Murphy's alma mater), the Phoebe Hearst Museum of Anthropology at UC Berkeley, and the Peabody Museum of Archaeology and Ethnology at Harvard University.

Murphy wanted the world's cultures to be represented by fine examples and presented with respect, in a manner to invite serious scholarship. His insistence applied to the Western heritage as well. As a Getty trustee, he urged that the Getty Trust, at that time planning its new hilltop center, confine the museum collection to European art before the twentieth century and acquire the finest works possible. For his birthday celebration friends at the Getty Museum offered a symposium on medieval illuminated manuscripts, which of course brought to Murphy's mind the early years with the original trustees who were wealthy cronies of J. Paul Getty. He could still chuckle over the argument he had contrived to convince the oilmen that illuminated manuscripts are art: think of them as medieval paintings, he had told them.

Not to be outdone, LACMA's trustees and curators selected a special painting for the museum's popular Masterpiece in Focus series of gallery tours. They picked a work that they knew was meaningful to Murphy, Rembrandt's *The Raising of Lazarus*. The painting evoked memories for him of Howard Ahmanson and the many evenings he had spent in Ahmanson's library alternately in companionable jesting and earnest conversation about plans for the city. The painting, which had seemed foreboding hanging above Ahmanson's mantel, now took on a new aspect in its gallery location. Rather than gloom, it seemed to represent hope for the future. Murphy thought it a particularly appropriate gift to have come from the estate of the ebullient Ahmanson, whom he still missed greatly.

The Department of Special Collections of UCLA's University Research Library had no difficulty picking books to highlight. Of course, the choice would be the Renaissance collection. A tour and reception was staged to feature the Elmer Belt Library of Vinciana and the Ahmanson-Murphy Aldine Collection of Renaissance books.

As the date of his seventy-fifth birthday came and went—only partly into the series of Franklin Murphy birthday parties—Daniel Belin teased, "You're 76! When do we stop? Passover lasted only eight days!"[4] Events followed at the William Andrews Clark Memorial Library and at the California Institute of the Arts, where Murphy and Roy E. Disney were to be honored with the Trustees' Medal for Distinguished Service to the Arts. Next came a symposium, "Chancellor/Scholars: The Formation of America's Great University Research Libraries," which honored Murphy's achievement in bringing UCLA's library into the circle of distinguished institutions. The Huntington Library mounted a display of Renaissance treasures that included Albrecht Dürer's famed woodcuts from the *Apocalypse* series.

Murphy still owned the print from the series that he had purchased when he was a cash-strapped teenager, making weekly payments to the bookseller.

Murphy's birthday celebration continued. He was treated to *Renaissance to Risorgimento: An Exhibition of Italian Books and Manuscripts in Honor of Franklin D. Murphy,* organized by Victoria Steele (later head of the Department of Special Collections at UCLA). In keeping with Murphy's interest in Renaissance printing, Steele had gathered a display of Italian drawings, sketches, books, and manuscripts, including a group of papal bulls dating from 1559 to 1644 that particularly engrossed Murphy. A symposium, "Celebrating American Collectors of Rare Books and Manuscripts," was cosponsored by UCLA and the Getty Trust to highlight manuscripts once owned by American collectors. Present to participate were many of Murphy's colleagues who shared his passion for art, books, and scholarship, including Robert L. Middlekauff, Deborah Gribbon, David Zeidberg, and Nicholas J. Barker.

The next-to-last event was a candlelit black-tie dinner at the Huntington Library. The guest list included avid book collectors, civic leaders, foundation heads, academics, journalists, and arts patrons. Welcoming remarks were offered by Robert A. Skotheim, Huntington president, and Robert Erburu, chairman of the board of trustees. In a moment that would not be forgotten by anyone in the audience, Vartan Gregorian, president of Brown University, delivered a fitting tribute to the honoree. Underlining Murphy's extraordinary money-raising skills that funded his role as culture broker, Gregorian told the guests, "He's been a Medici at your expense." Amid the laughter and applause Murphy rose to acknowledge the accolade. As for loosening purse strings, he said, "The Irish are not without verbal charm."[5]

The final event was a reception in the Murphy Sculpture Garden at UCLA to open the *Twenty-fifth Anniversary Exhibition.* The trees had matured and cast shade over the knolls and pathways—just as Murphy had pictured in his mind so many years before—inviting students and visitors to meander, linger, and enjoy the garden and the sculpture. Murphy and his fellow septuagenarians rested on the curved concrete benches installed like banquettes in the garden. He noticed that the students preferred to sprawl on the grassy slopes with their books and sandwiches. All about him he could see the familiar sculptures—among them works by Alexander Calder, Gaston Lachaise, Jacques Lipchitz, Henri Matisse, Jean Arp, Isamu Noguchi, David Smith, Francisco Zuniga, and Henry Moore. He knew the story of how each had arrived, seventy in all, a remarkable collection. The first eleven were from the David E. Bright estate. Some of the others he had acquired through hard negotiations; some were unexpected, such as the gift of a sculpture by Aristide Maillol from Henry Ford II. Auguste Rodin's *Walking Man,* a favorite with the students, was contributed by the Alumni Association and a secret donor as a tribute to Murphy in 1966. Murphy loved to repeat the story of the young couple who once approached him and confessed that their first child had been conceived on a balmy night in the moonlit garden, where Moore's *Two-Piece Reclining Figure* was their trysting place.

Murphy was both exhilarated and exhausted as the nearly two-year celebration came to an end. He penned his letters of appreciation, thanking in particular Robert Ahmanson for his involvement. He told Ahmanson that he and Judy had been entranced by the various events and deeply moved. The celebration had evoked memories for him of struggles, successes, and some defeats, and had brought him together with many friends made over the years.

CHAOS AT THE COUNTY MUSEUM

In April 1992 trustees at the National Gallery selected Rusty Powell as its new director. Powell's ginger-hued hair, which accounted for his nickname, had turned "moon-white," but the forty-eight-year-old Powell was believed to have the energy and drive to run one of the world's great museums as it entered a new century.[6] After twelve years as the director of the Los Angeles County Museum, Powell and his family had grown attached to the Pastel Empire. "It's a very bittersweet move," Powell's wife, Nancy, told the *Times.*[7]

In Washington on October 2, National Gallery Chairman Murphy joined seven hundred guests to bid farewell to retiring director Carter Brown and welcome Powell to his new post. At the event in the Gallery's East Building Brown predicted great success for Powell, whom he described as someone with passion for art but with his feet planted firmly on the ground. "When he went to Los Angeles, he burned up the track. He moved that institution into glory," Brown said.[8]

In Los Angeles Michael Shapiro, chief curator of the St. Louis Art Museum, was chosen as LACMA's new director. Selection of the New York–born, Harvard-educated scholar ended a four-month search and endless speculation. As the 1990s gave way to a national recession, the resources of the museum were stretched thin. The museum managed to keep the doors open but not without considerable anxiety; there was a general sense of dread that the ax would fall at any moment.[9]

Budget tightening was the order of the day when Robert Maguire was appointed museum president. Maguire, the managing partner of Maguire Thomas Partners, a major downtown development firm, first joined the LACMA board when the museum was thriving. The museum now faced its worst fiscal crisis as philanthropic dollars shrank and corporate donations to the museum reached an all-time low. The Ahmanson Foundation, the museum's largest supporter, continued its tradition of annual holiday gifts of European masterworks, contributions that had great appeal to the public. With $1.2 million provided by the foundation, the museum acquired *The Last Supper,* a majestic painting by the late-fifteenth-century Spanish artist Pedro Berruguete, which was put on view in the Renaissance Gallery of the Ahmanson Building. The foundation also disbursed a seven-figure sum for acquisition of a revered Florentine altarpiece (by the Master of the Fiesole Epiphany).[10]

Shapiro shocked Murphy and other museum trustees when he suddenly resigned in August 1993, less than one year after his appointment. The institution's pressing financial problems were cited as the main reason for his departure. About the county cutbacks of more than $2 million and a minuscule endowment, far less than most major metropolitan museums, Shapiro told the *Los Angeles Times,* "It stinks. The cuts took the guts out of the place in terms of how we operate it."[11] He had been forced to dismiss twenty-three employees and accept the resignation of five curators during his brief tenure. One museum observer remarked that only a masochist would take on the role of museum director under the chaotic conditions at the time.

Maguire put the best possible spin on the crisis facing the museum, telling reporters that the twenty-eight-year-old museum was fighting its way out of difficulty and getting a grip on the future. The problems Maguire was forced to manage included a lengthy dispute with Joe D. Price, who had donated the funds for the striking Japanese Pavilion but was now suing the Museum Associates for the return of some of his loaned artworks; and a $100 million lawsuit (undertaken with Stanford University) against the First Church of Christ, Scientist, concerning a potential bequest. Looking ahead, Maguire took note of the vacant Wilshire Boulevard property adjacent to the museum owned by the May Department Stores Company and envisioned the property developed to serve as additional space and as a potential source of revenue. Working closely with Murphy and members of the board, Maguire resolved to see the museum's $21 million endowment increased to $200 million. Maguire received constant counsel from Murphy, now a senior trustee; Murphy had been present during the optimistic days of LACMA's founding and had seen the institution through successive crises, but he would not live to see the museum emerge from the lingering, decade-long cloud that now enveloped it.

SHIFTING LEVERAGE

Franklin Murphy, watching on television, cheered along with the crowds at the track as Paul Mellon's thoroughbred, Sea Hero, won the 1993 Kentucky Derby. It was a grand moment for Mellon. Mellon, eighty-five and in declining health, shouted in delight as his horse and jockey, adorned in the gray and yellow Mellon silks, defeated the race favorite by two and a half lengths.

A little more than four months later, on September 29, 1993, Murphy retired as chairman of the National Gallery. His final speech was short and tinged with sadness that this day had come. "And so, as is always the case in human and institutional affairs," Murphy told the gathered guests at his farewell banquet, "there must be an end and there must be a beginning."[12] His voice was strong, but his face looked sallow, and the truth was that he was suffering quietly from a throbbing pain in his jaw, neck, and upper back. He appeared to have aged ten years. Those who had not been in his recent company were shocked by his appearance. But he worked the room as always, maintaining his network, laying yet more plans. Photographs show him hunched over his dinner plate absorbed in deep conversation with others in attendance, leading figures in American arts.

Behind the scenes Murphy had planned a transition that would satisfy both Mellon's desire for a family representative on the board and his dislike for the continued service of two longtime trustees who had married. John R. Stevenson stepped down as a trustee, and the board elected his wife, Ruth Carter Stevenson, to succeed Murphy as chair. She was the first woman chair of the institution. To fill the vacancies left by Murphy and Stevenson, the board named Robert Erburu and Louise Whitney Mellon as trustees. By this artful arrangement Murphy created an opening for a Mellon family member to join the board. He had every confidence that Ruth Stevenson would prove a capable leader. As the outgoing chair he felt he was leaving a board now in harmony and ready to proceed. Stevenson lived up to his expectations and led the Gallery with her unique style, and in less than ten years Erburu, mentored through the years by Murphy, would be held in such estecm by the trustees that he, too, would be elected chair.[13] Rusty Powell thrived in his post as director, earning the respect and admiration of his staff and museum officials.

· · · · ·

At the age of seventy-seven Murphy was ready for a new generation to take charge. As 1993 came to a close, many of Murphy's handpicked "mentees," as he called them, were in position to contribute their best talents to a host of institutional boards and cultural venues. Murphy had great faith in Erburu's potential. He followed in Murphy's footsteps as a trustee of the National Gallery of Art and continued his challenging role at the Huntington Library, serving as chairman from 1991 to 2001. As a board member of the Ahmanson Foundation, Erburu supported grants to Murphy-inspired cultural programs and institutions. Murphy saw his protégé succeed to the chairmanship of the enormous J. Paul Getty Trust in July 1993. Erburu's leadership at these distinguished cultural institutions furthered Murphy's ambitions for Los Angeles and the nation even after he was gone.

The year 1993 marked the fortieth anniversary of Murphy's service to the Kress Foundation and the thirtieth anniversary of the Kress Fellowship Program. Marilyn Perry had proved a talented administrator and was thriving as president of the Kress Foundation. During the year she had ably overseen the distribution of nearly $4 million for conservation of European art and architecture. The once-stodgy Kress Foundation had been invigorated and empowered by her dynamic leadership and was now recognized worldwide. In 1994 John Fontaine, then president of Knight-Ridder, Inc., would replace Murphy as the foundation's chairman. As a young associate at the law firm Hughes, Hubbard and Reed, Fontaine worked on corporate matters for the Kress Foundation, and Murphy had invited him to join the Kress board.[14]

The benefits of Murphy's guiding hand were also apparent at UCLA where as chancellor Chuck Young steadily met goals Murphy had set. National polls ranked UCLA among the top ten U.S. universities in terms of its resources, faculty, research, and student body. Decades after Murphy's tenure, former university president Clark Kerr gave Murphy full credit for the transformation of UCLA into a world-class university. Through Murphy's efforts, Kerr indicated, "UCLA and the Los Angeles metropolitan community got what they were entitled to: one of the great university campuses of the nation and of the world and one well integrated into the surrounding community."[15]

The role of paterfamilias appealed to Murphy in his later years, more than might have been expected. He enjoyed family gatherings with his grand-children. After fifty years of smoking he resolved to give up cigarettes. He could not reverse the damage he had done to himself, but he wanted to steer his grandchildren away from the habit. He resolved to quit—and did so cold turkey. The family finances had stabilized, but Judy continued to suf-fer bouts of anxiety. Her continued alarm and sadness over her daughter Joyce's deteriorating condition plunged her periodically into a state of de-pression. Martha stepped forward more frequently to take charge, especially during her father's absences.

In fall 1993 Murphy learned from his doctors that the chronic pain he suf-fered was due to acute cancer of the mouth and jaw. He organized his records and asked Erburu to serve as executor of his estate. He confided to Martha that the family would need her help and worried that he detected early symptoms of Alzheimer's disease in Judy's behavior. He spent his last few months at home but occupied every minute with work he wanted to finish. Erburu came frequently to visit and to be whatever help he could. Murphy, in his robe and slippers, continued to spin out ideas and plans.

Even as his health declined he continued to take pleasure in dispensing grants as a trustee of the Ahmanson Foundation. The last grants he awarded included funds for UCLA's Clark Library, UCLA's Center for Medieval and Renaissance Studies, the World Monuments Fund, and the Los Ange-les County Museum of Art. It was a great disappointment to him that he was not able to travel to the international conference in Florence, Italy, that summer to join scholars from around the world to mark the quincentenary of Renaissance printer and publisher Aldus Manutius. He had hoped through the spring that he might be able to go.

The cancer spread to his lungs, as he knew it would, and when pain re-lief could not be managed any longer at home, he consulted his physician son about his options. Murphy died in his hospital bed at the UCLA Med-ical Center on June 16, 1994. At the moment of his death he was holding Robert Ahmanson's hand. "Bob, there is so much left to do," he said.[16] Pur-suant to his wishes, his ashes were interred at Mount Washington Ceme-tery in Independence, Missouri, alongside the remains of his brother, Dr. George Murphy, his mother, Cordelia Murphy, and his father, Dr. Franklin E. Murphy.

In Florence, the conference host, Walter Kaiser, director of the Harvard

University Center for Italian Renaissance Studies at Villa I Tatti, had planned the conference as a way to honor Murphy's lifetime of promoting study of the Renaissance. Murphy was to have given the final address at the closing dinner on the evening of June 17, but that day news of his death reached Florence. Kaiser announced his passing in a moving tribute as scholars at the symposium joined in a moment of silence. "Nullum quod tetigit non ornavit" (He touched nothing that he did not adorn). Kaiser later sent Judy a poignant letter of condolence:

> One of the great American citizens of this century, few people have done more to enrich the lives of so many people than he. His intuitive understanding of the value of culture and his enlightened determination to share culture with everyone have quite simply, changed the mental landscape of our country. Few people can claim to have done so much. . . . There on the last day [of the conference] word came of his death; all of us were completely devastated. Yet there was also a very strong feeling that we were doing, each one of us, exactly what Franklin would have wanted us to be doing—and so we carried on until the end with the sense of his benevolent spirit presiding over us.[17]

A volume on the history of Aldus Manutius, produced by the conference and containing the best of current Aldine scholarship, was dedicated to Franklin Murphy.

· · · · ·

The memorial service for Murphy took place at UCLA, near the grassy berms of the Franklin Murphy Sculpture Garden. At the service Charles Young, Robert Erburu, Daniel Belin, and Franklin Lee Murphy delivered the eulogies. "To know Franklin was to sense his determination, his fairmindedness, his confidence, his uncommon common sense, and his optimism . . . and to want to be a part of all that," Erburu said. "It was to recognize a brilliant mind that was never lost within itself, but which directed its energies to pragmatic and productive ends." Erburu spoke of Murphy's reputation as a Renaissance man—maybe so—"but you had the feeling that whether he had been placed in the fourteenth century or the twentieth, his remarkable abilities would have won him a position of high service."[18]

The *Los Angeles Times* paid tribute to Murphy with lengthy articles describing his contributions to the city. In copy from the editorial desk the sad news was headlined, "A Death in the L.A. Family." William Wilson, the *Times* art critic, who had reported on the city's major art events over the years and had observed Murphy's guiding hand, wrote that Murphy was a civilizing force in a town where glitzy pop culture reigned. The *Times* editorial called attention to Murphy's invigorating confidence and knack for convincing others: "When you were with Murphy, you knew that there was a solution. (You might even be the solution.) For a will like his, there was always a way."[19]

There was soon to be more sadness for the Murphy family. Joyce Murphy Dickey died on December 21, 1997, at the age of fifty-five. Judy Murphy, deeply torn after her husband's death and disconsolate about Joyce's death, died in January 1998; the Murphy's second daughter, Martha Murphy Crockwell, died on June 24, 1999, also at the age of fifty-five. It had been capable, practical-minded Martha who cared for her mother in her last difficult years and looked after her affairs. For the surviving children, Carolyn and Franklin Lee, more tears followed with the death of Willia and Ted Roberts. Though the couple had no children of their own, their obituary, composed by Franklin Lee, credited them with four children—three girls and a boy whom they had spent their lives raising.[20]

· · · · ·

Murphy's death marked the end of an era. Within a decade, many of his fellow cultural architects also would be gone. Robert Vosper, with whom Murphy said he shared the most rewarding relationship of his professional life, died on May 14, 1994, just weeks before his friend. At the time of Vosper's death the great Ahmanson-Murphy Aldine Collection comprised more than seven hundred Aldine volumes and some two thousand additional items of Italian printing from the period 1465 to 1600. Moreover, the UCLA library—the great labor and joy of the Murphy and Vosper team—ascended to the number two spot among all American university libraries in 1997. (Chancellor Young had helped further Murphy and Vosper's dream and had protected the library during the financial hardships of the 1990s.)

Edward Carter, the powerful regent who had conceived the prototype for modern suburban retailing and had led the campaign for the Los Angeles County Museum, outlived Murphy only two years; he died in Los Angeles on April 23, 1996. He was survived by his wife, Hannah. In September 2003 Hannah Locke Carter donated the couple's magnificent painting collection of seventeenth- and eighteenth-century Dutch masterpieces to LACMA.[21]

After years of isolation in her second-story bedroom at Los Tiempos, Dorothy Chandler died at the Garden Crest Convalescent Hospital in Hollywood on July 6, 1997. Her death certificate stated she had suffered from senile dementia for the previous five years; the cause of death was listed as heart disease. According to Otis Chandler's biographer, when her obituary was sent to him for his approval, he changed the line crediting his mother with engineering his role as publisher in 1960 and added the attribution "she said" to the sentence. Otis Chandler's memory differed from his mother's on the manner in which the "sacred trust" had been passed.[22] In accordance with her wishes, her ashes were turned over to her son for final disposition. There was no public memorial, but numerous poignant tributes were published in the weeks and months following her death. Before Los Tiempos was emptied and sold, several neighbors watched as an office crew hired by Otis Chandler spent days shredding the remaining Chandler family documents.[23] Lost perhaps was an archive that could tell engrossing details of one hundred years of Los Angeles history from the perspective of four generations of the Chandler dynasty.

Walter Annenberg, who achieved such satisfaction through his art, died at his home in Philadelphia on October 1, 2002. He was interred in a mausoleum at Sunnylands, his magnificent property in Rancho Mirage. The billionaire publisher and philanthropist left half his fortune to his family, his personal collection of impressionist and modernist masterpieces to the Metropolitan Museum of Art in New York, and the remainder of his estate to charity. There had been considerable ambiguity in their relationship, but on hearing of Murphy's passing Annenberg told Robert Erburu, "He was a great citizen."[24]

Paul Mellon did not live to see the turn of the century. He died on February 1, 1999, at the age of ninety-one. He bequeathed $75 million and more than one hundred of his favorite artworks to the National Gallery of Art, the largest gift in the museum's history. "What he has done," Director Powell told the *Washington Post,* "is leave us a whole museum of French and American art."[25] In memorial tributes to the passionate collector who had devoted himself to the National Gallery, speakers recalled Murphy's description of Mellon as a man who simply wanted "the highest quality of everything."[26]

J. Carter Brown died on June 17, 2002, at the age of sixty-seven; he had been hospitalized following treatment for multiple myeloma. Memorial services were held in Providence, Rhode Island, and at the National Cathedral in Washington, D.C. In his eulogy, Vartan Gregorian, now president of the Carnegie Corporation, told the gathering of more than one thousand mourners that Brown had led the National Gallery of Art to international stature with grace and flair for four decades. "Carter . . . believed that art was everybody's business."[27]

· · · · ·

A year and a half after Murphy's death, in January 1996, Robert Erburu stepped down as chairman and chief executive officer of the Times Mirror Company. He was sixty-five. One of his last company transactions involved the sale of its cable operations to a new venture headed by Cox Enterprises of Atlanta that resulted in a $1.6 billion gain for Times Mirror. His successor was Mark H. Willes, an executive of General Mills who had played a key role in the Minneapolis food company's diversification strategy. In accordance with his mandate to boost dividends for the Chandler family, Willes imposed strict cost-containment policies. His directives to "slash" jobs brought an uproar from the news staffs, who tagged him "Cereal Killer" and "Cap'n Crunch." At first the stock price more than tripled, but then it fell by a third.[28]

In winter 1999 it was revealed that Willes and the new publisher, Kathryn Downing, had entered into a profit-sharing arrangement with a downtown entertainment arena known as the Staples Center. Disclosure of the breach of the customary wall between news and commerce "set off a newsroom revolt" over what was considered a blatant ethical lapse. The gaffe brought a public censure from Otis Chandler, who broke years of silence: "One cannot successfully run a great newspaper like the *Los Angeles Times* with executives in the two top positions both of whom have no newspaper experience at any level."

In March 2000 the citizens of Los Angeles were stunned by the announcement that the Chicago-based Tribune Company had acquired the *Times*. The $8 billion acquisition of the Times Mirror Company was done without the knowledge of Times Mirror chairman Willes. The Chandler family had grown increasingly uneasy with the company's direction under Willes, and the moment for merger was ripe. City leaders as well as citizens feared the loss of a uniquely Los Angeles point of view in the acquisition of their paper by a midwestern publisher. From his long study of the attraction of California, Kevin Starr called it nothing less than a recolonization, the latest invasion and capture of Los Angeles by midwesterners, much like the arrival of immigrants from the Great Plains by the thousands a century earlier.[29] The sale greatly enhanced the fortunes of the Chandler family and ended the publishing dynasty. Mark Willes also became rich, earning $90 million for five years of work; for her share in the drama, Kathryn Downing earned $10 million.

Maverick newspaper publisher Otis Chandler died on February 27, 2006, at the age of seventy-eight. The *Los Angeles Times* featured an unprecedented tribute about his life and his role at Times Mirror. Dean Baquet, then editor of the newspaper, praised the editorial staff for the poignant tribute. "I was proud of this paper," he said. "Otis Chandler got the send-off he deserved, from a paper he made great."[30]

· · · · ·

As fate would have it Murphy was not to attend the opening of the Skirball Center and see the realization of Moshe Safdie's architectural achievement. The public dedication of the handsome complex took place in April 1996. Jack Skirball's death preceded the center's opening as well, but support continued through his widow, Audrey Skirball-Kenis, and the Skirball Foundation. Murphy also did not live to see the debut in December 1997 of the J. Paul Getty Center on its crest in the Santa Monica Mountains. The collection of monumental limestone buildings could be seen for miles by travelers on the freeway through the Sepulveda Pass that joins the valley side of Los Angeles to the coastal side. Murphy had hoped that the geographic artery would be a symbol for the Getty Center's aim to reach out and welcome all sectors of the sprawling city. Uri Herscher offered the invocation at the opening, an event brimming with enthusiasm for the projects ahead as the separate programs of the Trust took up their quarters in the multibuilding complex. Harold Williams, still anticipating the synergy that the programs would engender once they were in proximity, retired in January 1998, turning over installation of the programs to the new president, Barry Munitz. An enthusiastic public embraced the Getty Center with record crowds and steady attendance. Construction of the mammoth project had been a fourteen-year drama that cost nearly $1 billion.

Harold Williams had masterfully supervised construction of the hilltop buildings, ably balancing the competing goals of the architect Richard Meier and the desires of the Getty's professional staff. With the Center's opening, Williams stepped down, but he left the Getty Trust in excellent financial shape. During his tenure its assets had grown an astounding 89.3 percent, reaching a staggering $6.5 billion, second in size only to the Ford Foundation.[31] As for J. Paul Getty's surviving sons, they had long since gone their separate ways. After Gordon Getty dismantled the Getty Oil Company in the 1980s, he was reportedly worth $1.5 billion. The majority of his time was spent in support of the San Francisco Opera and composing music. J. Paul Getty Jr. conquered his addiction to drugs and became one of England's most eminent philanthropists; he was awarded an honorary knighthood by Queen Elizabeth. He died in 2003. As the new century began J. Paul Getty's grandson, Mark, declared his intent to rebuild the Getty family fortune by bringing the scattered inheritances in the hands of Getty heirs into a cohesive investment plan.

At the Ahmanson Foundation Robert Ahmanson and Lee Walcott dispensed an astonishing stream of grants to benefit education, human services, and culture. Ahmanson credited Murphy with having been the most influential figure in his adult life, and he continued many of Murphy's goals for the foundation even as its assets neared the $1 billion mark. By the close of the decade Ahmanson would be able to disburse nearly $50 million annually in grants to Los Angeles institutions and agencies.

The enormous resources at his disposal were the result of the financial genius of the foundation's founder, Howard Ahmanson, and the advice and counsel of Franklin Murphy whose stewardship and skill at warding off legal claims and regulatory attack preserved the fortune for the future benefit of the public. In 2003 Walcott announced that in its fifty-year history the Ahmanson Foundation had disbursed over twelve thousand grants totaling a staggering $550 million.[32]

AFTERWORD

The Mosaic City

WHAT STANDS OUT AS THE MOST important aspect of Franklin Murphy's legacy is the trajectory he created for the institutions he fostered. His desire to see cultural centers as a home for the humanities merged with his belief that building steadily on cultural awareness was part of the path to civic harmony. "The humanities, in my view, are for the long haul of civilization," he told the President's Committee on the Arts and Humanities. "They are not designed to solve the immediate problems of this society. The humanities maintain our memory as a civilization."[1] Murphy's preoccupation with the humanities and his insistence on the establishment of distinct cultural centers turned out to be the right prescription for the city of Los Angeles.

By the time Murphy reached the peak of his influence, the idea of a melting pot, with homogeneity as a goal for immigrant assimilation, had been abandoned in favor of the image of the salad bowl. But Murphy rejected that image as well. The tumbled and tossed salad was a polyglotism that satisfied no one, he said. He envisioned distinct groups, side by side in a mosaic, all parts of the larger design. To that end, he promoted and supported centers in which each group could display the very best of its art and culture. In 1980 when Murphy was asked to make recommendations for the billion-dollar bequest of J. Paul Getty, he urged that the trust be devoted exclusively to the humanities. (Only a few American foundations had such a focus; most were concerned with medicine, science, and social issues.) In addition, he envisioned the Getty Museum as a sanctuary for art of the Western heritage, in keeping with his desire for distinct but outstanding venues for displaying the artistic gifts of individual cultures.

Los Angeles's cultural diversity is lauded as the city moves into prominence in global finance and trade, but it was not a foregone conclusion that diversity would be one of its characteristics. When Murphy arrived in 1960, a large portion of the population resisted the idea of multiculturalism, holding fast to their belief in Los Angeles as a white, largely Protestant, Anglo-Saxon city. Many removed themselves to suburban enclaves to control their social environment, and there they maintained their determination to keep the city "Anglo" by opposing immigration, rescinding fair housing laws, and pressuring the Board of Education to fight racial integration. In spite of the inhospitable attitude to cultural difference, Murphy immediately undertook to establish at UCLA a series of centers for cultural research, starting with centers for Armenian and Japanese American studies.

In coming to California, he had thought he would be leaving behind the provincialism, racism, and religious paranoia of the plains, but he soon found that midwesterners had come to the touted Pastel Empire in sufficient numbers that midwestern practicality and chronic suspicion of art held sway; adding to the rigidity of the local mind-set was the fear of communism that had a stranglehold in a city of defense-related industries. Murphy believed the country was well buttressed against the threat of communism, and he saw no danger in the social revolution of the 1960s. What he found missing was the public spirit, identity, loyalty, and civic cohesion that cultural institutions can bring to a city. Los Angeles was fragmented both geographically and psychologically. The defense industry, which was avidly courted, built sprawling factories and hangars at the city's outer rim, where housing tracts for workers became self-contained communities distant from the civic core. In the history of the city's development, small independent communities sought annexation to Los Angeles and brought their own identities and their own "downtowns." Contributing further to fragmentation were the all-white, planned communities that used the "Lakewood plan," which allowed developers to pay for select city services without participating in the total cost of city operations.[2] But the isolation and homogeneity of such townships kept them remote from the mixture of people in neighboring Los Angeles. After 1953 when courts ruled race-restrictive covenants unenforceable, whites fled neighborhoods as African American, Hispanic, and Asian families moved in. The Proposition 14 campaign in 1968 to rescind the state's Open Housing Act fanned resentment. In ordering Los Angeles to integrate the public school system, the court cited municipal policies that had fostered residential segregation. The strenuous resistance of many white families to school integration brought yet more racial division in the city.

By the time Murphy reached mandatory retirement age and left the corporate boards on which he served, he had seen the effects of the 1960s revolution ripple through social, political, and corporate life. Changes were evident not only in civil rights achievement but also in outreach for diversity, in community responsibility and environmental policies. The greatest change of all had been the burst of creativity that gave rise to the region's high-tech era. Instant communication made fast-paced global trade the basis of a new economy for Los Angeles. As globalization gained speed at the opening of the twenty-first century, researchers found that societies of multiple, diverse cultures were more stable and had greater economic vitality than either one-culture or dual-culture societies. Economists point out that groups who understand one another's wants and desires and their culturally dictated preferences are better positioned for the fast-paced design and marketing required in global commerce. Immigrant entrepreneurs have become a noticeable part of Los Angeles's economy, and because of their international ties, they provide another advantage in global trade relations.[3] In the long run Los Angeles, located on the Pacific Rim and already deeply involved in media and communications, was better positioned than other cities to restructure itself; but as a cold war industrial city, it was faced with upheaval in moving from Fordism to flexibility and adjusting to the demands of a new economic model. The transition for Los Angeles was not smooth. Even as international companies leased offices in the new glass-sheathed towers, marginalized, underserved, and neglected segments of the population became ripe for confrontation. Murphy saw Los Angeles explode in the two most violent episodes of civil unrest and racial violence in U.S. history.

When defense plants closed in the 1990s, unemployment, loss of status, and cultural misery descended on white working-class as well as minority communities. The city of Lakewood was described by cultural observer Joan Didion as a pocket of disillusionment: It was hard for Californians, notorious dreamers, to accept "that the trend was no longer reliably up."[4] As Los Angeles made the transition into a new economic pattern, urban commentators noted that the city, ignored for so long as "aberrant, idiosyncratic or bizarrely exceptional," was paradoxically becoming the prototype for the global era.[5] Los Angeles's failure as a modern city made it a superb candidate for a rethinking of the urban environment. The Chicago school of urban planning had set the standard for the design of cities based on concentric circles of development around a central core. Los Angeles's sprawl and multinucleated development put it out of the running as such a model. Urbanists now point out that American cities that are growing are doing so in the way Los Angeles has grown.[6] Such cities are devising for themselves a position in the worldwide economy with global movement of capital, labor, and information. But they are not without problems: they contend with competing interest groups battling over land use and density; they have to provide for increasing immigrant populations; and, like Los Angeles, they struggle to achieve a sense of community in a fragmented, urban setting. City leaders confronting these challenges do so without the old utopian optimism of the modernist faith in structured solutions; but, in studying the future they face, they are open to a wider range of options and receptive to more diverse views than in the past.

Murphy had expected to be among the civic leaders who would bring Los Angeles into maturity as a modern city, but instead he helped to guide Los Angeles though an era of radical change that rejected the creed of the modern. In the years after Murphy's death the effect of his influence has continued. The city now operates with a Cultural Master Plan that makes provision for arts of diverse groups: traditional art shares venues with popular art, city-sponsored street festivals and outdoor stages proliferate, and support continues to flow to the city's cultural life from Murphy-guided private institutions and philanthropies. The fragmented metropolis is coming together—coalescing into a world-class city that validates Murphy's high expectations.

Perhaps the greatest symbol for Los Angeles's transformation is the Walt Disney Concert Hall, which opened in fall 2003; it is a dramatic expression of the evolution from Dorothy Chandler's Music Center—a pristine, modernist home for high culture that put Los Angeles on the cosmopolitan map—to a state-of-the-art venue of tumultuous design equipped for music of all kinds in a mature, multicultural city. The inspiring new concert facility, designed by Frank Gehry, has been received as a "powerful and madly exuberant work," one in which the layered stainless steel surfaces of multiple soaring planes appear "violently torn apart and gently pieced back together"—a rich reflection of the transformed city, fragmented but coming together after all.[7]

ACKNOWLEDGMENTS

Of all things, I love Los Angeles. It is my home. It is my city. It has been a privilege to write the biography of the man who may have done more to shape the cosmopolitan cultural image of Los Angeles than any other person of his generation. This book was six years in the making. I am extremely grateful to the Ahmanson Foundation, the J. Paul Getty Trust, and the Skirball Cultural Center for their generous support that enabled me to write this book.

I am also deeply indebted to Jack Miles, Victoria Steele, and Suzanne Muchnic. I gratefully acknowledge Robert Ahmanson, Daniel Belin, Gina De Roma Bowles, Charlotte Brown, Francis Chung, Jim Clark, Paul Conrad, Nicholas A. Curry, Maygene Daniels, Robert DeKruif, Robert F. Erburu, David Farneth, Peter Fernald, Joseph Alexander Gallego II, Uri Herscher, Genevra Higginson, Clark Kerr, Deborah Marrow, Dennis McDougal, Jack Meyers, Barry Munitz, Phyllis Pavon, Marilyn Perry, Earl A. Powell III, Anne G. Ritchie, Stephen D. Rountree, Carmela Speroni, Lori Starr, Harold Williams, Lee Walcott, Charles E. Young, and David S. Zeidberg.

I must extend my deepest appreciation to my mother, Catherine Davis, for her editorial contributions and insights. I greatly appreciate the talents of Sally Berman, Richard Willett, and Rachel Winfree. I am especially thankful to the family of Franklin Murphy: Cordelia Ennis, Lyman Ennis,

Franklin L. Murphy, and Carolyn Murphy Speer. I am extremely indebted to my sponsoring editors at the University of California Press, Sheila Levine and Randy Heyman, and to Sue Heinemann and Sheila Berg, who brought considerable skill and insight to the preparation of the enormous manuscript.

NOTES

PREFACE: ART OF THE TRUSTEE

1. Kevin Starr, conversation with the author.

2. As quoted in Nancy Kellogg Harper, "Higher Education Leadership: Franklin D. Murphy in Kansas, 1948–1960" (Ph.D. diss., University of Kansas, 1995).

3. Earl A. Powell III, interview with the author.

4. Robert Vosper's introductory remarks in Franklin D. Murphy, "My UCLA Chancellorship: An Utterly Candid View," interview by James V. Mink, 1973, transcript 1976, Oral History Collection, Dept. of Special Collections, University Library, UCLA. Also see Robert G. Vosper, "Libraries and the Inquiring Mind," interview by Dale E. Treleven, 1990–91, transcript 1994, Oral History Collection, Dept. of Special Collections, University Library, UCLA.

5. Clark Kerr, interview with the author.

6. See Judith Murphy, "Chancellor's Spouse," interview by Dale E. Treleven, 1995, transcript 1997, Oral History Collection, Dept. of Special Collections, University Library, UCLA.

7. *Los Angeles Times,* Oct. 2, 1992.

8. *Time,* July 15, 1957.

9. Franklin D. Murphy interview, undated transcript, J. Paul Getty Trust Oral History Project, J. Paul Getty Institutional Archives, Los Angeles, p. 6.

10. FDM to Otis Chandler, Robert F. Erburu, and Phillip L. Williams, memo, Mar. 21, 1983, Papers of Franklin D. Murphy, Dept. of Special Collections, University Library, UCLA.

1. Franklin Murphy's great-grandfather, Patrick Murphy, of County Cork, Ireland, was Roman Catholic. He wed Martha Flanagin, a Protestant widow with three children. The familial pressures on Patrick and Martha, based on the conflicting religious beliefs of their parents, became so intense that the couple decided to leave Ireland. Ostracized by communicants of both churches, they resolved to go to America, start life over, and reject church affiliation of any kind. The family settled on a farm in Scott County, Indiana. See Franklin D. Murphy, "Family Background of Franklin D. Murphy," pp. 1–3 (manuscript, May 3, 1956).

2. Cordelia A. Brown was the daughter of Adolphus H. Brown and Tryphosa M. Beals. The family lived in Massachusetts, then relocated to Colorado, and later moved to Kansas City, Missouri. Murphy, "Family Background of Franklin D. Murphy," p. 3.

3. *Kansas City Star,* Nov. 20, 1949, p. IE.

4. Murphy, "Family Background of Franklin D. Murphy." See also Franklin D. Murphy, "My UCLA Chancellorship: An Utterly Candid View," interview by James V. Mink, 1973, transcript 1976, Oral History Collection, Dept. of Special Collections, University Library, UCLA; and Nancy Kellogg Harper, "Higher Education Leadership: Franklin D. Murphy in Kansas, 1948–1960" (Ph.D. diss., University of Kansas, 1995).

5. See Franklin D. Murphy, interview by Deborah Hickle, Jan. 19, 1990, University of Kansas School of Medicine Oral History Project. Also see Harper, "Higher Education Leadership," p. 18.

6. Cordelia Murphy Ennis, interview by the author.

7. *Kansas City Star,* Nov. 20, 1949, p. IE. Also see Harper, "Higher Education Leadership," p. 23.

8. Ennis, interview.

9. Harper, "Higher Education Leadership," p. 24.

10. Ibid., pp. 27–31.

11. Ennis, interview.

12. FDM to Mrs. Franklin E. Murphy, letter, Nov. 18, 1936, Papers of Franklin D. Murphy, Dept. of Special Collections, University Library, UCLA (hereafter cited as Murphy Papers).

13. Murphy, interview by Deborah Hickle, p. 4; *Kansas City Star,* Apr. 18, 1948. Murphy could find no further trace of Rein. See Harper, "Higher Education Leadership," p. 24.

14. FDM to Mrs. Franklin E. Murphy, letter, Nov. 18, 1936, Murphy Papers.

15. Murphy, interview by Deborah Hickle, p. 5. Also see Harper, "Higher Education Leadership," p. 40.

16. Murphy, interview by Deborah Hickle, p. 26.

17. See Judith Murphy, "Chancellor's Spouse," interview by Dale E. Treleven,

1995, transcript 1997, Oral History Collection, Dept. of Special Collections, University Library, UCLA.

18. FDM to Dr. Charles Mayo, letter, Nov. 24, 1959, Murphy Papers.

19. Murphy outlined the three major features of the Kansas Rural Health Plan for readers in the *Saturday Evening Post,* May 16, 1951:

1. It called for expanding the faculty, hospital and laboratories at the University of Kansas Medical Center . . . to permit us to take in 100 instead of 80 freshmen, and thus to increase the output of medical graduates by 25 percent.

2. It sought to help rural communities plan the kind of "medical workshop"—office, examining rooms, small diagnostic x-ray room and small clinical laboratory—that we knew would attract good doctors. These were facilities our students and young graduates had told us they would like to have but could not afford to buy in one lump sum. We felt that a town could, as a community project, build and equip such a workshop, which the incoming doctor could then rent or purchase out of current income at little or no interest.

3. It provided for a broadening of our postgraduate-education program, both the short refresher courses held at the Medical Center and the "circuit course" of lectures given in towns throughout the state. This feature was designed to keep rural physicians in constant touch with new developments in diagnosis and treatment. Fear of becoming medically isolated and turning into mere "pill rollers" had deterred many young doctors from taking practices in remote parts of the state.

20. Franklin D. Murphy, Inaugural Address, University of Kansas, Sept. 17, 1951.

21. See Harper, "Higher Education Leadership."

22. Kenneth S. Davis, *Kansas: A Bicentennial History* (New York: W. W. Norton, 1976), pp. 187–88, citing Karl A. Menninger, *Kansas Magazine,* 1939, pp. 3–6.

23. See David Halberstam, *The Fifties* (New York: Villard Books, 1993), chaps. 1 and 2, for a vivid description of the psychological climate of the time.

24. Murphy, Inaugural Address.

25. The Riemenschneider was a gift from the estate of Myrtle Elliott Thurnau. It was sculpted in 1499. Also see Harper, "Higher Education Leadership," pp. 247–50.

26. For an extensive analysis of Murphy's action and lack of action on racial integration, see Harper, "Higher Education Leadership," pp. 100–101. Harper credits the research of Heidi Pitts, "Racism and Reformation with Franklin Murphy" (manuscript, May 13, 1992).

27. Murphy, Inaugural Address.

28. When she gave a concert at the university, Ella Fitzgerald had no place to spend the night because local hotels refused to rent rooms to African Americans.

Fitzgerald slept at the university guesthouse, one of Murphy's first capital improvements as chancellor.

29. Murphy spent three weeks in the USSR in 1958. See Franklin D. Murphy, "Our Dangerous Complacency," *NEA Journal,* Nov. 1959. Also see "Educational and Cultural Affairs—A Fourth and New Dimension in Foreign Policy" (speech delivered at the UCLA Charter Day ceremonies, Mar. 22, 1961).

30. *Time,* Apr. 6, 1953.

31. *Time,* Apr. 6, 1953. See A. Whitney Griswold to FDM, letter, Nov. 18, 1952; and FDM to A. Whitney Grisold, letter, Nov. 29, 1952, University of Kansas Archives. Also see Harper, "Higher Education Leadership," p. 170.

32. Murphy, "My UCLA Chancellorship," p. 3.

33. Ibid., p. 2.

34. Ibid., p. 3.

35. Ibid., p. 4.

36. "Ike Sat at His Feet," *Time,* Oct. 27, 1952; "Docking Jabs at Murphy," *Great Bend (Kans.) Tribune,* Feb. 28, 1960.

37. Murphy, "My UCLA Chancellorship," p. 11.

38. "The Mad Governor and Nero," *Romancer,* Oct. 1960, University of Kansas Archives; see also Harper, "Higher Education Leadership," p. 191.

39. Murphy, interview by Deborah Hickle, p. 32.

40. "KU Undergoes Growth under Murphy," *University Daily Kansan,* Mar. 17, 1960.

41. "Tribute to Dr. Murphy," *Topeka Daily,* May 26, 1959; "Speedup," *Time,* July 16, 1951.

42. Harper, "Higher Education Leadership," pp. 291, 245–327.

43. Robert G. Vosper, "Libraries and the Inquiring Mind," interview by Dale E. Treleven, 1990–91, transcript 1994, Oral History Collection, Dept. of Special Collections, University Library, UCLA, pp. 359–60.

44. Raymond Nichols, quoted in Harper, "Higher Education Leadership," p. 200. When Murphy was KU chancellor he accompanied Joyce C. Hall, president of Hallmark Cards, Inc., on a visit to meet Winston Churchill at Chartwell. Joyce discussed the presentation of Churchill's watercolor paintings as Hallmark greeting cards. Murphy was subsequently able to be of service to Churchill and to galleries in the Midwest by arranging a tour of Churchill paintings.

45. Murphy, interview by Deborah Hickle, p. 30.

46. Marcellus M. Murdock to FDM, letter, Oct. 3, 1958; FDM to Marcellus M. Murdock, letter, Oct. 7, 1958. Murphy Papers.

47. FDM to Alvin McCoy (editor of *Kansas City Star*), letter, Sept. 8, 1959, University of Kansas Archives. Also see Harper, "Higher Education Leadership," pp. 234–35.

48. FDM to Ray Evans, letter, Mar. 12, 1960, University of Kansas Archives.

He added: "The time has come when I must express my resentment at this shameful performance on the part of a man who has the responsibility of giving not only administrative and political but moral leadership as well to the people who have elected him to high office."

49. See Murphy, interview by Deborah Hickle.

50. In accepting the challenge to move forward with the region, Murphy lent his support to numerous civic organizations; he also accepted appointment to the board of trustees of the Menninger Foundation of Topeka and to the board of Kansas City's Nelson-Atkins Museum of Art. In 1953 he had been tapped for the board of trustees of the Samuel H. Kress Foundation of New York. Through these strategic relationships he was able to direct philanthropic resources to the prairie states.

Organizations that Murphy served at this time included the board of governors of the American Red Cross, the Veterans Administration, the American Council on Education, the State Universities Association, the National Council of the Boy Scouts of America, the Ford Foundation Committee on the University and World Affairs, the Carnegie Foundation for the Advancement of Teaching, the Menninger Foundation, the Eisenhower Exchange Scholarship Program, and the U.S. Advisory Commission on Educational Exchange of the Department of State. He also served as a member of the American Board of Internal Medicine and the American College of Physicians.

ONE: INTO THE PASTEL EMPIRE

1. The description of the student demonstration has been drawn from "Kansas Loses Murphy," *University Daily Kansan Extra,* Mar. 17, 1960; and "Faculty 'Mourning' Greets Resignation," *University Daily Kansan,* Mar. 17, 1960. Also see Franklin D. Murphy Scrapbook, Chancellors' Papers, Kenneth Spencer Research Library, University of Kansas; Nancy Kellogg Harper, "Higher Education Leadership: Franklin D. Murphy in Kansas, 1948–1960" (Ph.D. diss., University of Kansas, 1995), p. 243. Hear the "Rock Chalk" chant at www.ur.ku.edu/KU/traditions/cheers.html.

2. Clark Kerr to FDM, letter, Mar. 29, 1960, Papers of Franklin D. Murphy, Dept. of Special Collections, University Library, UCLA (hereafter cited as Murphy Papers).

3. *Los Angeles Times,* Mar. 16, 1960, p. A1.

4. FDM to Edwin W. Pauley, letter, Mar. 21, 1960, Murphy Papers.

5. FDM to William E. Forbes, letter, Mar. 22, 1960, Murphy Papers.

6. "Statement of Dr. Franklin D. Murphy," undated, Murphy Papers.

7. Edward W. Carter to FDM, letter, May 13, 1960, Murphy Papers. At the time Asa Call was the president of the Pacific Mutual Life Insurance Company.

8. Leonard Pitt and Dale Pitt, *Los Angeles A to Z* (Berkeley: University of California Press, 1997), p. 271.

9. Among films using Bunker Hill locations were *Kiss Me Deadly, M* (1951 remake), *Criss Cross, Reckless Moment,* and *Act of Violence.*

10. *Los Angeles Times,* Jan. 29, 1956. Bernard Halbig, "The Planners and Bunker Hill," *California Sun Magazine* (Department of Journalism, UCLA), pp. 9–10. Though the plans and financing would undergo changes in the next few years, the thinking of the Community Redevelopment Agency in 1960 was that with a combination of loans from the Housing and Home Finance Agency and grants from the Eisenhower Slum Clearance Program the city could buy the 136-acre hilltop, relocate the residents, demolish the buildings, level and grade the crest, and prepare a thirty-block area for sale to private developers.

11. Downtown leaders feared competition from new business parks. The 20th Century-Fox studio lot on the west side of town was being turned into a 176-acre high-rise development of office towers, apartments, hotels, entertainment centers, and shopping malls. Welton Beckett was hired in 1957 to design Century City. Construction was planned to begin in 1961.

12. William Deverell, *Whitewashed Adobe: The Rise of Los Angeles and the Remaking of Its Mexican Past* (Berkeley: University of California Press, 2004), pp. 3–7.

13. *Los Angeles Times,* Sept. 18, 1960, p. H1.

14. The Master Plan for Higher Education in California was signed into law on April 27, 1960. Clark Kerr, *The Gold and the Blue,* 2 vols. (Berkeley: University of California Press, 2001–3), 1:182.

15. *Life,* Oct. 19, 1962.

16. The tier was defined as the top 12.5 percent of graduating students. State colleges were later called "state universities" and the junior colleges became "community colleges." For a comprehensive description of the Master Plan for Higher Education in California, see Kerr, *The Gold and the Blue,* 1:172–91.

17. Kerr, *The Gold and the Blue,* 1:172, 182.

18. *Los Angeles Examiner,* Sept. 22, 1960. Also see Kerr, *The Gold and the Blue,* 1:173.

19. Sales and earnings of Broadway-Hale Stores, Inc., reached record levels in 1960: sales increased 13 percent to $179 million (*Los Angeles Times,* Apr. 22, 1960).

20. Clark Kerr, interview by the author. Also see Kerr, *The Gold and the Blue,* 1:332.

21. Kerr, interview. Also see Kerr, *The Gold and the Blue,* 1:197, 331–32.

22. In 1960 the seven UC campuses were Berkeley, Los Angeles, Santa Barbara, Davis, San Francisco, Riverside, and San Diego. All except for San Francisco had general-campus status; San Diego opened in 1958 as the Institute of Technology and Engineering and achieved general-campus status in 1965. See Kerr, *The Gold and the Blue,* 1:app. 3, pp. 470–71.

23. Charles E. Davis Jr., "Southern California's Cultural Status Rises," *Los Angeles Times,* May 20, 1062, p. J1.

24. In 1961 the museum was split into the Los Angeles County Museum of History and Science and the Los Angeles County Museum of Art. In 1965 the history and science museum was renamed the Museum of Natural History and the art museum opened new facilities at 5905 Wilshire Boulevard. See Pitt and Pitt, *Los Angeles A to Z,* p. 288.

25. *Los Angeles Times,* July 1, 1960.

26. *Time,* Dec. 18, 1964.

27. Kerr, *The Gold and the Blue,* 1:140–41.

28. Ultimately, the Supreme Court ruled such oaths unconstitutional and the dismissed professors were offered their jobs back. The year 1960 had opened with Pauley and Kerr in a celebratory mood over achieving consensus for the Master Plan for Higher Education. Pauley had been helpful in gaining the much-needed support of Democratic Governor Brown for the plan.

29. *Time,* July 15, 1957, p. 31.

30. Franklin D. Murphy, "My UCLA Chancellorship: An Utterly Candid View," interview by James V. Mink, 1973, transcript 1976, Oral History Collection, Dept. of Special Collections, University Library, UCLA, pp. 14–15, 24. Allen came to UCLA in anticipation of being appointed president when Sproul retired, and thinking he would soon be called to Berkeley, he reportedly felt little reason to take an interest in Los Angeles (Kerr, interview by the author). Also see Kerr, *The Gold and the Blue,* 1:47–51, 196, 254–55, 334–35.

31. Anita J. Klaz, "An Oral History of Dorothy Buffum Chandler" (M.A. thesis, California State University, Northridge, 1981), p. 118. Also see Murphy, "My UCLA Chancellorship," pp. 21–22, 73–74, 243

32. Murphy, "My UCLA Chancellorship," p. 22.

33. Ibid., pp. 21–22.

34. Klaz, "Dorothy Buffum Chandler," p. 148.

35. George Sternlieb, *The Future of the Downtown Department Store* (Cambridge, Mass.: Joint Center for Urban Studies of the Massachusetts Institute of Technology and Harvard University, 1962), p. 10, cited by Lizabeth Cohen, *A Consumers' Republic: The Politics of Mass Consumption in Postwar America* (New York: Vintage Books, 2004), p. 265.

36. In 1886 the Times Mirror Company (founded in 1881) published the *Los Angeles Times* and operated the Mirror Printing Office and Book Bindery, which published the *Weekly Los Angeles Mirror* (founded in 1873). The *Mirror* folded, but the name was revived in 1948 when Norman Chandler created the *Los Angeles Mirror,* an afternoon tabloid, which became a broadsheet renamed the *Los Angeles Mirror News* in the mid-1950s but struggled financially and closed in 1962. See "Our Place in History: The Story of the Los Angeles Times Building" (manuscript, Archives, *Los Angeles Times*); also Pitt and Pitt, *Los Angeles A to Z,* pp. 296–97, 503.

37. FDM to Ray Evans, Chairman, Kansas Board of Regents, letter, Mar. 17,

1960, Murphy Papers. Murphy describes his membership on the U.S. Advisory Commission on Foreign Exchanges in the letter. In an address delivered on February 24, 1961, "The American College and University in World Affairs," Murphy described additional assignments he undertook to promote foreign exchanges as a member of a Ford Foundation committee asked by the State Department to make recommendations on the role of higher education in world affairs.

38. Franklin Murphy, "Educational and Cultural Affairs—A Fourth and New Dimension in Foreign Policy" (speech, UCLA Charter Day ceremonies, Mar. 22, 1961).

39. Murphy, "My UCLA Chancellorship," p. 10. See Robert G. Vosper, "Libraries and the Inquiring Mind," interview by Dale E. Treleven, 1990–91, transcript 1994, Oral History Collection, Dept. of Special Collections, University Library, UCLA. "Murphy Heads West after Docking Feud," *Daily Bruin*, Mar. 18, 1960.

40. Judith Murphy, "Chancellor's Spouse," interview by Dale E. Treleven, 1995, transcript 1997, Oral History Collection, Dept. of Special Collections, University Library, UCLA.

41. See Harper, "Higher Education Leadership," p. 331.

42. See Vosper, "Libraries and the Inquiring Mind."

43. "A Letter to Judy Murphy," *Lawrence Journal World,* Mar. 18, 1960.

44. FDM to Edward W. Carter, letter, Mar. 21, 1960, Murphy Papers.

45. See FDM to Frank C. Moore, Chairman, Board of Trustees, State University of New York, letter, Jan. 14, 1959, Murphy Papers, in which Murphy declines the post of president. Also see Murphy, "My UCLA Chancellorship," pp. 1–26.

46. Norris Leap, "UCLA Chancellor Envisions New Era," *Los Angeles Times,* Sept. 18, 1960, p. H1; Dick Turpin, "Master Plan Called UCLA Road to Future," *Los Angeles Times,* Apr. 29, 1962, p. I1.

47. Josiah Royce, *California from the Conquest in 1846 to the Second Vigilance Committee in San Francisco [1856]: A Study of the American Character* (Boston: Houghton Mifflin, 1886).

48. Carey McWilliams, *Southern California: An Island on the Land* (Salt Lake City: Gibbs M. Smith, 1946, 1973), pp. 273–83, 314–29.

49. Ibid., pp. 96–104, 205–9.

50. In 1896 Colonel Griffith J. Griffith, a mining millionaire and land baron, gave the city 3,500 acres in the Hollywood Hills, but the chaparral-covered foothills remained undeveloped until the Works Progress Administration and Conservation Corps programs of the depression era put in facilities to create Griffith Park. ("Former Foes Unite Behind a Proposal to Turn Old Reservoir Site into Park," *Los Angeles Times,* Jan. 15, 2004, p. B3.) Los Angeles has fewer parks than other major cities.

51. McWilliams, *Southern California,* p. 377.

52. D. J. Waldie, *Holy Land: A Suburban Memoir* (New York: St. Martin's Press, 1996), p. 62.

53. Ibid., pp. 1, 7.

54. Joan Didion, *Where I Was From* (New York: Alfred A. Knopf, 2003), p. 109. Waldie, *Holy Land,* p. 109.

55. D. J. Waldie, *Where We Are Now: Notes from Los Angeles* (Santa Monica, Calif.: Angel City Press, 2004), pp. 83–93. Waldie gives a poignant account of his family's preparation for death in the event of nuclear attack.

56. Orange County Research Institute, *Orange County Newsletter,* reprinted in *Orange County Industrial News,* Oct. 1961. Quoted in L. McGirr, *Suburban Warriors: The Origins of the New American Right* (Princeton: Princeton University Press, 2001), p. 52.

57. *Time,* July 15, 1957.

58. Murphy, "My UCLA Chancellorship," pp. 21–22, 60, 64–65, 73, 74, 87, 119, 135–36, 137, 161, 163, 169, 243. Also see Klaz, "Dorothy Buffum Chandler."

59. FDM to Mrs. Norman Chandler, letter, Apr. 9, 1960, Murphy Papers.

60. Welton Beckett, "A Contemporary Expression of Classic Architecture," *Los Angeles Times,* Dec. 6, 1964.

61. Description of the lease-back arrangement is taken from an untitled memo, Papers of Dorothy Chandler, Dept. of Special Collections, University Library, UCLA. Also see *Los Angeles Times,* Apr. 1, 1960.

62. *Los Angeles Times,* June 4, 1960, p. B4.

63. Robert Gottlieb and Irene Wolt, "The Power Broker Behind the *Times,*" *New West,* Sept. 26, 1977.

64. Harrison Gray Otis was made a lieutenant colonel at the end of the Civil War; in 1899 President McKinley boosted his rank to brigadier general, and he left for the Philippines, where he was among the commanders of the occupying force at the end of the Spanish-American War. Also see Dennis McDougal, *Privileged Son: Otis Chandler and the Rise and Fall of the L.A. Times Dynasty* (New York: Perseus, 2001), p. 32.

65. "Otis Chandler New Times Publisher," *Los Angeles Times,* Apr. 12, 1960, p. A1. Otis Chandler, "A Responsibility," *Los Angeles Times,* Apr. 12, 1960, p. A1.

66. Ibid.

67. Ibid.

68. Lally Weymouth, "The Word from Mamma Buff," *Esquire,* Nov. 1977, pp. 156, 202; Klaz, "Dorothy Buffum Chandler," p. 123.

TWO: UCLA IN WORLDWIDE TERMS

1. Franklin Murphy, "My UCLA Chancellorship: An Utterly Candid View," interview by James V. Mink, 1973, transcript 1976, Oral History Collection, Dept. of Special Collections, University Library, UCLA, p. 46.

2. Hansena Frederickson, "UCLA Administration, 1936–1968," interview by James V. Mink, 1966, transcript 1969, Oral History Collection, Dept. of Special Collections, University Library, UCLA, pp. 40, 50, 92.

3. See Murphy, "My UCLA Chancellorship," p. 32.

4. The Democratic National Convention was held in Los Angeles, July 11–15, 1960.

5. *New York Times,* Jan. 21, 1966, p. 29.

6. FDM to Clark Kerr, letter, May 12, 1960, Papers of Franklin D. Murphy, Dept. of Special Collections, University Library, UCLA (hereafter cited as Murphy Papers).

7. Franklin D. Murphy, interview by Verne A. Stadtman, for "The Centennial Record of the University of California 1868–1968. Included in Murphy, "My UCLA Chancellorship," appendix, p. 289.

8. Ibid.

9. *Los Angeles Times,* July 11, 1960.

10. Endorsements by the *Los Angeles Times:* 1960 Richard Nixon, 1964 Barry Goldwater, 1968 Nixon, 1972 Nixon for reelection. In his biography of Otis Chandler, Dennis McDougal states that Chandler reluctantly issued the endorsement of Nixon in 1972 in deference to his father, who was terminally ill with cancer. A group of *Times* reporters and employees published a letter of dissent, saying they were voting for McGovern. On September 23, 1973, Otis Chandler announced that in the future the *Times* would not endorse candidates for president, governor, or senator. See Dennis McDougal, *Privileged Son: Otis Chandler and the Rise and Fall of the L.A. Times Dynasty* (New York: Perseus, 2001), pp. 479 (n. 20:5), 480 (n. 23:3).

11. Murphy learned later that Kerr had been hospitalized with a respiratory condition.

12. Murphy, "My UCLA Chancellorship," pp. 31, 41.

13. "Inaugural Speech of Franklin D. Murphy," Sept. 23, 1960.

14. *Time,* Oct 21, 1966.

15. The warning regarding the Academic Senate came from Robert Vosper, who was familiar with UCLA operations from his years there before being enticed to KU by Murphy. Also see Murphy, "My UCLA Chancellorship," pp. 25–29, 33–34, 49, 173–82, 186–89, 215, 218, 235.

16. Murphy, "My UCLA Chancellorship," pp. 35–36. Murphy said his relationship with Chuck Young was the most effective working relationship he had ever experienced.

17. *Los Angeles Times,* Mar. 6, 2003, Calendar, p. 1.

18. Murphy, "My UCLA Chancellorship," p. 35.

19. In various comments to the press Murphy used figures that ranged from $120 million to $150 million.

20. Gene Blake, "Blue Book Guides Anti-Red Society," *Los Angeles Times,* Mar. 6, 1961.

21. "Agency Offers Prof Watchers," *Daily Bruin,* May 18, 1961.

22. "God-Loving Americans" (letter from alumni), *Daily Bruin,* Apr. 27, 1961.

23. "Murphy to Aid Corps," *Daily Bruin,* Apr. 4, 1961 (quoting *New York Times*).

24. See Charles Speroni, "Dean, Mentor, Colleague: Bridging Humanities and Fine Arts at UCLA," interview by Bernard Galm, 1980, transcript 1988, Oral History Collection, Dept. of Special Collections, University Library, UCLA.

25. See Clark Kerr, *The Gold and the Blue,* 2 vols. (Berkeley: University of California Press, 2001–3), 1:345, rankings by the National Research Council.

26. Andrew Hamilton and John B. Jackson, *UCLA on the Move: During Fifty Golden Years 1919–1969* (Los Angeles: Ward Ritchie Press, 1969), p. 138. The undergraduate library was named the Lawrence Clark Powell Library, and later the new University Research Library became the Charles Young Research Library.

27. Frederickson, "UCLA Administration," pp. 203–4.

28. Murphy, "My UCLA Chancellorship," p. 50.

29. *Time,* Oct. 17, 1960, pp. 58–69.

30. The account of this conversation is taken from Murphy, "My UCLA Chancellorship," p. 65.

31. Clark Kerr, interview by the author; see also Kerr, *The Gold and the Blue,* 1:214.

32. *Women's Wear Daily,* Mar. 18, 1975.

33. Gene Blake, "The John Birch Society: What Are Its Purposes?" *Los Angeles Times,* Mar. 5, 1961.

34. Gene Blake, "Birch Program in Southland Told," *Los Angeles Times,* Mar. 8, 1961.

35. McDougal, *Privileged Son,* p. 230.

36. Otis Chandler, "Peril to Conservatives" (editorial), *Los Angeles Times,* Mar. 12, 1961.

37. Lisa McGirr, *Suburban Warrior: The Origins of the New American Right* (Princeton: Princeton University Press, 2001), p. 173.

38. *Daily Bruin,* undated clipping, Murphy Papers.

39. Twenty-two UC Berkeley history professors joined their colleagues from forty universities across the country in signing a letter to Kennedy condemning U.S. intervention in Cuba. "Profs Write to JFK," *Daily Bruin,* May 19, 1961.

40. "Not Fooled" (editorial), *Daily Bruin,* Apr. 4, 1961; "Regents Set up New Committee," *Daily Bruin,* Apr. 24, 1961.

41. Michael R. Beschloss, *The Crisis Years: Kennedy and Khrushchev, 1960–1963* (New York: HarperCollins, 1991), p. 129.

42. Murphy, interview by Verne A. Stadtman, p. 278.

43. *Los Angeles Times,* July 25, 1966. See also Murphy, "My UCLA Chancellorship."

44. Kerr, *The Gold and the Blue,* 1:334.

45. Carter was also a trustee of the Brookings Institution and Occidental College as well as a director of the Stanford Research Institute. In addition to a seat on the board of regents, Carter served on the boards of the San Francisco Opera and the Southern California Symphony Association.

46. *Los Angeles Times,* Nov. 10, 1961.

47. *Time,* Apr. 14, 1958.

48. Ibid.

49. *Newsweek,* Apr. 5, 1965.

50. The dates of Howard Ahmanson's gifts to the county museum were reportedly October 1, 1958; November 28, 1958; and December 9, 1958 (untitled memo, Papers of Dorothy Chandler, Dept. of Special Collections, University Library, UCLA; hereafter cited as Dorothy Chandler Papers).

51. *Time,* Dec. 18, 1964.

52. "Dr. Murphy Heads Art Fund Drive," *Los Angeles Times,* Nov. 9, 1961.

53. Robert M. DeKruif, interview by the author.

54. Kenneth Lamott, *The Moneymakers: The Great Big New Rich in America* (Boston: Little, Brown, 1968), p. 132; *New York Times,* June 18, 1968; *Los Angeles Times,* June 18, 1968.

55. Howard Ahmanson was active in the Republican Party's National Finance Committee (Lamott, *Moneymakers,* p. 132).

56. LACMA Collections, Online, Center for European Art, European Painting, http://collectionsonline.lacma.org/mweb/about/europ_about.asp.

57. DeKruif, interview.

58. Franklin D. Murphy, Inaugural Address, University of Kansas, Sept. 17, 1951.

59. John F. Kennedy, Address to the Nation, Oct. 22, 1962.

60. Campus civil defense instructions described in "Civil Defense Program: Road to Survival," *Daily Bruin,* Apr. 24, 1961; and "Fallout—Nuclear Rain of Terror," *Daily Bruin,* Apr. 28, 1961.

61. Murphy's views on defeating Communism can be found in various speeches, including his Inaugural Address. Murphy's criticism of "Cold War foolishness" is reflected in his speech "From Birth to Maturity in 200 Years: An Oversimplified Analogy" (Nov. 5, 1974, in anticipation of the U.S. bicentennial).

62. Murphy, "My UCLA Chancellorship," p. 104.

63. *Los Angeles Herald Examiner,* Apr. 27, 1962, and Sept. 30, 1962; *Los Angeles Times,* Apr. 29, 1962, May 7, 1962, and Sept. 12, 1962.

64. The term for regents was later changed from sixteen to twelve years.

65. *Los Angeles Times,* June 23, 1974.

66. The regents had voted in 1958 to establish three new campuses at Irvine,

Santa Cruz, and San Diego. Four of the existing six campuses (Davis, Santa Barbara, Riverside, and San Francisco) were undergoing substantial construction, in addition to the expansion at Berkeley and Los Angeles.

67. Anita J. Klaz, "An Oral History of Dorothy Buffum Chandler" (M.A. thesis, California State University, Northridge, 1981), p. 118.

68. Charles Young, interview by the author.

69. Kerr, *The Gold and the Blue,* 1:202.

70. *Los Angeles Times,* June 23, 1974.

71. Kerr, *The Gold and the Blue,* 1:244.

72. Marvin Garson, *The Regents,* rev. ed. (Berkeley: Independent Socialist Club, 1967).

73. *Los Angeles Times,* Mar. 8, 1961, Mar. 11, 1961, Nov. 11, 1962.

74. *Los Angeles Times,* Nov. 24, 1960.

75. Dorothy Chandler to Mrs. John F. Kennedy, letter, Mar. 3, 1962, Dorothy Chandler Papers.

76. *Time,* Dec. 18, 1964.

77. *Los Angeles Times,* Nov. 11, 1962.

78. *Los Angeles Times,* Nov. 11, 1962. Taper's initial gift was $1 million.

79. *Los Angeles Times,* May 16, 1965.

80. Robert Gottlieb and Irene Wolt, "The Power Broker Behind the *Times,*" *New West,* Sept. 26, 1977.

81. See *Los Angeles Times,* Feb. 18, Mar. 13, and Mar. 20, 1962.

82. *Los Angeles Times,* Apr. 24, 1962.

83. *Los Angeles Times,* May 31, Sept. 11, Nov, 1, and Nov. 9, 1962.

84. Pauley was a dedicated Democrat and avid supporter of President Johnson, whereas Murphy felt that the "Great Society" concept "demonstrated more compassion than economic sense" (Murphy, "From Birth to Maturity in 200 Years").

85. Coach Wooden is considered one of the finest coaches the game has ever seen. See Hamilton and Jackson, *UCLA on the Move,* pp. 184–85.

86. As early as 1949 various groups had attempted to raise the funds to build a 10,000-plus-seat, multipurpose indoor arena.

87. FDM to Edwin W. Pauley, letter, Apr. 4, 1963, Murphy Papers. Also see Murphy, "My UCLA Chancellorship."

88. The first two NCAA basketball championships were in 1964 and 1965, before Pauley Pavilion opened. The other eight won by UCLA teams under Coach John Wooden were 1967 to 1973 (seven straight) and 1975.

89. Young, interview. Also see Murphy, "My UCLA Chancellorship," p. 205.

90. The dolphin photo is in the Murphy family album owned by Cordelia Murphy Ennis.

91. Kerr, *The Gold and the Blue.*

92. Chancellor Franklin D. Murphy, "Memorial to President John F. Kennedy" (Los Angeles Sports Arena, NBC Television, Nov. 24, 1963).

93. Young, interview.

94. Harry R. Wellman, "Teaching, Research, and Administration, University of California 1925–1968," interview by Malca Chall, 1972–73, transcript 1976, Regional Oral History Office, Bancroft Library, University of California, Berkeley, p. 135. The regents named Wellman acting president of the university in 1967.

95. Kerr, *The Gold and the Blue,* 1:215.

96. Young, interview.

97. Kerr, *The Gold and the Blue,* 1:214.

98. Young, interview.

99. FDM to Clark Kerr, letter, Mar. 17, 1964, Murphy Papers. In his letter Murphy opened with objective comments on campus issues but soon revealed his perception of the heart of the conflict with Kerr. "In all frankness, I believe that some of whatever problem we have had stems from our personal past experiences," he wrote. (Under the Kansas system, chancellors reported directly to the board of regents; there was no intermediary administrative head.)

100. Ibid. The letter reads in part:

Before coming to my present post, I was for nine years involved in an administrative mechanism where, as far as my position was concerned, things were precise, clear and quite manageable. Thus, at UCLA, I have had to make adjustments and concessions in the direction of accepting more control and less authority. In short, for reasons of past experience, some of the ground rules under which I now must function seem less satisfactory than those to which I had become accustomed.

"What do you want in a Chancellor at UCLA?" Phrased differently, the answer always came back approximately the same: "We want a strong leader—one who can improve administrative practice and efficiency—build faculty, alumni and student morale—bring the university into closer and warmer relationships with the city and the area—and, in the process, make a contribution toward building this into one of the most important university campuses in the world."

I was constantly reminded by many people, both here and in other parts of the country, that I was stepping into somewhat of an administrative vacuum. The sad story of Provost Dykstra's cruel disillusionment, an interim period when the campus was presumably run by a triumvirate of deans, Ray Allen's lack of decisiveness, all adding up to a great many years of administrative weakness, I was told required now a strong and vigorous person who could pull things together and into focus. I was also told that all of the necessary tools to do this particular job were available or would be made available if not then existent. I should add that I was advised by a good many people in other parts of the country that I really should not accept the post if offered, that it represented an administrative impossibility with a man caught between the long and deep tradition of faculty control of certain matters on one hand, and an over-all super administration on the other. I chose, nevertheless to come for the following reasons:

1. The great impression you made upon me as a man of vigor, ability and visions.
2. The quality of the Regents I met.
3. The excitement of Los Angeles and Southern California.
4. The enormous potential which UCLA had and continues to have.
5. The commitments, albeit general ones, that the tools would be forthcoming to do the job.

In retrospect, I suppose, I should have asked many more detailed questions than I did, but I rather thought that it would have been demeaning for all involved for me to get into such details; I took much on faith. Thus, you may understand my perhaps disproportionate shock when I was first told that it was not the custom for the chancellor to award the degrees in courses on the campus.

In any event, I came to UCLA with enthusiasm and as a result of a *positive choice* (not to escape a temporarily unpleasant situation as some may have thought). I will now tell you, for example, that only a month or two before I had turned down the vigorous and repeated invitation of the Regents of the university of Minnesota to come and engage in definitive and final discussions with them at the time of Lew Morrill's retirement.

I still retain my enthusiasm and belief that UCLA is destined one day to become one of the great university campuses of the world while, at the same time, being a part of a multi-university which already is unprecedented in all of the history of higher education. I have had to make personal adaptations, and sometimes this has been difficult, but I have tried very hard. Members of the regents, leaders in the Los Angeles community, mature and honored members of this faculty and alumni leaders have repeatedly told me that these past four years have been good ones at UCLA. I have built a staff which I believe is competent and loyal and wherein there is deep mutual respect and affection as well. In short, in terms of what I thought was expected of me, I believe I have succeeded in some modest degree. And I have from the beginning believed that if I could make a contribution to the distinction, visibility and appreciation by Los Angeles of UCLA, I would have made a major and practical contribution to the ongoing development of the statewide university of California.

101. Kerr, interview.
102. Kerr, *The Gold and the Blue,* 1:338.
103. *Los Angeles Times,* Apr. 25, 1965.
104. *Los Angeles Times,* Mar. 15, 1991.
105. Lamott, *Moneymakers,* p. 128. Also see *Los Angeles Times,* June 18, 1968; *New York Times,* June 18, 1968.
106. It was said that the editor's inspiration for the flag-flying signal was not

Buckingham Palace but rather Dorothy Chandler's policy of running up the flag when she was at home at Los Tiempos (Frederickson, "UCLA Administration," p. 189).

107. Ibid.

108. Murphy, "My UCLA Chancellorship," p. 244.

109. FDM to Irving Stone, letter, Apr. 15, 1969, Murphy Papers.

110. Ibid. The private donor was Theodore Cummings.

111. *Daily Bruin,* May 11, 1961.

THREE: TURMOIL AND GOLDEN MOMENTS

1. *Time,* Dec. 18, 1964.

2. Leonard Gross, "Soul of the Center," *Westways,* Feb. 1975; Charles Champlin in *Los Angeles Times,* Dec. 6, 1965, p. D1.

3. FDM to Dorothy Chandler, letter, Dec. 8, 1964, Papers of Dorothy Chandler, Dept. of Special Collections, University Library, UCLA (hereafter cited as Dorothy Chandler Papers).

4. *Los Angeles Times,* July 31, 1997, Home section, p. M1.

5. Ibid.

6. *The Music Center Story: A Decade of Achievement, 1964–1974,* ed. James W. Toland (Los Angeles: Music Center Foundation, 1974), p. 123.

7. *Time,* Dec. 18, 1964. It was a singular American honor to grace the cover of *Time,* but friends who knew Dorothy Chandler said that the cover illustration by Henry Koerner did not do her justice. Chandler must have been disappointed to see herself depicted as a matron with wrinkles. Norman Chandler, whose own likeness had been painted by the same artist for the cover of *Time* in 1957, was quick to soothe her. "Henry, you know, never flatters," he told her. In his portrait Norman looked every inch the Silver Fox that his wife often called him. After finishing her portrait, Koerner confided to Dorothy Chandler his belief that the true essence of the painting "will be seen only in hundreds of years." Koerner, who completed over fifty covers for *Time* of the world's most newsworthy figures between 1955 and 1967, viewed his assignments with some awe, calling his portraits "a hole through which I can see God."

8. *Los Angeles Times,* Dec. 6, 1964, Special Issue *Sunday Magazine.*

9. Charles Young, interview by the author.

10. *Time,* Jan. 1, 1965.

11. Hedda Hopper to Dorothy Chandler, letter, undated, Dorothy Chandler Papers.

12. "Address by Mrs. Norman Chandler before the San Francisco Junior League," Jan. 28, 1966, Dorothy Chandler Papers.

13. The Lytton Building would be renamed for Armand Hammer after Lytton was unable to fulfill his pledged donation.

14. Suzanne Muchnic, *Odd Man In: Norton Simon and the Pursuit of Culture* (Berkeley: University of California Press, 1998), p. 111.

15. *Newsweek,* Apr. 5, 1965.

16. See LACMA, *X, a Decade of Collecting, 1965–1975* (Los Angeles: LACMA, 1975); the names of early collectors who made important contributions to the museum are listed in the introduction. For the "Jugs and junk" description, see "Drawing the Line in L.A.," *Newsweek,* Nov. 22, 1965, p. 98. For comments on Hearst's contributions, see Mary L. Levkoff, Curator of European Sculpture, "William Randolph Hearst," *At the Museum: The Magazine of the Los Angeles County Museum of Art,* May 1999.

17. "Drawing the Line in L.A."

18. Millard Sheets, interview by Paul Karlstrom, Oct. 28, 1986, transcript, Archives of American Art, Smithsonian Institution, http://archivesofamericanart.si.edu.oralhist/sheets.86.htm.

19. *Los Angeles Times,* June 12, 1963, p. E8.

20. *Time,* Sept. 6, 1963; *Los Angeles Times,* Nov. 14, 1985. Also see *Current Biography Yearbook,* 1979.

21. Henry Seldis, "Dr. Brown Quits Art Museum Post," *Los Angeles Times,* Nov. 7, 1965.

22. "Los Angeles Art Museum Head Quits after Denouncing Trustees," *New York Times,* Nov. 8, 1965.

23. "Drawing the Line in L.A."

24. "Broken Harness," *Time,* Nov. 26, 1965.

25. "The Art Wagon," *Nation,* Dec. 13, 1965.

26. *Artforum* was founded in San Francisco in 1962, and the magazine moved to Los Angeles in 1965. After 1967 it was based in New York.

27. *Time,* Nov. 26, 1965.

28. Ibid.

29. Lisa McGirr, *Suburban Warriors: The Origins of the New American Right* (Princeton: Princeton University Press, 2001), p. 40.

30. Statistics quoted from "Watts Riots," a page of the website for *A Huey P. Newton Story,* www.pbs.org/hueypnewton/times/times_watts.html.

31. Dennis McDougal, *Privileged Son: Otis Chandler and the Rise and Fall of the L.A. Times Dynasty* (New York: Perseus, 2001), pp. 271, 478 n. 2.

32. See in the *Los Angeles Times:* "1,000 Riot in L.A.: Police and Motorists Attacked," Aug. 12, 1965, p. A1; "Eight Men Slain: Guard Moves In: Scores of Fires Rage Unchecked, Damage Exceeds $10 Million," Aug. 14, 1965, p. A1; "Guard Force from 40th Armored: 2,000 Move In: 3,000 More Wait in Nearby Counties," Aug. 14, 1965, p. A1; "Password Gains Safe Passage: 'Burn, Baby Burn' Slogan Used as Firebugs Put Area to Torch," Aug. 15, 1965, p. A1; "Causes of Riots Assessed by City," Aug. 22, 1965, p. A1; "Parker Warns Disrespect for Law Perils

US," Aug. 22, 1965, p. A1; "Viewpoint of Rioters Hard to Find," Aug. 22, 1965, p. A1; "President Warns Other Cities of Riot Dangers," Aug. 27, 1965, p. A1.

33. George Lipsitz, "Cruising around the Historical Block: Postmodernism and Popular Music in East Los Angeles," in *Time Passages: Collective Memory and American Popular Culture* (Minneapolis: University of Minnesota Press, 1990), p. 137.

34. See D. J. Waldie, *Holy Land: A Suburban Memoir* (New York: St. Martin's Press, 1996).

35. Lipsitz, "Cruising around the Historical Block," p. 137 n. 10.

36. Bruce Henstell and Bob Gottlieb, "He was the Most Powerful of Them All," *Los Angeles Magazine,* Sept. 1985.

37. Clark Kerr, *The Gold and the Blue,* 2 vols. (Berkeley: University of California Press, 2001–3), 2:220.

38. Todd Gitlin, *The Sixties: Years of Hope, Days of Rage* (New York: Bantam Books, 1993), p. 291.

39. "The Chancellor—An Interview," *Graduate Reporter,* Mar. 27, 1963.

40. Franklin D. Murphy, "My UCLA Chancellorship: An Utterly Candid View," interview by James V. Mink, 1973, transcript 1976, Oral History Collection, Dept. of Special Collections, University Library, UCLA.

41. Kerr, *The Gold and the Blue,* 1:211.

42. Ibid., 1:204–18.

43. William Trombley, "UCLA Autonomy Fight Believed Won: Chancellor Murphy Cites Shift of Authority to Campus Level," *Los Angeles Times,* July 25, 1966, p. A1. Also see Kerr, *The Gold and the Blue,* 1:218.

44. Clark Kerr, interview by the author; Kerr, *The Gold and the Blue,* 1:210.

45. Franklin Murphy, "Dissent, the Law and the University" (commencement address, UCLA, June 14, 1967).

46. Young, interview. Young credited Murphy with the courage to permit the event to take place on campus despite the opposition of key regents and threats of violence.

47. *Daily Bruin,* Feb. 24, 2000.

48. The list of new campus buildings completed during Murphy's chancellorship under the scrutiny of Bill Young was astounding: Boelter Hall, Brain Research Institute, Davies Children's Clinic, Dickson Art Center, Graduate School of Business Administration, Hedrick Hall, Knudsen Hall, Macgowan Hall, Medical Center Health Science Computer Facilities, Neuropsychiatric Institute, Rieber Hall, School of Dentistry, Social Sciences, Space Sciences Building, Stein Eye Institute, William C. Ackerman Union, University Activities Memorial Center (Pauley Pavilion), and the University Research Library. Murphy consistently consulted experts for specialized advice—in particular, for the Space Sciences Building, regarding which Murphy's knowledge was limited.

49. Richard Kent Nystrom, "UCLA: An Interpretation Considering Architecture and Site" (Ph.D. diss., UCLA, 1968), p. 154.

50. *Time,* June 16, 1967.

51. *Santa Monica Evening Outlook,* June 13, 1967.

52. Ibid. For the student in a troubled world, wrote reporter Camilla Snyder, the garden could "prove more salubrious than a psychiatrist's couch, any number of drinks or even a check-bearing letter from home. Magnificent sculpture has a way of making personal problems seem minuscule."

53. Cordelia Murphy Ennis, interview by the author.

54. Franklin Lee Murphy, interview by the author.

55. Ibid.

56. *Thirteenth Report of the Senate Fact-finding Subcommittee on Un-American Activities* (Sacramento, 1965) (known as the Burns Report), June 18, 1965, nos. 52, 65, 66, 67; Kerr, *The Gold and the Blue,* 2:59, 70. The June 1965 report accused Kerr of fostering an atmosphere at Berkeley that "welcomes Communist organizations, throws the portal open to Communist speakers, and exhibits an easy tolerance of Communist activists that defies all reason." The report claimed that to find out "how a minority of Communist leaders managed to bring this great educational institution to its knees, it is indispensable that we know something of the background of the man who was in command when the rebellion occurred." One explanation offered was that Kerr's earlier career in labor relations had brought him in contact with subversive elements.

57. Murphy, "My UCLA Chancellorship."

58. Ibid., pp. 135–36.

59. Kerr, *The Gold and the Blue,* 2:282.

60. Murphy, "My UCLA Chancellorship," p. 139.

61. The McCone report was titled *Violence in the City—An End or a Beginning: A Report of the Governor's Commission on the Los Angeles Riots,* State of California, Dec. 2, 1965.

62. See Oral History interview with H. R. Haldeman, interview by Dale E. Treleven, transcript 1991, Oral History Collection, Dept. of Special Collections, University Library, UCLA.

63. See Kerr, *The Gold and the Blue,* 2:288.

64. McGirr, *Suburban Warriors,* pp. 187–211.

65. Murphy, "My UCLA Chancellorship," p. 130.

66. Kerr, *The Gold and the Blue,* 2:295.

67. Ibid., 2:290.

68. Ibid.; Kerr, interview.

69. Kerr, interview. The account of the secretary blocking his entrance is from *Los Angeles Times,* Sept. 24, 1997.

70. Lally Weymouth, "The Word from Mamma Buff," *Esquire,* Nov. 1977, p. 154; Kerr, *The Gold and the Blue,* 1:304.

71. Kerr, *The Gold and the Blue,* 2:308.

72. *Los Angeles Times,* Sept. 24, 1997. Question and Answer Interview with Clark Kerr.

73. Kerr, *The Gold and the Blue,* 2: 298; *Los Angeles Times,* Sept. 24, 1997. No public discussion of this negotiation existed in Dorothy Chandler's oral history or was found in her surviving personal papers.

74. *Los Angeles Times,* Sept. 24, 1997. Question and Answer Interview with Clark Kerr. Also see Kerr, *The Gold and the Blue,* 2:102. Kerr writes, "There was a student uprising, not Communist dominated, in support of the civil rights movement and other issues. This insurrection could be channeled and absorbed successfully. It would take patience and some concessions, not police suppression."

75. Murphy, "My UCLA Chancellorship," p. 164.

76. Rosenfeld had fought the FBI through a lengthy legal battle to obtain the documents when finally the Ninth Circuit Court of Appeals ordered release of 200,000 pages under the Freedom of Information Act.

77. Seth Rosenfeld, "The Campus Files," *San Francisco Chronicle,* June 9, 2002.

78. FDM to Edward W. Carter, letter, Feb. 17, 1967, Papers of Franklin D. Murphy, Dept. of Special Collections, University Library, UCLA.

79. *New York Times,* June 17, 1994, p. B8.

80. *Time,* Sept. 27, 1968.

81. *Time,* Feb. 3, 1967.

82. *Daily Bruin,* undated clipping.

83. *Los Angeles Magazine,* month not specified, 1967.

84. *Time,* Apr. 21, 1967.

FOUR: 1968—YEAR OF CRISIS

1. *Daily Bruin,* Nov. 14, 1967.

2. *Daily Bruin,* Nov. 15, 1967.

3. *Daily Bruin,* Jan. 11, Jan. 24, and Jan. 25, 1968.

4. *Daily Bruin,* Mar. 1, 1967.

5. At both UCLA and Berkeley students inaugurated a vigorous campaign against university officials and the board of regents that focused on the personal wealth of the regents and their interests in the war industry. Pamphlets circulating on campus listed the interlocking corporate relationships of regents, accusing them of illegal conflicts of interest. When President Johnson announced plans to discontinue deferments for graduate students, UCLA administrators panicked at the prospect of losing both graduate students and teaching assistants. Adding to the tension was the revelation of a covert relationship between the CIA

and the National Student Association whereby the CIA provided financial support and provided secret briefings to student leaders.

6. At a rally sponsored by the American Federation of Teachers (AFT).

7. *Daily Bruin,* July 18, 1967.

8. *Daily Bruin,* Feb. 7, 1967.

9. *Daily Bruin,* Nov. 14, 1967.

10. *Daily Bruin,* Nov. 10–13, 1967.

11. Franklin D. Murphy, Guest Editorial, *Saturday Review,* Jan. 13, 1968; reprinted in *Daily Bruin,* Jan. 16, 1968.

12. Franklin Murphy, "Over 50 Looks at under 30" (address, distributed by the board of directors of the American Society of Corporate Secretaries, 1971).

13. Charles Young, interview by the author.

14. Franklin D. Murphy, "My UCLA Chancellorship: An Utterly Candid View," interview by James V. Mink, 1973, transcript 1976, Oral History Collection, Dept. of Special Collections, University Library, UCLA, p. 167.

15. This version of events as described by Murphy in Warren Bennis, "Starting Corporate Life at the Top," *Directors and Boards,* fall 1982, p. 27.

16. John M. Mecklin, "Ambitious Acquirers," *Fortune,* Sept. 1, 1968.

17. See Anita J. Klaz, "An Oral History of Dorothy Buffum Chandler" (M.A. thesis, California State University, Northridge, 1981), pp. 123–27.

18. Dennis McDougal, interview by the author; also Dennis McDougal, *Privileged Son: Otis Chandler and the Rise and Fall of the L.A. Times Dynasty* (New York: Perseus, 2001), p. 275.

19. *Lawrence (Kans.) Daily Journal World,* Feb. 21, 1968.

20. *Daily Bruin,* Feb. 15, 1968; *Santa Monica Evening Outlook,* Feb. 17, 1968.

21. *New York Times,* Feb. 17, 1968; *Daily Bruin,* Feb. 16, 1968.

22. *Daily Bruin,* Feb. 23, 1968.

23. *Daily Bruin,* Feb. 26, 1968.

24. *Daily Bruin,* Feb. 16, 1968.

25. *Daily Bruin,* Feb. 17, 1968.

26. *Daily Bruin,* Feb. 19–20, 1968.

27. Henry Ford II was a firm supporter of Lyndon Johnson and Johnson's Great Society. Ford felt that Johnson had been ill served by advisers who led him into the quagmire of the Vietnam War. He blamed in particular former Ford president Robert S. McNamara, who was secretary of defense in the Kennedy and Johnson administrations. See Douglas Brinkley, *Wheels for the World: Henry Ford, His Company, and a Century of Progress, 1903–2003* (New York: Penguin, 2004).

28. *Daily Bruin,* Apr. 2, 1968.

29. FDM to Thomas Bradley, letter, May 31, 1973, Papers of Franklin D. Murphy, Dept. of Special Collections, University Library, UCLA (hereafter cited as Murphy Papers).

30. *Los Angeles Times,* Apr. 22, 1968.

31. Richard Nixon to FDM, letter, Feb. 20, 1968; Nelson Rockefeller to FDM, letter, Feb. 20, 1968. Murphy Papers.

32. Grant Holcomb to FDM, letter, Feb. 22, 1968, Murphy Papers.

33. Murphy, "My UCLA Chancellorship," p. 326.

34. Andrew Hamilton and John B. Jackson, *UCLA on the Move, during Fifty Golden Years, 1919–1969* (Los Angeles: Ward Ritchie Press, 1969), p. 132.

35. Franklin Murphy, "The State of the University" (commencement address, UCLA, 1968).

36. Murphy, "My UCLA Chancellorship," p. 170.

37. Ibid., p. 168.

38. *Los Angeles Times,* June 18, 1968, p. A1; *New York Times,* June 18, 1968, p. 47.

39. *New York Times,* June 18, 1986, p. 47.

40. Margaret Bach, "The Ahmanson Foundation: Forty Years of Building Community, 1952–1992" (manuscript, June 1993), p. 15 (courtesy of Robert Ahmanson). Also see *New York Times,* June 18, 1968.

41. In addition to the $2 million he had committed for construction of LACMA, Howard Ahmanson supported a pioneering research facility at USC, later known as the Ahmanson Center for Biological Research; he served on the board of trustees at USC, his alma mater, where he had earned a bachelor's degree in economics in 1927; and he had donated millions of dollars for construction of the Ahmanson Theatre at Dorothy Chandler's Music Center.

42. *Los Angeles Times,* June 18, 1968. Also see H. F. Ahmanson Co., "Announcement to Employees," June 1968, Ahmanson Foundation Library.

43. *Los Angeles Times,* June 18, 1968.

44. Articles of Incorporation, the Ahmanson Foundation, Dec. 15, 1952. Also see Bach, "The Ahmanson Foundation," p. 15.

45. *The Ahmanson Gifts: European Masterpieces in the Collection of the Los Angeles County Museum of Art* (Los Angeles: Museum Associates, 1991), p. 9.

46. Robert DeKruif, interview by the author.

47. *Los Angeles Times,* June 18, 1968.

48. Kenneth Lamott, *The Moneymakers: The Great Big New Rich in America* (Boston: Little, Brown, 1968).

49. *Business Week,* July 1, 1961 p. 78; Bach, "The Ahmanson Foundation," p. 12. Robert DeKruif, Ahmanson's close friend and protégé, shedding light on Ahmanson's achievement, asserted, "[Ahmanson was] the most perfect combination of financial genius and sales genius that I've ever seen. He was a planner, approaching problems as to what's urgent, what's necessary and what's desired" (DeKruif, interview).

50. Bach, "The Ahmanson Foundation," p. 12.

51. According to the *Los Angeles Times,* Howard Ahmanson was principal owner of Home Savings and Loan Association, with assets of some $2.6 billion. Through his holding company, H. F. Ahmanson and Company, he also owned Ahmanson Bank and Trust Company, National American Insurance Company of Omaha, and Southern Counties Title Insurance Company, among others. See *Los Angeles Times,* June 18, 1968; *New York Times,* June 18, 1968.

52. It was Murphy's idea that at Washburn University young Ahmanson could earn academic credit toward the completion of his bachelor's degree already under way at Occidental College in Los Angeles.

FIVE: THE CHANCELLOR BECOMES CEO

1. "Our Place in History: The Story of the Los Angeles Times Building" (manuscript, Archives, *Los Angeles Times*).

2. Warren Bennis, "Starting Corporate Life at the Top," *Directors and Boards,* fall 1982, p. 27.

3. Dorothy Chandler felt it was imperative that the company's buildings and the company's image in general make an important statement.

4. Peter Fernald, interview by the author.

5. *Fortune,* Sept. 1, 1968.

6. *Newsweek,* Feb. 26, 1968.

7. *Time,* Feb. 23, 1968; Sept. 20, 1968.

8. Fernald, interview.

9. The plans had been devised by management consultants McKinsey and Company. Documents in the papers of Dorothy Chandler suggest that she selected the firm after working with them on early proposals concerning the Music Center.

10. *Fortune,* Sept. 1, 1968.

11. Times Mirror Annual Report 1969, Statement of Norman Chandler, Chairman of the Executive Committee.

12. *Fortune,* Sept. 1, 1968.

13. Bennis, "Starting Corporate Life at the Top," p. 26.

14. *Fortune,* Sept. 1, 1968.

15. Times Mirror Annual Report, 1968.

16. FDM to Walter H. Annenberg, letter, Oct. 31, 1968, Papers of Franklin D. Murphy, Dept. of Special Collections, University Library, UCLA (hereafter cited as Murphy Papers).

17. See Judith Murphy, "Chancellor's Spouse," interview by Dale E. Treleven, 1995, transcript 1997, Oral History Collection, Dept. of Special Collections, University Library, UCLA. Oral History Department Interview, 1995. "It all came together," Franklin Murphy said. "It was a business job, it was in Southern California; and it was in a field that I had a great interest in—publishing, which is,

in a sense, a different kind of educational process. So it was just like everything fitting together in an almost unpredictable and remarkable way." See Franklin D. Murphy, "My UCLA Chancellorship: An Utterly Candid View," interview by James V. Mink, 1973, transcript 1976, Oral History Collection, Dept. of Special Collections, University Library, UCLA, p. 169.

18. It was a prime piece of real estate situated near the enormous Greystone mansion once owned by the son of the oil tycoon Edward L. Doheny. A portion of the Doheny estate had been developed into a tract of expensive homes known as the Trousdale Estates. See Margaret L. Davis, *Dark Side of Fortune: Triumph and Scandal in the Life of Oil Tycoon Edward L. Doheny* (Berkeley: University of California Press, 1998).

19. FDM to Dorothy Chandler, letter, Sept. 24, 1968, Murphy Papers.

20. As distinguished from the President's Foreign Intelligence Advisory Board, which Murphy later joined during the Nixon administration.

21. Franklin Murphy, "Over 50 Looks at Under 30" (address distributed by the board of directors of the American Society of Corporate Secretaries, 1971).

22. Ibid.

23. Judith Murphy, "Chancellor's Spouse."

24. *Medical World News,* Sept. 11, 1970.

25. [Name omitted] to FDM, letter, Sept. 28, 1968. FDM to [name omitted], Oct. 2, 1968. Murphy Papers.

26. FDM to H. R. Haldeman, letter, Nov. 27, 1968, Murphy Papers.

27. FDM to H. R. Haldeman, letter, Nov. 20, 1968, Murphy Papers.

28. Franklin D. Murphy, interview by Deborah Hickle, Jan. 19, 1990, transcript, University of Kansas School of Medicine Oral History Project, p. 36.

29. Ibid., p. 35.

30. At one point Dorothy Chandler claimed that she helped Nixon become vice president. "I was the one who threw Nixon's name in the ring," she recalled about the time she persuaded John S. Knight, publisher of the *Chicago Daily News,* to print the news that Nixon would be named Eisenhower's running mate. See *Brill's Content,* May 2001; and Dennis McDougal, interview by the author.

31. After his defeat Nixon worked at the law firm of Nixon, Mudge, Rose, Guthrie & Alexander.

32. *Los Angeles Times,* Sept. 23, 1952.

33. Lisa McGirr, *Suburban Warriors: The Origins of the New American Right* (Princeton: Princeton University Press, 2001), pp. 127–29.

34. Ibid., pp. 172–75.

35. Lyndon Johnson to Dorothy Chandler, letter, Feb. 25, 1964, Papers of Dorothy Chandler, Dept. of Special Collections, University Library, UCLA (hereafter cited as Dorothy Chandler Papers).

36. Joe McGinnis, *The Selling of the President* (New York: Penguin Boooks,

1988). Also see American Museum of the Moving Image, "The Living Room Candidate," http://livingroomcandidate.movingimage.us.

37. At the time Governor Edmund G. Brown was a partner in the law firm of Ball, Hunt, Hart & Brown of Beverly Hills.

38. Edmund G. Brown to Dorothy Chandler, letter, Dec. 12, 1968, Dorothy Chandler Papers.

39. Anita J. Klaz, "An Oral History of Dorothy Buffum Chandler" (M.A. thesis, California State University, Northridge, 1981), p. 137. However, she claimed that Catherine Campbell Hearst, wife of *Examiner* publisher Randolph Hearst, provided repeated "scoops" to her family's San Francisco newspaper. Hearst had been appointed regent in 1956 by Governor Goodwin J. Knight and served for twenty years. Regents Hearst and Chandler had crossed swords during the height of the Free Speech Movement. (Sadly, Catherine Hearst would pay a heavy price for her tenure as regent, for her daughter Patricia "Patty" Hearst would be kidnapped in 1974 from her Berkeley apartment; the kidnappers cited Hearst's voting record on the board of regents as one of the reasons for the abduction.)

40. James Wrightson, quoted in unidentified newspaper feature, Dec. 1968, Dorothy Chandler Papers.

41. Ibid.

42. Clark Kerr to Dorothy Chandler, letter, 1968, Dorothy Chandler Papers.

43. Clark Kerr, interview by the author.

44. *Washington Evening Star,* Jan. 3, 1976.

45. Diana Mitchell, "Speaking of First Ladies," 1969, Dorothy Chandler Papers.

46. *Women's Wear Daily,* Dec. 14, 1967.

47. *Women's Wear Daily,* Mar. 18, 1975.

48. Ibid.

49. *Women's Wear Daily,* Dec. 14, 1967.

50. FDM to Norman Cousins, letter, undated, Murphy Papers.

51. The title of the organization established in 1956 by President Eisenhower was the President's Board of Consultants on Foreign Intelligence.

52. Richard Nixon to FDM, letter, Mar. 20, 1969, Murphy Papers.

53. Excerpt from "Presidential Statement of March 14 [1969] on the Anti-Ballistic Missile Problem," Murphy Papers.

54. Victor Marchetti and John D. Marks, *The CIA and the Cult of Intelligence* (New York: Alfred A. Knopf, 1974), p. 334. See also Charles D. Ameringer, *U.S. Foreign Intelligence: The Secret Side of American History* (Lexington, Mass.: Lexington Books, 1990).

55. Excerpt from "Presidential Statement of March 14 [1969] on the Anti-Ballistic Missile Problem."

56. "ABM Spotlight Beginning to Focus on Advisory Board," *Washington Post,* Apr. 24, 1969.

57. FDM to Henry Kissinger, letter, June 26, 1969, Murphy Papers.

58. FDM to H. R. Haldeman, letter, Aug. 19, 1969, Murphy Papers.

59. FDM to Maxwell D. Taylor, letter, undated, Murphy Papers. In the letter FDM stated:

As you know I am Chairman of the Board and Chief Executive Officer of the Times Mirror Company. One of our major properties is the Los Angeles Times which is the dominant newspaper in the Western United States. However, as chairman of the Board of the Company I have no direct responsibility for the newspaper. That is delegated to the Publisher, Mr. Otis Chandler. That is to say, Mr. Chandler and his colleagues are fully responsible for the day-to-day operation of the newspaper.

I could never take on a responsibility which would require either directly or indirectly any inhibition on the Los Angeles Times or its staff for the collection and publication of any information. I have made it quite clear to Mr. Chandler and his colleagues that any government advisory position I might take must not influence their normal operation of the newspaper one way or the other.

It is of course, quite possible that the large and competent investigative staff of the Los Angeles Times both here and abroad might, through their own sources unearth information which is not yet in the public domain. This, as you know, occurs from time to time with all good newspapers and good newspapermen. Obviously if such information is required and thought fit for publication in the best judgment of the staff of the Los Angeles Times it will be published.

The foregoing makes it necessary for me to say the obvious, namely that as I take on this advisory responsibility I understand quite clearly the necessity of serving the President and the Government not the Los Angeles Times. Therefore you can be sure that information which comes to me as a result of service on the Board will not be shared with anyone. If such information might ever appear in the Los Angeles Times it will appear only by virtue of its having been acquired from someone other than myself.

Finally, I should make it quite clear that if at the end of a reasonable period of time there appear to be any real conflicts of interest between my responsibilities as head of a company which, among other things owned a major newspaper on the one hand, and my role as a member of the Board on the other, I would clearly understand the necessity of retirement from the Board.

60. Richard Helms to FDM, letter, Mar. 11, 1970; FDM to Richard Helms, letter, Mar. 16, 1970. Murphy Papers.

61. FDM to Richard Helms, letter, Mar. 16, 1970, Murphy Papers.

62. FDM to Dorothea Gordon, letter, Aug. 17, 1971, Murphy Papers.

63. FDM to Robert O. Anderson, letter, Aug. 8, 1974, Murphy Papers.

64. FDM to Sally Fleg, letter, Aug. 22, 1974, Murphy Papers. Murphy was unrelenting about preserving the wall separating editorial and commercial interests. It had been the practice of the *Times* to permit its staff to receive complimentary tickets, but Murphy made the unpopular decision to eliminate all complimen-

tary tickets to avoid any possibility of conflict of interest, real or imagined, in reporting the news. Apparently, the scrupulous executive was not past sharing information obtained from giants in the world of newspaper publishing with White House officials when it came to secrets for weight loss. Included among Murphy's papers was a note in which he forwarded a grapefruit diet sent to him by Arthur Ochs "Punch" Sulzberger, publisher of the *New York Times,* to key presidential aide John Ehrlichman. Murphy warned Ehrlichman not to forget the water. "Curiously, the eight glasses of water are essential," he said. Arthur Ochs Sulzberger to FDM, letter, undated; FDM to Ehrlichman, letter, undated. Murphy Papers.

65. Otis Chandler to Albert V. Casey and Dennis C. Stanfill, memo "March Planning Conference," Mar. 6, 1969.

66. "Cultural Los Angeles: A Quiet Revolution," *TWA Ambassador,* undated, Murphy Papers.

SIX: THE CHANDLER EMPIRE
IN THE WATERGATE YEARS

1. Times Mirror Annual Report, 1971; FDM, Script for the Annual Meeting of Shareholders, Wed., May 26, 1971, p. 13.

2. FDM to Otis Chandler, letter, July 20, 1972, Papers of Franklin D. Murphy, Dept. of Special Collections, University Library, UCLA (hereafter cited as Murphy Papers).

3. FDM to Paul Conrad, letter, Mar. 25, 1977, Murphy Papers.

4. FDM to Jack Smith, letter, Aug. 26, 1971, Murphy Papers.

5. *Los Angeles Times,* July 2, 1992. Also see David Halberstam, *The Powers That Be* (New York: Alfred A. Knopf, 1979).

6. FDM to Nick Williams, letter, Aug. 26, 1971, Murphy Papers. Smith used his column for a moving farewell, leading Murphy to borrow Williams's phrase, "You done superb" (*Los Angeles Times,* Aug. 22, 1971).

7. Dennis McDougal, *Privileged Son: Otis Chandler and the Rise and Fall of the L.A. Times Dynasty* (New York: Perseus, 2001), p. 333.

8. Franklin Murphy, "Some Thoughts on the Current State of the Society" (speech, undated, Murphy Papers).

9. FDM to H. R. Haldeman, letter, undated, Murphy Papers.

10. FDM to H. R. Haldeman, letter, undated, Murphy Papers.

11. *Washington Post,* Nov. 10, 1988.

12. McDougal, *Privileged Son,* p. 272.

13. *Wall Street Journal,* Aug. 11, 1972, p. 1.

14. McDougal, interview; also see McDougal, *Privileged Son,* p. 301.

15. McDougal, interview; also see McDougal, *Privileged Son,* p. 307.

16. Lally Weymouth, "The Word from Mamma Buff," *Esquire,* Nov. 1977, p. 206.

17. Dennis McDougal, "Nixon and the Chandler Dynasty," *Brill's Content,* May 2001, p. 135. Also see H. R. Haldeman, *The Haldeman Diaries: Inside the Nixon White House* (New York: Putnam, 1994). The extent of White House involvement in the GeoTek affair remains unclear. The only specific reference to GeoTek seems to be an entry in Haldeman's diaries recording that Nixon told Haldeman that if Chandler's *Los Angeles Times* jumped on a story of campaign irregularities making the rounds, Chandler was to be reminded that when he was under attack because of GeoTek, Nixon had ordered "hands off."

18. Weymouth, "The Word from Mamma Buff," p. 206.

19. *Washington Post,* Oct. 10, 1972.

20. Richard Milhous Nixon, Second Inaugural Address, Jan. 20, 1973.

21. *Washington Post,* Nov. 13, 1993.

22. FDM to Councilman Thomas Bradley, letter, May 31, 1973, Murphy Papers.

23. FDM to H. R. Haldeman, letter, May 1, 1973, Murphy Papers.

24. FDM to Lawrence Higby, letter, May 31, 1973, Murphy Papers.

25. FDM to Theodore H. White, letter, Nov. 25, 1974, Murphy Papers.

26. FDM to Robert Vosper, letter, June 1, 1973, Murphy Papers

27. FDM to George Anderson, letter, June 15, 1973, Murphy Papers.

28. FDM to President Richard Nixon, letter, undated, Murphy Papers.

29. Carolyn Murphy Speer, interview by the author.

30. Although the wide expanse of glass walls that enclosed the executives' offices was modern, the exposure came to present a problem. Otis Chandler reportedly had bulletproof glass installed after receiving a series of violent threats about Conrad's editorial cartoons (David Margolick, "The Chandler Mystery," *Vanity Fair,* Sept. 1996).

31. FDM to Charles Kratka, letter, undated, Murphy Papers.

32. *Interiors,* undated, Murphy Papers.

33. Franklin Murphy, "The Necessity of Beauty in Urbanized Environment" (address to Town Hall, Jan. 14, 1964).

34. Franklin Lee Murphy, interview by the author.

35. FDM to Katharine M. Graham, letter, July 6, 1973, Murphy Papers.

36. FDM to Gov. Nelson A. Rockefeller, letter, July 23, 1973, Murphy Papers.

37. FDM to Baron Guy de Rothschild, letter, Oct. 5, 1973, Murphy Papers.

38. FDM to Walter Annenberg, letter, Oct. 8, 1973, Murphy Papers.

39. Franklin Murphy, "To Norman Chandler," undated, Murphy Papers.

40. *Los Angeles Times,* Oct. 21, 1973, p. 1.

41. McDougal, *Privileged Son,* p. 307.

42. Anita J. Klaz, "An Oral History of Dorothy Buffum Chandler" (M.A. thesis, California State University, Northridge, 1981), p. 134.

43. David Halberstam, "The California Dynasty: Otis Chandler and His Pub-

lishing Empire," *Atlantic,* Apr. 1979, p. 74; original emphasis. Also see Halberstam, *The Powers That Be.*

44. FDM to Honorable and Mrs. Nelson Rockefeller, letter, June 24, 1974, Murphy Papers.

45. Albert Casey with Dick Seaver, *Casey's Law* (New York: Arcade, 1997), p. 124.

46. FDM to Craig Crockwell, letter, Aug. 5, 1975, Murphy Papers.

47. FDM to Lee Iacocca, letter, Oct. 24, 1973, Murphy Papers.

48. FDM to Henry Ford II, letter, June 13, 1974, Murphy Papers.

49. FDM to Henry Kissinger, letter, Aug. 22, 1973, Murphy Papers.

50. FDM to Henry Kissinger, letter, Oct. 17, 1973, Murphy Papers. Kissinger won the prize in October 1973. The prize was shared by North Vietnam's President Le Duc Tho, who made history as the only Nobel laureate ever to decline the coveted honor.

51. McDougal, *Privileged Son,* p. 302.

52. McDougal, interview; McDougal, *Privileged Son,* p. 302.

53. FDM to John Lawrence, letter, Aug. 15, 1974, Murphy Papers.

54. Theodore White to FDM, letter, Jan. 7, 1975, Murphy Papers.

55. FDM to Theodore White, letter, Nov. 25, 1974, Murphy Papers.

56. FDM to Reese R. Milner, letter, Mar. 19, 1975, Murphy Papers.

57. The work of grassroots environmental organizations that sprang from the social commitment of the 1960s revolution was now producing far-reaching legislation. In California the Coastal Commission was created in 1972, and in the mid-1970s the South Coast Air Quality Management District was formed. The Santa Monica Mountains Conservancy came into being in 1979, dedicated to creating parklands and nature reserves.

58. Introductory remarks by J. Carter Brown preceding FDM speech, "Arts and Public Policy," Mar. 18, 1992, audio recording, Archives, National Gallery of Art.

59. McDougal, interview; McDougal, *Privileged Son,* p. 310.

60. Weymouth, "The Word from Mama Buff," p. 204.

61. "A Headliner's Full Life: Mrs. Chandler Is a Force in Journalism, Politics, Civic Affairs," *Life,* Dec. 24, 1956.

62. Ibid.

63. Margaret Sanger to Dorothy Chandler, letter, July 16, 1952, Papers of Dorothy Chandler, Dept. of Special Collections, University Library, UCLA.

64. Robert Erburu, interview by the author.

65. Al Casey quoted in Weymouth, "The Word from Mamma Buff."

66. Peter Fernald, interview by the author.

67. Ibid.

68. Halberstam, *The Powers That Be,* p. 97.

69. Klaz, "Oral History of Dorothy Buffum Chandler," pp. 127, 111.

70. Bob Gottlieb and Irene Wolt, "The Changing of the Guard," *Los Angeles Magazine,* undated clipping, p. 199, Murphy Papers.

71. Joan Didion, "Will Power," *Los Angeles Times,* July 13, 1997.

72. FDM to Mrs. Norman Chandler, Western Union Mailgram, May 19, 1975, Murphy Papers.

73. FDM, typed notes, Times Mirror Annual Meeting, May 1976, Murphy Papers.

74. FDM to Mrs. Norman Chandler, letter, June 3, 1976, Murphy Papers.

75. Weymouth, "The Word from Mamma Buff," p. 204.

76. Fernald, interview.

77. Gottlieb and Wolt, "The Changing of the Guard," p. 199.

SEVEN: POWER AND PHILANTHROPY

1. *New York Times,* Oct. 11, 1963.

2. John Hohns, "Power Brokers! Pinpointing the Most Powerful Californians and What They Do," *PSA Magazine,* Dec. 1975, p. 46.

3. *Los Angeles Times,* May 26, 1987.

4. Dennis McDougal, *Privileged Son: Otis Chandler and the Rise and Fall of the L.A. Times Dynasty* (New York: Perseus, 2001), p. 175.

5. FDM's first mention of the Bohemian Grove was in a letter to Michael Belmont of Cazenove & Co. of London (FDM to Michael Belmont, July 24, 1969, Papers of Franklin D. Murphy, Dept. of Special Collections, University Library, UCLA [hereafter cited as Murphy Papers]).

6. Imogene Butterfield to FDM, note, Sept. 9, 1975, Murphy Papers.

7. For 1975. Times Mirror net income now amounted to $69.5 million or $2.05 per share, up sharply 47 percent from 1975. A sense of serenity and confidence was reflected in Murphy's face when he was photographed with Robert Erburu and Otis Chandler for the company's 1976 Annual Report.

8. Times Mirror Annual Report, 1977.

9. *Business Week,* Feb. 21, 1977.

10. Ibid.

11. Times Mirror Annual Report, 1977. Revenues from newspaper publishing increased from $433.3 million to $510.7 million, and operating profit reached $81.3 million, up 58 percent. Newsprint and forest products operations also generated record revenues.

12. FDM to Otis Chandler and Robert F. Erburu, memo, Mar. 17, 1977, Murphy Papers.

13. One such story involved the murder of Eula Love, a black woman from South Central who was shot eight times by police. The attention-grabbing story amid the city's continuing conflicts between the police and the black community had been completely ignored by the *Times.* See *Time,* Aug. 13, 1979.

14. Jim Bellows, interview by the author; also see Jim Bellows, *The Last Editor: How I Saved the New York Times, the Washington Post, and the Los Angeles Times from Dullness and Complacency* (Kansas City, Mo.: Andrews McMeel, 2002), p. 226.

15. Anthony Cook, "Crown Prince of the Press," *New West*, Dec. 5, 1977, p. 59.

16. Murphy told the journalist and author Bob Gottlieb in an interview for *Los Angeles Magazine* that the *Times* wanted to bring in new blood and avoid stagnation. "The hiring of Tom Johnson," he said, "was the first move, of which there will be several over the next few years." Johnson came to Otis Chandler's attention when he was an executive at the Texas Broadcasting Company, owned by the family of Lyndon Johnson. (Times Mirror had acquired Austin television station KTBC from the Johnson family.) Tom Johnson was a graduate of Harvard Business School and a former White House assistant press secretary. Chandler had hired Johnson to revamp the *Dallas Times Herald,* and four years later he created the new position at the *Times* in which Johnson would serve as president.

17. McDougal, *Privileged Son,* p. 337.

18. As quoted in David Margolick, "The Chandler Dynasty," *Vanity Fair,* Sept. 1996, p. 230.

19. In 1977 company vice-chairman Otis Chandler's Times Mirror take-home pay was $355,910; Robert Erburu received $340,370.

20. Otis Chandler to FDM, letter, Aug. 30, 1978, Murphy Papers.

21. Robert Erburu to FDM, letter, Sept. 1, 1978, Murphy Papers. Erburu wrote, "Revenues in 1968 were $434.8 million. . . . This year the company's revenues should be about $1.4 billion and net income should exceed $120 million."

22. George F. Getty to FDM, letter, Dec. 17, 1969, Murphy Papers.

23. Franklin D. Murphy, interview by David L. Lewis, Oral History for the Ford Motor Company, Ford Corporate History Program, Oct. 26, 1989, p. 23.

24. Ibid.

25. FDM to Henry Ford II, letter, Jan. 16, 1976, Murphy Papers.

26. Lee A. Iacocca to FDM, letter, Jan. 12, 1976, Murphy Papers.

27. FDM to Henry Ford II, letter, Jan. 21, 1976, Murphy Papers.

28. FDM to Henry Ford II, letter, June 11, 1976, Murphy Papers.

29. Murphy, interview by David L. Lewis, p. 23.

30. Ibid.

31. FDM to Henry Ford II, letter, Mar. 14, 1980, Murphy Papers.

32. Section 4941, Internal Revenue Code.

33. FDM to Dorothy G. Sullivan, letter, May 18, 1973, Murphy Papers.

34. The state of California took the position that the exchange constituted an act of self-dealing. (The transaction involved 987,500 shares of H. F. Ahmanson and Company stock that Sullivan had donated to the foundation from 1952 to 1968, stock that brought more than $20 million when it was sold in October 1972.)

35. Robert Ahmanson, interview by the author.

36. Ibid.; also see *Los Angeles Times,* June 17, 1994, p. A34.

37. FDM to Robert H. Ahmanson, letter, Jan. 3, 1975, Murphy Papers.

38. Ibid. Murphy added, "From the very beginning I have had only one interest—namely, seeing that these problems were worked out legally, in good faith, and fairly."

39. FDM to William H. Ahmanson, letter, Sept. 3, 1975, Murphy Papers.

40. FDM to William H. Ahmanson, letter, Dec. 29, 1975, Murphy Papers.

41. The 99 nonvoting shares had previously been given to the Ahmanson Foundation. Through this elaborate structure one voting share of Ahmanco was entitled to vote the 600 voting shares of H. F. Ahmanson and Company, and the 600 voting shares of H. F. Ahmanson and Company were entitled to vote the stock of Home Savings.

42. *Los Angeles Times,* Mar. 19, 1979.

43. Daniel Belin, interview by the author. Also see Daniel N. Belin, "Evelle J. Younger v. The Ahmanson Foundation, The Ahmanson Foundation v. U.S." (unpublished memorandum, courtesy of Daniel N. Belin).

44. FDM to Honorable Robert J. Dole, letter, July 29, 1982, Murphy Papers; original emphasis. Murphy added, "The estate of the late Howard Ahmanson was extremely complicated and by the time the Foundation could be aware of exactly what it possessed from the estate due to Internal Revenue Service and California Attorney General technical questions, a number of years lapsed and by that time, because of the sad state of savings and loan associations, the value of the stock had eroded enormously."

45. Belin, interview; also see Daniel N. Belin, "Dr. Franklin D. Murphy" (memorial service address, June 30, 1994).

46. Ahmanson, interview.

47. Uri Hersher, interview by the author.

48. Margaret Bach, "The Ahmanson Foundation: Forty Years of Building Community 1952–1992" (manuscript, June 1993), p. 19 (courtesy of Robert Ahmanson).

49. FDM to Robert Ahmanson, letter, Oct. 23, 1980, Murphy Papers.

50. "Unconventional Couple: Rich Eccentric Howard Ahmanson Jr. Encounters His Life Partner Roberta," *Orange County Register,* Aug. 9, 2004.

51. FDM to Howard Ahmanson Jr., letter, Jan. 29, 1982, Murphy Papers.

52. FDM to Robert Ahmanson, letter, June 22, 1987, Murphy Papers.

53. FDM to President Gerald R. Ford, letter, undated, Murphy Papers. In this letter Murphy listed Rockefeller's government positions as Director, Office of Inter-American Affairs (1940–44); Assistant Secretary of State for Latin-American Affairs (1944–45); Chairman of the President's Advisory Committee on Government Organization (1953–58); Special Assistant to the President for

Foreign Affairs (1954–55); and member of the President's Foreign Intelligence Advisory Board.

54. Ibid.

55. FDM to Nelson Rockefeller, letter, Oct. 25, 1974, Murphy Papers.

56. FDM to Nelson Rockefeller, letter, Nov. 18, 1974, Murphy Papers.

57. *The Rockefellers* (2000), a segment of the PBS television series *The American Experience,* online at www.pbs.org/wgbh/amex/Rockefellers.

58. FDM to Nelson Rockefeller, letter, Dec. 20, 1974, Murphy Papers.

59. FDM to Happy Rockefeller, letter, undated; Happy Rockefeller to FDM, letter, undated. Murphy Papers.

60. FDM to Erin Crockwell, letter, Sept. 17, 1981, Murphy Papers.

61. FDM to Erin Crockwell, letter, June 10, 1983, Murphy Papers.

62. Cordelia Murphy Ennis, interview by the author.

63. FDM to Robert M. DeKruif, letter, July 23, 1979, Murphy Papers.

64. FDM to Franklin Lee Murphy, letter, May 27, 1981, Murphy Papers.

65. FDM to Franklin Lee Murphy, letter, undated, Murphy Papers.

66. FDM to Dr. and Mrs. Franklin Lee Murphy, letter, Aug. 6, 1982, Murphy Papers.

67. FDM to Franklin Lee Murphy, letter, June 13, 1983, Murphy Papers.

68. FDM to Franklin Lee Murphy, letter, Mar. 23, 1981, Murphy Papers.

69. Carolyn Murphy Speer, interview by the author.

70. Warren E. Burger to FDM, letter, Apr. 9, 1980.

71. "Fat Times in Los Angeles," *Newsweek,* Sept. 22, 1980.

72. McDougal, *Privileged Son,* p. 342.

73. FDM to Tsuneo Tanaka, letter, Apr. 2, 1982, Murphy Papers.

74. Tom Johnson to FDM, letter, Dec. 31, 1980, Murphy Papers.

75. Bellows, interview.

76. Bellows, *The Last Editor,* p. 167.

77. Robert Erburu to FDM, letter, Sept. 1, 1978, Murphy Papers.

78. FDM to Anthony Day, letter, Oct. 24, 1980, Murphy Papers.

79. See John van der Zee, *The Greatest Men's Party on Earth: Inside the Bohemian Grove* (New York: Harcourt Brace Jovanovich, 1974).

80. *Chicago Tribune,* Feb. 5, 1986.

81. FDM to Robert F. Erburu, Phillip L. Williams, Tom Johnson, memo, "Los Angeles Times—Bohemian Grove," July 21, 1981, Murphy Papers.

82. Daniel Boorstin to Charles E. Young, letter, 1981. Other letters came from county museum benefactor Anna Bing Arnold, county museum founder Ed Carter, Director of the Huntington Library James Thorpe, and Harvard President Derek Bok.

83. FDM to Dortch Oldhman, letter, Jan. 16, 1976, Murphy Papers.

84. FDM to George H. W. Bush, letter, Nov. 24, 1980, Murphy Papers.

85. Ibid.

86. FDM to James Baker II, letter, undated, Murphy Papers.

87. FDM to Peter O'Malley, letter, undated, Murphy Papers. "A great triumph for you, the players and the city!" an enthusiastic Murphy wrote O'Malley after the surprise finish.

EIGHT: THE LOS ANGELES COUNTY MUSEUM OF ART

1. FDM to L.A. County Supervisor Ernest Debs, letter, 1971, Papers of Franklin D. Murphy, Dept. of Special Collections, University Library, UCLA (hereafter cited as Murphy Papers).

2. FDM to L.A. County Supervisor Ernest Debs, letter, June 18, 1970, Murphy Papers.

3. John Walker to FDM, letter, July 22, 1971; FDM to John Walker, letter, Aug. 3, 1971; FDM to John Walker, letter, Nov. 17, 1971, Murphy Papers.

4. *Los Angeles Times,* Nov. 14, 1971.

5. FDM to John Walker, letter, Mar. 23, 1972, Murphy Papers.

6. Suzanne Muchnic, interview by the author. See also Suzanne Muchnic, *Odd Man In: Norton Simon and the Pursuit of Culture* (Berkeley: University of California Press, 1998), pp. 118–21; FDM to Robert McFarlane, letter, June 16, 1972 (courtesy of Suzanne Muchnic).

7. Henry J. Seldis, "Armand Hammer Wills $10 Million in Art to County," *Los Angeles Times,* Dec. 20, 1971, p. A1. The painting by van Gogh was *Hospital at Saint-Remy.*

8. Statement by Dr. Franklin D. Murphy, memo to the press, Dec. 16, 1971, Murphy Papers.

9. Paul Richard as quoted in Robert A. Jones, "Battle for the Masterpieces: The Armand Hammer–County Museum Deal: A Saga of Art, Power and Big Misunderstandings," *Los Angeles Times Magazine,* May 22, 1988, p. 16.

10. Jones, "Battle for the Masterpieces," p. 16.

11. John Walker to FDM, letter, Oct. 6, 1970, Archives, National Gallery of Art. See also John Walker, *Self-Portrait with Donors: Confessions of an Art Collector* (Boston: Little, Brown, 1974), p. 207.

12. Jones, "Battle for the Masterpieces," p. 16.

13. *Los Angeles Times,* June 13, 1973. The exhibition was at LACMA June 13–July 8, 1973. Also see www.nga.gov/past/date/exh377.shtm.

14. "Statement of Franklin D. Murphy, President of the Los Angeles County Museum of Art in Connection with the Exhibition of Paintings from the Soviet Union" (undated).

15. FDM to Edward W. Carter, letter, Oct. 18, 1973, Murphy Papers.

16. John Pastier, "Sculpture Garden a New Beginning," *Los Angeles Times,* July 1, 1974, p. E1.

17. *Los Angeles Times,* undated clipping, Murphy Papers.

18. FDM to Norton Simon, letter, undated, Murphy Papers.

19. Richard Sherwood, a partner in the law firm of O'Melveny and Myers, had been a museum trustee since 1966.

20. LACMA, *X, a Decade of Collecting, 1965–1975* (Los Angeles: LACMA, 1975), p. 10.

21. Burton B. Fredericksen to FDM, letter, Nov. 8, 1974, Muphy Papers.

22. FDM to Kenneth Donahue, letter, Aug. 29, 1973, Murphy Papers.

23. *Los Angeles Times,* Apr. 6, 1975.

24. *Apollo* magazine, undated clipping, Murphy Papers.

25. "Art Museum Opens Sculpture Garden," *Herald Examiner,* June 19, 1975.

26. FDM to Mrs. Freeman Gates, letter, Jan. 21, 1975, Murphy Papers.

27. *Los Angeles Times,* March 31, Apr. 9, Apr. 13, 1975.

28. *Newsweek,* Apr. 21, 1975.

29. Draft letter to *Newsweek,* Apr. 17, 1975, Murphy Papers.

30. FDM to Philippa Calnan, letter, Apr. 17, 1975, Murphy Papers.

31. *Herald Examiner,* June 19, 1975.

32. Dr. Armand Hammer to FDM, letter, Nov. 7, 1975, Murphy Papers.

33. "Hammer Calls Occidental Payments 'Insignificant,'" *Los Angeles Times,* May 22, 1976, p. C8.

34. *Los Angeles Times,* Jan. 12, 1980, p. C7.

35. FDM to Dr. Armand Hammer, letter, Feb. 3, 1980, Murphy Papers.

36. *Los Angeles Times,* Feb. 3, 1980, p. M1.

37. William Wilson, "A Somebody in LACMA Post," *Los Angeles Times,* Feb. 3, 1980, p. M1.

38. *ARTnews,* Jan. 1981.

39. *Los Angeles Times,* Feb. 3, 1980.

40. FDM to Eli Broad, letter, Aug. 7, 1980, Murphy Papers.

41. FDM to Eli Broad, letter, Dec. 22, 1980, Murphy Papers.

42. The French artist Honoré Daumier (1808–79) was known as a great lithographer and social critic, with a genius for gesture and facial expression in his observations of daily life.

43. John Walker, *National Gallery of Art,* foreword by J. Carter Brown (New York: Abradale Press, Harry N. Abrams, 1995).

44. See Jones, "Battle for the Masterpieces," pp. 8–12.

45. Richard Sherwood to Franklin Murphy, Edward Carter, and Mrs. Frost, memo, "Subject: Armand Hammer," Mar. 15, 1979, Murphy Papers.

46. Jones, "Battle for the Masterpieces," p. 11.

47. Agreement, May 27, 1980, Armand Hammer, Armand Hammer Foundation and Museum Associates. See also Linda J. Srassle for O'Melveny and Myers to Daniel N. Belin, "LACMA—Hammer Agreement Chronology," Jan. 26, 1988.

48. Edward Jay Epstein, "The Last Days of Armand Hammer," *New Yorker,* Sept. 23, 1996, p. 36. Epstein described Hammer's security provisions for the

manuscript: "After Hammer took possession of the codex, he had it dismantled and cut into 72 separate pages. He then had each page mounted in a free-standing display case so that it could be exhibited. He announced that he had retained a squad of elite commandos, trained in Asian martial arts and armed with Uzi machine guns, to guard the codex day and night. Though no actual commandos were guarding it—and it had once been left unattended in two crates on Hammer's plane at an airport—the purported security arrangements caught the interest of the media. With great fanfare the 'Codex Hammer' traveled to fifteen countries and attracted more than a million visitors."

49. FDM to Dr. Armand Hammer, letter, Dec. 15, 1980, Murphy Papers.

50. FDM to Dr. Armand Hammer, letter, undated, Murphy Papers.

51. *Los Angeles Times,* undated clipping, Murphy Papers.

52. FDM to Kenneth Hahn, letter, July 28, 1980, Murphy Papers.

53. FDM to R. Stanton Avery, letter, June 5, 1981, Murphy Papers.

54. *Los Angeles Times,* June 17, 1994 (William Wilson).

55. FDM to Kenneth Hahn, letter, June 1981, Murphy Papers.

56. FDM to Howard P. Allen, Norman Barker Jr., Edward W. Carter, Mrs. F. Daniel Frost, Earl A. Powell III, and Morton J. Goden, memo, Mar. 22, 1982, Murphy Papers.

57. FDM to Supervisor Edmund D. Edelman, letter, Mar. 22, 1982, Murphy Papers.

58. FDM to Howard P. Allen, Norman Barker Jr., Edward W. Carter, Mrs. F. Daniel Frost, Earl A. Powell III, and Morton J. Goden, memo, Mar. 22, 1982, Murphy Papers.

59. *Los Angeles Times,* Mar. 25, 1983.

60. *Los Angeles Times,* July 1, 1983.

61. FDM to Earl Powell III, letter, Mar. 25, 1983, Murphy Papers.

62. *New York Times* and *Chicago Sun Times,* undated clippings, Murphy Papers.

63. *Los Angeles Times,* Nov. 19, 1986.

64. *Los Angeles Times,* May 23, 1986.

65. FDM to Earl A. Powell III, letter, Dec. 3, 1986, Murphy Papers.

66. *Los Angeles Times,* May 23, 1986.

67. *Los Angeles Times,* Nov. 4, 1987.

68. *Daily News,* Nov. 1, 1987.

69. "Statement Regarding Loan to Director of Los Angeles County Museum of Art," Nov. 3, 1987, signed by Daniel N. Belin, President, Board of Trustees, LACMA.

70. FDM to Richard E. Sherwood, letter, Feb. 26, 1986, Murphy Papers.

71. FDM to Earl A. Powell III, letter, Mar. 6, 1986, accompanied by "Draft of Letter for Signature of Dr. Earl A. Powell III," Murphy Papers.

1. Murphy's service on the board of the National Gallery would total twenty-nine years (1964–93).

2. Franklin Murphy, interview by Alfred C. Viebranz, Jan. 24 and May 2, 1990, National Gallery of Art Oral History Program, p. 47.

3. *Washington Post,* May 4, 1985.

4. Ibid.

5. "Remarks by the President of the United States, John R. Stevenson, J. Carter Brown and Paul Mellon, National Gallery of Art," May 3, 1985, Archives, National Gallery of Art.

6. As president of the institution, Stevenson was actively engaged in day-to-day details of the museum with the various committee and patron groups in concert with the Gallery director.

7. Phillip Kopper, *America's National Gallery of Art: A Gift to the Nation* (New York: Harry N. Abrams, 1991), pp. 287–88.

8. FDM to Walter Annenberg, letter, Nov. 11, 1980, Papers of Franklin D. Murphy, Dept. of Special Collections, University Library, UCLA (hereafter cited as Murphy Papers).

9. Walter Annenberg to FDM, letter, Nov. 17, 1980, Murphy Papers.

10. FDM to the Honorable John R. Stevenson, letter, May 6, 1985, Murphy Papers.

11. FDM to Tom Christie, letter, Mar. 19, 1986, Murphy Papers.

12. J. Carter Brown to FDM, letter, May 8, 1985, Archives, National Gallery of Art.

13. Franklin D. Murphy, Nancy Hanks Lecture on Arts and Public Policy, Mar. 18, 1992.

14. "The Trustee: Franklin D. Murphy," *Art Newspaper,* Jan. 1991, p. 1.

15. Note that under the Gallery's original bylaws, the chief justice was, ex officio, chairman of the board. In 1979, when Warren Burger decided that he was too occupied with court duties to continue to serve as chairman, the bylaws were amended and Paul Mellon was elected chairman. Stevenson succeeded him as president. See Elizabeth A. Croog, National Gallery of Art Secretary and General Counsel, to Robert Erburu, National Gallery of Art, Chairman of the Board, letter, Jan. 22, 2003.

16. Murphy, interview by Viebranz, p. 16.

17. Regarding the issue of indemnification: "One of his [Brown's] most important achievements was to persuade Congress to indemnify art on loan from abroad. This relieved American museums of the burden of insuring borrowed art and enabled him to mount 'Treasure Houses of Britain,' a vast and opulent display of five centuries of glorious, if not uniformly tasteful, extravaganza" (*Daily Telegraph,* June 21, 2002).

18. *Los Angeles Times,* Nov. 4, 1985.

19. *Washington Post,* Nov. 12, 1985.

20. "Revised Comments for Delivery by Dr. Murphy on Evening of Oct. 31, 1985," Archives, National Gallery of Art.

21. Ibid.

22. "The Trustee: Franklin D. Murphy," p. 1.

23. "Armand Hammer Bequeaths Collection of Master Drawings to National Gallery," National Gallery of Art press release, Apr. 23, 1987, Archives, National Gallery of Art.

24. Previously owned by Thomas Coke, First Earl of Leicester, the master drawing had been inherited by the Viscount Coke (Holkham Hall). The National Gallery of Art's purchase gave the Gallery the first Raphael "cartoon" ever to leave Europe.

25. J. Carter Brown to FDM, letter, Oct. 17, 1986, Murphy Papers.

26. *Washington Post,* Apr, 24, 1987.

27. Ibid.

28. FDM to Francis S. Hodsoll, letter, Nov. 4, 1985, Murphy Papers.

29. Barnabas McHenry to Robert F. Erburu, letter, June 24, 1988, Murphy Papers.

30. Robert DeKruif, interview by the author.

31. Arthur Ochs Sulzberger to FDM, letter, June 11, 1987, Murphy Papers.

32. *Washington Post,* Oct. 29, 1997.

33. Amon G. Carter Sr. was a popular civic leader and longtime owner and publisher of the *Fort Worth Star-Telegram.* See "The Carter Legacy: Daughter Recalls Man Who Made Museum Possible," *Fort Worth Star-Telegram,* Oct. 21, 2001.

34. "Board Elects New Chairman, President and Two New Trustees," National Gallery of Art press release, Sept. 29, 1993, Archives, National Gallery of Art.

35. Paul Mellon to FDM, letter, Feb. 6, 1991, Murphy Papers.

36. Ibid.

37. Description of Hoving by Murphy. FDM to J. Carter Brown, letter, undated, Murphy Papers.

38. *New York Times,* undated clipping, Murphy Papers.

39. Grace Gleck, "Met's New Annenberg Center Stirs Controversy," *New York Times,* Feb. 27, 1977.

40. Pete Hamil, "Heir to a Soiled Fortune Buys a Museum's Soul," clipping from unidentified newspaper, Mar. 2, 1977, Murphy Papers.

41. *Washington Post,* May 23, 1989.

42. Catherine Barnett, "A Very Private View inside Walter Annenberg's Personal Paradise," *Art & Antiques,* Mar. 1989, p. 94.

43. FDM to the Honorable Walter H. Annenberg, letter, Nov. 18, 1976, Murphy Papers.

44. William Wilson, "Walter Annenberg Surveys the Land; In Art as in Politics, the Collector and Former Diplomat Knows What He Likes," *Los Angeles Times,* Aug. 12, 1990.

45. Peter Fernald, interview by the author.

46. Murphy, interview by Viebranz, pp. 42–43.

47. *Chicago Tribune,* June 27, 2002; *Boston Globe,* June 19, 2002.

48. *New York Times,* Jan. 25, 1992; *Daily News,* Jan. 25, 1992.

TEN: THE SAMUEL H. KRESS FOUNDATION

1. "50th Anniversary of Hallmark Cards Inc." (remarks by Franklin D. Murphy, Oct. 26, 1960).

2. Nancy Kellogg Harper, "Higher Education Leadership: Franklin D. Murphy in Kansas, 1948–1960" (Ph.D. diss., University of Kansas, 1995), p. 68.

3. Franklin Murphy, interview by Alfred C. Viebranz, Jan. 24 and May 2, 1990, National Gallery of Art Oral History Program, p. 2.

4. See Chiyo Ishikawa, with essays by Marilyn Perry and Edgar Peters Bowron, *A Gift to America: Masterpieces of European Painting from the Samuel H. Kress Collection* (New York: Harry N. Abrams, 1994).

5. John Walker, *Self-Portrait with Donors: Confessions of an Art Collector* (Boston: Little, Brown, 1974), pp. 137–38.

6. See Ishikawa, *A Gift to America.*

7. Despite his poor health, Samuel H. Kress still retained the title of chairman. See Carl Reiser, "S. H. Kress: Who's In Charge?" *Fortune,* Nov. 1957, p. 170.

8. Murphy, interview by Viebranz, p. 3.

9. Walker, *Self-Portrait with Donors,* p. 153.

10. Joyce Appleby, *Telling the Truth about History* (New York: Norton, 1994), pp. 161–97.

11. Ishikawa, *A Gift to America,* p. 26.

12. Walker, *Self-Portrait with Donors,* p. 153.

13. By September 1956 the company had cut its dividend rate from $3 to $2, resulting in a fast and steep decline in the stock price.

14. Reiser, "S. H. Kress," p. 170.

15. Rush Kress's personal holdings were approximately 5 percent of the 2,381,734 outstanding shares of common stock. See Reiser, "S. H. Kress," p. 170.

16. FDM to R. H. Kress, letter, Sept. 25, 1957, Papers of Franklin D. Murphy, Dept. of Special Collections, University Library, UCLA (hereafter cited as Murphy Papers). The full text of Murphy's letter reads as follows:

> This summer, Mrs. Murphy and I and our two older daughters spent about six weeks motoring through Germany and Austria. Among other places we spent a few days in Nuremberg. Of course, we visited the great Cathedral. I was simply amazed to see the extraordinary restoration that has taken place. Only then did I realize what a significant gesture you made in providing for this restoration.

We of course saw the Kress plaque on one of the pillars of the church, and altogether it was quite an inspiring experience.

I also want you to know that the postgraduate medical program at the University of Kansas continues to expand both in size and quality. With literally thousands of physicians coming from all states of the middle west to a whole variety of programs, it can properly be said, and has been so documented by the American Medical Association, that this is one of the most significant postgraduate medical programs in the country.

Next year will be the last year of committed support from the Kress Foundation for this program. As I advised you a few years ago, we have taken cognizance of this fact, and after the next contribution by the Foundation has been made we shall have our affairs arranged so that we can finance it locally without in any way compromising the quality of the program. Not only the university, but thousands of people in the Middle West who are the ultimate beneficiaries of this program are deeply in your debt.

You will recall that on May 25, 1957 I regretfully submitted my resignation as a member of the Trustees of the Foundation. Since I have not heard from the Foundation I presume the resignation has not been accepted. The whole matter developed rather suddenly and I have not had time to reconsider the whole situation carefully. In spite of the limitations of time and distance, I feel very close to the Foundation. You and your staff must surely know that both personally and officially I feel deeply indebted for this wonderful constructive support that the Foundation has given the University of Kansas and to me and which has made possible some permanently constructive developments throughout the whole Middle West.

In view of this, I should like at least to serve out my term as trustee, which would mean one more year. Somehow, I do not feel right about withdrawing from the Board at this time and consequently I should like to and hereby do withdraw my resignation. I will try to work out means by which I can personally appear at the foundation from time to time to give effect to the deep personal interest I feel in its affairs and all of you who guide them.

17. *Wall Street Journal,* Feb. 14, 1958.

18. *New York Herald Tribune,* Feb. 24, 1958.

19. FDM to Harold H. Helm, letter, Feb. 24, 1958, Murphy Papers.

20. *New York Times,* Feb. 24, 1958.

21. Rush Kress told the trustees, "I believe we can work together in and through this foundation in its chosen fields of art, medicine and other public service, which are our main purposes, to create a lasting monument to my brother and to render a service of outstanding importance to the people of this country and of the world."

22. In his remarks President Kennedy hailed the extraordinary contribution to the nation's art resources as "an enduring memorial to the industry, foresight and generosity of the Kress family and of the Samuel H. Kress Foundation."

23. Ishikawa, *A Gift to America,* p. 15.

24. In the course of assembling a diverse and talented group of trustees, Murphy brought on board Clarke Wescoe, who had succeeded him as chancellor at KU. It was an example of Murphy looking after those he mentored as well as an instance of his desire to expand eastern consciousness by increasing the midwestern presence on the board.

For his labors in guiding the foundation's work, Murphy received $20,000 each year. In 1984, when he became chairman, this was reduced to $10,000.

25. Modestini, a renowned restorer of Italian paintings, worked his wonders at Huckleberry Hill in Pennsylvania, a wooded estate in the Poconos where the foundation maintained a fireproof laboratory and storage vaults. "There was nothing ever like this in the whole of art history of this country; never will be again, I'm sure," Murphy said of that rarefied art factory (Murphy, interview by Viebranz, p. 9).

26. Murphy, interview by Viebranz, p. 11.

27. FDM to Dr. Marilyn Perry, letter, July 20, 1981, Murphy Papers.

28. FDM to Mary Davis, letter, Dec. 15, 1981, Murphy Papers.

29. FDM to Dr. Marilyn Perry, letter, Dec. 28, 1981, Murphy Papers.

30. Franklin D. Murphy, interview by Deborah Hickle, Jan. 1990, transcript, University of Kansas School of Medicine Oral History Project.

31. *Time,* Apr. 27, 1987.

32. *Wall Street Journal,* Apr. 16, 1987.

33. The twelve-year, $3 million cleaning project had been financed by the Nippon Television Network of Tokyo.

34. *Dallas Morning News,* Mar. 14, 1987.

35. Also invited were Dianne Dwyer, a private conservator of old master paintings, formerly in the Department of Paintings Conservation at the Metropolitan Museum of Art; Mario Modestini, formerly curator and conservator of the Kress Collection; and Leonetto Tintori, a Florentine who specialized in restoring frescoes.

36. "Joint Statement by Conservators on the Restoration of Michelangelo's Frescoes in the Sistine Chapel," Apr. 16, 1987.

37. *Los Angeles Times,* Apr. 18, 1987.

38. Franklin Murphy, "Conserving Our Cultural Heritage: A Personal Perspective" (remarks delivered at Collections, Monuments and Architecture at Risk: A Forum for Southern California Decision Makers, Feb. 27, 1989).

ELEVEN: THE J. PAUL GETTY TRUST

1. In 1968 *Fortune* reported that J. Paul Getty tied with Howard Hughes for the title of richest man in America.

2. See Robert Lenzner, "The Great Getty," series and book excerpt, *Houston Chronicle,* Apr. 13–18, 1986. Also see *The Gettys: A Tragedy of Riches* of the A&E television series *Biography.*

3. *The Gettys: A Tragedy of Riches.*

4. *Wall Street Journal,* Apr. 14, 1987.

5. Lenzer, "The Great Getty," *Houston Chronicle,* Apr. 18, 1986. Also see Franklin D. Murphy interview, undated transcript, J. Paul Getty Trust Oral History Project, p. 6.

6. Information on ranch house museum from Suzanne Muchnic, "A Getty Chronicle: The Malibu Years," *Los Angeles Times,* July 6, 1997; John Walsh and Deborah Gribbon, *The J. Paul Getty Museum and Its Collection: A Museum for the New Century* (Los Angeles: J. Paul Getty Museum, 1997), p. 21.

7. The Ardabil Carpet is considered one of the most finely designed and executed carpets in the world.

8. "European Itinerary for Dr. and Mrs. Franklin D. Murphy, September 1 to October 1, 1971," Murphy Papers.

9. Murphy, interview, Getty Trust Oral History Project, p. 4.

10. Ibid., p. 7.

11. *Chicago Sun-Times,* Apr. 6, 1986.

12. Ibid.

13. The painting's exhibition label was later changed to read: "Workshop of Peter Paul Rubens, ca. 1615."

14. Murphy, interview, Getty Trust Oral History Project, p. 6.

15. Details of exploration of Herculaneum from *The J. Paul Getty Museum* (Malibu, Calif.: J. Paul Getty Museum, 1974); Norman Neuerburg, *Herculaneum to Malibu: A Companion to the Visit of the J. Paul Getty Museum Building* (Malibu, Calif.: J. Paul Getty Museum, 1975); Amedeo Maiuri, *Herculaneum and the Villa of the Papyri* (Novara: Istituto Geografico de Agostini, 1973). Also see Walsh and Gribbon, *The J. Paul Getty Museum.*

16. Burton Fredericksen to FDM, letter, Oct. 20, 1971, Papers of Franklin D. Murphy, Dept. of Special Collections, University Library, UCLA (hereafter cited as Murphy Papers). This notion was later rejected. Fredericksen had been appointed curator at the museum in 1965, a role expanded to chief curator in 1971 when additional curators were engaged for the various collections in preparation for the transition to the new museum.

17. Murphy, interview, Getty Trust Oral History Project, p. 8.

18. *Chicago Sun-Times,* Apr. 6, 1986.

19. George F. Getty to FDM, letter, Dec. 17, 1969, Murphy Papers.

20. *Los Angeles Times,* Aug. 28, 1973.

21. *Chicago Sun-Times,* Apr. 13, 1986.

22. *Wall Street Journal,* Apr. 14, 1987.

23. See Lenzner, "The Great Getty."

24. Ibid.

25. Murphy, interview, Getty Trust Oral History Project, p. 33.

26. Ibid., p. 13.

27. FDM to J. Paul Getty, letter, June 26, 1973, Murphy Papers.

28. See Lenzner, "The Great Getty."

29. *The Gettys: A Tragedy of Riches.*

30. Walsh and Gribbon, *The J. Paul Getty Museum,* p. 48.

31. Handsome re-creations of room settings were devised to display the furniture and decorative pieces, but the paintings were crowded into rather airless, utilitarian galleries. The walls of the colonnaded porticoes were painted with illusionist murals in vibrant shades of pink, yellow, and green that seemed garish to many visitors, although such walls in ancient Rome had presented an even bolder palette.

32. *Daily Express,* July 10, 1976.

33. In his will Getty provided a modest income for his son Ronald, who purportedly had been slighted by Sarah Getty in anger over his mother's divorce settlement.

34. Gillian Wilson, quoted in *The Gettys: A Tragedy of Riches.*

35. Walsh and Gribbon, *The J. Paul Getty Museum,* p. 64.

36. Ibid.

37. Otto Wittmann was director of the Toledo Museum of Art from 1959 to 1977.

38. Murphy, interview, undated transcript, Getty Trust Oral History Project, p. 32. Also see interview with Otto Wittmann, conducted by Eric Abrahamson, J. Paul Getty Trust Oral History Project, Sept. 24, 1999, p. 32.

39. Franklin Murphy, "Draft Memorandum to the Trustees of the J. Paul Getty Trust," Aug. 18, 1980.

40. FDM to Derek C. Bok, letter, Oct. 6, 1980, Murphy Papers.

41. The other names Franklin Murphy recommended to lead what was later called the J. Paul Getty Trust were Ted Pillsbury, Henry Rosovsky, and David Alexander (Murphy, interview, Getty Trust Oral History Project, p. 22).

42. Murphy was first a member of the board of McCall's Corporation. He became a director on the Norton Simon board after the consolidation that in 1969 brought Hunt Food and Industries, Canada Dry Corporation, and McCall's together as Norton Simon, Inc., chaired by Harold Williams.

43. Harold M. Williams served as dean and professor of management of the Graduate School of Management at UCLA from 1970 to 1977. (In 1987 the school was renamed the John E. Anderson Graduate School of Management.) Franklin Murphy had left the chancellorship to join the Times Mirror Company in 1968. He claimed to have assisted in the selection of Williams by the university, but the record does not support any formal involvement in Williams's recruitment.

44. Williams was named chairman of the board of Norton Simon, Inc., in 1969.

45. Harold Williams, interview by the author.

46. Ibid.

47. Murphy, interview, Getty Trust Oral History Project, p. 32. Not only did Murphy push for the selection of Williams, he did the research necessary to determine a fair compensation package. Murphy spoke with Walter A. Haas Jr. (chairman of the board of Levi Strauss and Company), who was a trustee of the Ford Foundation, about the benefits packages afforded the chief executive officer of the Ford Foundation. He also asked John R. Stevenson for confidential details of the compensation package provided by the Mellon Foundation for their chief executive officer. The initial salary for the Getty's new executive leader was $181,583.

48. In February 1983 Harold Williams obtained court approval to change the organization's name from the J. Paul Getty Museum to the J. Paul Getty Trust.

49. Williams, interview.

50. Eric John Abrahamson, "The J. Paul Getty Trust: A Brief Institutional History" (draft, Oct. 8, 2001, courtesy of the J. Paul Getty Trust).

51. Otto Wittmann, interview by Lynda Jenner, undated transcript, J. Paul Getty Trust Oral History Project, p. 47.

52. Williams, interview. Also see 1981 Annual Report, J. Paul Getty Trust.

53. 1981 Annual Report, J. Paul Getty Trust.

54. Williams, interview.

55. See Murphy, interview, Getty Trust Oral History Project.

56. Williams, interview.

57. See Wittmann, interview, Getty Trust Oral History Project.

58. See Murphy, interview, Getty Trust Oral History Project.

59. J. Paul Getty Trust, Program Review, 1981–85.

60. Williams, interview. Description of seven centers in 1981 from Getty Annual Report.

61. Deborah Marrow, interview by the author.

62. *Globe and Mail,* Mar. 15, 1982.

63. *Wall Street Journal,* Apr. 14, 1987.

64. Debra Whitefield, "The Deal: How Getty Ended up with Texaco," *Los Angeles Times,* Jan. 19, 1986.

65. *Wall Street Journal,* Apr. 14, 1987.

66. Williams, interview.

67. *Wall Street Journal,* Apr. 14, 1987.

68. Williams, interview.

69. Murphy, interview, Getty Trust Oral History Project, p. 31.

70. *Los Angeles Times,* Apr. 30, 1995.

71. Ibid.

72. Gribbon was made deputy director and chief curator of the J. Paul Getty Museum in 1998. In October 2000 she succeeded John Walsh as director and vice president. Press release, J. Paul Getty Trust, June 19, 2000.

73. *Los Angeles Times,* Dec. 7, 1997 (Christopher Knight).

74. Walsh and Gribbon, *The J. Paul Getty Museum,* p. 67.

75. Ibid.

76. Ibid.

77. Jake Zeitlin to FDM, letter, Mar. 3, 1982, Murphy Papers.

78. "The Trustee: Franklin D. Murphy," *Art Newspaper,* Jan. 1991.

79. *Los Angeles Times,* Apr. 30, 1995.

80. Ibid.

81. Early possibilities for locations included the Ambassador Hotel near downtown Los Angeles and the Veterans Administration Medical Center in Westwood, but both locations had problems and limitations. For a history of the Getty Center's site selection, see Rocco C. Siciliano, *Walking on Sand: The Story of an Immigrant Son and the Forgotten Art of Public Service* (Salt Lake City: University of Utah Press, 2004), pp. 241–50.

82. Suzanne Muchnic, "Getty Center Is More than Sum of Its Parts," *Los Angeles Times,* Nov. 30, 1997, p. A1. This article appeared in a series titled "The New Getty."

83. The trustees embarked on an international search for an architect for the proposed center, and by February 1984 the field was narrowed to three: Richard Meier of New York, Fumiko Maki of Tokyo, and James Stirling of London.

84. Walsh and Gribbon, *The J. Paul Getty Museum,* p. 84.

85. *Los Angeles Times,* Oct. 13, 1993.

86. Suzanne Muchnic, "A Windfall for the Arts from Getty," *Los Angeles Times,* Oct. 16, 1984. Also see Christopher Knight, "Generous Getty Gives $8.5 Million to Area Institutions," *Los Angeles Herald Examiner,* Oct. 16, 1984; "Getty Trust Drops Ban," *New York Times,* Oct. 17, 1984.

87. Nancy Englander to FDM, letter, Oct. 17, 1984, Murphy Papers. Also see Franklin Murphy, Chairman, Grants Committee, Draft Comments, Board of Trustees Meeting, Oct. 26, 1984; "Getty Trust Announces New Grant Program," J. Paul Getty Trust, press release, Oct. 11, 1984.

88. FDM to Harold Williams, letter, Aug. 13, 1987, "Local Grant Program" (chart) attached, Murphy Papers.

89. Murphy, interview, Getty Trust Oral History Project, p. 29.

90. Marrow, interview.

91. Abrahamson, "The J. Paul Getty Trust," pp. 33–34.

92. Williams, interview.

93. Frederick Rose, "Wealth of Woes: J. Paul Getty Museum in Los Angeles Is Beset by Critics, Uncertainty," *Wall Street Journal,* Apr. 16, 1987.

94. Murphy, interview, Getty Trust Oral History Project, pp. 33–34.

95. Marrow, interview.

96. Williams, interview.

97. FDM to Harold Williams, letter, May 20, 1987, Murphy Papers.

98. Christopher Knight, "Art Commentary: Lifting the Veil: Richard Meier's Design for the Getty Center Will at Last Put a Unified Face on a Far-Flung and Sometimes Confusing Art Empire," *Los Angeles Times,* Oct. 27, 1991.

99. Williams, interview. Also see Abrahamson, "The J. Paul Getty Trust," p. 25.

100. *Los Angeles Times,* Aug. 24, 1997.

101. Siciliano, *Walking on Sand,* p. 246. Rountree had deep family roots in the Los Angeles area. He completed his undergraduate degree at Occidental and later served as the college's director of personnel and assistant executive vice president. His wife, Carol, was an assistant dean. After he obtained his master's degree in management at the Claremont Graduate School in 1976, Rountree was hired by the Getty Museum in Malibu.

102. Stephen D. Rountree, interview by the author.

103. Ibid.

104. Paul Pringle, "High Art for LA: Getty Center Seen as Antidote for City's Inferiority Complex," *Dallas Morning News,* Nov. 10, 1997, p. 1A.

105. Murphy, interview, Getty Trust Oral History Project, p. 31.

106. *Los Angeles Times,* Sept. 11, 1988.

107. FDM to J. Carter Brown, letter, undated, Murphy Papers. Also see Suzanne Muchnic, "Don't Hate Him Because His Museum Is Filthy Rich; John Walsh Has Run the Museum since 1983. What Has He Learned about the Art World That He Didn't Know Before? Not Much about the Art Part," *Los Angeles Times Magazine,* Apr. 30, 1995.

108. *Los Angeles Times,* Oct. 27, 1991.

109. Daniel Wood, "Bold Museum Plan Given by Getty Trust; 110-Acre Cultural Campus to Be Built on Mountaintop," *Christian Science Monitor,* Oct. 21, 1991.

110. The Getty Center for the History of Art and the Humanities was established in 1983. In 1997 the name was changed to the Getty Research Institute for the History of Art and the Humanities, and in 1999 it was renamed the Getty Research Institute.

111. Wood, "Bold Museum Plan Given by Getty Trust."

112. Williams, interview.

113. *Los Angeles Times,* Nov. 30, 1997, p. A1.

114. Murphy, interview, Getty Trust Oral History Project, p. 45.

115. Williams, interview. Also see *The Economist,* Oct. 12, 1991; *Christian Science Monitor,* Oct. 21, 1991; *Los Angeles Times,* Nov. 30, 1997.

TWELVE: THREE THAT GOT AWAY

1. Kevin Starr, conversation with the author.

2. *Arts and Antiquities,* summer 1987. Murphy pointed out that Hammer memorialized the same promise in his autobiography: Armand Hammer with Neil Lyndon, *Hammer* (New York: Putnam, 1987).

3. Armand Hammer to Daniel Belin, letter with enclosure, July 23, 1987, Papers of Franklin D. Murphy, Dept. of Special Collections, University Library, UCLA (hereafter cited as Murphy Papers).

4. FDM to Earl Powell III, letter, Sept 9, 1987, Murphy Papers.

5. *New York Times,* Jan. 22, 1988; *Los Angeles Times,* Jan. 22, 1988; *Wall Street Journal,* Jan. 22, 1988.

6. *Los Angeles Times,* Jan. 27, 1988.

7. Robert A. Jones, "Battle for the Masterpieces: The Armand Hammer–County Museum Deal: A Saga of Art, Power and Big Misunderstandings," *Los Angeles Times Magazine,* May 22, 1988, pp. 18–19.

8. See Box 65, Murphy Papers.

9. Charles E. Young, interview by the author.

10. FDM to William F. Thomas, letter, Feb. 4, 1988, Murphy Papers.

11. J. Carter Brown to FDM, letter, Feb. 10, 1988, Murphy Papers.

12. *New York Times,* undated clipping, Murphy Papers.

13. Christopher Knight, "Hammer's Exercise in Superfluousness," *Los Angeles Times,* Nov. 25, 1990.

14. *New York Times* review, quoted in *Los Angeles Times,* Nov. 19, 1986, p. S1.

15. FDM to Robert O. Anderson, letter, June 10, 1988, Murphy Papers.

16. FDM to Robert O. Anderson, letter, June 28, 1988, Murphy Papers.

17. *Los Angeles Times,* July 21, 1988.

18. *Los Angeles Times,* Mar. 13, 1989.

19. Paul Conrad cartoon, *Los Angeles Times,* Box 65, Murphy Papers.

20. See Mona Gable, "The Bitter Legacy of Armand Hammer," *California,* Apr. 1991; "Hammer's Will Power," *National Law Journal,* Sept. 28, 1992; Jay Epstein, "The Last Days of Armand Hammer," *New Yorker,* Sept. 23, 1996, pp. 36–37.

21. Boxes 63–66, Murphy Papers. Wedged in the voluminous files are copies of legal complaints, work products connected with various civil actions, depositions, courtroom transcripts, stipulations and releases, compromises and settlements, newspaper and magazine clippings, and extensive personal correspondence between Hammer and Murphy.

22. Jonathan L. Kirsch, "Art, Law and Ego," *California Lawyer,* Sept. 1990, p. 30.

23. Walter Annenberg to FDM, letter, Feb. 4, 1991, Murphy Papers.

24. Box 65, Murphy Papers. In one of the Hammer file boxes Murphy deposited the available biographies and nonfiction books published about Armand Hammer. "Also in th[is] box are copies of two books," Murphy wrote. "One book is titled *Red Carpet* by Joseph Finder. It has become a very rare book in that when it was published Hammer arranged to have all of the copies he and his agents could get their hands on here in Southern California and elsewhere bought up and destroyed. The other book called *Armand Hammer, the Untold*

Story by Steve Weinberg again reveals many aspects of this man which he does not wish to have revealed." Murphy described the libel suit Hammer brought against Weinberg and his publisher in an effort to discredit the book. The book had been praised, and reviewers had noted the considerable contrast with Hammer's autobiography written with Neil Lyndon. Author Weinberg spent five years writing about the elusive tycoon and his contradictory life, interviewing over six hundred of Hammer's friends, enemies, and associates and studying hundreds of thousands of pages of documents (Steve Weinberg, interview by the author).

25. Murphy included in his materials on Hammer an article from the *Manhattan Lawyer,* noting in particular: "Like most pardons Hammer's is based on forgiveness rather than the finding of innocence that he long sought. It does not clear Hammer of his 1976 conviction—a fact overlooked by his chief counsel in its press release declaring victory." "Furthermore," Murphy added, remarking on the misleading spin Hammer was putting out about the pardon, "this is fairly typical of the way Hammer has operated all of his life."

26. Earl A. Powell III, interview by the author.

27. J. Carter Brown to FDM, letter, June 6, 1988, Murphy Papers.

28. William Wilson, "The March to Boutique Museums," *Los Angeles Times,* Jan. 22, 1988.

29. *ARTnews,* Nov. 1990.

30. Edward Jay Epstein, "The Last Days of Armand Hammer," *New Yorker,* Sept. 23, 1996, p. 36.

31. *Los Angeles Herald Examiner,* Jan. 31, 1988; *Apollo,* Mar. 1991.

32. *Vanity Fair,* Mar. 1991, p. 112.

33. Ibid. ·

34. Gable, "The Bitter Legacy of Armand Hammer," p. 92.

35. John Richardson, "Hammer Nailed: As an Art Impresario, Armand Hammer Was More P. T. Barnum than Lorenzo de' Medici," *Vanity Fair,* Mar. 1991, p. 112.

36. Epstein, "The Last Days of Armand Hammer."

37. *Chicago Tribune,* undated clipping, Murphy Papers.

38. *Los Angeles Times,* June 24, 1990.

39. Suzanne Muchnic, interview by the author. See also Suzanne Muchnic, *Odd Man In: Norton Simon and the Pursuit of Culture* (Berkeley: University of California Press, 1998), p. 6.

40. *Los Angeles Times,* June 24, 1990.

41. FDM to Norton Simon, letter, Sept. 7, 1988, Murphy Papers.

42. *Los Angeles Times,* Oct. 2, 2002, p. A1.

43. Paul Richard, "The Impeccable Pictures of Walter Annenberg," *Washington Post,* May 22, 1989.

44. FDM to Walter Annenberg, letter, Jan. 25, 1988, Murphy Papers.

45. Walter Annenberg to J. Carter Brown, letter, June 9, 1988, Murphy Papers.

46. William Wilson, "Walter Annenberg Surveys the Land," *Los Angeles Times, Calendar,* Aug. 12, 1990.

47. Ibid.

48. William Wilson's feature read in part: "Annenberg's charmed life has in fact been punctuated with tragedy, criticism and controversy. His ambassadorial appointment was roundly drubbed as a political payoff to an unqualified crony. His handling of the inquiry was scorned as manipulative and self-serving. Shortly after his first wife divorced him, his son, a schizophrenic, committed suicide. Earliest and worst, his tough, German-Jewish immigrant father, Morris Louis Annenberg, was indicted for tax evasion and bribery. He had realized the American dream from ground zero, struggling up through the unsavory Chicago newspaper wars until he purchased the Inquirer in 1936. The indictment came in 1939. Annenberg immediately pleaded guilty to avoid the threatened implication of his son. He was released from prison in 1944, after serving three years. A month after his release he was dead" (*Los Angeles Times,* Aug. 12, 1990).

49. Walter H. Annenberg to Robert F. Erburu, letter, Aug. 13, 1990, Murphy Papers.

50. Robert F. Erburu to Walter H. Annenberg, letter, Aug. 13, 1990, Murphy Papers.

51. Walter H. Annenberg to Robert F. Erburu, letter, Aug. 14, 1990, Murphy Papers.

52. FDM to Walter H. Annenberg, letter, Aug. 14, 1990, Murphy Papers.

53. *Washington Post,* Feb. 3, 1991.

54. Muchnic, interview. Also see Suzanne Muchnic, "$1 Billion in Annenberg Art for N.Y.," *Los Angeles Times,* Mar. 12, 1991, p. A1.

55. Muchnic, "$1 Billion in Annenberg Art for N.Y."

56. Suzanne Muchnic, "Annenberg to Give L.A. Art Museum $10 Million," *Los Angeles Times,* Mar. 14, 1991, p. B1.

57. *Washington Post,* Mar. 15, 1991.

58. Ibid.

59. Handwritten notes, Franklin Murphy speech, "Andrew W. Mellon Medal," undated, Murphy Papers.

60. Anonymous observer, interview by the author.

THIRTEEN: CHANGING OF THE GUARD

1. Times Mirror Annual Report, 1984, p. 59.

2. *Los Angeles Times,* June 17, 1994.

3. Robert F. Erburu, interview by the author.

4. *Columbia Journalism Review,* May 2000, p. 16.

5. Erburu, interview.

6. Cordelia Murphy Ennis, interview by the author.

7. Franklin D. Murphy, typed memo, "Family Background of Franklin D. Murphy," May 3, 1956, Papers of Franklin D. Murphy, Dept. of Special Collections, University Library, UCLA (hereafter cited as Murphy Papers).

8. FDM to Charles M. Thompson, M.D., letter, Nov. 23, 1987, Murphy Papers.

9. "Dr. George Murphy" (obituary written by Norman Cousins, undated), Murphy Papers.

10. Franklin D. Murphy, interview by David L. Lewis, Oct. 26, 1989, Oral History for the Ford Motor Company, Ford Corporate History Program, p. 57.

11. FDM to William Clay Ford, undated, Murphy Papers.

12. Murphy, interview by Lewis, Oral History for the Ford Motor Company, pp. 55–59.

13. FDM to David Mahoney, letter, Dec. 23, 1987, Murphy Papers.

14. FDM to Irvine O. Hockaday Jr., letter, Dec. 9, 1987, Murphy Papers.

15. FDM to Donald Kennedy, letter, Dec. 15, 1987, Murphy Papers. Dickey was accepted as a student at Stanford University and graduated in 1991.

16. *Forbes,* Apr. 12, 1993.

17. *Los Angeles Herald Examiner,* Dec. 12, 1984.

18. Richard Riordan, in conversation with the author.

19. William Wilson, "Franklin D. Murphy; A Civilizing Force for the City," *Los Angeles Times,* Calendar, June 17, 1994, p. F1.

20. Franklin D. Murphy, interview transcript, J. Paul Getty Trust Oral History Project, p. 43.

21. Robert Ahmanson, interview by the author.

22. Uri Herscher to FDM, letter, Aug. 20, 1986, Murphy Papers.

23. Frank J. Adler, *Roots in a Moving Stream: The Centennial History of Congregation B'nai Jehudah of Kansas City, 1870–1970* (Kansas City, Mo.: Congregation B'nai Jehudah, 1972), chap. 8, "1928–1945: Rabbi Samuel S. Mayerberg." See also "Governor's Bid Spurned: Kansas City Rabbi Will Testify on Police Only to Grand Jury," *New York Times,* Apr. 26, 1950 (referring to Mayerberg's activities against Pendergast in the 1930s).

24. Jody Jacobs, "Hebrew Union College to Celebrate," *Los Angeles Times,* Feb. 7, 1985.

25. Uri Herscher, interview by the author.

26. FDM to Uri Herscher, letter, Feb. 1, 1988, Murphy Papers.

27. FDM to Walter Haas Jr., letter, June 6, 1989, Murphy Papers.

28. Herscher, interview.

29. Franklin D. Murphy, "The Role of the University in a Troubled Society" (address to Town Hall, 1967), p. 15.

30. FDM to Russell Shank, letter, Nov. 27, 1981, Murphy Papers. Murphy insisted on building strong relationships between the center's new director, Gerald Yoshitomi, and UCLA university librarian Russell Shank. As chancellor at

UCLA Murphy had established the Japanese American Research Project in the Department of Special Collections, which contained a rich depository of personal papers from the Issei, Nisei, and Sansei generations. The collection contained correspondence, diaries, oral histories, and other primary sources that constituted the most extensive archive relating to Japanese immigration and wartime internment. The archives of the U.S. War Relocation Center at Manzanar, California, and rare photographs of the center by Ansel Adams were also in the collection. "Given the strong collection of Japanese materials at UCLA," Murphy told Shank, "it would be useful for the University to develop a relationship with the Japanese American Cultural Center which is supported by all of the significant Japanese Americans in Los Angeles."

31. FDM to Robert O. Anderson, letter, Apr. 17, 1980, Murphy Papers.

32. The rare honor was bestowed in recognition of Murphy's distinguished services "in the cause of strengthening the bonds of friendship between the United States and Japan, particularly in the realm of cultural exchange" (FDM to Tsuneo Tanaka, Japanese consul general, letter, Mar. 26, 1982, Murphy Papers). See also Consulate General of Japan, "Japanese Government to Confer Decoration on Dr. Franklin D. Murphy," press release, Oct. 28, 1982.

33. Franklin D. Murphy, "My UCLA Chancellorship: An Utterly Candid View," interview by James V. Mink, 1973, transcript 1976, Oral History Collection, Dept. of Special Collections, University Library, UCLA, pp. 62–64, 239–47.

34. *Los Angeles Times,* July 20, 1983.

35. Clark bequeathed the library to UCLA, which has since added more than seventy thousand books and manuscripts, mostly pre-1640 English literature. The bequest to UCLA stipulated that the collection could not be moved and was to be maintained in the beautiful building and scholarly setting that Clark had created.

36. "The Library, Their Legacy," *UCLA Librarian* 47, no. 2 (Winter–Spring 1995): 10. Also see *The Aldine Press: Catalogue of the Ahmanson-Murphy Collection of Books by or Relating to the Press in the Library of the University of California, Los Angeles, Incorporating Works Recorded Elsewhere* (Berkeley: University of California Press, 2001).

37. Daniel N. Belin, interview by the author. Also see "The Library, Their Legacy," p. 10.

38. "The Library, Their Legacy," p. 10.

39. FDM to Professor Mortimer Chambers, letter, date not specified, Murphy Papers.

40. FDM to Robert Vosper, letter, Aug. 24, 1981, Murphy Papers.

41. FDM to Chancellor Charles E. Young, letter, Nov. 18, 1981, Murphy Papers.

42. FDM to Lee E. Walcott, letter, Feb. 15, 1989; FDM to Robert H. Ahmanson, letter, Feb. 15, 1989, Murphy Papers.

43. One poignant letter from O'Casey, in simple words of deep compassion, concerned the assassination of President John F. Kennedy; he wrote Murphy at UCLA in 1963, "We cry out here against the terrible thing that has happened to you American people—this stupid, foul cutting down of a vigorous, flowering, and fruitful young American tree. Words become drunken things when they go to tell the hatred of this ill deed, or the sorrow filling our hearts over the death of your lovable young leader. Whatever hand fired the shots, it was the hand of a bloodier villain than terms can give out." Sean O'Casey to FDM, letter, undated, Murphy Papers.

44. FDM to Mrs. Sean O'Casey, letter, Sept. 22, 1964, Murphy Papers.

45. "This was no victimless crime," wrote columnist Patt Morrison of the *Los Angeles Times* about the devastating fire. "It was an assault on the city family." Patt Morrison, "4 Years after the Library Burned: A Continuing Saga," *Los Angeles Times,* Apr. 30, 1990, p. A1.

46. Paul Ong and Evelyn Blumenberg, "Income and Racial Inequality in Los Angeles," in *The City: Los Angeles and Urban Theory at the End of the Twentieth Century,* ed. Allen J. Scott and Edward Soja (Berkeley: University of California Press, 1996), p. 319.

47. Murphy, "The Role of the University in a Troubled Society," p. 15.

48. James D. Wolfensohn, Opening Keynote Address, in *Culture Counts: Financing, Resources, and the Economics of Culture in Sustainable Development: Proceedings of the Conference Held in Florence, Italy, October 4–7, 1999* (Washington, D.C.: World Bank, 2000).

49. The institution's endowment was inadequate for the needs of its operation. Huntington Library president Robert A. Skotheim told the *Los Angeles Times* that the institution could be compared to an impoverished dowager who sat in her crumbling mansion rather than vulgarize her lifestyle by getting a job. "Here we are in an elegant building but the irrigation system is antiquated and the roof leaks," he said. Skotheim's predecessor, Robert Middlekauff, author and former provost of the University of California at Berkeley, had taken on the challenge of balancing the budget over the course of his five-year directorship, but the distinguished library still faced years of acute shortfalls in operating income without the cushion of a sufficient endowment. Suzanne Muchnic, "Garden of Hope: Heading off a Projected Shortfall, the Huntington Is Finding Ways to Boost Revenues, including Increased Membership and Mandatory Entrance Fees," *Los Angeles Times,* Aug. 13, 1995, Calendar.

50. The Ahmanson Foundation, Organization Profile Report, Henry E. Huntington Library and Art Gallery, Nov. 21, 2002. Robert Ahmanson called the works in the Huntington Library "invaluable resources" that need "not only the community's but the nation's attention in bringing them to a state where their true capacity can be realized."

51. Franklin Murphy, "Pluralism and Philanthropy—The Uniquely American

Tradition" (address to Chancellor's Club Dinner, University of Kansas, Dec. 12, 1978), p. 12.

52. *Los Angeles Times,* June 25, 1991.

53. "He [Erburu] has, in fact, been the leading fundraiser in the institution's history," observed the Huntington's Robert Skotheim. The Huntington Library, Art Collections, and Botanical Gardens, *Calendar* for Mar.–Apr. 2001.

FOURTEEN: THE DOGE OF LOS ANGELES

1. The opening of the long-awaited museum was acclaimed by the *Los Angeles Times* as coming at a time when cultural diversity was emerging as a major issue in American education.

2. *Los Angeles Times,* Sept. 27, 1992. The *Times* capsulized the long road to the Fowler Museum's creation:

> Twenty-nine years after then–UCLA Chancellor Franklin D. Murphy established the museum as the Museum Laboratories of Ethnic Arts and Technology; 25 years after the last of 30,000 objects in Sir Henry Wellcome's ethnic art collection were donated to UCLA; 17 years after Chancellor Charles E. Young appointed anthropologist Christopher B. Donnan director of the museum and charged him with fundraising for a new building; 14 years after the museum's interim home opened in the basement of Haines Hall; 9 years after the Regents of University of California approved a new museum facility; eight years after the museum's principal benefactors, Francis E. Fowler II, Phillip F. Fowler and the Francis E. Fowler Jr. Foundation, made the lead gift of construction; 5 years after ground was broken; and four years after the last exhibition was held in Haines Hall, the university is opening what Young hails as "the premier cultural facility in the Los Angeles area dedicated to non-Western artistic traditions."

3. Franklin D. Murphy, "My UCLA Chancellorship: An Utterly Candid View," interview by James V. Mink, 1973, transcript 1976, Oral History Collection, Dept. of Special Collections, University Library, UCLA, pp. 230–32. *Los Angeles Times,* Oct. 16, 1992.

4. Daniel N. Belin, interview by the author.

5. *Calendar,* Huntington Library, Art Collections and Botanical Gardens, Jan.–Feb. 1993. "As befits a modern Medici, the evening began with the viewing of early Renaissance printed treasures," gushed the *Times.* "The literary art works included the first printing of Dante's 'Divine Comedy,' Albrecht Durer's famed prints from 'The Apocalypse' and an original edition of John Milton's 'Areopagitica.'"

6. National Gallery of Art, "Board of Trustees Elects Earl A. Powell III New Director of the National Gallery of Art," press release, Apr. 28, 1992. In Los Angeles Powell had assumed the directorship of the county museum at a moment when the institution was far from world class and its board was locked in battle with its professional staff. He had managed to increase the museum's budget over

twelve years from $8.5 million to $31 million; he doubled the museum's attendance and membership and successfully completed the museum's $80 million capital campaign.

7. *Los Angeles Times,* Oct. 2, 1992.

8. Ibid.

9. *Los Angeles Times,* Sept. 3, 1991.

10. *Christ on the Cross with Saints Mark, John the Baptist, Vincent Ferrer and the Blessed Antoninus* (Master of the Fiesole Epiphany).

11. Suzanne Muchnic, "Art, History and the Real World," *Los Angeles Times,* Oct. 3, 1993.

12. Handwritten notes, Franklin Murphy, speech, National Gallery Banquet, Sept. 29, 1993, Papers of Franklin D. Murphy, Dept. of Special Collections, University Library, UCLA (hereafter cited as Murphy Papers).

13. Murphy did not live to see Erburu's appointment as chairman at the National Gallery, which occurred in 2000.

14. Fontaine joined the Kress Foundation board in 1975.

15. Clark Kerr, interview by the author.

16. Robert Ahmanson, interview by the author.

17. Walter Kaiser to Judy Murphy, letter, July 15, 1994, Murphy Papers.

18. "Remarks by Robert F. Erburu at the Memorial Service Honoring Dr. Franklin D. Murphy," June 30, 1994. (Courtesy of the Ahmanson Foundation.)

19. "A Death in the L.A. Family" (editorial), *Los Angeles Times,* June 14, 1994; William A Wilson, "Franklin D. Murphy; A Civilizing Force for the City," *Los Angeles Times,* June 17, 1994.

20. Carolyn Speer, interview by the author; Franklin L. Murphy, interview by the author.

21. *Los Angeles Times,* Sept. 25, 2003.

22. Dennis McDougal, *Privileged Son: Otis Chandler and the Rise and Fall of the L.A. Times Dynasty* (New York: Perseus, 2001), p. 433.

23. Anonymous observer, interview by the author.

24. "Remarks by Robert F. Erburu at the Memorial Service Honoring Dr. Franklin D. Murphy."

25. Paul Richard, "Paul Mellon's Final Gifts," *Washington Post,* Feb. 11, 1999, p. A1.

26. Dr. Marilyn Perry, interview by Alfred C. Viebranz, Mar. 6, 1995, Oral History Program, National Gallery of Art, p. 16.

27. *Washington Times,* June 20, 2002, p. A20.

28. It has been reported that Times Mirror stock went from $23.25 on the day Mark Willes arrived to a high of $72.63. But the stock price fell 35 percent from that high to $47.94 by winter 1999.

29. *Independent,* Mar. 19, 2000 (Andrew Gumbel).

30. Dean Baquet to editorial staff, *Los Angeles Times,* e-mail, Feb. 28, 2006.

31. *Los Angeles Times,* Dec. 4, 1997, p. A1 (Michael Hiltzik).

32. The Ahmanson Foundation, Annual Report, 2002.

AFTERWORD: THE MOSAIC CITY

1. Franklin Murphy, "The Practical Value of Humanistic Study" (speech, Plenary Meeting XVII of the President's Committee on the Arts and the Humanities, Mar. 31, 1988).

2. See D. J. Waldie, *Holy Land: A Suburban Memoir* (New York: St. Martin's Press, 1996).

3. James Flanigan, interview with the author. (From his forthcoming book to be published by Stanford University Press.)

4. Joan Didion, *Where I Was From* (New York: Alfred A. Knopf, 2003), p. 129.

5. E. Soja, "It All Comes Together in Los Angeles," in *Postmodern Geographies: The Reassertion of Space in Critical Social Theory* (New York: Verso, 1989), pp. 190–221.

6. Michael J. Dear, *The Postmodern Urban Condition* (Oxford: Blackwell, 1999), p. 143, citing J. Garreau, *Edge City: Life on the New Frontier* (Garden City, N.Y.: Doubleday, 1991), p. 3.

7. *Los Angeles Times,* Oct. 19, 2003, p. A1 (Nicolai Ouroussoff).

FRANKLIN D. MURPHY'S
POSITIONS AND AFFILIATIONS

EMPLOYMENT

1948–51   Dean of the School of Medicine and Associate Professor of
           Internal Medicine, University of Kansas
1951–60   Chancellor of the University of Kansas
1960–68   Chancellor of the University of California, Los Angeles
1968–81   Chairman of the Board and Chief Executive Officer, Times
           Mirror Company
1981–86   Chairman of the Executive Committee, Times Mirror Company
1986–94   Director Emeritus, Times Mirror Company

CORPORATE BOARD DIRECTORSHIPS

Bank of America
Ford Motor Company
Hallmark Cards, Inc.
McCall Corporation
Norton Simon Inc.
Times Mirror Company

CULTURAL FOUNDATIONS AND INSTITUTIONS

Chairman
Samuel H. Kress Foundation
Los Angeles County Museum, Board of Trustees
National Gallery of Art

President

Samuel H. Kress Foundation
Los Angeles County Museum, Board of Trustees

Trustee

The Ahmanson Foundation
California Museum of Science and Industry
The J. Paul Getty Trust
Los Angeles County Museum, Museum Associates
National Gallery of Art
Skirball Cultural Center, Honorary Posthumous

Fellow

Royal Society of Arts

Member

Museum of Archeology and Anthropology, University of Pennsylvania, Board
   of Overseers
Presidential Task Force on the Arts and Humanities
President's Committee on the Arts and Humanities

CIVIC, PUBLIC AFFAIRS, EDUCATIONAL,
AND SCIENTIFIC ORGANIZATIONS

Chairman

American Council on Education
Carnegie Foundation for the Advancement of Teaching, Board of Trustees
Commission on Intergovernmental Relations, Study Committee on Federal
   Aid to Public Health
Council on Higher Education in the American Republics
President's Biomedical Research Panel

President

State Universities Association

Trustee

Carnegie Institution of Washington
Eisenhower Exchange Scholarship Program
Institute of International Education
Salk Institute
University of Pennsylvania

Fellow

American Academy of Arts and Sciences
American Association for the Advancement of Science

Member

Alpha Omega Alpha

American Board of Internal Medicine

American College of Physicians

American Council of Education, Committee on Institutional Research Policy
and Committee on Problems and Policies

American Legion, Medical Advisory Commission

American Medical Association, Council on Medical Education and Hospitals

Beta Theta Pi

Boy Scouts of America, National Council

College of Physicians of Philadelphia

Federal Commission on Government Security

Foreign Intelligence Advisory Board

Institute of Medicine, National Academy of Sciences

National War College, Board of Consultants

Nu Sigma Nu

Peace Corps National Advisory Council

Phi Beta Kappa

President's Task Force on Private Sector Initiatives

Sigma Xi

United States Advisory Commission on International Educational Cultural
Affairs

United States Air Force, Board of Visitors to the Air University

Urban Institute

Veterans Administration, Special Medical Advisory Group

Woodrow Wilson National Fellowship Foundation

SELECTED BIBLIOGRAPHY

A NOTE ON SOURCES

Franklin Murphy had a reputation for tossing out papers and giving no attention to preserving a record of his achievements. His longtime associates thought there would be little material surviving in his private files. But they were wrong. Murphy, in fact, preserved an astounding record of his life and activities. The collection of Murphy's papers is unusual in terms of its size, scope, and contents. It spans the years 1944–94 and consists of ninety-one boxes containing more than ten thousand documents (90 linear feet). Murphy's carefully preserved correspondence, something of a who's who of the twentieth century, reveals the extent of his influence on the cultural arts and the personal satisfaction he took in his lifelong activities.

The surviving personal papers of Dorothy Chandler have only recently been made available. They were donated to the University Library's Department of Special Collections at UCLA by her family in 2002. Although the files have seemingly been purged before their disposition, the files (twenty-one boxes, or 10.5 linear feet) are still a rich revelation of details connected with Chandler's involvement with the Los Angeles Music Center and other civic endeavors. In addition, I was able to locate the only known oral history given by Dorothy Chandler, conducted in 1981 by Anita J. Klaz, a graduate student at California State University, Northridge. In the complete transcript of the interview Mrs. Chandler provides a surprisingly lengthy and candid discussion of her work for the Times Mirror Company as well as her thoughts and feelings about her role.

The university archives at both UCLA and the University of Kansas contain a rich resource of documents and correspondence concerning Murphy's tenure as chancellor. The texts of Murphy's many speeches, spanning the years 1946–94, cover a broad range of issues and ideas and shed a great deal of light on his evolving interests and points of view. A multitude of sources, including numerous oral histories, manuscript collections, letters, diaries, office files, memoirs, newspapers, periodicals, and interviews, are listed in the bibliography.

INTERVIEWS BY THE AUTHOR

Ahmanson, Robert. Beverly Hills, Jan. 29, Feb. 27, Mar. 5 and 26, 2002; Aug. 16, 2004.

Belin, Daniel. Beverly Hills, Apr. 18 and June 26, 2001.

Chung, Francis. Beverly Hills, Jan. 29, Feb. 27, Mar. 5 and 26, 2002.

Clark, Jim. Los Angeles, Oct. 2, 2002.

Daniels, Maygene. Washington, D.C., June 5, Oct. 3 and 4, 2001.

DeKruif, Robert. San Marino, Feb. 25 and Sept. 23, 2002.

Ennis, Cordelia. Pasadena, Feb. 13, Mar. 7, 13, and 31, and Oct. 6, 2002.

Ennis, Lyman. Pasadena, Mar. 7 and 13, 2002.

Ennis, Rebecca. Pasadena, Mar. 31, 2002.

Erburu, Mrs. Lois. Beverly Hills, Dec. 22, 2001.

Erburu, Robert F. Beverly Hills, Apr. 17, May 30, Aug. 8, Oct. 3, Nov. 6 and 28, 2001; Sept. 5, 2002; Jan. 22 and 23, 2003.

Farneth, David. Los Angeles, Sept. 21 and Dec. 11, 2001.

Fernald, Peter. Pasadena, May 3, 2001; Jan. 16, 20, and 27, and Feb. 3, 2003.

Herscher, Dr. Uri. Los Angeles, Apr. 4, Oct. 31, Nov. 12 and 13, 2001; May 27, 2002.

Higginson, Genevra. Washington, D.C., Oct. 4, 2001.

Kerr, Clark. Berkeley, Sept. 25, 2001.

Marrow, Deborah. Los Angeles, Dec. 11, 2001.

McDougal, Dennis. Los Angeles, May 29, 2001; May 23, 2002.

Meyers, Jack. Los Angeles, May 10, 2002.

Muchnic, Suzanne. Los Angeles, Apr. 11 and Sept. 17, 2001; Sept. 18, 2002.

Murphy, Franklin L. Los Angeles, Mar. 8 and Oct. 15, 2002.

Pavon, Phyllis. Beverly Hills, Apr. 16, 2001.

Perry, Marilyn. Los Angeles, Sept. 10, 2002.

Powell, Earl A., III. Washington, D.C., Oct. 3, 2001.

Ritchie, Anne G. Washington, D.C., Oct. 3, 4, and 5, 2001.

Rountree, Stephen D. Los Angeles, Nov. 14 and 20, 2001.

Speer, Carolyn Murphy. Brentwood, Apr. 9, Sept. 11 and 13, and Oct. 30, 2002.

Speroni, Carmela. Brentwood, Jan. 10 and 24, 2002.

Starr, Lori. Los Angeles, Apr. 4, 2000; Apr. 31 and Aug. 6, 2001.

Steele, Victoria. Westwood, Jan. 28 and 29, 2003.

Walcott, Lee. Beverly Hills, Nov. 26, 2001.

Williams, Harold. Los Angeles, Oct. 1, 2001; Oct. 10 and 17, 2002.

Young, Charles E. Westwood, Dec. 20 and 27, 2001; Sept. 16, 2002.

Zeidberg, David S. San Marino, Aug. 7 and Sept. 18, 2001.

ORAL HISTORIES

Byrne, Jerome C. "Oral History Interview with Jerome C. Byrne, Special Counsel, Special Forbes Committee of the Regents of the University of California, 1965." Interview by Dale E. Treleven, June 3, 8, and 15, 1993. Oral History Program, University of California, Los Angeles, and State Government Oral History Program.

[Chandler, Dorothy Buffum] Klaz, Anita J. "An Oral History of Dorothy Buffum Chandler." M.A. thesis, California State University, Northridge, 1981.

Frederickson, Hansena. "UCLA Administration, 1936–1968." Interview by James V. Mink, 1966. Transcript, 1969. Oral History Collection, Department of Special Collections, University Library, University of California, Los Angeles.

Haldeman, H. R. Interview by Dale E. Treleven. Transcript, 1991. Department of Special Collections, University Library, University of California, Los Angeles.

Kerr, Clark. "University of California Crises: Loyalty Oath and Free Speech Movement." Interview by Amelia Fry, Sept. 29, 1969. In "Earl Warren: Views and Episodes: Oral History Transcript." Earl Warren Oral History Project, Regional Oral History Office, Bancroft Library, University of California, Berkeley.

———. Interview by David Turney (professor of education, Indiana State University), Mar. 23, 1982. In "Interviews with 18 University Presidents: Oral History Transcripts, 1981–1982." Regional Oral History Office, Bancroft Library, University of California, Berkeley.

Kerr, Clark, and Morton Meyer. "Interviews with Clark Kerr and Morton Meyer: Eyewitnesses to UC Campus Turmoil in the Mid-1960s." Interviews by Nancy M. Rockafellar, May 2, 1995. Transcript, 1996. UCSF Oral History Program, Archival Interview Series, no. 13. Oral History Program, University of California, San Francisco.

Mellon, Paul. Interviews by Robert Bowen, July 26–27 and Nov. 10, 1988. National Gallery of Art Oral History Program.

Murphy, Franklin D. "My UCLA Chancellorship: An Utterly Candid View." Interview by James V. Mink, 1973. Transcript, 1976. Oral History Collection, Department of Special Collections, University Library, University of California, Los Angeles.

———. Interview by David L. Lewis, Oct. 26, 1989. Oral History for the Ford Motor Company, Ford Corporate History Program, Dearborn, Michigan.

————. Interview by Deborah Hickle, Jan. 19, 1990. University of Kansas School of Medicine Oral History Project.

————. Interview by Alfred C. Viebranz, Jan. 24 and May 2, 1990. National Gallery of Art Oral History Program.

————. Interview, undated. The J. Paul Getty Trust Oral History Project.

Murphy, Judith. "Chancellor's Spouse." Interview by Dale E. Treleven, 1995. Transcript, 1997. Oral History Collection, Department of Special Collections, University Library, University of California, Los Angeles.

Perry, Marilyn. Interview by Alfred C. Viebranz, Mar, 6, 1995. National Gallery of Art Oral History Program.

Sherwood, Foster H. (UCLA vice-chancellor, academic affairs). Interview by James V. Mink, 1987. Transcript, 1989. Oral History Collection, Department of Special Collections, University Library, University of California, Los Angeles.

Speroni, Charles. "Dean, Mentor, Colleague: Bridging Humanities and Fine Arts at UCLA." Interview by Bernard Galm, 1980. Transcript, 1988. Oral History Collection, Department of Special Collections, University Library, University of California, Los Angeles.

Strong, Edward W. "Philosopher, Professor, and Berkeley Chancellor, 1961–1965." Interview by Harriet Nathan, 1988. Transcript, 1992. Regional Oral History Office, Bancroft Library, University of California, Berkeley.

Vosper, Robert G. "Libraries and the Inquiring Mind." Interview by Dale E. Treleven, 1990–91. Transcript, 1994. Oral History Collection, Department of Special Collections, University Library, University of California, Los Angeles.

Wellman, Harry R. "Teaching, Research, and Administration, University of California 1925–1968." Interview by Malca Chall, 1972–73. Transcript, 1976. Regional Oral History Office, Bancroft Library, University of California, Berkeley.

Williams, Arleigh. "Dean of Students Arleigh Williams, the Free Speech Movement, and the Six Years War, 1964–1970." Interview by Germaine LaBerge, 1988–89. Transcript, 1990. Regional Oral History Office, Bancroft Library, University of California, Berkeley.

Wittmann, Otto. Interview by Lynda Jenner, undated. The J. Paul Getty Trust Oral History Project.

Young, Charles E. (Not yet released, no date or interviewer indicated.) Courtesy of Chancellor Charles E. Young.

COLLECTIONS

Administrative Subject Files for Chancellor Franklin D. Murphy, 1935–71. Lawrence Clark Powell Library, University of California, Los Angeles.

Archives of the Ahmanson Foundation, Los Angeles.

Chancellor's Papers, University Archives, University of Kansas, Lawrence.

Letters of Teddy Kollek. Courtesy of Teddy Kollek and Uri Herscher.

Letters, photographs, and memorabilia of Franklin D. Murphy owned by Dr. Franklin Lee Murphy.

Letters, photographs, and memorabilia of Franklin D. Murphy owned by Carolyn Murphy Speer.

Letters, photographs, and memorabilia of Carmela Speroni, Los Angeles.

Los Angeles Archival Collection of Nicholas A. Curry, Pasadena, Calif.

Papers of Dorothy Chandler. Department of Special Collections, University Library, University of California, Los Angeles. Cited below as Dorothy Chandler Papers.

Papers of Franklin D. Murphy. Department of Special Collections, University Library, University of California, Los Angeles. Cited below as Murphy Papers.

University Archives, University of California, Los Angeles.

University Archives, University of Kansas, Lawrence.

ANNUAL REPORTS

The Ahmanson Foundation. Courtesy of Robert Ahmanson.

The J. Paul Getty Trust. Courtesy of David Farneth, Getty Research Institute.

The Samuel H. Kress Foundation. Courtesy of Dr. Marilyn Perry and Daniel N. Belin.

The Times Mirror Company. Courtesy of Robert F. Erburu.

ARCHIVAL MATERIAL

Abrahamson, Eric John. "The J. Paul Getty Trust: A Brief Institutional History." Draft, Oct. 8, 2001. Courtesy of the J. Paul Getty Trust.

The Ahmanson Foundation Officer and Trustee History. Courtesy of Robert Ahmanson.

Bach, Margaret. "The Ahmanson Foundation: Forty Years of Building Community, 1952–1992." Manuscript, June 1993. Courtesy of Robert Ahmanson.

Belin, Daniel N. "Evelle J. Younger v. The Ahmanson Foundation, The Ahmanson Foundation v. U.S." Memorandum. Courtesy of Daniel N. Belin.

Hamilton, Andrew. "Some Curious and Relevant Facts about UCLA's University Residence." Dec. 19, 1968. University Archives, University of California, Los Angeles.

Mitchell, Diana. "Speaking of First Ladies." Senior Project, California State Polytechnic College, 1969. Dorothy Chandler Papers.

Murphy, Franklin D. "Family Background of Franklin D. Murphy." May 3, 1956. Murphy Papers.

Pitts, Heidi. "Racism and Reformation with Franklin Murphy." May 13, 1992. University Archives, University of Kansas, Lawrence.

Rountree, Stephen D. "Reflections on Franklin D. Murphy as Chair of the J. Paul Getty Trust Building Committee." Courtesy of Stephen D. Rountree.

BOOKS, ARTICLES, DISSERTATIONS

Adler, Frank J. *Roots in a Moving Stream: The Centennial History of Congregation B'nai Jehudah of Kansas City, 1870–1970.* Kansas City, Mo.: Congregation B'nai Jehudah, 1972.

The Ahmanson Gifts: European Masterpieces in the Collection of the Los Angeles County Museum of Art. Los Angeles: Museum Associates, 1991.

The Aldine Press: Catalogue of the Ahmanson-Murphy Collection of Books by or Relating to the Press in the Library of the University of California, Los Angeles, Incorporating Works Recorded Elsewhere. Edited by Nicolas Barker et al. Berkeley: University of California Press, 2001.

Aldus Manutius and Renaissance Culture: Essays in Memory of Franklin D. Murphy: Acts of an International Conference, Venice and Florence, 14–17 June 1994. Edited by David S. Zeidberg with the assistance of Fiorella Gioffredi Superbi. Florence: Leo S. Olschki, 1998.

Alexander, Christopher, Sara Ishikawa, Murray Silverstein, with Max Jacobson, Ingrid Fiksdahl-King, and Shlomo Angel. *A Pattern Language: Towns, Buildings, Construction.* New York: Oxford University Press, 1977.

Ali, Tariq, and Susan Watkins. *1968, Marching in the Streets.* New York: Free Press, 1998.

Ambrose, Stephen E. *Nixon: The Education of a Politician, 1913–1962.* New York: Simon & Schuster, 1987.

Ameringer, Charles D. *U.S. Foreign Intelligence: The Secret Side of American History.* Lexington, Mass.: Lexington Books, 1990.

Asseyev, Tamara Constance. "The Development of the Los Angeles Music Center Project." M.A. thesis, University of California, Los Angeles, 1968.

Bellows, Jim. *The Last Editor: How I Saved the New York Times, the Washington Post, and the Los Angeles Times from Dullness and Complacency.* Kansas City, Mo.: Andrews McMeel, 2002.

Bernstein, Carl, and Bob Woodward. *The Final Days.* New York: Simon & Schuster, 1976.

Beschloss, Michael R. *The Crisis Years: Kennedy and Khrushchev, 1960–1963.* New York: Edward Burlingame Books, 1991.

Books Included in the Ahmanson-Murphy Collection of Early Italian Printing (through 1600) at UCLA. Los Angeles: Department of Special Collections, University Research Library, University of California, Los Angeles, 1992.

Brodie, Fawn M. *Richard Nixon: The Shaping of His Character.* Cambridge, Mass.: Harvard University Press, 1983.

Buccellati, Giorgio, and Charles Speroni, eds. *The Shape of the Past: Studies in Honor of Franklin D. Murphy.* Los Angeles: Institute of Archaeology and Office of the Chancellor, University of California, Los Angeles, 1981.

Burlingham, Cynthia, and Elizabeth Shepherd, eds. *In the Sculptor's Landscape:*

Celebrating Twenty-five years of the Franklin D. Murphy Sculpture Garden. Los Angeles: Frederick S. Wight Art Gallery, University of California, Los Angeles, 1993.

Cannell, Michael. *I. M. Pei: Mandarin on Modernism.* New York: Carol Southern Books, 1995.

Cannon, Lou. *President Reagan: A Role of a Lifetime.* New York: Simon & Schuster, 1991.

Clifford, Griffin S. *The University of Kansas: A History.* Lawrence: University Press of Kansas, 1974.

Cohen, Lizabeth. *A Consumers' Republic: The Politics of Mass Consumption in Postwar America.* New York: Vintage Books, 2004.

Coll, Steve. *The Taking of Getty Oil: The Full Story of the Most Spectacular—& Catastrophic—Takeover of All Time.* New York: Atheneum, 1987.

Dallek, Robert. *Ronald Reagan: The Politics of Symbolism.* Boston: Harvard University Press, 1984.

Davis, Kenneth. *Kansas: A Bicentennial History.* New York: Norton, 1976.

Davis, Margaret Leslie. *The Biltmore Hotel: Host of the Coast.* Los Angeles: Archetype Press, 1998.

————. *Dark Side of Fortune: Triumph and Scandal in the Life of Oil Tycoon Edward L. Doheny.* Berkeley: University of California Press, 1998.

————. *Rivers in the Desert: William Mulholland and the Inventing of Los Angeles.* New York: HarperCollins, 1993.

Dear, Michael J. *The Postmodern Urban Condition.* Oxford: Blackwell, 1999.

Deverell, William. *Whitewashed Adobe: The Rise of Los Angeles and the Remaking of Its Mexican Past.* Berkeley: University of California Press, 2004.

Didion, Joan. *Where I Was From.* New York: Alfred A. Knopf, 2003.

Erie, Steven P. *Globalizing L.A.: Trade, Infrastructure, and Regional Development.* Stanford: Stanford University Press, 2004.

Finley, David Edward. *A Standard of Excellence: Andrew Mellon Founds the National Gallery of Art at Washington, D.C.* Washington, D.C.: Smithsonian Institution Press, 1973.

Fisher, Michael P. "The Turbulent Years: The University of Kansas, 1960–1975, a History." Ph.D. diss., University of Kansas, 1979.

Fogelson, Robert M. *The Fragmented Metropolis: Los Angeles, 1850–1930.* Berkeley: University of California Press, 1995.

Franklin D. Murphy Sculpture Garden, University of California, Los Angeles: An Annotated Catalogue of the Collection. Los Angeles: Frederick S. Wight Art Gallery, University of California, Los Angeles, 1984.

The Franklin E. Murphy, M.D., Fund: A List of Books Acquired by the History and Special Collections Division of the Louise Darling Biomedical Library: From the Inception of the Fund to the Present, 1975—1991. Los Angeles: University of California, Los Angeles, 1992.

Garson, Marvin. *The Regents.* Rev. ed. Berkeley: Independent Socialist Club, 1967. [Originally printed by the Free Speech Movement in 1965.]

Garvin, Alexander. *The American City: What Works, What Doesn't.* New York: McGraw Hill, 1996.

Gottlieb, Robert, Mark Valliantos, Regina M. Freer, and Peter Dreier. *The Next Los Angeles: The Struggle for a Livable City.* Berkeley: University of California Press, 2002.

Greene, Robert, and Joost Elfers. *The 48 Laws of Power.* New York: Viking, 1998.

Halberstam, David. *The Fifties.* New York: Villard Books, 1993.

————. *The Powers That Be.* New York: Alfred A. Knopf, 1979.

Hamilton, Andrew, and John B. Jackson. *UCLA on the Move, during Fifty Golden Years, 1919–1969.* Los Angeles: Ward Ritchie Press, 1969.

Harper, Nancy Kellogg. "Higher Education Leadership: Franklin D. Murphy in Kansas, 1948–1960." Ph.D. diss., University of Kansas, 1995.

Heirich, Max. *The Beginning: Berkeley, 1964.* New York: Columbia University Press, 1968.

Ishikawa, Chiyo. *A Gift to America: Masterpieces of European Painting from the Samuel H. Kress Collection.* With essays by Marilyn Perry and Edgar Peters Bowron. New York: Harry N. Abrams, 1994.

Jasper Johns to Jeff Koons: Four Decades of Art from the Broad Collections. Los Angeles: Los Angeles County Museum of Art in association with Harry N. Abrams, 2001.

Judis, John B. *The Paradox of American Democracy: Elites, Special Interests and the Betrayal of Public Trust.* New York: Pantheon Books, 2000.

Kerr, Clark. *The Gold and the Blue: A Personal Memoir of the University of California.* 2 vols. Berkeley: University of California Press, 2001–3.

Klabin, Israel. "The Intrinsic Value of Heritage." In *Culture in Sustainable Development: Investing in Cultural and Natural Endowments: Proceedings of the Conference on Culture in Sustainable Development—Investing in Cultural and Natural Endowments at the World Bank in Washington, D.C. on September 28–29, 1998,* ed. Ismail Serageldinn and Joan Martin-Brown. Washington, D.C.: World Bank, 1999.

Kopper, Philip. *America's National Gallery of Art: A Gift to the Nation.* New York: Harry N. Abrams, 1991.

Los Angeles County Museum of Art. *X, a Decade of Collecting, 1965–1975.* Los Angeles: LACMA, 1975.

Lamott, Kenneth. *The Moneymakers: The Great Big New Rich in America.* Boston: Little, Brown, 1968.

Lankford, Nelson D. *The Last American Aristocrat: The Biography of Ambassador David K. E. Bruce.* Boston: Little, Brown, 1996.

Marchetti, Victor, and John D. Marks. *The CIA and the Cult of Intelligence.* New York: Alfred A. Knopf, 1974.

Marts, Arnaud C. *Philanthropy's Role in Civilization: Its Contribution to Human Freedom.* New Brunswick, N.J.: Transaction Publishers, 1991.

Mason, Alexandra. "Vosper and Murphy in the Great American Desert." Paper presented to the Conference of the Rare Books and Manuscripts Section of the Association of College and Research Libraries, San Francisco, June 25, 1981.

Mayer, Jane, and Doyle McManus. *Landslide: The Unmaking of the President.* New York: Houghton Mifflin, 1988.

McDougal, Dennis. *Privileged Son: Otis Chandler and the Rise and Fall of the L.A. Times Dynasty.* New York: Perseus, 2001.

McGirr, Lisa. *Suburban Warriors: The Origins of the New American Right.* Princeton: Princeton University Press, 2001.

McWilliams, Carey. *Southern California: An Island on the Land.* Salt Lake City: Gibbs M. Smith, 1946, 1973.

Mellon, Paul, with John Baskett. *Reflections in a Silver Spoon.* New York: William Morrow, 1992.

Muchnic, Suzanne. *Odd Man In: Norton Simon and the Pursuit of Culture.* Berkeley: University of California Press, 1998.

The Music Center Story: A Decade of Achievement, 1964–1974. Edited by James W. Toland. Los Angeles: Music Center Foundation, 1974.

Nielsen, Waldemar A. *Golden Donors: A New Anatomy of the Great Foundations.* New Brunswick, N.J.: Transaction Publishers, 2001.

———. *Inside American Philanthropy: The Dramas of Donorship.* Norman: University of Oklahoma Press, 1996.

Noonan, Peggy. *What I Saw at the Revolution: A Political Life in the Reagan Era.* New York: Random House, 1990.

Nystrom, Richard Kent. "UCLA: An Interpretation Considering Architecture and Site." Ph.D. diss., University of California, Los Angeles, 1968.

Ong, Paul, and Evelyn Blumenberg. "Income and Racial Inequality in Los Angeles." In *The City: Los Angeles and Urban Theory at the End of the Twentieth Century,* ed. Allen J. Scott and Edward Soja. Berkeley: University of California Press, 1996.

Pitt, Leonard, and Dale Pitt. *Los Angeles A to Z.* Berkeley: University of California Press, 1997.

Reeves, Richard. *The Reagan Detour.* New York: Simon & Schuster, 1985.

Rosenfeld, Seth. "Reagan, Hoover and the UC Red Scare." *San Francisco Chronicle,* June 9, 2002.

Royce, Josiah. *California from the Conquest in 1846 to the Second Vigilance Committee in San Francisco [1856]: A Study of the American Character.* Boston: Houghton Mifflin, 1886.

Savio, Mario, et al. *The Free Speech Movement and the Negro Revolution.* Detroit: News & Letters, 1965.

Schmidt, Ronald J., Jr. *This Is the City: Making Model Citizens in Los Angeles.* Minneapolis: University of Minnesota Press, 2005.

Siciliano, Rocco C. *Walking on Sand: The Story of an Immigrant Son and the Forgotten Art of Public Service.* Salt Lake City: University of Utah Press, 2004.

Starr, Kevin. *Embattled Dreams: California in War and Peace, 1940–1950.* New York: Oxford University Press, 2002.

―――. *Endangered Dreams: The Great Depression in California.* New York: Oxford University Press, 1996.

―――. *Inventing the Dream: California through the Progressive Era.* New York: Oxford University Press, 1985.

―――. *Material Dreams: Southern California through the 1920s.* New York: Oxford University Press, 1990.

Stuckey, Mary E. *Playing the Game: The Presidential Rhetoric of Ronald Reagan.* New York: Praeger, 1990.

Thomas, Bernice L. *America's 5 & 10 Cent Stores: The Kress Legacy.* New York: John Wiley & Sons, 1997.

van der Zee, John. *The Greatest Men's Party on Earth: Inside the Bohemian Grove.* New York: Harcourt Brace Jovanovich, 1974.

Waldie, D. J. *Holy Land: A Suburban Memoir.* New York: St. Martin's Press, 1996.

―――. *Where We Are Now: Notes from Los Angeles.* Los Angeles: Angel City Press, 2004.

Walker, John. *National Gallery of Art.* Foreword by J. Carter Brown. New York: Abradale Press, Harry N. Abrams, 1995.

―――. *Self-Portrait with Donors: Confessions of an Art Collector.* Boston: Little, Brown, 1974.

Walsh, John, and Deborah Gribbon. *The J. Paul Getty Museum and Its Collection: A Museum for the New Century.* Los Angeles: J. Paul Getty Museum, 1997.

Weinberg, Steve. *Armand Hammer: The Untold Story.* Boston: Little, Brown, 1989.

White, Theodore H. *Breach of Faith: The Fall of Richard Nixon.* New York: Atheneum, 1975.

―――. *The Making of the President, 1960– .* New York: Atheneum, 1961.

Williams, Harold M., Ada Louise Huxtable, Stephen D. Rountree, and Richard Meier. *Making Architecture: The Getty Center.* Los Angeles: J. Paul Getty Trust, 1997.

Williams, Harold M., Bill Lacy, Stephen D. Rountree, and Richard Meier. *The Getty Center: Design Process.* Los Angeles: J. Paul Getty Trust, 1991.

Wolfensohn, James D. "Opening Keynote Address." In *Culture Counts: Financing, Resources, and the Economics of Culture in Sustainable Development: Proceedings of the Conference Held in Florence, Italy, October 4–7, 1999.* Washington, D.C.: World Bank, 2000.

SELECTED SPEECHES OF FRANKLIN D. MURPHY

(Listed chronologically)

Inaugural Address, University of Kansas, Lawrence, Sept. 17, 1951.

Address on the Occasion of a Dinner Celebrating the 71st Birthday Anniversary of President Harry S. Truman, May 8, 1955.

Comments on the Occasion of the Opening of the National Fund-Raising Drive to Build the Eisenhower Library at Abilene, Kansas, Feb. 27, 1958.

"The American College and University and World Affairs." Western College Association Meetings, Los Angeles, Feb. 24, 1961.

"Education and Cultural Affairs—A Fourth and New Dimension in Foreign Policy." Mar. 22, 1961.

"Education, World Affairs, and People to People." Aug. 13, 1963.

Memorial to President John F. Kennedy, Los Angeles Sports Arena, NBC Television, Nov. 24, 1963.

"The Necessity of Beauty in an Urbanized Environment." Address to Town Hall, Jan. 14, 1964.

Statement to Congressional Committee concerning the International Education Act of 1966.

"The Role of the University in a Troubled Society." Address to Town Hall, 1967.

"Dissent, the Law and the University." Commencement address, University of California, Los Angeles, June 14, 1967.

"The State of the University." Commencement address, University of California, Los Angeles, June 14, 1968.

Address, 51st Annual Meeting of the American Council on Education, Oct. 10, 1968.

"Some Thoughts on the Current State of Society." 1970.

"Over 50 Looks at under 30." Address distributed by the board of directors of the American Society of Corporate Secretaries, 1971.

"From Birth to Maturity in 200 Years: An Oversimplified Analogy." Nov. 5, 1974.

"Pluralism and Philanthropy—The Uniquely American Tradition." Address, Chancellor's Club Dinner, University of Kansas, Lawrence, Dec. 12, 1978.

"The Practical Value of Humanistic Society." Plenary Meeting XVII of the President's Committee on the Arts and the Humanities, Mar. 31, 1988.

"Arts and Public Policy." Mar. 18, 1992. Audio recording. Archives, National Gallery of Art.

Hoving, Thomas P. F., 217, 255–57, 314–16, 333, 334
Hughes, Howard, 322, 435n1
Hughes, Langston, 10
Hughes, Robert, 331
Hughes Aircraft, 37
Hughes, Hubbard and Reed, 381
Hulten, Pontus, 217, 223
Humphrey, Hubert, 115, 130
Hunt Foods and Industries, 56, 71, 210, 437n42
Huntington, Henry Edwards, 370
Huntington Library, Art Collections, and Botanical Gardens (San Marino), 244, 302, 307, 363–64, 370–72, 376, 377, 381, 446nn49, 50; American Gallery, 235
Huxtable, Ada Louise, 316

Iacocca, Lee A., 156, 178–81
illuminated manuscripts, 302
immigrants, 25, 43, 83, 362, 390, 392; children of, at UCLA, 43; Jewish, 358–59, 443n48
impressionist paintings, 56, 203, 210, 213, 216, 278, 339; see also specific artists
Independent Colleges of Southern California, 182
Indian art, 210, 216
Individual Trustee Responsibility Fund (ITRF), 186
Ingres, Jean-Auguste-Dominique, 322
Institute of International Education, 124
integration, 9–10, 367; opposition to, 390, 391
Internal Revenue Service (IRS), 124, 125, 144, 183, 184, 187–91, 194, 199, 235, 287, 306, 426n44
International Association of Bibliophiles, 366
International Fund for Monuments (IFM), 270
International Herald Tribune, 315
international style, 75
Irvine, University of California at, 97, 108, 407n66
Irvine Foundation, 63, 230, 363
Islamic art, 216

isolationism, 10, 53
Isozaki, Arata, 234
Italian Renaissance art, 263, 268, 272, 361; see also specific artists

Jackson, Bob, 159
Jacobs, Jody, 218
James, W. H. ("Tex"), 152
Janss family, 42
Japanese American Cultural and Community Center (Los Angeles), 307, 356, 362–63, 445n30; Franklin D. Murphy Library, 363
Japanese American Cultural Center (New York), 363
Japanese Federation of Economic Organizations, 325
Jarvis, Howard, 124
Javits, Jacob K., 152, 162
Jerusalem Committee, 358
Jews, 10, 32–33, 331–32; culture and heritage of, 317, 358–62; immigrant, 358–59, 443n48; at UCLA, 43
John Birch Society, 49, 52–54, 88, 129
John Paul II, Pope, 270
Johns Hopkins University, 205; Hospital, 350
Johnson, Lyndon B., 45, 68–69, 84, 99, 106–8, 129–30, 135, 176, 407n84, 414n5, 415n27, 425n16
Johnson, Tom, 176, 177, 200–202, 425n16
Jones, Robert A., 213, 323
Jorgensen, Mr. and Mrs. Earle, 204
Juan Carlos, Prince of Spain, 163
Judaica, 374

Kaiser, Walter, 382–83
Kandinsky, Wassily, 210
Kansas, University of (KU), see University of Kansas (KU)
Kansas City Star, xii, 2, 12, 15, 34–35
Kansas City Star Company, 173
Kansas City Symphony, 261
Kansas Rural Health Plan, 7, 12, 59, 397n19
Kansas State College, 14
Kantor, Paul, 219
Kaufman, Gordon B., 119
Kaufman, Martha, 327–28

Mellon, Ailsa, *see* Bruce, Ailsa Mellon
Mellon, Andrew, 71, 239, 241, 244, 246, 251, 254, 342–43
Mellon, Bunny, 240
Mellon, Louise Whitney, 380
Mellon, Paul, xii, 108, 114–15, 163, 203, 244, 281, 380; death of, 385; and National Gallery, 71, 114, 239, 243–46, 253–54, 261, 264, 341–43, 431n15; retirement gala honoring, 240–41
Mellon family, xi, 253
Mellon Foundation, 244, 246, 270, 289, 370–72, 438n47
Mencken, Henry L., 29
Menil, Dominique de, 330
Menil Collection (Houston), 330
Menninger, Karl, 8
Menninger Clinic, 115, 125
Menninger Foundation, 399n50
Messer, Thomas M., 217
Metropolitan Museum of Art (New York), 217, 286, 287, 301, 314, 315, 317, 333; Annenberg and, 255–57, 335, 336, 340–43, 385; Department of Paintings Conservation, 271, 435n35; Kress Collection donations to, 267; Lehman collection at, 321; Program for Art on Film, 306
Mexican Americans, 25, 103
Michelangelo, 74, 250, 270–71
Middle East crisis, 157, 158
Middlekauff, Robert L., 377, 446n49
Mies van der Rohe, Ludwig, 80, 149
Milken, Michael, 355
Miller, Arthur, 133
Miller, Paul, 152
Milner, Reese Llewellyn, II, 145, 148
Milton, John, 447n5
Minnesota, University of, 409n100
Mississippi Summer voter registration drive, 86, 87
Mitchell, John N., 141, 143, 159
Mitchell, Silberberg and Knupp, 322
Modestini, Mario, 192, 268, 435nn25, 35
Monet, Claude, 257
Monet Museum (Giverny), 256
Moore, Henry, 91, 210, 219, 377; *Two-Piece Reclining Figure,* 378

Morgan, Julia, 105
Morgan, Pierpont, Library, 267, 302
Morisot, Berthe, *The Pink Dress,* 256
Morrill, Lew, 409n100
Morris, Willie, 176
Morrison, Patt, 446n45
Mosby, C. V., Company, 139, 175
Mosher, Samuel B., 63
Mount Sinai School of Medicine and Medical Center, 335
Mozart, Wolfgang Amadeus, 105
Muchnic, Suzanne, 305, 333, 341
multiculturalism, 358–63, 390, 391
Munitz, Barry, 387
Murdoch, Rupert, 334
Murdock, Marcellus, 12
Murphy, Annette (sister-in-law), 152, 350
Murphy, Carolyn (daughter), *see* Speer, Carolyn Murphy
Murphy, Cordelia (sister), *see* Ennis, Cordelia ("Cordie") Murphy
Murphy, Cordelia Antoinette Brown (mother), 2–4, 187, 382, 396n2
Murphy, Franklin D.: adolescence of, 2–4; as Ahmanson Foundation advisor and trustee, 112, 124–25, 181–94, 206, 319, 356–58, 388, 426n44; Ahmanson's friendship with, 57–59, 72–73, 100, 110–15; and Annenberg Collection, 335–343; arrival in Los Angeles of, 23–26, 35–39, 41–44, 390; on Bank of America board, 124, 273, 362, 373; birth of, 2; book collection of, 123–24, 365–67; boyhood of, 1, 2; and brother's death, 349–51; cultural exchange advocated by, 10, 33, 402n37; and daughter Joyce's illness, 351–53; death of, 382–86, 392; departure from Kansas of, 21–22, 34–35; education of, 3–5; elder statesman role of 355–56; in Europe, 4–5, 72–73, 128, 152–53, 398n29, 433n16; family background of, 1–2, 396n1; family life of, 6, 51–52, 73, 91–92, 123, 126–27, 148, 151–52, 196–99, 382; on Ford Motor Company board, 71–72, 124, 157, 162, 163, 178–81, 206, 351, 373; on Foreign Intelligence Advisory Board, 134–35, 141,